THE CORRESPONDENCE OF

William Carlos Williams

and Louis Zukofsky

THE CORRESPONDENCE OF

William Carlos Williams

& Louis Zukofsky

EDITED BY BARRY AHEARN

Wesleyan University Press MIDDLETOWN, CONNECTICUT

Published by
Wesleyan University Press,
Middletown, CT 06459

5 4 3 2 1

Grateful acknowledgment is made to the Ezra Pound Literary
Property Trust for permission to use previously published or
archival material.

Library of Congress Cataloging-in-Publication Data

Williams, William Carlos, 1883–1963.
The correspondence of William Carlos Williams and Louis
Zukofsky /edited by Barry Ahearn.
    p.   cm.
ISBN 0-8195-6490-7 (cloth : alk. paper)
Includes index.
1. Williams, William Carlos, 1883–1963—Correspondence.
2. Poets, American—20th century—Correspondence.
3. Zukofsky, Louis, 1904–1978—Correspondence.
I. Zukofsky, Louis, 1904–1978. II. Ahearn, Barry. III. Title.
PS3545.I544Z483 2003
811'.5209—dc22   2003016103

CONTENTS

This volume contains the surviving correspondence between William Carlos Williams (1883–1963) and Louis Zukofsky(1904–1978). It consists of 565 letters and cards from Williams to Zukofsky, 161 letters and cards from Zukofsky to Williams, and two letters from Florence Williams to Louis and Celia Zukofsky. One additional letter, which Zukofsky wrote but decided not to send to Williams, is included as Appendix A. Of the 565 letters from Williams to Zukofsky, a few (especially in the last few years of Williams's life) were written mostly by Florence Williams. Internal evidence from Williams's and Zukofsky's letters suggests that a substantial number of letters from Zukofsky to Williams were lost or discarded. It may be that they exist uncataloged in some archive, but this seems unlikely. Seven of Williams's letters to Zukofsky have been published before, one (4 December 1929) in facsimile in the *William Carlos Williams Newsletter* (Fall 1976), the six others in John C. Thirlwall's edition, *The Selected Letters of William Carlos Williams* (New York: McDowell, Obolensky, 1957): 23 March 1928, 2 April 1928, Easter [7 April]1928, 5 July 1928, 18 July 1928 and 21 June 1942. Thirlwall, however, silently normalized Williams's spelling. Furthermore, Thirlwall changed some of the details in Williams's letter of 21 June 1942. Readers were not alerted to the changes.

Williams's letters to Zukofsky are principally in two locations: the Beinecke Library at Yale University (435 items) and the Harry C. Ransom Humanities Research Center at the University of Texas at Austin (129 items). A handful of letters from Williams to Celia Zukofsky are at the McKeldin Library of the University of Maryland at College Park. These letters concern Celia's setting to music of two poems by Williams: "The Pink Church" and "Turkey in the Straw." Portions of some of these letters are included in this edition. In the McKeldin collection there is one letter (17 September 1948) from Williams to Louis Zukofsky. The bulk of Zukofsky's letters (109) to Williams are at the Beinecke Library. A considerable number (47) are in the poetry collection of the Lockwood Memorial Library of the State University of New York at Buffalo. Four letters from Louis Zukofsky to Williams are at the Lilly Library of the University of Indiana: 1 February 1943, 19 October 1946, 3 June 1949 and 21 December 1951. The Lilly letters also include six letters from Louis Zukofsky to Florence Williams, all written after her husband's death. There are not printed in this edition. One letter's (27 June 1960) current location is not known to me.

At one time it was in the possession of the late William Eric Williams, who sent a photocopy to me in 1977.

My intention is to present—as closely as possible—a faithful version of the letters as they were received by the two poets. Spacing, spelling, punctuation, and other physical characteristics of the words in the letters have been reproduced as they appear in the originals. Where the editor has felt it necessary to intrude with an explanation or amplification, such intrusions are placed between square brackets. The appearance of ellipses between square brackets in Williams's and Zukofsky's letters indicates a word or words have been deleted by the editor. These few, minor omissions were requested by Paul Zukofsky. Williams's and Louis Zukofsky's own afterthoughts and additions are placed within angle brackets.

The form and number of pages of the letters are indicated at the head of each. For example, TLS-2 indicates a typed letter signed by the author, consisting of two pages. Other abbreviations used are ALS—autograph letter signed; ACS—autograph card signed; TCS—typed card signed; TL—typed letter unsigned; AL—autograph letter unsigned; AC—autograph card unsigned; TC—typed card unsigned. Signatures are located on the pages as closely as possible to the same position in the originals. At times Williams and Zukofsky omitted the date or the place at which they were writing. But it has often been possible to assign a probable date and place. Where the editor has done so, such data are inside square brackets. Where Zukofsky noted the date on a letter from Williams, it was the date on which he received it. In most cases it appears that subtracting a day or two from the date received gives the date on which Williams composed the letter.

Wherever possible, notations at the end of each letter inform the reader about people, books (including Williams's and Zukofsky's own works), journals, organizations and the like that Williams and Zukofsky refer to. In a few cases the references remain unidentified. Readers wanting further information about some of the people mentioned by Williams and Zukosky should refer to the Biographical Notes.

I am indebted to authors who have gone before me. In Williams's case, I made extensive use of Paul Mariani's *William Carlos Williams: A New World Naked* (New York: McGraw-Hill, 1981). This work proved indispensable. Other necessary aids were Emily Mitchell Wallace's *A Bibliography of William Carlos Williams* (Middletown, Connecticut: Wesleyan University Press, 1968), Neil Baldwin and Steven L. Meyer's *The Manuscripts and Letters of William Carlos Williams in the Poetry Collection of the Lockwood Memorial Library, State University of New York at Buffalo: A Descriptive Catalogue* (Boston, Massachusetts: G. K. Hall, 1978), John C. Thirlwall's *The Selected Letters of William Carlos Williams* (New York: McDowell, Obolensky, 1957), and two volumes edited by

Hugh Witemeyer: *Pound/Williams: Selected Letters of Ezra Pound and William Carlos Williams* (New York: New Directions, 1996); and *William Carlos Williams and James Laughlin* (New York: W. W. Norton, 1989). With respect to Zukofsky, I often had recourse to Celia Zukofsky's *A Bibliography of Louis Zukofsky* (Los Angeles: Black Sparrow Press, 1969) and Marcella Spann Booth's *A Catalogue of the Louis Zukofsky Manuscript Collection* (Austin, Texas: Humanities Research Center, 1975).

I am deeply grateful to all the research librarians who helped me. Special thanks go to Patricia Willis, Curator of the Collection of American Literature at the Beinecke Rare Book and Manuscript Library (Yale University); Cathy Henderson, Associate Librarian at the Harry C. Ransom Humanities Research Center (the University of Texas at Austin), Beth Alvarez, Curator of Literary Manuscripts at the McKeldin Library (University of Maryland); Saundra Taylor, Curator of Manuscripts, the Lilly Library (Indiana University), and Robert J. Bertholf, Curator of the Poetry/Rare Book Collection (State University of New York at Buffalo). For their generous assistance I also am indebted to Pamela Gray Ahearn, Richard Caddell, Hilda Zacharia Colletti, Jonathan Gill, James A. Gray, Willard Goodwin, Ellen Mankoff, Alec Marsh, Dr. Maressa Hecht Orzack, Sam Ramer, Sylvia Roder, Mark Scroggins, G. Thomas Tanselle, Arnold Wand, Paul Williams, Hugh Witemeyer, Don Zacharia, Paul Zukofsky, and Daniel Zukowsky. My apologies to anyone whom I may have inadvertently forgotten to thank. Suzanna Tamminen of Wesleyan University Press has seen this volume through every stage of its progress.

Research for this volume was aided by a grant from the George Lurcy Charitable and Educational Trust.

Autobiography
   William Carlos Williams. *The Autobiography of William Carlos Williams.*
   New York: New Directions, 1967.
Baldwin and Meyers.
   Neil Baldwin and Steven L. Meyers. *The Manuscripts and Letters of William Carlos Williams in the Poetry Collection of the Lockwood Memorial Library, State University of New York at Buffalo: A Descriptive Catalogue.* Boston:
   G. K. Hall, 1978.
CP1
   The Collected Poems of William Carlos Williams, Volume 1 (1909–1939). A. Walton Litz and Christopher MacGowan, eds. New York: New Directions, 1986.
CP2
   The Collected Poems of William Carlos Williams, Volume 2 (1939–1962). Christopher MacGowan, ed. New York: New Directions, 1988.
CSP
   Louis Zukofsky. *Complete Short Poems.* Baltimore: Johns Hopkins Univ. Press, 1991.
EP/LZ
   Pound/Zukofsky: Selected Letters of Ezra Pound and Louis Zukofsky. Barry Ahearn, ed. New York: New Directions, 1987.
EP/WCW
   Pound/Williams: Selected Letters of Ezra Pound and William Carlos Williams. Hugh Witemeyer, ed. New York: New Directions, 1996.
Mariani
   Paul Mariani. *William Carlos Williams: A New World Naked.* New York: McGraw-Hill, 1981.
Prepositions +
   Louis Zukofsky. *Prepositions +: The Collected Critical Essays.* Middletown, Conn.: Wesleyan Univ. Press, 2000.
Recognizable Image
   A Recognizable Image: William Carlos Williams on Art and Artists. Bram Dijkstra, ed. New York: New Directions, 1978.
SE William Carlos Williams.
   Selected Essays. New York: Random House, 1954.

SL

The Selected Letters of William Carlos Williams. John C. Thirlwall, ed. New York: McDowell, Obolensky, 1957.

Something to Say

Something to Say: William Carlos Williams on Younger Poets. James E. B. Breslin, ed. New York: New Directions, 1985.

Wallace

Emily Mitchell Wallace. *A Bibliography of William Carlos Williams.* Middletown, Conn.: Wesleyan Univ. Press, 1968.

WCW/JL

William Carlos Williams and James Laughlin: Selected Letters. Hugh Witemeyer, ed. New York: W. W. Norton, 1989.

INTRODUCTION

William Carlos Williams (born 1883) and Louis Zukofsky (born 1904): the dates alone tell part of the story. Williams was quick to see his encounter with the budding poet as an instance of generational succession. Soon after they met he wrote, "I did not wish to be twenty years younger and surely I did not wish you to be twenty years older. I was happy to find a link between myself and another wave of it. Sometimes one thinks the thing has died down. I believe that somehow you have benefitted by my work. Not that you have even seen it fully but it proves to me (Christ, god damn this machine) that the thing moves by a direct relationship between men from generation to generation. And that no matter how we may be ignored, maligned, left unnoticed, yet by doing straightforward work we do somehow reach the right people" (7 April 1928). Meeting Zukofsky became for Williams another instance of something he valued most highly—contact. His words had reached out and drawn in one of "the right people."

Williams's remarks also touch on one of his familiar complaints: the American writer struggles against a culture that complacently prefers the conventional and the familiar. For two decades Williams had fought to bring his work to a wide audience. He wanted popular success for a number of reasons: it would bring in some needed cash; it would prove there was a market for the kind of writing he represented and championed; it would make it possible for other, worthy authors to find an audience. Zukofsky, only twenty-four years old when they met, had not yet experienced this struggle to publish. Zukofsky might well have presumed that the work of the poets of the generation before (Pound, Williams, Eliot, Cummings, Stevens, Moore) had laid the groundwork for the succeeding generation, which, building on their example, would find a receptive audience and willing publishers. Indeed, in 1931, when Zukofsky compared *Spring and All* to Wordsworth's preface to *Lyrical Ballads* as a work that might begin "a century of writing" (*Prepositions* +, 198), he anticipated he would be part of a new movement in the poetry of the twentieth century comparable in its influence to that of Romanticism in the nineteenth century. Zukofsky's career did begin well. He placed his work in *The Exile, Hound and Horn, Poetry, The Criterion*, and other journals, was named editor for the "Objectivists" issue of *Poetry,* and edited the *"Objectivist" Anthology.* There were good reasons for Zukofsky to be sanguine about his prospects. Yet

Williams reminded him from time to time that "the sons of bitches that run theaters and publishing houses" (12 May 1928) still blocked the way. Eventually Zukofsky would no longer need reminding. By the time he had turned forty he was well aware that little or no market existed for his work. He indicated to Williams that the absence of an outlet discouraged his art: "I'm certain I'd write more if the possibility of publication drove me to it" (25 December 1945). Near the end of their correspondence, he wondered if his worth would be recognized in his lifetime: "The older I get the more I fall back quietly on my work for solace and don't expect miracles for another how many years, if— from society" (29 June 1960).

When faced with public apathy, writers sometimes console themselves by reflecting that at least someone—another writer—acknowledges their talent. Williams often found merit in fellow writers who otherwise met with ridicule or silence. This was the case in his friendship with Zukofsky. Various examples of his generosity to the younger poet run through the letters. The first letter in the collection finds Williams happy to have Zukofsky venture out to 9 Ridge Road in Rutherford for a visit and dinner. He had not yet met Zukofsky or seen any of his work. All Williams had to go on was the letter (not located) in which Zukofsky introduced himself. (We can tell from Williams's response that Zukofsky had reported that Pound had urged Zukofsky to "look up" Williams.) Williams tempers his welcoming response with his recurring complaint that Pound thought him too provincial. Learning from Zukofsky that Pound recommends Williams as the "best human value" on Pound's American visiting list, Williams quickly assumes this praise of his character is a polite way of saying that Williams "can't write" (23 March 1928).

Williams also helped Zukofsky in other respects. Williams urged his new friend to meet others in his circle of acquaintances, such as Robert McAlmon and Nancy Cunard. When Williams thought Zukofsky might somehow profit from such meetings, he would dash off a note. Williams also frequently alerted Zukofsky to opportunities for publication. As soon as a new literary magazine swam into Williams's ken, he would tell Zukofsky about it. Williams was also happy to recommend Zukofsky, whether to the Guggenheim Foundation, the University of Wisconsin, or to friends who might be able to offer Zukofsky a job. During the first fifteen years of their friendship, the problem of finding work for Zukofsky becomes one of the minor themes of the correspondence. Williams was well aware during the 1930s that Zukofsky was pressed by economic difficulties. When Zukofsky remarked that he wanted Williams to hurry and send along one of his manuscripts, so that "the publishing business may start & I may have the 2¢ sooner to send you another letter" (27 October 1931), he was being only partly facetious. Perhaps it was the thought that Zukofsky was verging on homelessness that prompted Williams a few years later

(23 February 1934) to offer him one dollar for answering the phone at the Williams home one evening.

Zukofsky repaid the older poet by editing his work. From the beginning of their friendship, Williams depended on Zukofsky's criticism. One of the most remarkable features of the Williams-Zukofsky relationship was how soon and how consistently Williams sought his younger friend's editorial advice. In February 1929, for example, Williams sent him a copy of his poem, "The Flower," urging him to "Do your woist." Zukofsky's tinkering pleased Williams. After examining the suggested revisions he wrote again, "Many thanks for [y]our good offices: the poem is improved . . ." (12 February 1929). Williams found Zukofsky's critical abilities useful for a variety of genres. He submitted his critical prose for Zukofsky's emendation. When Williams was preparing his essay on Gertrude Stein—"The Work of Gertrude Stein"—for Richard Johns's magazine, *Pagany,* he turned to Zukofsky for help. Zukofsky obliged, as Williams's letter of 22 November 1929 demonstrates, "Many, many thanks, by the way for your very valuable notes on the Stein piece. I made many corrections throughout the whole improving it greatly." Thus began a decades-long editorial practice. Williams would produce a poem or essay; Zukofsky would then comment on it. The most extensive record of such a procedure still extant is a draft of *The Wedge* that Zukofsky read and commented on (see Appendix C). Even more surprising is how boldly the youthful Zukofsky advised Williams about the shape of his literary career: "I don't think it is any use publishing a miscellany of poems, those of your poems i.e. which never before appeared in a volume. And again, just a collection would be a step back <rather> than forward" (26 September 1929). No document survives suggesting that Williams rebuked Zukofsky for butting in with advice about what poems of his should next be published. Perhaps he considered that Zukofsky would learn soon enough that getting a volume published at all was no light matter. Even when Zukofsky had learned that, however, he was still inclined to offer unsolicited advice to Williams, in one case suggesting how he should be more judicious about selecting his material when reading poems over the radio (22 February 1937).

At first glance, it appears strange that the customary relationship between an older and a younger poet, in which the older serves as a mentor to the younger, would be reversed when it came to the question of editing. The reason for the reversal may lie in the two poets' differing approaches to the art. Williams tended to emphasize inspiration, while Zukofsky emphasized craft. Williams found his inspiration in events in the "real" world, in glimpses of nature or humanity. His letters often refer to scenes and people he finds moving. Zukofsky, on the other hand, was inspired by works of art: Bach's *St. Matthew's Passion,* Williams's and other poets' poetry, his own poetry ("Mantis: An Interpretation"), and motion pictures. Williams's awareness of this distinction between

Zukofsky and himself appears in his afterword to *"A" 1–12*. There he posits as an important difference between his art and Zukofsky's that he (Williams) was seeking to put an image on paper (something external that was seen and recorded), while Zukofsky was more interested in arranging words and sounds (which may be done with minimal reference to external phenomena).

The process of editorial suggestion seems to have worked strictly in one direction: from Zukofsky to Williams. We find little indication in the letters that Williams ever provided detailed comments about Zukofsky's work. The reason for this probably lies in Williams's recognition that his young colleague operated in a way that was frequently beyond Williams's comprehension. From the beginning Williams confessed he had difficulty with the logic of Zukofsky's poetry. Although he liked Zukofsky's poem, "Memory of V. I. Ulianov," he lamented, "Sometimes though I don't like your language. It probably is I and not you who should be blamed for this. You are wrest[l]ing with the antagonist under newer rules. But I can't see "all live processes" "orbit-trembling" "our consciousness" "the sources of being"—What the hell? I'm not finding fault I'm just trying to nail what troubles me. It may be that I am to literal in my search for objective clarities of image. It may be that you are completely right in forcing abstract conceptions into the sound pattern. I dunno" (25 July 1928). As the relationship developed, Williams did not trust himself to make specific recommendations about Zukofsky's craftsmanship. From the beginning he had a somewhat restrained attitude about *"A"* and its difficulties. On 18 January 1931, he commented, "Well, I've read the "A" and be God—it's not tawdry. Its movement calls up a world of sound in which things coccur in unused relationships—almost filed out with a file they show such marks of making on them." This note of praise mixed with an air of mystification was reiterated when Williams encountered further installments of the poem. Whenever Williams commented on the portions of the poem, he found himself praising it, but with an air of one who struggled to designate its exact excellence: "If one look for matter among the variety of statements he'll go astray. It is the wholeness and unity that gives the form—I can't name it" (4 March 1937). One striking aspect of Williams's reaction to *"A"* is the absence of constructive criticism. With only one or two exceptions, Williams has no advice to give Zukofsky about how to improve *"A,"* whereas Zukofsky readily suggests improvements in Williams's work. Eventually, when Williams was called on to write a short essay to accompany the publication of *"A" 1–12*, his remarks about the poem, which by that time (1957) he had seen in various forms for almost three decades, indicated that reading it was an exercise in bafflement. He recognized that Zukofsky was up to something important, but Williams could not quite wrap his mind around the whole. Typically, Williams submitted his essay to Zukofsky, and, as usual, the younger poet edited it.

Few artistic friendships are without their periods of disquiet, estrangement or conflict. The Williams-Zukofsky relationship was no exception to this rule. The most serious threat to their mutual regard arose from Williams's obsession with a project dear to his heart, the proposed opera on George Washington, *The First President.* No Williams scholar today considers this one of Williams's major works, but the degree to which Williams's letters in the mid-1930s refer to this project shows that it loomed large to the author. For example, even though Williams writes that, "My inclination to write has been low," he feels compelled. "I must drive myself to the finishing of this libretto the best way I can. If only I had a clear notion of what Serly wants it might rekindle my interest. I feel that I'm fighting a fog. If you can help, go to it" (5 June 1934). Zukofsky went to it, but friction arose. The creation of an opera is a collaborative act, but in this case Williams seems to have found collaboration irksome. Williams had hoped that George Antheil would compose the music for *The First President,* but, after a long delay, Antheil went on to other projects. Williams was bitterly disappointed. The next composer to express serious interest in the libretto was Tibor Serly, whom Williams had met through Zukofsky. Serly's initial interest, however, was followed by delay and eventual abandonment of the project. And it was not only the failure to find a composer who would carry on and complete the project that troubled Williams. He had his vision, or thought he had his vision, of what Washington meant to the country, but when he sought help in expressing it, contributions by others seemed only to muddle the issue. On 17 July 1934 he wrote to Zukofsky asking for his and others' assistance with a portion of the opera: "I'm curious to know what your reaction to the plan of the ballet will be. Let the others in on it if they are around. We are doing this as a group." Zukofsky's reply, however, displeased Williams (letter of 7 August 1934). Eventually, after years of much thinking, revision, and commentary from all involved, Williams grew quite wildly frustrated: "Eight years of that God damned opera and the fiddling and fussing that went with it just about had be ready for the psycho-pathic ward" (January 1936). The trouble over the composition of *The First President* clouded relations between Williams and Zukofsky, at least temporarily. Tibor Serly, after all, had been Zukofsky's friend. But something seems to have cleared in the air between Williams and Zukofsky once Williams dropped the opera. A letter of 4 February 1936 shows Williams looking forward to a return to friendly relations: "I think we both rather deliberately looked away from each other for a time—as any ape, rat, elephant or baseball player shoud, now and then—if he care for his companion." *The First President* seems to have been the sole project for which Williams found his friend unsuited. Perhaps it came down to the fact that Williams was concentrating on Washington the man while Zukofsky preferred to filter Washington through other concerns, principally economic ones. Yet the ruptures between Williams and Zukofsky were infrequent and never irreparable. Writing of the estrangement much later, Zukofsky professed to be hazy about its fundamental cause: "You know, I remember the squabble of a few years ago and the reason it happened was that I felt you really didn't care to see me much, and well I never like to make a nuisance of myself if I'm smart enough to catch on" (1 February 1943). Williams's reply, two days later, minimized the rift: "If anything happened between us "years ago" for my part it was, if I remember anything at all—it was that I began to feel restless at your critical position, as I used to feel with Pound at times when he would press me too hard. I wanted to break away (probably from something inside myself) and felt, perhaps, that you represented certain critical restraints that acted as a check upon me. There is a certain meticulousness about your position that I respect, in you, but which doesn't agree with my particular kind of irritabliltiy after the first ten years. I wanted to get off on the loose and see what a different sort of treatment would do for me." Williams dismisses the estrangement, variously finding it to be (a) of little consequence, (b) his fault, and (c) necessary for his artistic health. Williams had long since returned to feeling comradely; a few months later he sent Zukofsky the draft of *The Wedge* to work on.

One telling moment in their relationship came with the publication of Williams's *Autobiography*. Williams's discussion of his life and his literary friends omitted Zukofsky. By this point, Zukofsky had been editing Williams for twenty years. Yet not a hint of this important service appears in the *Autobiography*. Zukofsky might well have taken umbrage at being reduced to a non-person in Williams's life. How can one square Zukofsky's absence with such earlier statements by Williams as, "Anyhow, your poem is a beauty, you are fast becoming the most important and neglected poet of our time and place" (3 April 1941)? Yet Zukofsky expressed no disappointment. On 30 September 1951, he wrote, "I've been reading your Autobiography—as relief from getting into the grind of the academic year. I've told my chairman, the dean, and my colleagues that you mention Bklyn Poly—it flatters them, I hope to the extent of adding to the sales of the book." Perhaps Zukofsky's reference to Williams's mention of Brooklyn Polytechnic tacitly rebukes Williams for not stating the reason Williams had come there—to lecture at the invitation and arrangement of Zukofsky. Nevertheless, none of Zukofsky's letters to Williams explicitly complain about anything Williams has done or failed to do; they never contend that Williams has done Zukofsky a wrong. Quite to the contrary, Zukofsky finds in Williams and his art, he says, matter for inspiration. In the same letter in which Zukofsky mentions reading the *Autobiography,* he indicates that reading it has returned him to his own work: "Sitting up late alone—after a hundred pages of your book <i.e. Part I—tho' I find myself

reading all thru as the "subject" strikes me when I thumb pages>—I turned to A-12 again last night."

One aspect of their relationship that helped keep them amicable was their similar attitude toward political issues. Both Williams and Zukofsky were keenly aware of political developments. Williams's poetry, which revealed a generally leftist sympathy, led to his being denied the post of Consultant in Poetry at the Library of Congress in 1952. (Had Zukofsky risen in the early 1950s to similar fame, no doubt the post would have been denied him even more rapidly.) Williams's letters reveal that during the 1930s and 1940s he thought well of the Soviet Union. At least some aspects of life there seemed to him to represent the promise of a better future. Williams recognized that Russia was not a utopia, but he thought it might be moving toward a society in which all strove for the common good: "I have been reading the Dean of Caterbury''s, The Soviet Power. He's an old man and I didn't like the way he acted toward Eddie the King and his Moll—but if you haven't glanced into that book, do it. To let such an enlightenment as Russia represents no matter how failingly be blotted <out> by the brutality of Nazidom would be the final disgrace" (6 October 1941). Williams's sympathy with left-wing causes was hardly based on a consistent ideological commitment. He was simply casting about for a solution to human problems he saw and commented on, as he did in a letter of 23 February 1949: "It must be the lowdown district of Newark for we ran into 5 Sunday afternoon bums that really hurt. I can't have anything to do with tramps. I can't take it. What in hell is one to do? Become a bum oneself? I can't see any other answer. Anything else is a complicated lie. These men in their 40s or so, big broken nosed wrecks either out to be taken out and shot or be sheltered and fed and loved, God damn it. It distresses me more and more as I get older. I fell dirty and cowardly. I can only avoid looking at them." Eventually Williams judged that the early promise of the Soviet experiment had failed. After the Cold War had been underway for several years, and after the failed revolt in Hungary in 1956, Williams lamented that there was, "nothing much to hope for any more from Moscow, a stone hung on a rope round our necks" (16 June 1957).

Zukofsky's leaning toward the left was somewhat different. Where Williams sought practical solutions to such problems as the "broken nosed wrecks," apparently an inevitable byproduct of capitalism, Zukofsky's interest in communism and Russia were always interwoven with his commitment to art. One of Zukofsky's early letters to Williams waxes enthusiastic about one aspect of Soviet life, their motion pictures. His praise of them, however, says nothing about politics, but instead returns to his and Williams's art: "I mean for God's sake don't miss these Amkino films. Seeing them you'll forget Al Smith and vote for yourself, and Spring and All especially Song No XV (it took this night to see what you were getting at <was a song>) and the fact that you're alive" (22 October 1928). Indeed, his remark suggesting that Williams "forget Al Smith" suggests that political action as Williams conceives it is a waste of their time. So far as Zukofsky was concerned, "action" was action to get deserving authors published. In 1932 this action took the form of Zukofsky proposing that Williams, he, and a number of other writers form a collective publishing company, one in which expenses and profits would be shared by all. After much hesitation, Williams finally conceded that the "scheme as outlined has the earmarks of feasability, the best yet! I am grateful to you for your vision and persistence, I'll back you in every way possible. To begin with you may count on me for the first hundred toward my book. I'd pay it all but I decided long ago not to. And I'll go after Maranne and Wallace Stevens at once" (September/October 1933). Zukofsky's proposal eventually became the Objectivist Press, which published a handful of titles but never lived up to Zukofsky's ambitions for it.

It was typical of Zukofsky's approach to politics that he felt moved to join others only when it involved writing and publishing. Zukofsky seemed to feel that since poetry was his forte, then the promotion of poetry was where his energies should be focused. It was up to other people, possessing other talents, to manage and promote other aspects of human improvement. At one point Zukofsky thought he had found the appropriate vehicle for his talent. The 1935 assembly of the American Writers' Congress led to the formation of a League of American Writers. Williams was only moderately interested in the League, but Zukofsky became a member of the committee that was formed to found a new magazine to represent the League. He subsequently asked Williams for a submission to the fledgling publication, but the magazine never saw the light of day. Clearly Zukofsky was looking for a position of authority with a publication whose political stance he could be comfortable with, but this hope was never realized. In 1940 he tried again to make a place for himself in literature and politics as co-editor of a journal. Together with his friend René Taupin, he began planning a quarterly to be called *La France en Liberté,* but it never appeared. The magazine would have been, among other things, a vehicle in which French anti-fascist exiles could publish. It would have provided Zukofsky with an opportunity to strike a blow in the war effort as well as publish.

The war had various unexpected effects on Zukofsky. Since he turned thirty-eight in January of 1942, he was not the right age for joining the service. Zukofsky doubtless felt that his talents as a communicator were what should be put to use; he would have been simply in the way on the battlefield. He did come close to getting into the background of the battle, though. As he tells Williams in a letter of 10 November 1942, he had applied for a commission in the U.S. Army, and a Major Crawford had contacted him to see if he could speak fluent French. Had Zukofsky been able to do so without any further training, he might have been sworn in and sent to North Africa to help smooth relations between the invading Allies and the French colonial authorities. Since he could not acquire fluency overnight, Zukofsky was sent back home and the Army never availed itself of his talents. The war, however, did have the effect of providing employment for Zukofsky in jobs related to it. He eventually found himself writing technical manuals for radio equipment.

At least Zukofsky made some contribution to the war effort. Williams faced the problem of being powerless to help, even as his sons went off to fight. Both boys served in the armed forces and were often far away and out of touch. One indication of Williams's anxiety about his sons appears in a letter of 15 September 1942: "Bill is on some island south of the Equator and west of the Date Line, that's all we know. We haven't heard from him now in two weeks. I try not to think about it." Although Williams chafed at his inability to participate directly, he did his best to contribute in the few ways he could. In the same letter he dramatizes his struggle to retrieve scrap iron: "I've been crawling under my office today collecting scrap, a hell of a dirty place to look for old pieces of iron pipe, old wire, anything at all. I got a throat full of muck—but what is that to what the kids are getting? I take a masochistic pleasure in whatever I can force myself to do." In some small way, Williams's suffering under his house was offered up to the gods of war as a token of his solidarity with the embattled younger generation. Like Zukofsky, of course, Williams sought to engage the war with his writing. He found that one other home front contribution—the victory garden—was comparable to his own activity in assembling the manuscript of The Wedge: "Have changed my mind for the third time, today I cut the book by about twenty three pages and that is final. So you won't have to do anything but put it in the drawer, at ease. I feel much better. I had almost to get a fever to do it—in fact I was helped by an article on gardening which said that the victory gardneers next year, it is hoped, will profit by their errors next year. That if you plant too much and have not the hardihood to weed out what you cannot use or that you have not the place for,the overabundance of no matter what you have growing is a WEED! Tear it up" (April 1943). The gradual realization that his own art could be considered a contribution to the Allied cause culminated in the introduction to The Wedge, where Williams argues that his writing is part of the struggle of the free nations.

As Williams's concern about his sons at war indicates, one of the continuing themes of the letters is family life. Williams tends to discuss his family more than Zukofsky. Part of the reason for this is that he had more family: a mother who lived at his home, a wife, two sons, daughters-in-law and grandchildren. Zukofsky did not marry until the correspondence had been underway for a decade. Of course the musical career of Louis and Celia's son, Paul, becomes central to the letters in the final decade, but overall it was Williams who dwelt most on family. His sense of identity seemed inextricably and significantly bound to the shape of his family's history. In one letter Williams reports, "This afternoon I went with my mother to our old house where my brother now lives and he and I dug through a half dozen old trunks and large portfolios at random looking for what we might find. I found leters addressed to my mother at several New York, Brooklyn, West Indian and Parisian addresses, some of them written by my father. There were stacks of small photographs which my mother later identified mostly Spaniards and Frenchmen withe their wives, children and all the rest of it." Despite the sorting through the trove of memorabilia, Williams expresses disappointment at finding "nothing new about the family history" (26 November 1933). In part the letters from Williams become a chronicle of the lives of the Williamses, even down to the grandchildren. Occasionally Williams even dramatizes domestic conversation, as he does in his letter of 23 February 1949, where Floss catches him preparing to mail a rare book to Ezra Pound's disciple, Dallam Simpson, and assures him that the book is *not* leaving the house.

One melancholy but unavoidable aspect of the relationship between Williams and Zukofsky came about as a consequence of the long decline in Williams's health that began in the late 1940s. Williams frequently noted his various setbacks. He would bemoan his state of mind, health, or career; Zukofsky would reply and attempt to cheer him. Writing on 14 April 1960, Williams remarked that, "The winter in Florida without a typewriter was not such a good idea. I all but ~~but~~ forgot where the keys were on the board, really. It gave me a fright." Williams added that he was "slowly getting control of myself again but I'm getting so far behind on my writing that I'm about ready to quit. In fact if it weren't for Floss to read to me I feel as though I might as well quit the game. Seriously." He ended by saying that he feared his mental faculties were becoming impaired: "It's my memory, even my mind, which is a fear that is faliling me." Zukofsky quickly replied that Williams's fears were exaggerated. "And if you will please let me be the doctor—since I'm the only poet of our time, who fair as he has tried to be to the un-progress of science, has never missed a typewriter—there is no crisis! And as for stopping to write, I am really waiting for a time when—and that's not hard to imagine having gone thru what we have—life, and <u>that</u> is the poem, will be no poorer even when poetry is not being written. Because that's when it's written, and even literally gets written down" (15 April 1960). Zukfosky also pointed out that there were few errors in Williams's letter, but the truth is that many of Williams's letters from the last ten years of their correspondence show more than the usual number of typos. Williams was never an immaculate typist, but the letters from the last ten years of his life painfully reveal his physical deterioration. Williams's decline is sadly recorded in the misspellings and awkward spacings.

Even though Williams in his last years was apt to dwell on his discouragement ("So that there is nothing left for me but to acknolge my defeat, another defeat in the mounting field of defeats that I have had to accept of late" [11 February 1959]), neither he nor Zukofsky allowed despair to predominate. A poetic triumph by either one became a cause for celebration. In the midst of his troubles, Williams still responds with enthusiastic delight to Zukofsky's poem, "4 Other Countries": "I don't care if I never write another line and hope not to do it after Floss has just read me the 4 Other Countries which she has just finished reading me and at her own request reading it over again. That is a pleasure I never hope to live through again—and when I looked over her shoulder to see the pages as she was and saw those quatrains unrolling before her—my mouth literarlly fell open at my own amazement" (23 October 1958). After thirty years of friendship, Williams was delighted to find his long-standing faith in Zukofsky's talent fully justified. Zukofsky, for his part, pointed out to Williams the beauties he found in *The Desert Music*: The Idyl is lovely (sound lovely if you wish with the tone of Floss whenever she uses that word of something—it has that way always struck me as final)" (14 March 1954). He also praised the portions of *Paterson* as they appeared, as he did on the occasion of the publication of *Paterson: Book V*: "The image of the unicorn is most fortunate and holds the contrapuntal material together—so that I never feel a symbol, but the whole poem at once as it moves, or tho it moves" (28 December 1957). Zukofsky at one time even planned to bring more of Williams's writing to the world by making good on his earlier plan to publish some of Williams's letters (see Appendix B). As he wrote to Williams on 15 October 1960, he had tentatively arranged with the University of Texas Press to have a volume of letters published. The volume would consist of selected letters written to Zukofsky between 1923 and 1955. Although that volume never appeared, the present one fulfills Zukofsky's long-delayed desire to see Williams's letters published. It also eloquently testifies to the personal and literary bond connecting Williams and Zukofsky, a bond between (as Florence Williams says in the last letter) "treasured friends."

The Letters

1. TLS-1

March 23, 1928

My dear Zukofsky:

By "human value" I suppose Ezrie means that in his opinion I can't write. Damn it, who can write isolated as we all find ourselves and robbed of the natural friendly stimulae on which we rest, at least, in our lesser moments? But undoubtedly the old ant eater didn't mean anything at all other than that he'd like me to make your acquaintance, and you mine.

So you are responsible for EXILE now. Is that so? Come over to this suburb some Tuesday, Friday or Saturday evening for a country meal and a talk and explain to me what all has taken place in "the center" while I have been rusticating. I'd like greatly to see you since you come with an introduction from my old friend. But do call up first since I am a laborer and my time must be arranged to fit the adavent of a guest. I have a good cook. What do you like especially to eat?

      Yours

      W. C. Williams

"human value": Pound wrote to Zukofsky on 5 March 1928, "Do go down an' stir up ole
    Bill Willyums, 9 Ridge Rd. Rutherford (W. C. Williams M.D.) and tell him I tole you.
    He is still the best human value on my murkn. visiting list" (*EP/LZ*, 7).

EXILE: The *Exile,* Pound's little magazine that appeared for four issues in 1927–28. In his
    letter of 5 March 1928, Pound had proposed that Zukofsky select work by Williams for
    publication in the *Exile.*

2. TLS-1

March 28 [1928]

Dear Zukofsky:

Neither am I of "the center". Lucy just likes to know what people especially fancy when she cooks for them so as to be sure, if possible, to please them. Nothing elaborate here.

Unfortunately I will not be at home this Saturday evening. What about Sunday? I am coming in to the Philharmonic concert. Perhaps I could meet you between half past five and six somewhere in the city and you will have supper with me there.

It is funny that I am being interviewed and having my caricature done at five o'clock by some strangers at the Park Central Hotel, a Miss Herrman and Mr. P. – I didn't exactly catch his name over the phone. Could you not rescue me there, Room 2550 at 5.30? Drop me a note here or just arrive there and ask for me at the time stated above.

> Yours
> W. C. Williams

Lucy: Lucy Wooton, who for many years served as housekeeper and cook for the Williamses. She had previously worked for Florence Williams's mother.

concert: On Sunday, 1 April 1928, the New York Philharmonic Orchestra performed works by Bach, Monteverdi and Franck, but the main offering on the program was Beethoven's Ninth Symphony.

Miss Herrman and Mr. P.: Eva Herrman's caricature of Williams appeared in the *Dial* 85: 11 (November 1928), facing page 396. Mr. P.: Unidentified.

3. TLS-1

> 9 Ridge Road
> Rutherford, N.J.

March 28/28

Dear Zukofsky:

Fortunately I just picked up your letter and saw, "East 111 St." An hour or two ago I sent you a note to West 111St.

In that note I said that I would not be at home this Saturday evening and asked you to meet me in New York on Sunday at 5.30 at the Park Central Hotel, Room 2550. I'm damned if I know where the hotel is but it should not be hard to find – somewhere around 57th. St. I think.

The fact is that I am going to the place mentioned to be interviewed by some fellow who is writing a book about modern literary persons. A woman named Herrman is to do a caricature. It would be nice if you would rescue me there at the time mentioned, we could then have supper together and talk of Pound.

> Yours
> W. C.Williams

some fellow: Unidentified.

4. TLS-1

> [Rutherford, N.J.]

Monday [2 April 1928]

Dear Zukofsky:

Yes, yes. You have the rare gift. As with everything else there are flaws – the tripping rhythm – but not always the tripping rhythm – just sometimes. It spoils the adagio effect. It is noteable that the lines have such an excellent internal necessity that they must be read slowly. It is thoughtful poetry, but actual word stuff, not thoughts for thoughts. It escapes me in its analysis (thank God) and strikes against me a a thing (thank God) There are not so many things in the world as we commonly imagine. Plenty of debris, plenty of smudges.

This has been a pleasure, i.e. the reading of your poem. You make me want to carry out deferred designs. Don't take my throries too,seriously. They are for me not you – or for you of course, or anybody.

I'd give my shirt to hear the Mattaus Passion this week but I doubt if it can be done. If I do get there in spite of everything I'll cast an eye around for you.

But your work's the thing. It encourages me in my designs. Makes me anxious to get at my notes and the things (thank God) which I did not tell the gentleman. Thanks for the supper. As soon as work lightens a bit for me here in the suburbs I want you to come out. I tell you what I'll do. I'll invite Cummings out also, just like that. I'll tell him I wnat him to see your poem and that you want to talk to him – and that I also would like to talk to him. It would be amusing to see what happens: I congratulate Pound on his luck in finding you. You are another nail in the Dial coffin. Damn fools.

>Yours
>Williams

your poem: Probably "Poem Beginning 'The.'"

Mattaus Passion: Johann Sebastian Bach's *St. Matthew Passion,* performed at Carnegie Hall on 5 April 1928. Zukofsky attended and recalled the performance at the beginning of "A."

Cummings: E. E. Cummings (1894–1962), American poet.

5. TLS-1

[Rutherford, N.J.]

Easter [7 April 1928]
Dear Zukofsky:
Was the Matthäuspassion well sung? I wish I could have been there.

What meeting you meant to me was at first just that Pound had admired your work. I was amazed to see you, nothing like what I had imagined. Then just reticence. Finally your poem thrilled me to the middle and back again.

I did not wish to be twenty years younger and surely I did not wish you to be twenty years older. I was happy to find a link between myself and another wave of it. Sometimes one thinks the thing has died down. I believe that somehow you have benefitted by my work. Not that you have even seen it fully but it proves to me (Christ, god damn this machine) that the thing moves by a direct relationship between men from generation to generation. And that no matter how we may be ignored, maligned, left unnoticed, yet by doing straightforward work we do somehow reach the right people.

There must be an American Magazine. As I have gotten older I am less volatile over projects such as this (a magazine) less willing to say much but more determined to make a go of it finally – after I am 70 perhaps. And you seem to me to posess things which I can never touch and which would be invaluable to such a project. Perhaps it will crystallize soon.

I'll write to you telling you when it will be possible to have you out here for some of Lucy's cooking! It has been a real satisfaction to read you poem. I'll not forget it soon. Let me see more of your work. I will return anything you ask me to with the greatest care. Also I'll let you glimpse work of my own as soon (my God) as I have time to prepare any to be submitted to you.

    Williams

6. TLS-1

Rutherford, N.J.

April 16, 1928

Dear Louis:

Come out on Friday, between five and six. If you come a little early you avoid the commuter crowd. Take a bus either at 36th St. and 6th Ave. beside the old Herald Building or <one> behind the Hotel Astor. Take a Passaic-Paterson bus stopping at Rutherford. I live only two or three blocks from the station. Ask anyone.

Glad you liked Spring and All. I have renegged on inviting Cummings: when I said what I did I did not know he wa a popular playwright.

Drop me a line.

    Williams

Spring and All: In "Sincerity and Objectification I–III," Zukofsky called *Spring and All* "a work most indigenously of these States . . . beginning perhaps a century of writing, as Wordsworth's preface began it in 1800 in England," (*Poetry* 37 [1931]: 279). *Prepositions* +, 198.

7. TLS-1

[Rutherford, N.J.]

April 27, 1928

Dear Louis:

Your Cummings is good, brief criticism. The Dial would have done well to print it. Is that your own, about philosophy, the "dreampistol"? Wonderful if it is, and fine anyway. I hope it's yours.

The poems are nowhere up to the poem "The". I like a line here and there but they do not get going. But I'll read them again.

I'm driven with work as usual – rather unexpectedly at this season however – Just now I have the novel again in my hands going over it finally before it will be sent to the printer. I am just dolling it up, pulling out unneeded words, phrases, paragraphs, etc.

Williams

Your Cummings: Zukofsky's essay, "*Him.*" *Prepositions* +, 84–85. Williams refers to this
    sentence, "His is not (or at least very rarely and then unfortunately) the dreampistol
    of philosophy which goes off bang—into flowers and candy."
the poems: Probably "18 Poems to the Future," a collection of short poems later incorpo-
    rated into *55 Poems* (1941).
the novel: *A Voyage to Pagany* (New York: Macaulay, 1928). Wallace A10.

8. TL-1

[Rutherford, N.J.]

[12 May 1928]

Dear Louis:

Come Sunday at noon. Tell me if it is impossible. Nathan Asche and his wife may be here. Do you want to bring your girl? Do so if you care to. I'll get Lucy to make some kind of a lunch for us.

And don't neglect to bring back my loose scripts. It makes me ill not to have them under my hand. I don't care about the novel, keep that as long as you like.

I must confess that I wrote to Cummings inviting him to spend a day with me. He came, a week ago. I told him no one else would be here. It's just as well. I left him alone most of the time: a real New Englander, not I but he.

Saw Strange Interlude last night. Someone gave me a ticket. It's a fine play. My delight that O'Neil has risen to his pr[e]sent eminence because of his faults which saved him from a commercial production is not the least of my thrills. He is so god damned rotten that he is good. He is so biassed, deformed, ampu-tated that he has been able to drive his thin rigid point through the crust of – no that covers feeling. It is because of his faults that he has got on. The sons of bitches that run theatres and publishing houses should have their balls cut out and chopped up for salami. But I never realized the functions of our faults so clearly before as I did last night watching O'Neil cavorting about (in imagina-tion) there on the stage, unable to handel a situation, unable to write dialogue, unable to delineate character or to do anything surely – as surely as a Sat. Ev. Post writer – but by Jesus – doing it anyway by virtue of his colossal faults. It is great.

And he knows (or must know) the value of his distortions, the things that save him from realism. I wonder if he does? He will someday if he doesn't now. It is a frank convention, how work, as much so as the opera or OEdipus Rex. Abnormal people become normal on the stage. They must wear figurative masks. They must be deformed to show normality. Normal people on the stage are sick. It would be the way to show sickness. The great theoretical fuckable American Girl on the stage all stripped and powdered is so grotesquely sick that no one can see it.

Shit

I must go
Williams

Asche: Nathan Asch (1902–1964), Polish-born American novelist.
Strange Interlude: Eugene O'Neill's play opened in New York on 30 January 1928.

9. TLS-1

Rutherford, N.J.

[12 May 1928]
Dear Louis:

Did I mail you the right letter or did I put my wife's letter into your envelope? I had a queer feeling after the things had dropped into the box.

In case she is to get what was intended for you, may I repeat that I'd like to see you out here Sunday for lunch. The Nathan Asche's will probably be on hand. etc. I'll tell you the rest later.

Perhaps it's just a dream of mine that things went wrong.

Yours
Williams

You know I may have sent the other letterto 111 E. 57th St. I'm crazy

10. TLS-1

[Rutherford, N.J.]

May 17, 1928
Dear Louis:

I have marked among your poems which I like. I cannot do more. I think you have gone past these things, the images seem clouded with words, the authenticity of the feeling struggles with the expression, the inversions check my pleasure. And yet, even when the rhythm is completely choked up with words, I do find something good. Yet I'm sure you have left all this behind.

Hell, it makes me feel rotten.

What you had to say about the novel did me much good. I felt that you had hit on some very raw spots. Oh well, I can't quite bring myself to throw the thing away though I wanted to do so after you had left.

I've not yet had time to read the Henry Adams.

There's mother calling me to supper.

So long. I'm anxious to see what you're doing now.

And your suggestions conerning the novel have been invaluable. More another time. See you in the city some day soon.

> Yours
>
> Bill

the novel: *A Voyage to Pagany*.

the Henry Adams: Zukofsky's essay, "Henry Adams: A Criticism in Autobiography"
   (*Prepositions +*, 86–130).

11. ALS-2

[Rutherford, N.J.]

Friday [Zukofsky's notation: "May 28/28"]

Dear Louis

's all typed, finished at 11:30 last night.

See you in the city at your own place (telephone) next week. I'll write again.

Before that I'll send <you> stuff to forward to lb.

> Bill

Cheer up, you're good. Can't say that about many.

's all typed: Probably *The Descent of Winter*.

12. ALS-1 [fragment]

[Rutherford, N.J.]

[Zukofsky's notation: "May 31/28"]

The 2nd line about the Street organ

Shams

not Shame

Next Sunday afternoon I'd like to run up to your place.

> Bill

Street organ: Williams refers to an entry in "The Descent of Winter," dated 10/29 and beginning, "The justice of poverty" (*CP1*, 300–01).

[Rutherford, N.J.]

Sunday [25 June 1928]

Dear Louis:

I knew something must have been wrong. I am really very sorry to hear that your sister has been ill and hope that she may recover – or may have recovered – completely.

The 1st of July is no good for a visit. I'm going to drive my Ma up to the shore. The Fourth seems to be my first free day. Come then if you care to, glad to see you.

The page proofs of my novel-novel have been returned to the printer. I suppose it will cost me a small fortune but I went to it and slashed away at the thing in whole hearted style. In the main I think the work has been much improved – thanks to your suggestions and those of two others, my stenog and a good scout of a woman who used to teach English in Hight School. Also I myself did some tidying up here and there. On the whole, yes, just that, the book looks about as presentable as I can make it. I cut out a lot about the Rhine! which should give you a special pleasure.

Must quit now. I have to go out and make a bouquet (an old fashioned one – all squeezed up in rings of colors) to present to a couple who are having a house warming tonight. God knows it's hot enough already.

Family home in three weeks! I'll be glad.

 So-long

 Bill

Contact – inspired you – good.

your sister: Fanny Zukofsky Wand (d. 1972).

[Rutherford, N.J.]

July 5/28

Dear Louis:

A most enjoyable argument – rare as snakes feathers. Most talk and argument is crap, foot-ball.

Here are a few notes I jotted down this a.m. – sorry they are not favorable comments – but I think I see you more clearly than formerly and in so doing there is a better light upon your verse. I have been looking for the wrong things. Evenso I do not find the scripts I had worthy of you.

 Bill

Poems are inventions richer in thought as image. Your early poems even when the thought has force or freshness have not been objectified in new or fresh observations. But if it is the music even that is not inventive enough to make up for images which give an overwhelming effect of triteness – as it has been said. The language is stilted "poetic" except in the one piece I marked.

Eyes have always stood first in the poet's equipment. If you are mostly ear – a newer rhythm must come in more strongly than has been the case so far.

Yet I am willing to grant – to listen.

Bill

15. TLS-2

[Rutherford, N.J.]

July 12 [1928]

Dear Louis:

I enclose a letter from Pound. If you can find it convenient to see the people he speaks of, do so; it is hopeless for me to attempt it. As to the reading of proof, however, I stand ready to do my part at any time. Read the letter, tell me what you think of it and return it, if you please.

If you care to bring the letter with you and come out this Sunday afternoon, I will be here practically alone all day. Not that I can promise any conversation as interesting as our last, this time – or should I say not that I expect any – but we'll just sit around, if you care to.

Monday morning my family should arrive; they will arrive, that is sometime on Monday, probably in the morning. I want you to meet them all a little later.

I finished the "Henry Adams" yesterday before breakfast. It interested me greatly both as an introduction to the life of an American of extra-ordinary significance to my way of thinking – which is not putting it half firmly enough – and as the work of another American – Oh hell, my mind is thick this morning: I enjoyed your work. All through the reading I came upon lines of real distinction – without attempting to analyse them just now. To me your thesis shows a worthwhile subtlty of style indicative of a mind of fine grain and selective power of thought which is unusual – Christ! what in hell am I saying. And it is true besides. Anyhow I liked your work. It impressed me. You seemed to hold the damned subject up from the table as a whole with clean hands. That's the gist of your power to me. I don't feel any shit – smell, would be better. You have power that is real, penetrant and (so far) flexible enough not to crack irritably the way the thing usually does in the people I have to do with most often.

Anyhow I read the thesis.

Drop me a line.

    Yours

    Bill

a letter: Enclosure lacking. Letter not located.

16. TLS-1

[Rutherford, N.J.]

July 22, 1928

Dear Louis:

I'm teaing with I.M.P. of the Herald-Tribune Book Section on Tuesday this week. After that, if you're around, we might get together somewhere. God know where one meets in N.Y., a stupid place. Let's start a sidewalk cafe. Is ti the dirt or the weather or what that would make it a failure?

Isn't there some place at which I could call you up when I am through with the lady?

Marianne is willing but she suffers from the terrific weight of indifference under which all labor in these here United States just as we do. I am glad she has accepted your poems. All the good that comes from such a success is, however, the cash you will pocket. The Dial to me is about as dead as a last years birds nest. One must believe in spiders -

I have heard again from Ezrie, he speaks of the proffs of my stuff, etc. which Covici is supposed to have ready for us in a short time. Do you know anything of this?

Last week's heat laid me low. In another eight days I'll be off for a rest. But for the moment the art of writing seems very hypothetical in importance and probablility of existence, but it is only a momentary decline; still I cannot believe in the prose style of – the rest of them.

    Yours

    Bill

I.M.P.: Isabel Paterson (1885–1961), novelist and critic. In her literary column she wrote, "We met William Carlos Williams this week, too . . . He is the author of 'Voyage to Pagany,' which will be published soon . . . He has an immense enthusiasm for the critical acumen of Ezra Pound, and the musical genius of George Antheil . . . You may remember that Antheil is the composer of the 'Ballet Mecanique,' scored for sixteen electric pianos and other deadly instruments to suit . . . A steam riveter, probably . . . As we did not hear the Ballet when it was produced over here, we have no right to an opinion about it; and Mr. Williams has . . . He says it soothes him . . . " "Turns With a

Bookworm," *New York Herald Tribune*, 5 August 1928, XII, 16. On 11 August 1928, Williams wrote Pound about the interview (*EP/WCW*, 92–93).

Marianne: Marianne Moore

your poems: Four poems: "tam cari capitis"; "Song theme to the last movement of Beethoven's Quartet in C-sharp minor"; "Some one said, 'earth'"; "The silence of the good," the *Dial* 85:12 (December 1928), 458–459. The first two poems are in *CSP*, 33–34.

Ezrie: Letter not located. The "proffs" would be proofs of *The Descent of Winter*, published in the *Exile*, no. 4.

Covici: Pascal Covici (1888–1964), American publisher and editor. He had taken over responsibility for publishing the *Exile*.

17. TLS-1

[Rutherford, N.J.]

July 25 [1928]

Dear Louis:

Certainly the "Lenin" outdistances anything in the earlier book of poems as the effect of a "thing" surpasses ~~the thought of it~~ all thought about it. It is the second poem of yours that I like, the first being the long one. In some ways this poem is your best work (that I have seen). It has a surging rhythm that in itself embodies all that it is necessary to say but it carries the words nevertheless and the theme helplessly with it. The word "continual" at the end in fine.

It is this, the thing that this poem is, that makes you what you are today – I hope you're satisfied! No doubt it is the underlying th me of whatever feeling we have for each other – It seems to me surely the contra-bass for everything else we may do. If there is not that under our feel (though I realize that you are speaking of a star) then we cannot go on elaborating our stuff.

Sometimes though I don't like your language. It probably is I and not you who should be blamed for this. You are wresting with the antagonist under newer rules. But I can't see "all live processes" "orbit-trembling" "our consciousness" "the sources of being" – What the hell? I'm not finding fault I'm just trying to nail what troubles me. It may be that I am to literal in my search for objective clarities of image. It may be that you are completely right in forcing abstract conceptions into the sound pattern. I dunno. Anyhow, there you are.

I will say that in this case the abstract, philosophic-jargonish language is not an obstruction. It may be that when the force of the conception is sufficiently strong it can carry this sort of thing. If the force were weaker the whole poem would fall apart. Good perhaps. Perhaps by my picayune imagistic mannerisms I hold together superficially what should by all means fall apart.

Good for you, nevertheless. It's a good poem. I congratulate you.

>   Yours,
>   Bill

"Lenin": Zukofsky's poem, "Memory of V. I. Ulianov" (*CSP*, 21–22).

18. TLS-1

[Monroe, New York]

August 22, 1928

Dear Zukofsky:

I won't change that to "Louis" – too much labor, by which you may see that my vacation is agreeing with me.

How is your job holding out? I'm sorry for you in there in the city roasting to death. Yet it's heat that hatches the eggs, maybe you're getting your new poem into shape. We found four turtle eggs on a small island in a lake yesterday, the first I had ever seen.

My typewriter has not been idel. (again I refuse to correct) Just this morning I succeeded in elucidating a certain passage of thought in the opening chapter of my new book on the Humanization of Knowledge. I'm am determined to go through with it before next April and to submit it in the Forum contest.

For the most part, however, I have done very little during the past few weeks but to eat, sleep, visit friends here and there and receive letters. Today it is raing hard. Yesterday I swam with my boys and a little girl across a lake to the island mentioned above, about a quarter of a mile.

Any news from Covici, Pound's last letter seemed anything but encouraging? Drop me a line, I'll be glad to hear from you.

>   Yours
>   Bill

your job: Unidentified.

my new book: *The Embodiment of Knowledge* (New York: New Directions, 1974).

Forum contest: Williams hoped to win the Francis Bacon Award sponsored by *Forum Magazine.*

19. TLS-1

August 30, 1928

Dear Louis:

Congratulations on having finished the job!

Yes, I received the Mt. Saint Michel but have not read it; also the other books which I have read. Many thanks.

To hell with Pound'd collective schemes. In that mood he gives me a pain in the ass. Let him come over here and do some grubbing before he starts that with me. I could go on for three pages giving historic reasons. It is too much of a bore.

I've done two more poems – three in all which I have sent to Marianne.

I count on seeing the beginning of the Poem beginning "A". It is the logical completion of your original idea and you alone should do it.

As soon as I am settled at home I'll write again. Be sure to wear your new suit when you come.

Best luck
    Yours
        Bill

Mt. Saint Michel: Henry Adams's *Mont Saint Michel and Chartres* (1904, 1913).

collective schemes: On 12 August Pound had written to Zukofsky that he should "form some sort of gang" to influence publishers (*EP/LZ*, 11–15).

more poems: "On Gay Wallpaper," "The Lily" and "The Source," the *Dial* 85:5 (November 1928), 391–94. Wallace C124. *CP1*, 285; 286; 286–88.

20. TLS-1

Wednesday [Zukofsky's notation: "Oct 4/28"]

Dear Louis:

Coming home from my vacation I fell into a flurry of work which has not let up until today. At last I am able to look around and orient myself a little. Where in hell are you, where have you been and what have you been doing? For myself I've been flat.

However I have followed my plan to compete with the rest of the intellectual lights of the world for the Francis Bacon Award. Just today I have received the prospectus. Now the chapters must be forced into a gallop. I am counting on you to help me later on.

That aside, I have done nothing but chase the devil around a bush according to the habits of my profession. But only yesterday Floss said, What about your friend Zukofsky?

I don't know how you feel or how you're fixed but I'd like to see you some-time next week. I have nothing to show and damned little to say but it would be fun to get together for an hour or so. Maybe you could arrange to come out to supper. I'll name a date later. Would next Tuesday be convenient?

Morley Callaghan has been in the city recently. He's a nice guy to talk to. I've just finished reading his Strange Fugitive. I understand Pound is doing me for The Dial. There isn't a word to say about my book. The reviews seem timorous but respectful. Anyhow the wild radicals, i.e. myself, are drawing attention. Lord, Lord, give me time!

Best luck. Drop me a line telling me what you're at.

Yours
Bill

P.S. What in hell does Pound mean when he says Covici isn't going to print us for a year? Does that refer to Exile? That's a hell of a note.

Did you see Rebecca West on Joyce in The Bookman? Somehow it made me mad all through. I have written asking them if I may answer her. More later.

W.

Francis Bacon Award: Sponsored by *Forum Magazine.*

Callaghan: (1903–90), Canadian novelist whose first novel, *Strange Fugitive*, was pub-lished in 1928.

Pound is doing me: Pound's essay, "Dr. Williams' Position," appeared in the November 1928 issue of the *Dial.*

reviews: Four reviews of *A Voyage to Pagany* are reprinted in Charles Doyle, ed., *William Carlos Williams: The Critical Heritage* (London, Boston and Henley: Routledge and Kegan Paul, 1980).

Pound mean: Williams seems to refer to a letter from Pound to Zukofsky that I have not been able to locate.

West on Joyce: "The Strange Case of James Joyce," *Bookman* (London) 68 (Sept. 1928), 9–23. The essay was reprinted in West's *The Strange Necessity* (London: Jonathan Cape, 1928).

21. TLS-1

Rutherford, N.J.

October 10 [1928]

Dear Louis:

I'm damned sorry I had to leave in that way. It was a pity to make you take the long trip here and back for that. Why the devil didn't you come to supper at least?

Of course, what the hell? Such things just are. Your criticism is valuable to me, as soon as I shall have had it typed I'll send you a copy with whatever comment I have to make at the time. At present it seems to promise more value to me in almost a private way than it can hold for any outsider. It seems too specially selective in its view of my work to be suitable for even The Dial's pages. Who knows? Let Marianne decide.

Damn it though I'm real sorry we had to be rushed that way. I wanted to see the beginning of your new poem, though you may not have brought it with you.

At a more favourable opportunity I'll come at you again, we'll have supper together somewhere in N.Y. á la Pound. Anyhow we did get together. I'll write again soon. If there's anything interesting to hand I'll ship it forward. Do the same. Yours

> Bill

your criticism: Probably Zukofsky's essay, "Beginning Again with William Carlos

Williams," *Hound and Horn* (Winter 1931), 261–64. Reprinted with revisions as part of

"William Carlos Williams" (*Prepositions* +, 45–53).

new poem: Probably "A."

22. TLS-1

[Rutherford, N.J.]

[Zukofsky's notation: "Oct17/28"]

Dear Louis:

What a swell idea you have hit on with which to open your poem. I was thrilled at once. Why is it you have unerringly struck a major note in your two longer poems whereas I find nothing of it in the earlier shorter things? I dunno. Pound says I'm wrong – to some extent at least, to the extent that your earlier work is better than most of the truck Harriet prints in Poetry.

Anyway, I was thrilled by your beginning – and from that moment to this I have been nearly torn apart by the exigencies of my practice. No use going into detail. As soon as I shall find a moment to do it in I'll read what you have written carefully and write again.

Everything pertaining to writing has gone by the board in the rush.

One thing you may be amused in doing, I dunno. I received a letter from a little Jew corner-stand-news vendor one Zacharia whom I knew in Rutherford years ago as a news-boy – I received the letter today – you may care to look him up at his stand, 116th St. and 7th. Ave. I gave him one of my books, Al Que Quiere. He works half a day and reads good books the other half. Tell him you are my friend and that you'll pinch hit for him when he has the grippe. Now don't tell me I never gave you a tip! Anyhow you may just like to stop by and talk with him whether or not you wish to mention me or not. It's strange for him to have remembered my name. Some day I'll go up there with you and talk to the guy.

Ain't the weather oppressive.

    Yours

    Bill

Vote for Al Smith!

your poem: "A" 1–2.

Harriet: Harriet Monroe, editor of *Poetry*.

Zacharia: Zachy Zacharia (1890–1976), whose poems appeared in two New York Yiddish newspapers, the *Freiheit* and the *Tog*. See Don Zacharia, "My Legacy," *Kenyon Review* 7:1 (Winter 1985), 97–110.

Al Smith: Alfred E. Smith (1873–1944), the Democratic nominee for president in 1928.

23. TLS-1

                                                       [Rutherford, N.J.]

Oct. 18 [1928]

Dear Louis:

Fine! though I don't as yet know what it is all about any more than I do of some of Pound's best things – or my own, for that matter. It is, however, fully up to your best work. In places it leaps up as alive as anything on the earth. It is impossible for me to go into detail now. Nor do I wish to give the impression that I am satisfied to take the meaning for granted any more than I am with Pound's work or my own. I find invariably however that when the instnct has clicked the mind will come lumbering after.

The thing is that when you are at your best there is a beauty all over the work that comes out of the words as an emanation comes out of a woman to us at times. I find you the very opposite, let us say, to Isidore Schneider who remains so much cold fish to me. Maybe it's this maybe it's that. What the hell. I am an ignorant man in these things. Maybe it's your use of grammar. Maybe Rebecca West could nail it in a phrase (Maybe not also) God knows whether it has anything to do with the past or the future but somehow (and I am not in the least satisfied in saying it) you have made the thing happen for me.

That's a hell of a lot of help to you. Someday though after my fashiuon I'll dig out a few seeds – in time. I know now however that the search will be fruitful so that's that. There ain't so much work that has more than a dead smell to it. You know how one smells it! It's why a faint touch of musk (which is quite foul when strong) pleases the ladies.

Some women are delicious to smell, like buckwheat and some – reek! Jesus! I can hardly sit in the office with them. Though I imagine some men will be attracted by that which repells me. It is acid, fulminous. And should they get hot, hot that is where it counts. Boy! I look toward the wall for the chemical fire extinguisher. But when a sweet one comes in my virtue exists like a small flower on a loose piece of earth above a precipice. And isn't it a fine day.

Yours

Bill

Just received (£5.5s od) Pounds second book of Cantos. When you want to see it speak up. Yrs.

what it is all about: *"A"* 1–2.

Schneider: (b. 1896) American proletarian poet and novelist. Boni and Liveright published his *The Temptation of Anthony and Other Poems* in 1928.

second book: *A Draft of the Cantos: 17–27* (London: John Rodker, 1928).

24. ALS-2

[57 East 111th Street, New York]

Oct 22–28

Monday 1 A.M. and

Dear Bill!

I've just come home from there – The Cameo Theatre, 42nd St. btwn 6th Av. & Bway – South side of 42nd very important! And seen, I've seen the Amkino presentations – A Shanghai Document and 3 Comrades and 1 Invention. I'm drunk, How shall I say it? Two movies together making our St. Matthew Passion – our Passion – <of today I mean> the movies became, well, became, just became <Art!> You wouldn't believe it. I'm crazy. But I'm not crazy. If I could run these films in your house, if I could run them for all the Williamses, if I could take them to Ezrie in Rapallo, if I could show them before Antheil! We've had intimations of this, but really we just didn't know. Hard to think I might I have missed this just as blindly as I dropped in on it.

Your praise of the first two movements of "A" meant O so much to me, but now I almost feel I didn't deserve it. Almost – because I now see I didn't know what I was at, tho I thought I knew. I now see that I don't know what I'm at, but after this evening with Amkino, I can't help but know that I will know what I am at. You get me. I'm just nuts. I mean I couldn't flunk an examination at college if only I read the table of contents of the books. There's a cretin for you.

I mean for God's sake don't miss these Amkino films. Seeing them you'll forget Al Smith and vote for yourself, and Spring and All especially Song No XV (it took this night to see what you were getting at <was a song>) and the fact that you're alive. And maybe you'll care to see me after that, and maybe

19

you won't – but for your own sake take a few hours off and run into New York and straight to the <u>Cameo</u>, some time <u>this</u> week. Americans, we just don't know – but we gotta

> Yours and again yours
> Louis.

Amkino presentations: The Amkino Corporation, based in New York, distributed Soviet films in North and South America.

Shanghai Document: A 1928 documentary directed by Yakov Blyokh. It showed the daily life of ordinary Chinese workers in Shanghai, but also focused on the idle pastimes of resident Westerners.

Three Comrades: A 1928 comedy directed by Alexei Popov (1892–1961). It followed the attempts of three factory workers to successfully demonstrate their box making machine.

Antheil: George Antheil (1900–1959), American composer. Zukofsky attended performances of Antheil's works in New York. Zukofsky's poem, "Critique of Antheil," appeared in the fourth issue of the *Exile*. It is not collected in *CSP*.

Song No XV: Later titled by Williams, "Light Becomes Darkness." *CP1*, 213–14.

25. TLS-1

> 9 Ridge Road
> Rutherford, N.J

Oct. 26/28.

Dear Louis:

Good luck to you. In Hartford look up Wallace Stevens of whom you have heard. He is a friend. You will find him at his office in the Hartford Accident and Indemnity Corporation Building. Do not fail to go to him at the earliest possible moment as he may be of assistance as a reference. Tell him you are my friend.

I will type the review of my book this week. I like it but I find it too special in appeal. It should not be lost however as it links up the thing I am doing with its proper historical background. The only thing is, who in hell cares about that but myself – and you. I'll type it out and send it to the Yale Review!

I shall have to miss the pictures. I'm sorry. I intended to go this afternoon but someone gave me two tickets to The Front Page for tonight and I cannot go to both places the same day.

Best luck in Hartford. I hope you land the job.

> Yours
> Bill

Hartford: In "For Wallace Stevens," Zukofsky discusses his trip to Hartford, his failure to get a job with the Hartford Accident and Indemnity Company, and his discovery that Stevens was away. See *Prepositions +*, 31.

the review: "Beginning Again with William Carlos Williams."

The Front Page: This play by Ben Hecht and Charles MacArthur opened in New York on
14 August 1928.

26. ALS-1

9 Ridge Road
Rutherford, N.J.

Friday [Zukofsky's notation: "28 Oct/28"]

Dear Louis,

Its all logical enough, what Ezra writes, but I refuse to be this good. Let him
come over here and risk his hide. That alone can put such a scheme across.

I've been drowned in work, an epidemic of childish shits.

Come over any time. I mean it. If I'm out I'll return. Glad to see you

Bill

Ezra writes: Pound had urged Zukofsky to launch a cooperative publishing venture.

27. ALS-2

[57 East 111th Street, New York]

Nov 2/28

Dear Bill –

If nothing of moment results, then maybe a few minor poems.

The first three were written on the train (up and back), the last three on the
Staten Id. Ferry. Will minor poems become a matter of swift sketching with me?
I don't know, but I'm scared to write them these days. I copy them out for you.

No news, as yet, from Hartford.

Ezra writes that Cov. is bringing <out> No 4 this month. For the rest the
Exile is suspended; "in case of absoloot woik of cheenius that no one will
touch, I can always issue a special number in france austria or elsewhere, even
in Italy."

Haia! wake the flute and the drum!

The Prophet, the Prophet is come!

'Eel tellum! But he's the kindest prophet who ever lived!

Louis

P.S. I also saw Zacharia – and again I'm grateful to you (Is there or isn't there
something wrong here about the grammar. It sure is as you say my use of
grammar!) Enough. But think of it the Jews read us religiously – I mean you.
And you've been not traduced but translated – as something is just translated
on a level or even to heaven – you, and Ezra, and Cummings, and Eliot, and
Wallace Stevens, and Mina Loy (all these names don't mean the same thing to

me of course but I'm trying to outline the effort for you). And the fellow who did it – one Licht – asked me to ask you to forgive him for not asking your permission! If a half dozen read his work and understand it as Yiddish I'll be – but it is Yiddish and literature too!

Sure I want <to see> the Sec. Book of Pound's Cantos, but don't you trouble, I'll take them <home> myself when I come to Rutherford again. Let me hear from you soon.

Louis

minor poems: Enclosures lacking.

Ezra writes: In a letter to Zukofsky of 21 October 1928 (Texas).

Licht: Michel Licht (1893–1953), who published a book of Yiddish translations of contemporary American poetry in New York in 1932.

Sec. Book: *A Draft of the Cantos: 17–27* (London: John Rodker, 1928).

28. ALS-1

657 Main Avenue
Passaic, N.J.

Nov. 21/28

Dear Louis:

You guessed it. I've been harassed (spelling?) to the point of hari kari recently by – the things. No time for anything.

If, when, as soon as – we can see Macaulay I'll do my part – but I am hopeless of fruits.

Yours
Bill

Macaulay: The publisher of *A Voyage to Pagany*. In a letter of 3 November 1928 (Texas), Pound had suggested to Zukofsky that he approach this publisher and propose that it publish inexpensive editions of works by Williams, McAlmon, Zukofsky, Marianne Moore, and others.

29. TLS-1

[Rutherford, N.J.]

Sunday [2? Dec. 1928]

Dear Louis:

No use talking, time grows scarcer as the days grow shorter. I undertake too much. It is perhaps a sort of mania not to be idle. The result is that my free afternoons and evenings have disappeared entirely. Now I have begun a translation of a novel by Phillipe Soupault. My first thought was to give mother an occupation. I planned to speak of this to no one but to go about the task in a leisurely way without thought of having the work published – unless it should just happen. But Jospehson found me out, through his wife so that now I am bound to finish the work in time for fall publication, 1929. Crazy, crazy.

The Humnaization of Knowledge will have to go on also. What else will be doing I cannot say. Practice will probably drive me wild. I promised Hart Crane two months ago to let him know when I should be free to see him. Why all this blather?

I want to use your short thesis on my book. I do like the things you say there, it is important to me. I have not touched it. It would make an excellent foreword to a second volume of In The Am; Grain – if ever written.

In the appreciation which I have written for The Dial and which will appear in January – notice the last paragraph. I squeezed it in in order to make a talking point for you or any of us in our attempt to put over Ezra's program. It is not much but it can be referred to. I believe Matthew Josephson who seems to be connected in some way with Macaulay & Co would be the proper person to approach when we are ready.

The Rebecca West article took too much out of me for nothing for me to go on with it properly. Either I should have worked it out minutely over fifty pages, taking three months to complete it or – She did not seem worth killing. Anyhow I grew bored. I almost threw the thing away. I got into a nervous fit over not having time to play with the points and arrange them. When Sylvia Beach wrote that she was bringing her brochure out on Joyce I offered what I had. She cabled acceptance. I slammed my random shots together and – so it always seems to go. More mania.

Heaven knows you must have lost faith in my honesty or something of the sort by this time. I hope not.

The New School banquet? Forget it. Bad enough to have to talk in private. Nothing annoys me more. In public we usually act like fools. I just get excited, rave over nothing that means a thing to me and end by disgusting myself and my intimates. You're right to keep away. God, what I really need is a little quiet. Come out and sit around when you care to. If you'll get here late, say 8.30 any fine evening I'll drive you back to 42nd. St. around mid-night.

> Yrs
> Bill

What about the final <u>Exile</u>?

a translation: *Last Nights of Paris*, by Philippe Soupault, translated by William Carlos
  Williams: New York: The Macaulay Company, 1929. Wallace A11.
Jospehson: Matthew Josephson (1899–1978), American biographer and historian. Josephson was an editor at Macaulay.

your short thesis: "Beginning Again with William Carlos Williams."

In The Am; Grain: Williams's *In the American Grain* (New York: Albert and Charles Boni, 1925). Wallace A9.

the appreciation: Williams's essay, "Kenneth Burke," appeared in the January 1929 issue of the *Dial*. His comment about the "last paragraph," however, suggests that he has in mind his essay, "A Point for American Criticism," (*SE*, 80–90).

West article: Williams's response to West's "The Strange Case of James Joyce."

Sylvia Beach: American bookseller and publisher in Paris (1887–1962). Williams contributed "A Point for American Criticism" to her publication on Joyce, *Our Exagmination round his Factification for Incamination of Work in Progress* (Paris: Shakespeare and Company, 1929). Wallace B11.

New School banquet: Zukofsky wrote to Pound on 19 November 1928 that the New School for Social Research would be "running a Dinner for young writers" on 8 December.

final Exile: The fourth and final number of the *Exile* had already appeared in October.

30. TLS-1

9 Ridge Road
Rutherford, N.J

[December 1928]

Dear Louis:

There is hope! A brand <new>, gritty clean magazine is about to see the light of day in Mississippi. I am to be a contributing editor. An outlet at last. I want your poem beginning "A" for it if The Dial isn't large enough. They are to pay (I think) well. I'll let you know more when I know more but it sounds hopeful – as I have said. It is to be called BLUES: An anthology of American writing. I want to guard myself concerning the pay part of it, however, since I am not too certain about that though it looks good.

I refuse to return the review of my book. I will though of course in a few days. Not yet.

Yes, meet me after the banquet of worms – or, as you say, caterpillars. I hope I'll not disgrace you there. I don't know when the thing will end – or begin either for that matter.

Yours
Bill

BLUES: Edited by Charles Henri Ford from February 1929 until the fall of 1930.

the review: "Beginning Again with William Carlos Williams."

9 Ridge Road
Rutherford N.J.

Dec 20/28

Dear Louis:

Your poems received – and I'm trying hard to get inside. Of them all, so far I like the last two of the small group and – <u>not</u> the beginning of "A" – but later where it gets swinging.

"Commerce will not complete anything"

But, nothing I see here comes up to "The". Is it I or you who is muddled? I cannot <u>see</u> at all. or I see only spots that are you as I know you. Otherwise I am batting around in the air knocking against things that bewilder me.

Why "thousand" in the first line. It seems loose, unconnected, not a necessary number?

Too much stage setting on 1st page.

Why repeat "black, black"?

The images on this first page come too fast, they joggle and nothing is distinctively set set down save "white matronly flounces"

Something simpler more subdued, or disciplined more "Bach" must come out of that first page.

and the second. (to the middle)

From the middle of page 2 it begins to move though how related to the beginning and to Bach is not clear.

"The immature pants that filled chairs" – does not, in kind, appear often enough.

———

Part I p. 9 to 10 splendid. but where you turn to Bach again what I'd do is throw out the whole concept of the poem as a theme and put the patches of "poetry" here and there together. I think you're trying to imitate your success with "The" – and you are thus merely imitating.

When you forget all about your damned theme you justify yourself.

Basta for tonight

yours
Williams

3.

Florence likes your small pomes – God knows why. She likes "guys" – says it's no worse than a lot of my own "triumphs"

Am reading 'em over in a careless, unstudying mood maybe they are "honest" as writing which so many pleasant fol de rol aint? "If you get what I mean"

<u>W</u>

poems received: Williams cites passages ("Commerce will not complete anything") from
   song 4 of "29 Poems" (*CSP*, 23–24) and from the first Movement of *"A."*
"guys": Unidentified.

■ 42. TLS-2

[Rutherford, N.J.]

Jan. 4, 1928 [1929]
Dear Louis:

Listen! your stuff in Exile 4 has again about it the something I like. What in hell is the matter with me? I can't for the life of me see anything in much of the stuff you send me. Then unexpectedly I am convinced that you are exceptional, about as good as there is, and that first rate.

Is it that I must have the authority of the printed page and Pound's stamp upon your work before I am convinced? I can't quite believe that myself.

I like the Cumming's thing much more now that I see it printed than I liked it typewritten. Have you worked on it since I saw it? Or is this exactly what I had before me. I am really curious.

Well do I know that the best work is very hard indeed to see, by which I mean really to see. It is new and simple and offers no explanation of itself. Ones eyes have to grow accustomed to it, have to be built up to it slowly or they will see nothing at all. Eyes themselves never see anything but what they are used to, anybody's eyes, but mine especially. First I sense a thing blindly, later I see it – if ever.

And I like Preface – 1927. You do know English, something of which I was not thoroughly convinced in the new Bach bit. I like your constructions, they have a convincing ring of thought thought to a purpose. "To escape it would be laughable".

Now I want to get out your criticism of myself.

What I propose is that we bring out Exile V (Spring 1929) at my expense. I want you to see Covici Friede at once. Get a line on what it would cost. Don't mention me quite yet but say you have a friend who is interested. If possible say we would guarantee any deficit. Ask them what the deficit on the present iss ue would be or is.

In that issue we could put your first part of the Bach – revised! and your thing on me. I have several things I could use and we could dig up – this man Gould in N.Y. Cummings if we can get him – Pound would be glad to send us something.

Go to it. I won't say how much I'll be good for but I like Exile. It is really something and I'd like to see your new stuff printed. Damn it I'd like very much to see it printed.

I'm going to carry out my threat of last year, I'm going to invite Cummings out here, I'm going to mention you and Exile and put it up to him squarely (relatively) to come and meet you or – do as he pleases.

>Best luck
>Bill

your stuff: "Mr. Cummings and the Delectable Mountains" (later retitled "Him"), "Preface—1927," "Critique of Antheil," "Constellation," and "A Preface."

Bach bit: "A"-1.

Gould: Joseph Ferdinand Gould (1889-1957). Legendary Greenwich Village Bohemian. A portion of his "Oral History of the World" was published in the *Exile*, no. 2. See Joseph Mitchell's memoir, *Joe Gould's Secret* (1965).

43. TLS-1

>9 Ridge Road
>Rutherford, N.J.

January 25, 1929

Dear Louis:

While tearing around tending the sick I've composed a Novelette in praise of my wife whom I have gotten to know again because of being thrown violently into her arms and she into mine by the recent epidemic – though not by the illness of either of us, quite the contrary. Anyhow I'm giving the thing – just fifty pages that I scribbled at night after hours in order to relax my faculties before sleep – to The Caravan. It is as it is.

My proposal was to pay for one more Exile, or rather to be responsible for any deficit – in order to have your new thing in it, etc. But if Covici is off the whole thing so am I.

Eke the Philadelphia proposal. It will be, as you say, just another place for us to fire at. Like Blues.

Life is growing less violently tremulous again – just beginning to quiet down – a little – today. Cummings did not answer my letter. I heard from McAlmon that T.S.Eliot has turned definitely to Anglo-Catholicism of late. Djuna Barnes is in N.Y. Perhaps I'll have a chance tosee her before she returns to Paris.

Must go out and deliver a new truck driver now.

>Yours
>Bill

Novelette: Published in *A Novelette and Other Prose (1921-1931)* (Toulon, France; To Publishers, 1932).

The Caravan: *The American Caravan,* an annual of contemporary writing. Williams had appeared in both the first and the second in the series. Wallace B9 and B10.

Philadelphia proposal: Zukofsky wrote to Pound on 28 Jan. 1929, "a printer, name Kay of
   Philadelphia, will sponsor a quarterly to be called The States and sponsor it for at least
   an annual run (Yale)."
McAlmon: Robert McAlmon (1896–1956), American writer and publisher. He and
   Williams founded the little magazine *Contact*. McAlmon's Contact Publishing Com-
   pany published *Spring and All* in 1923.
Barnes: Djuna Barnes (1892–1982), American novelist.

44. TLS-1

9 Ridge Road
February 3/29 Rutherford, N.J.
Dear Louis:

Put the enclosed over on your brother editors if you can. The style is called
"slippers in the mud". Good luck to you.

As soon as I get up from this seat I'm going to look for your criticism. If it's
not enclosed in this letter it's because I couldn't find it. That doesn't mean it's
lost either.

Work is letting up a little but there is so much catching up to do that I won't
feel the lull until perhaps another rush intervenes so that I'l enjoy only a rest
that might have been – in retrospect. Yet I have had time to sweat over the en-
closed today. Doesn't look it, does it?

I went to Philadelphia last Thursday to give a talk at the New Students
League on modern literature. Left here (Newark) on the 6.08, composed the
spiel on the train during supper, talked, caught the 10.25 from West Philadel-
phia and landed in bed at 12.30. How's that for stepping? A kind friend took
down my remarks short-hand. When I see them I'll pass them on to you for
your magarzine. Maybe. If they aren't too foolish.

No time yet for a trip to the city.
　　　Yours
　　　Bill

enclosed: Enclosure lacking.

45. ALS-1

9 Ridge Road
Rutherford, N.J.

Feb. 7/29
Dear Louis:

Here she is. I'd like to see her in print. I had put her away so carefully it took
me two days to find her.

And will you be so genteel as to scribble me down (on the script) the changes you so generously have suggested. I'm for 'em – i.e. the changes. Then send the thing to me to be recopied – I'll cross my heart I'll return it pronto.

> Yours
> W.

she: Possibly "A Note on the Art of Poetry," *Blues* 1:4 (May 1929), 77–79. Wallace C132.

46. ALS-1

[Rutherford, N.J.]

<u>Friday</u> [February 1929]

Dear Louis:

Here y'are. Do your woist. I'm drowned in the translation, woiking night and day.

See when I can come up into the light.

> yours
> W.

Here y'are: Zukofsky's notation: "enclosing 'The Flower' MS." "The Flower," *U.S.A* 1 (Spring 1930), 31. *CP1*, 322–25.

translation: Williams's translation of Philippe Soupault's *Last Nights of Paris*. Wallace A11.

47. ALS-1.

[Rutherford, N.J.]

Feb. 12/29

Dear Louis:

Many thanks for our good offices: the poem is improved – looks a little like John Donne: I said "a little."

You'll have to call up when you want to come out. I'm dated up – mostly – for the week end. Maybe I can meet you in N.Y.

Write

> Yours
> Bill

When (if) I get the Phila. talk notes I'll slip 'em to you.

poem: Probably "The Flower."

9 Ridge Road
Rutherford, N.J.

[Zukofsky's notation: "19 Feb/29"]

Dear Louis:

For spontaneousness and the rhythm this seems to me about the best of your short poems. The images are not cut out and stuck on as they so often are in short poems but take part in the shuffle, all one. Yes, I like this.

Someone would say it is like some of the pieces in Spring and All. Well, so it is: came off the same tree. Fine. It is then a confirmation of the vitality of my own work for it is quite unlike my own work in the coloration and mood. Anyhow I like it.

Best luck. Did you see the cracks they took at you in Salient?

Yours
Bill

this: Probably either—or both—of the two poems ("Tibor Serly" and "D.R.") combined under the title "Two Dedications." Both were composed in early February 1929. *CSP*, 37–39.

Salient: Mavis McIntosh, "A Critique of Poor Reasons," *Salient* 2:3 (February 1929), 34– 36. McIntosh criticized four reviewers, one of whom was Zukofsky: "In *The Exile No. 4*, Louis Zukofsky reviews E. E. Cummings' play *Him:* 'That Mr. Cummings will himself walk the Delectable Mountains one can but prophesy. It depends more on the times than on Mr. Cummings.' It seems to us that it will depend more on the times than on anything else. 'But that if Mr. Cummings continues his work the artist in him will more and more write with all his five senses about the man and man's deliverance in general is as certain as that he has mastered the dark in these lines: "Where I am I think it must be getting dark: I feel that everything is moving and mixing, with everything else."' Mr. Cummings says it is getting dark, Mr. Zukofsky says Mr. Cummings has mastered the dark, and for us it is all very dark."

[Rutherford, N.J.]

March 4/29

Dear Louis:

We have a new President. Have you heard? Here's the poem, final version. Use it and weep - or what you will.

I can't send the Novelette just now. I'm supposed to be working on a dull place in the middle of it and, who knows ? maybe I may do so one of these days perhaps possibly.

Anyhow the translation of Soupault's novel must be in my April 15 which means that I must do at least two pages every day from now to then.

Well.

Well?

> Yours
> Bill

new President: Herbert Hoover.

the poem: Unidentified. Possibly "The Flower."

50. ALS-1

Rutherford, N.J.

March the 22nd (29)

Louis XVII:

Thanks for the phrasing – almost sounds living.

Reserve evening of April 7th Come with me to Carnegie Hall.

Fine work on (the States)

> yours
> Williams

April 7th: On Sunday, 7 April 1929, at 8:30, John McCormack sang at Carnegie Hall.

(the States): The proposed periodical to be published in Philadelphia and partly edited by Zukofsky.

51. TLS-1

[Rutherford, N.J.]

May 7 [1929]

Dear Louis:

I have a sort of malicious pleasure in reading that you're working all day long, a slave to circumstances in the same old beautiful way! Thus one is led to admire the grafters and so forth.

I've got to have a talk with Charles Reznikoff. I've read most of the Five Groups of Verse and most of the New York piece. His work gives me a feeling of great honesty, as you have said, and a sturdy resistance to a cheap art. What is lacking is design and the clarity of a comprehensive form. But then, who else has anything at his command to boast of along that line? I like the man's work seriously, he seems to me to be an important link in the chain we are all working at: the chain that is which will allow us to – To hell with that figure.

There is a stale successful conception of writing practiced and lauded and backed by the dull wits in the "great academic tradition" and their pimps like

Mencken. Then there is the so called "modernist" tendency which always goes on dragging its tradition of failure and inability to "put itself across". I suppose it's purely a matter of time, the space of years between "success" of some one man and the time it takes the rest of the world to catch up to him. The academic never moves. The modernist tendency must always "fail" as it is always moving and must always move to keep out of its own shit – so to speak, to keep alive – a thing the static academic does not need to bother with since its "life" is purely a question of aesthetics and not actuality.

But goddamit why must the new always be considered an outcast measure? Can't it be put over, not some one piece of work, but can't it be put over that the new is the living coral that leaves the academic, the classic so called, behind – sometimes. Must new work always be considered a failure if it does not measure up to the "perfection" of a few exquisite (dead) somnets or hexameter lines? There should be a new measure. We should not try to measure the new by static academic measures which do not apply to it except finally of course. Is it alive and moving to a relative perfection – which has been attained in the past and which it __may__ attain. If the possibililtym the drive is there new work is good. That is its measure. And a whole contemporary movement must be measured in the same way.

And if we say that, then never was art more healthy than it is right today. And Reznikoff as a place in this "chain".

Call up this week end. We can talk.

   Yours
   Bill

Five Groups of Verse: Published by Reznikoff in New York in 1927.
New York piece: Probably the short story, "Evening in Greenwich Village." Zukofsky sent
 this and another story, "Passage-at-Arms," to Ezra Pound in March 1930.
Mencken: Henry Louis Mencken (1880–1956), American journalist and editor.
living coral: Williams recalls his poem, "It Is a Living Coral" (1924). *CP1*, 255–59.

52. TLS-1

[Rutherford, N.J.]

May 15, 1929
Dear Louis:
Read the enclosed letter and then, if you will, send my Novelette to this man Posselt, c/o the publishers mentioned – by registered mail with a note attached giving my address. Let me have the receipt.

Nothing may come of the small venture but someone may as well be seeing the manuscript.

Rain.

On Sunday I went with Floss and Paul to see her parents forty miles back in the country. It brought all the old delight in the delicacy, profusion and color of nature back to me. What can we ev[lacuna in ms.] that? The hills on which the grass has not yet grown too long were blue with short stemmed violets and yellow with cinquefoil; the woods were full of singing birds, of all colors, blue, scarlet and black. I saw a grouse, a rabbit, a woodchuck. I love it (as anyone must) and wonder at myself for being where I am – neither in the city nor, really, out of it. Oh well, the country is there, if I should live to be old and choose not to kill myself by debauchery as I sometimes think I may – all things being equal. But probably not. In any case the violets are there.

> Yours
> Bill

enclosed letter: Enclosure lacking.

Posselt: Unidentified.

her parents: Paul and Nannie Herman.

53. TLS-1

[Rutherford, N.J.]

August 5 [1929]

Dear Louis:

A friend of yours wrote asking for instructions relative to the acquisition of my works. I wrote – after some delay – and sent him a copy of The Tempers.

Today my letter returns to me. I enclose it.

How's tricks? I'm off again for a vacation, taking Mt. St. Michele & Chartres along. I didn't finish it last year and have had no chance to read it since. Shit – up to my neck. It is at such moments and after such confessions as this that I believe it is so.

Well –

> Yours
> Bill

a friend: Unidentified.

The Tempers: Published by Elkin Mathews in London in 1913.

my letter: Enclosure lacking.

Rutherford, N.J. [Vermont]

August 23, 1929

Dear Louis:

I'm here in Vermont on Florence's uncle's farm. It's just the place to remain forever – if such a thing were possible without nostalgia for the others with all their aches and other distempers. Anyhow, here I am, typewriter and all for another ten days or so.

Yes, use my name and be blessed. One of the Giggenheims is treasurer of my college club but what good that may do is more than I can imagine. Influential friends are not in my posession.

The Novelette is still in the air. I am having it looked up by Mavis McIntosh. Hillman still seems somehwat interested but you know what that means, in most cases, nothing. Still, I stick on, hoping that he may print it for should he do so it will be well printed.   ·

Printing anything ourselves seems a mad idea to me just now. I may quicken to it later however. We'll see. Yes, it may be the only way.

We'll be home Sept. 10. The house is being redecorated while we are away. Call up some time after the middle of the month and plan to have supper with us, we are always glad to see you.

I'm not sying anything about "A" until I see it finished, then I'll be eager to read it after which we'll have a talk or two.

Here's hoping you do get that scholarship. You would profit by it and so would the country! It is therefore a patriotic duty for old Gug to do you a favor, and may Yaveh send him sense.

The Hound and Horn accepted a poem! Tha's all that's new. Oh yes, heard some good records on the Victrola recently, Helen (?) Kane among others.

Best of luck,
        Yours
        Bill

---

uncle's farm: The Haslund farm in Wilmington, Vermont. It is sketched in the final chapters of *White Mule* (1937).

One of the Guggenheims: William Guggenheim (1868–1941), youngest son of Meyer Guggenheim, who had graduated from the University of Pennsylvania in 1889.

McIntosh: A literary agent (with the firm of McIntosh and Otis) and wife of John Riordan, the editor of *Salient*.

Hillman: Unidentified.

that scholarship: A Guggenheim Fellowship. Williams's copy of his letter of recommendation follows his letter to Zukofsky of 3 November 1929.

a poem: "Rain," *Hound and Horn* 3:1 (October–December 1929), 78–81. Wallace C138.

Helen (?) Kane: Helen Kane (1904–1966), popular American singer. Zukofsky refers to her in two letters to Pound (*EP/LZ*, 98–99).

55. TL-1

[Rutherford, N.J.]

Wednesday [15 September 1929]

Dear Louis:

It occurs to me: if you do not sell your the-this or nothing, why not let Richard John, who is slowly going through a long period of gestation with his magazine PAGANY, have it. He lives Boston, unfortunately, but he is coming to N.Y. the middle of October, I met him this summer. He is a young man who has miraculously paid me twenty dollars for my Stein article which I sent to him in the form of a manifesto, he (telephone!) – never mind that.

I can't make out this John. He is very slowly getting his magazine together, a quarterly which he describes as native; Pagany, a native Quarterly. He says I am its inspiration and that the name originated in my Voyage to Pagany. I reminded him that his metaphor is mixed (in a way) since the Pagany in my do do de o doo applies to Europe and not to anything native.

Anyhow, there you are. Think of this. The man may perhaps have an idea, he is deliberate enough about it in any case to warrant watching and helping. I'd not let Pound know of this just yet as he might unbalance the effort. Later he should come in – if he will. He won't, of course, unless he can father-mother-bugger it – the new Trinity.

Yes, again, Pound is simplicity and the age is as you say. But I'd like to see you press down a little hard on the MORAL key. But why? I like your work and if my croticism seems insistent it is the insistence of Mother telling sonny to "Button up your overcoat" but why, you are right in insisting, counter-insisting, should one seek to "Put anything over"? What you have said is THERE, then that is enough. I am wrong.

No, you are neither pure nor gentle. Or, yes, you are pure but you are not gentle. Even your face shows it of late. You have grown ten years older since 1928.

Bob McAlmon is coming to N.Y. Leaves France Sept. 28. That will be interesting, though what he will be like this year I cannot guess. Last time he tried to act bored, with me at least. He was good in spots but it's ridiculous to be taht way in this era. He may have improved. Anyhow I'll be glad to see him.

Without undue enthusiasm I enjoy these signs of a small change in the current of events in our favor – if any.

Enclosed you'll find a better copy of the Stein with a note from BOOKMAN attached. And so such turds float down the sluices to sea breeding mosquitos as they go. Damn such shits to hell.

There's life stirring more than ever here (in me and in my place) and I'm delighted to find you with your purity -

Yes, complexity is not the word. Yet it will serve in one sense if thru a pseudo-complexity Pound's moral simplicity of beauty shines.

Yes, my collected things need to come out for us all!

Richard John: Richard Johns (1904–1970) had written to Williams in April 1929, requesting material for his forthcoming periodical, *Pagany: A Native Quarterly.*

Stein article: "The Work of Gertrude Stein," *Pagany* 1:1 (Winter 1930), 41–46. Wallace C142.

Voyage to Pagany: Williams's novel published by Macaulay in 1928.

note: Enclosure lacking.

56. TLS-1

[Rutherford, N.J.]

Friday [20 September 1929]

Dear Louis:

Come Saturday for supper. Bring the Pound essay and the Cantos. I have finished the Mt. Saint Michel and Chartres, it was delightful though I could not go the long descriptions of the windows. Possibly one should have the book and the windows before one simultaneously for that.

Yes, Pound wrote me, in his usual sly way, asking what the prospects of your Philamadeelphia venture were likely to be; meanwhile (apparently) writing you of his other ideas. Sometimes that guy gives me a pain in the hemorrhoids.

Well, there you are. We'll be glad to see you. Congratulations re. the job (that your are about to lose it). What other benefit have we to ask from life than that?

> Yours
> Bill

Pound essay: Zukofsky's "Ezra Pound: His Cantos," first published in translation as "Ezra Pound: Ses Cantos," *Echanges* 1:3.

Pound wrote: Letter not located.

venture: The proposed quarterly, *The States.*

the job: During 1929 and the first half of 1930, Zukofsky appears to have been working as a substitute teacher in the New York City high school system as well as doing "free lance writing (reviews and translations)," Carroll F. Terrell, ed., *Louis Zukofsky: Man and Poet* (Orono, Maine: National Poetry Foundation, 1979), 62.

[Rutherford, N.J.]

Sunday [22 September 1929]

Dear Louis:

Fine. I like your thesis. It calls for a magazine in which to publish it. It should in fact set the critical tone for the magazine which seems never to be born in this bum pump a dum!

But that isn't the half of it. You really have a style. The last american one is in Alcove 23, Case 9. And what you have to say is original work, nicely maintained.

Now. You are sometimes too light in your touch. You make a splendid point at the beginning in calling attention to Pound's moral quality, beauty and order and of course you do show how Pound's complexity (in the Cantos) can never properly be less than it is, that it is inherent in the age as contrasted, let us say, with Dante's. But I do not find the original A of the A B A scheme which seems to be invoked strongly enough returned to, with the addition of the complexity, which would force the thing home with a greater force.

Oh well, it's nothing. I like the work and I am sure Pound will also.

Best luck to you. It was a pleasure having you here. See you again soon.

Yours
Bill

your thesis: "Ezra Pound: His Cantos."

bum pump a dum!: Williams cites phrasing from "A"-7.

57 East 111 St. New York

Sept 23/29

Dear Bill:

I don't <know> the page in the typescript but it is the third sentence in the third paragraph above the quotation "It'z a animal Signori, you go and enforce it": please change <the beginning of> that sentence from "The Complexity of Pound's contemporary world" to "The lack of argumentative <piety> in Pound's contemporary world." It was that word complexity was ailing me all the time and like the M.D. that you are you diagnosed it.

No. It's not complexity which is my point but Pound's essential simplicity, which is his morality which is his nature not more—nor less. The word complexity which, as far as I can make out looking the essay over, I used only once was (cut it out, bless you) one of those blind lapses when the sense of the thing just doesn't see all the way thru and obliges itself with makeshift.

What I mean to say all thru is that Pound is <u>not</u> complex. Our age because it makes use of the cinema rather than the miracle play does not thus assume the characteristic of complexity which for the present purpose we'll set against the simplicity of immediacy. Both the cinema and the miracle have this latter quality – the difference is perhaps one of time elapsed. —I guess that's when Hen Adams' contrast of our multiplicity against 13 cent. unity falls out i.e. excepting (and accepting) that his own personal equation of the matter is still valid, but to a man like Lenin our age must have been overwhelmingly simple. Joyce is simple, if anything. So are you. So am I, when I know what I am talking about, or rather when the words talk about me by the way.

And so are the Cantos. Fullness, inclusiveness is not complexity. For that matter, Dante may be more "complex" i.e. fuller, more enumerative than Pound.

What I really tried to show thru the entire thing is that this kind of simplicity is not grasped by the ordinary word-monger (my thesis, that word sure is the bum pump a dum at its dumbest, is all of a parcel with "A".) i.e. the order and moral backbone of words as Pound uses them is not the immoral slop of people with fifth rate idears. Tell them that Ezra's moral because he is a poet and they'll think you're crazy, because in order to be moral you must either be a neo-catholic or a Wailing Wall of Jerusalem or a reader of Spengler's Decay. It's for this reason that I turned at the end from even Pound's mildly theological opinions to pure aesthetics <(exposition of the entirety of the order)> which is the morality of the business since the poetry has a body, a spirit, a simplicity of intercourse, and intelligent savoir faire de penis with a direction, a what is it that's necessary for complete creation which the half-embryos can't recognize. Do you wonder? Ain't got no faculties.

Anyway, let me know whether the omission of <u>complexity</u> doesn't <or does>save me from some of my own punishment.

For the rest, I want to forget this and get down to reading you for the "Collected Definitive." (To begin by pasting <together> yours on Gertrude.)

Let me know when you're free again and I'll come out pure and gentle as ever.

        Yours

        Louis

O yes, let me know on what page of the typescript <u>complexity</u> occurs, so I can write E.P. & ask him to correct his copy. Thanks.

---

the typescript: "Ezra Pound: His Cantos."

Spengler's Decay: Oswald Spengler (1880–1936), German philosopher. His *Der Untergang des Abendlandes* (1918) argued that civilizations inevitably fall and rise in cyclic patterns. A translation, *The Decline of the West,* was published by Knopf in 1926.

"Collected Definitive": Zukofsky planned to edit a collected edition of Williams's works. yours on Gertrude: "The Work of Gertrude Stein."

59. ALS-3

57 E[ast] 111 St. N.Y.

Sept 26/29

Dear Bill:

Thanks for returning the Pound, tho there was no need to – I told you to keep it. I'll be glad to get in touch with Rich. Johns, tho I'd like to wait till I hear from Papa. What bothers you I suppose is that he's always wanting to button your overcoat – as you say – but after all he has a beard, and that's his privilege. Somehow my allegiance – if I have any – is all your old friend's – after all, he told me to get in touch with you – not that you don't know all this – yes. Mebbe we can let Dick John have parts of A? What's his address? Or let me know if you care to recommend me to him. Tho' that's a bother. Le' us wait.

Some of your carbon for "The Somnambulists" didn't take, so the copy I have is incomplete (bottom of pg 3 etc). That's an important part, evidently, about the matter of the book itself. What you have to say of Emily Dickinson, however, and K.B. herself is analysis of character worthy <of> another Ameri-can Grain. In her connection with your challenge to the great and blackguardly American publishers why not subtitle the essay "A Manifesto" transferring this from the Gertrude Stein, since you drop it (and I believe advisedly) from the Bookman copy. <Keep the Kay Boyle book for me – I'd like to read it.>

The "Bookman copy" does wonders of correlation with the first page as you had it originally. The essay itself is excellent, no faults except that it is perhaps too pithy: pg 6, for example, the business of movement, knowledge, truth, the relation of the old logic to "transition" – all in one, is a little knotty even for me who's willing to read you 3 and 4 times to get your point. It's there, and I'm the last to kick about such things myself, but I'm thinking of the publick. Well, screw them! – Somewhere on pg 7 I'd put down what Gertie herself said in Transition 14 (i.e. of Tender Buttons): "It was my first conscious struggle with the problem of correlating sight, sound and sense, and eliminating rhythm; some of the solutions in it seem to me still alright, now I am trying grammar and eliminating sight and sound. And connect this with the "progression," and perhaps the "repetitiousness," also emphasizing more that Stein's art is her ar-ticulate parallel to the U.S.A. as subject matter, the ground parallel, by quoting from Useful Knowledge, a very pertinent book to this matter.

The letter from Seward Collins is funny as hell, letting the sweet pussie out of the bag so openly. Well it's to be expected. At first they are more veiled with one, send him bare rejection slips, then offer him $15 a month to live on, when his talent is recognized, and if thinking of his work he doesn't tell them where they come off, they hate him openly. Big crap.

What's interesting to me out of all of this is the general agreement in your work on Stein with Kaigh's Paper and my Pound: His Cantos or such matters as the "professional stool," its logic, and the shitification of the work as is. Considering the differences of our natures, professions etc., the similarity of thought regarding these things says something about the mentality of one little region in America.

Which takes me back to your own work. I don't think it is any use publishing a miscellany of poems, those of your poems i.e. which never before appeared in a volume. And again, just a collection would be a step back <rather> than forward. The need is for the best in you – and to pick that one must start from a point of vantage – Spring in All, The Gt. Am. Novel, the best in In the American Grain, the Descent of Winter. What comes up to this should be included, whether written previous to or after these. I should even suggest, since our need is for us all rather than for repetition of groups of poems which have already appeared in a volume, or volumes, to break up some of your old things in Al Que Quiere etc and include the shining parts as appendix to your (my) collection. What I mean is it is important for you as well as your studious reader (the hurried ones can go to hell) that Spring and All be included complete, while a poem like Rain should be represented by <only> a line like every open object of the world. This line with others may go into an appendix; it is at least final in itself and <is> you. Still it is not a complete poem as "The pure products" is. Your autobiographical you goes out, but since people can look the old volumes up if they want to, the process of collecting the "real" you should be worth more than the loss. My essay (I'm going to write it – give me time) will explain all this. For the present I'm rereading my subject matter.

   Yours Louis

"The Somnambulists": Williams's review of *Short Stories* by Kay Boyle. It was included in *A Novelette and Other Prose.*

K.B.: Kay Boyle (1902–92), novelist and short story writer. Boyle discusses Williams in her revised, expanded edition of Robert McAlmon's *Being Geniuses Together* (1968). Her *Collected Poems* (1962) is dedicated to Williams.

Transition 14: "Tender Buttons: Objects—Food—Rooms," *transition* 14 (Fall 1928), 13–55.

Useful Knowledge: Published in New York by Payson and Clarke in 1928.

Seward Collins: Co-editor, with Burton Rascoe, of *Bookman.* Later editor of *the American Review.*

Kaigh's Paper: An essay by Zukofsky's friend, Irving Kaplan. For an account of this essay's history, see Andrew Crozier, "Paper Bunting," *Sagetrieb* 14:3 (Winter 1995) 45–74.

"The pure products": Williams's poem "To Elsie." *CP1,* 217–19.

[Rutherford, N.J.]

Tuesday [1 October 1929]

Dear Louis:

Work comes down with a flooding reality sometimes which obliterates everything else, that is what has happened since the receipt of your last letter.

Please, since you have a copy, return the Pound pages to me. I should like to have them to read over from time to time. My only reason for returning them was that I thought you had said you wanted them.

You may have the Kay Boyle book at any time. There has also arrived a long unfinished poem, printed in paper-covered book form, by Bob McAlmon. I am sending you a copy of it for you to keep. <When you're out here sometime> I have five. To me, it is the best that Bob has evolved, the best poem and for wholeness of conception and thoughtful work the best fabrication of any sort. I have not, of course, seen his long prose account of modern times, perhaps three full volumes.

What you say of my Stein thing seems to me valuable, there is need of quotations from her own statements but it is exactly that which is hard for me because I am not a great reader and the pat sentence or phrase which I know exists and which I want often I cannot find. I'm going to read over what she says about Tender Buttons, etc. now – as soon as I am able to.

Sunday we brought Mother down from the country and have her now installed in her own demesne on the north side of the house.

Things look as if they are going to be crowded for me until after the middle of the month. I have not even read the "Paper" you left with me. Today I hoped to get up early and go to it – but the time didn't occur. Nor the Lenin –

Keep me posted, I'll do the same for you.

Yours

Bill

Pound pages: "Ezra Pound: His Cantos."

Boyle book: Kay Boyle, *Short Stories* (Paris: Black Sun Press, 1929).

unfinished poem: "North America, Continent of Conjecture." A portion was published in *This Quarter,* issue four.

prose account: *The Politics of Existence.*

Stein thing: "The Work of Gertrude Stein."

"Paper": See Zukofsky's letter of 26 September 1929.

the Lenin: Probably Zukofsky's poem, "Memory of V. I. Ulianov." *CSP,* 21–22.

■ 61. TLS-1

[Rutherford, N.J.]

Wednesday [2 October 1929]

Dear Louis:

Forgot. Yes, by all means make (if you will) a collect definitive of my work. It is precisely what I should like to see, for after all I have never had any great interest in a mere collection of what I have put on paper.

It would be a great service on your part to undertake such a work.

Yours

Bill

■ 62. TLS-1

Rutherford, N.J.

Oct. 22, 1929

Dear Louis:

Things are just beginning to clear again – for a while. Bob McAlmon has been in N.Y. for two weeks. We've seen a little of each other. If you'll be free some evening next week, say (rooughly) Tuesday let's try to get together though where in hell we can go for a talk is maore than I know and they call New York a city. Shit.

Why wouldn't it be possible to have an indoor plaza on the fortieth floor of some building with cafes about the sides of it and open spaces in the walls of the building to let in sunshine and rain? It outght to pay well.

And what do you think of this for a lovely thought. Women should have photos of their private beauties made, then reduced in size by photographic methods to be made into miniatures which could be worn in a locket about the throat for ready reference. No?

Well, poetry is alive with me but still. And say I am to be a judge of work to be accepted by a large publishing house in N.Y. And I'm going to fight like hell for a book of your containing "The" and "A" so get them all set for I have a hunch they are going to be accepted. Can't tell details yet but it seems good. Odd that I am asked to be judge and assistant editor (almost) when I can't even get a book of my own work accepted. Well, well.

Cheer up (or not) it's raining or as it may be and so, it – goes / ¾

Yours

Bill

Oh yes, will you indicate, as fully as convenient the additions to be made to my Stein essay & send the whole business back to me. W.

So The States is really coming out!

publishing house: Liveright.

57 E[ast] 111 St. N.Y.

Oct 23/29

Dear Bill:

Decorating you with this nice new colon, left lapel, buttonhole, I've been writing and re-writing my application and plans for work for the Gug fellowship – it's a scream. And writing letters to old profs to set me up a peg – the integer Zookawfsky breaking into fractions. Well, it'll be over soon.

I may also get a translation from the Yiddish – this puts me in a class with Isaac Goldberg I suppose – but I need the money so badly (maybe I'll tell you the mess when I see you – and mebbe I won't – no, it's not a curetage) – I'm preparing a sample chapter.

Curfuffle infortunée regarded especially as so much time taken away from my thochts about your work. However, you'll want to hear some of the things I have in mind on Sour Grapes and the unprinted stuff – which is all I've tackled so far. And you should see what we've made out of the St. Francis Einstein – unless I'm wrong. This needs at least a day with you alone.

I've indicated my additions to the Stein lightly in pencil so you can erase them. Get Billy to do it. – Which reminds me one of the kids last week wrote about a policeman chasing a thief with his gun out. And all the bastard faculty (whenever I see 'em, I don't sub regularly – as you know) is reading The Privy or whatever it is by "Chic" Sales. Pace Gertrude Stein, I tried to Analicize the kid by saying: Whose gun was it? The policeman's or the thief's? O, in that case you mean, "A policeman with gun in hand was chasing a thief." Who also had his gun in his hand.

No, your idea of pussie in a locket is still redolent of fetish and totem. To take yourself out of 'om Eliot's class, you must advocate with me easeful distribution on a large scale – throw a penny in the slot and out she comes. That's A meri can! But your idea of an indoor plaza on the 40ieth floor is better. Now, if you were the business man I am not –

———

The States coming out? Who told you? As far as I know never in connection with the Phila. dastard. At any rate all the mss. have been returned to me including your revised "The Flower".

———

Pound has not yet read my essay, which I'm sending to This Quarter – but P's letter on the Gug. application is a gem.

———

getting back to my decoration at the beginning – who is the publisher? If this is successful you'll be doing wonders for us yet. As for my book (by the way, someone at Liveright wants to see it) there's "The" and "A," and if you're a good fellow you'll help me chuck away all the shorter bunk I don't want and make an arrangement of what's good. An arrangement not merely chronological or aperitive – that's what always results when I do it. That there is a lot of truck I don't need to warn you. That omitted (the truck) <u>you</u> can <u>publish</u> it.

That's that. I'll keep every night next week, except Friday, open for you and McAlmon (you didn't send me his book as you said you would, that's allright, give it to me when I see you). Tuesday would be excellent. I'll meet you where you say. When I get a place, it will be different. At least I hope that much. Drop me a line or telephone any morning before 8:30. University 2476.

      Yours—Louis.

colon: Zukofsky drew an arrow from the word "colon" to the colon after "Dear Bill."

Isaac Goldberg: (1887–1938), American author of numerous articles and books on music and literature.

St. Francis Einstein: Williams's poem, "St. Francis Einstein of the Daffodils." First published in *Contact*, number four, in 1921. Wallace C64. *CP1*, 130–33; 414–15.

Billy: William's son, William Eric Williams.

the faculty: Zukofsky worked as a substitute teacher in the New York City school system.

"Chic" Sales: Charles Partlow "Chic" Sale (1885–1936), American actor and humorist. His short book, *The Specialist* (1929), concerns one Lem Putt, a specialist in the construction of outhouses.

This Quarter: The Paris literary journal did not publish "Ezra Pound: His Cantos."

P's letter: It is unclear whether Zukofsky refers to a Pound letter about Zukofsky's Guggenheim application or Pound's letter of recommendation. I have not been able to locate a letter from Pound to Zukofsky that would fit the first possibility. Pound's recommendation in the archives of the Guggenheim Foundation noted that Zukofsky "seems to be one of the people for whom the endowment was expressly made. And he is one of the very few men in America, if any, writing anything I can read with interest. One of the very few capable of producing anything save stock size commercial stuff." Pound went on to say of Zukofsky's prose that, "It is very solid criticism of a kind that is bound to bring him international reputation in time."

Liveright: Zukofsky wrote to Pound on 17 December 1929 that Liveright found his work "Not commercial" (Yale).

9 Ridge Road
Rutherford, N.J.

Oct. 24, 1929

Dear Louis:

Thanks for returning the Stein thing. I haven't looked at your pencilings yet but I'll get to that later.

For Jesus sake do get Liveright to do your book if you can, my editorship may prove a flop. But I will not pass anything I do not like, they'll take what I will have or out I goes. I may have given you the idea that I was to be handed McMillan or Doubleday on a silver platter. Not, it's not that good but I may be able to get something over for all that.

Just finished reading "Paper". It is excellent. <u>Pagany</u>, will publish it I know. Send it on to Johns if you will.

Enclosed is a letter from a Phila. venture which I carelessly took to be The Staes. How about sendingthis new crowd my "Flower". Do it for me, will you? Or send it back or – if you want the thing for Pound's new toy – it's yours. Or as you please.

Did you once ask me for a letter relative to the Gug Fellowship? I have a dim recollection of your mentioning some such wild idea. Tell me again, if I can be of use, use me.

What's the money needed for, if not a curettage it must be a gift to the Lying Inn.

Where will you be on Sunday? I may want to call you up in the afternoon. I'll do so, of course, if things work out for a free evening – if you have aother plans pay no attention to what I have just said. Tuesday, then, if all goes well.

> Yours
> Bill

Yes, I am keeping McAlmon's poems for you.

Enclosed: Enclosure lacking. Williams probably refers to the little magazine *U.S.A.*, which published "The Flower." Wallace C143. *CP1*, 322–25.

Pound's new toy: Probably Samuel Putnam's *New Review*, of which Pound was an associate editor. Its first issue did not appear until January 1931,

■ 65. TLS-1

9 Ridge Road

October 28, 1929 Rutherford, N.J.

Dear Louis:

As usual Tuesday is not to be the day on which I visit New York. But will you call up McAlmon at the Hotel Lafayette. He will wait in to hear from you. God knows waht you'll have to say to each other but I do want you to meet and it may happen through the beneficent agency of that peace which passeth all understanding that you will not be antagonistic to each other. Please do call Bob and go down to see him. You'll hear from me again later in the week. Must rush now.

>Yours
>Bill

■ 66. ALS-1

57 East 111 St. N.Y.

Nov. 3/29

Dear Bill:

Saw McAlmon yesterday and, as far as I can tell, it will be allright for the three of us to get together sometime. When you can.

Which reminds me – I've been trying to remember this everytime I've seen you in the last half year: a very dear friend – the mother of two children etc – dreamt that you visited her in blue stockings (Prussian blue) with pink toes and pink heels, and forthwith set yourself to playing a gramophone record upon her where you ought not to. This is literal: and, what more, she has never read a line of yours, or mine either, for that matter. Now – perhaps you'd want to meet her, too, for been with her you have.

Get in touch with me.

>Yours,
>Louis

dear friend: Probably Katherine Hecht, the wife of Theodore Hecht (1905–72), a close friend of Zukofsky.

67. ALS-1

9 Ridge Road
Rutherford, N.J.

Nov. 3/29

Dear Louis:

Your notes have been of great assistance to me in revising the Stein thing.

Look up Kathleen Tankersly Young (y:z) 605 W. 118th St. N.Y.C. Phone: Monument 9834. She has enjoyed your work. Do this. She wants to see you.

Something else, can't think what. Must wait till you come out – when? Work is going into second speed. I'd like to see you muchly soon tho' I have nothing to communicate.

Yours
Bill

Young: Kathleen Tankersley Young, American poet.

68. TLS-1

[Rutherford, N.J.]

[1929]

Dear Louis:

This is what I says:

REPORT: I am convinced after a two year's friendship with Mr. Louis Zukofsky during which I have carefully made myself familiar with his literary work, that he is endowed with a rare insight into the conditions, difficult for many to realize, surrounding modern writing; and that he has shown by work already accomplished high literary ability in bringing several of his conceptions in the modern manner to a realization. That his work is somewhat difficult for the general reader, giving it little popular appeal, has been for me a good sign.

I have read Mr. Zukofsky's Master's thesis dealing with the writings of Henry Adams. I have read other critical essays of his notably one concerning the poetry of Ezra Pound. I have read his poem of length beginning "The" which appeared in "Exile," a periodical, as well as parts of the new poem beginning "A" – which I think to be his best work to date – from all of which I gather one satisfying impression, that these are evidences of a united mind and spirit spending itself as a unit for the single purpose of creating works whose intent is to raise, dignify and elucidate some kind of a life worth realizing and living today in a world very much overtaxed with shoddy. Mr. Zukofsky's talent is somewhat satirical but only so to a secondary and unimportant degree. I believe he has a very positive contribution to make in the substance of poetic form to modern life.

From what Mr. Zukofsky has already done I sense the approaches of a distinguished mind expressing a truly liberated aesthetic which one might daringly call american and which has fascinated me by its strength, its tolerance, its evidences of being capable of a large organization, its musical subtlty and its sobriety.

Because I have been impressed by what to me is the curious aesthetic force of Mr. Zukofsky's writing – as well as his delightful personality – I have sought him out, invited him to my home where my family has enjoyed him as much as myself. He and I have spent many hours during the past two years discussing poetry and its place in a heightened literary life in New York City and the U.S. in general. It is in this way that I have come to know Mr. Zukofsky. He has brought his work to me and I have read it with pleasure.

Mr. Zukofsky needs help such as the Guggenheim Foundation can give; with that help I believe him to be in a position to make an original contribution to american letters of distinction and worth.

> $ in hoc signum vincis!
> meself meself meself and
> thensum! Mammy Alma,
> Mammy Alma! O won't you
> cum back to MEEEEEEEE! $

Well anyway.
    Yours
    Bill

69. TLS-1

[Rutherford, N.J.]

Nov. 22, 1929
Dear Louis:

Can you? will you? we should like you very much to come out Sunday afternoon for supper with us.

Bring your mind.

And your appetite, though for no special reason – though we shall have plenty to eat – or at least sufficient (to eat – of course).

Not that there is anything that I have to show you.

John Herrmann was circumsised last week. He is six feet three in his stockings (cotton). Odd, isn't it.

And so off and sew up.

Many, many thanks, by the way for your very valuable notes on the <u>Stein</u>

piece. I made many corrections throughout the whole improving it greatly. I have not kept a corrected copy (save the corrected copy which is somewhat illegible) but you'll see the beautiful thing in PAGANY first issue – unless I find myself dished. Which

Has happened before. But I don't think so.

I never do. Thus it cannot have been.

Oh yes, TRANSITION is here. I mean the latest TRANSITION which I have not read. And BIFUR #3 with a terrific grotesque of chinese corpses reproduced from a photograph.

You know, those damned Gugg Fellowship people did you a great favor. They sent me to blank to fill out and at the same time informed me that it had to be in their hands the second day following. Thus I went to it half sore and wrote the thing off with a will at one swoop. To hell with them.

> Yours
> Bill

Now I remember what it was I wanted to put into my last letter – what is the name of the second hand book dealer on Fourth Ave. who bought the remaining copies of In the Am Grain? I want to get a few more of them – to keep handy. W.

John Herrmann: American novelist and labor activist (1900–1959).

pagany: "The Work of Gertrude Stein" appeared in the first issue.

BIFUR #3: The photograph (facing p. 105 and titled "Chine 1929") shows seven naked, decapitated bodies, with their heads nearby. Williams was listed as one of the "Conseillers Étrangers" of *Bifur*. Williams had contributed a short essay to the previous issue of *Bifur*, "L'illégalité aux États-unis." Wallace C135.

70. TLS-1

Rutherford, N.J.

Dec. 4, 1929

Dear Louis:

Many thanks for your critical survey of my poems, I have been tremendously interested in what you have done, it has revivified the whole field for me, so much so that I shall not rest now until the "collect definitive" which you have foreshadowed in published. It is for this that I have waited, and might have waited in vain to realize.

I'm trying an experiment. I'm sending the Elsie poem to Scribner's telling them that it has been published in a book privately printed in Europe but never in the U.S. and that since I consider it one of my best works I should greatly like to see it appear in my own country. We'll see what happens.

There's nothing else of new. But when you have typed out what you had written on that card and which I didn't even half understand when you were reading it I'd like to see it.

The correction for the Stein article was here bright and early Monday A.M. I sent it off instanter to the home of the bean and the cod.

This has beena grey day, inside and out and within and without. Me Lord, a lady awaits without. Without what, slave? Without victles and clothes, me Lord. Feed her and bring her in. – Wha, wha, wha! I liked the Reznikoff bit. He is, as you say, a straight shooter.

Best luck – for a job – or what'll you have.

  Yours
  Bill

Scribner's: *Scribner's Magazine,* which published nothing by Williams.

Elsie poem: William's poem, "To Elsie."

Reznikoff bit: Unidentified. Possibly another copy of one of the items Zukofsky sent to
  Pound on 22 November 1929: *Rashi, Coral, Meriwether Lewis,* "Editing and Glosses"
  (poems), and other poems from *Five Groups of Verse.*

71. ALS-1

            57–that's my number . . .

So late in Dec. [postmarked 10 December 1929]
Dear Bill:
O.K. re-Johns.

Been down in the dumps again. Lonely here, as hell. It gets so close you bump into every door jamb. A kind of blindness. But if I had a telescope, I couldn't see my way out of it – Jerrymiuh.

Haven't heard from anybody excepting Ezra who quotes Edmund Wilson on Eliot: "The poet of The Waste Land making water – " Of course E. W. didn't stop there. What your gwine tu du?

Let's compose:

O emunctory, head's in a sorry state

When ass is head and both prevaricate!

A plaintive dulcimer and won't console anybody.

Did you hear from Scribner's – mebbe there's cheer that way. Call me up, won't you, if ever you're in town. – Me Villonaud: Hole, Skoal!

  L etc.

Ezra who quotes: In an unpublished letter of 25 November 1929 (Yale), Pound refers to
  Edmund Wilson's article, "T. S. Eliot," which appeared in the *New Republic* for 13 No-
  vember 1929, pages 341–49. The sentence Pound cited is on page 345: "The water for

which he longs in the twilight desert of his dream is to quench the spiritual thirst which torments him in the London dusk; and as Gerontion, 'an old man in a dry month,' thought of the young men who had fought in the rain, as Prufrock fancied riding the waves with mermaids and lingering in the chambers of the seas, as Mr. Apollinax has been imagined drawing strength from the deep sea-caves of coral islands — so the poet of 'The Waste Land,' making water the symbol of all freedom, all fecundity and flowering, of the soul, invokes an April shower of his youth, the song of the hermit thrush with its sound of water dripping and the vision of a drowned Phoenician sailor, sunk beyond 'the cry of gulls and the deep sea swell,' who has at least died by water, not thirst."

72. TLS-1

[Rutherford, N.J.]

Dec. 11, 1929

Dear Louis:

When in doubt, come on out! If I happen to be busy or want to do something else I'll say so. Give Floss a ring – and speak a little louder so Mother can hear you! and ze'll all be happy. (You don't need to give fFloss a metal ring – but just a metallic one, on the phone)

This damned machine writes z when I want it to write w: you see!

As it happens, though, this week would not be so good for a visit since Floss has been in the hospital a couple of days having her tonsils out and will only arrive home again this A.M. She's a game kid. I'll tell you why when I see you.

As I've told you in the past – or maybe I haven't I'm building a studio, or country store, in my attic. I'm doing it myself, that's why it is so long in the making. But someday it will be done and a stove will be in it and then you'll have a place where you can go to – besides to hell – and sit down and work for an hour or so when every other place palls. It won't be long now.

This studio is going to be good.

So come out next week and – sit around. I have a few things to say but – not much. I'm lucky to have a job. Oh that was funny. I met an Associate Editor of the Sat. Eve. Post the other afternoon at tea out here in Rutherford, a nice chap, who congratulated me on my luck in life on being able to write what I please and tell the world to go to hell. Boy oh boy! If he only knew how slowly that perfection has been making! I can still see little Willie, a meeical soph at Penn, walking the dark streeets of Philie and zondering how he could get a job as a stage hand – anything to get rid of medicine. And then suddenly the light! "I'm a writer? Right now. What difference is it what I'm doing? I'll practice medicine and use that as a stick to get down the plum I want." And then the battle began.

And so, zitness the enclosed letter – and weep. "Paterson" is as thoroughly incomplete a poem as I have ever printed. Makes me itch with disgust. Yet the poem itself (which I have never been able to get at to finish) is one of my most favored children.

Now to medicine.

Yours

Bill

enclosed letter: Enclosure lacking.

"Paterson": First published in the *Dial* 82:2 (February 1927), 91–93. Wallace C108. *CP1*, 263–66.

73. ALS-2

57 E[ast] 111 [Street, New York]

12–12–29

Dear Bill:

There's always a way out: the <u>States'</u> stationery, for example.

For yourself, I suggest a volume of unpublished work placed with Scribner's might lead them to take the Collected later on. The Novelette – probably won't go? How about a volume of essays – the Stein etc. Of course, you might get 64 pages of poetry together, but it would be a shame to spoil our idea of the Collected Definitive. Tho' that's only my idea – and maybe not so sensible. Witness: "The," "A" etc rejected by Liveright – poems not commercial. Three of the edtrl. stiffs liked 'em, and how many didn't?

Send Chawrlie, "Paterson" – what's the 'arm done, good advertising. Chawrles, by the way, is an old college classmate. Used to stand before the altar in the empty Columbia chapel at night and yell: Kee-rist! God!! A good feller, but might as well have a toy instead of a mind.

Yeh, cure that attic of yourn, and maybe we can open a laboratory for thought and attendant processes up there. I'll say we'll make a more forceful two than M.V.D. and Chawrles!

Your story of Ben Franklin walking the unprotected streets of Philie, Willie au lieu d'un lightning rod, his sole propeller, should inspire any American boy (or girl) aspiring to be a stage hand. Me too, but would they – the scene-shifters – believe it, looking at muh? Suzh-a a bespectacled lad – compound him.

He'll bus it to Rutherford next week if he can.

Hope Floss will be entirely well, sooner than I can say it.

Yours

Louis

stationery: This letter is written on the reverse of a sheet of stationery headed, "the STATES[,] a Quarterly."

Chawrlie: Charles Abraham Wagner (1899–1986), American poet. He edited *Prize Poems,*
1913–1929 (New York: Charles Boni, 1930). Wallace B13. Williams's poem, "Paterson,"
was included in the volume.

M.V.D.: Mark Van Doren. (1874–1972), American poet, teacher and editor. Zukofsky had
studied under him at Columbia University. Van Doren wrote the Introduction to
Prize Poems, 1913–1929.

74. TLS-1

Rutherford, N.J.

Dec. 22, 1929

Dear Louis:

Ya didn't come out last week.

Awright. Make it next year then, this week is going to be crowded. Pray for
snow, the kids have a vacation and want snow.

And, to keep you employed, won't you help me by taking care of this com-
mission which the fateful Ezra has shot at me? Please.

Nothing new. McAlmon sems to be out of luck as usual, after bright pros-
pects of being published by someone or other his hopes have been dashed
once more. I have reason to believe that it has hurt him severely this time. Shit.
Christ. Goddam. Meanwhile Hemingway is becoming the modern Playboy.

I was thinking about that this morning. McAlmon is a better writer than
Hemingway. I believe that though it would be hard to prove. But the gist of it
rests in this, that Hem is a clever manipulator of phrases and dramatic effects
whereas McAlmon is fixed as the North Star on a quality in words that he be-
lieves to be "true".

Let's hope it doesn't end in a tragedy – though the tragedy is already
present, only the catastrophy fails. Perhaps I shall try to do for Bob, as I see
him, what I did in the Stein thing for her (not that she gives a good goddam).
But what will anything I have to say benefit Bob? He needs to be published at
once.

So do you for that matter – though you can afford to wait, just now, better
than Bob can.

> Yours
> Bill

this commission: Enclosure lacking. Perhaps Williams refers to Pound's request, in a let-
ter to Williams of 5 November 1929 (*EP/WCW,* 98–99), that Williams produce an
essay distinguishing the important contemporary writers from the unimportant ones.

75. TLS-1

Rutherford, N.J.

Dec. 27, 1929

Dear Louis:

Many thanks for the books. They will be disposed as you have directed, some in Flossie's bookcase and some others in mine, we very much appreciate your thoughtfulness and good feeling toward us.

Your letter sounded like a stanza from the "Testament" of that other poor student Villon. Jesus! I dunno. Nothin' much happens from age to age, does it? And it's little use seeking something to blame.

And here I am able and willing and there aint no employment for me either, not even to the extent of five dollars.

> Yours nevertheless
> Bill

And the guy who got your job at the Rutherford High School is called Mr. Pappenfuss!

Ra ra ra!

Yes. Sunday Jan. 4th.

> W.

76. ALS-1

1051 Tiffany St. N.Y.

1/8/30

Dear Bill:

The enclosure is for your bairn.

R'cd 1.25 for the cactus from Richard Johns

and

am substituting (for a cow – he is an excellent one) for 3(!) days.

I must be foreshadowing a rising market – or is it just sympathetic magic – the playful ardors of the Menner baby in Washington and his cohorts.

> To –
> Louis

Enclosure: Enclosure lacking.

the cactus: Zukofsky's poem, "cactus, rose-mauve and gray, twin overturned," *Pagany* 1:1 (January–March 1930), 79. Later collected as poem 22 of "29 Poems." *CSP*, 33.

Menner baby: Unidentified.

1051 Tiffany St N.Y.

1/14/30

Dear Bill

Please return the enclosed with your answers.

Ezra goes on for a bit longer on: "the utility of plain Uniform format for porpoises of distribution of new authors" Advises also to "print and NOT bind."

The story of this affair is: Reznikoff has a press as you will note from the books of verse and plays which he himself set (vide your bookshelves). R. is willing to lend us the press, equipment, type etc and share rental and moving incidentals involved in setting up the press in some loft or office (or maybe we can save rent if someone has a cellar or an attic); he also offers to teach us – to the extent of his capacity and our susceptibilities – the secrets of composing and pulling the lever. However, he thinks the individual (and each one shd. decide his own worth for himself i.e. whether he merits the ink or not) shd cover the cost of paper and binding and shd. get back what he makes. He thinks binding can also be learned i.e. stitching, especially of paper covers.

– In short, Reznikoff supplies the press, and we find free upkeep for it or share expenses, and whoever prints pays for his own paper, ink, binding, does his own work, selling, and reaps the profits and the glory.

If you think Bob etc (anyone you please) will be interested perhaps we can arrange a meeting of all of us. If you think the idea is nonsense, say so, but (perhaps) better get in touch with Bob anyway.

       As ever,

       Louis

Who's miss Bitch?

Ezra goes on: In a letter of 31 December 1929 to Zukofsky (Texas).

Bob: Robert McAlmon.

miss Bitch: Sylvia Beach, so referred to by Pound in his letter to Zukofsky of 31 December 1929.

78. TLS-1

9 Ridge Road
Rutherford, N.J.

Jan. 14, 1930

Dear Louis:

Time is the element Ezra has not figured into his calculations. It is the thing which excludes me absolutely from all thought of such a proposal as he advances. But if there is anyone who has the time to fool with the business I'll give whatever script I have. ~~for a share in the venture~~ Naturally, if you get the Gug'Ship it's all off anyway.

In short I'm interested but not able to help, what's more I don't think much of the scheme. The Miss Bitch, or Sylvia Beach, Ezra speaks of would certainly not pay for unbound sheets. She is sold on Joyce and has not time to bother with other matters – besides she's been ill.

As for Bob, he's spent ten years having his own and other people's work printed privately and now finds himself in a position where he must either sell or quit. He certainly is the last one to approach ~~on the proposal~~ re. the scheme just now.

Maybe it's the weather or something else that has be headlocked but I can't see light in hand-press editions today. Nancy Cunard may be playing with the game but what elese has she to do? not a damned thing. Then there's the Black Sun Press. But all those people have at least a million dollars behind them – and time to burn.

To me the privately printed route can only be travelled by someone who loves the game for itself and has an income which makes him independent. Then he will sit down to it and wait for time to bring slow rewards. It is not an outlet for us.

Maybe we could put the press in a window on Fifth Ave and have ezra work it from 9 to 5 in billiard-cloth green overalls. I'd pay to see that too.

's a dark day.

  Yours

   Bill

What price some broken down old printer, some old guy who would be willing to do it in his spare time and glad to get the cash. Ad. in the N.Y. World?

Cunard: (1896–1965), English poet and publisher. In 1928 she had purchased the types and press that William Bird had used for his Three Mountains Press. For the next three years she published—under the name of Hours Press—books by Richard Aldington, Louis Aragon, Norman Douglas, Samuel Beckett, Robert Graves, John Rodker, George Moore, and Ezra Pound.

Black Sun: The Black Sun Press had been founded in Paris in 1927 by Harry and Caresse Crosby. Among its early publications were works by D. H. Lawrence, Hart Crane, and James Joyce.

1051 Tiffany St N.Y.

Sunday [late January 1930]

Dear Bill:

Ezra writes "Hours Press starting again. says it will print a pocket edtn of 30 Cantos sometime within the year at reasonable price"

Also wants to print "The."

"also ready to take a book by Bill Wms. I suggest that you make it poems and that you consult with Bill and get 16 or 20 pages of poems or other unpublished and unprinted matter.

"Hours has the Three Mts type etc and can work best on short vols printed large; also for profits etc

"Of course if there is a reason for larger vol. by Bill it can be excogitated, but knowing the firm I think best results can be got from short works. 16 to 32 pages.

"My Cantos are an exception, but they have a reason fer being done in one wad rather than in 2.

"Re Bill, it wd. be better to use something not available in one wad; also as Hours is using "The" as reprint from Xile 3; better not at once reprint Bill's stuff from Xile 4."

– – –

I've written Ezra about the Collect definitive we were planning – if you still want me in on it. The preface can be done when the collection is ready.

There's also the Novelette?

But why not a collected edition of the works of Wm. C. Wms. – pocket ed. 1 vol.

If you want to see me next Sunday about this, I'll "save" a dollar and come out?

      Yours,

        Louis.

P.S. Bob McAlmon shd be in an Hours.

Ezra writes: In a letter to Zukofsky of 10 January 1930 (Yale).

Three Mts: The Three Mountains Press of Paris, founded by William Bird. In 1923 it had published Williams's *The Great American Novel.*

9 Ridge Road
Rutherford, N.J.

Jan. 27, 1930

Dear Louis:

Next ~~Sunday~~ <Saturday evening for supper> will be all right, ~~come toward the end of the afternoon as a cousin with his wife and baby will be here earlier in the day.~~

That's good news from Pound and a much better scheme for publishing our works than the-hand-press-in-New York route. I wonder if this is the Press that Nancy Cunard is financing. She is said to have purcahsed Bill Bird's outfit.

Decidedly do I want to have them do a book of mine. The one that would give me greatest pleasure to see between covers is the novelette. But TRANSITION may have it in the next issue. Would that debar it from consideration by "Hours"?

A new book of poems would be my next choice but here too enters the question of previous publication for nearly all the poems will have appeared in some magazine or other by this fall. Nevertheless as a book the collection of new verse would be an original volume.

The Collect Definitive would be all right but it would contain much old stuff rewritten it is true, but old for all that. And a complete collection of my verse with the new stuff added would be by far too bulky for the present purpose.

The novelette seems the best bet, provided previous publication (?) in TRANSITION is not a disqualifying factor. It is also the choice nearest my heart.

Scribner's has accepted and paid ($65.) for a poem of mine! The Miscellany, 26 W. 9th St. is a new sheet worth looking into. Well printed. Send them some work.

My Mother fell on the ice a week ago and broke her left hip and elbow. She will be in the hospital for a month and a half. As far as we can tell her condition is satisfactory. A most unfortunate accident.

Well, see you Sunday.

Yrs.

Bill

TRANSITION: Portions of *A Novelette* did appear in *transition* 19–20 (June 1930), 279–286. Wallace C149.

a poem: "Wedded Are the River and the Sky," later retitled "A Marriage Ritual." *Scribner's Magazine* 88:1 (July 1930), 59. Wallace C150. *CP1*, 349–50.

The Miscellany: It published Williams's poem, "Birds and Flowers, I–II." *The Miscellany* 1: 1 (March 1930), 8–10. Wallace C145. *CP1*, 326–28.

9 Ridge Road
Rutherford, N.J.

Jan. 31, 1930
Dear Louis:

Saturday is the day.

Bring anything of mine which you have and may be looking over as somehow or other I lose track of my work sometimes and then – what t'ell, it's gone.

It was my impression that Pound wanted new work or rather work that had never appeared elsewhere for his HOURS venture. The Primavera thing will appear in part at least in the new Imagist Anthology. BUT the poem in a complete form will still be available.

As TRANSITION is to publish parts of the novelette in a coming issue –

Let's get both the poem and the novelette ready and send them both to Pound. In many ways I should NOW prefer to see the poem under or between covers.

Well, bring anything of mine that you have. and I'll be glad to see THE published.

Yours
Bill

Primavera: The sequence of poems titled "Della Primavera Trasportata al Morale." Wallace B14, A15, A20, A36. *CP1,* 329–49.

Imagist Anthology: *Imagist Anthology 1930* (New York: Covici, Friede, 1930). Several other poems by Williams also appeared in the *Anthology.* Wallace B14.

■ 82. ALS-1

Rutherford, N.J.

Feb. 13/30
Dear Louis:

'ere 'tis. <separate cover> If you wish to comment, comment. Mark up the script ad lib – I have two other copies. Delete poems, sections of poems, lines, words the whol woiks or nothing as it may happen to suit your fancy or conscience. Then let's 'ave 'em back.

Floss is doing the same. God save the poet . . .

Yours
Bill

'ere 'tis: Zukofsky to Pound, 14 February 1930 (Yale): "Bill is preparing for Hours—a. The Novelette, b. Primavera (new poems)."

[Rutherford, N.J.]

Feb. 20 [1930]

Dear Louis:

It can't be this Saturday since we have a social engagement that night.

Next Tuesday we are going to see the Chinaman do his stuff. Wang-Tang-Lang – or whatever. He is said to be a marvel. I am preparing to see him with humbleness at heart.

Floss hasn't a thing to say about the poem except that she thinks it's swell. I though she might object to a line or two here aor there.

Your suggestions seem to me mainly good. I'll cut out the crap, etc.

Sure I can do better. Wait till you see. Anyhow I can do more, and I'm gonna too. Plenty more. Books and books more, and then some. Till there isn't a wiggle left in my waggler.

Haven't had a chance to really weigh your pencillings but, as always, I thank you profoundly.

> Yours
> Bill

the Chinaman: Mei Lan-Fang (1893–1961), renowned Chinese opera performer who was
    best known for his female roles. He toured the U.S. in 1930.
the poem: Probably "Della Primavera Trasportata al Morale."

1051 Tiffany St
New York

2/21/30

Dear Bill:

Re – the inclosure – I've written to Otto H. Kahn etc, so will you write to Sandburg and forward the dread edict to McAlmon. Of course, if you have any old Graphics around etc etc send 'em on to Ezra. Unfortunately, I'm too highbrow.

If you haven't shipped the Novelette and Primavera, this is the time and with your fauxteagraph.

If – ef – you know the proper approaches, maybe you can get Eduard Estlang Kewmangs' foteegraphff

——

One Ezra is enough?

——

Butt I really got a lot of stuff myself – not my own – as I'll tell you when I see you.

The Hound & Horn has accepted my review of your Pagany to run as a postscript to the Henry Adams which they intend to print in 4 installments, the first beginning in the April number. All right?

———

Beat you to Mei Lang-Fang-Whang!! Hopsingooliong Tong!!! – Helen is tyking me tonight.

     Yrs

        Louis

inclosure: Enclosure lacking. On 6 February 1930, Pound sent a letter (now at Buffalo) to
    Zukofsky which he was to pass on to Williams and McAlmon. Pound listed a number
    of items he wanted for an American number of the Belgian magazine *Variétés*, in-
    cluding tabloids, newspaper headlines, and photographs of representative Americans,
    machines, and architecture. Zukofsky sent these items to Pound on 6 March 1930.
Hound & Horn: "Henry Adams: A Criticism in Autobiography," appeared in three suc-
    cessive numbers of the *Hound and Horn*: 3:3 (April–June 1930); 3:4 (July–September
    1930); 4:1 (October–December 1930). The review of *Pagany* appeared as "Beginning
    Again with William Carlos Williams (Postscript to "Henry Adams'), *Hound and Horn*
    4:2 (January–March 1931).
Helen: Possibly Helen Dechar, sister of one of Zukofsky's friends, Eddie Dechar.

85. TLS-1

[Rutherford, N.J.]

Feb. 28, 1930

Dear Louis:

When you called the other day I was in the midst of a hot argument which made it difficult for me to answer your collectedly. I felt afterward that I had spoken disconnectedly and unintelligibly. You must take my word for it that I was in no mood to be pleasant or polite or even friendly at the moment. And that's that.

What I would have said – or should have said, had I been able, is that I was thrilled at the acceptance of your Adam's (pardon slips in spelling and the rest) by H. & H. It is most pleasing to me to have you subjoin your note on my work (to the Adams, naturlich) Fine all around, congratulations.

I've been over your notes on my Primavera. Some suggestions I have accepted, others I've thrown out. Flossie stands out for the pricks, she wants them in. No doubt wer anoth r writing my poem,or had another written it, all your suggestions would be pertinent and improvements on the texts. But inasmuch as I have certain things to say, in my own way – I don't feel that I want to trim much, for any purpose.

Yet, your suggestions, at least 50% of them, are real improvements and I have adopted them. Many, many thanks.

As to Pound's new thrust: I'm for it. I'll do my part. But whether or not I have anything suitable for his purposes I am far from certain – or something to that affect, I'll send the two things. The Primavera and the Novelette, I'll send them next week.

I'm sorry your improvements in the two shorter poem came too late to be incorporated in the printed text. Miscellany printed the one and Scribner's has had my corrected proof on the other for a month. The birds and flowrs thing is rotten. I'm sorry I ever let it go. Shit. Never mind.

I'm delighted, let me say it again, that the Horny Hound has your Adams in tow. It is a real milestone in our very questionable progress to whatever.

Work is swamping me. This is the first I have applied word to paper in a week. No chance to see you now. Mei is was and forever shall be superb. It made me feel that all I have ever done has been hacked out with a stone axe.

> Yours
>
> Bill

two shorter poem: "Birds and Flowers, I–II" and "Wedded Are the River and the Sky,"
    later retitled "A Marriage Ritual."
birds and flowrs: "Birds and Flowers, I–II."
Mei: Mei Lan-Fang.

86. TLS-1

[Rutherford, N.J.]

April 3 [1930]
Dear Louis:

Congratulations on the appearance of your "Henry Adams" in H & H. I haven't read it yet – in fact do not posess a copy of the mag. but – congratulations just the same. Pound, Burke, Sheeler – splendid. But I felt keenly disappointed that they did not use my "Sea Elephant" in the same issue. It seems to be my time for – a sensing of dregs.

Floss' father accidently, as far as we know, killed himself with a shot-gun last Thursday. Floss has been torn apart by it all. She has been away for some days.

The "last imagists anth." will be out on the 10th. They have a partial, early lot of my "Primavera" in it. I hope "Hours Press" comes through and saves me later, though I expect nothing.

I'd like to see you but I don't want to just now. For one thing I am sick with work. It's that more than anything else that has me crushed. Don't even write me, unless you have something of your own plans or accomplishments you want to tell.

It was a real delight to see your work in the H & H – that was my reason for scribbling tonight.

> Yours
> Bill

Pound, Burke, Sheeler: Publications in *Hound and Horn* 3:3 (April–June 1930) by Ezra Pound, "Cantos XXVIII, XXIX, XXX," Kenneth Burke, "Ninth Declamation," and Charles Sheeler, "Four Photographs: Ford Plant."

"Sea Elephant": "The Sea-Elephant." First published as "Love in a Truck or, The Sea-Elephant," the *Miscellany* 1:5 (November 1930). Wallace C155. *CP1*, 341–43.

Floss' father: Paul Herman died on 26 March 1930 "of a self-inflicted gunshot wound at his home in Monroe" (Mariani 304).

87. TLS-1

[Rutherford, N.J.]

Friday [Zukofsky's notation: "Apr? 1930"]

Dear Louis:

Your work in H. & H. is delightful – delightful prose – and in Pagany your poetry, your poems, or poem – equally so. And I mean precisely delightful. Your give pleasure ~~to me~~ give it ~~to me~~. It is the generosity of excellence. Good and thanks. I have a weak feeling,in seeing "1924" beside your poem, that I may have missed much that you put plainly on the page for me in that lot of verse which you gave me to read.

However, I do not think so. I think this, in Pagany, is the best short poem of yours that I have seen – perhaps it too was in that lot.

See you soon, I hope. You'll hear from me again. If possible go to see the "Paul Klee" show at the Neumann Gallery, 9 w. 57th Call up ~~to~~ first to see when it will be on.

The Anthology is even worse than I imagined it would be. Errors!

– " – and Spring

is yeomen in! &%$# jesus@_*

What a cocksucking mistake THAT is!

> Yours
> Bill

Pagany: Zukofsky's three poems, "It Is Well in This June Night," "And Looking to Where Shone Orion," and "Only Water." *Pagany* 1:2 (April–June 1930), 21–22. The second and third poems are in *CSP*, 29.

[Rutherford, N.J.]

Friday 7 A.M. (by the whistle) [9 May 1930]

Dear Luois:

I've never been so hellishly distraught in my life as during the recent past – I can't even tell you precisely why this has been so – I mean to say, I do not my-self exactly understand it – but it has been so.

Meanwhile I have taken ten and twenty minutes stabs at writing – just the same. But it has been only that with a result of loose ends, waiting letters, etc. which you can imagine for yourself.

Importuned for prose or verse by this or that small publication or individual I have been on the point, several times of asking you to let one of them have the birth-of-the-baby thing. But each time I have squirmed away.

I have sent a poem to This Quarter, which What's His Name has accepted. I'm sending three, no four poems to Caravan – on shortest notice – one of the poems had been scribbled on prescription blanks the day before, another I found in a drawer – I had completely forgotten it and two others I had done last summer and never looked at after first flinging them on paper. This is fool-ish practice – but then I'm a foolish person – at times – and not half fool enough at others. Paganyhas two poems. What else?

Ezra speaks well of your services to him re. the Variété. I'm very curious to see the result. I tried to buy the sheet at Brentanos (I mean an earlier copy) but the woman at the desk said, No, we don't handle it. One should, I think (I might have said) For they must, after all (to look at most of them)

Just now the front door bell rang by weight of the enclosed – Shall I say, in reply, what? Born, died, resurrected in Rutheford, N.J. Collector of Infant's Cock Cheese

This letter has degenerated – it's what happens when one relaxes – some-times, often with me. But I have been extremely ragged.

No direct news about the Primavera thing from Hours Press. Hope that too doesn't fail.

And the hot weather.

All I started to do was to communicate – and this is what it has come to.

Yours

Bill

"birth-of-the-baby": Probably Williams's short story, "A Night in June," *Blast* 1:5 (Octo-ber–November 1934), 2–4. Wallace C212. Reprinted in *Life Along the Passaic River.*

This Quarter: "Child and Vegetables," *This Quarter* 2:4 (April–June 1930), 685–686. Wal-lace C146. *CP1*, 328–29.

What's-His-Name: Edward Titus (1870–1952), owner and editor of *This Quarter* 1929–
    1932.

Caravan: "Sunday" and "A Crystal Maze" appeared in *American Caravan IV* (New York:
    Macaulay, 1931). Wallace B15. *CP1*, 353–54; 396; 354–56.

two poems: "Flowers by the Sea" and "Sea-Trout and Butterfish," *Pagany* 1:4 (Fall 1930), 5–
    6. Wallace C154. *CP1*, 352; 378; 353.

Ezra speaks: Pound to Williams, 26 March 1930: "Zuk iz doin nobl fer the Variétés num-
    ber" (Buffalo).

enclosed: Enclosure lacking.

89. TLS-1

[Rutherford, N.J.]

May 27, 1930

Dear Louis:

Your letter and one from the U. of Wisconsin asking me my opinion of you and your ability as an instructor of English arrived in the same – or by the same mail. Which is correct Professor? I'm answering both at once.

Yes, let's get together next week. I'm sorry to hear that you are planning to leave this vicinity tho' if the past six months can be taken as an index of that which I am to expect in the way of leisure for conversations with my friend and a half it will make little difference in my own small life.

Conrad Aiken won the So and So Prize. Some think Crane should have had it.

There is nothing in my drawer worth your attention. What there is is no more than a much divided note on what might have been done and may still be done when there is time to do more than make notes. If ever. I received back the rapid jot I referred to in my last and sent to Caravan. They took two other poems however, an old one called Sunday and a new one, quite forgotten, called A Crystal Maze – about the difficulty and problematical worth of screwing a black haired virgin – it would be the only kind I could stomach – There should be a secret hour added to every 24 for amorous rendezvous.

I'll reserve Tuesday next. WE8ll meet in N.Y. I know a superbly dirty and hidden away speak easy where we may eat and enjoy the best beer I have touched to my lips and poured down my gullet in ten years. The test of it is in the hours that succeed the drinking. It does not dope one as is thecase with most of the slops sold in recent times.

Oh yes, Nancy and Hours Press, have turned me down. My poem will not be printed in Europe. Aint it a shame. Or in other words: Shit.

It's all right for Aldington to say he wants to do thi and that but in the first place The Four Seas Co. have refused to let me use the copyrights to my poems without coming across to the tune of five hundred dollars first, and in the second place – I doubt the word of anyone who wants to print my poems.

Wasn't the Paper Books Collection of Prize poems beautifully printed and arranged? Grand.

I'm out of my slump – in a way. But our family affairs are still in bad shape.

See you soon.

Bill

U. of Wisconsin: Zukofsky taught English at the University of Wisconsin for the academic year 1930–31.

Aiken: Conrad Aiken had won the Pulitzer Prize for his *Selected Poems* (1929).

Crane: Hart Crane (1899–1932), American poet.

Sunday: "Sunday" and "A Crystal Maze."

Aldington: Richard Aldington (1892–1962), British novelist and poet. He edited *Imagist Anthology 1930*, which included poems by Williams. Wallace B14.

Four Seas: The Four Seas Company had published *Al Que Quiere!* (1917), *Kora in Hell* (1920), and *Sour Grapes* (1921). For Williams's difficulties with publisher Edmund Brown regarding copyright, see Mariani 299–300.

Paper Books Collection: *Prize Poems 1913–1929*, ed. Charles A. Wagner (New York: Charles Boni, 1930). Williams was represented by "Paterson." Wallace B13.

◼ 90. TLS-1

[Rutherford, N.J.]

June 9, 1930

Dear Louis:

It's all off for next Sunday, better so.

No news. Just the usual time eating machine of no consequence. It's a curious phenomenon. I must say I don't quite understand it though in my own case it seems to be lack of – no, rather too much "pity" that causes the breakdown.

TRANSITION, they say, is finishing its career. Again, best so. It's time had come.

Taupin seems a good sort. He did not send me his book, of that I am sure now. I sent him a wire to the ship telling him it was not here.

See you some day soon again though when it is hard to say. I brought Mother home Sunday. She is doing reasonably well though as yet she is unable to stand up or to walk.

Yours

Bill

Taupin: René Taupin (1904–1981), Franco-American critic and educator. Williams refers to Taupin's *L'Influence du symbolisme français sur la poésie américaine (de 1910 à 1920)*

(1929). Zukofsky's review ("Imagisme," the *New Review* 2 [May–June–July 1932], 160–61) notes, "Mr. Taupin's book should be translated into English. With the essays on the French symbolists and the new poetry in Pound's 'Pavannes and Divisions' and 'Instigations,' whose influence M. Taupin acknowledges, and the pertinently fired improvisations in Williams's 'Spring and All' and other of his occasional critical assaults, it forms perhaps the only printed literature worthy of respect in this matter, which, after all, is: what is poetry?"

91. TLS-1

[Rutherford, N.J.]

July 2, 1930

Imagine, it will be July 4th. pretty soon – and still no appreciation of what it means to be alive in America

Dear Louis:

All you do (no not all, of course) is to make me sad. I cannot quite make out all that you say, I wish it were not I about whom you are writing. It seems too like a country I have always wished to live in and shall never find – not even when I am dead for I shall have to leave it behind. Hell, I feel that this sounds foul with sentimentality. Not at all.

This latest of yours is impossibly prose, it is surely the unthinkable thing, the comprehension – more intuition than truth – I am not the person you think, I have not done the work you say I have. But it is the truth that I have wanted to say, to make, to make visible.

It is rather yourself who has imagined the scene and fitted our work, of a somewhat earlier generation, to your imaginings. But you have created something which we at least cannot let disappear.

I don't know what else to say, especially today when after fumbling with a stupid paragraph I feel completely beaten.

You've gathered something, precious to us at least. It should be tremendously noted, eagerly grasped, – but it ends merely with one or two.

I can't believe that no one will want to print this thesis, or writing, that it means nothing to them. You see it has hit me hard. It seems pathetic to me. It wakes too much of that which was so confident in me when I was writing. Things that seemed monumentally important. It digs up causes, personal impulses, it is true.

Anyhow, get it printed and let me have a copy.

No let up yet, I confess I feel downcast, unwilling to see anybody. Either I'll have to write again – my head is teeming with projects – or never show my face to anyone. There is less and less time for anything, I grow frightened that it will continue this way – and I seem powerless to escape.

You'll have to come out before the 19th. I don't know when but propose some day – it'll be all right.

> Yours
>
> Bill

all that you say: Probably Zukofsky's essay, "American Poetry 1920–1930," a copy of which Zukofsky sent to Pound on 18 June 1930.

92. TLS-1

[Rutherford, N.J.]

July 8, 1930

Dear Louis:

Bring Taupin and come along Thursday evening, after eight or anyhow after supper as I have office hours from seven on and won't be free until later.

You get me wrong about your essay. But no you don't after all since you say that if I think it beside the point nobody else unless it be Pound and Taupin will think otherwise. Exactly.

Exactly.

I do not think it is beside the point, I find it amazingly true and penetrating – and still it makes me unhappy. God damn it, we're sunk, can't you see that? as far as any present day acknowledgement of our work is concerned.

It is the very excellence of your criticism that depresses me.

But helll, I'm not depressed as all that. What you have said is true and important – even if it does have to do with me in major part. I'll have to stand that.

In fact what you say is amazingly true especially of my own writing. If I say you have imagined the whole business it is because I doubt, often, that what I want to <say> really gets on the page. I fear that you have learned to know me and so have projected an excellence into my written work which really only exists in my desires. etc. etc.

Balls. Where the hell are you going to get with your damned criticism? And who the hell ever said you wanted to get anywhere with it.

You're amazing alert to what I believe is the finest there is in the life about us. You're about as rare as a virgin without cramps in her thighs. Or what have you? Anyhow, anyhow, anyhow – I ain't depressed today.

Come on out.

> Yours
>
> Bill

93. ACS

[Postmarked Chicago, Illinois]

[Postmarked 23 July 1930]

Dear Bill:

That's either iris or maize said the urban poet to himself on the way to Chicago.

Louis

94. ACS

[Utah]

[Postmarked 25 July 1930]

Dear Bill, Good practice out here! Louis

Good practice: The postcard depicts numerous infants and toddlers, with the caption: "Utah's Best Crop, One That Never Fails."

95. ALS-1

1110 Miller Av., Berkeley, Calif

Sept 2/30

Dear Bill:

The enclosure's what I'm playing with. It is from a bitch who wears a dog's collar and she won't give me her opinion of the flower.

"A" 6 and 7 – about 40 pages – completed.

Will be in Madison, Wisc. on or about Sept. 17 and expect to hear that you won the Scribner prize when I get there.

My best to Floss and your mother.

As ever,

Louis.

Enclosure: A lock of red hair and a stem of a plant with small leaves and flowers.

Scribner prize: *Scribner's Magazine* had announced it was beginning a "$5,000 Prize Contest" for short novels. Entrants whose stores were printed included James Gould Cozzens, John Peale Bishop, W. R. Burnett, and Marjorie Kinnan Rawlings.

[Rutherford, N.J.]

Sept. 9 [1930]

Dear Louis:

The cards marking your trail across Vinland arrived through the usual courtesy of the Post Office Dep't: maize and babies.

And then the hair and the flower. Now how did the flower get so caught in the hair that you had to cut the hair to disentangle the flwoer. And how did she come to be lying on her stomach on the flower instead <of> upon the flower of American manhood? And just which location yielded such hair. It has the curl of strange places. But the color is perfect. I insist on adding that I caught no compromising odor. Thanks for sharing with me such a tender souvenir. Your college year must – cannot fail now to – succeed.

Since the Scribner's Contest does not close until Sept. 2d and since I have not yet sent in my story – I have not yet won the prize. One great success I have had so far in this category however: the requirement is for a short novel of from 15,000 to 35,000 words. After terrific effort I succeeded in writing 15,007 words. I was knocked semi-conscious by the count. That is, the count is accurate if you count contractions such as "can't"as two words. Haw, haw!

We had a splendid eight days at Gloucester where we all four of us enjoyed the hospitality of Richard Johns and a lady friend. He is a curious phenomenon, this Dick Johns. God help him I think he has something worth while to do, perhaps even something to say. But it is the doing which will count. He is an enthusiast in a quiet persistent way for modern writing, his very quietness and sensual approach bodes well for his future, he loves writing, reads it (an almost unprecedented accomplishment) apparently in preference to writing. An odd fish but very likeable, one that can swim.

> Yours
>
> Bill

<and love from me too – Florence>

Contest: The *Scribner's Magazine* "$5,000 Prize Contest" for short novels.

writing 15,007 words: "Old Doc Rivers," eventually published in *The Knife of the Times and Other Stories* (New York: The Dragon Press, 1932). Wallace A13.

[Rutherford, N.J.]

[After 9 September 1930]

Dear Louis:

D'ja get my letter finally? If not write to California for it. But I think you must have it by now.

Good news about "A" (that you are getting on with it) and about the Indice (EYEtalian I presume for Index). I'll await a copy with interest and get my brother to read it to me. MAYBE.

At last I have finished my room in the attic. Floss carried up a glass vase full of verbenas as the sign and signature to it all. It's a great room, long amd rather low and full of light (dust also for the moment). I am there now at 5 P.M. after a swim in the nearby pool with my kids. What a place this is, what a place this is, what a place this is for writing.

But don't broadcast its existence to the world just yet. When you are here-about you may spend one night in it, maybe two, maybe more if I do not grow jealous. What more could a man offer? What more could a man have to offer?

As I said a moment ago it is a grand room. To which I can only add that it's a wonderful room.

Now that the construction has been completed the furnishing must be thought of. Then everything related to writing (my writing) must have a place. Finally every common convenience to the act itself must be found and inaugurated. I want to be able to write sitting, standing, lying down and perhaps standing on my head - surely often kneeling.

Anyhow its a grand room. There is a door to it with a key in the lock.

Be nice to the professors, remember they do not mean to harm you and that they have wives and children very often.

Is it a co-ed institution?

> Yours
> Bill

Indice: Zukofsky's essay, "The Cantos of Ezra Pound," was translated by Emanuel Carnevali and published as "Cantos di Ezra Pound," *L'Indice* (Genoa) in three numbers: 10 April, 25 April, 10 May 1931.

my brother: Edgar Irving Williams (1884–1974). Edgar studied architecture for three years at the American Academy in Rome.

[Rutherford, N.J.]

Sunday [October? 1930]

All right Dear Louis:

I'll send you the story then. You'll get it in a day or two.

Yes, come and spend a day in the attic. But it may be cold there in December. But Post hoc propter hoc, maybe you'll Villon it and with freezing ink do a Testament there. I hope to do more than that.

Don't get married right away. Wait a year and then, as my pathologist friend once told me (he's now the Chief of the working division of the N.Y. Board of health – Krumwiede by name) propose in the morning, just after breakfast. I did.

Mark the MSS. – slash it, cut it, reject it or leave it lay. I'll be glad to hear from you.

My room (attic) is not like the one in the hotel (with bath) which was shown to the farmer boy from up state whose bride awaited his pleasure in the lobby. "No," he said to the clerk, "that aint no fit room for a man to take his bride to, why there's a privy connected with it and there'd be people comin' in and out all night long." There's no such such comvenience here.

> Yours
> Bill

the story: Probably "Old Doc Rivers."

Villon: François Villon (1431–c. 1463), French poet. Zukofsky refers to his poetry in line 21 of "Poem Beginning 'The.'" *CSP*, 9.

get married: I have not been able to determine how serious the prospect of marriage was, or whom Zukofsky might have wed.

Krumwiede: Charles Krumwiede, whom Williams depicts in chapter 16 of his *Autobiography*.

657 Maine Avenue, Passaic, N.J.

Oct. 9/30

Dear Louis:

In my Passaic office; you're invaluable, you've lifted a ton off my chest. you're criticism is a proper dose for me, it cured me of an illusion.

Its ridiculous for me to aim at prizes – or at pleasing any one or at conforming to what I think one should think were he to think.

The first part of my story should have been buried before you saw it – but I had to <u>fake</u> a number of things in order to save my skin. I had to place the incidents elsewhere than at home.

Well that's over and I feel clean again – thanks to you. And many thanks.

They blush, Louis, not from shyness but from <u>guilt</u>. They know God damn well what they have been feeling and what <u>teaching</u> – and what they should have been doing.

My regards to the So. A. – chosen pair and good luck.

yours Bill

my story: "Old Doc Rivers" (see following letter).

So. A.—chosen pair: Unidentified.

100. TLS-1

[Rutherford, N.J.]

Oct. 15 [1930]

Dear Louis:

Certainly you have not compromised, it is precisely because you have not that it succeeds. There are battles ahead with the communists or is it beside them? the Steins, the neo-Parisians, the Muscovites – possibly the negros of the future. You stand down through more layers than most moderns choose to consider important, you are with Pound in this – but you have not compromised.

You're right too, one can never be certain that he is alive. But I am he who should worry today.

It is precisely the assurance I received from you in your criticism of the Old Doc Rivers thing, the lopping away of a worry, an affirmation by subtraction, an assurance that I was alive again which exhillerated me. Something has been wrong recently. Perhaps it has been a feeling that I waste my time on – that I compromise when I write to make things to suit a committee – I didn't like that composition but couldn't come out of it.

Today, in the same mail with your letter, the Old Doc Rivers has been returned to me finally, declined. Good. I'll slash it about and perhaps get it into shape to lead off a book of short stories as originally intended. But this time I'll aim to please no one.

Better to quit writing entirely. But even that isn't an answer. When one dies he is dead and soon stinks quite apart from his own willing or otherwise.

It's splendid news about the acceptance of the essay by Symposium.

As to the Poetry debauch, good God! I'll get after McAlmon. I believe I even have a poem of his here parts of which are splendid tho' I roasted it to him recently. By some curious trick of the imagination I have persistently kept the Alphabet of Leaves thing for just the purpose you want it for. When you want it, yell.

And congratulations.

> Yrs.
> Bill

the essay: "American Poetry 1920–1930," *The Symposium* 2:1 (January 1931). *Prepositions +*, 137–51.

Poetry debauch: Harriet Monroe had asked Zukofsky to edit the February *Poetry*.

Alphabet of Leaves: "The Boticellian Trees," *Poetry* 37:5 (February 1931), 266–67. Wallace C158. *CP1*, 348–49.

101. TLS-1

[Rutherford, N.J.]

Oct. 31 [1930]

Dear Louis:

Have you heard from McAlmon? I have told him to communicate with you. But do not forget that Poetry has published him already – some years ago.

Enclosed you'll find the Alphabet thing.

Hound & Horn have written that they are going into the publishing game instanter. What the hell does that mean? As soon as anyone makes that decision he makes a subtler one under the breath, so to speak, to try to find books that will <u>sell</u>. No wonder the French use that word (sel!) to indicate salt. It's a salty tale for me. Or who threw the overalls in Mrs. Murphy's chowder?

Anyhow, I sent in my novelete. 'Twill serve, 'twill serve.

Nothing else to say. I'm having my piles treated. He sticks a needle up me arse and squirts me full of whatever he has in the syringe; probably the wine of Circe. Or what have you?

Mother drifts along, I have picked up some good pages from her conversation recently. I'm getting the knack.

> Yours
> Bill

102. ALS-1

419 Sterling Place, Madison, Wis

11/28/30

Dear Bill:

Here at last is a copy of the thing. Will show you <u>6</u> in Rutherford, Xmas vacation. Not a clean copy to read from, but –

Hear Ezrie warned you not to contribute to my number on the grounds that well – why repeat – He's wrong this time – whatever he means. Your poem is the best (I'm not kiddin' either!) in my issue and I have some splendid material by Rakosi etc etc. Bob McAlmon, too. Was very nice about it & splendid all around. Saw Harriet on a week-end trip to Chicago. She said you were handsome. There! Tell, Ezra! Also saw a Renoir which you'd have probably help<ed> me steal – too big tho – <u>Les Danseuses</u>.

For the rest working like a bastard 14 hours a day and more – being an editor – and a conscientious one – is no cinch, etc etc.

Probably 10 below zero outside (has been for several nights now) but <u>hot</u> in the room till you open a crack in the window and one's – become Xmas tree decorations. Oi!

My best to Floss et all – Let me hear from you

    Louis –

the thing: Possibly "A"-7. The "6" may refer to "A" 1–6.

Rakosi: Carl Rakosi (b. 1903), American poet. Zukofsky placed his poem sequence, "Before You," first in the "Objectivists" issue of *Poetry.*

McAlmon: His poem, "Fortuno Carraccioli," was in the "Objectivists" issue of *Poetry.*

Harriet: Harriet Monroe (1860–1936), founder and editor of *Poetry.*

<u>Les Danseuses:</u> I have not been able to determine which Renoir Zukofsky saw.

  103. TLS-1

[Rutherford, N.J.]

Jan. 4, 1931

Dear Louis:

Here's one Mother handed me, it is in the French patois of Haiti:

Macaque connati qui bois li monter.

It means – the monkey knows which tree to climb – or in present day mode: He knows his palm trees (onions).

Then there's this – thanks to you:

To

    a child (a boy) bouncing
    a ball (a blue ball)

    He bounces it (a toy racket
    in his hand) and runs

    and catches it (with his
    left hand) on a green

> rhomb seven floors straight
> down which is the old
>
> back yard –

Best luck to you for the new year: my thick dome is being penetrated grad-
ually by your non e't sonnet sequence. I think I'm going to like it after a while.
>   Yours
>   Bill

To: First published in An *"Objectivists" Anthology* (1932), with minor changes. Wallace
    B18. *CP1,* 362.
sonnet sequence: "A"-7.

104. ALS-1

>   TO Publishers, 214 Columbia Heights, Brooklyn, N.Y.
>   [419 Stirling Place, Madison, Wisconsin]

Jan. 6/ 31
Dear Bill:
How many of the enclosure can you use to advance sales? Important for the
existence of To that you speak up for yourself as much as you can, get started
on intensive publicity – i.e. see that all the wise-guys on newspapers and mag-
azines will be informed. Books will be off the press before the middle of Janu-
ary, Oppen writes. We can't afford to give away free review copies unless we're
sure of reviews. If you will handle Kenneth Burke, Isabel Paterson etc etc, I
will handle the rest. And I shd. be seein' ya 'baht this – Friday aft. maybe?
>   Best to all – Louis

enclosure: A card with a printed text. "THE NEW REVIEW EDITIONS, Paris, France, will
    publish in the winter of 1931, or the spring of 1932, an unpretentious paper-back book
    known as the Objectivist's Anthology and edited by Louis Zukofsky. The publisher
    will pay each poet a nominal fee of not less than $5 for his work in the volume, and
    after the cost of production and distribution has been deducted, all receipts from the
    sale of the book are to be divided proportionally (per page) among the contributors.
    Contributions are invited for consideration till October 15, 1931. Address: Louis Zu-
    kofsky, 50 Morton Street, New York, N.Y." On the card Zukofsky wrote, "I'll selektum
    from the volume – & you kin approve."
Burke: Burke had published essays in the *New Republic,* where his friend Malcolm
    Cowley had been literary editor since 1929.

[Rutherford, N.J.]

Monday [15 January 1931]

Dear Louis:

You'll have a copy of the thing (after Floss gets here) if two can be found in the region. I'm sure four must be in the posession of our families – if only we haven't destroyed them. I'm starting an intensive search. There is one on file in the library of Congress and the old boy who printed the thing has a copy. But he won't even let me so much as see it.

But if everything else fails I'm determined to have a reprint made – of which you shall have one especially bound in gold leaf and ivory.

Surely you're the only one who would be thoughtful enough to write me such a letter about my first effort. And you're right, Joyce had nothing whatever to do with my development. Even when I seem to resemble him most (in The Gt. Am. Novel) – Oh well, but you know all this perfectly.

About yourself – I'll read the "A" within the next few days, tho' the print is bad. But already I begin to get the feel of it much better.

Don't call this year unbearable. It may be hell, in a sense, out there, but that will be only the spur to a better critical evaluation of what we have here about us, than could have been possible otherwise. And it will make you articulate when you have been disinclined to be so. I don't mean in print – but round and about.

McAlmon's story in Morada (which arrived today has a velvety quality that shows him on his way to being the finest prose aritist we have ever produced in America. I'm delighted. It looks as tho' it's coming, Mr. Critic.

The Buntings, Floss, Bob and I had a supper in Brookly last week. They (Bob and Bunting) flayed me for my reverence of a greek "beauty" which they insisted the Greeks never in the least realized or thought of. It may be tehy are right. I spoke of the temple to Poseidon at Paestum in its awe inspiring present condition. Sure, said they, the Greeks had a sense of neatness and balance, they were craftsmen but all this Hildadoolittlehermes stuff is the bunk. So is Pound's Artemis cult. The Greeks were plain dirty and aimed for the hole – and that's that.

Aw' right, says I, that's where I'm aiming too so maybe I'll be beautiful. – But no doubt I have a hangover from other years, an adolescent tendency to grovel to unearthliness – call it beauty, call it what you will. Anyway we had a good talk – it cleared the atmosphere nicely for me in several respects. I' m hard at work on the continuation of White Mule.

Yours Bill

the thing: Williams's *Poems* (1909). Wallace A1.

McAlmon's story: "New York Harbour," the *Morada* 5 (December 1930), 8–13. Reprinted in *Post-Adolescence: A Selection of Short Fiction*, ed. Edward N. S. Lorusso (Albuquerque: Univ. of New Mexico Press, 1991).

Artemis: Williams may have read Pound's remark ("I would erect a temple to Artemis in Park Lane.") in his "Credo," *Front* 1:1 (December 1930), 11.

106. TLS-1

[Rutherford, N.J.]

Jan. 18 [1931]

Dear Louis:

I can say this for the justice of your statements concerning my work: that you have expressed precisely what I wished should be contained therein. Thus it must be that I have succeeded to some extent in doing what I set out to do.

Pagany was to be a clearing of the ground preparatory to beginning. And yes, the line forms arose just out of a dissatisfaction with the looseness of vers libre.

But you have contributed heavily toward the next step in bringing to my attention the word "quantity". You're quite right, that's where much if not all of the release lies. I have in my duller hours (and weeks – and years) worried over accent. But I have not thought much of quantity. Lucky for me it didn't come more to my attention earlier when it might have interfered with my practice of it!

Symposium has asked me (Your doing?) to review Pound's XXX Cantos. I'll do it – then read Dudly Fitts, who seems to know what he is talking about – from the few snatches that I read.

You're going to have one of the Poems 1909 – on one condition: that you review it somewhere and quote one of the sonnets! God Help you . . . But of course there are no conditions whatever attached to the gift. In a week or two I'll send the thing on.

Also I received a request from Columbia that I send in my statement as to your qualifications. A good joke would be to clip your two recent statements about me and pin them to the letter without further comment. But of course they woudn't have the wit to be pleased. I'll do it in the conventional way. Good luck.

Well, I've read the "A" and be God – it's not tawdry. Its movement calls up a world of sound in which things occur in unused realtionships – almost filed out with a file they show such marks of making on them. It's an exciting poison, too. It ties up bundles not used to being together. I think its a new state in which things wear button holes instead of clothes; . What I get, then, is a feeling. So far I get no story – and want none – the sea and very hot "names," hot from filing, tell of the incidents of creation. I'll not read it again until it is in print. It's like nothing else, a hard necessitous form – which is the substance. We'll see.

   Yours
   Bill

Symposium: "Excerpts from a Critical Sketch: The XXX Cantos of Ezra Pound," *The Symposium* 2:2 (April 1931), 257–63. Wallace C161.

Fitts: Dudley Fitts (1902–1968), American poet, critic and educator. Williams probably refers to "Music Fit for the Odes," *Hound and Horn* 4:2 (Winter 1931), 278–89.

recent statements: "Beginning Again with William Carlos Williams (Postscript to "Henry Adams"), *Hound and Horn* 4:2 (Winter 1931). "American Poetry 1920–1930," *The Symposium* 2:1 (January 1931).

107. TLS-2

             [Rutherford, N.J.]

Sunday [2 February 1931]
Dear Zuke:
Sorry not to have sent the script of "A" back to you sooner. Impossible to think in this rush save of the immediate necessity. Had a bad cold too which gave me an opportunity to get the review of Cantos blocked out – had to be in bed some hours longer than usual. I'll let you have a glimpse – ask your assistance maybe.

The Poetry makes a splendid stabs for intelligence – I begin to see the world being recreated again as it has not been since 1913. You have managed uncannily (if one didn't know it was from a clear purpose and a beliefe 'faith' in it) to ride up forward. All sorts of projecys are surging in my head – wish I could write them down more fully.

But it's true with me that the wind whips the water and the water whips the rocks. When I am busiest with my trade as a physician (consequaently have the least time for writing) I have the swiftest, most abundant stimulus to write and get the most done. It is amazing but true. It is the only way in which I can work with mad speed. It has to be and it is. It is lucky maybe – maybe I lack the inhibitions which would make me stop when I had done – and need a physical knife to cut me o f from the paper –

The review in H.&H. – makes me dizzy. Man you mustn't speak of me as you do. It doesn't hurt me, it isn't that – it doesn't mess me up. But Yesus! I ain't that good. Yes, I am!

Anyhow, I know perfectly well that it isn't I that is being talked about – it is that for which we both care and insist on forwarding that is being talked about: and you have a sharp eye.

Symposium, too. I have read it all. Good work. You clip it off sometimes too much but – sometikes it is the clipping that makes the point clear.

Your best work, to me, is your demonstration (and discovery) of the work of Reznikoff. That's splendid. Your selections are thoroughly convincing. As a critic it is the biggest feather in your cap. You've done a fine thing. You've done something for him too.

I haven't read the short poems in Pagany yet. But I have enjoyed your short poems so much recently that

(next day)

Monday: I'll write again when I can – soon.

     Yours

     Bill

review: "Beginning Again with William Carlos Williams (Postscript to "Henry Adams")." Symposium: Zukofsky's essay, "American Poetry 1920–1930."

your demonstration: Zukofsky's essay, "Sincerity and Objectification: With Special Reference to the Work of Charles Reznikoff," *Poetry* 37:5 (February 1931), 272–84. *Prepositions +*, 193–202.

short poems: "Buoy—No, How," "(Awake!) Propped on the Earth," "Tall and Singularly," "Passing Tall," *Pagany* 2:1 (January–March 1931), 89–90. All but the second poem are in *CSP*, 23–24; 31; 27.

108. TLS-1

[Rutherford, N.J.]

Feb. 17, 1931

Aw ri' Louis:

I return the Iliad – you must be looking for work. Though I'd like to see a few pages of it – a few well chosen pages.

Yezzir, I'll send the – Sketch for a Chriticism of the XXX Cantos of Exra Pfound. It'll have to be a "sketch" since I simply cannot find time for more. I wish I might be able to do a well considered article but – can't be done. Any suggestions (on the script when I send it to you will be carefully perused and swiped if possible).

When will the Gugg be decided. Any news? Any hope or soap or anything?

I liked your poems in Pagany – pity to waste work on this land of worms on rainy sidewalks. I should say – The delicacy of flavor which each one of us posesses to some degreee is lost here. It is in us, we use it as it were squirting an atomizerful of perfume out the window to stop the stenches of the stock yard.

You have it. I have it. Balls have it – you may rub it hard you may scrub it well (as he sez to the girl) but you can't get rid of that cod fish smell. But what the hell good does it do us – or the stock yard.

Any how I like your short poems as amended during the past year or so. And there y'are. Nothing new. All well. Rain. Mud.

> Yours
> Bill

Iliad: Probably "*A*" *1–7*.

Sketch: "Excerpts From a Critical Sketch: The XXX Cantos of Ezra Pound."

poems: "Buoy—No, How," "(Awake) Propped on the Earth," "Tall and Singularly," "Passing Tall."

109. TLS-1

[Rutherford, N.J.]

Feb. 23, 1931

Dear Louis:

'ere it is – good or bad – I'm through with it – come what may. I don't want to see it again. Read it – chuck it away – keep it. Or send it on to Pound if you care to. I won't.

Symposium has the original. I wrote making it easy for them to reject the script if they want to.

The goddam thing almost tore my heart out – first reading the text and then scribbling what I had to say on street corners – the backs of letters – prescription blanks – and transcribing at 1 A.M. holding my eyes open (one at a time) with my right hand while I typed with my left.

It says in places much that I want to say but who in Christ's world will take the trouble etc. etc.

Now Pound wants me to select poems (of my own) for an anthology – and type them out clean I suppose for him. And me with more ideas in my head than a garbage can has slops –

Well, here's how.

> Yours
> Bill

'ere it is: "Excerpts From a Critical Sketch: The XXX Cantos of Ezra Pound."

anthology: *Profile* (Milan: Giovanni Scheiwiller, 1932). Pound's anthology included four poems by Williams: "Hic Jacet," "Postlude," "Portrait of a Woman in Bed," and "The Botticellian Trees." Wallace B17. *CP1*, 15–16; 3–4; 87–88; 348–49.

[Rutherford, N.J.]

March 9, 1931

Dear Louis:

After battling back and forth with Wheelwright I have been allowed to make use of eight pages, on which to present an excerptfrom my "Sketch" – no, ten pages. It's the same old game. But it was either that or let the thing rot so I pulled a few bits out here and there and let it go at that. It may possibly do Pound some good – but there is no flair to the thing now at all.

I'm glad you liked it though, your praise enlivened me for – still does. Should the thing as a whole appear I'll incorporate your suggestions.

Why not make whatever notes you have to make in the script you have and send that on to Ezra? But if you really still want to keep the thing say so as I have an extra copy here which Ezra may have. Speak up.

White Mule goes on. I have a long installment for the next Pagany – if Johns uses it all.

On March 20th. I am to talk on, The Logic of Modern Letters, at a book shop in N.Y. : Moss & Kamin, Hotel Geo. Wash. Lexington & 23d. It's a nice room (full of big wooden columns) But anyhow, it helps me to formulate my thoughts to have to do things like this occasionally. Hope I feel able on that day. I'm not preparing a paper, just thinking it out. I'll probably read some verse – Marianne Moore, Wallace Stevens – etc. talk about Stein, Joyce, etc. Finish by reading a few of my own -

Bob McA. is in Paris getting a new quarterly started – these same book shop people – he wants a couple of my short stories.

Nothing else much save that it is March and wasn't that a son of a bitch of a storm we had yesterday – you had it a day or teo previously I think. Our rose trellis blew down.

>   Yours
>   Bill

No. Keep your script I'm sending Ezra mine (I have 2) today

Wheelwright: Philip E. Wheelwright (1901–1970), co-editor of *The Symposium*.

"Sketch": "Excerpts From a Critical Sketch: The XXX Cantos of Ezra Pound."

installment: "White Mule" [To Go on Being], *Pagany* 2:2 (April–June 1931), 80–95. Wallace C160.

Moss & Kamin: David Moss and Martin Kamin (1897–1976), booksellers.

new quarterly: Moss and Kamin were interested in reviving *Contact*, but McAlmon's participation in the venture may have been in doubt from the beginning. Sanford J. Smoller states that McAlmon "would have nothing to do with their [Moss and

Kamin's] idea to publish a quarterly." *Adrift Among Geniuses: Robert McAlmon, Writer and Publisher of the Twenties* (University Park and London: Pennsylvania State Univ. Press, 1975), 238.

111. TLS-1

[Rutherford, N. J.]

Mar. 13/31

Dear Louis:

The part which I have cross-checked will not appeal in Pagany – not in the finished story. It was just an idea I had which I have discarded. But you may be interested anyway.

No opinion to give you as yet on the poem. I always need time, my mind is a vegetable.

Yours

Bill

I've been plugging away at my lecture! all inside, no writing It almost wrecks my stomach is turned my sleep is getting lurid. For I think I have something to say! Odd

the poem: Unidentified.

112. ACS.

[Madison, Wisconsin]

[Postmarked 16 March 1931]

[Zukofsky's wrote in the margins of a card advertising the appearance by Williams "at the Fortnightly Forum in the Lounge of the George Washington Hotel, 23rd Street and Lexington Avenue, Friday, March 20th."]

Didn't get the Guggenheim – you can say that at the lecture. Anyway, the Post Office might as well know you'll be there. My best – Louis

Will write again soon.

113. ALS-2

419 Sterling Place, Madison Wis
viz-Siberia

Apr. 16/31

Dear Bill:

Nothing except a bitter (?) aside: document untitled Immature Pebbles and beginning with a quotation from Thorstein Veblen's Vested Interests: "An

Imponderable is an article of make-believe which has become axiomatic by force of settled habit. It can accordingly cease to be an Imponderable by a course of unsettling habit."

And the rain brought this nicer (?) child yesterday – you'll find Proposition LXI – in Spinoza's Ethics \<Book IV\>:

Prop. LXI
(The Strength of the Emotions—Ethica ordine geometrico demonstrata)

> Confute leaf –
> Point's water with slight dropped sounds, –
> Turn coat, cheat facts, say for the spring's bloom's fall
> The tree's trunk has set the circling horn-branch
> To cipher each drop – the eye – shot in the rain around.
>
> So cheated well
> Let the fallen bloom-wet clutter down, and into . .
> And the heart (fact . .) holds nothing, desire is
> No excess, the eye points each leaf
> The brain desire, the rain (cheat.) recites
> 　　　　　　　　their brief.

Incidentally, Prop LXI is – Desire which arises from reason can have no excess.

It's the application wich counts?!

O.E.D. – the rain. Le-et it ra-ain!!

You have not congratulated me on my not getting the Gug. I see our dread competitor, Hart Crane etc – I hope my friends in a body weren't too much for you at the meeting some Fridays ago – did they knock out a communehiss? I told 'em to be your bodyguard – not that you need 'em but it's always safer when you lecture to people who hear talk and talk back.

Well, write me anyway – tell me what to do beg. June, for instance – I've been offered a reappointment here at $1000 – same salary to starve on, so I'll starve among friends – i.e. I'll probably resign. My best to Floss, mother and whoever –

> Louis

Has Simposiume come out with the Note on E.P.?

Immature Pebbles: Number 2 of "29 Poems." *CSP*, 41–42.

Vested Interests: Thorstein Veblen, *The Vested Interests and the State of the Industrial Arts* (New York: B. W. Huebsch, 1919), 8. The quotation is from the essay, "The Instability of Knowledge and Belief."

Prop. LXI: Number 3 of "29 Poems." *CSP*, 42.

Crane: Hart Crane was awarded a Guggenheim Fellowship.

Note: "Excerpts From a Critical Sketch: The XXX Cantos of Ezra Pound."

114. TLS-1

[Rutherford, N.J.]

April 2?, 1931

Dear Louis:

Nearly sent you a telegram yesterday but after paying $2.50 for the April Criterion decided not to. Your criticism of Pound's Cantos was the cause. It is excellent. Tired as I was I felt the old blood mounting to my head as no play that could ever be written could make it mount. It is a true divertissement of the intelligence writing such as that – of which there aint much. In the center of the writing there is true fervor, it leaps ahead with power – complex power that is only simple in its movement. Fine. I like it. It is convincing, enheartening. It is remarkable too that you have come where you are through study and reading (tho' that ain't quite true). I mean that study has not hurt you. Most it simply castrates. That's a fine augury.

You start clumbsily (as you have a tendency to do – thank you!) You try to cram in too much. It probably comes from cutting too heavily; your starts are your worst feature. But when you hit the pace and get the sense of distance – distance to go – well in mind the thing moves with authority.

It is curious to note the resemblances and dissimilarities between your treatment of the theme and mine. On the whole we agree with a sureness which indicates something solid and new underneath our observations.

Would it not be possible for us to assemble a book touching Pound's Cantos? It says that your essay is a long one; shall we take what Eliot wrote in The Dial, your essay and mine (touched up and straightened out), and shall we invite Dudly Fitts to come in? Mind you, I have not read the Fitts thing. I am asking you, simply, shall we? But it might be wise to have him in even tho' we disagree or even think him bad for if he is bad some will agree with him and buy while those who reallymatter will see better than ever that he is bad. Meanwhile it will give the book a complementary balance within itself. Anyhow, what do you think?

Went to the Met. Museum yesterday to see the new French paintings. Instead I chiefly admired a portrait head by El Greco and his View of Toledo. After that most things look dull. The American work in the museum is pretty poor. Six or eight living men whom we know paint much better. Isn't it a shitting crime that a big stone heap like that should sit on life and keep it under. God damn them to hell, the lousy cancerous bastards with their stolen fortunes and dust bins of heads. The French work is fine, no doubt, but very uneven and by no means as powerful as we used to imagine.

Yours

Bill

Your criticism: "The Cantos of Ezra Pound (one section of a long essay)," the *Criterion* 10:40 (April 1931), 424–40.

what Eliot wrote: "Isolated Superiority," the *Dial* 84:1 (January 1928), 4–7.

Fitts thing: "Music Fit for the Odes."

115. TL-1

[Rutherford, N.J.]

[29 April 1931]

Dear Louis:

Yea, I've heard the same complaint from Bob McA. that I have looked at manuscript or type-script without enthusiasm – and then admired the same work when in print. Can't help it, 's the way me mind works. I always want to see my own work printed before I finally make up my mind about it. The only excuse is that most modern work is written to be printed and cannot be considered to exist until it is so. Then, there's a'nother reason – esp. with your rotten scripts: I can't read 'em half the time!

As to the Pound Book: maybe you'd make a little more ordered list of what should go into it than appears in your letter – with sources (what mags. etc.) I'll do the rest – as far as possible. Has Bob written anything about him?

Had supper with Moss & Kamin (Moscowitz und Kaminsky, perhaps) last night and the wife of the latter. A queer trio. Kamin I think the most civilized, the most cultured the most irresponsible, as he is the most charming of the three. Moss is a vegetarian, knows a lot of facts about books, recent books and writers, but is futilely eccentric – but <is> the business insister. Mrs. K: "Sally" is the glue. <I like them. They are not bastards. Rather naive – with reservations> They have bought the remainder of the Contact books. Bob, the damned fool, sent all the books in a big case in one lot: result, the customs have held everything up indefinitely awaiting Consular Invoices, etc. Again – and again: shit, this, hits, sith – and finally shit.

the wife: Sally Kamin.

[419 Sterling Place, Madison, Wisconsin]

May 3/31

Dear Bill:

An "ordered" list of Contents – Pound Book –

1. Your essay complete
2. My essay complete. My review. (I'll send copies later on). Meantime, refer to Criterion, Apr. 1931.
3. Cantos d'Ezra Pound par. Louis Z – Echanges Numero 3, Juin 1930.
4. T. S. Eliot – Pound's Cantos. The Dial Jan 1928 (or maybe it was Dec. 1927).
5. Dudley Fitts – Music Fit for the Odes – The Hound & Horn Winter 1931 – corrections of misprints in Hound & Horn Spring 1931.
6. I've written to Zabel. – You'll hear from me soon.
7. John Gould Fletcher – The Criterion – vol viii – no xxxii – Apr. 1929 – I'm not for including this – however.
8. Ezra's note to Cantos XXVIII–XXX – Hound & Horn Spring 1930.
9. Ezra's Credo – Front No 1.

L'Indice (Genova) Apr. 1931 – IX – has just come out with a trans. of mine into wop done by E. Carnevali – only part 1 – but no need to print me in every language. Unless you want to help E. C.

Bob hasn't written since he left the U.S.A. Ad. of Moss & Kamin on last page of Spring, Pagany – looks good – but only the Lord god knows the heart and veins of N.Y. booksellers.

Thanks a lot for your present of Symposium. Nothing: except I note I'm a bum calligrapher.

Acknowledged etc

Louis

Your essay: The unabridged version of "Excerpts From a Critical Sketch: The XXX Cantos of Ezra Pound," *The Symposium* 2:2 (April 1931), 257–63. Wallace C161.

My essay: "Ezra Pound," *Prepositions* +, 67–83 . Part 3 of this essay appeared as "The Cantos of Ezra Pound (one section of a long essay)," the *Criterion* 10:40 (April 1931), 424–40.

Cantos d'Ezra Pound: "Ezra Pound: Ses Cantos," *Échanges* 1:3 (June 1930).

Eliot: "Isolated Superiority."

Fitts: "Music Fit for the Odes."

Zabel: Morton Dauwen Zabel (1902–1964), American editor, educator and author. Associate editor of *Poetry* 1928–1936.

Fletcher: (1886–1950), American poet. Fletcher reviewed three books: *Ezra Pound:*

Selected Poems, ed. T. S. Eliot; *A Draft of XVI Cantos; A Draft of the Cantos XVII to XXVII*. The *Criterion* 8:32 (April 1929), 514–24.

Ezra's note: An untitled note of eight lines. *Hound and Horn* 3:3 (Spring 1930), 358.

Ezra's credo: "Credo," *Front* 1:1 (December 1930), 11.

trans. of mine: "Cantos di Ezra Pound," *L'Indice* (Genoa), April 10, April 25, May 10 1931.

Ad. of Moss & Kamin: The announcement in *Pagany* 2:2 (April–June 1931), indicated that "Contact Editions . . . is to take up publishing again, in America, under the auspices of Moss & Kamin. Robert McAlmon . . . will continue his editorship." The announcement also indicated the editorial policy of the venture. "Contact editions are not concerned with what the 'public' wants. There are commercial publishers who know the public and its tastes. If books seem to us to have something of individuality, intelligence, talent, a live sense of literature, and a quality which has the odour and timber of authenticity, we publish them." The same issue of *Pagany* contained Zukofsky's poem, "Blue Light," 79–80. The poem eventually was collected as number 27 of "29 Poems" in *55 Poems. CSP*, 36.

117. ALS-1

[Rutherford, N.J.]

July 2, 1931

Dear Louis:

Yes, come out Tuesday evening for supper. Glad you're back. But there's nothing to tell you. Somehow the recent poop has been so much garbage. But come and sit around. That's probably the height of intelligent behaviour for the moment anyway.

Paul's at camp. Bill's on a boat at this moment approaching the Panama Canal on its way to San Francisco – he's working, a "bellhop"

Yours

Bill

Paul: Williams's son, Paul Herman Williams. "Paul had gone up to Camp Enajerog in Vermont" (Mariani 315).

Bill's: Williams's son, William Eric Williams. "Bill Jr. had sailed for San Francisco via the Panama Canal as a bellhop on a steamer on June 27" (Mariani 315).

118. TLS-1

[Rutherford, N.J.]

Thursday [July 1931]

Dear Luois:

It's an inspiration to have you home. And you look better for having lived through the year – you don't, I mean, look exactly corn fed, in fact you look somewhat transparent – but that only adds to what I said in the first place: you look better. It's an aura of that out of which springs written poetry.

Nativity (a rotten name) contains a good poem of yours, very good. One of the best of the short ones since it tackles the one subject most neglected (as you say) and deals well with it, the major sight of these parts.

Even I came to life and did a short poem this A.M. – enclosed.

That room of yours looks good to me. Don't not get it. It should be worth a winter at least – and this winter must be a good one. I want to see Taupin soon, I feel that I have not taken the time to value him, I regret my resentment against that which he probably didn't say. But he'll have to take his xhances with the rest of us in this neglecting barrel bottom.

But imagine if one could work again, at that excellent prescious and rare thing poetry! My blood sings with it – as I might see it real. It's good to see you released from your year on the frontier – makes one think of the old Chinese who were always going to or returning from the remote provinces. How rare it is to find and to have a croonie – in the special sense I mean.

W.

good poem: "N.Y. 1927," *Nativity* 2 (Spring 1931), 20.

New York, my city,
Now song once
From the fluent single man
Finds not a voice for the new day's dawn, —
From Insufficiency more than one man together
Must, as in Egypt once,
Labor to give last littleness a norm if not a song,

Build them high walls, hugeness
Like Memnon
That sings an isolated note at dawn.

So may, two-footed,
Find strength in common and reach where
Up—gullies of air
Each new day thirds
Tall companies
Of newly risen pyramids
(Structures in mass instead of song)—

Propitious the rays of sun,
Sand-color, on each new tower that prinks
You, city, as with a giantship of sphinx.

Then, what if before the single and once singing heart

A winter lies, a dispersed festival,

For the walkers, steel-shifters, thru canyons on parade,

The sun may be summery!

And you, New York,

Your buildings, morning-glories of over night,

For the mourner of past Song

    grace

           the adornment of a worn cravat—City! . . .

short poem: Enclosure lacking.

119. ALS-3.

50 Morton St

July 10/31 New York

Dear Bill –

The Colored Girls of P. – o & n – goes.

For the other – I don't know what reception <u>others</u> will give it, but I think it <u>shd</u>. be printed – as a document, or if you will a poem.

I make several suggestions on the MS – which I'd be glad to have when you're thru with them. The main flaw – and it is Ezra's as well as yours – is that you both hang on to the Democratic Dogma – which Henry Adams & his brethren saw was no use because the <u>facts</u> were infinite & against <u>that truth</u> (or myth – or whatever served Jefferson & no longer will serve us).

But what interests me – and the others can go hang – comrades & all – is that of <u>your place</u> you've "bred" the first two distiches (?) on top of pg 4 – "Whiskey Rebellion, we may end where we began."

True, however, what'll serve Russia won't <u>exactly</u> serve us, but industrialism shd. make it something <u>near</u> that. So I've suggested <u>A</u> <u>Party</u> <u>Poem</u> – not "a Democratic Party Poem" – and certain omissions – passages which seem somewhat suburban – the U.S.A. is after all a nation, an entity related to international affairs. And other omissions – where the personal skin is too tender. The idea is to give no one a chance to press a finger into it. The arrows → point the parenthesis – [ ] – these suggest the omissions.

On pg 6 I've added 2 words and substituted one. I think they'll work in – mental music if you will – <& rather ironic – >connecting with <u>section 3</u>.

That's that. Let me know.

It was good to be with Floss & you on Tues. – It's hard to tell you how much. Anyway I thanked Floss before going – which was silly – as if it were the first time.

René is grateful for Spring & All – & well – he'll probably write you himself.

Drop me a note at 50 Morton next week or the week after & come up. There are two chairs – & some other salvage – but I guess it'll be alright.

    Ever Louis

Colored Girls: Williams's story, "The Colored Girls of Passenack, Old and New," *Contact* 1:1 (February 1932). Wallace C168.

the MS: "A Democratic Party Poem." Williams had composed it in 1928. See Mariani 268–69. In a letter of 25 May 1931 (Buffalo), Martin Kamin had indicated that he and David Moss intended to publish the poem.

Democratic Dogma: Brooks Adams's *The Degradation of the Democratic Dogma* (New York: Macmillan, 1919) relates how the history of the United States demonstrated the failure of "the advent of perfection through the influence of democracy" (vi). The sentence also echoes a passage in *The Education of Henry Adams:* "The student had nothing to say. For him, all opinion founded on fact must be error, because the facts can never be complete, and their relations must always be infinite" (410). This passage also appears in "A"-8 (82).

120. TLS-1

                                  [Rutherford, N.J.]

Wednesday [Zukofsky's notation: "July 15/31]

Dear Louis:

Would you accept my acceptance of all your suggestions save one? That one being the inclusion of (Democratic) in the title in parenthesis. To remove that word entirely removes much of the immediate attractiveness of the printed book as it lies on the stand for sale. Or am I wrong? But putting parentheses around gives the meaning which you suggest and which I accept. And it is definitely a Democratic Party poem.

Yes, you are right again, no doubt, the major fault of the thing stands, a tardy belief in the practicability of the old myth. But the writing occured and has so become objective to me. I, after all, remain objectified to myself by the poem. Certainly I should never write that way again – And so perhaps it may step up a reader to impossibilities of thought. In fact I at one time had a new ending to the thing in mind, to make it definitely ironic. But I rejected that. I wanted to say: If this is all impossible, as you may see at once that it is, what then? –

    I understand that you want the script so I am enclosing it. See you soon.

    Bill

the script: Enclosure lacking.

121. TLS-1

[Zukofsky's notation: "July 17?/31]
Friday A.M.
Yes, you're right. I'll tell them, at once to return the script to me for further consideration. I should be careful though I detest being so. The thing was written loosely but, as you suggest, I have no way of commanding the sort of attention it requires – and the vulnerability of my position needs no bush.

Many thanks. I'm glad Taupin

Yes, no doubt Pound and I are wrong. But that isn't quite the point in this "document" or relative to this document, which has to say – Here's this? You do not even take it seriously when you pretend to. For what it is here is what might be done with it.

Well. One should be reasonably alert, you're right, in his own defense.
    Bill
What furniture do you need? a chaise lounge?

122. TLS-1

[Rutherford, N.J.]

July 18, 1931
Dear Louis:
Yes, I can come in Wednesday evening <8:30 at 50 Morton St with my car. if that is ok> ~~but I~~ doubt if I can make it much before nine. And yet why not? Send me another note saying you want me at a certain time and I'll be there.
    Chatto & Windus sent me the enclosed. <Can't find it. Just turning me down tha's all.> I sent the blue ball (sounds like a disease) poem to H. & H.
    I'm going over all the verse I have lying about with a view to submitting it to someone possibly toward the end of this month. Don't you think it would be best to give the script into the hands of some agent – some established name? Anyhow the work goes on – and, for your satisfaction, the suggestions you scribbled on some of my papers a year ago and which were not too acceptible to me then seem cogent now and very much to the point. Not that you would expect me precisley to adopt your wordings.
    Floss will not be with me on Wednesday, but she thanks you for your thought of her.
    Yours
        Bill
Nothing doing on a new mag:

blue ball: "To."

[Rutherford, N.J.]

Saturday [Zukofsky's notation: "July 25/31"]

Dear Louis:

This last week before my vacation is going to be so hectic that I doubt if I shall be able to do anything at all about my poems. But if I find it possible to whip them into any kind of shape before then (I've been working on them for weeks now) I'll see you next Friday afternoon in N.Y. But if Friday is included in your week end span say so frankly and we'll forget the matter for the present.

You see, I don't want to begin working on selection and order until I have the individual poems in the precise shape I want for them. Just drop me a line.

Don't be silly, I couldn't have expected you to pay for my supper. Besides I have plenty of money for such things. You haven't the money and I have, so I pay. Do you want Later on you can give me a banquet or send me a wreath or something – when you are rich – or something.

Yes, the anthology – that, I'll tend to. And the letters to Bob and Marianne Moore. Preface? Why not use Eliot's – No. That goes into the body of the book. Don't let's have a preface, just start in and say what we have to say and let it go at that. I have some new poems which I sent to the Horn & Hound yesterday. When I have time to make some copies of them I'll send them to you. Kirstein wants to print a group – some day! Yesus – someday.

I like your room. Hope to see much of you there in the fall – or is ti Fall. But these days I am rushing on toward the end of something or other so that I don't know where to get in a few extra breaths even.

My regards to Taupin. I want to see him again. I mean I want to know him better. It will occur now, next winter should be interesting.

    Yours
    Bill

anthology: The proposed anthology of essays on Pound's *Cantos*.

[Rutherford, N.J.]

July 29, 1931

Dear Louis:

Nothing doing for Friday, I can't make it. Thus the thing will have to wait until the Fall – and much better so. Meanwhile, I'm having the poems typed. Maybe it will be possible to send you a full script of them before I leave. In that case, look them over, make any notes that you care to and put them aside for me.

Address me here during August should you feel impelled to write – the letter will be forwarded. And so, fare thee well. I'm writing to Bob and the others about the Pound book today.

>Yours as ever

>>Bill

Bob's address is – as always – 12 rue de l'Odeon. Iasked him to write you about new poems.

I'll try to remember to mark unpublished poems in the batch I'm sending you – for the anthology.

>If I get the things typed in time. My typist has the shits.

125. TLS-1

>[Rutherford, N.J.]

Sunday [Zukofsky's notation: "Aug 2/31"]

Dear Louis:

We're in luck as the enclosed letter testifies. Read and return it to me here in Rutherford – it will be forwarded to me.

See you in September.

The poems have not been typed as yet but may be ready tomorrow – if so etc. etc.

If not –

>Yours

>>Bill

Oh yes, we had Nancy and Henry Crowder here last week – or this week or whenever the damned week begins or ends or what the hell – He is <u>good</u>, I like him immensely. Why don't you look them up at the Something Hotel up on St. Nicholas Ave. It's on the right hand side going north at about 120th. St. The Gondola (no, not really) but something like that.

>>Grampion

>>182 St. Nicholas

enclosed letter: Enclosure lacking.

Nancy Cunard and Henry Crowder: Henry Crowder (*ca.* 1895–1954), American musician.
He and Cunard lived and worked together from 1928 to 1935. Williams's short story,
"The Colored Girls of Passenack, Old and New," appeared in *Negro Anthology Made
by Nancy Cunard 1931–1933* (London: Wishart, 1934). See also Henry Crowder (with
Hugo Speck), *As Wonderful as All That? Henry Crowder's Memoir of His Affair with
Nancy Cunard, 1928–1935* (Navarro, Calif.: Wild Trees Press, 1987).

126. ALS-1

Aug. 3/31

Dear Bill –

Here y'are – returned. Floss & you must be sailing – how's it? Send the verse if you can – if not the fall'll do. Putnam is still sick – and I've had no written word from him yet.

Thanks for Nancy's address – maybe I'll go see them if the heat's hot enough. What'll I say to them – life or letters? Do you think they want to be called on?

      Best

      Louis

Putnam: Samuel Putnam (1892–1950), American editor, essayist and translator.

127. TLS-1

[Rutherford, N.J.]

[August 1931]

Dear Louis:

If you call on or up Nancy just mention your interest in her symposium Color and she will be glad to see you and talkwith you.

Under separate cover and by registered mail I am sending you the collected poems, that is, all new poems as yet unpublished, etc. etc. If you have no time for them please, at least, put them aside for me since I always have the fear that the scripts may be accidentally destroyed. I have two others however so do not be unduly impressed.

There will be things in this script of which you do not approve, check them in pencil freely and as you please. Some of your suggestions I'll probably adopt later. But in general I want this book to appear more or less as it has now taken form. It represents work done over a ten year period and should not be too rigorously pared.

My original idea was to send the book to Brandt & Brandt (if that's their name) and have them shoot it around for me. Perhaps I'll do that in the end. In the meantime if you can find a reputable N.Y. publisher for me why should you not have the commission. Do you care to take on the job? I'd suggest you see Conrad Aiken first. After that, do as you please. But please do not put yourself out. I speak of this simply because it came into my mind this morning, my object in sending you the poems was not that at all but to give you pleasure – if possible – and to benefit by your advice.

No use trying to write me for several weeks unless you want to write to

Rutherford as usual whence letters will be forwarded to us as we are able to send for them.

Best luck to you – and many thanks for alll your kindnesses.

Yours

Bill

Color: *Negro Anthology Made by Nancy Cunard 1931–1933* (London: Wishart, 1934).

collected poems: Williams's selection of poems written between 1921 and 1931. Eventually published as *Collected Poems 1921–1931* (New York: Objectivist Press, 1934).

Brandt & Brandt: A New York literary agency.

128. ALS-1

50 Morton St

N.Y.

Aug 11 [1931]

Dear Bill

Yr. poems here and will be watched carefully till you come back.

First reaction:

"He certainly knew his stuff – did Uncle Bill"

If I felt rotten before the volume came (and I did), I've been overhauled now for 2 days.

I am reminded of what you said of Mei – Paraphrase: You make me (as a poet) feel like the aboriginal cave-man.

Whatever suggestions I'll have later – shd. merely be pleasant.

One suggestion now – while I ponder the MS. suppose you send a copy to Ezra and have him ponder it too. Then let's see if our 2 critical nuts (E's & mine) come together. If you don't like this suggestion, forget it – &, of course, I'm not saying anything to anyone.

I don't know Aiken – but if, outcast that I am, I can do anything in the way of preparing a possible publisher for you – you know I will.

My etc to you & Florence wherever you are

Louis.

Please write me when you come back.

what you said of Mei: See Williams's letter of 28 February 1930.

129. ACS [copy in Zukofsky's hand]

Montreal, Quebec

Aug 11/31

Did you get the script? I sent it by registered mail. We start this eve on a small steamer northward. But we're enjoying the winds.

 Bill

130. ACS

[Postmarked at Woodmont, Connecticut]

[Postmarked 27 August 1931]

> Not Ezrachen!
> What's to be
> decided shall
> be " here.
> Mark up the
> script ad lib.
> Home Monday. Bill

be " here: The quotation mark is intended as a ditto mark, repeating "decided."

131. ALS-1

50 Morton St
N.Y.

Aug 28/31

Dear Bill –

na – na – no Ezrachen –

Even if he is a good tennis player.

Think I've sold some poems of yrs. to H & H, and told 'em if they're good they'll get a better group than you showed them.

Will be away from the city Aug 31 – <to> Sept 3, but if you can see me the aft. Friday, Sept 4 – it would be i.e. as nice as I might expeck!

Otherwise, suggest some night or eve. of the week of Sept 6 – maybe Labor Day (for poets?)

 Best to Floss and all

  Louis.

some poems: The only poem by Williams published in *Hound and Horn* after this date
 was "In the 'Sconset Bus," 5:4 (July–September 1932), 540–41. *CP1*, 362–64.

[Rutherford, N.J.]

Tuesday [Zukofsky's notation: "Sept 2/31"]

Dear Louis:

Yes, Friday – come to supper with me, I'll call for you around mid afternoon – say at three or thereabouts. Naturally I won't expect you to have supper at that time. Perhaps we'll be able to have a look at the script and to talk – and to talk. What have you been doing to H. & H. that they write asking me for my opinion as to their make up, general tone and policy? Or what?

Anyhow we're home again.

> Yours
> Bill

[Rutherford, N.J.]

[Zukofsky's notation: "Rcd Sept 8/31]

Dear Louis:

The more I think of it the more I have been impressed by the friendliness of your gesture toward me in working over my things as you did. It is all the more unusual and delightful to me in that I find myself willing even eager to accept nearly every suggestion you have made.

On Saturday I went to look up Nick McKnight. As he was not at homeand his house solidly closed I wrote him a letter – in order not to lose time – to be forwarded to him wherever he may be. As soon as I hear from him I'll communicate. But I told him that it might be better if he wrote you direct.

I was glad to meet the lady. In fact you'd have a battle for her on your hands if such things were possible – which they aint. She's good. So is the smaller one – in a very different way: wine and vinegar – but quite delicious vinegar too.

Poems enclosed. See you some time.

> Yours
> Bill

And the latest of all – souvenir de Labrador. Hope it goes.

The thing is almost finished – but not quite. I sent off the original arrangement to somebody or other (address somehwere) but didn't keep a copy (except of notes) This needs perhaps some slight touching up of the lines – dividing. But here it is for you anyway. It has something I think – and know.

McKnight: Nicholas McDowell McKnight (1899–1982), American educator who held a
 series of deanships at Columbia College from 1931 to 1957.
souvenir: Perhaps "The Cod Head." *CP1*, 357–58.

50 Morton St
N.Y.

Sept 17/31

Dear Bill –

Thanks for the typescript of <u>March</u>.

Now send the others.

If Geo. Oppen goes into the publishing business – paper covers 35¢ a volume, and I'm his advisory staff, wd. you care to be the first published – Say the Collected Poems, or maybe a collected Prose wd. be a better idea. Assuming i.e. a N.Y. Pub. will grab at your poems 1921–31 –

Hear from McKnight?

Going to lecture for Putnam?

If all goes well I'll have an occasional review of books I don't want to review in the N.Y. Eve. Sun.

– Eve. allright – S.O.Bitchy –

As ever,
Louis

<u>March</u>: Williams's poem, "March." Wallace A5 and C13. *CP1*, 137–41.

[Rutherford, N.J.]

[17 September 1931]

Me 48 today! O yea?! Sept 17, 1883

looks queer

What is wrong with this picture?

Brandt & Brandt have the script of the poems –

I have a copy. Bernice Baumgarten is

apparently interested.   <u>W.</u>

Baumgarten: A literary agent with Brandt and Brandt.

50 Morton St
N.Y.

Sept 18/31

Dear Bill–

Nothing wrong with that picture <1883> – we'll see each other when you're 96 & more vigorous than G.B.S. To the Nobel Prize! For you! And then – me!

Thanks for the McKnight letter. I've been around to Columbia myself & I suppose it's useless. But then we've done, we're doing, all we can.

Who's Bernice Treegarden? Bring the other copy of the poems the next time you see me – or keep it till I see you – remember, tho, I must have my selections for the anthology by Oct 15. How about seeing each other one of these next three Fridays?

Louis

■ 137. TLS-1

Friday [September 1931]

Dear Louis:

Reply: Bernice Baumgarten is the prick of Brandt&Brandt, literary agents; she has shown a business interest in my poems, which she has – tho' I have no final word from her as yet. McKnight says there is nothing for you at Columbia but that he is bringing pressure to bear elsewhere – with what results time will tell. Next Friday I'll bring in the copy of I have of the collected poems properly marked up as to where each has been published, etc. No, I'm not expecting to lecture for Putnam or any one else. Yes, if Geo. Oppen goes into the publishing business he may have the collected prose.

That requires a new paragraph: he may have the collected miscellaneous prose which I have roughly slapped together long since. Or he may have the volume consisting of Spring & All. The Gt. Am. Novel and the new novelette – a book I am most eager to see printed. Or he may have both. If the poems find no publisher he may have that too, but we'd better wait a while for that.

I'm working today on the Homage to Pound. I have Marianne Moore's new bit which is to come out in Poetry shortly etc. etc.

Why in hell didn't you tell me about your Third and Fourth Movements (as I often say to the nurse about my baby patients) they seem the best yet? Just by chance I happened to get hold of The New Review. Much more coherence, smoothness – pleasure! Naturally I don't expect you to tell me about these things but I'm glad I came upon the thing. Very fine – really lovely (there's not much loveliness about) and why not - for a change. You need more continuity to your things from the reading viewpoint sometimes. Your theme is so difficult – at times – tho' it may be simple to you that you don't allow the reader to get started. Sometimes. I know what it comes from and that it can't be different – but it's nice to feel you working smoothly as if your were more married into the slippery slot. There's pleasure there too. Rape aint everything.

I'm forwarding a paper with a bit by Pound that is worth noteing.

> Yours
>
> Bill

Oppen: Zukofsky wrote to Pound on 15 October 1931, "Geo Oppen is planning a publish-
ing firm – To, Publishers, and I'm the edtr. We'll probably begin with Bill's uncol-
lected prose – or at least – Bill's been spoken to" (Yale).

Homage to Pound: The planned book of essays on Pound.

new bit: Moore's review of A Draft of XXX Cantos. "The Cantos," Poetry 39 (October
1931), 37–56.

Third and Fourth Movements: "A"-3 and "A"-4, New Review 1:2 (May–June–July 1931).

a paper: Enclosure lacking.

138. TLS-1

[Rutherford, N.J.]

Tuesday [Zukofsky's notation: "Sept 30/31"]

Dear Louis:

Nothing doing Friday. I may come in to the city, I'll tell you why, but my
time will all be sewed up while I am there. Kamin wants to start a jew (ya, ha! a
slip of the finger!) new quarterly and he wants me to be Editor with Nathanael
West as my first assistant to do all the work. And I says yes, damn fool that I
am. So on Friday (after three postponements) I am to meet the men (I've never
met West) and talk the thing over.

Anyhow I've had the lazy good for nothin' sit and fart away the hours blues
of late so nothing's been done about the Homage to Pound. Besides I've had
not a word from Putnam that he really wants the thing. I don't know where he
is or anything about him save that we talked together that night. Perhaps that's
at the back of my indifference.

Meanwhile Marianne Moore's review is a beauty – in the next Poetry: but
better in the galley proofs, so excellently fitted to her continuous style: not a
bad name for a literary paper, by the way: Galleys. Or do you want to have sup-
per with me Ftiday just for an hour? I could call for you about six, leave the
pomes and then go up to see Kamin. In the afternoon I'll be busy out here.

> Yours
>
> Bill

New Transition editors: Putnam & Jolis

soon to appear

West: (1903–1940), American novelist. He and Williams edited the second series of Con-
tact for three issues.

Putnam: Samuel Putnam, editor of the *New Review,* published seven books under the New Review imprint, none of which were produced by Williams or Zukofsky. Among the Williams papers at Yale, however, is a card with a printed text: "Tribute to Ezra Pound / Edited, and with an Introduction, by William Carlos Williams. / New Review Publications / 42 *bis, rue du Plessis* / Fontenay-Aux-Roses / Seine, France."

review: Moore's review of *A Draft of XXX Cantos,* "The Cantos."

Jolis: Eugene Jolas (1894–1952).

■ 139. ACS

50 Morton St New York

Wed. [postmarked 30 September 1931]

Dear Bill:

I'll wait for you here Friday at 6 (5:30–6:30) in case you decide to come and bring the poems. Wd. be nice if you cd. manage it without trouble –

Yes, M.M.'s review of E. is a beauty even if she flavors the Cantos with old-maidishness and yet doesn't think he shd. use cuss words. But it is a rarity.

Neither 've I 'eard from Putm. But let us work & 'ope. – Interesting: yr. editing a new mag. but what pub.'s to be trusted? Tell me that and I'll tell you why I'm making use of the open forum of a postcard & more. Etc.

Yours Louis

review of E.: Moore's review of *A Draft of XXX Cantos,* "The Cantos."

■ 140. ACS

[Postmarked Rutherford, N.J.]

[Postmarked 1 October 1931]

To save time meet me at Gray's Rest. East 18th St. at 6.30. I'll bring in what I have & leave it with you – a fairly large bunch. No new works – B & B are trying out Viking Press on the script.

W.

B&B: Brandt and Brandt Literary Agency.

script: Williams's manuscript of his *Collected Poems 1921–1931.*

[Rutherford, N.J.]

Oct. 8, 1931

Dear Louis:

I corrected "trubid" in the script which is still at sea. Thanks tho'. And I do like your selections and the arrangement. Nathanael West is a tall chap whom I saw only for a moment that night – as I had to rush away to deliver a cheeild as usual. But I liked him, he's no Gentile! A stange thing, he looked like an uncle, or half uncle of mine who I admired in some ways – tho' he died of cerebral syphilis contracted in the West Indies from a nigger when he was fourteen or so; It made a difference. Tho' I didn't tell West. He really is a very curious type, straight (I think) and capbale of discriminating enthusiasm. Gord knows what else. He even seems to want to work. He'll have to for I won't. We are to do the quarterly.

And in the first issue as a feature about which I am most enthusiastic, we plan to print a complete bibliography of the "small magazine" (american) since 1900. It's a whale of a job but West wants to do it and I'm helping as I can. It's his idea. I think that's the kind of stuff comes of a real interest. More later when I know more. And I'm the editor! Yasuz. But I am just the same as you'll see. Please do not as yet communicate this information to Ezrie. Plenty of time for that.

Don't tear the script apart – the book of scripts that is, keep it for your amusement. I'll send copies of the poems – also the thing of Bob's you want – and by the 12th. surely. You can count on it. (May not arrive till 13th.) I'll look over "opalescent sahadows" et al. We'll see.

Meanwhile, it finally rained. I was beginning to curse the skies.

Best luck (if any)

Bill

I'll let you have the Dream Life of Balso Snell when I see you soon

W

"trubid": A word in line 61 of "This Florida: 1924." Zukofsky included the poem in An "Objectivists" Anthology. Wallace B18. *CP1*, 359–62.

an uncle: Godwin Wellcome, whom Williams recalls in chapters 2 and 6 of his *Autobiography*.

Dream Life: Nathanael West's novella, *The Dream Life of Balso Snell* (New York: Contact Editions, 1931).

"opalescent sahadows": A phrase in line 9 of "A Morning Imagination of Russia." Zukofsky included the poem in An "Objectivists" Anthology. Wallace B18. *CP1*, 303–06.

[Rutherford, N.J.]

Friday [9 October 1931]

Dear Louis:

'Sconset is a small cluster of houses on the ocean side of Nantucket, an old artists' colony now more than a little run down – but still lovely.

No, the poem you want did not appear in Poetry but in Little Review.

I'm shooting the present batch of scripts to you at once, use them as you please. But they'll have to be checked against the versions in your posession – they need it.

By early next week you'll have the Morning Imag. of Russia (which I'd like you very much to use) and the McAlmon thing.

Best luck. See you soon. I'm not coming in today, must go see Bill play socker, he's just been elected captain of the team and he wants me there. Also there is plenty to do – with a lot of old shingles to carry in to the cellar, a roof to paint, a quarterly to edit and Yasus knows what all. Oh yes, I'll have to get Mother's tropical plants in from the garden soon (today) or one of these fine mornings we'll wake up to find them frost nipped.

(And there's another poem, beginning "I'm not coming etc.) Oh Yes? But It's as much of a one – Oh hell.

     So long

     Bill

'Sconset: Williams refers to the title of his poem, "In the 'Sconset Bus."

the poem you want: Probably "To Mark Anthony in Heaven" (Wallace C47). Retitled

    "Mark Anthony in Heaven" in An "Objectivists" Anthology. CP1, 124–25.

Morning Imag.: "A Morning Imagination of Russia."

McAlmon thing: Two poems by McAlmon appeared in An "Objectivists" Anthology,

    "Child-Blithely" and "Historical Reminiscence."

[Rutherford, N.J.]

Oct. 19, 1931

Dear Louis:

Enclosed you will find a ticket for the Rodeo to be used next Tuesday evening, we will be there – we shall be there – or Floss will and I probably shall also. this seems to be the better way to have you join us as we are not coming in to supper.

But if you cannot manage to be present shoot the ticket back at once so that I may have it by Tuesday morning.

They tell me it says in the papers that I have won a prize out Chicago way for my poem the "Botecelli Trees". Now aint that somethin'. Hope it's true as I can well use the hundred for this and that.

Good luck. See you Tuesday maybe.

Yours

Bill

Rodeo: During October, 1931, a rodeo was presented at Madison Square Garden for the benefit of the Broad Street Hospital.

a prize: Williams had been awarded *Poetry* magazine's Guarantor's Prize of $100.

144. TLS-1

[Rutherford, N.J.]

Oct. 25, 1931

Dear Luois:

Nothing much to say except that the new mag. is slowly shaping up. And that I have had no word from either Putnam or my script of poems.

The chief reason for this letter, tho', is to tell you that I regret having told you to let that stuff of Roskolnikoff's (can't think of the correct spelling just now) go to the H.& H. without my taking what I wanted first. Don't let them have it too long. Hurry them a little. Thus maybe they'll miss the point. I doubt it tho'.

The mag. is to be very plain, no stunts or decorations. Naturally this will cut down the fun but I can't see clearer than that for the moment. Wish we could compete with the sur-realistes but we can't unless we do it for one issue, one issue – the last! For God's sake, tho' we aint goin' in for the "marble halls" stuff either, don't get me wrong – just what we take to be CONTACT – a contact as exemplified in the words. And that ain't journalism either which never did contact with anything between the tear ducts and the nerts and not even with them – just tickled them a little. I can see no function for myself outside of selection and to keep down a tendency to prettification with an eye to "business".

But I wish I had that legal chronicle stuff and that the H. & H. would go take a crap for themselves.

Yours

Bill

legal chronicle stuff: Charles Reznikoff's adaptation of court proceedings, published as *Testimony* (New York: Objectivist Press, 1934). It appeared in *Contact*, however, under the title, "My Country 'Tis of Thee."

214 Columbia Hts, Brooklyn, N.Y.

Oct 27/31

Dear Bill:

Reznikoff, you New Jerseyite – R-E-Z-N-I-K-O-F-F! What makes you re-member how to spell my name?!

Well, you kin 'ave the MS – or what wdn't I do for you? At any rate, H&H – Mr. Cockstein – hasn't answered my letter when they want to see me about the excellent script of the legal chronicle – and when they do I can say a publisher became interested in Mr. Reznikoff's MS.

It wd. be a good idea for you to print the thing entire – serially – or at least one whole section of it that way – or in one issue of Contact (how many pp. will the mag. contain?) My choice of a few pages out of the end of Parts I & II shdn't bother you & you can use 'em if you wish – & I think you shd. I've persuaded R to omit the Lincoln halters at the beg. & end. & also changed the introductory quotation from Ephesians magnificently – as only the great ar-ranger of the age – meet L.Z. – can do those things!

But you will have to come and see me at my houseboat or where you say (this Friday or when?) to get the MS. It will cost too much to send first class, Registered – and I need the money which I still haven't to mail the Anthology to Putnam in Paris. His American editress Junya Lass tells me he sailed last Friday.

Re – the Homage suggest you send him a letter <(c/o The New Review Paris)> and the list of MSS you showed me – or better the MSS what you have, & tell him to hunt up what you can't find or buy, all arranged as you want it for publication with a title page bearing your name first & mine last. Better insist than do nothing – it, action, on our part, will at least make the bastard feel sheepish if he has gone back on us.

Have added Mary Butts & T. S. Eliot's Mariana to the Anthology. It's done – & some class!

Say lissun! Hurry up typin that there prose of yrs. In fak' please bring it along the next time you see me. Geo. wants it by Dec 1. But the earlier you do it, the quicker this publishing business may start & I may have the 2¢ sooner to send you another letter.

See you Friday? Regards

Louis

Cockstein: Lincoln Kirstein.

Lincoln halters: Evidently quotations from Abraham Lincoln. Printings of *Testimony* have no such quotations.

quotation: Ephesians 4:31, "Let all bitterness, and wrath, and anger, and clamour, and
  railing, be put away from you, with all malice."
Anthology: An *"Objectivists" Anthology.*
Homage: The planned book of essays on Pound.
Butts: Mary Butts, "Corfe," An *"Objectivists" Anthology,* 36–39.
Mariana: T. S. Eliot, "Marina," An *"Objectivists" Anthology,* 160–61.

146. TLS-1

[Rutherford, N.J.]

Oct. 29, 1931

Dear Louis:

Not tomorrow (Friday), I'll have to be out here all day. But more important
than that is that the script you want will not be ready before Monday. I'll bring
it over to you some day next week – as soon as I can get off. It amounts to a
hundred pages!

I'm delighted that the Reznifkoff script is still available, I'll go over it with
you when we meet. If possible I'll print it all but that will have to wait for a de-
cision until I can tell what else there is to go in, etc. However I'll print every bit
of it if it can be done.

A letter at last from Bob, he'll be in Munich for a while. He's sending a poem
which he wrote in Mexico two years ago but which he has now finished. He
says also that his Politics of Existence is about ready to be shown – or will be by
spring.

As to the Homage to P. affair, I'll write to Putnam if you say so but I'd rather
wait until we know definitely as to whether or not he is going on with the An-
thology. If he turns that down he can go to hell before I'll get any book ready
for him – even tho' it might be a graceful compliment to Pound. Bob says he
has nothing to say about Ezra, nothing, that is, which he finds it possible to say
just now. His letter saying that however and a few other things might be used.

Never mind about postage I'll see that you get some stamps – I have some
left over from some local political work I've been interested in. I'll send them
to you – in this letter maybe – if I think of it after addressing the envelope.

Oh yes, the new quarterly begins to look as if it might begin to look like
something if somebody doesn't do something to it when I'm not looking. But
if they do you can bet they won't have my lyrical cognomen marking the cover
of the second issue – or any work of mine in it either.

Yours
Bill

Reznikoff script: *Testimony.*

a poem: Probably "Farewell to Alamos," *Contact* 1:3 (October 1932), 88–91.

Politics of Existence: A novel on which McAlmon had been working since 1928. Only a portion of it appeared in his lifetime. "*The Politics of Existence:* 2 Extracts From – ," *This Quarter* 1:4 (Spring 1929), 17–32.

147. ALS-1

214 Columbia Hts, Bkyn

Oct 31/31

Dear Bill,

Thanks for the Two's – tho' maybe you should have kept 'em for the next local political campaign and refrained from obliging 14 Objectivists to a political party. Poets must be kept pure you know etc

See you next week in town where and when you say. Bring the MSS.

Nothing new – except that I hear Reznikoff is very ill.

Yours

Louis

Two's: Two-cent postage stamps.

148. TLS-1

[Rutherford, N.J.]

[Zukofsky's notation: "Nov 4/31"]

Dear Louis:

I just obtained the script last evening. I'm sending it to you by ~~express, insured~~ <mail>. I can't see you this week – I have to talk with West over the first issue of Contact which is coming on fairly well. Perhaps when we are fairly launched it will all be easier, I hope so at any rate.

No further word from Bob. Wish I had the Resnikoff thing at hand but I'll have to wait till I can get to Brookly for that I suppose. I'd say come out Sunday and send you a ten trip ticket (may do that yet) but we shan't be home Sunday. Paul playing football has us on edge I fear – Saturdays that is. Well, time is long (enough) if one has the ability to absorb the punishment.

Anyhow, look for the script which I have not even read over – aside from the first page – which interested me all over again.

Yrs.

Bill

Bob: Robert McAlmon.

Resnikoff thing: The manuscript of *Testimony*.

[Rutherford, N.J.]

[Zukofsky's notation: "Nov. 8/31"]

Dear Louis:

Yesterday West and I made up our first issue of Contact. The extensive bibliography idea we found to be impossible as it would take up all our space. So we are printing just a concise list of the small mags since 1900 – (American and English-printing-Americans) with a one sentence descriptive note in each case.

The only other items aside from poetry and fiction will be a brief "comment" by myself on the critical position of the mag.

The rest of the space will be taken up with the following.

A story (or poem – if it arrives) by McA.

2 poems by L.Z.

Short Story – Shapiro (a good one – too)

The colored girls etc. W.C.W.

Scenario – Perelman (the one who did the lst Marx bros. thing)

2 (or more) poems – e. e. cummings

Reznikoff – ? ? (a big piece of it – as much as possible –)

(This is the final order.)

Send me at once the name of Reznikoff's works – and his correct full name. I'll see you for the stuff later.

   yours

    Bill

The following: The contents of the first issue (February 1932) of the second series of *Contact* were: "Comment by the Editor," Four Poems" by E. E. Cummings, "My Country 'Tis of Thee" by Charles Reznikoff, "Ballad of the Talkies" by Ben Hecht, "Ferry" and "Madison, Wis. [,] Remembering the Bloom of Monticello" by Zukofsky, "Scenario" by S. J. Perelman, "Idiot of Love" by Parker Tyler, "The Colored Girls of Passenack – Old and New" by Williams, "Miss Lonelyhearts and the Lamb" by Nathanael West, "It's All Very Complicated" by Robert McAlmon, "The Advance Guard Magazine" by Williams, and "Bibliography of 'Little Magazine' compiled by David Moss. Julian Shapiro's story, "The Fire at the Catholic Church," appeared in *Contact*'s second issue (May 1932).

■ 150. ALS-1

[214 Columbia Heights
                                                Brooklyn, New York]

Monday 5:30 P.M. [9 November 1931]
Dear Bill,
Charles Reznikoff, and the name of the work is <u>My Country 'Tis of Thee</u>.
Might have used the enclosed in my anthology – <if it weren't for the dedi-
cation – > instead I used something K.R. dedicated to Ivor Winters.
Ergo, it wd. be nice if you could use the enclosure by Rexroth in yr. first
number.
Can see you Friday between 3 and 6 (not after 6) – if you're in town.
Thurs. wd. be fine.
Ms. for Geo Oppen r'cd.
will write again late tonight.
        Yuss
        Louis.

enclosed: Enclosure lacking.
K.R.: Kenneth Rexroth.

■ 151. ALS-1

                                                [Rutherford, N.J.]

[Zukofsky's notation: "Nov. 9/31"]
Dear L -
I'm completely and God damned tired – added to which a disgust at being
unable to find a copy of the poems I got together this summer – shit take it.
You have the carbon of the bastardly botch. Have the shitty mess transcribed
somewhere at my expense will you? <I don't care what it costs: on good paper
too please> I'd like an extra carbon too so I can lend it to friends – in this life.
The enclosed of Cummings Viva to appear in Contempo – maybe.
        <u>W</u>

enclosed: Enclosure lacking. No poem from W [ViVa] (New York: Liveright, 1931) ap-
peared in Contempo.

[Rutherford, N.J.]

[15 November 1931]

Dear Louis:

Nov. 15, 1931:

Were it not for Reznikoff's thing I'd quit the Kamin quarterly at once, as it is I'm holding on only long enough to see if I can put over the first issue. Maybe I won't even last as long as that. The more I think of it the more certain I become that it's the wrong lead for me.

The book from which I quoted is, The Sylvan Year, Leaves from the note book of Raoul Dubois, by Philip Gilbert Hamerton (author of "The Intellectual Life," "Etching and Etchers," etc. Boston: Roberts Brothers. 1876. The same volume also contains another book, The Unknown River. The Latin quotation is from Virgil's Ecologues X. There is a picture of the old boy himself on the front. Glancing through the book I find that he was at home in Paris and London. He has a good eye and a very pleasant literary style. Geez! he knew Greek and Latin and quotes them all over the map. But it doesn't seem to have spoiled his eye. A curious, well printed old book.

"Now whatever a good artist paints is sure to be harmonious, for the simple reason that he makes it so:" How's that?

The corrections I'll send you in a day or so but this is just to ask you to stick to your decision and to cut out the Mc A. thing, the Three Letters and the Improvisations. Don't even send them to Open) Oppen?) – please.

     Yours

     Bill

Latin quotation: The epigraph on the title page of *The Sylvan Year:* "Non canimus surdis: respondent omnia silvae" (*Eclogue X*, line 8).

"Now whatever . . . : "Now whatever a good artist paints is sure to be harmonious, for the simple reason that he makes it so; and there is no doubt that any first-rate landscape-painter who chooses to paint a spring scene will get a harmony out of it (as he will out of any thing in the world), which may be used afterwards as a critical argument in favor of the 'year's pleasant king'" (*The Sylvan Year*, 65).

Mc A. thing: "Robert McAlmon," an essay intended for *A Novelette and Other Prose*. Never published, the manuscript is in the Williams collection at the University of Buffalo. Baldwin and Meyers B87.

Three Letters: "Three Letters" is a story Williams originally planned to include in *A Voyage to Pagany*. It was then intended for *A Novelette and Other Prose*. Never published, the manuscript is in the Williams collection at the University of Buffalo. Baldwin and Meyers B87.

Improvisations: Probably not those in *Kora in Hell: Improvisations*, but ones published by

Williams since its appearance. See Wallace C99, C111, C116 and C117. The improvisation, "A Memory of Tropical Fruit" (Wallace C111) was reprinted in *A Novelette and Other Prose*.

■ 153. ALS-3

214 Colum[bia Heights],
Brooklyn, N.Y.

Monday Nov 16/31

Dear Bill –

Yees, yeas, I'll make the cuts as you say – including i.e. excluding from the volume Danse Pseudomacabre also. What's the title of the book?

A Novelette and

and

Other Prose

(19 ? – 1931)   1920   1921   19what?

<u>Tear out the Gertrude Stein from Pagany & send it to me.</u> Maybe there'll be room for it.

Please. Etc. The Sketch on E. P. shd. also go in, but I'm still hoping Putin-ham will write us – In any case, these here To, Publishers won't stop with only one volume of Wool Willy Woolums – let's say they'll have coin for another in 1933?!

& please send the corrections right away.

Thanks for the information on Raoul Dubois – I'll want to borrow the book when I see you –

And you're absolutely right about E. E. Cs – as ever.

Louis

Danse Pseudomacabre: A short story by Williams. The *Little Review* 7:1 (May–June 1920), 46–59. Wallace C48.

Gertrude Stein: "The Work of Gertrude Stein," *Pagany* 1:1 (Winter 1930), 41–46. Wallace C142.

Sketch on E.P.: "Excerpts From a Critical Sketch: The XXX Cantos of Ezra Pound."

Dubois: The fictitious narrator of Philip Gilbert Hamerton's *The Sylvan Year: Leaves from the Notebook of Raoul Dubois* (Boston: Roberts Brothers, 1876). Hamerton (1834–1894) was a British author, art critic and etcher. *The Sylvan Year* is a study of people and nature in the French countryside.

154. TLS-1

[Rutherford, N.J.]

[November 1931?]

Dear Louis:

You might say that I showed you the letter then ask the man to come clean and direct. I told him you were all right but of course that means nothing.

Anyhow, please return the letter.

    Bill

See you Tuesday or Friday.

the man: Yvor Winters, whose negative review of Taupin's *L'influence du symbolisme français sur la poésie américaine* appeared in *Hound and Horn* 4:4 (July–September 1931), 607–18. Zukofsky to Pound, 11 November 1931: "But Ivory has just writ Bill Wooly a writ, sayin: 'Your pet bull-pup, Zukofsky, is getting on my nerves; one of these days I am going to kick his teeth out past his tail. . . .' Sweet old Bill – he sayz – re Ivory: 'You might say that I showed you the letter then ask the man to come clean and direct.' (!!) Haw!" (Yale).

155. TLS-2

[Rutherford, N.J.]

[18 November 1931]

Dear Louis:

The script of the Human Body thing is very faulty having been compiled from my first loose notes when the article was written. I tried to get hold of the finished review but was told <at the newspaper office> that there were no more on file. However you can, I am sure, get the original at the N.Y. Public Library or the Brookly Library. In fact you would do me a great favor if you would have a public stenog do it at my expense. Do it at once, please. And one carbon for me to keep.

It appeared in Canby's: Saturday Review of Literature Dec. 10, 1927.

I'd suggest that you leave 5 or 6 pages blank in the script you send to Europe, saying that the <above> script will follow for I believe I'd want to see the thing again before letting it go on.

I can't send you the Stein thing either as it came out in the first issue of Pagany and I only have one copy of that. But I'll have that typed out too for you in a day or so.

Now please get the other for me.

And perhaps after all I am going on with Contact – I dunno for sure yet. <yes, I'm going on with it.> It's like the weather.

    Yours

        Bill

Corrections:

A Novelette – VIII –

The work that is being done by many writers is so much of one – The sound of her book etc. etc.

(incomplete sentence)

Miss Moore –

Poe in his most read first essay quotes Nathaniel Willis' poem, The Two Women, admiringly and in full and one senses at once the reason: there is a quality to the feeling there that affected Poe tremendously. This mystical quality that endeared Poe to Father Tabb, the poet-priest, still seems to many the escense of poetry itself. It would etc etc.

Thickcake –

(I can't make it out myself – but we're not going to use this one so it doesn't matter)

The Venus –

p. 66 (near bottom) and top of p. 67 –

When I saw you I saw something unusual, I am never mistaken. I saw something different from what I see every day, neither throwing away nor taking hold to the old horrible handle, all filthy – Is it America? I asked, but you tell me nothing.

The Human Body –

p. 89 –

It is wonderful to read in these pages of the intestinal flora, the bacillus etc. etc.

Human Body: "Water, Salts, Fat, etc.," Williams's review of Logan Clendening's The Human Body (New York: Knopf, 1927) appeared in A Novelette and Other Prose. It was first published in the New York Post, 31 December 1927.

Canby's: Henry Seidel Canby, editor of the Saturday Review of Literature. Clendening's book was reviewed in the issue Williams specifies, but the reviewer was Percy G. Stiles.

Stein thing: "The Work of Gertrude Stein," first published in A Novelette and Other Prose.

■ 156. ALS-1.

[214 Columbia Heights, Brooklyn, N.Y.]

Friday 11/20/31
Dear Bill:
ok, you're going on with Contact!!
Changes in MSS. entered.
Spent about an hour yesterday trying to hunt up the "finished review" of

The Human Body – at Bkyn Public Lib. & the N.Y. Pubic Library. Nothing at the Bklyn. Lib. N.Y. Pubic: The Sat. Rev. of Lit. and Books, N.Y. Her. Trib. have reviews of the book in their issues of Dec. 10 (11?) 1927 - but not by W.C.W. Also looked up the Lit. Rev. of N.Y. Eve. Post & nothing at all in that. Now where do you think the review appeared? If your date is wrong, it's hardly possible that they printed 2 reviews of the same book – one by you & one by someone else? Figger it out –

I don't see what's wrong with the review as it stands (in the typescript). Do you? Or did the newspaper version slick it up?!

The main point is we're late! I'd like all of the MSS. to reach Buddy <(Geo Oppen)> by Dec 1 or soon after. Can you send the Stein thing by Monday? And I'll mail the whole thing (omissions mentioned to you excepted) on Monday.

C'mawn, le's hurree –

Louis

Stein thing: "The Work of Gertrude Stein."

157. ALS-1

[Rutherford, N.J.]

[Zukofsky's notation, "Rcd Nov 21/31"]
The Kay Boyle thing is important.
– many thanks for what you are doing.
I'll let you know when I am free again
– Contact going on has me tied again   W

Kay Boyle thing: "The Somnabulists."

158. ALS-1

[Rutherford, N.J.]

[Zukofsky's notation: "Rcd Nov. 29/31"]
Oh yes, an ~~opportunity~~ offer to print the novelette – came the day after you sent it to Europe – Ha, ha.

Send this on if you will – I've touched it up here and there.

Nothing new. Expect to have an argument before Contact is finally made up. I'll write when there is anything happening.

W

offer to print: Publisher unidentified.
this: Enclosure lacking.

[Rutherford, N.J.]

Dec. 6, 1931

Dear Louis:

Hectic days these, but Contact is going ahead. I must ask you, however, to tell Reznifkoff that I cannot use all of his first section in the first issue. I have cut it in half and shall use the first half only. If it is well received I'll use the second half in the next issue and then go on and finish the book in subsequent issues. To have given well nigh half the present issue to him would have thrown everything else out of balance. I stuck to my point until last night but deemed it wise finally to give in. I intend to open with R. Though unless we put Cummings first, in which case R. will come second – after C.'s poems. I hope this will be satisfactory.

You'll hear from me very soon again.

    Bill

Had a bid from Knopf (keep it under your hat) on the volume of poems. Don't know how it will come out.

I'll write you if they accept.

Want you out here soon -

    yrs
    Bill

Contact: The second series of *Contact*. The first issue appeared in February 1932.

[Rutherford, N.J.]

Dec 8/31

Dear Louis:

Haven't had time to decipher Oppen's letters as yet but am delighted that he is going ahead.

Of course you're in the 1st Contact. Who the hell said differently.

And I'm putting in the two poems you enclosed – if not too late. In 2nd if so. Thanks for the news etc

    yours
    Bill

I like immensely the tone (it isn't exactly that) of the Oppen letters. A man like that can <be trusted to> do anything he decides on as necessary. You're lucky to have him to work with.

    <u>W</u>

two poems: Two poems by Zukofsky appeared in the first issue of *Contact:* "Ferry" and "Madison, Wis. [,] Remembering the Bloom of Monticello." Two more poems appeared in the third issue: "Song 9" and "Song 10," *Contact* 1:3 (October 1932), 75–76. *CSP,* 24, 27, 40–41.

161. ALS-1

> [On printed letterhead of To Publishers,
> 214 [December 1931] Columbia
> Heights, Brooklyn, N.Y. and France: Le
> Beausset Ivar]

Continue to address yr. mail to L. Zookawfsky
      but!
- just to show you where <u>we</u> are in the world.
'N how'z Contack?
   Louis

162. ALS-1 [fragment]

> [214 Columbia Heights
> Brooklyn, New York]

[December? 1931?]
And when I see, I'll show you the rest of Geo. Oppen's letter which is some of the best, if not the best criticism of yr. work, I've seen.

  Guess we're fortunate!
   Yrs.
   Louis

P.S. Please rush yr. answers.

163. AL-1

> [Rutherford, N.J.]

Monday [December? 1931?]
Dear Louis:
You will receive the additonal material by separate packet. Use it. Never mind the projected Symposium on Pound.

  Glad to hear Oppen is going on to his criticism – should I see it soon – do I need it, perhaps? badly – or is it – flowers? No, it can't be a wreathe. Anyhow I'd like to know.

  Correcting.

Symposium: The planned collection of essays about Pound.

[Rutherford, N.J.]

[Zukofsky's notation, "Rcd/ Dec 22/31"]

Unique copy of the Pound thing: do not alter it (in sense or correct it – other than for syntax or grammar) it is a sketch –

Pound thing: "Excerpts From a Critical Sketch: The XXX Cantos of Ezra Pound."

■ 165. ALS-1

[Rutherford, N.J.]

[December 1931]

Dear Louis:

I want that Oppen phrase (in his letter) about sincerity being not in the writer but in the writing. I hope you haven't destroyed it. Send it to me please. I want to make use of it no matter how for the present.

And is the Putnam anthology coming out?

Bill

P.S. I have copy of the Boyle thing I'll send you when I have had it clean typed again – soon.

I want to see you but I'm – no, between Xmas & New Year – I'll surely let you know.

Contact is coming fast now. I have the dummy

Looks good

Bill

Putnam anthology: The planned collection of essays about Pound.
Boyle thing: "The Somnambulists."

■ 166. ALS-1

[Rutherford, N.J.]

1/7/32

Dear Louis

Come tomorrow eve. at about 8 o'clock – or phone me and I'll come in – phone at about 1 P.M.

I'd say come to supper but am uncertain about everything.

Phone anyway and then I'll see.

yrs

Bill

167. ACS

To Publishers
214 Columbia Heights, Brooklyn N.Y.

Mon. [18 January 1932]

Have you an extra copy of January I can see?

Dear Bill:

See by the piepers (Mon. Her. Trib.) you don't know what To, the dative of the Noun means. Our name – a noun – To. The dative wd. be to To or for To. to or for To, drinking to it or directed to it, you will discover sumpn. Hence: "discovery".

Good publicity. And now, please send yr. list of 100 – 200 – Yrs. Louis

January: The title of the novelette in *A Novelette and Other Prose.*

Her. Trib.: "Doctor-Author Calls Writing Balance Wheel," *New York Herald Tribune,* 18 January 1932, p. 11. Zukofsky was responding to this part of the article: "Dynamic, restless, nearing fifty years of age, he has explanations for most things, but not for the name of the house that will publish his book – 'To,' of 214 Columbia Heights, Brooklyn. 'Discover the dative of the noun – To?' he observed sitting in his consulting room. 'What's the dative of anything? Ask me another. However, I'm grateful to anyone who brings out my books.'"

168. TLS-1

[Rutherford, N.J.]

[*ca.* 20 January 1932]

I never knew "To" was a noun. Gosh all hemlock, I'll have to look that up. Any way it's not a bad name for publicity – nobody can understand it or keep from thinkin' about it once they see it.

Yes, I have another copy of the novelette but I hate to let go of it. Naturally, I know the book is coming out – but if it doesn't and if that script is lost. Do you want it just for fun or for some special reason? I'll send it if you insist. The same for the Kay Boyle thing: I have another copy but it leaves me without any if I let that go and that always gives me an uncomfortable feeling. Have it if you like tho' – but the book should be out so soon now.

Nothing else new. As always the issuing of Contact will be delayed – I suppose—for weeks. Too damned bad but it must be so – printers - etc.

Here's your list.
Yours
Bill

Kay Boyle thing: "The Somnabulists."
your list: Enclosure lacking.

169. TLS-1

[Rutherford, N.J.]

Jan. 22, 1932
Dear Louis:
I'm returning some things herewith: keeping the Nancy Cunard poem and Frances Fletcher's: Being Exclusive.

Yes, January is the name of the novelette. But I may have forgot to mention it. 's too bad. And I hope Oppen does include the Pound and Boyle things but if not – why then not.

Contact should be coming along by the end of the month.

Nothin' new. Got a lot of stuff to return to people so will have to cut it short.

Floss says your circular 's amusin', I like it, says she.

And here are a couple of new addresses (keep the other list, I don't want it back):

Ruth Bingham, 269 W. 11th. St. N.Y.C.
Edw. J. O'Brien, 118 Banbury Road, Oxford, England
T. S. Eliot, Harvard! Rah! Rah!

    Yrs.
    Bill

Cunard poem: Probably "Collect," which appeared in *Contact* 1:2 (May 1932).
Being Exclusive: Frances Fletcher (1894–1972), American poet. Zukofsky published her poem, "A Chair" in *An 'Objectivists' Anthology*. "Being Exclusive" is a short story. It did not appear in *Contact*.
Pound and Boyle things: "Ezra Pound" and "The Somnambulists."
circular: An advertisement announcing the publication of *A Novelette and Other Prose*.

170. TLS-1

[Rutherford, N.J.]

Jan. 27, 1932
Dear Louis:
Now you <u>have</u> got me scared. What is this manuscript you want returned? I've looked in the usual places and find nothing of yours. What form is it in, printed or what? I can't seem to remember. And have you no copy of it?

Well, write again giving me a better description of the thing. If it's here it hasn't been lost and I'll find it but for the moment I can't place it.

I had a nice letter from Reznikoff, I like his hand writing, his letters are of the same stuff as the poems. And it's odd that his hand writing is somewhat like Wallace Stevens'(es) – or what kind of language is it anyway?

Sorry if my carelessness has delayed you in any way. If it is carelessness.

Yours

Bill

manuscript: Zukofsky's essay, "Ezra Pound: His Cantos."

171. ALS-1

[214 Columbia Heights
Brooklyn, New York]

Jan 29/32

Dear Bill:

The manuscript you "can't find" – or maybe have found by now: a typewritten essay, on regular typewriting bond, light weight paper, about 25 pp. entitled Ezra Pound: His Cantos; probably a carbon, but the only copy I had. You took it last fall for the Tribute to Pound volume (see Putnam's announcement in this number of The New Review) and you had <it> in a bag or envelop with your own Sketch for E.P.'s Cantos, Front No 4, The Hound & Horn containing Fitts' review etc. Maybe you folded the essay into one of the magazines.

Well, here's luck to your finding it.

Louis

Putnam's announcement: In the fourth number of the New Review (November–December–January 1931/2), a number of future publications were announced, but none of them were a tribute to Ezra Pound.

Sketch: "Excerpts from a Critical Sketch: The XXX Cantos of Ezra Pound."

Front No 4: Louis Zukofsky, "Ezra Pound's XXX Cantos," Front 4, 364–69.

Fitts' review: "Music Fit for the Odes."

172. TLS-1

[Rutherford, N.J.]

Feb. 3, 1932

Dear Louis:

Unpalatable as it is for me to have to admit it, I am forced to admit for all that that I cannot find your manuscript. I have looked in all likely places for it but to no avail. I may yet find it but I don't think that likely. Have you no way of recreating it from notes? This is all very annoying but I can't do more just now than tell you the fact. Damn it. I hope you can forgive me.

There's no news other than that Contact will be out this week.

    Yours

    Bill

173. ALS-2

[214 Columbia Heights

Brooklyn, New York]

Feb 5/32

Dear Bill:

Too bad – but that's that if it's lost. Forget it, unless it turns up.

I don't know where the original long hand ms. is. Putnam possibly has a copy of the thing. Are you sure you didn't forward it to him?

Impossible to recreate it – since I don't keep notes. There's the French translation, but I could no more <re->translate the thing into English than say Dudley Fitts can.

Have you a copy of The Criterion April 1931, which contains the 3rd section of the essay?

Let's see: considering the enclosed circular wd. you write to Putnam and ask him what he intends to do, and if he has a copy of the essay on hand to include it in the volume, or if the appearance of the last is a fabulous idea to return it? Thanks, if you care to do this.

Saw Reznikoff yesterday, & he seems gratified by your note

Anxious to see Contact & yrself when you can find time.

    Yrs

    Louis

French translation: "Ezra Pound: Ses Cantos," *Échanges* 1:3.

3rd section: "The Cantos of Ezra Pound (one section of a long essay)," the *Criterion* 10:40 (April 1931).

circular: Among the Williams papers at Yale is a card with a printed text: "Tribute to Ezra Pound / Edited, and with an Introduction, by William Carlos Williams. / New Review Publications / 42 *bis, rue du Plessis* / Fontenay-Aux-Roses / Seine, France."

174. ACS

[Postmarked Rutherford, N.J.]

[Postmarked 5 February 1932]

I found the script at last. Did you say you wanted it or shall I keep it? No, I did not see the notice in the current New Review. Contact should be out today. Nothing new but letters from this one & that one.

    Bill

657 Main Avenue

Passaic, N.J.

Feb. 14/32

Dear Louis:

It looks as though it were going to be impossible for me to see Taupin before he leaves for France. Please tell him that I wish him luck for his trip. I have been thinking a good deal about his critical attitude toward American poetry of late and trying to evaluate his services to letters – especially American letters. I'd like him to realize that I for one greatly appreciate the work he has done – even tho' I cannot agree with him in all he says. He is a bitter pill for us to swallow sometimes – he makes us look a rather negative lot. But most tonics are bitter.

The thing is that he too often appears to be <no more than> a Frenchman looking only for that which is French – a sort of French Scout in the pay (one might almost say) of France to organize her literary colonization.

This leaves out of his consideration everything <almost> not French in our work and so his attacks look to me to be pretty negative and that complexion is cast over much that he does.

Mind you, I say this because he is intelligent and will welcome it.

I should much like to see less of the french stress in what he has to say. He's been in America long enough for us to claim him, if ever so slightly, as our own. I'd like to have him draw a parallel between certain of the stresses in French literature and our own, recognizing the two to be cousins and not nearer relations.

His revelations concerning Eliot, the more they show Eliot influenced by French writing the more they make him worthy <of> no critical mention at all.

Give him my best wishes for a good trip, as I have said, and say I wish it were possible for us to talk together more often.

No news of any sort – just the same stalemate.

Yrs

Bill

revelations concerning Eliot: In *L'influence du symbolisme français sur la poésie américaine*, Taupin argues that Eliot was indebted to Theophile Gautier, Tristan Corbière, Remy de Gourmont, Jules Laforgue, Jean de Bosschere, and André Salmon. Taupin also published in 1932 *4 essais indifférents pour une esthétique de l'inspiration* (Paris: Presses universitaires de France). Although not discussing Eliot in this volume, he does include an essay, "La Poésie D'Ezra Pound," in which he refers to "Louis Zukofsky, le critique le plus intelligent de Pound" (231).

176. TLS-1

[Rutherford, N.J.]

Feb. 17/32

Dear Louis:

Shit and double shit for Putnam. I enclose your script herewith. As soon as the book arrives let me know so that I may drive over there or have you out here or as it may happen.

I'd like to have seen Taupin, wanted to very much, maybe we can have an afternoon together later. I feel he is not really friendly to American writing but perhaps I'm wrong. But friendly or not he is valuable. Only how shall we use him? I wish I knew more of the past.

Get hold of the recent Fifth Floor Window, a small mag. There's a readable article on Surrealism in it.

Contact should be out today. There are two good photo shows going on: at Steiglitz's, An American Place and at the Julien Levy Gallery.

Yours
Bill

your script: Enclosure lacking.

article on Surrealism: Henry Bamford Parkes, "Notes on Dada and Super-Realism," *Fifth Floor Window* 1:3 (February 1932), [5–10]. Parkes (1904–1972), British-born teacher and author, emigrated to the U.S. in 1927 and joined the faculty of the History department at New York University in 1930.

photo shows: Stieglitz's An American Place was showing photographs by Stieglitz.

Julien Levy Gallery: The gallery was exhibiting surrealist paintings by Herbert Bayer, Cocteau, Dali, Max Ernst, Charles Howard, Picasso, and Pierre Roy.

177. ALS-1

[Rutherford, N.J.]

March 14, 1932

Dear Louis:

Yes Contact is out – down and out in so far as I am concerned: the first issue is the cheapest sort of a subterfuge for good faith in carrying out an agreement. I'll try to get you a copy, thurs., forget it.

Let's hope the books get here before you start West. No news other than that medicine keeps me humpbacked.

Yours
Bill

books: Copies of *A Novelette and Other Prose*.

[214 Columbia Heights
Brooklyn, New York]

Mar 16/32

Dear Bill:

Yes, the books should be here any day now. Got a consular invoice yesterday, stating 500 copies had been shipped on March 4. Ezra has already seen a copy & doesn't seem to think that the printing is too de luxe; Oppen says they're nice – the volumes – & regrets misprints about 1 to every four pages, he says there were seven times as many before his 8 proofreadings – you see the printer didn't know English. On the other hand, Ezra's idea of good printing may be somewhat exaggerated. Not on this hand.

Also r'cd 2 checks from Oppen yesterday, each for $100 – one of which is definitely yr. royalties – the other, I'm not sure I can make out his handwriting, for To's American expenses. He asks me to send on yr. check immediately. But there's something phoney about the checks, tho the receiving teller at my bank didn't seem to notice it: both of them carry the same number, but one of them says original, duplicate unpaid and the other says duplicate, original unpaid. They were sent by Buddy's bankers, Thos. Cook & Son, so yr. royalties are safe, but I think there was some mix up & the wrong drafts were sent on to me. I'd send your $100 any day, right now, if I were certain that my bank won't notify <me> of the mistake. If it does, however, I haven't enough cash of my own to cover. You won't mind waiting, then, two weeks or so, till I am sure that the bank has definitely collected? In any case, if the checks sent were correctly made out, it's not your publisher who's keeping you waiting but your best friend, I'm afraid!

Lowenthal brought his copy of Contact around the other day to show me. Moskowitz & Kaminsky's job sure looks poor. They spaced my first poem wrong, & there are misprints in both. Haven't bought a copy yet, since I'm trying to exist on $100 a month, paying my rent, & helping my father, brother and a friend all out of work, and this month I had to pay $15 of outstanding debts besides. <I don't suppose Contact's contributors are getting paid?>

What about the second issue? All made up? Or could you use the preface to An "Objectivists" Anthology I once read to you in Grey's restaurant? Or Movements 1, 5 and 6, or any one of em, of "A"? Or is Number 2 not coming out?

& I'm still woikin. But lissun if you can't find any immediate date to drop in on a pore lonely bastard (all I have you see is this fancy stationery!) please reserve the afternoon of Friday, April first for me, and fool me by seeing me before I go west on the fifth.

My affections, reverence etc to the family & yr self

Louis

books: Copies of *A Novelette and Other Prose.*

Lowenthal: Jesse Lowenthal (1899–1963), a friend of Zukofsky. Zukofsky had published one of his poems in the "Objectivist" issue of *Poetry.* Lowenthal was an English teacher at Stuyvesant High School in New York City.

Moskowitz & Kaminsky's: David Moss and Martin Kamin, the publishers of Contact Publishing.

my first poem: "Ferry." *CSP,* 24.

179. ALS-1

> 657 Main Avenue
> Passaic, N.J.

March 17/32

Dear Louis:

Take your time about the check. It's good news that the books have arrived. Anxious to see them.

The book of short stories is here also – a fine printing job. I'll send you a copy at once.

Yes, I'll reserve Friday April 1st or sooner.

> yours
> Bill

Contact is in the balance.

> Mar 17/32

to continue:

I don't think I'll use anything of yours in the next issue – if there is one.

But if the second, or next, issue shows any kind of improvement over number 1 then -

I'll use your new Cantos of A in the third

At present I am holding back the material for no 2 until I have some assurance that I shall not be disgraced again.

Were practice not so violently active now I'd write more fully but March will not allow me peace – never has – my flesh, even, seethes my cock burns – I am more potent – but harassed.

> Yrs
> Bill

the books: Copies of *A Novelette and Other Prose.*
book of short stories: *The Knife of the Times.*
new cantos: "A"-5 and "A"-6.

180. ACS

[Postmarked Rutherford, N.J.]

[Postmarked 30 March 1932]

Friday – at your room – I'll come early – about 2 or a little after. Lots of news this time. Perhaps I can help at the application office – at once [.] I'll try to phone today.

Yes, write. Now is the time I am sure.

> My best
> Bill

181. ALS-2

[Rutherford, N.J.]

<u>Monday</u> [April 1932]
Dear Louis:

Don't be dumb – it's a swell book. Floss is delighted – ain't that enough?

Just your asking about <u>Paterson</u> started me off and I finished it – so to speak. That is I sketched it out to the end and nailed the last few lines. I'll be finished – really in the next year or so – with your help maybe: not too much but –

Then you can have it if you want it. I'm really delighted with the <u>Novelette</u>. Send me the 50 at once – Take out the cash ad lib. For Ezries libro.

> Best luck
> Bill

swell book: *A Novelette and Other Prose.*
Ezries libro: A copy of *A Novelette and Other Prose* for Ezra Pound.

182. AL-1

[Rutherford, N.J.]

[Zukofsky's notation: "Apr 5/32"]
Ask at the N.Y. Public Library – I suppose – about copyright.

———

or write and send 2 copies to the Library of Congress
> Something like that.

[Rutherford, N.J.]

April 11, 1932

Dear Louis:

I like Reisman's criticism of the novellette and other writings & he does see
– which I don't always. I feel along too often only once in (idle) moments com-
ing up into the light. I mean criticism of my work when it is from someone
who sees helps me to see and I like it.

I can't use the writing but I'm sending it on to Contempo.

They want someone to do a note on – I enclose the letter. I gave them your
name & Reisman's no others.

I'm not keen about autographing the books. But send me a dozen then if
they go for a fortune! We'll incorporate. Yes, send me a dozen & I'll return
them signed, pronto.

The Buena Vista sounds swell. But what evening – it has to be a Tues. Fri. or
Sat. I'd like to do it very much – maybe on the 19th

Goo' luck

yrs

Bill

Reisman's criticism: His review of *A Novelette and Other Prose* appeared in the *Lion and
Crown* (Fall 1932), 44–46. See the Biographical Notes, page 556.

the letter: Enclosure lacking.

Apt 11 – 2130 Leavenworth
San Francisco, Calif

May 28/32

Dear Bill

I'm afraid I deserve myasskickedoff (pace my 4 yr. old nephew) – acting as
unreliable as all the other publishers. But as you may have guessed, I've been
broke till today. I'll send the balance of $35 as soon as I can when I get back.
And, in fact, I'm starting out on the 6th of June on an extended hitch thru the
north – i.e. Montana, N.D. Minn etc and maybe up to Ottawa, Canada, for a
week, before New York. Jerry seems to have a lady there he wants to see.

Wa-all Points West is Points West, & we've had enough. And after a lapse of
30 days after our stop in Mexico, we still don't seem to need medical advice.

The poems for Contact if you want 'em – tho I'd rather you print 5 or 6 of
"A" if you want that. Otherwise return the enclosures in your next – i.e. the
poems, make sure to use the check.

Try and send me an AIR Mail to reach me here before June 6 (air mail takes 2 days) – but if you can't manage write me P.O. Box 3, Station F, New York City.

And: what you been doin' & what this summer?

My regards to Floss & all

Louis

nephew: Arnold Wand (b. 1927).

enclosures: Enclosures lacking. The Zukofsky poems appearing in the third issue of *Contact* were "Song 9" and "Song 10." *CSP*, 45.

185. TLS-1

[Rutherford, N.J.]

June 1, 1932

Dear Louis:

It was damned nice to hear from you. I like the poems and will use them in #3. It hasn't done you any harm to travel. Hope you don't catchum syphilis after all. It takes six weeks you know to develope, not 30 days. The treatment is very effective – and painful and disgusting. Well . .

Hot here. Had the 3d floor roof ringed with a raining today – at last. 's very pleasant out there. My Alps!

The check will pay for the teak of which the railing is made and there will be fifty cents over to apply on the carpenter's bill. But then, one does not live to learn. Teak is teak.

Really, it gave me a very happy feeling to hear from you. When you go away now a value goes away – somewhere, not accessible any more – something that one relied on. It was very reassuring, also, to read Marianne Moore's first poem in the New (perhaps the last) Poetry. I read the other two poems of M's but – perhaps I'm tired.

Contact #2 will be out in a week or so. Then we start on #3. The damned thing seems to have a root – I vary from disgust to confidence

Floss is well. The boys too. Eke Mother

Bill

Marianne Moore's: The three poems by Moore were "The Steeple-Jack," "The Student," and "The Hero." *Poetry* 40:3 (June 1932), 119–128.

[Rutherford, N.J.]

June 14, 1932

Dear Louis:

Glad you're back. There's nothing startling to tell. Contact #II should be out in a week – I hope it looks better than #I – but as I've not seen proofs I cannot say.

Speaking of proofs I had a yard or two of them from Oppen – poems of mine, for an anthology I presume; I'd lost track of the thing completely. Corrected and returned them.

Also received an anthology <u>Profile</u> by Ezra. Well integrated and not a little surprising in makeup. Well printed. I liked it, tho' cannot quite justify either his inclusions or omissions. Yes, some sort of idea is evident.

A considerable quantity of good material for Contact continues to come in – quite surprising stuff at times. Short stories mostly – very little if any good poetry of course.

Our 3d floor balcony has been completed, a great success – you must come out soon and tell us about the trip – next week, perhaps Tuesday next – or almost any time. This week end – Sat. eve?

Hard thought has never been so imperatively necessary to me – leading to some kind or kinds of decisions.

     Yours

        Bill

Bill takes College Entrance Latin soon. Then boys to camp. Floss at home all summer – no long vacations this year.

The opera's at a standstill. Paterson untouched . . nothing new to show. Perhaps my piles! (not enlightening)

anthology: *An "Objectivists" Anthology.*

<u>Profile</u>: *Profile: An Anthology Collected In MCMXXXI* (Milan: Giovanni Scheiwiller, 1932).
    Zukofsky was represented by "Poem Beginning 'The.' " Williams's poems were "Hic Jacet," "Postlude," "Portrait of a Woman in Bed," and "The Botticellian Trees." *CP1*, 15–16; 3–4; 87–88; 348–49.

[Postmarked Rutherford, N.J.]

June 21/32

Dear Louis:

Not Tuesday after all. I hope this isn't going to start a series of impasses – but practically every day this week is taken: boys to camp, mother to the shore

– last looks at friends who're leaving etc. & Bill's college <entrance> exams (creating tension) etc. etc. Next week should spell easier times.

> Yours
>> Bill

188. TLS-1

[Harriman, N.Y.]

July 4, 1932

Dear Louis:

There's been nothing to say and much to do. And I felt very much disinclined to see anybody. What's the use of a mere formal meeting, even of friends, under such circumstances. I didn't even write. In fact there's nothing to say now.

Floss and I are here at her mother's farm for the weekend. We're going home this afternoon. This about finishes up our planned doings.

Contact appeared last week. It's better than the first issue but costs too much. Nor can much be done about that. The price per issue to produce it still ranges above any possible sales price. Still, Kamin wants to go ahead so ahead we'll go. I think the new cover at least pleases the eye. You'll see that we've taken liberties with Reznikoff's contribution. If you should hear from him I'd like to know what he says. And I'd appreciate your own reaction. The cuts are from a book of about the time the incidents in his collect occured and do set off his findings rather nicely – in my opinion. If he wants to use the cuts in his book as it will later appear I'll be glad to let him have them. I hope at least that he will not take exception to what I have done.

Billy was accepted by Williams College. He's pleased.

As you have probably surmised, the opera did not go through. I learned a few things concerning what is needed, wrote a few concise scenes and then everything went to sleep. I do, however, mean to finish the composition this summer. Or have I told you all this before.

I'm taking no vacation this year. Were it not that I feel so listless I'd welcome the summer's quiteness. But somehow – well, I go on working, more or less.

Hope to see you soon,

> Yours
>> Bill

Reznikoff's contribution: Charles Reznikoff, "My Country 'Tis of Thee," *Contact* 1:2
   (May 1932), [99]–108.
cuts: Nineteenth century illustrations of "Oratorical and political gestures," "Simple bodily pain," "Love," "Gratitude" and "Simple laughter."
the opera: Williams's projected opera about George Washington.

P.O. Box 3, Station F
New York

July 16/32

Dear Bill:

I was waiting for you to write. And here is your letter, which you missent to my old Brooklyn address, which was forwarded to San Francisco and back again. I'm sorry – I should have got in touch with you before.

Telephoned you yesterday (Friday) but you were out.

I thought I might get a cheap shack somewhere near the sea for the summer – but there are no cheap ones [. . .] The room at 214 Columbia Heights is still vacant as I left it, but I may as well continue to hope that it will be till September when I intend to take it, and try to save that extra rent money towards what I still owe you. I'm sorry – again- to mention it, but it does bother me off and on. You see none of the money coming to me came and won't be, if it is, for months, but I'll pay you on or about Aug. 1.

Nothing new, except To's publication of E.P.'s How to Read & Spirit of Romance part I, a copy of which I'll give you when I see you. Also the Anthology I edited is expected any day now.

I should like to see you and Floss, and will come to supper, or as you say, when you say. Or if you prefer, why don't you and Floss meet me at the Buena Vista some night next week and have beer with me alone [. . .] Let me know. Better not make it a week-end day perhaps, but any week night.

Haven't seen Contact, but Reznikoff seemed pleased in a letter. I haven't seen him, in fact have seen almost no one.

[. . .]

    As ever,

      Louis

To's publication: Ezra Pound, *Prolegomena: How to Read, Followed by the Spirit of Romance* (Le Beausset (Var), France: To Publishers, [1932]). Published in June 1932, this was in-
tended as the first in a series of volumes that would collect Pound's critical writings.
anthology: *An "Objectivists" Anthology*.

[Rutherford, N.J.]

July 18/32

Dear Louis:

The trouble was ~~that~~ I lost your P.O.Box address and so found myself forced to write to Columbia Hts. ~~Next~~ This week I'll be driving in, Wednesday or

Thursday – Hell, I'll pick you up in front of the N.Y. Public Library this Wednesday at 5.45. If you aren't there I'll know you haven't been able to make it.

Never mind about the cash, use it for licherachure (i.e. ham sandwiches)
Yours
Bill

191. TLS-1

[Rutherford, N.J.]

July 23/32
Dear Louis:

Glad to have seen you [. . .] more serious talk will have to wait for cooler weather – if it will.

In writing to Hobs and-or Butts mention Dr. Allen as having suggested their names. The place is Upton Lake, Clinton Corners, N.Y. It is in the sticks north of Poughkeepsie. A small RURAL – poetry should look interesting Greek -

The cottages are small, I'd stress the point that being a teacher, professor, instructor – you are looking for an inexpensive place where you can read and be quiet – otherwise they may jump the price on general principles;

Good luck. I've seen the little lake. It's pretty
Yours
Bill

192. ALS-1

[Rutherford, N.J.]

[Zukofsky's notation: "7/26/32"]
Dear Louis:

Whatever you decide is satisfactory to me. Yes, send me the 5 copies 'stead of the 3 bucks. I can't wait to see them. I boost ~~them~~ it in Contact (i.e. the Anthology)

Our Arcadia'd like to have you come out for a few days – if – when – as – to (dative)

yours
Bill

I'm next to hopeless about Contact. a dull chore – not enough good work or too much. I can't tell which: a quarterly can't be just amusing, must be weighted – if to be excused.

anthology: An "Objectivists" Anthology.

193. ALS-1

P.O. Box 3, Station F
New York City

July 30/32

Dear Bill:

Sending 6 copies of the Anth. under separate cover. Check or M.O. for $35 will follow as soon as I get my Aug. check – in a few days. Thanks, I'm glad you helped me decide that. Build a canvas awning over your roof!

Will be at South Beach, S.I. all August – my lumbago which went but has returned needs the sun. If the Choimun lady who rented out the rooms doesn't act grouchy maybe you & Floss wd. care to come out on the beach – if you know a way of getting there from Jersey. Will let you know, if you want to, if the Choimun lady is grouchy or not.

Send a copy of Contact 2 – if you can spare it, & maybe I'll have something to say when we talk next. Incidentally, Ezra wants to know why you don't send <u>him</u> a copy.

Thank Floss for the invitation. Maybe in Sept. if the "business" permits, & if it's still Arcadia – i.e. no one home yet.

The tips about up state arrived late. Thanks again, anyway. The address if right alright – only make your F (Station F) clearer when you send the praises for the Anthol. – if praises they will be.

> Yrs
>
> Louis

Marianne Moore ordered a copy of The Novelette to E. P. last week.

Anth.: *An "Objectivists" Anthology.*

Ezra: "Why don't that old ASS Bill grumpus von Vilhelm strasse send me his bleating
lamb of a maggerzeen . . ." (*EP/LZ*, 126).

194. TLS-1

[Rutherford, N.J.]

Aug. 1/32

Dear Louis:

All right, I'll watch my Fs.

By the way, didn't I lend you the small volume of Pound's Cantos? Or was it the new edition of Personae? Look it up.

Yes, we'll run over to Staten Island some day.

Contact #2 goes forward tomorrow morning. I await eagerly the arrival of the Anthology. And I'll have a copy of C. sent to Ezra instanter – in fact have also tended to that.

The current issue of Eng. Review contains my letter on Anglo-American literary relations. I have only the one copy, should I receive others I'll forward one.

I shall not waste the thirty five since you want me to have it. Thanks.

No news otherwise.

But there will be at least one more issue of Pagany. And so one more chapter of White Mule. Maybe many more chapters, who snows?

I am salting away all new projects that come up to the extensive surface of my well surfaced brain for I will not give myself up to the new now, too much depends on digging in. For a year at least, maybe two I have promised myself to do nothing but clean up the shop. I have gently told Kamin that after this year there will be no Contact (in all probability) for little Willie.

> Yours
> Bill

small volume: Probably the Hours Press edition of *A Draft of XXX Cantos* (1930).

new edition: Originally published by Boni and Liveright in 1926, a fourth impression of
Personae was issued by Horace Liveright in May 1932.

Anthology: An *"Objectivists" Anthology.*

my letter: The *New English Weekly* 1:14 (21 July 1932), 331. Wallace C178.

195. TLS-1

[Rutherford, N.J.]

Aug. 5, 1932

Dear Louis:

's a wonderful book, a distinguished object, and the preface is like the Bible for impressiveness and impenetrability – it's a veritable glass miggle for slipperiness. But the most impressive feature of the whole is that it is a whole and like nothing else I have ever observed. It is splendid that your long poem and Rexroth's long poem should lie side by side – or stand side by side. I think those two are the feature of the whole show.

I haven't read much yet, just corrected the errors – where possible and browsed about here and there. Later on I'll have more to say. I think you should get some reactions.

> Yours
> Bill

wonderful book: An *"Objectivists" Anthology.*

your long poem: *"A"* 1-7.

Rexroth's long poem: "Fundamental Disagreement with Two Contemporaries," 79–86.

■ 196. TLS-1

Aug. 24, 1932

Dear Louis:

We're using the two poems of yours, sent from Arizona, in the next issue of Contact. Can you help me to get work of Rakosi, at once? Perhaps you have something of his to hand. If he can't be reached quickly it's no use bothering.

As to our visiting you . . when? I simply can't get away for other than family matters. It may be, however, that I, alone, may be able to sneak off next week for a few hours. We'll see.

Wish I had a job to offer you for the winter. But I ain't.

     Yours

     Bill

two poems: "Song 9" and "Song 10."

Rakosi: Williams used two poems (with a joint title) by Rakosi: "African Theme, Needle-work, Etc.," *Contact* 1:3 (October 1932), 35–36.

■ 197. TLS-1

[Rutherford, N.J.]

Sept. 10/32

Dear Louis: If you can make out what I was driving at in the enclosed go to it. I can't work over it now. But feeling inclined to put the thing down I did so.

Mark it up, chisel it apart – do what you please with it. And maybe send it to Lesitscistchsky for his New Broom if you want to – or back to me for final labor (and labor it will be for me if I have to work over it)

Anyhow – that's what you set going by your damned Anthology /

Contact 3 is made up. Out in a month or whenever – I'm busy as hell trying to get going and cleared of letters – etc

     Yrs

     Bill

enclosed: Enclosure lacking. A draft of Williams's review of An *"Objectivists" Anthology*.

Lesitscistchsky: James G. Leippert, editor of the new periodical, the *Lion and Crown*.

   Theodore Leschetizky (1830–1915) was a Polish pianist, teacher and composer.

P.O. Box 3, Station F
New York

Sept 12/32
Dear Bill:

Thanks. I get it. "Collaboration" in this case will have to be limited to

(pg1–¶4) the omission of commas after "whole" & "truths," and if I get
your meaning the introduction of commas around "as excellence."

(pg1 ¶6) suggestion that you add the word "obviously" since the mass of
Rexroth's poem is cumulative rather than impaired (by its length,
let's say).

(pg1 ¶6) if you don't want to say "this work" or "this book" – "this" will
be enough – the next paragraph of your note explains.

(pg 2 ¶3) suggest you add "almost" since Rexroth does say "we ferry the
Skagit" (a river in the west) etc, "I take places, I take scenes," but I see
your point, I think (from the next paragraph) & so I've added the
distinction (difference) in pencil & you can appropriate it or think
about it & revise.

(pg2 ¶6) I wdn't delete "also", but maybe it's King's English by
Compulsory.

And now as to where to place it: I think it would be useless in Leippert's –
especially since Jerry has promised him a review of it – and Jerry needs the
practice of sitting down to write and gettin' to it.

If Contact 3 can use it, L.Z. wd. be gratified. Better, if you can get the Horny
Hound or the Chimpanzee (Symposium) & make some money <on> it, L.Z.
wd. be tickled. Especially – since the screws I think will never bother to find a
reviewer for the book. I know the fine waste of spirit involved in correspond-
ing with the bastards, but if you care to find the leisure to bother

Wut else? O yuss. Did you get the M.O. for $35 that I sent on Aug 2. One I sent
to someone else some years ago went & got lost & ever since I'm uncertain –

For the rest, I can't find a place to live in, nor does a job seem to be coming
my way – Hell is on the rise.

Yrs – & to Floss
Louis

Rexroth's poem: "Fundamental Disagreement with Two Contemporaries."
Leippert's: The *Lion and Crown*, edited by James G. Leippert. No review of *An "Objecti-
vists" Anthology* appeared in *The Lion and Crown.*
Horny Hound: *The Hound and Horn.*

Symposium: *The Symposium*, ed. James Burnham and Philip Wheelwright, printed
   Williams's review. *The Symposium* 4:1 (January 1933), 114–16. Wallace C185. Reprinted
   in *Something to Say.*

199. TLS-1

[Rutherford, N.J.]

[September 1932]
Dear Louis:
Thanks. I'm doing the thing over – lightly, using all of your suggestions and
adding a word or two of my own for additional clarity. Then it goes to Sympo-
sium – this afternoon. After that I'll see.
   Wish I could find work for you.
      Yrs.
      Bill
~~Send your copy to H & H. if you care to — if~~ both ~~accept — what t'ell.~~ We'll
~~choose~~
Yes, I received the check

200. ALS-1

[Rutherford, N.J.]

Saturday 9/24/32
Dear Louis:
Symposium took the criticism but they say it came in too late for the Octo-
ber issue. They will bring it out in January. That's late but it will be worth while.
   I couldn't say a thing about it in Contact as it has been against our feeling to
do book reviews. I did however bring it in under your name in the Contribu-
tors Notes!
   Contact is in bad shape (morally) I am afraid. Kamin is away <in Europe>
and Moss seems paralyzed – full of objections – no good. I wonder, even if
there will be an issue this fall. Probably there will be one (badly printed) in De-
cember???! je ne sois rien. I'm doing almost no writing. What with Bill's going
away to college, practice picking up and the general hell of life as I live it – time
exists only in ostrich stomachs along with the pebble-diamonds they swallow.
   But I ain't weakening – and only hope that you may be able to live.
      yours
      Bill

Contributors Notes: The third (and final) issue of *Contact* contained no information
   about contributors.
Bill's: William Eric Williams.

. . .

Sept 28/32

Dear Bill

Glad about the Symposium acceptance. (and – too bad about Contact).

Guess Leippert wrote you about my suggested compilation (what!) from or of your letters. I though it might have more point than another say by me on you – nobuddy being interested anyway. Well, I'm enclosing it. Please cut out what you will and send the rest to him & have him type it (I'm dropping him a note saying he'll hear from you. Alright?)

You'll note I confined my selection to the year 1928 – i.e. far enough away to be – History. Also, that I've tried to make it funny in spots. Also, to display you as a critic of manners (!) as well as woids. That I happen to be the subject is not my fault?

[. . .]

     Yrs as ever

     Louis.

P.S. What's this new prose & verse of yrs. Leippert mentions?

P.S.S. I feel I ought to be seein' you more. Maybe you can manage it when I get my own place?

     Louis

and the cat should eat the rooster's bloody comb

compilation: For a planned Williams issue of the *Lion and Crown*. Leippert had written
    to Williams on 30 August 1932 that he intended to make "the last issue of the first year
    a William Carlos Williams number . . ." (Yale). No such issue was published.
new prose: See the following letter.

[Rutherford, N.J.]

Monday – 5.35 P.M. [4 October 1932]

Dear Louis:

I've been swamped again with work and petty affairs. I enjoyed your selections from my letters, there's nothing to be deleted. I'll have the typing done myself in order to check errors.

The new work I'm sending to Leippert will be a prose caterpillar on French painting – using it as an example to say what I want to say about American writing: an allegory in essay mode – only that's too literary sounding. It's just the stuff about French painting which I've had in my head since my mother went to school in Paris and which Taupin wouldn't believe was real. It's all written but not copied out and corrected. I'll send you an advance copy.

Then there's a group of poems, things that I had half written as much as a year ago but never showed to anyone for the reason that they were unsatisfactory to me: perhaps three poems – nothing overwhelming you may be sure.

Boy! I'm tired tonight – for no especial reason unless it be that I came near being unreasonably ill last week. I caught a cold and for a day or two I was worried lest it get me in the lungs for on top of it all I had to deliver a baby with forceps in the middle of the night. I was frankly scared for an hour or so. It would be inconvenient to be ill now.

Yes, we ought to get together. The best way would be for me to come in some day when you are settled – if ever. And if not you will have to come out here. Perhaps we can fix it so that you can spend a few days or a week here before it gets too cold. I'll let you know. You can have the whole top of the house with porch, typewriter et al (some latinist, eh what!) How about it? You haven't something you'd like to work on? You would have hours of freedom.

This man Parkes who writes essays was out her yesterday for a talk. I like him. Sometimes I fall for the British as though they were God's chosen people. I suppose it's my old man in me that does it. Anyhow Parkes is nice. I enjoyed talking to him for I had been lonesome and he wanted me to talk so I talked my head off all about the things I like and the things I don't like including Eliot. But he's such a cool reasonable but well directed person that I couldn't make myself angry. I especially enjoyed his having come to America out of Europe deliberately because of the odor of decay there. That's the true American spirit. He's an American – with a British accent. He's all right. Teaches history or some sort at N.Y.U. Lives on East Houston St. because he feels alive in the stir there.

Yours
Bill

prose caterpillar: Among the Williams manuscripts at Buffalo are four fragmentary writings on art, one of which is titled: "French Painting and Modern Writing" (Baldwin and Myers C8). I have found no completed essay that matches Williams's description in this letter. "French Painting" in *RE* is an extract from *The Embodiment of Knowledge*.

203. TLS-1

[Rutherford, N.J.]

Monday [Zukofsky's notation: "10/10/32"]

Dear Louis:

Your new address noted, I'll be seein ya over there some day within the month. I've met this fella Foster in fact he's sent me work for Contact. I'll remind him that he owes you a bill.

I've had an invite to talk to The Vagabond's of Greenwich Village some evening. I may do it a week from tomorrow (Tuesday) evening. Also The Literary Club of Stuyvesant High S. wants me to talk to them some Thursday at 1 P.M. May do that too if encouraged. Just plan to get up unprepared and spill whatever is inside or alongside me. I refuse to take time to get up a lecture.

Your extracts from my letters is being typed now, ready tomorrow along with a new chapter of White Mule for Pagany.

Nothing much else except that there is to be a new issue of Contact after all – I think, for I have had no concrete evidence of it but they say it has been in the hands of the printer for two weeks past. It may possibly happen that there will even be a fourth issue but as far as I'm concerned that will positively be the last – if I get that far.

> Yours
> Bill

Foster: Harvey N. Foster, author and editor. Co-editor of *Fifth Floor Window*. Foster submitted poems to Williams for consideration for publication in *Contact*.

204. TLS-1

[Rutherford, N.J.]

Oct. 17, 1932

Dear Louis:

– and did you see the roasting I got in The New English Review by someone signing himself Professor Austin Warren. Do you know of any such person? I answered his attack at once but they may not give me space. It's of no importance, however.

Yes, to hell with the Vagabonds and the School and all that sort of crap. I've decided not to talk.

I hear nothing from Contact. It may come out and it may have been buried, I dunno.

Never mind about Winters, he surely is insane.

But what do you mean, the Dep't of Taxes has assessed your personal estate at $5000. ? And do you mean you really want me to come quick to see you? I'll be there on Wednesday for at least an hour if you really mean it.

> Yours
> Bill

roasting: Austin Warren, "Some Periodicals of the American Intelligentsia," *New English Weekly* (6 October 1932), 597 (reprinted in *William Carlos Williams: The Critical Heritage*). Warren dismisses Williams, *Contact*, and the writers represented in it. Williams replied to Warren shortly thereafter in the *New English Weekly* (10 November 1932), 90–91. Wallace C184.

Winters: Yvor Winters. His review of An *"Objectivists" Anthology* in *Hound and Horn* 6:1 (October–December 1932), 158–160, condemned almost every aspect of the work. Winters concluded, "The book . . . is encouraging in one respect: none of the talented writers of Mr. Zukofsky's generation are included, and the theories that Mr. Zukofsky struggles hopelessly to express, the methods of composition that he and his friends have debauched till they no longer deserve even ridicule, seem to be sinking rapidly to lower and lower literary levels; they should be in a few more years no serious cause of consternation."

▓ 205. TELEGRAM

Rutherford, N.J.

28 October 1932

MEET ME DOWN TOWN GALLERTY THIRTEENTH ST NEWYORK TWO PM LUNCH—
BILL.

DOWN TOWN: The Downtown Gallery was exhibiting paintings by Marsden Hartley.

▓ 206. ACS

[Postmarked Rutherford, N.J.]

[Postmarked 2 November 1932]

Come early on Thursday – I mean before 6 P.M. as we want to have supper ahead of the usual time. Floss has a date later in N.Y. . Thanks for the quotation.
Bill

▓ 207. TLS-1

[Rutherford, N.J.]

Nov. 9, 1932

Rall right Louis,

I'll return the stuff you want back as soon as I have finished mt quoting – which I aint done yet – but in a day or two I'll be finished. Haven't looked at Jerry's things yet nor will I just yet, can't stop to think or evaluate just now. But I'm using him in No. 4 and you too – so help me.

Glad you liked the reading. I liked it myself, that's the reason it sounded good. I'd like to read more but dread the stodginess of it when forced or formalized. It's an art – no,a pleasure which I'd mightily enjoy cultivating or havijg someone near me cultivate. It has a future. In fact without a delevopment of the art of reading it is unlikely that the best of our work will even become know to ourselves. I often think of it. I have even wanted to pay someone to come and read to me. But who? No woman, surely. Some man, some grey haired man (Homer!) myself perhaps as you suggest. It would be a relief after music, too much music which ofetn leaves me brutalized, numb, gone out.

Yesterday I had to deliver a brat in a nearby hospital when I wanted to be home for supper. Looking around for some reading matter I found a copy of Shakespeare in the drawer of the dresser in the doctors rest room. I dove into Twelfth Night – whole pages seemed uninteresting – made to order – careless ramblings to fill in the space and time. The art in that case was in the life of the man who was writing I am sure. Oh well. Just amusing

This is just to tell you I received your letter and will tend to things soon. Oh yea, the thumb's swell (swollen! still a little)

> Yours
> Bill

No. 4: No fourth issue of *Contact* appeared.

208. TLS-1

[Rutherford, N.J]

[Zukofsky's notation: "11/14/32"]

Dear Louis:

The papers you desire I return herewith. I have rewritten the review completely, made it much simpler, shorter with sufficient quotations to bring it back to about the original length. When it has been typed out clean I'll send you a copy – maybe in this letter. I did not use your suggestions re. your own work as you will see.

I have read with interest a short thesis by Gottfried Benn in the last Transition (the new T. #21) on the nature of the ego – sounds rough but it's well done. I've known vaguely much of what he writes about but never had it so well systematized for me before. It's curious, too, in the world how one's intimate thoughts have foretold all the discoveries and dilemmas of science. When we read of some age long work which has come to a triumphant climax we can almost always say, Why, certainly, anyone could have told him that. No doubt, though, we'd say the same if the work had come out differently. But it is great to read of the stratification of the consciousness – the self – down through the middle brain into the nerves and the very glands. It is the basic stuff of poetry, the "depth" which peaople speak of in a writer is really more of a depth than anyone has heretofore realized. Lautreamont and the others become more valuable is this light. Prose, most prose, becomes as we have always known it to be – just the patter of the intelligence, the almost negligable forebrain. Anyhow, I enjoyed what I read. Must tell Jolas so. One should always tell a man he has been enjoyed – his work is assisted.

No new writing.
Best luck
Bill

review: Williams's review of *An "Objectivists" Anthology*.
short thesis: Gottfried Benn, "The Structure of the Personality," *Transition* 21 (March
    1932), 195–205.
Lautreamont: "Comte de Lautréamont" was the pseudonym of the French poet Isidore
    Lucien Ducasse (1846–1870), best known for his prose cantos collected under the title
    of *Les Chants de Maldoror*.
Jolas: Eugene Jolas, editor of *Transition*.

■ 209. ALS-1

[Rutherford, N.J.]
Nov. 29, 1932
Dear Louis:
I am getting in touch with McKnight. Hope you like #3 There will be a #4
and then (as far as I'm concerned) it's all off
See you some day soon
Bill

■ 210. ALS-1

39 Sidney Place
1932 (still) Brooklyn, N.Y.
Like spring, for Dec. 1st
Dear Bill:
Thanks in re – McKnight.
Haven't seen Contact #3 – yet. I suppose McK will send a copy.
I enclose 4 more poems – 2 of Oppen's, 2 of mine – you can have 'em for
Contact 4 or return 'em – as you decide. Merely want to give you more to se-
lect from.
    See you in town when you come in, when you say. May have something to
talk about – a writer's union which I've proposed to Bunting & asked him to
transmit the plan to Ezra. But don't mention the idea to anyone – till after I've
spoken to him.
        Yours
        Louis

4 more poems: Enclosure lacking.
union: Zukofsky elaborated on his plan in a letter (23 December 1932) to Pound, "We the
    Writers Extant, W.E., WE, should therefore engineer for ourselves, & out of our re-

sources, to clarify the general mess, to centralize the marketing of our products (and so to get ourselves published without obligation to a price system) and to support the Writers Extant as much as possible with our limited means" (Yale).

211. ALS-1

[Rutherford, N.J.]

Dec. 5/32
Dear Louis:
Sorry but though there may be a 4th Contact (still doubtful tho') we'll have to use the batch of material already on hand.
No word from McKnight – nor from the stars – only the moon, I'm afraid
    yours
    Bill

212. ALS-1

[Rutherford, N.J.]

Dec. 12, 1932
Dear Louis:
's finished – as far as I am concerned. Contact 4 will be the last (?) but even thaat will be under the editorship of a "group" – proletarian in feeling.
Enclosed are several enclosures – selfexplanatory.
Nothing more to say just now.
    yrs
    Bill

Enclosed: Enclosures lacking.

213. TLS-1

[Rutherford, N.J.]

12, 15, 1932
Dear Louis:
Nope! I'm out, completely out – so am returning the poems herewith. The one about the sink is the best to my taste and an excelent composition, perhaps you'd care to send it to "Contact #4" directly.
Nothing new other than more or less vague plans and petty irritations – it were better to have been Aristotle or any of the excellent dead.
    Yours
    Bill

about the sink: "To My Wash-stand" (Song 22 of "29 Poems"). *CSP,* 52–53.

[Rutherford, N.J.]

FEB. 1, 1933

Dear Luis:

(Geez! is it going to be one of <u>those</u> letters, two mistakes already) – not that I have anything to say but I have been cleaning up after myself re. Contact and these poems of Oppen's have to be dealt with. As he may have moved since sending me his last address I am taking the liberty of sending the poems to you.

That's about all.

However, Leippert asked me to be Associate Ed. of his mag. which I had to refuse to be. No <u>sir</u>, not twice in the same trap. I am only beginning to feel alert again. What a mountain of ashes buries one when he tries to really do anything. The task becomes titanic. Contact goes on as indicated in my last. They have made Macleod editor – with my full consent.

Nothing else – unless – Oh yes. One of the Benets asked me to send a poem for an anthology: one short favorite poem. Perhaps you know about the project – God help them – instead of getting behind something. But who does (who has the means) at this late date.

It is so easy to fall into this mood of regret and Mediterranian moonlight. But it's not easy to give a haul or a shove in a much too hot sun. I can never write fast or well enough to please myself.

Kenneth Burke has a scheme for publishing scripts by a photostatic process. If you have anything of novel length for him send it to 280 Bleecker St., N.Y.C.

I work at White Mule – but it is slow to grow. It makes me ill that Pagany does not appear when Johns has two chapters and never answeres letters while of one of the chapters hurridly corrected and forwarded I have no other copy.

And Antheil never has answered my inquiries.

Screaming with chagrin, disappointment and anger would be needless to say useless. But I wish to build for you my prison walls.

     Yours
     Bill

his mag.: The *Lion and Crown*.

Macleod: Norman Macleod (1906–1985), American poet, novelist and editor. Editor of the *Morada* (1929–1930) and American editor of *Front* (1930). No further issues of *Contact* appeared.

an anthology: *Fifty Poets: An American Auto-Anthology,* ed. William Rose Benét (New York: Duffield and Green, 1933). Wallace B20. The poem Williams selected was "The Red Wheelbarrow."

Antheil: During 1932 Antheil was enthusiastic about writing the music for the Washington opera. Antheil, however, never produced any.

215. TLS-1

[Rutherford, N.J.]

Feb. 10, 1933

Dear Louis:

Toward a Commune of Letters! – in the mind. And an Aristocrasie of Manners. Read the enclosed and if you have any comments to make, make them. I don't feel competent.

Practice is plumb shot to hell. Hardly a call any more. And when there is it's: I can't pay you today, doctor. Result. I have time to write. But the mood is difficult. Resignation won't do. Action lacks a reasonable direction both on physical grounds (How can I live?) and spiritual (to include the moral and aesthetic). Hope seems out of date. One can nevertheless work – as self criticism.

I have an offer to have White Mule published by a N.Y. firm. But I have scarcely finished a fifth of it and it is not a thing which can be unrolled like toilet paper. It requires invention and that takes time. However I enjoy the task.

Your Ibsenesque house-maid was swell.

Best luck (food and bed)

  Bill

an offer: Possibly from Donald Friede of Covici-Friede, who had expressed interest in *White Mule* in 1932.

Ibsenesque house-maid: Whether Zukofsky was quoting an actual person or an imaginary one is unclear. See the following letter as well.

216. ALS-1

[39 Sidney Place
Brooklyn, New York]

Feb 12/33

Dear Bill,

Don't know Y.W. well enough to call him Professor, but I hope Carl accepts the suggestion. Also if Y.W. has any mss. he would want me to put some pabulum into, he may send 'em via The Hound & Horn & I'll send the bill to Kirstein's department store papa.

The arguments with Y.W. are not to be used. Doing this work of gentle critical suggestion (I don't say correction and clarification), my mind is sidetracked from its own work & grows avid for justice another form of clarity &

definition. But no use getting too serious about it – so if Carl and you get an occasional laugh out of the "arguments", maybe what I did is worthwhile.

My comments, for Carl, on the paper are confined to brackets [ ], which mean omit the passages or words in brackets & continue as is. <u>Not to be confused with</u> <u>Yvor Winters</u> parenthesis () and his pedagogical peremptory "meaning?" Also, wherever I offer actual words, I don't mean for Carl to incorporate dogmatically, but to present my opinion of what the facts are, determined by my knowledge of yr. work & (I suppose it can't be helped) by the character you yourself have presented (to me).

Continuing the Ibsenesque housemaid – "It's terrible, my dear, it's terrible, the things one hears and reads nowadays."

Hope practice picks up, & that you can finish <u>White Mule</u> anyway. Who offered to publish it? And has any one taken <u>Script</u>?

> Yrs
> Louis

Y.W.: Yvor Winters.

Carl: Possibly Carl Rakosi, whose essay on Williams, "William Carlos Williams," appeared in *The Symposium* 4:4 (October 1933), 439–47. Rakosi begins, "The manuscripts of sixty-five poems by Williams written between 1921 and 1931 (including selections from *Primavera* and *Spring and All*) and nine others of prior date have recently been collected under the title *Script*." Rakosi goes on to quote from various poems while comparing Williams's work to that of his contemporaries, particularly Marianne Moore.

arguments: See the note to Williams's letter of 17 October 1932.

217. TLS-1

[Rutherford, N.J.]

March 3, 1933
Dear Louis,

Can you help me to locate the Guggenheim Foundation people. Where do they hang out? And what are Moe's initials? No. I'm not looking for a fellowship, just information.

Nothing new.

> Yours
> Bill

Moe's: Henry Allan Moe (1894–1975), secretary of the Guggenheim Foundation.

[Rutherford, N.J.]

3/7/33

Yes, not even jokingly should one use their language. Thanks. But I have several counter-irritants for you when we shall get together. The hardest task is to prepare the material for a typist – often I'd rather do the work myself and that is laborious. I'll see you Friday (D.V.) I'll drive over arriving about two thirty or three and bring my tools. Have R. there. Organization would help but isn't it like trying to fit together five pieces of a forty foot mosaic? See you Friday.

> Bill

the material: Probably the manuscript for *Collected Poems (1921–1931)*.
R.: Charles Reznikoff.

▪ 219. TLS-1

[Rutherford, N.J.]

[8 March 1933]
Dear Louis:
Just a little exercise to get me back into thought of poetry –

For the first time in a year I've felt like a man again – Antheil's perfidy knocked me cold – then Contact hit me before I was on my feet – Then – other things. Finally they began to press me for White Mule. I didn't have enough of it to show a publisher so I had to get to work. Now I've finished the baby's first year. Seven chapters which you have

not seen. At least amusing.

And now I can – if I can – go to hell in my own way once more. It's great!

Flores has more or less dumped me re. my poems. What the hell is the matter with people? So, I'm at those once more, trimming, rearranging, etc. etc. preparatory to trying another agent.

Hope you like the sonnet – more truth than poetry maybe.

> Yrs; Bill

Antheil's perfidy: Presumably a reference to Antheil's early enthusiasm for the project
   and subsequent silence about it.
Flores: Angel Flores (1900–1992) published *The Knife of the Times and Other Stories.*
the sonnet: Enclosure lacking. In all likelihood, however, the sonnet referred to is "Our
   (American) Ragcademicians" (*CP1*, 364). A copy of the poem in the Zukofsky papers
   at Texas bears Zukofsky's notation, "Enc. 3/8/33."

[Rutherford, N.J.]

March 14, 1933

This may not be
<u>correct for Italy.</u>

Dear Louis:

Here are "twenty pages" of verse for Ezra's anthology. They have been se-
lected with a purpose which may or may not be apparent but unless you have
some very strong reason for excluding any one of them or for putting some-
thing you may like among them I'd rather the group stands as it is. After all,
what is the sense of your telling me what to send and me telling you. If we
don't know what we want to represent us it's about time we learned – or took
the consequences.

However, here are the verses – a few of them you have not seen before, as al-
ways I'm open to criticism from you. If you will I wish you'ld send them on to
Ezrie for me when you have done with them – as soon as possible. Postage en-
closed. Send on your selections from your own work if you will, I'd be glad to
see them and to send them on if you want me to.

I do nothing but punch the typewriter these days – that is when I'm not de-
livering the usual quota of week-end babies (I don't mean that they're all girls)
– tho' it saves money to have girls nowadays – they don't have to be circum-
cised. My eyes are heavy as lead – one should say "gold" perhaps.

     Yours
     Bill

Ezra's anthology: *Active Anthology,* ed. Ezra Pound (London: Faber and Faber, 1933). Wal-
    lace B21. See Williams's letter of 15 March 1933 to Pound (*EP/WCW,* 134–35).

[Rutherford, N.J.]

Saturday [1933]
<u>in time</u>
Dear Louis:
    Here.

       yrs
       Bill

[Rutherford, N.J.]

March 22, 1933

Dear Louis,

I sent Zabel nothing you haven't seen excepting the enclosed – of which I'm not particularly proud. It, the exception, has only the virtue of being conversational in tone which is (now comes the dark secret) the way I want Paterson to be – just a lot of talk - made or broken by the way it hits and not the way it addresses itself to the target. I think you saw a long skinny poem called, The Locust Tree in Flower. That also may possibly be new to you but I don't think so. It's odd but, off hand, I don't know which the hell the other nine are – anyhow they're not new to you – some of them fully a year old but as yet unprinted. I was keeping them for Leippert but decided not to, finally.

Don't neglect that face of yours. If the pain continues an xray of the maxillary sinus on that side should be taken. You may know of some clinic such as The Cornell Clinic where it can be done skillfully and at next to no expense. Use my name as having recommended you to them. Or if it gets worse and you don't want to go to a clinic tell me and I'll fetch you out here to one of my friends. Then again maybe it's a tooth.

Tell Reznikoff that I thought you were a little hard on my nice Foot-note and that I thank him for rescuing it!

I've been driving myself hard making a clean copy of the script-volume of poems which I want to get off to Maxim Liever next week along with the "first year" of White Mule, the bait for the poems. I have the poems ready now, not verydifferent from what you saw last year – in fact not different at all other than for the inclusion of five or six new things such as Sluggisly, The Flowers Alone and – hell, I dunno what, not much. I revised two or three old things too, drastically revised them, such as The Bells – at your suggestion (by the way, that's one of the ones I sent to Poetry) My friend, Mrs. John, is typing out the White Mule stuff. On that I'm going to try to get an advance royalty! O yea? – in or der to able to hire a typist and really work at the thing.

No, I haven't see Moe yet or done a thing about it all, no time, but I shall write to him today and try to date him up for a talk early next week.

    Best luck

    Bill

Zabel: Morton Dauwen Zabel (1901–1964), associate editor of *Poetry.* A group of poems appeared under the title, "That's the American Style," *Poetry* 43:1 (October 1933), 1–8. Wallace C191. The poems were: "The Flowers Alone," "The Locust Tree in Flower,"

"Tree and Sky," "The Centenarian," "4th of July, I–III," "An Old Song" (later retitled "Song") and "A Foot-Note." *CP1*, 365–66; 366–67; 385; 367–68; 368–69; 369–70; 370.

enclosed: Enclosure lacking.

nice Foot-note: "A Foot-Note," *Poetry* (October 1933). Zukofsky to Pound, 21 March 1933, "Bill's selection his own – except I thought <u>A Foot Note</u> shd. Be omitted & Bill agreed (he not bein' in a particularly Bull mode (I mean mood, I suppose), but I'm sending it anyway, since I think <u>you</u> ought to decide" (Yale).

Maxim Liever: Maxim Lieber (1897–1993), a New York literary agent.

Sluggisly: "Sluggishly" was first published in *Active Anthology. CP1*, 370–71.

The Bells: "The Catholic Bells," first published in *An Early Martyr and Other Poems* (New York: Alcestis Press, 1935). Wallace A16. *CP1*, 397–98.

Mrs. John: A Mrs. Johns typed much of Williams's work during the 1930s. See Mariani 308 and 350.

223. TLS-1

[Rutherford, N.J.]

March 24, 1933

Dear Louis,

Poem I couldn't enclose in last letter (no time to type it) enclosed in this.

Please return enclosure. And please, by return mail, let me have some information about your white hope: his name, age, present position and condition. I must be prepared to give a few details to Moe – not too many. I'm going in on the afternoon of Tuesday next. Here's hoping.

Letters from Ezra in nearly every mail, you too in all probability. His english publisher "seems serious". E.P. now wants 28 additional pages of verse from me.

The volume of verse together with the first 15 chapters of White Mule go to Lieber also on Tuesday.

> Best luck
>> Yours
>> Bill

Poem: Enclosure lacking.

white hope: Tibor Serly (1900–1978), Hungarian-American violinist and composer.

[Postmarked Rutherford, N.J.]

[Postmarked 31 March 1933]

No time since seeing Moe to write – and none now. After this week end I'll give you the details. it's a fairly long story. Can you get me Serly's home address?

Bill

[Rutherford, N.J.]

April 2, 1933

Dear Louis:

I know you're more or less waiting for this letter, perhaps more than less, I dunno. Perhaps not. Anyway, I saw Moe (as I told you) last week. We had a long talk the upshot of which is that to his knowledge (?) Antheil is working on the opera. The only evidence, real evidence, I have of this is that he, Moe, walked out of the room during our conference "to look up the information", coming back after a moment to say, "Yes, he is working on the opera." What he did while out of the room I cannot say as he did not tell me. Perhpas he took a piss.

The real information is that the Gug People want the opera and they want Antheil to do it. I have reason to believe that if he has done nothing about it they want him now to commence inasmuch as they have just extended his endowment. Moe says that he himself is going abroad in June and that he will see Antheil. I'm not completely satisfied that the matter will go forward but it would be foolhardy for me to make a fight just now; I intend to leave the nect step up to Moe and to Antheil.

About Serly Moe had much more to say. He listened to my account of the man, a very brief statement of the essentials which you supplied me with after which he, Moe, asked me for Serly's address saying, "He has all the preliminary requirements and we are looking for another qualified musician." Apparently, while he wants Antheil to go on with my opera he at the same time seems willing to give Serly serious consideration for whatever other project may be in the wind. And this is as accurate an account of my hour with Moe as I can give you. Please let me have Serl's home address at once if you have not already amiled it.

Yours

Bill

the opera: *The First President.*

226. ALS-1

[Rutherford, N.J.]

[1933]

Good. Omit the last sheet of script – just tear it up. Also thanks for the corrections which please make: "Banks" for "Nanks" – I have written Antheil an ultimatum. <(more about this later)> For the pain use <u>Pyramidon</u>, a five grain tab. Get a dozen anywhere.

Bill

"Banks": One line near the end of "It Is a Living Coral" is "Banks White Columbus." The poem was published in *Active Anthology*.

227. TCS

[Postmarked Rutherford, N.J.]

4/12/33

Friday's the day: 2.30 or 3 P.M. for an hour at least. Nothing new except the snow and maybe the apocalypse at hand.

Yrs.

Bill

228. TLS-1

[Rutherford, N.J.]

April 28, 1933
Dear Louis:

What the hell can I say about Writers Extant? I don't see how it can be done. I think your prospectus is too complex. Where in hell is one to begin?

It's all very well to name off twenty or more names of those you'd like to see members of such an organization but can you get them and can you keep them and can you manage them when you have them? I doubt it very much.

Personally I could at a pinch give up a couple of hundred dollars, but why? For two hundred dollars I could in all probablility get my poems published and although that is a most selfish viewpoint yet it <is> one which must have weight with me since a sum of that sort is not easy for me to detach from my ordinary expenses. And unless I gave it I wouldn't take a thing from the organization.

It is possible that we might get a book that would sell and so bring us in a profit. But don't imagine for one minute that if some book were profitable it wouldn't be taken away from us damned quick by the author or the firm to which he would sell out his rights.

Without names, though, there can't be any thought of beginning: Who are they?

The enclosed letter may interest Serly. As soon as I receive the papers from the foundation I'll forward them to you. My thought is that S. should offer something, not the opera, as his thesis – so to speak – after which – should he get the award – we can do as we please, as Moe indirectly suggests.

Very dull days for me.

     Yours

     Bill

your prospectus: Not located.

enclosed letter: Enclosure lacking.

229. TLS-1

May 6, 1933

Dear Louis:

I have had word from Serly that he is sailing on Wednesday next. That makes the time very short, especially since he says he is tied up on Tuesday. Because of this I want you to come out with him Monday for supper at 6.30. I'll have office hours during the evening but that doesn't matter. Later on I'll have Mrs. Spence down and we can make some music.

For the rest: Having thought (waited!) doubtfully with your "Writers Extant" in mind I have come to the conclusion that there's no other way out of our difficulties. It is basically the only way for us to proceed. BUT I do not think we have as yet hit upon either the correct name for the venture nor upon the proper method or proceedure.

You have made a start and the motion is not lost. We are all searching for the phraseology. Part of the next step and it may take some time to develop it, come what may, is for you to see the men involved, personally. It will not be until after that that a program can be put down on paper. When you have done this (supposing for the moment that you are the permanent secretary indicated in your project) and after you have seen certain theoretical scripts, including my White Mule. Then we can band together, publish one book, the best we can find, and then, with some solid ground under our feet and a snarl in our voices we can begin. LAST will come what is written down as a contract – after we have had some experience. Everything else must be tentative up to that time.

Now, to be thoroughly candid, Serly has let me know of Pound's offer. By adding two and two, and to hell with you if you don't grab at it, I'm willing to put a hundred dollars into the pot for the good to all that may come out of it.

Take Pound up. Go to Europe as soon as you can. Look around. Make notes. Learn whatever there is to learn over there – and when the cool weather come again we may all be the wiser.

But come out Monday night anyway. Monday for music. Put off the other till some Tuesday.

> Sincerely yours
> Bill

Mrs. Spence: Madeline Spence, who, with her husband, Andrew Spence, were Rutherford friends of the Williamses.

Pound's offer: Pound had written to Zukofsky on 28 April (Texas), encouraging him to come to Europe that summer. To pay for his transportation, Pound offered Zukofsky a check for $112.

230. ALS-1, TLS-1

[Rutherford, N.J.]

[Zukofsky's notation: "5/6/33"]

Show this to Serly – I think the name is better than yours.

a few paragraphs may be added: Reznikoff can take care of a proper arrangement of the items.

————

Not more than 2 pages in all

THE WRITERS PUBLISHERS, Inc.

1. Membership in the group is limited to those writers who have in actual possession an available and complete book manuscript of high quality which is unacceptable to the usual publisher.
2. Manuscripts to be published by the group are to be selected (with advice) by a Director who shall be elected by a majority of the group members for the term of one year.
3. The business end of the group activities will be under the direction of a paid Secretary-Treasurer, under bond, who shall occupy the office indefinitely—or until removed by a two thirds vote of the existing membership at any time.
4. Initial funds are to be contributed by the charter members as may be agreed upon, to be added to later as the business of the group may prove profitable.
5. The first membership will be made up of a selected, voluntary group who by a majority vote, after the first requisite is satisfied, will add to their numbers from time to time.

6. Resignation from the group may take place at the discretion of the member by which he is absolved from further financial responsibility at the same time relinquishing any claim he has had upon the group's resources.
7. Dissolution of the group as an organization will be consitional upon an equal distribution among the members of all funds and other rights enjoyed by the group under its incorporation.
8. Further additions to these rules will be made from time to time.

Show this: Zukofsky to Pound, 11 May 1933, "I enclose a copy of Bill's 'revision' of the prospectus. I don't think he gets the real purpose of the original prospectus. But maybe you can do better in an idle moment. I mean tho his draft wd seem to be more business-like than mine he doesn't see how he's trapped himself again in the 'highbrow licherary circle of viciousness'" (Yale).

231. TLS-1

[Rutherford, N.J.]

Tuesday [Zukofsky's notation: "5/16/33"]

Dear Louis:

Come out this Thursday afternoon if you can manage it. Plan to arrive at about three o'clock. We shall then have plenty of time for talk. It's been impossible to see you earlier, rushing about, one thing and another. By the way, Katherine, one of our best friends is on the verge of death from a growth in the abdomen.

Nothing to report. I've written nothing, planned nothing – save as one plans in a semi-conscious way while he dashes from point to point of his daily routine.

Started to read a book two days ago: Pity is Not Enough – by Josephine Herbst. The first pages reveal some good writing – how flat that sounds! One feels at least that the prose has been made out of SOMETHING. Out of words, presumably.

The opera is constantly in my head. Serly was of considerable help to me in clarifying what I must do. I will take up the next step in a few days.

Drop me a card if you're coming.

    Yours

    Bill

Katherine: Katharine Sheeler (1881–1933) had married the painter Charles Sheeler in 1921. She died of cancer in June 1933.

Pity is Not Enough: Josephine Herbst, *Pity Is Not Enough* (New York: Harcourt, Brace, 1933). Williams recalls Herbst (1897–1969) and her husband, John Herrmann, in his *Autobiography*. He also includes a letter from Herbst in *Paterson: (Book V)*.

[Postmarked Rutherford, N.J.]

[Postmarked 16 May 1933]

Having written you a note this morning I have to cancel it. Thursday I have to lecture to the nurses from 4 to 5. So come Wednesday, if you can, or come Thursday anyway, we can talk before and after the lecture but it doesn't leave much time. Wednesday would be better if the notice isn't too short. and "the rain it raineth every day".

    Yrs.
    Bill

■ 233. TLS-1

[Rutherford, N.J.]

May 24, 1933

Dear Louis:

I've tormented my soul long enough over our Writer-Publisher proposal: I think it's no go and we should give it up. As far as you personally are concerned I think it would be an excellent thing for you to get to see Pound this summer. I'll be glad to contribute my bit to assist you as agreed with Serly. I believe we'd all derive some benefit from it by clarifying our present more than a little muddled thinking. Go and take a look. In the fall we can appraise the situation again if we want to.

And don't forget that with every advantage in their favor large publishing houses are going broke. While even such a venture as Angel Flores' Dragon Press has cost its sponsor two or three thousand dollars which he'll never see again. It can't be done today. Pound said it over and over again in his letter. We've got to heed such evidence.

The only possible way out of our difficulties, aside from hoping against hope, would be to print a series of six books at our own expense and then give someone like Harcourt, Brace 15% to market them – as others have done before us. But could we find six saleable new books? I doubt it. And even if we could find them, where would the next six come from? No, I can't see it.

    Yours
    Bill

his letter: Perhaps Pound's letter of 28 April 1933 to Zukofsky, in which Pound said, "On the whole wd/ be simpler to earn some money and spend it printing an occasional book" (Yale, Texas).

[Rutherford, N.J.]

May 31, 1933

Dear Louis:

It means this: I saw West and <he> would have nothing to do with a self publishing venture. Quite correctly I think, he pointed out that no book should be self-published until it had been the rounds of all the commercial publishers. This would take a year. And if all of them turned it down you could be reasonably sure that it would not sell fifty copies under any circumstances. We should simply lose our money.

Besides, there are not twelve books in the country that would be available for our uses.

As for Josephine Herbst: she is about to become a successful author. Under those circumstances I refuse point blank to approach her. What for? To ask her for money? Never. To ask her for a script? Insane.

Stevens is under contract to Knopf.

It's simply an impossible situation.

The Apollinaire is a valuable piece of work. I read the 3d. part of the script and am now tackling the first two. But it's worse than algebra to me. It's all I can do to decipher a meaning from the few chisel cuts you have put in that rock. This however is real. I wish that it might still be possible for you to bring Taupin out here for an evening later in the month.

A short note from Serly saying he is still interested in the opera. And did I tell you that I had heard from Antheil? I think I did tell you that. Serly shall have the libretto as soon as it will be finished.

> Yours
> Bill

West: Nathanael West.

Stevens: Wallace Stevens.

The Apollinaire: Zukofsky's *The Writing of Guillaume Apollinaire*. Translated by René
    Taupin, it was published as *Le Style Apollinaire* in France.

opera: *The First President.*

■ 235. TLS-1

[Rutherford, N.J.]

June 20, 1933

Dear Louis:

You must forgive me. I can't talk to anyone or see anyone these days. I want to come in to Brooklyn before you leave – and I will make good my promise of the check – but it seems impossible for me to move. I am trying to write the libretto for Serly without success, I have labored at it until my eyes are almost hanging out – but nothing gets on the paper – or nothing that is of interest. I don't know what has come over me but at times I'm pretty well convinced it is the end of me as far as writing is concerned. Perhaps it is extreme fatigue – though I look well enough. It is heartbreaking to toil at something and feel one's interest grow less and less the more he works – panic finally. But you make a mistake if you take this to be pathetic. I'm not making excuses. All I mean is that when I can't write any longer then I'll be through with writing. Though I confess there's nothing else.

    Yours
    Bill

libretto: *The First President.*

236. TLS-1

June 25, 1933
Dear Louis:

Give Ezra my regards and ask him, for me, if he still drops his voice at the end of a poem when he is reading it so that nobody can hear the last three lines. Or are the last three lines of any poem not worth listening to; now there's a new school! The Penultimates.

Lord knows what you'll see in Europe. My guess is that it won't be poetry.

A card from Serly saying he will write later.

Took my mother to the shore today (yesterday) and Paul leaves for camp tomorrow. Formerly this meant that I started writing at once as though someone had shot off a pistol. But this year – I'm thinking. I don't call it thinking though. I call it waiting. My brain is surely a vegetable.

My chief occupation is the reading of U.S. history. I start looking something up and then discover what I am really interested in. An hour later I find I have been very neatly amusing myself.

I have, meanwhile, designed five or six second acts for my opera. No, my libretto. An opera is something you pay six dollars to hear, isn't it. By I love my libretto his tale is so long and if I don't hurt him he'll do me no harm.

Finally it begins to penetrate unto me that I can very well amuse myself without the world. They call it jerking off.

Don't be sea-sick. It is a very nasty experience. There is no preventative.

Drop me a card from the great beyond and, if you have time, try and put some news on it. Most letters one gets refer to the health of the Prince of Wales or state that the wine is excellent or that the trains carry one from place to place over there much as they do here. You will positively not see the Grand Canon of the Colorado is Provence.

Remember me to Mr. and Mrs. Oppen, I enjoyed meeting them and hope that they will look us up, call us up sometime in July, we plan to remain right here. Or if they are to remain in Sidney Place I'd enjoy running in there – when?

Come back wiser or not at all! (With your shield ot on it!)

Best wishes Bill

libretto: *The First President.*

237. TCS

[Postmarked Rutherford, N.J.]

6/26/33

Tuesday is impossible for me. But I think I can make it Wednesday. I won't have much time but I'm fairly sure of being there between three and four. I'll have to leave by five thirty at the latest. It would save me an additional trip to the city if you can have someone buy me, at some second hand bookshop, three or four copies of my V. to P. I'll pay you for them if you can have them there. If not convenient though, forget it. Do you want the Appolinaire now? If so mail a card to that effect so I shall get it Wed. A.M. Maybe the opera egg is hatching, hope so. It may be china though, or merely rotten.

Bill

V. to P.: *A Voyage to Pagany.*

238. ALS-1

[Rutherford, N.J.]

July 20, 1933

Dear Louis:

Thanks for the letter. My regards to Idaho Ezra if he's still around. The rest of this letter you may consider padding, as far as news is concerned.

Reading Mencken's <u>American Language</u>. best thing he ever did – should have stuck to scholarship and not attempted interpretations: he has a flair for "going places" though for what reason I cannot say.

The person who wants to do my poems (have I told you this?) still wants to do them as soon as he finishes having a nervous breakdown – said the gellatine splitting in half.

Nothing doing <just now> on the opera. Perhaps Ezra will have a few ideas as to how I should not proceed! I can imagine!!

Just hot weather, enough to kill a snake.

It can't be pleasant being in Paris, an American, these days. But it is possible that popular disfavor may prejudice the Surrealistes in our behalf. And what the hell good would that do us?

> Yours
> Bill

Disregard imbecilities as usual, if you please.

Better take a trip out to the catacombs while in Paris! It is a very <u>wise</u> thing to do? Then go up in the Eiffel Tower. Thus you will see all of Paris – oh shit!

American Language: Williams corresponded with Mencken about *The American Language,* and Mencken even solicited Williams's advice in preparation for the fourth edition (1936). Although Mencken did not use any of this advice, Williams reviewed the new edition favorably: the *North American Review* 142:1 (Autumn 1936), 181–84. Wallace C243. Reprinted in *Selected Essays.*

the person: Probably Maxim Lieber, literary agent.

opera: *The First President.*

239. TLS-1

[Harriman, N.Y.?]

[August 1933]

> August the August
> Rainy Day
> Year of the World n

Dear Louis the Louis:

It's raining. Has been raining for several days. I'm on my vacation recovering from my vacation. Nothing else that I can think of off hand.

So to continue. Chopped down two apple trees in blighted fruit yesterday. Chopped them up putting the wood suitable for heating purposes in one pile, the leafy branches in another, greater one for the flame. This preliminary to the construction of a lawn tennis court.

Rain drove me indoors where I took up my review, reviewing after ten years Mencken's The American Language which is a book worth reviewing, ten years after the publication of his third edition. Didn't get very far. Just gathering up the stray ends of what I had begun to write a month ago.

Thanks for your nice long letter, I was glad to receive it. Glad Serly is surviving. Regards to me old frien' Ezra. Please tell him how much I enjoyed his Canto XXXIV in Poetry: easy long lines without strain – almost a revolution in itself. I envy him his excellence. And the material of them, the Mearly Merican – so well understood and utilized. Nothing much better to be seen anywhere – nothing better anywhere. Wish history were less yesterday and today better history – and better written.

Can't say that I'm burning up with enthusiasm for my own personal future. Don't know what it is but I want awfully to run like hell. Much, even, as I'd enjoy success in whatever literary project might appear – perhaps I'd enjoy more a devastating dose of nonentity.

Floss is well. It's a real pleasure to me to have my boys around – and not trying to murder each other at sight. They seem to have begun to discover the world of ease, culture and the all embracing twat – though I doubt seriously that they quite know twat it's for just yet.

Maybe I could – twat? I's one solution but no proper end.

> Yours
> Bill

Canto XXXIV: In *Poetry* 42:1 (April 1933), 1–10.

240. TLS-1

[Rutherford, N.J.]

Wednesday [20 September 1933]

Dear Louis,

It was good to hear from you, that you're back and on the job again. Hope you enjoyed your trip, and I mean "enjoyed" it; possibly there'll be some profit, huh?

Serley called me up two days ago, said he was pressed for time and wanted to see me. I arranged to meet him in N.Y. Saturday afternoon – if possible. I'll probably be able to make it. We'll talk, have supper somewhere and then I'll drive him over to your place in the evening. I'd rather have a go at him alone first. I think I can get his "feel" better that way, as to what's going to happen about the Washington thing. I haven't touched it since early summer. Couldn't.

I've written a long "thing", ten pages, this summer, done a criticism of Mencken's Am. Language for The New English Review, read some books, swum, rested, acquired a small dog, reacquainted myself with my boys and that's all. The "thing" is a completely new venture, a poem, if you want to call it that in five line sentences (more or less) about the low-life of these parts. Sent it to Poetry. No word. Probably stunned them. They are about due to return it any day. I haven't a clean copy. Poetry is publishing a group of poems of mine (you've seen them all) in October. Rakosi has had a critical appreciation of my script of poems accepted by Symposium, to come out forthwith. No work from the nervous breakdown guy. No progress. That's the news.

Seee you Sat. eve post haste – for better or for wurst about 8 or earlier.

> Yrs.
> Bill

Wus 50 last Sunday.

Washington thing: *The First President.*

a long "thing": "Life Along the Passaic River," *The Magazine* 1:2 (January 1934), 47–51. Wallace C194.

a criticism: Williams's review appeared in the *North American Review* 242:1 (Autumn 1936), 181–84. Wallace C243.

group of poems: See Williams's letter of 22 March 1933.

critical appreciation: Carl Rakosi's essay, "William Carlos Williams."

nervous breakdown guy: See Williams's letter of 20 July 1933.

241. TLS-1

[Rutherford, N.J.]

Thursday [Zukofsky's notation: "9/28/33"]

Dear Louis:

Even up to 8.45 I thought we might be able to get away but then something happened that absolutely handcuffed us. What happened? Sorry to have missed it.

> Yours
> Bill

P.S. Just to give you an idea: Wednesday night at midnight I was wakened to go out and open a child's inflamed ear. At 5 A.M. I went out again to deliver a baby at the hospital. I put in a day's work after that and then sat in the office all evening till 8.45, chaffing at the bit, damning telephone callers by the dozen and then – when I could at last tear myself away I went in to pick up Floss and found a masseur, whom I had asked to come some time, who expected me to consult with him over Mother's inability to walk. While I had in my mind all along that I must get up Thursday, this, morning early in order to be 1/2resent at the removal of a tumor of the brain from a patient of mine at the Medical Center, 168th. St. N.Y.

> Bill

[Rutherford, N.J.]

Monday [Zukofsky's notation: "10/2/33"]

Dear Louis:

It probably won't be possible to come in the week. But I'll have the poems to you by Friday.

That scheme as outlined has the earmarks of feasability, the best yet! I am grateful to you for your vision and persistence, I'll back you in every way possible. To begin with you may count on me for the first hundred toward my book. I'd pay it all but I decided long ago not to. And I'll go after Marianne and Wallace Stevens at once.

Never feel that you have to explain delays to me.

Reznikoff's Testimony will have a heavy backer in Kenneth Burke whom I saw yesterday. It is wisdom to bring that out now. A fine selection of material.

Yrs.

Bill

Synopsis of suggestions discussed and general agreements arrived at at meeting Sept. 24th. Writers-Publishers to be incorporated:

1. A possible list of subscribers to 1 book of poems to be circularized and approached by whatever means possible. The book to sell at $2. and to be the most saleable we can find.

2. This book to be published on the basis of whatever advance subscriptions are obtained.

3. The proceeds, if any, from this sale to be divided, 60% to the author, 40% to the group which 40% is to be used to publish book #2 and to pay the Executive Secretary who will be the sole officer of the group.

4. On this basis books are to be continued to be printed and sold as often and for as long a time as practicable.

_____

Notes: When the first book is advertised it will be put forward as one of a series of four which will all be published and offered, separately, for subscription during the first year.

The original suggestion of E.P. to be rewritten to conform to this plan.

As a feature of the plan distinguished (?) modernists of the day will write introductory pages to these books – their names (with consent) to be given out when the first notices appear: such names as Marion Moore, T.S.Eliot, Wallace Stevens, etc etc. This in effect will be a sponsoring Committee without putting too much of a burden on names.

Harriet Monroe and Poetry to be approached from the first with intent to get as much backing from that source as being the <u>official</u> (?) poetry organization in U.S.

Mr. Zukofsky be named to Executive-Secretary etc. etc. with power to keep records, see individuals, arrange for publishing, correct proofs ? ? ? select format, wrote letters, devise lists, compose advertising matter, push sales, etc. etc#
– God help him!

243. TLS-1

[Rutherford, N.J.]

Thursday [Zukofsky's notation: "10/5/33"]
Dear Louis:
The script goes forward under separate cover. It is not registered so look for it. I have been over it carefully, whatever it's virtues or defects may be I want it printed in full as I have selected and arranged it. As there is a table of contents I did not number the pages.
     Yours
     Bill

244. ALS-1

[Rutherford, N.J.]

10/5/33
Dear Louis:
Marianne refuses – except to back <u>me</u> personally. No use insisting further – unless you want to use her to "move" my poems.

The only possible name of any accuracy for us is <u>Cooperative Publishers.</u> – leaving out all "thes" and "Incs".

Thus ends the 1st inning.
     Bill

245. TLS-1

[Rutherford, N.J.]

Tuesday [1933]
Dear Louis:
Should I find it impossible to get to N.Y. on Wednesday the enclosed will speak for me. However, I'll be there ifI can. There has been some progress as the enclosed page will reveal. It looks as if it's merely up to us to show whether we really have anything or not.

The names I'd suggest for the first year would be my own (not because I wish it so but because the general opinion seems to be that my book would be a good one to start with) the Zukofsky, Bunting, Rakosi. I believe we'll have our hands full trying to get a book out every 3 months.

See you Wednesday.

Floss and Mother both thanks you for the little gifts and send you their affectionate greetings which they will themselves enlarge upon at another time.

Sincerely yours
Bill

the enclosed: Enclosure lacking.

246. ACS

[Rutherford, N.J.]

[1933]

1. R's The O's Press is satisfactory to me—perfectly. Very good.
2. I'd welcome suggestions from you for cuts in my script—in fact I urge you to enumerate them at once—beginning, no doubt, with <u>all</u> the old Egoist stuff. But I reserve the right to decide finally. your reasons for action would interest me.
3. I'll communicate with K.B. at once.
4. If possible (for various sentimental & practical reasons) I'd like Wallace S. to do my introduction
5. Shall not be home next Sat. before 6 P.M. Come then.
   Bill

R's The O's Press: Reznikoff's The Objectivists Press.
K.B.: Kenneth Burke
Wallace S.: Wallace Stevens.

247. TLS-1

[Rutherford, N.J.]

Sunday [1933]
Dear Louis:

Yr right. A shorter more carefully selected book ud be better. Cost of composition must be got down to two hundred. Find out how many pages they'd set up for two hundred and we'll cut it down to that, regardless.

Stevens has consented to try his hand. If I don't like it he's given me leave to omit it. i.e. Preface.

I can see you in the city next week for an hour or so in the afternoon. Which day? Or better, which day not?

With luck I may be able to swing entire cost of setting up my book but I've got to earn it outside my practice. In any case, though, the hundred dollar guarantee still stands.

> Yrs
> Bill

shorter . . . book: Zukofsky to Pound, 23 October 1933, "Bill's book (500 copies, 180 pages is estimated to cost $468). We have half of the money promised, & are assured of getting the rest. It is possible—even probable—that Bill's book may cost less if he's willing to cut down on the contents, which wdn't harm it at all - & he says he is willing" (Yale).

248. ACS

[postmarked Rutherford, N.J.]

[Postmarked 17 October 1933]

Stevens has my other clean copy of script. So not this week, next. Will write again. Tell me when Ives returns original. No news.

> Yrs
> Bill

249. TLS-1

[Rutherford, N.J.]

Wednesday [Zukofsky's notation: "10/25/33"]

Dear Louis:

Friday then, rather early in the afternoon, as close to 2 o'clock as possible. I'll come to your room. I've been working over the cuts on an incomplete script which I have here and - I think I may have gone too far. It was gloomy weather yesterday anyway and nothing looked good. I kept cutting and cutting until it got into my spirit and I wanted finally to cut my own head off and let it go and that. It's hard to know where to stop. Too much cutting makes the book just an inhuman skeleton and too little makes it fat and flabby. Finally we'll strike the athletic mean. If there is an athletic body in the thing. Too much by myself.

Yes, let Ives do it. I can't quite see how we are to go forward without all the money in hand and I simply can't put it up - but we must go ahead and I presume that my book is more or less in line as an opener. I don't care a rap though where you put me if you want to open with something else. I'll come out of it no doubt but for the last few days I've been down.

> Yours
> Bill

Ives: *Collected Poems 1921–1931* was printed by J. J. Little and Ives Company, New York.

[Rutherford, N.J.]

Oct. 29, 1933

Dear Louis:

Your assistance has been invaluable, the book assumes a shape. Within a day or two the script will be again in your hands. As soon as you have the new estimate which should include some extra pages for the introduction, let me know, and I'll forward my check.

Yesterday there was a letter from Kenneth Burke saying he was ready to go ahead with the Reznifoff book? I hope R. accepts the offer. And, please, make certain that R's book comes out under our imprint, as one of our series. You seemed uncertain of his intention to cooperate with us in this – that he might be intending to go on alone. That would defeat everything we have planned. It should be definitely understood that his book and mine are numbers 1 and 2 in a series which we intend shall go on indefinitely. No use thinking of my book unless he comes in. Both books should be advertised simultaneously.

Enclosed is the script I've been peddling around. Hope it doesn't torpedo you entirely. I'm still hoping to sell it but the chances of doing so grow dimmer and dimmer. There ain't no market for such things in this land of revolution-aries and anti-revolutionaries. I'll be printed though. Sooner or later. No doubt I'll have to give it away.

What a crappy cold I have, just one continuous stream of liquid snot. Can't think or do more than get out of my own way. Blow, blow, thou bloody snoot!

There is this: we have Bill's room unoccupied – for a month or two you can sleep and eat with us: January, February, March. That should kill the winter. That is, if the worst comes to the worst. We're going ahead somehow.

    Yours

    Bill

I'll let you know about coming out for supper later in the week.

    <u>W</u>

script: Probably "Life Along the Passaic River."

[Rutherford, N.J.]

Nov. 1, 1933

Dear Louis:

Next week then, I'll let you know.

It's fine news that Reznikoff is willing to play ball with Burke. A good pol-icy, I think, this of having forewords by someone not directly on our team.

I'd like to have the enclosed poem included in the <u>first</u> section of my book if you can find a place for it. That's up to you but, on short notice, I feel that the thing belongs and belongs there – even adds something there which is needed, reinforces something I want to say.

Glad you find something in the script.

See you later.

Yours
Bill

enclosed poem: Enclosure lacking.
script: Probably "Life Along the Passaic River."

■ 252. TLS-1

[Rutherford, N.J.]

Friday A.M. [Zukofsky's notation: "11/10/33"]
Dear Louis:
Your letter just here. I've been promising myself every day that I'd write telling you to come – as we had agreed – but death and destruction stood in the way. I've been caught in the traffic. Not a moment to turn around in. I think it ended last night when I gave an address to the Poetry Club at N.Y.U. Didn't have the heart to tell you I was going to do it. Pretty useless I'm afraid.

It's splendid and to some extent – well, it was damned fine of the others to come in. You may count on me for the $250, at once with the understanding that the final $150. will be returned at an early date. I'll write to Stevens today. Yes, let's get going.

Better not come tomorrow evening. I'll get in to N.Y. next week when I can. You'll come out here when it happens, perhaps for some sort of celebration when the book goes to press – or as it may happen.

Fine letter from Rakosi. There's other news but I can't write more now.

Yours
Bill

■ 253. TLS-1

[Rutherford, N.J.]

Nov. 15, 1933
Dear Louis:
Here is the revised Preface and the revised Table of Contents (~~minus the term "Preface" which must be inserted somewhere~~). Go ahead. If Stevens balks we can make readjustments later but I don't think he will.

Send the book to the printer for a final estimate at once. As soon as his figure is given and you're ready to go I'll mail you my check as agreed.

I think I have solved Serly's first act!

    Yours
    Bill

my reiterated thanks for your thoughtful assistance

revised Preface: Zukofsky to Pound, 16 November 1933, "Bill's book will probably go to the printer's for final estimate next week, as soon as we have Wallace Stevens' approval of Bill's & my cuts of his originally very monocled myopic preface – now very readable & even very cunning" (Yale).

first act: Of *The First President.*

254. TLS-1

Nov. 26, 1933

Dear Louis:

Check enclosed for $250, as per agreement, the $150. to be returned at an early date, when possible. As I understand it, should the books sell, realizing, let us say, $700. gross, I am to get 15% of that as my ultimate share. Is that correct? As I understand it as soon as the 500 copies have been printed the type will be redistributed. Is that also correct?

Relative to the advisability of having had the book printed more cheaply: Under the circumstances, no. But, had Reznikoff had his book done with a less expensive firm it seems to me it would have been wiser. Then I could have followed suit and the rest of us the same in due order. It would be bad, on the other hand, to have to resort to cheaper printing as we go along. That's in the past now. No regrets. The books will be a better buy for the ultimate consumer.

It has been a strange day for me today. I delivered a male child, 8 lbs. 13oz. at 2 A.M., go to bed at 3. The morning was spent running about working. This afternoon I went with my mother to our old house where my brother now lives and he and I dug through a half dozen old trunks and large portfolios at random looking for what we might find. I found letters addressed to my mother at several New York, Brooklyn, West Indian and Parisian addresses, some of them written by my father. There were stacks of small photographs which my mother later identified mostly Spaniards and Frenchmen withe their wives, children and all the rest of it. Many other things turned up among them charcoal drawings made by my mother at the college in Paris, some oil paintings of hers, water colors of flowers. Later Mother told the rambling story of this

woman who committed suicide, of that one who died of tuberculsois, etc. etc.
What a world!

I even found a penicl drawing made by my father at the age of twelve. An
oak tree! Anyhow, a tree. But nothing new about the family history.

We'll be working on my bibliography for the jacket but how I'm to dig up
blurbs is more than I can say. Can't there be something new written? I could, of
course, quote from letters but would that be fair? Your stuff that you once got
together for that guy at Columbia might do. Do we have to do that?

When shall we get together? Not Thursady in any case. Friday? Saturday?
Best wait for the proofs, then write me and I'll fetch you hither, we should be
able to spread out better here.

Yours
Bill

guy at Columbia: James G. Leippert, editor of the *Lion and Crown*. The "stuff" Williams
refers to included a compilation of letters from Williams to Zukofsky written in 1928.
See Appendix B, pages 543–48.

■ 255. TLS-1

[Rutherford, N.J.]

Nov. 29, 1933
Dear Louis:

The reason I mentioned the 15% was that you yourself had spoken of it in a
letter this fall. Let it rest. As for the copyright, take it out in the name of the
press as you please. No need to make further inquiry relative to the forms for
my book. The type had better be redistributed. I brought these matters up
solely for my own information.

The long this I sent you several weeks ago has been taken by The Magazine,
California. I have received a check for twenty five dollars for it. Take notice!
Every little bit helps.

If you are out here Saturday drop in. Bill is home from college but there is
nothing especial on the programme, we'll be glad to see you. It is not likely that
you'll have the galleys in your hands by then but if you do we may be able to go
over them Saturday evening.

Now for the first act of that libretto. I want to devote the spare time in the
month of December to that.

Yours
Bill

long this: "Life Along the Passaic River."

[Rutherford, N.J.]

Dec. 6, 1933

Dear Louis:

You should receive the corrected galleys simultaneously with this letter. There were few errors in setting up. I made only one insignificant change.

In one place where the printer had made four errors, I think, in the spelling of "rime" I began to change the spelling of the word back to "rhyme" but then realized that I was wrong. It occured in, This Florida: 1924. You will see the place. I may be wise to speak in detail of this when the galleys go back though I believe my final notes are lucid enough.

In Stevens' introduction the word "surrealiste" occurs. I place an <u>accent aigue</u> over the e – which would be correct in french but I (inadvertently) left an e on at the end of the word which really makes the ending feminine. Perhaps what had best be done would be to anglicise the word and spell in without the accent "surrealist". Will you take care of that.

These have been particularly hellish days. Next Saturday afternoon might be a good time for getting together but only if there is some-thing urgent to be done. Write me. I'll reply to your letter by phone using the telephone address you have given me.

The book looks to be well printed. The most curious effect I received was from the beginning of the Primavera, the long fragmentary passage: it some-how has coherence and to me effectiveness. The whole book has a definite shape now, to me, seems to come up to the attention as a whole – appears to be a creation. That is the test of a book: Is it a book at all or just so many pages of printed matter. More and more one realizes that the creation of a book is a sudden miracle which happens, just like that, at the moment it is assembled – or it doesn't happen. I have – I got, suddenly a feeling that this was a book – a curious thrill of newness which I had not quite been prepared for.

Perhaps I could run in next Saturday afternoon. But write then I'll phone.

My ever present gratefulness to you for your time and attention.

Yours

Bill

This Florida: 1924: First published in *Collected Poems 1921–1931. CP1*, 359–62.

257. ACS

12/12/33

Let's meet at the Café Lafayette Univ. Pl & 10th St(?) Friday at 5 P.M. I may mail the proofs 1st Class before then – but meet me anyway. No use trying to do anything else – too pressed. I'll try to have ready: Bibliog. Blurb and Color Scheme (red)

Bill

Café Lafayette: In the Hotel Lafayette, on the east side of University Place, between Eighth and Ninth Streets. Greenwich Village artists and intellectuals gathered there.

258. ACS

[Postmarked Rutherford, N.J.]

[Postmarked 14 December 1933]

No proofs have arrived. I'll meet you as arranged, however, and if the proofs arrive tomorrow a.m. I'll corrected them at once and bring them.

Bill

259. TLS-1

[Rutherford, N.J.]

Tuesday [December 1933]

Dear Louis:

At two this morning I awoke realizing that the things in The Descent of Winter part of my book are improperly spaced. They have been printed too close together. The pages should be reset leaving about half an inch between each dated item of that section of the book. Not a hard job.

If there is still time to do it I'd very much like to have this taken care of. Please urge Reznifkoff to get in touch with the printer at once.

At the same time, if the final printing is under way and there would be much expense involved in this readjustment let it pass.

No other news.

Yours

Bill

260. ACS

[Rutherford, N.J.]

[December 1933]

I sent the material for the jacket early this week. Good Lord, you don't mean to say you haven't received it. It must be there somewhere. Look again for it or phone. reverse the charges if you want to.

      Bill

261. TLS-1

[Rutherford, N.J.]

Friday [Zukofsky's notation: "Dec 22/33"]

Dear Louis:

Did I, some time ago, lend you Hemingway's, Death in the Afternoon? If so, keep it, only, I want to know where it is. And I didn't, did I, let you have the script of White Mule? I'm fairly certain that you haven't had that.

Not having heard from you today I presume that the blurbs and the biography arrived. Even at some cost I hope you did finally fix up The Descent of Winter, damn it.

Not having heard from Serly but having heard that he is having troubles of his own I have not been able to do a thing with the opera. That is something which needs undivided attention whereas my attention is in the bowl and the chopper has been on it for months. I have solved the problem of the scenes but I have not attacked the words. Impossible to get going without some more definite objective than I have now.

I'm selling my book to the town, one at a time – by promises.

      Yours
      Bill

Death in the Afternoon: New York: Scribner's, 1932. Published in September 1932.
the opera: *The First President.*

262. ALS-1

9 Ridge Road
Rutherford, N.J.

12/27/33

Dear Louis:

I talked to Reznikoff over the phone last evening.

If the <re>spacing of the D. of Winter – can be done by prearranged estimate for five dollars or less – do it. It ought to be possible.

      Bill

I'll have something for Serly.

■ 263. ACS

[Rutherford, N.J.]

[1934?]

If I'm not there by tomorrow at 3 P.M. its because I'm stuck. No chance to come before this.

      Bill

■ 264. ALS-1

9 Ridge Road
Rutherford, N.J.

Jan. 6, 1934
Dear Louis:

Bunting is living the life, I don't know how sufficiently to praise him for it. But it can't be very comfortable to have to exist that way. I feel uneasy not to be sending him his year's rent and to be backing at the same time a book of my own poems. It's dog eat dog in the end I suppose anyway you look at it.

I've located the script of White Mule I was looking for. It was in Lieber's office all the while.

No word from Serly. not that I expected any.

What will be the publishing date now?

      yours
      Bill

publishing date: *Collected Poems 1921–1931* was published on 20 January 1934.

■ 265. ALS-1

9 Ridge Road
Rutherford, N.J.

Jan. 15, '34
Dear Louis:

Here's this. Rather well done. I enclose Miller's letter. If you want more let's utilize the forum.

No new news. Just work.

      yours
      Bill

this: Enclosure lacking.

Miller's letter: Enclosure lacking. Fred and Betty Miller edited the magazine *Blast*, in which several of Williams's short stories appeared.

[Rutherford, N.J.]

Jan. 23, 1934

Dear Louis:

Thanks for everything. The book is perfect in format and the cover distinguished. I'll show my appreciation for all you have done in more practical ways later.

The single copy arrived Sunday morning and the others, which I have not yet unpacked, a few hours ago. These are, I presume, my personal allotment. I shall need no more unless after a year, perhaps, I find that a few additional copies are necessary.

I intend to take orders and transmit them to you. I personally shall not take any money. Before I decided on this plan a friend of mine gave me two dollars for a book which I now enclose. Please send it to her: Mrs. C.V.Britton, 88 Prospect Place, Rutherford, N.J. Also, send 10 copies, C.O.D., to Dr. Ralph Gilady, 205 Union St., Hackensack, N.J.

I am putting a paid ad in the local newspaper this week.

It won't hurt you to be bored with your job! Though, naturally, you could better afford to be bored if you were better paid than is probably the case.

New small magazines are cropping up daily. Thier requests for a contribution have me dizzy. I'm sending nothing to anyone for the plain reason that I have nothing to send. There is one exception, The Magazine, 522 Calif. Bank Bldg. Beverly Hills, Calif. They want material and they pay. Get busy.

See you someday.

    Yours

    Bill

the book: *Collected Poems 1921–1931.*

The Magazine: *The Magazine* published chapters of *White Mule* in 1934 and 1935.

[Rutherford, N.J.]

Jan. 28, 1934

Dear Louis:

Send me two <of my> books to this address and one to my son Bill (William E. Williams, P.O.Box 1235, Williamstown, Mass.), check enclosed.

I started Reznifoff's Testimony and contrary to my first feeling discoverered that his careful editing of the material helps the effect. An excellent piece of work.

The telegram was the result of having heard that two people had had their letters returned from the address 10 W. 36. Hope I didn't upset you.

Did I tell you that The Magazine has, tentatively, as I take it, offered me the chance to have my White Mule published at a modest price month by month. But that's only a dream I'm afraid.

Wrote a two page blurb for the man Louglin, whom I do not know, "The Element of Time", advice to the unborn as it were telling the world (of them) that life is endless and consists mostly in ripping down the scaffolding from the Grace of God: to try and keep the proffs from ripping your pants off. Not that they need the advice tosay – of maybe more than ever. For the Harvard Advocate. But I advised him to throw it into the waste basket and maybe he'll do so. I didn't keep a copy.

> Best luck.
> Bill

Testimony: Charles Reznikoff's versions of court proceedings, published as *Testimony* (New York: Objectivist Press, 1934).

Louglin: James Laughlin (1914–1998), American publisher and poet.

"The Element of Time": The *Harvard Advocate* 120:4 (February 1934), 10. Wallace C196.

268. TLS-1

[Rutherford, N.J.]

Feb. 1, 1934

Dear Louis:

It might be wise to send me a list of those to whom you have sent review copies, individuals and periodicals. Have you, in particular, sent them to Harry Hansen, Mary Colum, Horace Gregory, D.G.Bridson (c/o The New English Review, with my compliments) and Kay Boyle, through her N.Y. publishers <Parker Tyler>.

The Magazine took the chapters of White Mule – until they go broke. I've sent the first installment which will appear in March. It happens to be one of the best I've written to date, the Christmas party. I should get about twenty five bucks for each chapter, more or less. It will at least cover the cost of the poetry.

No news from Serly. No matter, though. I've plenty to keep me occupied and the Second Act can be whipped into shape at any moment since it since most of it is already on the paper and the rest has been thoroughly mapped.

I'm writing to Gregory and Hansen now.

> Yours
> Bill

Hansen: (1884–1977), American journalist and editor. Literary editor of the *New York World-Telegram* (1931–1948).

Colum: (1887–1957), Irish-American literary critic. Wife of poet Padric Colum. She was in charge of the "Life and Literature" department of the *Forum*.

Gregory: (1898–1982), American poet, critic and teacher.

Bridson: Douglas Geoffrey Bridson (1910–1980), British poet and dramatist; later a writer and producer with the B.B.C. Zukofsky met him in London in July 1957.

Tyler: (1904–1974) American author and editor.

Second Act: Of the libretto for *The First President*.

269. ALS-1

9 Ridge Road
Rutherford, N.J.

Feb. 2, 1934
Dear Louis:
Enough copies have been distributed gratis. I shall not write to Reznikoff. Never mind about Kay Boyle and don't ask Reznikoff to send me a list of those to whom copies have been given.

I had a note from Harry Hansen, two lines, saying he hoped he could look at my book in the course of time. He has it on file. I wrote to one or two others. It is now just a question of waiting.

yours
Bill

270. ALS-1

[Rutherford, N.J.]

Feb. 2, 1934
Dear Louis:
Check enclosed. The address to which the book is to be sent will be found on the back of the check.

A certain Wilson, writing from Ann Arbor, says that he will have a review of the book in Canby's Sat. Review – against the poor C's better judgement. Let's offer a pair of brand new rubber balls to such dears as a prize.

Yours
Bill

Wilson: The *Saturday Review of Literature* published no review of *Collected Poems 1921–1931*.

Canby: Henry Seidel Canby (1878–1961), American literary critic. Editor of the *Saturday Review of Literature* (1924–1936).

9 Ridge Road
Rutherford, N.J.

Feb. 13, 1934

Dear Louis:

Not as many sales as I expected out here, it'll be slow work. Poetry goes down hard with most. Here's a check though for two more. Send one direct to Estelle Hegel, Nurses Home, Passaic General Hospital, Passaic, N.J. and the other to me – for Mrs. Carnevali, by the way.

The rush of medical work keeps me from reading anything so I'm not sending you the Harvard Advocate just yet, want to go over it a little more carefully first.

What is the use of Ezra sending us those assinine "reviews" from the English papers. They should be buried at his desk and a monument raised over them just there to warn away the unwary. The best reading to be found among them is on the reverse.

You've noticed the winter I suppose. But what is this about factories near Newark being requisitioned for the manufacture of munitions. Good God what next.

> Yours
> Bill

Mrs. Carnevali: Emily Carnevali, the wife of the poet Emanuel Carnevali.
winter: On 9 February 1934, the temperature in New York City fell to –14° Fahrenheit.

657 Main Avenue, Passaic, N.J.

Feb. 20, 1934

Dear Louis:

Check enclosed. Send the two books to me – for Hilair Hiler and his old man: they want me to put my name in 'em.

Not such a bad notice in The Times.

And please, unless there are reasons, check contents of letter also enclosed. Tried to reach Serly and Klenner yesterday but failed.

> Yrs
> Bill

Hiler: Hilaire Hiler (1898–1966), painter and author.
notice: Charles G. Poore, "The Poetry of William Carlos Williams," the *New York Times Book Review* (18 February 1934), 2. While Poore notes that Williams is not popular

because "he has written some of the most obscure poetry of our time," he concludes that Williams "knows that poetry only continues to flower when from age to age there are poets intransigent enough to give it new life. This book is one to stand beside the books of Ezra Pound, his friend, in that fine category."

letter enclosed: Enclosure lacking.

Klenner: (1890–1955), German-born American composer.

273. TLS-1

[Rutherford, N.J.]

Feb. 23, 1934

Dear Louis:

Provided your love life permits it I'd like you to accept a cold blooded business proposition: Floss and I have to go out tomorrow evening. We will have no one to mind the phone during that time. Were we to have someone come in for that purpose it would cost us a dollar. Enclosed is the dollar. You mind the phone.

This will give you a quiet evening during which you may read the articles you have wanted to see for several weeks or months. You will then have Bill's room for the night and remain here over Sunday. Sold?

Please plan to get here Saturday in time for supper. Or, if you find it impossible to come, let me know at once so that we may act accordingly. You can get a return trip ticket on the Erie for thirty five cents at the lowest. Take Brooklyn subway to Hudson Terminal. Shift there to Tube, Erie Station, Jersey City. Then train. Very easy.

I'll apply for Pulitzer if I can find out where to apply at. No, I had nothing to do with the Times review. He must just have liked the book. Seems odd but there y'are. Sorry Rezzy has been such a thorn in your flesh. I wrote acknowledging the check two days ago.

Floss sends greetings. See you soon.

     Yours

     Bill

Pee Pee S.

It is the publsher of the book who must make the application. Write to The Committee on the Pulitzer Awards, Columbia University, and say: We beg to call your attention <to> the Dr. Williams book of poems, which we published Jan. etc etc. and which has received such favorable comments in the daily press. We believe the book is of importance and because of its high quality merits your consideration for the Pulitzer Poetry Award. We enclose a clipping from The Lit Section of the N.Y. Times as evidence of what we say and should be glad to forward you a copy of the book or to take whatever steps are necessary to place this publication vefore you.

My information and the approximate draught of the letter come from Nick McKnight.

So get busy. And. –

Yours Bill –

Pulitzer: Williams was posthumously awarded the Pulitzer prize for poetry for *Pictures from Brueghel* in 1963.

274. TLS-1

9 Ridge Road
Rutherford, N.J.

Feb. 26, 1934

Dear Louis:

Sorry to bother you with this but I have not received the two copies of my book for which I sent you the last check – the books for Mr. Hiler. Or didn't you receive a check last week, with a note mentioning the Hilers?

I think I said that I wanted the books sent to me so that I could autograph them. In order to check on the matter I called Mr. H, a moment or two ago. He said that neither had he received the books. Please check all around and if the books have not been sent please send them. etc.etc. Thanks.

Serly, over the phone, sounds madder than ever. I hope he doesn't pass out before he does his job with me.

Yours
Bill

275. ACS

[Postmarked Rutherford, N.J.]

[Postmarked 27 February 1934]

Books rec'd this a.m. – I'll expect the other package shortly.

Bill

276. ALS-1

[Rutherford, N.J.]

March 13, 1934

Dear Louis:

Did I send you Gertrude Stein's Autobiography of Alice B. Toklas? Damn if I can't keep track of my books. If you have it O.K.

Card recd'd. I want one of Oppen's books. Glad to see E.P. has done the foreward. you next. Get ready, <u>be</u> ready.

>yours
>Bill

Autobiography: *The Autobiography of Alice B. Toklas* (New York: Harcourt, Brace, [1933]).
Oppen's books: *Discrete Series* (New York: Objectivist Press, 1934).

277. ALS-1

[Rutherford, N.J.]

March 19, 1934
Dear Louis:
Two books rec'd, haven't read it yet.

Letter enclosed. I went up to Masy's myself today and showed them the letter. They said they had sold out my book and were unable to get any more though they had written twice to renew their order. Please get after whoever is responsible as I am sending people to Masy's for the book every week.

Best wishes.

>yours
>Bill

Masy's: Macy's department store.

278. TLS-1

[Rutherford, N.J.]

March 28, 1934
Dear Louis:
Let me, in a small way, express my thanks to both you and Taupin for the valuable and interesting work you have done in your thesis (Taupin's you'll say) on the work of Appolinaire. It is something to which I have already referred, in private, several times and to which I expect to refer many times again. The reading is difficult but it is evident that the difficulty is essential to a correct exposition of the text. It is unusual in America for a magazine to give place to a thesis of this sort.

I'll be doing a notice, perhaps a criticism, on Oppen's book shortly. Perhaps I'll send it to the Westminster gazette.

Thanks for the Serly programme. I've been turning the matter of the libretto over in my mind, and over and over but without putting anything on paper. Several new thoughts are taking shape but it is impossible for me to work seriously at this when I feel that Serly is not (for the moment) ready to go ahead.

Will you cross a name off your mailing list: that of a Miss Hagel who is no longer at the Passaic General Hosp.

Nothing much else, just the weather.

> Yours
> Bill

thesis: *The Writing of Guillaume Apollinaire.*

a notice: "The New Political Economy," *Poetry* 44:4 (July 1934), 220–225. Wallace C204.

Serly programme: Probably the program for a concert referred to by Ezra Pound, "Last year his [Serly's] orchestration of the fantasy which Mozart wrote for a musical clock was performed under Dohnanyi . . . ," "Tibor Serly, Composer," the *New English Weekly* 6:24 (28 March 1935), 495. Zukofsky had evidently sent a copy of the program to Pound on 19 March 1934, "with the compliments of the dread Tibor" (Yale).

279. TLS-1

[Rutherford, N.J.]

May 10, 1934

Dear Louis:

Enclosed is the criticism of Oppen's book as well as the letter from Zabel. I'll send the criticism on to him anyway. After reading the carbon copy I'm sending you, give it to Oppen if he wants it or keep it yourself or do as you please with it. Should Poetry turn me down I'll have the thing published elsewhere.

See you Tuesday evening at Serly's. Bring the script of the libretto with you, the first version. I expect to have a "final" version with me that day but it would be just as well to let Serly have all the versions. He'll razz things around to suit himsefl anyway before he's through – which is perfectly all right with me. All I want is that the work get done. It should be a pillar of some structural value in spite of what others seem in advance to believe of it.

There's little life in me these days. I suppose the time of year and my time of year have much to do with it. "That time of year thou dost in me behold" – "bare ruined choirs where late the sweet birds sung". Maybe I just need a rest. Can't take it now. Must finish this bloody opera thing, that at least.

> Hasta luega, (Spanish)
> Yours
> Bill

9 Ridge Rd.

criticism: "The New Political Economy," *Poetry* 44:4 (July 1934), 220–225. Wallace C204. Reprinted in *Something to Say.*

letter from Zabel: Enclosure lacking.

"That time of year . . . : Lines from Shakespeare's Sonnet 73.

[Rutherford, N.J.]

May 21, 1934

Dear Louis:

The Bach Mass will be sung this Wednesday evening beginning at 7.30 at the Mosque Theater, Broad St., Newark. We shall leave here around 6.30. Come for a light supper at about 6 o'clock or meet us in Newark, as you please. But let me hear from you by Wednesday morning so that I may know what to expect.

There's been no congenial moment in which to think of the libretto since our last meeting.

> Yours
> Bill

9 Ridge Rd., Rutherford, N.J.

<u>better this way</u>

<u>P.S.</u> Ticket enclosed. Meet you at the theater. Take tube train at Hudson Terminal. Note the time! <u>7</u>.30.

Bach Mass: J. S. Bach's *Mass in B Minor*.

151 Remsen St
Brooklyn, NY

Tues. Morn. [postmarked 22 May 1934]

Dear Bill:

Thanks for sending this ticket, but I guess my bum luck's working even against yr. kindness. Been down with a cold since the Tuesday I saw you. It doesn't get better, & since yesterday has affected my sinus. And if I know my sinus there's about .5% of a chance (5/10) that I'll be fit enough to go to Newark tomorrow & listen to 3 to 4 hrs. of music. I feel terribly sorry and pretty much gipped, but I guess I'll just have to go home, since there's no use trying to be anything but the sick animal when one's in this fix.

I'm returning the ticket sp. del. – so you won't have to waste it.

I hope Floss, Mrs. Spence & you have a swell time.

You will of course – the B Minor, whatever the performance, is always wonderful.

~~Been doing~~ It's been all I can do to get to work every morning & get thru with the days.

But send the script of the libretto, when you're ready. I'll get down to it as soon as I can.

Thanks again.
                As ever,
                Louis

■ 282. TLS-1

                                                        [Rutherford, N.J.]
        June 1, 1934
        Dear Louis:
        I'll be sending the libreto, 1st Act, pretty soon. I haven't been able even to
think of it recently.
        Oppen says you didn't give him the second copy of my criticism of his book
which I sent you for him. Maybe you didn't receive it. Maybe you didn't know
I wanted him to have it. Maybe you ate it and swallowed it thinking there
might be nourishment in it.
        How are you anyway? Oppen says not so good. I can send you to a personal
friend, an excellent medico, at a good N.Y. hospital clinic for treatment at no
cost if you care to take me up. I mean for your so called sinus. Stop screwing
and eat more food. Why the hell do you want to die young, maybe your book
will be published sooner than you think. Come on, live awhile longer.
        Here's a new poem to cheer you up.
                Yours
                Bill
        9 Ridge Road

new poem: Enclosure lacking.

■ 283. TLS-1

                                                        [Rutherford, N.J.]
        June 5, 1934
        Dear Louis:
        What there is to send the wild Ted more than the lullaby at the end of the
first scene in the first act is more than I know. As a matter of fact I gave him the
works before he left, including the best of what you had. I can't even find a
clean copy of it among my things now.
        As I understand it you were to go over that same first act making sugges-
tions or rewriting whatever parts of it you cared to adding a lullaby at the end
of the first scene. I'll do a lullaby too, if I can think of anything that seems ap-
propriate. But I can't believe that I've let Serly get away with every copy of the
finished (?) script that I posess. I must look again.
        Meanwhile I'm enclosing what I have found so far.

My own main job will be to give him a detailed synopsis of the 2nd and 3d acts which I'll get at at once. I've had to do three new chapters of White Mule for The Magazine. My inclination to write has been low. But I must drive myself to the finishing of this libretto the best way I can. If only I had a clear notion of what Serly wants it might rekindle my interest. I feel that I'm fighting a fog. If you can help, go to it.

Yours
Bill

wild Ted: Tibor Serly.
enclosing: Enclosure lacking.

284. TLS-1

[Rutherford, N.J.]

June 8, 1934
Dear Louis:
Be careful with this copy as it is the sole remaining one I posess. Mark it up, of course, as you please but don't lose it.

Copies of The Magazine seem hard for me to get. White Mule goes on slowly. Someday when you are here you can sit down and read what I've done.

The libretto's the thing now.

Yours
Bill
9 Ridge Rd.

this copy: A copy of the libretto for *The First President*.

285. TLS-1

[Rutherford, N.J.]

June 11, 1934
Dear Louis:
We enjoyed your visit and wonder why you do not come oftener. The answers no doubt is "time and money".

Poetry is using my review of Oppen's book in the next issue, the full text. I'm pleased and know Oppen will be also. At the same time that I sent that review I enclosed a poem, An Elegy for D. H. Lawrence. They accepted that also – to be published in the fall. A bum (uncorrected) copy of it is enclosed. Please return it. The final work isn't much better.

You've kindled my interest in the libretto once more. I haven't had time for a dig at the thing yet since I've been rushed all day with work but the time is coming soon when I can throw myself into it.

It was a pleasure to see you looking so well.

> Yours
> Bill

my review: "The New Political Economy."

An Elegy: "An Elegy for D. H. Lawrence," *Poetry* 45:6 (March 1935), 311–15. Wallace C221.
CP1, 392–95.

(uncorrected) copy: Enclosure lacking.

286. TLS-1

Rutherford, N.J.

June 20, 1934
Dear Louis:

At last! I've been fighting (so to speak, no matter how pleasantly) through an underbrush of incidentals – waiting tell I should be able to sit down to our problem:

I'm going to try to write a version of the madrigal that is independent from yours to some degree. Your lines are excellent but I do think the whole too complicated. One thing, you have hit on an excellent idea and a perfect first line. That's something. If I can be of assistance to you in making the song simpler I think we shall have the perfect lyric for our purpose.

Get the rest of the act to me by the 28th if possible so that I may have it typed and made ready to ship to Serly early in July. This is imperative. Perhaps you can arrange to come out for that week-end. We've got to hurry a little now so as not to disappoint the guy. I had a brief word from him in Paris.

I'm going to get at the madrigal now.

> Regards
> Bill

Lets see the cuts in the Lawrence piece. It won't be published till the fall anyway – maybe I can incorporate some of your suggestions in it.

> W

madrigal: For the libretto for *The First President*.
Lawrence piece: "An Elegy for D. H. Lawrence."

[Rutherford, N.J.]

Tuesday afternoon [Zukofsky's notation: "June 1934"]

Dear Louis:

The carbon of the script I gave Serly has finally turned up – under my nose. It's virtually the same as the messy original I sent you (original in point of contents).

In this letter I'm enclosing a new version of the "lyric" I ended the first scene with in Serly's copy. My idea was not a lullaby but a bit of personal remembrance between the husband and wife "to give him something pleasant to think about while he is going to sleep". It would be somewhat silly to sing W. to sleep with a child's lullaby. If it must be a lullaby it should have at least some vague adult quality – unless it's some conventional sleeping song of the time none of which do I know or have I been able to find.

Why not send this letter to Ted with my enclosure telling him at the same time that we're working on a true lullaby such as he has asked for.

The thing is that the woman has asked the man to think <u>back</u> over his life. To think of something pleasant. She then tries to supply a pleasant personal memory. But he (as the whole opera is about to demonstrate) thinks of anything but pleasures. That is my point.

I feel better this afternoon than I did when I last wrote. From now on for as long as I can stand it with the vague aim we're trying to clarify I shall plug at this one point and the synopses of the two succeeding acts – developing them as fully as possible as I go along.

Get this off to Serly, to Ted, give me his address and let us, you and me, arrange some sort of conference – perhaps with John Klenner participating – soon.

Your comment on the verse I sent you will do.

    Yours

    Bill

Ted: Tibor Serly.

[Rutherford, N.J.]

June 29, 1934

Dear Louis:

Here's my transcript of the act. I have made certain slight changes here and there as you will discover. Along with it I send Jerry's script and the one we corrected together. Pencil up the carbon – the new one – and let me have it back at once so that I can send the final draught off to Serly before the 4th if possible. You can incorporate your note which came by card this A.M. in the text where you think it should go.

Please watch the first scene avoiding as far as you are able making it modern french, which I do not want. It is all right to give the dream quality, and we have done it, but we do not want to get too far away from the period and the characters, But do your stuff freely and I shall decide what nuance I can use. Serly will of course be the last judge – unless the stage director gets it into his hands as he must in the end.

Thanks for your great help. We are not through by any means as yet. As soon as I have finished the draughts of the last two acts – in synopsis – you'll have a chance to tackle them too.

We're coming on. Things are shaking into place. It begins to look like business.

> Yours
> Bill

(1) We can't use a "deep stage" at first – unless I'm mistaken – because we need the full stage for the 2nd scene and thus, the 1st must be set up in front of it to avoid delays between scenes. Or if you think the deep stage is essential, say so. I doubt it.

(2) What is Serly's precise address. Isn't it c/o some woman?

Jerry's: Jerry Reisman.

289. ACS

[Monroe, N.Y.]

[July 1934]

Here for a rest (work) for July. I sent off the 1st act. I'm about to attack the detailed synopsis of the other two now. Great weather since the rains. Birds sing me to sleep and wake me up. What singing! What luminous dumbells. Excrement (expletive)!

> Bill

c/o Mrs. P. Herman. Monroe, N.Y.

c/o Mrs. P. Herman
Monroe, N.Y.

Tuesday (I guess) [17 July 1934]

Dear Louis:

Here is the detailed synopsis <I am keeping a copy> of the 2nd Act which Ted wants. Look it over. If you have any important changes to make write them in and send the thing on to him. Let me have a copy of your suggestions. Or send the whole back to me for me to retype it. As you please. Only get it off as quickly as possible.

The 3d Act will follow within a week or so. I am at it in my head and have made important progress. It should be a wonder if properly digested.

I'm not doing much else, just farting around using a pick and shovel, reading a very little and running to town for mail and the necessary supplies. I enjoy it.

Well, let's hear from you. I'm curious to know what your reaction to the plan of the ballet will be. Let the others in on it if they are around. We are doing this as a group, I have nothing to sell -

Good, says Floss. You're getting to be a real something or other. Now if somebody can only <u>do</u> it. Real theatrics.

At last we're getting the idea, I think, blocking the stuff off in chunks so that the guy may be able to pick it up in convenient pieces and smear his stuff around them. At least I hope he'll agree that this is what we've done.

Best of luck, something may happen yet.

> Yours
> Bill

Ted: Tibor Serly.

151 Remsen St

Aug 1/34 Brooklyn N.Y.

Dear Bill:

I'm holding on to the synopsis of Act III. No use sending it to Ted at this stage of the game. He'll be just about starting back when it gets there, & besides he has enough to work on already.

Ничего (Rooshian for NOTHING DOING!)!!!!!

Washington as Jerry historically stated yesterday has got to be kept above politics. Probably won't do the <material> progress of the opera any good to bring up the Senatorial scandal. Besides that, I can't see - or, as an American (mind you!) bear to see – your Senator thinking of Washington (who was above politics, a unifier, mediator, etc) & mixing her up in his Limbo with the sordid love-life of his bimbo.

Of course, it's not the ideas a man holds, but the depth or strength of the emotions which retains them, but the synopsis, as you have it, is, as you've guessed, not convincing. One can't imagine the Senator dreaming just that way.

And, this is more to be feared, your historical character of Washington wd. vanish, his story, vanish completely, in your 3rd act. Which won't do – since the audience wdn't know what's happened to your opera of gen. Washington becoming, & dreaming before the night of the morning after of, The First President.

As I remember yr. original 3rd act it was pretty good. And I guess you better retain it. I haven't yet found the proper modern interruption which might suit Ted, but I think Jerry has, and I enclose his suggestion. The merits of it are: it won't interfere with your words & may be the thing Ted wants. The shots, by the way, as suggested appeared in a newsreel, more or less as Jerry has 'em, & wuz sponsored by the N.R.A. So I don't think you'd offend anybody. Besides that the reel is practically available so it won't cost much to produce. And you can add <&> or change or omit, any of the shots given, of course.

The difference between an immoral Senatorial tragedy possibly besmirching Washington's character & an apocalypse of the future of the U.S. revealed suddenly over Washington's inauguration is not to be passed over. I think the audience swept away by the sudden flashing on of the screen might even be gullible enough to take the anachronism quite naturally.

Let me know what you think, & if I can think up something else, I'll let you know.

I'd like to see yr. orig. synopsis for act III again.

Well, I'm drunk myself on some candy someone left here, so here's my love to Floss, by way of return etc – too bad there ain't no goldwasser.

I notice you're back – we ought to get together soon – don't know about this week end, [...]. But soon. And you can suggest a day.

> Yours
>> Louis

[Enclosure in Jerry Reisman's hand.]

Act 3

The act is developed according to original plan where Washington dreams back to his first love.

After taking the inaugural oath, Wash. assumes the posture given to his statue on the steps of the sub. treas. building, apparently beginning an oration. The light grows very dim so that the populace can hardly be seen, and Wash. keeps his pose thru' all that follows; a red or green light plays on his face, giving it a statue-like appearance.

Over the heads of the people, a series of news-reel shots is projected on a screen. These shots are chosen to give a very frank picture of the U.S. today, but they must offend no one, and they shall <u>not</u> give the effect of propaganda. Three or four times a shot of Washington's "sub. treas." statue is given, and the effect of the whole series of shots shall be that, tho' these are trying times, the spirit of Washington and what he stood for, is still with us, and will be our salvation. The series begins and ends with shots of the statue, perhaps taken from various angles. The last shot begins to fade away and the light on Washington's face disappears, the populace can be seen again, Washington begins to speak. Then Curtain.

<u>Note.</u> Serly can get his modern stuff in while the shots are given.

(over)

Suggested Shots

1. Wash. statue on sub. treas. steps.
2. Mid West farm. Wheat all the way to the horizon.
3. A modern hotel elevator. Going up, going down, with people.
4. A train going through a valley in the Rockies.
5. A row of harvesters cutting wheat in S. Dakota.
6. Chicago stock yards, showing cattle, image of tracks.
7. A large transatlantic steamer passing Statue of liberty—Close view.
8. Oklahoma oil-fields. A gusher.
9. Boulder dam being constructed.
10. A large office staff at work, showing typewriters, etc. Also executive in a spacious office.
11. Broadway at night.
12. Heavy automobile traffic, New York.
13. Coal miners at work and in their shacks, showing poverty.
14. Drought scenes in mid-West. Dying cattle and ruined crops.
15. Bonus marchers being evicted from Wash. D.C.
16. Breadline, Bowery, N.Y.
17. Wash. statue. It remains for a while, fades, and the real Washington begins to speak, etc.

Ted: Tibor Serly.

Ничего: The word more usually suggests lack, triviality or unimportance, rather than emphatic negation.

Senatorial scandal: No such scene survives in the published version of *The First President.*

N.R.A.: The National Recovery Administration.

his statue: J. Q. A. Ward's statue of Washington (1883) stands on Wall Street on the spot where Washington took the oath of office as President of the United States in 1789.

Boulder Dam: Renamed Hoover Dam in 1947, Boulder Dam was constructed on the Colorado River, 1930–1936, and is considered one of the great engineering projects of the age.

Bonus marchers: U.S. World War I veterans had been voted a bonus payment in 1924. The bonus, however, was not payable until 1945. In 1932, thousands of veterans encamped in Washington, D. C., and demanded immediate payment. Although many grew discouraged and left, a substantial number remained. Eventually Federal troops dispersed them, although during the operation one veteran was killed and several were wounded.

292. TLS-1

[Rutherford, N.J.]

Aug. 7, 1934

Dear Louis:

Arrived home Sunday evening. This is the first chance I've had to write. Come out when you get ready. Any time. Let us know and we'll make a place at table. Bring Jerry if you want to or the lady or as you please.

There's no finished synopsis of the third act as I had it at first. The thing was mostly in my mind and I just put it aside. But now I'll get at it again and do the thing as I wanted to with, perhaps, new slants which may or may not succeed.

I'm not satisfied with Jerry's scheme at this time. It would come as too terrific a shock if my original third act stands. The problem remains a problem with my vote for my own original idea of making the thing a purely "period" composition. Ted may want to incorporate his new ideas and the backers, if any, may want to force my hand – but I still believe the thing as planned is the correctscheme.

This is an idea which has occured to me: let the scene stay as I first planned it but let the music enter it doubt. There can come a time when the music breaks, tentatively starys a new mood and falters again just at the close of the third act or just before the final "coronation" scene. I'd like Ted's slant on what he could do along that line.

But I agree with you the "Senator" stuff is no good. You raised my hopes when you came out so strongly against it for I never wanted the damned mess that way.

No more now. Have you see the criticism of my book and the Objectivist attitude in Dynamo, a mag of revolutionary poetry. It was written by a man named Newman. It isn't bad, not ill natured but has a ring of fairness about it that at least allows it to stand.

The general depression, the unseen depression, is on me pretty strongly but in writing this, at least, I begin to pick up and wish to proceed. Repetition surely must stop. Some new step has to be taken and it can be taken, I at least can take part in it. Maybe it's André Gide. I want to look around. War may end everything and me. I hope not.

> Yours
> Bill

Jerry: Jerry Reisman.

Ted's: Tibor Serly.

criticism of my book: Charles Henry Newman, "How Objective Is Objectivism?" *Dynamo: A Journal of Revolutionary Poetry* 1:3 (Summer 1934), 26–29. Newman reviews Williams's *Collected Poems 1921–1931* and finds that "His poem is killed before it is born and remains an undeveloped foetus. In avoiding sentimentality, he reacts to an extreme, identifies sentimentality with emotion, and avoids becoming emotional. His poem remains the polished shell of a violin, its music unheard . . . Actually, the Objectivist has no objective, has no direction in the sense of movement towards a goal. His aim is really the aim of the camera, its lens focused upon an object, to snap a lifeless photograph. It is the act of the recorder and not of the creator, the man of purpose. . . . William Carlos Williams has made a definite contribution to American poetry but he is now fighting in an unworthy cause and the scars and the wreckage of his days are many. In remaining an Objectivist, pre-occupied with the external, he remains the dispassionate one, the non-partisan, without direction; he does not create with feeling; he is unable to probe profoundly into the conflicting social scene as he excludes a point of reference and maintains no true scale of values to weigh his opinions."

Gide: André Gide (1869–1951), French novelist and critic. Recipient of the Nobel Prize in Literature in 1947.

293. ALS-1

> 657 Main Avenue
> Passaic, N.J.

Aug. 16, 1934

Dear Louis:

Somewhat unexpectedly Floss was operated on this morning for a condition which has been bothering her for a number of months. She is in good condition. I believe it will materially improve her future health and well being.

This will change our plans to have you out this Sunday as I'll be camping out for the next eight to ten days.

Meanwhile I've had a letter from Serly which I enclose. As soon as thing steady themselves a little here, we'll start moving again on the opera project. It takes time to move heavy objects.

Best all around
>   yours
>   Bill

Please return Ted's lines. I have sketched a preliminary new scheme for the 3d Act.

letter from Serly: Enclosure lacking. Probably a letter of 3 August 1934, in which Serly said that he had "become fully convinced the piece can become a real Opera" (Buffalo).

294. ALS-1

> 151 Remsen St
> Brooklyn N.Y.

Aug 20/34
Dear Bill:

The mighty atom's letter returned to you with this. I suppose his authentic acceptance should shelve all of us into seventh heaven!

Please give my best love to Floss and all my wishes (and all our friend's wishes) for a speedy recovery, – tho' I haven't said anything about her being ill to all our friends. Sorry she has to bother with more than one representative of yr. profession . . .

Get in touch with me when you have had yr. peu de camping – as the French put it.

>   Yrs
>   Louis

atom's letter: See the note to the previous letter.

295. ALS-1

> 657 Main Avenue
> Passaic, N.J.

Tues. [22 August 1934]
Dear Louis:

Floss is coming along well. Thanks for the good word.

"The mighty atom" seems a little contrite, wondering whether or not we can do with him for our composer!

As the strain relaxes I'll be at the 3d act again. It won't be long before I'll have a tentative synopsis to show you.

Not much else. The sun, the rain – and the lack of one, both or the other are about the news.

Bill

"mighty atom": Tibor Serly.

296. TLS-1

9 Ridge Rd.
[Rutherford, N.J.]

Monday [31 August 1934]
Dear Louis:

No, I haven't been working much. I havent't been able to. Just today, however, with Floss beginning to eat as she should and the weather not so heavy my mind is beginning to click again. I have very roughly sketched out my third act as I want it. It may not please Serly at once but I believe I can convince him that it is the only possible solution to the problem as originally planned. If the sort of thing I have in mind isn't done the whole scheme falls down. The third act must be Washington's youth. It must be the "bottom" of his dream, deep within him. This may sound Freudian but that's just too bad. It can be done without marring the immaculate reputation of the man. It must be done. All we require is skill. And if we have the skill it will make a third act such as no third act has ever been in the past.

As soon as I am able to jot down the sequences, today if possible, I'll give you a preliminary look in.

Yours
Bill

297. TLS-1

[Rutherford, N.J.]

Labor Day [3 September 1934]
Dear Louis:

Here is the fated third act – a preliminary brief synopsis with a note. It must be done this way.

If you see Serly before I do please tell him I have a present for him in the form of a book, which he wants, for atmosphere and some of the details. I have bought it for him expressly. It is easy reading and amazingly instructive.

Floss is coming along slowly. She is home now. It's a rush and tumble world.

But the opera can be "grand" if only we have the genius for it.

Yours
Bill

book: Williams never specifies its title. Among the books from his library, the one closest
to fitting his description is Gaillard Hunt's *Life in America One Hundred Years Ago*
(New York and London: Harper Brothers, 1914). See "Descriptive List of Works from
the Library of William Carlos Williams at Fairleigh Dickinson University," *William
Carlos Williams Review* 10:2 (Fall 1984), 30–53.

■ **298. TLS-1**

[Rutherford, N.J.]

Friday [September 1934]

Dear Louis:

Pretty rotten but such as it is (for a starter) here it is. I ain't proud of it. I'd
rather have the original 3d act as I planned it.

Anyhow, won't you give it the once over. Take a stab at it, make any sugges-
tions you have in mind, hand it on to your pal Jerry and let's see what comes
of it.

I will say that, could we make it solid enough,it will be the answer. But can
it be made to have enough dignity to answer and can the symbolism be
brought into effect? I don't know. It's all to be acomplished.

Floss has had two good drinks and sends her love. She adds, Am I sober? No.
Anyhow, let's have a word.

> Yours
> Bill

O.S."The incident in Washington's young life" can be anything but is in-
tended to give me a chance to stick to my original plan anyway. That's the kind
of guy I am.

> W.

Better not send it on to Serly – unless to save time (with a letter from you)
Then you can write me – or as you please. Bill.

Jerry: Jerry Reisman.

■ **299. TLS-1**

[Rutherford, N.J.]

Sept. 17, 1934

Dear Louis:

It's all right for Friday. Come in the afternoon some time whenever you're
ready. No. Let me know what time to pick you up at Ted's. That was the ar-
rangement. Say at 4 o'clock?

Ted is absolutely right about that third act. We haven't hit the dynamic in-
tensity requisite as yet. I feel it there, now, very clearly but the facts haven't

been born yet. They will be, then everything will come out. I hope only that he knows that anything that is necessary can be done and will be done with the precision and power he wants . But he must give us the encouragement of believing in the theme. Without that we're sunk.

At the moment I'm inclined to agree, too, with Ted in his desire to limit the 2nd Act to two scenes , the first and the second, making the ballet the climax of the act. We could then use the final scene in the act as now written the first scene of the third act. It is something I have in mind. I'm not sure that this is what I want but it is worth thinking about at any rate.

No progress as yet on the weeping song. No time. The boys leave today and tomorrow. Floss is getting stronger.

> Yours
> Bill

Just received Bunting's criticism of my book, not bad. In fact he has done me a service that is of great value. Why not a world with a few more Bunting's in it? Damn 'f I know.

weeping song: See the following letter. The song is given to Benedict Arnold's wife in Act I, scene 2 of *The First President.*

Bunting's criticism: "Carlos Williams's Recent Poetry," *Westminster Magazine* 23:2 (Summer 1934), 149–54. Reprinted in *William Carlos Williams: The Critical Heritage.*

300. TLS-1

[Rutherford, N.J.]

Sept. 22, 1934

Dear Louis:

It did me a world of good to have you two here last evening. My mind is clearing. I am just about ready to begin to put on the pressure. I couldn't do so until I had a clearer notion of the finished scheme to work on. It's always so. I make all sorts of excuses to myself so as not to have to get to work. Then my own laziness becomes intollerable and action starts.

Your finding something to like in the poem about the old woman and the plums also did the trick. I got up this morning and finished the thing. I like it myself now though I was ready to throw it away yesterday. Muchas gracias (Spanish)!

Till next Friday, then, at John Klenner's – unless I hear from you or Ted to the contrary.

I almost forgot the most important thing of all, the weeping song. I have made a few passes at it without much success. Enclosed are a few suggestions which you can look over. A third verse might do the trick. I don't know.

My best to the others
            Yours
                Bill
If I can find it I'll stick in a bird poem I did this summer.

(Transcript according to Zukofsky)

He has left us here alone
    All alone,
In this wild place,
    Who loved us as his own.
(To the mercy of cruel men)

(Variation according to Williams)

Alone!
At the mercy of cruel men.
He has left us here alone
All alone
In this wild place
We shall never see him again.

Sorrow!
Sorrow, little child.
Weep, weep, sweet face.
There is no pity, pity for us
Alone in this wild place
At the mercy of unfeeling men

Alternative stanza endings:
    (1) <u>last line</u>: Who loved us as his own.
    (2) <u>last 2 lines</u>: omit "alone".   next page

[These two stanzas in Zukofsky's hand are on a separate card.]

He has left us here alone
    All alone,
In this wild place,
Who loved us as his own.
(To the mercy of cruel men).

Sorrow, sorrow, little child,
    Weep, weep, sweet face
He has left us here alone
    All alone
To die and not come again

the poem: "To a Poor Old Woman," *CP1*, 383

weeping song: Sung by Benedict Arnold's wife in Act I, scene 2 of *The First President.*

301. TLS-1

[Rutherford, N.J.]

Oct. 3, 1934

Dear Louis:

After mooning about for the past week, trying to think through "the encir-cling gloom" – mostly of my own manufacture – the perfect scene sequence for the second and third acts quite simply appeared to me, embodied in the sky.

What bothered me about the tentative plan as we had thought of it at our last meeting was the bad spot between the projected battle scene and the inau-guration scene. That was no good – and there were other smaller improprieties here and there. Anyhow, here's the answer:

The second act must be three scenes instead of two. The ballet has grown too large in our eyes. In the composition as planned it is one of the scenes only and must remain so. It is an important scene and must have its share of the time allotment but it mustn't be over stressed. You remember it follows the jocular, comfortable atmosphere of Scene 1. The ballet is a combination of deprivation, the cold and a dream. Then, as it ends in an icy, darkening atmos-phere, suddenly the scene is projected into a blinding light of summer noon. It is the midst of a battle, Washington appears in the flesh, heroically. This final bit of the second act is short, fast and full of sound.

The Third Act then opens with the Inauguration. This whole act is to be Maestoso. Not precisely pomp and ceremony but full of the dignity of office. A national consciousness as of power established. After this first scene there will be one other, as you suggested, at Mt. Vernon – prophetic. Here lies the opportunity for everything everybody has asked for. What the substance will be remains to be seen but it will have above everything else the sense of projec-tion into the future with the disturbance of uncertainty and strength strug-gling to maintain or undoe the work.

Please communicate with Ted – I never know where he is.

Yours
Bill

9 Ridge Rd., Rutherford, N.J.

Ted: Tibor Serly.

9 Ridge Road
Rutherford, N.J.

Oct 17 [?] '34
11:45 P.M.
Dear Louis:
I did it and sent it off to 420 Riverside, is that right? If not the P.O. will re-
turn it.

Bill

[Rutherford, N.J.]

Oct 30, 1934
Dear Louis:
The Mantis – needs to be read more carefully before a <proper> criticism
can be offered. To me, so far as I can tell after a first glance, it seems as tho the
form has made you do what you never would have done otherwise: stress too
heavily what should have been lightly touched – something you have done
elsewhere frequently. The ungainliness of the creature needs stating – that is,
to a person who has never seen it what you say brings no adequate picture – I
am taking random shots. I should say in a general way the composition should
go this way:

1. Descriptions – lightly – ungainliness with a grace unrelated to its sur-
rounding. then – 2. drop all direct reference to it (in the body of the poem)
then 3. bring it back at the close. What I remember of the poem being that the
end of it is the best.

I myself dread the implications of a too regular form – our world will not
stand it. The result of the implied comparison being unreality. This is usually
interpreted as falsity. Every time I try old forms I start with great interest and
end by abandoning everything except the feeling of the original which is a per-
manence. If you slashed, elided, opened up with spaces – a vitality germane to
today, to yourself, to the structure of our emotions of the present – would be
let in. You know this better than I.

2

The evening was an improvement on many of our past encounters over "the
opera". Ted has seen the light by contact with his practical friends of the stage. I
want to remain in the background and feed myself to him only so fast as he

wants me. He has the major part of the work to do. But now at last I begin to feel that the work is finding its manner of progress. John Klenner is going to be the key to our coordinations. I saw him for a few moments uptown last night.

We've all added something. Its very interesting and it is a very healthy sign that the thing has come from several men rather than one man. It gives it the broad base such a work should have.

Let the Mighty Atom be served is my motto. If we survive the ordeal we may find ourselves in an extremely advantageous position into which all that we have been battling for for the past ___ thousands of years – will fit solidly. That the work has the possibility in itself of such a critical quality is tremendously satisfying. It holds dynamite, for and against. Why bother with lesser critical statement while such things can go on. After all what else is good work?

Oh well, I got Ted his jelly.

> Yours
> Bill

Mantis: Written 27 October 1934. "'*Mantis,' An Interpretation,*" was written 4 November 1934. *CSP*, 65–66; 67–73

Ted: Tibor Serly.

Mighty Atom: Tibor Serly.

304. TLS-2

[Rutherford, N.J.]

Nov. 14, 1934

Dear Louis:

We'll talk of the poem, the notes, my possible book to come (when?) and all that another time. For the moment I have to concentrate on the opera and that, that, that . words fail me. What in hell he is at I swear I don't know. He hasn't read the script I am sure, hasn't studied the possible adaptation of a possible new recitative (of which he himself spoke two years ago) to the words as they exist . . But all that I take for granted. When however he misquotes me from a script which he thinks he has lost and then tells me that "for instance" this is the sort of "error" I have made . . Jesus Christ!

I'm inclined to think Dr. Pleasants may have a few helpful suggestions to offer if they are offered with proper humility and proper regard for the composition we have in hand. But if we are to have a new opera now he'd better write it himself. Ted doesn't seem to grasp that we are not trying to set the life of Washington to music. We are working on a composition by myself utilizing certain carefully selected scenes for an effect. That effect is my part of the problem. It is the original idea of the whole scheme. It is it's sole value. It has already been decided on. But if the composer does not even know what the purpose of the design is then it's all up.

I have read exhaustively into the life of Washington. Then what in hell can Ted be thinking of when he says that this or that character did or did not do this or that at such and such a time – because Dr. Pleasants says etc etc. Shall I send Ted to Irving Berlin to have him find out how to write his music? I know perfectly well that Lafayette is an attractive character, that Mad Anthony Wayne is the same, that Lee was perfect for opera. But I also know that the chief objective we have all had in mind has been to select, to cut down a thousadn possible scenes, to make it all fit into an hour and a half of playing time – and at the same time to make the dream sequence effective.

We have fought over these things time and time again until with your own useful suggestion for a change in the third act abd Ted's own suggestion for a slight alteration of the sequence in the second act everything is (roughly) in order. The only thing that remains is to make the words singable. That's where we need to work and not much anywhere else.

The one thing of use to us in this last letter of Ted's is the emphasis on Washington's love for Lafette and if I myself brought out anything forcibly in our last talk it was that. Let it be one of the main themes in the last act – as I myself had it an important scene in the second at until Ted himself discarded it because he everything shorter, more compact. I have worked hours at a time and over and over agin rearranging, cutting, rewriting – and this for years now – but, as I said before, Jesus Christ if no attention at all is paid to what I have put down and no effort is made to discover why it was done then we're sunk and that's all.

The opera has tremendous possibilities, it is a real opera in spite of all those European sons of bitches who havent yet learned how to sit on a toilet seat – and are so sure they know everything before they even see it – and who are so quick to discourage Ted. It has a design – it has been written with a purpose – Now, if Dr. Pleasants wants to pick out all the operatic characters of th e Revolutionary period and scramble them up to make a spectacle <[In Florence Williams's hand.] (It's a pageant!!!) Sure that's what he (Pleasants) wants – oh you artists. – Best to you all – Florence> – Ok with me but to hell with it.

I'll work, I'll be patient, I rewrite I'll listen to John Klenner, I'll adapt the words for singing – but for the love of God let's stick to our original purpose, let's try to mould our efforts to that – and don't let's spoil what has already been done by chance shots, by taking advice from people unfamiliar with the problem. For instance, if Ted had read the speech he quoted to Dr. Pleasants he would have realized that in speaking of Arnold and Morristown I mentioned that Washington decorated Arnold at Morristown for his valor etc. etc. which was exhibited anywhere else but there. But all this is ridiculous and has noting to do with the opera anyway.

I'll be at your service almost any time Sunday as well as next Tuesday evening when I'll have ready what I can get ready. Nor do I want Ted to gather that I would not like to talk with Dr. P but as I said above – Jesus Christ – I'm only the author of the piece what the hell do I know about it.

>Yours
>Bill

Dr. Pleasants: Henry Pleasants (1910–2000), American author and critic. He was appointed music editor of the *Philadelphia Evening Bulletin* in 1934.

Ted: Tibor Serly.

Irving Berlin: (1888–1989), American songwriter. His then recent musical revue, *As Thousands Cheer* (1933), introduced such songs as "Easter Parade," "Heat Wave," and "Harlem on My Mind."

Lafette: The Marquis de Lafayette (1757–1834) assisted the American colonies during the Revolutionary War.

Mad Anthony Wayne: (1745–1796), American revolutionary war soldier.

Lee: Charles Lee (1731–1782), British-born revolutionary war soldier. As a result of a dispute between Lee and George Washington, Lee was court-martialed in 1778 and suspended from the army for a year.

Arnold: Benedict Arnold (1741–1801), American revolutionary war soldier whose attempt to betray the post at West Point made his name a byword for treason.

Morristown: Morristown, New Jersey, where the Continental Army spent the winter of 1779–1780.

305. TLS-1

[Rutherford, N.J.]

Nov. 14, 1934

Dear Louis:

I am sorry to have to use you as intermediary but things are getting desperate now and something has to be done – even if it comes to imposing on a friend – or I don't know where we're going to land.

I want you to do this. No matter how important the detail of the first act may be to Ted we've got to ourselves decide the precise sequence of all the scenes in the whole opera before we waste any more time on details. I simply can't go on revising and revising and looking up this and that when the whole scene is going to be thrown out finally.

Now. Enclosed is a <u>new arrangement</u> which explains itself. I have adopted Dr. Pleasants' feelings about certain characters and I have put back into the running scenes that I had worked months on formerly. I think the result is the best yet. I want you to demonstrate this new sequence to Ted as I have no confidence at all that he will see it otherwise. I want you to do this as a preliminary to our general meeting if possible. Or just send it to him if you think best.

There are other changes in this new sequence which need no special mention but I feel that if this goes through we will after all have arrived somewhere. The greatest change is the doing away with the entire scene of the British in Phila and I think it is a good thing to be got rid of. It was oppressive, hard to stage and altogether too complex. The new scenes are all simple, all colonial and all important.

For God's sake do your stuff. And please give Ted my love and say that I'm with him like a Siamese twin – only I can't help saying to him, "Sit or get off the pot" I wanna do it too.

> Yours
> Bill

Not that I'm neglecting detail. I am not. If Ted like the 1st scene as arranged 's all right by me.

Ted: Tibor Serly.

new arrangement: Enclosure lacking.

■ 306. TLS-1

[Rutherford, N.J.]

Saturday [17 or 24 November 1934]
Dear Louis:

Thanks for the letter. I'll try not to bother you again – in the same way. I think I know my Tadj fairly well but at times it gets a little thick and I have to blow off. Forget it. I'm sorry. No need to show him my letter.

But I do wish you'd show him the other things, the revised sequence for the 2nd act and the revision of act 1.

I had a card from the apparition himself this morning telling me to hold everything, etc. etc. That I must meet Dr. P etc etc. And that Dr. P. was enthusiastic for the scheme and would help in every way possible, etc. etc. Fine. Looked at more calmly the addition of another talent to the already complex whole is perfectly acceptable to me. I had to laugh, though, when The Mighty Atom gave me the information (with a triumphant flourish) that the doctor was also a soldier during the recent war and therefore – Oh boy! oh boy! – what an assistant that makes him.

It'll go forward. And as you say, it will be the more formidable for the very curious manner of it's group-conception. Somebody's a whore somewhere in the ensemble.

Ted's card said he would call me up Tuesday. That means that any meeting before that is off. I can well use the time. One way to do that will be to go over your own composition.

Copious pages from Ezra. He's off again. This time he wants to back some new magazine which I suspect is connected with Yale Univ. Press. I don't know for sure as he didn't say. He seldom does. One hears of this or that in connection with him but – that's always been his way. Even when I was close to him for two or three years at a time there was always a well preserved mystery.

> Yours as ever
> Bill

Tadj: Tibor Serly.

a card: Tibor Serly. In the card, postmarked in Philadelphia on 16 November, Serly said,
> "Don't know if L. Z. mentioned my talk with Dr. Pleasants. Saw him again to-day and
> as he is writing what seems to be the most accurate history work on Washington I
> think it almost providential that he was thrown in our way and believe it wise that we
> all get to-gether before you go on with any more work. Dr. Pleasants is all exited [sic]
> over the work and willing to give all he's got incl. Manuscripts he gathered over half
> his life. Besides he is an experienced soldier (having been Col. in the army) which sh'd
> be of help too" (Buffalo).

Dr. P: Dr. Pleasants.

Mighty Atom: Tibor Serly.

new magazine: Letter not located.

307. TLS-1

[Rutherford, N.J.]

Nov. 26, 1934

Dear Louis:

It was impossible for me to come in last night. I was too worn out to move. Two thirty the night before with the fatigue of a days work piled on top of it doesn't go down as readily as it used to. I'm sorry, too, as I should have liked to meet the gang.

Ted wrote me saying the first act as I had cut and rearranged it was more as he wanted it and that he had given it to John Klenner. It may be that after John has reworked it it will do. If you hear any word of this shoot it on to me. I don't expect to hear about it from the others.

Ted wants me to go down to Phila before the first of the year and I'm going to try to do it. When I do I'll take the new version of the second act with me; if possible I'll send you a draught of it at the same time.

Nothing much else of new. Rather a dull drill most days. At the moment writing nothing at all. As soon as I hear finally from Ted though that the first act will do things will pick up again.

Wish I wuz in the West Indies taking it easy on one of the small islands pictured in the recent Geographic Magazine. No wonder the ordinary run of Macy employees and college girls loved that long book – I've forgotten it's name – that was a best seller recently. To let the mind wander on what old time mariners knew and had witnessed is close to delirium these days. We are closed in, choked, beshitted as we have never been in the past. In those days at least, if one did not live long, he had a chance for a wild death after one beautiful "ride". There are adventurers today but the mind can't go a long with them, it can't, it's just so much syphilis which is too easy to get close to home anyway. Still, I have wished for almost anything rather than the monotony of some of these days. Monotony and to have to live in the stench of those who need no theory of government to brand them as blackguards. Writing itself seems a cage to me at such moments.

I'll get over it (never).

Yours
Bill

Ted: Tibor Serly. Serly's letter of 22 November 1934 is at Buffalo.

Geographic Magazine: D. Fairchild, "Hunting Useful Plants in the Caribbean," *National Geographic Magazine* (December 1934), 705–37. This article has photographs of scenes on the islands of Tobago, St. Kitts, St. Lucia, and the Grenadines.

long book: Possibly either of two books by Charles Nordhoff and J. N. Hall, *Men Against the Sea* and *Pitcairn's Island*, both published by Little, Brown in 1934.

■ 308. ALS-2

9 Ridge Road
Dec. 1, 1934 Rutherford, N.J.
Dear Louis:

Just impossible to make it today. I'm sorry too.

If I don't see you early next week: the best way to go about taking care of a thyroid enlargement such as that of which you speak is to go direct to one of the large clinics – Medical Center (168th St & B'way) or Cornell (on East River) or Bellevue. Say I sent the patient. Preliminary study is essential to any advice as to treatment. And don't be backward about it.

I'm flat from too much running about during the last three days.

    yours   Bill

Sing God damn!

Sing God damn!: Williams echoes Ezra Pound's poem, "Ancient Music."

■ 309. ALS-1

149 East 37 St

New York

Dec. 1/34

Dear Bill:

Sorry about this afternoon. Don't know when you can see me next week except Wednesday night after six, or let's say five [. . .] & I'll turn up. I'd say Monday all day, but I can't any more. The administration thought it necessary to set us working 5 days instead of 4. Lord knows how long that will last.

[. . .]

Here I am troubling you, and you've been chasing about I suppose as usual. Sorry, but thanks for whatever you can or can't do.

    Best,

        Louis.

■ 310. TLS-1

[Rutherford, N.J.]

Dec. 10, 1934

Dear Louis:

Ted's letter enclosed. It's impossible for me to get into the city this week. Certainly not before Friday, if then. The only thing I can suggest is that you send me the script of the first act, at once, special delivery together with any comments you have to make. I'll then have it typed clean and returned to Ted by Thursday evening at the latest. He seems to think it is important.

The only other possible mode of procedure would be for you or John to have the thing typed at my expense. Let Ted have the original and send me the carbon – with whatever comments you or John have to make. Final corrections and alterations could be made later.

Drop me a line telling me what the decision has been. But in view of Ted's difficult position re. Stokowsky I don't want to disappoint him now.

For me the days are becoming hectic in the extreme. It looks as though I had started on the 14 hours a day, 7 days a week routine with which winter has made me familiar before this. I despise it but it's my living during some months in the year when I don't pay expenses. I don't know how long it will keep up.

> Yours
> Bill

2nd act. practically finished

3d act. shaping itself.

Ted's letter: Probably a letter of 2 December 1934 in which Serly proposed that Williams and he get get together to "clinch the 1st act" (Buffalo). A week later, a postcard from Serly postmarked 9 December 1934 said, "Dear Bill, Just looked over complete 1st act as gone over carefully by L.Z. & John. It looks in fine shape now. I don't know what will happen re- Stoki. But I want to have complete copy of 1st act typed (final!!!) to give to Stoki (if??) Will you please see Louis to once more check up before you make complete type. He has time best either Wed. & Thurs. from 5 p.m. Let me hear how you like it. Best Ted" (Yale).

Stokowsky: Leopold Stokowski (1882–1977), British-born American conductor. Musical director of the Philadelphia Orchestra (1912–1936).

311. TLS-1

[Rutherford, N.J.]

Dec. 14, 1934

Dear Louis:

Here it is, please send the copy, this copy, on to Ted as I want to keep the carbon for a record. One of these days the whole damned business is going to be lost. I haven't the least idea, for instance, where the final copy of the first scene is at the present moment. I suppose Ted has it but he's just as likely to leave it in a taxi or elsewhere as not. Not that I'm picking on Ted – I'm sympathysizing with him.

The end of the last scene in the act stinks – but let it. If we ever get going, really, that will straighten itself out. That aside you have improved the lay-out in many places.

It occurs to me that perhaps I haven't copied all that you intended should be copied in that last scene, it was impossibly confused what with the two pages, some of the material on one page, some on the other. In particular I couldn't make out whether or not you wanted the young officers and servants to come out of the house at the cries of Mrs. Arnold. If there are mistakes in the typing send the last two pages back with whatever notes you care to make.

For myself I'd like to see the bed-room scene returned. I don't care much though, so long as the transition from the preceeding scene (the figure of W.) is made in a convincing manner – which is <u>not</u> now the case. That going back and picking up an unannounced baby is ridiculous.

I tell you what I'll do: I'll write it to suit myself – though without the bed-room – and send that along with the rest as 6a and 7a.

Mrs. Spence is playing a Bach Piano Concerto, arranged for two pianos by Busoni. I think it's the D minor. Sunday at 4.30. I have given the Hechts tickets. If you are around I can get you one or more for friends.

> Yours
> Bill

Oh hell, let the last scene stay as it is – till a change is or is not forced on us later.

Ted: Tibor Serly

Busoni: Ferruccio Busoni (1866–1924), German-Italian composer and pianist.

312. TLS-1

[Rutherford, N.J.]

Jan. 2, 1935

Dear Louis:

Aren't you the little Secretary of State? Which state it would be hard to say but no doubt a state of mind not altogether this or that these days. I've written to Bill Bullitt – God knows how to spell it (Floss will know). Should I hear from him, either way, I'll let you know at once.

Hays has written me of the Westminster Quarterly. I didn't recognize my-self. But if I'm what he thinks then he's quite right, I ain't

> Yours
> Bill

Bullitt: William Christian Bullitt (1891–1967), American diplomat. Ambassador to the So-viet Union, 1933–1936. The nature of Williams's request is unclear. Bullitt wrote on 7 January 1935, "Dear Bill, Of course you may use my name in applying for just as many Pulitzer Prizes as you want. Good luck to you and every wish" (Yale).

Hays: H. R. Hays, "William Carlos Williams and the Chronicle Method," *Westminster Magazine* 23:3 (Autumn 1934), 179–82. Hays discusses *The Knife of the Times* and con-cludes, "Williams's universally receptive method means that only by accident will he ever hit upon material which has any great social importance. The charm of his writ-ing which lies in exact observation and great expression of detail is purely technical. He, too, writes for a limited audience. The episodes which he absorbs are in them-selves aimless details. It is significant that for all his desire to be an expression of America, he is in actuality appreciated by the esoteric few. Thus the full scope of his ambition remains unrealized and will so remain as long as he evades the problem of drama with which any literature profoundly expressive of a group must deal."

[Rutherford, N.J.]

March 1, 1935

Dear Louis:

Message from the Hechts received. Nothing much to report. I have a poem coming out in The New Republic during the next two weeks (probably). I don't know whether or not you saw it. The Yachts – imitative in technique but otherwise fairly satisfactory to me.

Ezra continues to bedevil and reward me. He has me sending him clippings and what not for The New English Weekly. He is doing a colyum – American Notes. Rather good at times but very brief: limited. I also send him most short comments I sould otherwise not write at all. It keeps me amused and does, possibly, no harm. I enjoy spilling over in a general way sometimes. I have evn sent him a few poems.

A mag. called Alcestis has two poems of mine in it. Just out. Somewhat Greek in spirit but not, so far as I can detect homosexually overweighted.

Poetry should have the D. H. Lawrence piece in this month.

Here I stand, so help me God! I can do none other.

What about yourself? I ain't seen nor heard hide nor hair of you for night onto six months or more. Wassa me? No soap? The only thing I did hear was that you and the Oppens had differed over this that or the other and had agreeed to disagree. I'm sorry for that. We were there one arctic evening to see the Terrible Ted just before he sailed for Europe and forgetfulness – I'm afraid. Hope not though but I'm completely resigned to anything that doesn't happen.

White Mule in the hands of an agent. It may be a day and it may be forever, Kathleen Mavourneen, the girl of me heart!

A guy back from Paris named Henry V. Miller has sent me (loaned me) a book of his, Tropic of Cancer, that is a whore with her pants off for purity and candor. A swell book. Floss and I are reviving our drooping spirits nightly with it and –

Jeez! I almost forgot. The Magazine of The Oxford English Club would be honored if the estimable Weelum Carloose Weelyums would honor them with a poem – And what a poem I sent them. It is short and bastardly. I doubt that they'll use it.

Give us a line.

Yours

Bill   (over)

Did you know that a Zukowsky was court poet during the rein of Catherine of Russia?

Hechts: Theodore and Katherine Hecht, mutual friends of Williams and Zukofsky.

The Yachts: "The Yachts," the *New Republic* 82:1066 (8 May 1935), 364. Wallace C225. *CP1*, 388–89.

American Notes: Pound published his "American Notes" in the *New English Weekly* from January 1935 to April 1936. They were devoted to the economic and political scene in the United States.

two poems: "Hymn to Love Ended (Imaginary Translation From the Spanish)" and "The Raper From Hackensack" (later retitled "The Raper From Passenack"), *Alcestis* 1:2 (January 1935), 2–4. Wallace C216. *CP1*, 391–92; 385–87.

Lawrence piece: "An Elegy for D. H. Lawrence."

none other: Williams echoes a sentence attributed to Martin Luther at the Diet of Worms (1521): "Ich kann nicht anders, hier stehe ich."

Terrible Ted: Tibor Serly.

Kathleen Mavourneen: A popular song, composed *ca.* 1838 by Frederick Nicholls Crouch (1808–1896).

Henry V. Miller: (1891–1980), American novelist and essayist. Williams discusses Miller in his poem "To the Dean," *Circle* 1:2 (1944). *CP2*, 48.

a poem: No poem by Williams appeared in the Oxford English Club's publication.

Zukowsky: Vasily Andreyevich Zhukovsky (1783–1852), Russian poet.

314. TLS-1

[Rutherford, N.J.]

March 10, 1935

Dear Louis:

"Beeoootiful" is the perfect criticism of our contributions to Poetry: a Magazine of Verse. Anyhow, they pay.

As soon as the weather improves I'll take you up on your suggestion and meet you at 125th St., letting you know a day or two in advance of the time at which I can be there. It's a good idea.

Today the Oppens and the John Klenners are coming out for tea and the evening. At that time I'm going to try to sound John out as to the possibility of going on with Act II. I have finished my draught of it and have Serly's approval of that. Only the "libretization" remains to be accomplished. The ballet, which comes at the end of that act, I wrote out in fullest detail and gave to Serly before he departed these shores. He seemed pleased. Then comes the 3d act which I have clearly in mind – at least for the first version to be written.

The chief stumbling block to the whole project is Serly's inability or disinclination to go ahead. I don't blame him for his slowness but – it is impossible for me to do anything about it. I still feel that now is the time to strike, that we have a great idea (if he <u>can</u> do the music) but there we stand. I am willing to take all the time needed for the work – but I can't proceed with not even a page of the music to inspire me or even to assure me that my time is not being wasted.

Still, I'll have the 3d act finished in my own way before Ted returns and the 2nd act will be in shape (if John consents to collaborate) but if the moosician won't play! we're still bogged.

I'll save anything there is in N.E.W. etc for you to look at but the only things of mine they have used so far have been the reprints from In the Am. Grain.

Best luck. There's nothing to get down about – and SSSSprrrrrinnnng! iz kummings, e e e e! Ezra seems to have heard about it too – of late. Hoffentlich not too late.

> Yrs.
> Bill

P.S. John has been here & assures me that all is well. He gave me plenty of hope again.

> W.

our contributions: In 1935 *Poetry* published two poems by Williams: "An Elegy for D. H. Lawrence" and "Item," 46:3 (June), 134. Wallace C229. *CP1*, 379.

N.E.W.: The *New English Weekly*. One reprint from *In the American Grain* appeared: "George Washington," the *New English Weekly* 6:9 (13 December 1934), 193–94. Wallace C215.

John: Probably John Klenner.

Ezra: No letter from Pound to Williams has been located that would explain this comment.

315. TLS-1

[Rutherford, N.J.]

Monday [29 April 1935]

Dear Louis:

Your note came this A.M. too late to do anything about the Writers' Congress – the sessions of which terminated yesterday if I am not mistaken.

I went to the public meeting at Mecca Temple on Friday and listened attentively without learning much of anything. Everyone was polite. On the other hand there was a plainness, a frankness and a good feeling prevalent that was most impressive. Curiously enough the speech that impressed me most was from a source I least expected it from: Waldo Frank. His learned terminology was putrid but he did have something to say. The audience was strangely annoyed and pleased. When, toward the end of his endless speech, he said he only had two more points to make and then he would quit,many laughed and applauded almost breaking up the continuity; but when finally he did finish the applause was greater than for that of any of the regular speakers on the program. He said, briefly that the place of the artist in the revolutionary movement was not in the over simplification of propaganda, the necessities are far more complex than that, but in conditioning the proletarian mind, making it ready for revolution.

I note that you will change your abode.

A card from Serly telling of his luck, that he will conduct a full concert of his own works in Budapest on May 13th. I am planning to cable him that morning wishing him success.

Did I tell you that the Alcestis Press, a guy named Latimer, is bringing out a small paper book of 30 of my newer (mostly) poems toward the end of May.

> Yours
> Bill

Writers' Congress: The call for the Congress was published in the *New Masses* (22 January 1935), 20. It said the Congress would cover "all phases of a writer's participation in the struggle against war, the preservation of civil liberties, and the destruction of fascist tendencies everywhere." The call also urged the Congress to assemble on 1 May 1935, but it was actually held on 26–28 April 1935.

Mecca Temple: At 135 West Fifty-fifth Street. The 27 and 28 April sessions—closed to the public—were held at the New School for Social Research.

Frank: (1887–1967), American novelist and critic. His address, "Values of the Revolutionary Writer," appears in *American Writers' Congress*, ed. Henry Hart (New York: International Publishers, 1935), 71–78. When the League of American Writers was established on the final day of the Congress, Waldo Frank was elected chairman of the League. Zukofsky wrote to Ezra Pound on 11 May 1935, "The League of American Writers having been formed at the recent American Writers Congress and a united front of writers being its intention you can join, or criticize, or in one way or another help put 'em straight" (Yale).

paper book: *An Early Martyr and Other Poems* (New York: Alcestis Press, 1935). Wallace A16.

316. TLS-1

[Rutherford, N.J.]

May 14, 1935

Dear Louis:

Pound has gone nuts, without a doubt. I shall pay no more attention to him.

Letters from various people say variously that the world is as it is. The best of these letters, curiously enough, was from Bob McAlmon in Cornwal, He seems to be happy, full of zest and at work on another novel – having first finished twenty of what he calls "short stories". They are uusally too long to be used by anyone in a magazine.

I had an evening with Ford Madox Ford and Mark VanDoren last week. Good talk and good food. Also I had an evening with Henry Miller and Hilaire Hiler. More good talk and good food – also drinks. This might lead you to think that I am much in the city. To prove it witness the enclosed pass to a burlesque show for two, use it if you want to.

I sent Serly a cable wishing him luck. I hope he received it in time as planned. If you see any comment in our papers on his concert I'd appreciate your sending me the clipping.

I'm writing nothing at all but an occasional letter. The opera moves – mostly in my head – but moves only. I did go in to the Public Library about a month ago but couldn't find what I was after. What a place! It is enough to turn a writer to paper.

Meanwhile the garden blooms and school and college are about to shower us with their products. Paul has the measles.

Yours
Bill

Pound has gone nuts: Probably a reference to a letter of 29 April 1935 (Texas) from Pound to Zukofsky, in which Pound urged Zukofsky and Williams to take control of the journal *New Democracy* from its editor, Gorham Munson. Zukofsky replied to this suggestion in a letter of 11 May: "I'll forward your letter to Bill – 'sall I can do – let his conscience awareness, etc. direct his mature age, I'm not responsible – if he can kick Munson out, & will print what I can to say frankly in New Dem, anything I wdn't be ashamed to sign my name, too, as a person who's lived 31 years – salright with me – but it's up to Bill – But I've looked at New Dem – & read a number of issues – & where you seen any room for any decent people in it, or any prospect of change for the milktoastists, or any possibility of inserting a live literary page in the outfit is beyond me" (Yale).

best of these letters: Letter not located.

an evening with: See Mariani 379.

317. TLS-1

[Rutherford, N.J.]

Sept. 6, 1935
Dear Louis:

Nothing much to say, if anything. Had a card from Ted mailed in Paris saying he was there on his way home. Maybe when he gets here a crisis will be reached. Who knows? I've worked long over the libretto with results satisfactory to me, the mechanics of the thing are in order in a very simple solution which, if Ted is willing to take hold, will be effective.

I have nothing to show you otherwise. I've been into the city twice recently to see Bob McAlmon who is here but without anything happening. He is drinking too much as usual – but time is passing and the aggregate of his drinking begins to show – though he would deny this. No matter.

I haven't wanted to see anyone, perhaps you've been the same. What the end will be – there appears to be something <u>else</u> in construction – not a five year plan in any case. Maybe nothing at all.

The book Alcestis is bringing out should be ready for inspection in another month. I saw the Westminster anthology and liked the gesture.

I guess that's enough of the "I's" for the present. Anyhow I wanted to let you know that I'm not dead yet. Mother's still at the shore but should be home soon. The boys are here getting ready to go back to college. I didn't take much of a vacation this year, just remained home and delivered babies. Also built a board fence in the back yard.

What are you doing? I haven't heard from anyone in an age.

  Yours

  Bill

Just ran across your excerpts from my letters to you; that was a very friendly thing for you to do. I wish they might have been printed somewhere.

  <u>W.</u>

Ted: Tibor Serly.

book: *An Early Martyr and Other Poems.*

Westminster anthology: *The Westminster Review* 24:1 (Spring-Summer 1935). Edited by
  Pound, John Drummond and T. C. Wilson, it contained contributions by Zukofsky
  ("Home for Aged Bomb Throwers"; "This Fall 1933 / American Banknote Factory";
  "To such of one body as one mind"; "3/4 time [pleasantly drunk]") (*CSP*, 46, 56, 57,
  58), and Williams ("Late for Summer Weather"; "An Early Martyr"; "Invocation and
  Conclusion"). Wallace C220. *CP1*, 384, 377–78, 387.

your excerpts: Typed copies of early letters (1928) from Williams to Zukofsky now in the
  Williams papers at Yale. See Appendix B.

[Rutherford, N.J.]

Oct. 15, 1935

Dear Louis:

Be seeing you soon now (if possible) now that the God damned opera has been put to bed. The principle purpose of this is to ascertain whether or not you're still living – at the same address. Mrs. Hecht, who was here yesterday, says you have become a man of the world, the business world. Pleased to hear it.

I've scarcely written a thing during the past year but the itch has returned with greater peace of mind. I have one or two poetic projects – even a couple of performances to show – to speak of. I'll let you know later.

What I started to say in the first paragraph is that I'm planning to send you my new book which has been out a week now. Treasure it, there ain't many of them. I'm not speaking of the writing.

> "Now the winter's wait is done
> Now we welcome back the sun"
> (He shits best who shits first!
> Act I – Scene 2)

Hope you're surviving and – thought of you in Phila. last month when I saw a mantis on Chestnut trying manouvre himself – or herself! – about the entrance to a tobacconists shop, poor thing.

Were the Oppens in a ship wreck or were they not?

Yours

Bill

new book: *An Early Martyr and Other Poems.*
mantis: *CSP,* 65.

[Rutherford, N.J.]

Oct. 18, 1935

Dear Louis:

As far as having anything to do with any new organization sponsored by Ezra is concerned, no. I'm willing to praise what I see of his that I find to be praiseworth – when I see it. But that's all. I wish you luck. And when the son of a bitch asks you next time if you think I'm still interested in prosody please neglect to relay any answer to him. I'm thoroughly fed up on his person. – with, might be a better word. What does he mean by writing in that manner? It means only one thing to me and that is that I'm not interested in having him mess over what I do. He's what I call a friend etc etc – forget it.

Enclosed you'll find 13 pages which you might care to look at. They were to be the last part of the Primavera. I dug them up the other day – a month ago and sent them (the originals) to Poetry. No reply. Your criticism would be appreciated – Oh I mean, if you have anything to say, spill it. Thought you might be amused.

Thanks for your hint to Ted. If he does the ballet it will be an advance for us all. Yes, the libretto shall be completed during the next month or two "in my fashion". You'll see. I have it rather clearly in mind now. When I am through with it I'll be completely through. If Ted wants to adapt it here and there he may, even getting a professional librettist to take a fling at it. If Ted finds it distasteful to go on and would rather drop the whole project it will be up to him to say so.

I saw your review in Masses.

The book goes forward with this letter. There are one or two things in it I wish had been omitted but in general it's as good as I could reasonably expect it to be. There's much I want to do but all sorts of hindrances keep my pace slow. I go, though, but it leaves little time for the amenities. I'm having a story which everyone refused to print published in the Harvard Advocate.

We'll get together soon but these things have to happen, they can't be forced. I've been oppressed and tormented and you've had your own troubles also. Tell me what you think of my poem. That will get us on our way again.

Best of everything to you.

Bill

new organization: On 29 September 1935, Ezra Pound's friends, Aldo Camerino and Carlo Izzo, had written to Zukofsky, Selwyn Jones (a Welsh poet), Basil Bunting, James Laughlin, and J. P. Angold (an English poet) proposing (at Pound's suggestion), "to establish a regular exchange of technical, mostly prosodic, information, suggestions, etc., between literary people of different countries." On 10 October 1935, Zukofsky wrote to Pound, "I propose that Bill Williams be asked to join as a medical consultant (Yale)."

13 pages: Not located. Subsequent letters indicate that this was a draft of "Perpetuum Mobile: The City."

Ted: Tibor Serly.

your review: "Lewis Carroll," *New Masses* 17:2 (8 October 1935), 24. Zukofsky reviewed *The Russian Journal and Other Selections from the Works of Lewis Carroll*, ed. John Francis McDermott (New York: E. P. Dutton, 1935). *Prepositions +*, 65–66.

The book: *An Early Martyr and Other Poems*.

a story: "A Face of Stone," the *Harvard Advocate* 122:3 (December 1935), 19–23. Wallace C236.

111 East 36 St
New York

Oct. 21/35

Dear Bill:

I've jotted down some notes in pencil – which you can erase easily when you're thru with 'em – on the MS. It's easier to "criticize" with the work before you – I hope I haven't spoiled your copy. For the rest of the form, i.e. pages 1–3, and again pp 10–13 and a page or so in the middle give the feeling of perpetuum mobile – a sense of a round like the Early English rounds or the Alisoun. The last is said in praise. If you will clarify the other things that don't seem clear to me, you will have the form plus: the classic appearing again in our time and clarifying it.

Thanks for the book – it's a good collection (whatever my differences) and a beautiful book. Not anybody can "perform accurately to a given end" these days and Flowers by the Sea, View of a Lake, Pig-Bank, To a Poor Old Woman, Proletarian Portrait (swell writing in spite of all my reservations), the effect of sky in Tree and Sky, To Be Hungry and The Auto Ride (espec. the last, we shdn't have omitted it from Collected Poems), The Wind Meaning focus, are swell writing.

It seems to me that Hymn to Love Ended would have been perfect with just lines 1 to 7 inclusive (omitting "as from an illness" line 4). – But then I don't know imaginary Spanish?

Why the revolution is not yet accomplished we can leave for when we get together again. When you say – now that I know what all the silence was about.

     Yours

        Louis.

Ted's 6 Dance Designs were performed at the end of the Friday and Sat. concerts of the Phila. last week. Ted conducting his score. I understand even old man Serly thought they were good – so they must be. I cdn't get out there unfortunately.

Alisoun: "Alysoun," is an anonymous English lyric of the early fourteenth century.

the book: *An Early Martyr and Other Poems.*

6 Dance Designs: *Six Dance Designs* was composed by Tibor Serly in 1932–33.

[Rutherford, N.J.]

Oct. 22, 1935

Dear Louis:

Mentally I'm feeling more and more "like myself" these days than I have- felt for a year or more. Unless I'm much mistaken it was the opera bug which had infected me to such an extent that I could not react normally to other things. I tried to subordinate myself completely to Serly but finally it began to get me. The whole thing had that about it which made me think that if the work could be put through it would have a direct effect in establishing us all on a sounder footing. It seemed in every sense a major project whose energy once generated could be tapped into by all of us. I still think the same but today I can look at the thing from a more detached viewpoint. It had become an obsession but an unfortunate one in that I myself could do nothing to bring it to fruition. I haven't given it up but at least I have regained the power to put it away from me at will – and I feel better. Later in the winter I think I'll be able to show you my own part of the work completed and in a form that I can then put aside finally.

Pardon me for speaking of myself first. What I meant to say was that I very much appreciate your pencil notes on the poem. They are valuable. I'll prob- ably take advantageof them all and the poem will be far better "realized" that it is at present. Yes, it has that feeling of perpetual motion. Poetry, by the way, turned the thing down with understandable if somewhat unconvincing rea- sons for doing so. I have now sent the original draft to a "contest" being held by some publication in N.Y. called – or the company is called The Ad Astra Pub- lishing Co. There is to be a book,the prize to be $25. For the best poem, no re- striction as to length! Imagine!

Every year we're different men, Louis, wiser, I hope, if every year shorn somewhat closer to the hide in the matter of what genius we had. Maybe that's a good thing. I think that in our friendship there's much more to come and I for one am in a better position to appreciate it today than I was yesterday. We were too damned close together for a while. That's no good. The most any one can do is to be a kind of mirror for the other. And the mirror had better be a clear one, not a tinted one, just clear.

I had a long letter from Marianne Moore the other day taking me to task for the matter of some of the poems in the new book. She admires Item most but, apparently, her teeth are on edge at some of my other compositions. I an- swered her that a book to me is a sort of confession. She had said that she couldn't understand why a man would put something in a book which he would be unlikely to say to another's face. I told her that was the reason.

Don't bother to come out here. I'll pick you up in N.Y very shortly and take you to Ticino's for supper. I'll get Floss to drive in with me.

It's swell that Ted got to have his Dance Designs performed at last and that it was a success. I don't see how they can refuse to give him the Gug – unless they're just a lot of cock suckers. We'll see. And after that we'll see some more. And after that –

I had a sucpicion that you wouldn't be pleased at the Norman Macleod thing. But, as I sez to Marianne, that's something over which I have no particular control. I am willing to be led along the right path just so long then I've got to go whoring. If I didn't I'd die of dry rot. And a book is my confessional – not half the confessional it should be at that. But that is another matter. Nothing I want to do more than just once before I did beshit everything in sight. It's burning to get out of me. I know that's an anti-poetic feeling. And that may be the answere: I'm either absolutely correct or else I'm anti-poetic. I can't stand the full restraint that Ezra, even in his wildest ravings, is willing to acknowledge. Maybe that makes him a better man than I am. My only answer to that is that there ain't no such animal. No one is "better", Anyone is only relatively perfect. It is this tolerance which I apply to others as well as myself which alone keeps me going. And the stink of it is that I must be the one to see and to acknowledge – and forgive while to such a man as Ezra – with some sort of pride of spirit – if you call it that – I remain only a half educated barbarian. That goes deep. Deep in me where hell will break loose. I deny their God damned papacy. Every tenet that can be called tenable, every scientific trend, every philosophic stab, every physical grasp of facts establishes the sort of tradition Ezra tries to hold up as false – empty, a boast like that of D'Artagnan or a stage hero. That's what I wish to avoid, to destroy. That's, for instance, the real underlying ground in my imagination of the character of Washington – or Shakespeare. There is something there, underneath the dynamo of intelligence – of life itself that is crude, rebellious – the lack of which, or the denial of which makes an Eliot and makes him an ass.

Pardon this incoherent tirade. It is offnesive in that it is not clear. But it may be permitted in a personal letter.

> Yours
> Bill

long letter: In the letter, dated 17 October 1935, Moore says, "I cannot see that art is in any way different from the rest of life, from conversation or from the strategies of solitude; and it is an unending query with me why a person would say on the page what he has never been known to say to your face" (Rosenbach). Williams's reply is in his *Selected Letters*, 155–56.

Ticino's: See Williams's letter of 19 December 1935.

Macleod thing: Norman Wicklund Macleod (1906–1985), American poet. Williams refers to "A Poem for Norman Macleod," first published in *An Early Martyr and Other Poems. CP1*, 401.

322. TLS-1

[Rutherford, N.J.]

[30? October 1935]
Dear Louis:

Thanks for the defense. I said I liked your notes to Mantis better than the poem. Forgive me.

I contributed this from the Spanish of Lupercio De Argensola 15??

CANCION:

Alivia sus fatigas
El labrador cansado,
Quando su yerta barba escarcha cubre,
Pensando en las espigas
Del Agosto abrasado,
Y en los lagares ricos del Octubre.

The tired workman
Takes his ease,
When his stiff beard's all frosted over,
Thinking of blazing
August's corn,
And the brimming wine-cribs of October.

Note: the third line of the Spanish is particularly fine
        Bill

Lupercio De Argensola: Lupercio Leonardo de Argensola (1559–1613), Spanish poet. Williams first published his translation in *Adam & Eve & the City* (Peru, Vermont: Alcestis Press, 1936). Wallace A17.

111 E. 36 St

n.y.c.

[postmarked 1 November 1935]

Dear Bill – Thanks for the copy of the Cancion and for sending it on with the rest. The internal rhyme resembles the Welsh Exhibit A at that. Anyhoo, the aphorismic quality probably does. A Spanish "Dick the shepherd blows his nail" with suggestion of grandam's saw? Would be nice in a workers anthology. And I'd like to hear you read it aloud sometime.

> Louis.

Welsh Exhibit A: Probably specimens of the poetry of Selwyn Jones circulated by Aldo
  Camerino and Carlo Izzo to a small number of friends of Ezra Pound.
"Dick the shepherd . . . : Part of the song, "When icicles hang by the wall," from *Love's La-*
  bours Lost (Act 5, scene 2).

■ 324. TLS-1

9 Ridge Road, Rutherford, N.J.

Dec. 19, 1935

Dear Louis:

Would you be able to join me tomorrow night, Friday, at, say, 6.30 for supper and a talk? I'm going into the city in the afternoon and intend to stop there for supper anyway. Come if you can and bring anyone else you want to if you want to. I don't mean to make it a party, just that I'd like to see you. I'll probably be alone.

If the first sentence hadn't got so complicated before the intended end of it I'd have added that the "there" referred to later was Ticinio's Restaurant on Thompson St. two blocks below Washington Sq. South. You'll find it; perhaps you already know it. Just a cellar joint but rather good. Electric sign in front.

Ted Hecht has been in once or twice recently. Also Taupin and Mimi who were here night before last to pick up some bits of furniture for their new-old house in Nyack.

Best luck. If you can't come just forget it, I have to eat anyhow. No need to send word.

> Yours
> W. C. Williams
> (absent mindedly)
>> Bill

[Rutherford, N.J.]

Jan. 23, 1936

Dear Louis:

My failure to answer your last letter promptly was only in part due to having to get that book ready for Latimer. In addition, I've been working hard at getting around to see my patients and seeing them and getting home again. It's been hard going. At nine thirty every evening I'm ready for bed and by ten I'm in it and asleep – more or less. I don't mind it but it doesn't leave much time for anything else. As a matter of fact these winter weeks every year, with hard work and the cold, are a superb tonic to me. My nerves are rested by the primitive life we have to live. Temptations of all sorts are shunted off automatically and we become the simplest sort of animals.

On the other hand I did finish the new book Latimer wanted. He has it and likes it and it has gone to the printer. As soon as I am able to get some clear carbons together I'll let you pass on the result of my recent labors. There was no time for dawdling. I wrote furiously, composing three longish poems at top speed with but a single revision in each case. I completely rewrote the thing you penciled for me: The City. Between the two of us it stands up much better now. Thanks again.

There has been no time to more than glance at Evan's work. The litttle I saw I understood and liked. I think both he and you are to be congratulated. Most people would have missed his value. Almost everyone sees only in grooves – especially the communistically inclined! A poet risks his life with them. Evans quality, whatever it may amount to, is his own; he does not owe it to any "cause" – though that may have pulled the latch. I want to meet him with you. The weather will have to soften, though, before I can get away from this ant-arctic.

Sure, I'll jern the Writer's League. I'm in the office now. When I Go into the house I'll read the prospectus over again. And I'll send whatever I have to send which at the present moment is absolutely nothing. No even a scrap. And I was happy as a lark over the fact that I didn't have to think writing for at least a month. Anyhow, I'll send when and what etc. etc. Also I'll see that Bob McAlmon gets your release.

Worst of all is that I've been invited to give three lectures, no less, at Hunter College. Fer God's sake help me out. You know, not that I want to be told what to say but – what the hell I can't start reading ten volumes of verse in the few hours I have at my disposal every week and then formulate anddigest them into a course of lectures. I may want your assistance. I'll let you know later what is to happen. Best luck. More another time.

Bill

the book: *Adam & Eve & the City.*

three longish poems: Probably: "Adam," "Eve," and "Perpetuum Mobile: The City" (*CP1*,
    407–14; 430–35). Other "longish" poems in the volume included "St. Francis Einstein of
    the Daffodils" and "The Death of See," both of which had been published previously.

The City: "Perpetuum Mobile: The City."

Evan's: Robert Allison Evans (*ca.* 1885–1943), American mining engineer and poet. In a
    letter of 18 January 1936 to Ezra Pound, Zukofsky mentioned that Evans was "50, has
    two sons like Bill, worked in Pennsylvania mines for a quarter of a century, wuz a
    mining executive at $10,000 a month till he set about telling the operators & distrib-
    utors like Burns brothers how the shits shdn't run their business . . . and wuz
    canned" (Yale).

Writer's League: The League of American Writers. See the following letter.

■ 326. TLS-1

[Rutherford, N.J.]

Sunday [26? January 1936]

Dear Louis:

Reading Evans in a free moment after dinner: why in hell don't you send
some of his stuff to Cowley of the New Republic. Is some stupid orthodoxy in
the way? Must it be the New Masses or some kindred fixation? Hasn't anyone
the sense to see that value is value without the blue rosette pinned next to the
ox ears? I think Cowley would use a poem or two here and there and Evans
might get a check.

I've decided not to speak at Hunter College. On the other hand I've given
them your name with my blessing – also your address. It would only send me
into a stew for the next three months and this is my rest period – or composi-
tion period. I want to be at liberty to do what I please this spring. Eight years of
that God damned opera and the fiddling and fussing that went with it just
about had be ready for the psycho-pathic ward. I'm going to speak at Dart-
mouth in April sometime; that will be just about enough.

And if Evans sends anything to Cowley ask him please to use my name. I'll
be in some Saturday or Friday soon – but not yet. I'm on duty at the hospital
through February. Maybe, though, I won't have to wait till March.

I'm having the carbons of the new book duplicated and made clean this
week.

Aw right, I'll attempt to answer the two questions and enclose the result. As
far as I can see it doesn't make the least bit of difference how a man answers
them so long as he keeps using his head where he happens to be and, if he is a
writer, writing with as keen a regard for form as his experience warrants. A
man's a man for a' that.

I'll wait for a bill before sending the five bucks.

>Yours
>Bill

And I'm writing to Latimer today. I'll speak of your book and Buntings.

opera: *The First President.*

new book: *Adam & Eve & the City.*

two questions: On 31 January 1936, Zukofsky sent Ezra Pound the following announce-
ment. He appears to have sent a copy to Williams as well. "The League of American
Writers, established at the first Congress of American Writers called in New York,
April 26, 1935, to oppose War and Fascism, will publish, on the anniversary of the
Congress, the first number of a literary quarterly tentatively entitled AMERICAN WRIT-
ING. The pages of this quarterly will be open to all American writers, non-League
members as well as League members, who are willing to co-operate as writers with a
magazine editorially opposed to all forms of reaction tending to stifle the freedom of
expression. We plan from time to time to conduct inquiries into various aspects of
the problem confronting American writers. At this time we are addressing to a num-
ber of American authors the two questions below: 1. Is the possibility of Fascism or
Communism anything for an American writer to worry about? 2. In view of your ex-
perience and observation of the contemporary American scene, does there seem to
you to be any value in any organization of American writers, particularly an organ-
ization "for the defense of culture." May we be favored by your response to our inau-
gural inquiry? EDITORIAL BOARD." Zukofsky was a member of the editorial board.

your book and Buntings: By this date Zukofsky had completed all the poems that were
eventually published in *55 Poems.* "Bunting's book" was a collection of his poems
made by Bunting in 1935 and titled *Caveat Emptor.*

327. TLS-1

[Rutherford, N.J.]

Jan 29, 1936

Dear Louis:

Keep the Poetry notice. Some day I'll show you the books or pamphlets, as
many of them as I have – two, I think.

I thought the questions were asked in good faith. So I answered them that
way. If they don't care to publish my replies it makes no difference to me.
Please don't try to protect me.

Inasmuch as Latimer has already sent my script to the printer, the book may
be out before any magazine can use whatever of the items in it have not al-
ready appeared. I am having a copy made of the script for you. It should be
ready within the week. I'll indicate the poems that have not been printed.

The snow does not seem to melt.

Yours

Bill

Poetry notice: Enclosure lacking.

questions: The editors of *Partisan Review* and *Anvil* had circulated a questionnaire to various writers. Williams's answers were published in the journal as part of "What is Americanism? A Symposium on Marxism and the American Tradition" (3:3; April 1936), 13–14. See Mariani, 388–89.

the book: *Adam & Eve & the City.*

■ 328. TLS-1

[Rutherford, N.J.]

Feb. 4, 1936

Dear Louis:

A fine letter, and many thanks. I know of no one who so steadily keeps the modern level in his criticism and in his thoughts. I confess envy and admire you. I feel sometimes like a bad boy just thrashing about with a stick to see what harm he can do. Not that I believe that of myself, quite the contrary, but at moments my feeling becomes so imperative that I damn thought and reason to hell – perhaps not even enough. But you do move along with me as you pull my fragementary attack together and I profit by it. You make me feel like a banker! Not a nice feeling. I get it for nothing – so to speak.

I want to get the affect of my book on you. Glad you kept it out of the letter. At the moment the snow a nd ice are making my life that of a recluse. But I'm coming in when I can. I think we both rather deliberately looked away from each other for a time – as any ape, rat, elephant or baseball player should, now and then – if he care for his companion. It's a dangerous subject.

I'm returning the answers which are better as you have left them.

The chap Laughlin has just sent a card saying he is in bed having broken his back skiing. A back injury involving a break is a serious thing. He is an awfully nice boy. And a good writer in the making. I hope he comes on well.

I haven't done a thing about Jerry's scenario and Joyce. Perhaps it's just as well. We have all of us a way to go by ourselves in such matters.

Yours

Bill

Wood Thrush and Chinese Toy came out in <u>Smoke</u>. The Rose in <u>Caravel</u> (published in Majorca by Sid Salt). Elder Poet to appear in *Poetry*. Pitch and Copper in the <u>mag Alcestis.</u> From "Paterson" didn't appear nowhere – I must have marked those 4 by mistake. I didn't send anything to Harriet after all. It's all yours to do with as you please and are able. I understand.

my book: *Adam & Eve & the City* (Peru, Vt.: Alcestis Press, 1936). Wallace A17.

Laughlin: Laughlin wrote to Pound on 22 January 1936, "I done skied into a tree and in consequence will be of aboslutely [sic] no use to you, myself or anybody else for the next two months. Three cracked vertebrae are the damage; however no permanent injury is foreseen" (Pound-Laughlin 54).

Jerry's scenario: A screenplay of Joyce's *Ulysses*. Never published, it is in the Harry C. Ransom Humanities Research Center at the University of Texas. See Joseph Evans Slate, "The Reisman-Zukofsky Screenplay of 'Ulysses': Its Background and Significance," *Joyce at Texas*, ed. Dave Oliphant and Thomas Zigal (Austin: The Humanities Research Center, 1983), 107–39.

Wood Thrush and Chinese Toy: "To a Wood Thrush" and "Antique Engine" (later retitled "A Chinese Toy"), *Smoke* 4:4 (Autumn 1935), 41. Wallace C232. *CP1*, 405, 407.

The Rose: "The Rose," *Caravel* 4 (Fall 1935), 1. Wallace C233. *CP1*, 406.

Salt: Sydney Salt (he also spelled his first name 'Sidney') and Jean Rivers co-edited *Caravel: An American Quarterly* (Majorca) from 1934 to 1936. Salt's *Christopher Columbus and Other Poems* (Majorca: Caravel Press, 1937) contained an Introduction by Williams. Wallace B29. The introduction is reprinted in *Something to Say*. Salt's poems appeared in *Poetry, Pagany, Transition*, the *New Review, Front* and *Caravel*.

Elder Poet: "To an Elder Poet," *Poetry* 49:2 (November 1936), 69. Wallace C244. *CP1*, 417.

Pitch and Copper: "Fine Work with Pitch and Copper," *Alcestis* 1:4 (July 1935), 15. Wallace C230. *CP1*, 405–06

From "Paterson": "From the Poem 'Patterson'" (later retitled "Unnamed: From 'Paterson'"), *Adam & Eve & the City*. *CP1*, 417–19.

329. TLS-1

[Rutherford, N.J.]

Feb. 7, 1936

Dear Louis:

Gettin' foxy, huh? Action speaks louder than kind words. So I got to work for the party after all.

Weel, the project interests me – greatly, only it's quite a job you're handing me. There's one thing I couldn't get from your letter: Do you want a book on the subject or a chapter in a book,a thesis?

When I understand clearly what is wanted I'll give you my answer. Just how many words?

And I thought I was settling down to a nice quite spring! You're a helluv a guy.

But the project is a thrilling one, something that needs doing.

     Yours

     Bill

the project: "The Writers of the American Revolution." It was eventually published in *Selected Essays* (New York: Random House, 1954). Wallace A40.

330. TCS.

[Postmarked Rutherford, N.J.]

[Postmarked 11 February 1936]

Sold! I'll have the thing ready for you by the end of March – or much sooner if possible. Thanks for the suggestions but the conditions of the situation and the facts will have to instruct me as to the final form.

     Yrs.

     Bill

Which of the poems are you taking? I want to know shortly.

     <u>W</u>

the thing: "The Writers of the American Revolution."

331. TLS-1

9 Ridge Road
Rutherford, N.J.

Feb. 27, 1936

Dear Louis:

So far it has been impossible for me to get at the article or chapter or whatever it may be called that you want of me. I'm beginning to worry about it. Practice has been heavy, twelve hours of it every day with night work added on occasion. I'll do my best but what if I'm not able to finish the thing? I'll do something but it may have to be done hurriedly without the proper amount of preliminary reading. If practice continues through March as it has been going this month – and the roads slow to improve – I don't know, I don't know.

Enclosed is – whatever it is. I tore it off under greatest pressure to read at a meeting of a Barnard College literary society which took place last Tuesday evening. I didn't want anyone ptresent, but Mimi came and brought René. I read them poems for an hour which they swallowed like so many pills. Not much satisfaction in it, save the experience to me. They are not ready for what I have to offer – unless I am at fault in the presentation.

Heard from Ted Serly who is giving a concert in Phily March 4. I can't go.

> Yours
> Bill

article or chapter: "The Writers of the American Revolution."

Enclosed: Enclosure lacking.

René: René Taupin.

332. ACS

[Rutherford, N.J.]

[17 March 1936]

Finished your g.d. compilations last pages at 10.30 & got my typist out of bed to receive it. She'll have it for me at noon on the 18th. I'll give it a final look & mail it to you that you may have it the a.m. of 19th. It was a h. of a job to string the stuff into a whole. If too long (20 pp) you'll have to cut it. work shd be easier now.

> yrs
> Bill

compilations: "The Writers of the American Revolution."

333. TLS-1

[Rutherford, N.J.]

March 27, 1936

Dear Louis:

The mag. probably won't be published. I think I can already smell the garlic. But the corrections and suggestions are quite satisfactory to me. In fact I value them highly. Did I understand aright that your article on Chaplin was to be in the same issue.

Old business: Yes, keep the Barnard speech.

No other news, just passing the time watching the flowers grow. What speed! To a modern they surpass in the rapidity of their development all human or understandable records of achievement. We are a sluggard race.

> Yours
> Bill

mag: Probably the proposed League of American Writers' magazine, *American Writing*.

article on Chaplin: "Modern Times," *Kulchur* 4 (November 1961). Reprinted in *Prepositions +*.

Barnard speech: See Williams's letter of 27 February 1936.

9 Ridge Road, Rutherford, N.J.

April 16, 1936

Dear Louis:

You don't mean to say I didn't acknowledge your Chaplin article? I can't believe it. I sat down and read it at once on its receipt and without stopping. I thought it extremely good and looked forward to its appearance in the mag that I might pass it around to others.

Anyhow I am returning it to you in this mail and only hope that the magazine materializes – though when things hang fire so long they seldom explode.

I get to New York almost not at all or if I go it is for so special a purpose, such as a visit to Bill's medical school or a look at Hartley's pictures, that I see no one. I don't know, I don't know. Yet I manage to write a little now and again. There'll come a break, please believe it.

> Yours
> Bill

Chaplin article: "Modern Times."
medical school: Cornell Medical College.

9 Ridge Road
Rutherford, N.J.

April 21, 1936

Dear Louis:

If you have the time look up a certain Mary Barnard, one of Ezra's string of ponies (he seems to like 'em long) now in New York from Portland, Oregon. She won the Levinson Prize this year – tho' I didn't know it when she told me (Jesus!) But she's all right if a trifle suppressed. Has a brain no doubt. We've got to make her welcome.

She lives at 148 W. 11th St. Drop in some time. She has s cript for a book but isn't over confident – which is a virtue. At that she may go ahead of many because of the more or less conventional surface of her work and it's maidently purity. Not as bad as that.

> Yours
> Bill

Barnard: (1909–2001), American poet. The announcement that she had won the Helen
Haire Levinson Prize appeared in *Poetry* 47:2 (November 1935), 107.

336. ALS-1

[Zukofsky's notation: "Apr. '36]

Dear Louis:

I may have sent a letter West 36th St.

I may have done it again yesterday. Hell, the daffodils are up – as always in the omelette I carry on my shoulder.

Bill

337. TLS-1

[Rutherford, N.J.]

May 5, 1936

Dear Louis:

Our ill luck in not getting together seems to continue. Ted Hecht whom I met on the street Saturday said you were coming out that night but I was all but on my way at that moment to see a friend in North Jersey with whom we stayed till near midnight.

A card enclosed explains itself. If you can help Larson to the addresses, help him.

I journeyed to Dartmouth last week to read to them as I had read to the Barnard girls. The idea contained in the first part of my essay went over no bigger than it did at Barnard. The prof there, at Dartmouth, disagreed with me on the use to which the sonnet form should be put. He thought I overstressed the necessity for a new and significant form. What the hell? That's that. But it all helps to clarify the mind of Whoever Che Wis. I agree, that if one wishes to cross the ocean there is no need to design a new sort of boat at each crossing, especially one with three ends to it. But does that hold good in crossing a continent with a 200 inch mirror on board? New ways must be found, sez I. Not necessary, sez he. Not of any great importance, adds he. Og the greatest importance, sez I. You're a good guy, sez he, but I differ with you. You're a good guy, sez I, you'll grow up in time. Or words to that effect. Dante wrote punk sonnets too, sez he. Villon used a form more suitable to his age, sez I. Villon dignified a popular form, sez he – and besides Villon is the one eternal contemporary. There ain't nobody else on earth like him. Which is beside the point, sez I but I agree wid you.

Can you help me locate a guy named Leippert who once wanted to edit a mag at Columbia. This is important. Did you know him? What has become of him? Any information will be greatly appreciated. I want to find some old scripts I sent him and which he never returned.

I've virtually stopped writing . It was the only thing to do. I want to read and I want to think. How long it will last I do not know but it will last until I ~~feel that~~ something has accumulated back of the damn face sufficient to break through of its own power.

Best luck.

  Yours

  Bill

Larson: Raymond E. Larsson (1901–1991), American poet. Enclosure lacking.

338. TLS-3

         9 Ridge Road
         Rutherford, N.J.

July 22, 1936

Dear Louis:

Your last letter received, yes, I had the same communication from Lowenfels. As the only corrected copy of the script mentioned was sent to you I'll let them keep it indefinitely on the chance that they may want it later. Perhaps they'll return it to me should the magazine project finally collapse.

Just corrected the galleys of my opera libretto and introduction which will appear in September. It looks interesting. If only I had a compser to work with. For this time I'm going thorugh if it carries me to the White House. Serly has not communicated with me since winter.

Glad you're at poetry again. Alcestis, via Leippert (alias Latimer) has postponed the appearance of my second book until September. Just as well. I may be enabled to sell one or two of the new things in it by then. Not likely though. Latimer wants to go on printing me, I can't see why, but I've decided to call a halt. He wants me to finish the <u>Paterson</u> poem. It would be a book in itself. Not now. He also wants to bring out a definitive volume of collected poems. That, I may accept – but not just yet. If he really means to that, say in about a year, it would be worth while. I don't want any small books though in the near future, not until he prints books by some others first.

I wrote two poems under the spur of the Nation's contest: $100. prize. Good poems too but not much chance of winning under the circumstances.

Social Credit induced me to write a paper on The Attack on Credit Monopoly from the Cultural Viewpoint. I read it at the Public Affairs Conference at the U. of Virginia. It was fun but hot as hell. We were regally entertained by some of the F.F.Vs. Charming people and better equipped to think than most of us up here. A little slow, perhaps, but they don't over-shoot the mark. Floss and I motored down slowly. Jeez! we almost died with the heat.

H.H.Lewis has a new book, or pamphlet, of poems out – or soon to be out.

He asked me to review it for New Masses. I have done so and sent him both the original and the carbon. If they use it you'll probably see it there. Naturally they may turn it down. Queer how they can think that is going to get them anywhere. In it the one bright though I was able to relieve myself of was that what we must have in poetry today is not propaganda for the proletariat – but a proletarian <u>style</u>.

Larrson in California wants to get up a new Objectivist Anthology, 1936. Rexroth is the instigator I believe. I sez, O.K. I'll send what I hev. R. Larsson, 1880 Turk St. San Francisco.

Two good short stories in the first issue of Green Horn. Also some punk stuff as will always be the case. Cut of a Jug and the one about the Italian farmer in Pennsylvania. Both well done.

My boy Bill is in Arizona picking up fossils and information about Indians and the rest of it. Paul at a camp in Vermont, working for his keep. Floss survives. Mother at the shore still finds that she is "no better". Amazing what hope can do for we poor broken dynamos.

Guess that's all. I think I'm alive still but don't feel very sure. When I bear down I can still make the phrases come – now and again. But there's no inclination to do the same things over. Maybe there's good work in the offing but I'm not too sure. Saw Three Men on A Horse, a two year old play, last night. Laughed myself sick. What the hell. Read Shakespeare's Winter's Tale. Not so hot, But there are good places.

      Best all around

      Bill

Lowenfels: Walter Lowenfels (1897–1976) was the chairman of the editorial board of the proposed League of American Writers magazine, *American Writing.*

the script: "The Writers of the American Revolution."

opera libretto: "THE FIRST PRESIDENT, Libretto for an Opera (and Ballet) in Three Acts: 1. Introduction for the Composer; An Occasion for Music 2. Opera Libretto," *The New Caravan,* ed. Alfred Kreymborg, Lewis Mumford, Paul Rosenfeld (New York: W. W. Norton, 1936). Wallace B26.

second book: *Adam & Eve & the City.*

two poems: No poems by Williams appeared in *The Nation* in 1936 or 1937.

a paper: "The Attack on Credit Monopoly from a Cultural Viewpoint" appears in *A Recognizable Image.* The conference Williams refers to took place in early July 1935.

F.F.Vs.: F. F. V.: "First Families of Virginia."

Lewis: H. H. Lewis, American poet who called himself a "Missouri farmhand." The book may be Lewis's *Midfield Sediments,* which only reached the proof stage.

Two good short stories: "Out of a Jug," by John C. Rogers; "The Stranger," by Alfred Morang, *Green Horn: A Herald of Coming Writers* (August–September 1936).

Three Men: A farce by John Cecil Holm and George Abbott. It ran for 835 performances at The Playhouse (New York), starting on 30 January 1935.

339. ALS-1

9 Ridge Road, Rutherford, N.J.

July 24, 1936

Dear Louis:

Keep the libretto if you want to. I wanted it close to home until it had been set up in print.

You'll hear from me again soon.

> Sincerely
> Bill

libretto: *The First President.*

340. ALS-1

111 E 36 St
NY

Oct 19/36

Dear Bill:

It looks as if the enclosure can be touched up for the present campaign and used alright.

Best luck with it.

> Yrs
> Louis.

enclosure: Although the enclosure is lacking, an archivist's note indicates it was "A Democratic Party Poem," written by Williams in 1928. A portion of it appears in Mariani, 268–69.

341. TLS-1

[Rutherford, N.J.]

Dec. 7, 1936

Dear Louis:

Here's this. What do you think? To me it means almost nothing. What in hell do I know about the no doubt very worth names of whome the Godjum speaks? And wouldn't it be worse than ridiulous for me to append my name to a screed of this sort just for form's sake?

Annie Howe, tell me what you make of it all. If you have reasons to advance, advance them. I'll be listening. Maybe you'd care to write direct to the Boss yourself. I'll write something or other myself.

Spoke at the Brooklyn Academy of Arts and Sciences last Friday evening together with Marianne Moore at a Poetry Symposium – to 30 people ina hall seating 300! A very nice time was had by all except that Floss said I swore and cursed too much. I forgtot to wear evening dress – so had to swear, I suppose, to make up for that.

Marianne was BEAUTIFUL! I found myself drifting off into the trance which only beauty creates, more than once. Floss agrees. There is a quality there which is unspeakably elevating – through all her frail pretences of being this or that by God, she IS. The modern Andromeda – with her greying red hair all coiled about her brows.

We don't seem to see each other any more. Perhaps it isn't necessary. Maybe it's even best that we go each his own way.

Well, that's that. My best as always.

> Yours
> Bill

This: Probably the "Manifesto" Williams had received from Ezra Pound. Williams wrote to Pound on 8 December 1936, "The Manifesto doesn't strike me as so hot. I've sent it along." *Pound/Williams*, 186.

the Boss: Either Pound or Benito Mussolini.

Poetry Symposium: Held on 4 December 1936. See Mariani 394.

342. TLS-1

[Rutherford, N.J.]

Dec. 9, 1936

Dear Louis:

Nerts. I said "as ever" and I meant as ever. We had a time together crabbing over this and that and then I wanted a time to myself. As far as any wish is concerned in the matter, that's been my wish. I got sick and tired of messing over the insides of poems or discussing them with anyone, you or anyone else. Yes, I wanted to be left alone.

The Brooklyn thing I mentioned to no one. I had no idea how it would come out. Marsden Hartley saw it advertised in the Brooklyn Eagle and rushed over at the last minute. He looks like a bald headed eagle himself.

There's nothing to be done. We'll meet when we meet. The same with all my friends, I see them almost never. But when we meet it's delightful. One thing I won't do I won't make a case of personal matters. I wish to God you could break loose and – what, I don't know.

I've been cracking my brains to know how I can get in to New York for a few hours shopping; I want to see Hartley; I want to see some of the magnificent shows at the various galleries; I want to see Hamlet; I want to go to the zoo; I'm burned up to do fifty things I can't get to.

Meanwhile I write what comes into my head and it's a pleasure – not that I can't think about it, often, and shouldn't like to talk to you about it such talk could occur easily. We always found much to say over such matters. Nor shall I let you break up the possibility of other talks later. Or any time. But that sort of thing can't be arranged.

My disappointment and very near disgust over the opera affair may have given me a momentary desire to clean out and start fresh. I dunno. I can't work that way.

Shit with it all. If we aren't as we were then we aren't at all. I see no change, only different circumstances which may change also – when they will. I'd like to see you and will make a try, somewhere for a drink – and a little ease. I can't stand anything else just now.

> Yours
> Bill

[In Florence Williams's hand.] P.S. This is a swell letter! Bill ain't got no domestic difficulties – just the crud! You being a Phi Beta Kappa should understand. – Lots of love – Flossie.

Brooklyn thing: See the previous letter.

Hamlet: John Gielgud (1904–2000) appeared in *Hamlet* in New York from October 1936 to January 1937.

343. TLS-1

9 Ridge Road, Rutherford, N.J.

Dec. 23, 1936

Dear Blooie:

Here's some poems for you to chew on. Send me some as good.

Mary Christ Muss to you and a Mrs. Simpson!

Me ol' mother joins me with the same. She says her right eye is practically useless and that if she could get rid of it she thinks she could see better with the left, maybe.

The boys have learned at college to fart at table during the meal.

So you see we're getting along.

Any news from Reznikoff. I liked his last book and told him so – but haven't got to see him.

Marianne Moore, following our talk had me printed up in the Brooklyn
Daily Eagle.

> Yrs
> Bill

some poems: Enclosures lacking.

Mrs. Simpson: Wallis Warfield Simpson (1896–1986), American socialite. Edward the
Eighth abdicated the English throne on 10 December 1936; he and Mrs. Simpson mar-
ried in June 1937.

his last book: *Separate Way* (New York: The Objectivist Press, 1936).

printed up: Moore reviewed *Adam & Eve & the City* in the *Brooklyn Daily Eagle,* 20 De-
cember 1936, section C, p. 16 ("A Vein of Anthracite"). On the same page was printed
Williams's poem, "Advent of Today."

344. TLS-1

9 Ridge Road, Rutherford, N.J.

Feb. 5, 1937

Dear Louis:

Shall be in the city this afternoon for a short time but not to stay later than
about six or so. Ford Madox Ford says he wants to write me up for some paper
in New York. I'm taking him some books which I can ill afford to lose. Hope he
returns them.

Did you hear of the Serly concert, the Philadelphia Orchestra performed
his Symphony a week ago? We phoned in for tickets and just about made it. I
looked all around for you but didn't see anyone but Serly himself wandering
about the audience during the intermission, unrecognized and as lost, in ap-
pearance, as ever. His wife was with him. His success probably puts me off for
an indefinite period.

Enclosed is Ezra's latest, in reply to my missive enclosing the Amdur book-
let. He thinks once more that he would like to come to America to reside for a
time and asked me where I thought he should stay. I suggested Key West.

Nothing else for the moment. Not a ppeep from Laughlin for several
months but that doesn't disturb me for there is one man that means what he
says – perhaps he can afford it.

Mother and I go on with the Quevedo translation thoigh very slowly, her
eyes are very bad now and her Englosh worse. It is often funny to see us strug-
gle over a passage. My back is broke leaning over the edge of her bed. Mrs.
John is at the same time transcribing many letters of Mother to me and all
sorts of notes I have made on Mother's conversation. By this you see that my

next offense against the world will probably be the biography. It should be a fascinating this to do if only I can keep my spirit up.

Poem drip from my pen like dirty water from a broken pipe. I am not proud of my recent quality but I let it go on rather than fix the leak. I don't know what is to come of it. Looks to me like the final break-up. Then a momentary flash will come. A transition perhaps. I'm not trying to guid it but weak willed let it dribble, all sorts of trash, sometimes in complicated rhyme.

Wish I could see you again. I count on a spring campaign of reacquaintance. I can't buck this shitty weather, the cold offends me to the quick. Some sort of clemency should be given.

> Yours
> Bill

Serly concert: A performance at Carnegie Hall on 26 January 1937. The Philadelphia Orchestra, conducted by Eugene Ormandy, performed Serly's First Symphony.

Ezra's latest: Probably Pound's letter of 24 January 1937 (*Pound/Williams*, 187–88). Williams had sent Pound Alice Steiner Amdur's *The Poetry of Ezra Pound* (Cambridge, Mass.: Harvard Univ. Press, 1936).

Quevedo translation: This collaboration was eventually published as *The Dog and the Fever* (Hamden, Conn.: Shoestring Press, 1954). Wallace A39.

the biography: Williams's account of his mother appeared as *Yes, Mrs. Williams* (New York: McDowell, Obolensky, 1959). Wallace A45.

345. ALS-1

> 111 E 36 St
> N.Y.

Feb. 7/37

Dear Bill,

Ted told me later Friday night about your having been there – I usually drop in there on Friday about 10.

Hope F. M. Ford does what he said he would and that we'll see it.

I was at Ted's concert – by some stroke of luck I got a ticket from a speculator in the lobby about a half hour before the performance. Sat in the last row of the gallery. It was as you say very good – tho' the piano score had led me to expect a work of greater scope. Hope he can get his later works performed now, & will keep on writing in spite of the constant drain this business of getting performed seems to make necessary. You know he's doing a ballet – commissioned etc. It seems only us poets can "afford" to do what we want – immediately. I still think if he can get himself established that he'll do the Washington – he's got too much of a sense of loyalty to just put things off –

but who knows what time & the business of living will make necessary for him.

You say "Enclosed is Ezra's latest" – but I guess you forgot to enclose it. You got my card on the Cendrars booklet? What does he say?

If he's really coming to America – that is news. It would be darn nice to have him around here – might give one a feeling again that something of an audience for literature can exist again. If he could afford New York City, don't you think he wd. prefer it to Key West? How about Staten Island – I think it has all the isolation (without the sham) of Monterey etc (aside from the fact that it's too near Edwin Markham) & all the convenience of being in the middle of things if & when he wants to be. If you agree, you might write him – I'm not saying anything to him, because maybe I'm not supposed to know, tho' we discussed his coming over in 1933, & the main drawback was money then.

Hope Laughlin does "White Mule". The Quevedo I'm sure will be one of yr. best things, judging from material along that line you've already done.

I think I'll have some more "A" for you to read later in week, & by the time you've read it maybe it'll be spring again. The weather has me, too. <My cold better, but still a handicap.>

So best & to Floss & all

Yours
Louis

Ted: Tibor Serly.

the Washington: *The First President.*

Ezra's latest: See the previous letter.

Cendrars booklet: Possibly Blaise Cendrar's *Vol à voiles* (Lausanne, Switzerland: Payot and Co., 1932).

Markham: Edwin Markham (1852–1940), American poet. Principally known for his poem, "The Man with the Hoe" (1899).

Quevedo: *The Dog and the Fever.*

346. TLS-1

[Rutherford, N.J.]

Feb. 10, 1937

Dear Louis:

Thanks for your letter I'll tell Ezra to go to Staten Island where, if the expense would not be too great, he could exterminate Markham before settling down.

I saw Ted again last Friday for twenty minutes on my way to sup with Ford. I don't know what Ford will d o about the article but I know he has a dowry in my books which I have lent him. I hope he reeturns them as I'll be sunk if he doesn't. He says that since I have gone to "such trouble" to get the books to him he'll try to do an article on me solo whereas formerly he had in mind only a general article on "neglected writers". Who knows what if anything will be done?

The Poetry Hour man, Sullivan, wants me to read on the air, "free", a week from Sunday at 4 P.M. I said I'd do it. He says he wants me to discuss some phase of the modern movement at the same time. Why not? I'll see whaT I can remember of the Brooklyn spiel. Maybe I can even improve it. My present purpose in all such sessions is to speak extempore. After a few hundred failures I'll be dead then it won't matter.

No word from Laughlin but I think he's going ahead.

McAlmon is looking forward to a W P A job on the West Coast. He was coming east but seems to have changed his mind now that he has something to do.

No, it isn't at all certain that the Quevedo book will be good. I hope it will be what I want it to be but the test will come in the writing or assembling. The continuity will be difficult to manage along with the fluidity which I am determined to preserve. But it does seem as though we are getting along, at last. The Translation is showing up a curious old script that is something entirely new to me. So far we have gotten to page 52 – out of a full 96. Inuendo, scandal, double meaning, obscenity, filth, contempt for woman, peasant humor, proverbs, anti-clericalism are blended into a hodge-podge of soup, goats, chamber pots until Gertrude Stein seems a simple, quiet mind beside them. So far all we have been able to do is the decipher the words in a rough manner. When it begins to trickle a little more easily I'll send you a script.

> Yours
> Bill

Ted: Tibor Serly.

Ford: Ford Madox Ford.

Sullivan: A. M. Sullivan (1896–1980), American poet. For several years he hosted a weekly radio program devoted to poetry.

Brooklyn spiel: Williams spoke at the Brooklyn Institute of Arts and Letters on 4 December 1936 during a symposium sponsored by *Poetry*. Mariani 394. See letter 341.

Quevedo book: *The Dog and the Fever*.

[Postmarked Rutherford, N.J.]

[Postmarked 17 February 1937]

Floss found the recently lost Pound letter which I'll send you soon. Did I say Feb. 21st at <u>noon</u> W.O.R. Anyhow it's to be at noon.

    Bill

Pound letter: See Williams's letter of 5 February 1937.

W.O.R.: The New York radio station which broadcast the Poetry Hour.

■ 348. ALS-2

[111 East 36th Street, New York]

Washington's Birth. [22 February] 1937.

Dear Bill

Beautifully spoken American English – beautiful talking – over WOR at noon yesterday, so that when you made yr. point about the relation of poetry & music, and the music of American speech, the whole talk was one thing.

I think it should have struck every body as very well done, even tho some of us may have been aware that you were new to talking over the radio. Your timing was excellent – the pace you took to read – and with a little more emphasis here & there on selection of material, contrast, rather than understatement (really very fine sequence of statement) you should be able to do this kind of thing perfectly in the future. You've a fine radio voice, and the next occasion shd. make it easier to be in even finer voice.

Probably the first decent thing said about poetry, Am. poetry, over the air. Damn it we shd. have more of this kind of broadcast. And it was entertaining & could be made that for a wide public.

Have you had a chance to look at A-8? Anxious to have your say on it – & would like to send it to Ez. as soon as you're thru with it. Send it with his lost & found letter as soon as convenient, please – & my thanks.

Just one more thing. A poem of Robert Allison Evans appears in New Republic of Feb. 17. It might help – shd. help – the literary situation in general if some one wrote into the editors, giving Evans credit for what he's worth, & urging 'em to print more as good. And I think yr. approval would help a little more than others'. <If it's convenient – etc.>

    Best to yourself, Floss & all –

    By the way, Ted, Alice, Jerry, also listened in yesterday.

        Yours

        Louis.

WOR at noon: See Williams's letter of 10 February 1937.

A poem: "Coal Cracker's Song," the *New Republic* 80:1159 (17 February 1937), 41.

Ted, Alice, Jerry: Tibor Serly, unidentified, Jerry Reisman.

■ 349. TLS-1

> 9 Ridge Road
> Rutherford, N.J.

Feb. 22, 1937

Dear Louis:

Just to enclose Ezra's letter of which I have spoken. Nothing else to speak of save that I have made a certain amount of progress with the translation. Due to the mild winter there are a number of green shoots showing in the garden. The same to you.

> Yours
> Bill

My hospital service ends March 1st.

Ezra's letter: See Williams's letter of 5 February 1937.

the translation: *The Dog and the Fever.*

■ 350. TLS-1

> 9 Ridge Road
> Rutherford, N.J.

Feb. 25, 1937

Dear Louis:

The lines from "A" up to whatever the page number was were received on time but until the last few days it was impossible for me to get to them. I'm sorry not to have acknowledged the receipt, though.

Two nights ago I began the reading. I was interested at once and recognized something I liked but my head fell forward on my chest and I had to quit. No use my trying to do anything when I'm in that condition. And the better the stuff the less am I able to continue. I did though find myself falling asleep in a peculiar condition. The was a sort of splintering of ideas and images with flashes of lights striking through. It came from your idea. You have apparently invented a form. It is one of the -poias, I don't know which. Perhaps, Logo. It is truly illuminating.

Tried again last night but couldn'make much headway. I've been very tired recently. It is partly spring, partly work and partly me. I waste myself without purpose or accomplishment at times – merely by breathing.

But to return to the script, it has a fresh effect on the mind, and a serious one. It is poetry – since it uses the form of ideas to place a meaning above the literal meaning of the component members. My first impression is one of en-lightenment, of a spread of light through various media into which it has not spread due to impedimenta: by organizing the material in a certain way the light is shown to go in where it has not been able to go before. It is a unity of idea that gives a form – that's what I'm trying to say. If that is poetry then this is poetry. But there is little if any melopoia. I can't say more till I have been able to read all.

I think you are doing an important thing and doing it with surprising skill and persistence. But don't expect the mountain to come to you – in the form of a public demonstration. I know you don't expect that.

I have your card about Amdur and will send it to Ezra with the suggestion. As to René, I don't know. I think he's going nuts. But this is said only in the most friendly manner. I fear for him. We'll see.

As to the hospital, all I meant is that I'll be free for the next two months.

"Energetic" eh? Tha's me! A nice note from Ted. More about the opera an-other time. I M not letting it sleep.

> Yours
> Bill

Enclosure just a fancy from my desk to show the Chaucerian mood as Aprille approaches.

-poias: In *How to Read* (1929) Pound defines three aspects of poetry: Melopoeia ("wherein the words are charged, over and above their plain meaning, with some musical prop-erty, which directs the bearing or trend of that meaning"); Phanopoeia ("a casting of images upon the visual imagination"); Logopoeia ("the dance of the intellect among words").

Amdur: See Williams's letter of 5 February 1937.

René: René Taupin.

Ted: Tibor Serly.

Opera: *The First President*.

Enclosure: Enclosure lacking.

351. ALS-2

> 111 E 36 St.
> N.Y.

Feb 26/37

Dear Bill:

Thanks for the Spec. Del.

Your finding the <u>logo</u> of the -<u>poia</u> of "A"-8 suits me alright. "Splintering of ideas and images with flashes of lights" especially relevant when considered along with next to last line of pg 29 of my typescript, & all in all again helps me to see my intention – gone into the writing, now that I'm thru with it – the germ of the first seven lines of this movement.

As for the <u>melo</u> of the <u>making</u> – I thought I'd been making her thruout the thing – but, even if I've succeeded, that shdn't be too evident till you've finished reading all the 41 pp. So I'm waiting for your verdict on the whole or hole etc. Take your time. No, I don't expect a public demonstration applauding my aplomb or the lines or what. Only when you're thru with it please return the MS. to me, so I can send it to Ezra. And that's about all of an immediate public I can try to take care of at present.

I get you as to René. I know – it's hard for me <too> to ask him to get back to criticism again, but I know he can do it & that it might even make him feel better all around – and tho that's a valid feeling, it still makes one feel foolish to ask him, considering how he's been feeling. Maybe Ezra himself shd. ask him – shd. be easy for Ezra to do since he doesn't know R's personal state. I'll see, maybe I'll suggest it casually when I send him my MS.

Maybe you can use the enclosure – since you've probably r'cd one like it yourself & may not want to go alone. Or if no one cares to go, & you decide to make it <yrself> anyway, & you're in the neighborhood of my house about 4 P.M. tomorrow, save the enclosure & we'll go together. I have an appointment at six, tho.

Well, two months away from a hospital is better than nuthn. Thanks for the Chaucerian button etc

> Yours
> Louis.

next to last line: The earliest surviving typescript of "A"-8 has for the next to last line of
  page 29: "Go splintered rondel as a nosegay to Bob" (Texas).
René: René Taupin.
enclosure: Enclosure lacking.
Chaucerian button: See the previous letter.

352. TLS-1

[Rutherford, N.J.]

March 4, 1937
Dear Louis:
Just coming up for air after another mole's dig through the mazes of my daily profession – it's been tough going for a few days. Arses to the right of him volleyed and thundered . . . "A" is getting to be truly impressive, this last section takes hold of me in a new way, more heavily than anything so far. A very curi-

ous effect it has on me. It's basic seriousness is what carries it bound up with the validity of the thought. So few things are serious. All day long, year in and year out, I put off the seriousness of my life. Everything is against one, beginning with the newspapers. Your ground is wholly opposed to that. It doesn't matter whether you are successful or unsuccessful or whether you are understood or not understood, the thing is that it is there.

To me it is the shuttling back and forth of the ideas that gives the music here and their persistence – that you discover the same thing everywhere under everyone's nose – always the same and always unnoticed and unseized. The two or three sentences from Lenin punctuate all of him in a manner that clarifies his whole intention. If one look for matter among the variety of statements he'll go astray. It is the wholeness and unity that gives the form – I can't name it.

I don't want to read this part again. It has a couple of soft spots in it – you probably know them better than I – just not quite solid enough for the rest – a little bitterness that has no place here – a side glance of no importance – an occasional overemphasis that needs no more than a blue pencil to correct it. What I want now is to see the thing whole. I'll return the two parts I have at once. I am very much impressed – more than I was by the first parts. But that's why I want to see the whole.

A letter today from Laughlin who is now back at Harvard. I very lightly touched on "A". Can't do more for the moment. When he's ready he'll react. I trust his intelligence and ability – as well as his good will. If there is any reaction in the near future, you'll hear of it. I want to see you next week. How about Tuesday evening? Drop me a card. Tried to get in to see Dr. Faustus last week but failed to gain admission.

See you soon.

Bill

sentences from Lenin: Williams probably refers to the sequence of statements in "A"-8, pages 90–92.

Dr. Faustus: Orson Welles's critically praised production of *Dr. Faustus* ran from 8 January to 29 May 1937 at the Maxine Elliott Theater in New York.

353. TLS-1

9 Ridge Road, Rutherford, N.J.

March 7, 1937

Dear Louis:

O.K. not Tuesday. And not Wednesday either, that's impossible for me. Let's say Friday afternoon, but I'll write again before then mentioning some place near you for a rendezvous. Or you write. Whatever you say.

Nothing else much except news from – Laughlin – or did I tell you about that? I'm inclined to repeat when there is so little to tell relative to the art. It is merely that he is at last getting White Mule printed. It will be in general appearance like any novel but well bound. I have agreed that he is to write a postscript to it – inasmuch as many will find the ending unssatisfactory. He wants to take a shot at the crew of publishers and say a word as to a possible continuation of the story. But nothing relative to all this will appear on the title page.

Up till 5 this morning on another delivery. I saw the <u>aube</u>, a faint coldest light rimming the east, as unlike the night glow of the city as innocence is from guilt.

Yours
Bill

news . . . Laughlin: See the previous letter.

postscript: Hugh Witemeyer notes in *William Carlos Williams and James Laughlin: Selected Letters,* "The first edition of *White Mule* carried a postscript by JL entitled 'White Mule and New Directions.' It combines praise for WCW's 'pure' novel with an attack upon publishers who 'have made literature a business' (8).

354. TLS-1

9 Ridge Road, Rutherford, N.J.

March 10, 1937
Dear Louis:

It wouldn't be possible for you to come out here next Friday, would it? The thing is, Mother fell again about an hour ago and seems to have broken something else. I don't exactly know what as yet. You could come for lunch, whenever you are ready either at twelve or two or any time between as I have no office hours that day. It is Floss' suggestion.

One way or another we are being pressed a little harder than usual in our living this spring. But boiled fresh cod tastes just as good as ever when Floss fixes it. Not that we expect to have that on Friday.

If you can't come or if the coming will inconvenience you let's still put our meeting off for a few weeks. It will keep. But I don't see how it will be possible for me to get away if Mother has to have a cast on with all the attendant rearranging of schedules which that will involve. If things turn out better than expected I'll send a special delivery tomorrow.

Yours
Bill

[Rutherford, N.J.]

March 12/37: 3.30 P.M.
Quiet way in front of a patients house, a girl 11 with pneumonia.
    W.C. Williams
Sun Shining!

356. ALS-2

111 East 36 St
New York

Mar. 15/37
Dear Bill:
"The Book of Prosody": sounds like "The Book of Ruth" or something to study: nice title. What is it to be, or rather how much more of it is there? It's something worth doing. The nice thing is that when I find myself taking exception to one thing or another you say, you take up the point in the next sentence or next paragraph and I've no cause for taking exception when you've said all you wanted to say. E.g. sensual qualities in ¶ one, & then yr. definition of what is & is not sensual on pg 2. Or, another example, I don't quite approve of the phrase "potential rather than direct meaning" – doesn't seem accurate for the moment. But the very next sentence improves it – makes the meaning accurate. The whole business of the simile is excellent analysis. The last paragraph on Pound while obviously unfinished is a fine configuration, the whole contour of a suggestion. I'd like to see more of this, and I hope you go on with it. – I feel that the "logic" you find inferior to "direct conviction" will eventually be qualified as "formal" <i.e. you will probably qualify it as such.> The logic, symbolic or whatever, the thought process, experimental approach etc of modern science, technics, gathering of factual data and presentation as system is a process not too far off from the poetic: but this is merely repeating what I've said in the poem in several places, espec. p. 41. By the way this is "A"-8 not the last movement – there ought to be 24 movements altogether if I live long enough, though yr. analysis of this bit is so final I feel posthumous already. Thanks a lot for the original & copy. You have another?

———

I hope your mother's injury isn't serious. How is she?
It was a good thing after all I made no arrangements to come out last Friday – I cdn't have made it even if I <had> wanted to. I still don't know what was the matter – probably nothing more than a slight ptomaine poisoning – but I didn't want to do anything on Friday anymore or for the next two days. Damn

nuisance & waste of a week-end. One of these days I'll make it a point to get the fragments together & take the train to Rutherford & knock on yr. door. Please drop me a line when you have time.

My best, & very best regards to yr. mother.

      Yrs

      Louis

"The Book of Prosody": An envelope in the Zukofsky papers at Texas is marked, in Zukofsky's hand, " 'A' - The Book of Prosody[;] Statement - Oxford Anth. [,] Sent from Rutherford N.J. [,] Mar 13, 1937 to L. Z. 111 E 36 St N.Y." The "Statement for THE OXFORD ANTHOLOGY OF AMERICAN LITERATURE, to accompany the poems selected above my name" (2 pages) remains with the envelope. Williams wrote above the statement, "Louis Zukofsky - with whom much of this has been developed - for what it's worth, huh?" The accompanying two-page document, headed "From THE BOOK OF PROSODY" is as follows: "As an example of the use of information in poetry as contrasted with prose, take the last movement of Zukowsky's [sic] 'A' in which many statements and quotations are placed in juxtaposition one after the other for 41 pages in all: The writing of it is not put down for the literal meaning of the individual items or their particular truth (though it is understood that they must be true to be used) but for their sensual qualities - sensed at a stroke by the mind - not dwelt on as in a consecutive and developing prose discourse. ~~in which meaning is supported on either side by its logical relationship to other meanings.~~ So by repeated sensual impacts one after the other and using new materials each time a conviction is born that this and this and this being true and being related in meaning the truth of each one of them is separately affirmed. This is purely a sensual matter related to art. It has nothing to do with logic but arrives irresistably [sic] by conviction. It is interesting and depends on the obvious tactile acceptance of each item as true or made of the truth. And so each item must be very judiciously studied not to fly out of line by false emphasis or feeling but needs only to be true: nothing must interfere with that or the whole structure will fall.

This has nothing to do with the value per se of the information imparted. That naturally is of primary importance. All that is touched upon above is the manner chosen for imparting that knowledge whether prose or poetry and if poetry how it has been in this case and what effect may be expected from such treatment.

A further definition of what is and what is not sensual is invited by the sort of material used. It should be noted that in this poem the principle of the simile is used rather than metaphor. What is being said is that all these things are alike and so each one gains in potential rather than direct meaning. This is the basic function of poetry, by use of form to impose a further meaning upon the literal significance. ~~of the words~~ So it seems that here by a thoroughly academic procedure modified to an enlarged use (the simile) an orthodox effect of poetry is obtained in a new way. Thus, the segments of information are to be understood to have a sensual quality rather than a logical one.

This is important for it again enlarges the poetic means – we see the same differently used in Pound's Cantos where bits of "prose" are used among conventionally moulded poetic lines – Added to the usual use of figures, the rose, the melody we must perhaps add the idea but the idea treated as a sensual object." "A Note on Poetry," which Williams contributed to *The Oxford Anthology of American Literature*, ed. William Rose Benét and Norman Holmes Pearson (New York: Oxford UP, 1938), 1313–14 (Wallace B34), bears little resemblance to this typescript.

357. TLS-1

[Rutherford, N.J.]

March the St. patric's. [17 March 1937]

Dear Louis:

That is all of the book there is. It came to a head as I was about to transcribe my notes with the realization that the notes were part of a book that I have for a long time wanted to have and to read. No one else writes it so we had better get started. It grows out of our own experiments and reasonings. We have developed, in Objectivism, an important step toward a full understanding of what modern poetry is attempting and must have attempted. It is the inevitableness of it that impresss me most; that is why I never care who writes anything so long as it gets written.

My idea has been for a number of years that we shall have to consolidate our position by a reasoned work is which shall be embodied all that modern times have learned about poetic constitution (I refuse to use the word technique: technique is inseparable from the constitution of a poem: there are only poems) The present notes merely give a tentative flavor. I'm delighted that they have caught on with you.

We should make an outline, two outlines and combine them, giving chapter headings, etc, covering the whole subject with a bibliography beginning from Aristotle! but with emphasis only upon today – and especially ourselves, using our own works and those of which we approve brazenly for our illustrations. Let it be such a defense that it will constitute an inevitability, therr won't be anything else left.

Thinking it over quickly (after ten or twenty years of brooding) I think you and I should do it. Let us take alternate or even duplicate chapters – it doesn't make any difference and build them up by mutual criticism and rewriting. When finished René will write a compreshensive introduction. It should make a book of some importance especially if well written. It needn't be too big either, just final. It's sickening to feel the dense ignorance concerning poetry in the minds of the usual magazine editor, or any editor, such as the late Harriet used to be. Sorry to have to say it.

If I can get in Saturday around mid-afternoon would you be around?

> Yours
> Bill

the book: See the previous letter.
René: René Taupin.
Harriet: Harriet Monroe.

358. ALS-1

> 9 Ridge Road
> Rutherford, N.J.

April 8/37
Dear Louis:

Shall by in N.Y. Friday. At about 3 or 3.30 I'll stop at your place. If you're not there I'll understand. Leave a note if you want to.

> yours
> Bill

359. ACS

> [Rutherford, N.J.]

[April 1937]

Don't wait later than 3.30 – and not even till then if it rains heavily – as the papers say it will. All right about the prosody thing – I'll let it write itself. We'll see.

> Bill

prosody thing: See Zukofsky's letter of 15 March 1937.

360. ALS-1

> 9 Ridge Road
> Rutherford, N.J.

5/6/37
Dear Louis:

They're having me for some reason or other, as "honored guest" – at the annual distribution of awards for student poetry at Columbia, Harkness Auditorium at 8 P.M. tonight. I don't know whether or not its a private affair or what. I've been translating Spanish revolutionary ballads – here's one –

> yrs
> Bill

revolutionary ballads: Enclosure lacking. Williams contributed one translation ("Wind of the Village") to *And Spain Sings*, ed. M. J. Benardete and Rolfe Humphries (New York: Vanguard Press, 1937). Wallace B28.

361. TLS-1

May 7, 1937

Dear Louis:

I was in dread lest perhaps you might by accident get to the occasion of my "honoring" after all. I think as many as fifteen men, women and children appeared – not counting myself – for the event. Professor Edman was rewarding though inclined to be a trifle professorial in a good humored way. He told two good anecdotes. One was of T.S.Eliot when he lectured at Columbia two years or so ago. In the character of a perfect Oxford Englishman Eliot first proclaimed, in drawling accent, that he didn't think he had ever before in public expressed his opinion of the poet Milton. The profs were by this time sitting openmouthed on the edge of their seats. Lycidas is, to be sure, a beautiful lyric poem. But Paradise Lost, exclaimed Mr. Eliot, I consider a failure! The audience collapsed. It is the first time I have ever admired Eliot.

The second anecdote has as its scene a tea in Cambridge at which Frost and Eliot were present. During the afternoon Eliot at one time turned to Frost and said, I think Mr. Frost will now read us one of his poems. To which Frost replied, Now, now Eliot. You read us a poem and I'll write one while you're doing it. Not too bad for Frost. What a shame we aren't all of us a bit more civil and civilized. We might, just might, see the beginnings of a life here.

The Spanish originals all are returned with the translations. I am sorry. My translations keep as close as posssible to the pace and meter of the Spanish. I have done them line for line and almost word for word. The originals are not in rhyme. Here's another. You may keep the carbons if you wish to – at least until the book is out, then destroy them.

I was asked to send something for the next issue of The Columbia Review – if possible a sketch of my talk – which had been given extempore – I had not realized that I was to be the speaker of the evening – I thought I had been invited merely to be honored. Anyhow, I sat down yesterday and tore off four pages for them. If it is printed I'll send you a copy of the mag which they promised to expedite to me. It came out brown on top like a bun or a cake.

It's wonderful living through a springtime without the urge to write a word about it. For the first time in years I'm having the time of my life just looking around. I feel no compunction, God is not driving me.

Yours

Bill

Edman: Irwin Edman (1896–1954), American philosopher and teacher.

Eliot: Eliot lectured on "The Verse of John Milton" at Columbia University on 21 April
   1933.

the translations: See the previous letter.

Here's another: Enclosure lacking.

something: "Poetry," *Columbia Review* 19:1 (November 1937), 3–5. Wallace C252.

■ 362. TLS-1

                                          9 Ridge Road, Rutherford, N.J.
June 6, 1937
Dear Louis:

Bob McAlmon is in N.Y. on his way to London where a book of his BEING
GENIUSES TOGETHER has just been accepted for publication. He leaves the 10th.
I'm going to try to see him Tuesday.

Meanwhile WHITE MULE is out – or will be released on the 10th. A copy
should reach you in a few days. It looks all right. Not too many typographical
errors and it reads along. Paul likes it.

My few spare moments are being taken up with the Chairmanship of the
Bergen County Medical Board to Aid Spanish Democracy. Why in hell do I
do it?

See you soon in spite of it.
       Yours
       Bill

BEING GENIUSES TOGETHER: Robert McAlmon, *Being Geniuses Together* (London: Secker
and Warburg, 1938). It appeared in the late summer of 1938.

■ 363. TLS-1

                                               [Rutherford, N.J.]
July 18, 1937
Dear Louis:

Nothing much to report except that I don't get into New York – once in a
month, to be exact – on more or less of an errand. Practice has been active and
exacting, hard cases with much close watching necessary. I do hope to have a
few consecutive days in there during the summer sometime. I want to follow
up some work in translating, at the Library.

The inside of my head's been active. Lord knows what will come of it. Two
books, at least, have taken final form and the Paterson thing isn't far off the last
alignment. All in my noodle. May they be born without the dismemberment
of "father". And Laughlin, as perhaps I told you, wants to do a "collected

shorter prose pieces", "If White Mule pays for itself", such a book to be issued this fall. I have a lady friend typing the stuff now – irregularly – but I think she'll go through. But I've written scarcely a word all summer.

White Mule is selling slowly, so I've heard. They're printing up – no, binding another 300, but that only makes 800 in all so far. That ain't many! But if it pays for itself I'll get another book and so it has always gone with me. It wouldn't be healthy at my age to burst suddenly into blatant bloom.

The enclosed letter from the inevitable and inimitable Ted came a few days ago. So he's going to be "in the money" again. He's funny the way he uses my life as an excuse for accepting a pay check. You might think he was blaming me for a seduction. What a pity it is that they don't ask Toscannini to kiss his foot in addition and promise him twenty years in a silken prison thereafter for his better ease and comfort. Don't misunderstand me. Ted's all right only he's "funny". If he doesn't watch out somebody is going to catch him and FORCE him to be a composer. I even think he may do my ballet some day if he doesn't watch himself carefully. And then what a world of success he's going to have dumped on him. It's a crime. But I'm going through with him or no one. It's fate.

So what about yourself? Any more auditions? Give us a tumble when you have time. Mother goes up to my brother's farm Aug. 1st. After that we may sneak off for a week or two. I wish it might be Nova Scotia – or the moon.

> Yours
> Bill

Two books: Perhaps one of these was the never completed "Book of Prosody."
Paterson thing: Williams worked on this project during 1938. In March 1939 he sent
   Laughlin a manuscript of poems titled "Detail and Parody for the Poem Patterson."
lady friend: Probably Kathleen Hoagland (1904–1984), teacher, author, and resident of
   Rutherford.
enclosed letter: Enclosure lacking.
Ted: Tibor Serly.
Toscannini: Arturo Toscannini (1867–1957), Italian-born operatic and symphonic con-
   ductor. Principal conductor of the New York Philharmonic, 1930–1931 and 1935–1036.
my ballet: *The First President*.
brother's farm: Edgar Williams had a "place in Connecticut" (Mariani 442).

364. TLS-1

[Rutherford, N.J.]

August 8, 1937

Dear Louis:

They'll be sending you the current issue of a professional magazine called The Writer. It contains a sort of article by me on the writing of White Mule.

There's no use my pretending I can go here and there as I may please. I don't know what's going to happen but unless there is a radical change of some sort in me or the world I'll probably withdraw more and more from New York and involve myself more and more with "Patterson" – if anything.

Mother is away at my brother's for a month and we're going down the coast for a two weeks vacation – if all goes well – on the sands. I haven't done such a thing in years.

Matters in general haven't gone so very well with us in recent months. Oh, nothing moral, ethical or anything of that sort but the burden of our elders has closed in on us pretty heavily. It takes the heart out of a person. And I'm a good deal of a problem besides to myself and to others.

I never hear from Ezra any more. Do you? See you in the fall. Hope you finish "A" this summer.

> Sincerely yours
> Bill

sort of article: "*White Mule* Versus Poetry," *The Writer* 50:8 (August 1937), 243–45. Wallace C249.

365. TLS-1

[Rutherford, N.J.]

Nov. 10, 1937

Dear Louis:

Strange things happening in the world and as strange to me – perhaps to you also. Whatever time I have at my disposal I use for writing. I have been writing at every available moment, furiously, of late. Part of it has been due to pressure from the outside which seems to be increasing as time goes on. I can't write fast enough for those who demand work of me, all sorts of things if seldom lucretive.

Laughlin suddenly insisted on a book of short stories which I had to dig out, arrange and retype in some instances. They are in proof form now, he intends to have them out by Christmas I think. He has consented to keep the price reasonably low, one fifty. The format will be the same as that of White Mule which continues to sell slowly. Nothing in it for me.

I had to make a choice between doing the second vol. of W.M. or finishing my mother's biography. I chose the latter. The old lady may not live much longer – though by her appetite and excellent digestion I think she'll live to be a hundred! – so I did not feel that it was fair to put off the tribute much longer. But it's a job! I'm at that stage when I feel submerged in the mass of material I've collected. I have an excellent outline prepared by the detail of retyping, shuffling material about and connecting this and that into a smooth narrative form has me groggy. My volunteer typist is a charming and efficient person but I have to wait for her to find the time to finish each piece of work that I give her before I can hand her something else. etc etc

Laughlin, if you will <permit> it, plans to bring out your poem entire next year. But I remember now that we have spoken of this before.

New Masses plans to print my article on H.H.Lewis in an early issue. The Oxford Book of American Verse is after me to write some sort of explanatory note to my things included there.

Had supper last night on the hill with René & Mimi. Oh, go and see the present show at the Steiglitz gallery, 509 Madison this month if you can – an interesting look backward. Don't miss it. Tell others if interested.

This is just a greeting. Glad you're back in the world! No use saying more, you know the answers.

     Yours

     Bill

Never a word from Ezra, no acknowledgement of White Mule!

book of short stories: *Life Along the Passaic River* (Norfolk, Conn.: New Directions, 1938). Wallace A19.

mother's biography: *Yes, Mrs. Willliams.*

volunteer typist: Probably Kathleen Hoagland.

your poem: "A"-8 appeared in *New Directions in Prose and Poetry 1938.*

my article: "An American Poet," *New Masses* 25:9 (23 November 1937), 17–18. Wallace C255.

explanatory note: "A Note on Poetry," *The Oxford Anthology of American Literature,* ed. William Rose Benét and Norman Holmes Pearson (New York: Oxford Univ. Press, 1938), 1313–14. Wallace B34.

René: René Taupin.

Mimi: Taupin's wife.

present show: "Beginnings and Landmarks," with works previously exhibited at Stieglitz's "291" gallery between 1905 and 1917. Artists represented included Matisse, Picasso, Rodin, Brancusi, Toulouse-Lautrec, Marin, O'Keefe, Dove, Demuth, Steichen, Maurer, Man Ray and Picabia.

9 Ridge Road
Rutherford, N.J.

Nov. 15 '37
Dear Louis:
Hell knows when but sometime . . .
Meanwhile
    Norman H. Pearson
        147 Cottage Street
           New Haven
                Connecticut
With my blessing.
    Bill

Pearson: Norman Holmes Pearson (1909–1975), American literary scholar and teacher.

[Rutherford, N.J.]
Oct. 31/38
Dear Louis:

Glad to get your card. I'll try to slip the Gug an earful but . . . they are, to my thinking, among the world's most to be prized sons of bitches. No hope without soap.

Saw #8 in New Directions as it passed under my nose but had no time to read.

The Collected Poems (mine) are out but not yet in my hands. I'm sending you one so act accordingly.

Saw Mother operated on last Thursday for cataract of one eye. She behaved well. The job was beautifully performed. She seems to be doing satisfactorily. The other eye still remains to be treated. Poor thing, she is brave – for what? Nothing much left of her: all she wants to do is put her papers in order before dying.

I'm not writing. Plenty of plans but no accomplishment. The life is like trying to thread a square yard of mosquito netting with one thread.

    Yours
    Bill

the Gug: The John Simon Guggenheim Memorial Foundation. Williams's recommendation is in the archives of the Foundation. He notes that "If I should have to choose one to whom to present the fellowship it would be Louis Zukofsky." Williams refers to "*A*" as an attempt by Zukofsky to synthesize "in a poem the multiple elements of the struggle of a potentially classless world to bring itself into a whole. He is treating his subject by an objective method of 'real' juxtapositions of the elements to 'make' a composition in the manner of Bach's greater musical compositions." Williams also found common ground with Zukofsky: "What Zukofsky is doing is very close to my own objectives in the field of poetry. It represents a great amount of thankless underground work, the building of foundations which I believe directly underlie the poetry of the immediate future."

#8 in New Directions: "A"-8 appeared in *New Directions in Prose and Poetry 1938.*

Collected Poems: *The Complete Collected Poems 1906–1938* (Norfolk, Conn.: New Directions, 1938). Wallace A20.

368. ALS-4

31 W. 11 St.
N.Y.

Nov. 2/38

Dear Bill:

I'll be very happy to get a copy of your Collected Poems. It'll be the first really new book I'll have seen in a long time.

I copy out from "A Test of Poetry," which I had typed up the summer of 1937 after letting it lie around for 3 yrs. in ms., an item which may interest you. There are about 150 pp. of this test in 3 parts, the first & third without comment, in which the reader is just given "juxtaposed" examples. I use you again in Test 3 – the song "I tried to put a bird in a cage" placed between the negro chain gang song "Forty-leben days gone by" & Marianne's "Poetry / I too dislike it." Keep the enclosure. I went the rounds of New York publishers with the ms. this last year, but no one wants it. So what? But it would be better to be able to send it to you as a book, printed, than in snippets.

I've been working on more "A". Slo-w –.

I hope your mother is much better.

I know the wear & tear on you, and hope you can get back to your work soon.

Thanks again for the Gug business. I gave the same three references I submitted the last long ago, Ez, Eliot & you. Do you think Norman H. Pearson would have any influence as a reference? He seemed to like my work when I sent it to him for the Oxford Book of Am. Verse, tho it didn't fall into his chronological scheme. Was the book ever published?

Give my best to all

Yrs

Louis

Examples 24a & b –

<table>
<tr><td>24a—</td><td>

I have a gentil cok
  Croweth me day;
He doth me risen erly
My matines for to say.

</td></tr>
</table>

	I have a gentil cok;
(1) descended	Comen (1) he is of grete (2)
(2) great (stock lineage)	His comb is of red corel
(3) jet	Itis tail is of get. (3)
	I have a gentil cok;
	Comen he is of kinde;
	His comb is of red corel,
(4) indigo	His tail is inde. (4)
(5) azure	His legges ben of asour (5)
	So gentil and so smale;
(6) spurs	His sporès (6) arn of silver white
(7) the skin of the slain	Into the wortèwale (7)
	His eynen arn of cristal
(8) set (literally <u>locked</u>)	Loken (8) all in aumber; (9)
(9) amber.	And every night he percheth him
	In mine ladyes chaumber.

Anonymous
15th century

<table>
<tr><td>24b—</td><td>

So much depends
upon

a red wheel
barrow

glazed with rain
water

beside the white
chickens.

</td></tr>
</table>

William Carlos Williams
Spring and All
1923.

Comment:

24a.—This is material for mosaic work, or stained glass, tho it *has* been treated in words.

24b.—But for the first four words, this description might have been painted.

Whatever the symbolic implication of 24a, if any, the attention of the poet seems to be taken up by sheer play; by the opulence of lovely, but artificial, conditions.

The white chickens of 24b are even more gentle than the mosaic 'cok' (24a) descended of gentility. The more than visual importance of the simple rural objects observed is only too evident in the short thoughtful cadences of this poem.

Note:

It may take only four words (see 24b again) to shift the level at which emotion is held from neatness of surface to comprehension which includes surface and what is under it.

Question:

1. Quote the four words of 24b referred to in the comment. _____

2. Do your prefer 24a to 24b?

   Yes _____ No _____

3. Do you think that 24b is not poetry?

   It is not _____

   It is _____

A Test of Poetry: Louis Zukofsky, *A Test of Poetry* (New York: The Objectivist Press, 1948). The most recent printing is by the Wesleyan University Press, 2000 (Volume I of the *Collected Works of Louis Zukofsky*). "I tried to put a bird in a cage" is the first line of Williams's poem, "The Fool's Song" in *The Tempers* (*CP1*, 5–6). It appears at the end of *A Test* (150). The examples Zukofsky sent to Williams also appear in *A Test* (100–101).

more "A": Zukofsky began work on the first half of "A"-9 in 1938.

Oxford Book of Am. Verse: *The Oxford Anthology of American Literature*.

369. TLS-1

[Rutherford, N.J.]

December 2, 1938

Dear Louis:

Just a word. I dropped in at your place the other evening on the chance I might see you but you weren't in – as I more or less expected. Just wanted to say I'm going to "read" at Gorham Munson's this Sunday afternoon at 4 P.M. or so. The whole business is a mess. Seventy five cents admission! Don't go. They sort of put it over on me – without conscious intention of doing so, fo course; I thought I was just gojng to read to a few dumb guys just for the fun of it. Perhaps no one will come anyhow. Forget it.

The Gug papers came day before yesterday. There were four seeking my sponsorship. I put you at the top. Here's hoping but, as I have said in the past, not one of those I have signed for during the past ten years or more has succeeded in landing the job.

The Oxford Anthology, which is out, is an awsome spectacle but a fine job and a very interesting book. It is even good reading.

Anyhow there it is. Hope you make the Gug. You deserve it if anybody does – which nobody does, of course. Nobody deserves anything, is what I mean. The tragedy of youth is that it still keeps some comparative sliding scale of worth in its mind and finds, too often, that there's another scale being used under the table. What is a Gug for anyone to deserve it. You're just lucky if you get it. So say your prayers like a good boy and read Silone's "Bread and Wine" as I am doing two years late. Not too hot as writing but with something like good black bread and good cheap Dago red wine too.

> Yours
> Bill

Gug: The John Simon Guggenheim Memorial Foundation.

four seeking: I have not been able to identify Zukofsky's three rivals.

Oxford Anthology: *The Oxford Anthology of American Literature.*

"Bread and Wine": Ignazio Silone (1900–1978), Italian novelist. *Bread and Wine,* trans. Gwenda David and Eric Mosbacher (New York: Harper & Brothers, 1937). Set in Fascist Italy at the beginning of the Italian war against Abysinnia, the novel tells the story of Pietro Spina, a communist agent who, returning in disguise to his native region, discovers that doctrinaire solutions are not what the Italian peasantry needs. As he remarks near the end of the novel, "Our love, our disposition for sacrifice and self-abnegation are barren if dedicated to abstract and inhuman symbols; they are only fruitful if carried into relations with our fellow-men. Morality can live and flourish only in practical life" (289).

■ 370. ALS-1

[41 West Eleventh Street, New York]

Dec. 3/38

Dear Bill:

I'm very sorry I was out the other night when you dropped around – if it was Thursday, I went uptown to see Basil. I'd enjoy it a lot, if you feel like it, if

you'd come here next Thurs. or the Thurs. after., I could make some supper –
and if you'd like to see Basil, I'll try and shanghai him. Let me know.

No, I won't go Sunday to the reading, but hope it turns out pleasanter than
you expect.

Thanks for your wishes for the Gug., & again many thanks for yr. say to
them – let it turn out as it may. As I said, it's a raffle.

How have the reviews been on yr. <u>Collected</u> – I haven't seen any, but I've
probably missed them. I'm not asking, but in case you sent a copy of the book,
it hasn't arrived. I should buy one and boost your sales – but it's no use for me
to think about buying things. On the other hand, if you have to pay for copies,
please don't send me one. I hate to pay for my own work, and hate to see any-
one else do the same. I'll get around to <u>Collected</u> somehow sometime.

What else? The short enclosures, you've probably not seen? The Postscript
to <u>Anew</u> 6 is really nobody's business, meant to be stuck at the end of a volume
of <u>Anews</u>, if & when, so people can read <u>6</u> and the <u>Postscript</u> together if they
wish – I don't mean to say the <u>P.S.</u> is in the poem.

Best to the home-folk.

 Yrs.

 Louis

Basil: Basil Bunting.

the reading: See the previous letter.

<u>Collected</u>: *The Complete Collected Poems 1906–1938*.

<u>Postscript</u> to <u>Anew</u> 6: A short collection of quotations from Cavalcanti, Dante, Marx, and
 Henrik Anton Lorentz, published in the notes to *Anew*, where "Anew 6" was retitled
 "Anew 29."

371. TLS-1

[Rutherford, N.J.]

Dec. 11, 1938

Dear Louis:

Thanks for the invitation to supper, that's fine. I'll let you know within a few
days when I can make it. You suggest a Thursday. I'll see what I can do for this
week. After all, a man has a right to cut his office hours occasionally, maybe it
can be done this week. I'd like very much to see him. But I'll have to let you
know. I may even have to wire you Thursday morning. I have no other choice.
Wait until you hear from me before counting the date final.

It's been more than a year now that I have been under a cloud as far as see-
ing people is concerned. Threre's been nothing to say, much to think
about,more to decide upon. Of late I've begun to live a little again, in my head,

so that now I again feel the necessity for <u>convivio</u> and talk. I'm beginning, that is, to feel the necessity.

Many things have happened not the least of which have been the acceptance of two writings which I spent much time upon and which have been delayed, delayed and delayed in getting toward publication. They have to be published. One is the thing Dorothy Norman will bring out in next spring's issue of her Twice a Year and the other is a study of Ignazio Lorca in relation to classic Spanish literature which has finally been accepted by the new Kenyon Review. I feel better now.

All sorts of incidentals have come in between. The latest is that they may, possibly, want me to take over, as Director, the Literary Project of the N.J. P.W.A. This is for your private ear. I should know by Thursday what the outcome is to be.

More important is that I've begun to think about poetic form again. So much has to be thought out and written out there before we can have any solid criticism and consequently well grounded work here. There are so many terribly limited minds posing as critics here. Edmund Wilson, for instance and any number of others. Ivor Einters and whole sections of polite literature surrounding such places as Harvard, Princeton and thr New York Sunday Supplements. They are, many of them, people of good will but they don't really know anything. I say this cooly and considerately but it is true. I have been amazed, of late, to begin to suspect what isn't known. Even our dear ol' Ezra is badly lacking in his adjustments. So it goes. This is what has been happening to me. My mind has been agog. I've felt beaten. All the varied phases of political action – getting on because undiagnosed SOON ENOUGH. All these things are from the same egg which WE should be hatching first.

So many things, so many things – to be said and done. I feel that I haven't the wit or the energy to tackle them and that there's no use in anything until they are tackled.

Yet, I sense a return to America recently. There is the same stir in the air there was in 1913, before the World War. Maybe it's the end, another calamity on the way. But what of that. The thing to do is to seize the opportunity while it lasts, get what there is to get and get it quickly. That is how I feel.

In other words I want to write again and I am writing. I'm not thinking much but writing. Anything. What there is to write. A woman on the Nation, Margaret Marshall who seems to be the right sort, has asked for small bits of prose, short story type of thing. I've done a few and sent them to her. People I have had to do with during the last twenty years.

Poetry hasn't moved forward as well as prose. I've jotted down many short notes, almost completed ltrics, with an intention to have them be true lyrics – if it can be done in our present day language.

If I can't make it this Thursday what about a week from Tuesday, or even this Tuesday? Tuesday evenings I have no office hours. I have no office hours Saturday evening either. Sundays too I have no office hours. What say?

Yours

Bill

I received your post script to the Canto you mention and have added it to the other scripts, or parts of scripts, which I have. No comment for the moment.

What about Evans? Can't I see him too some time. I mean the Pennsylvania Coal Mining engineer. Isn't his name Evans? I'd like to know him better.

two writings: "Against the Weather: A Study of the Artist," *Twice a Year* 2 (Spring–Summer 1939), 53–78. Wallace C272. "Federico Garcia Lorca," the *Kenyon Review* 1:2 (Spring 1939), 148–58. Wallace C270.

Norman: Dorothy Stecker Norman (1905–1997), American photographer, author, and social activist. Williams wrote to Pound on 6 April 1938, "A woman named Dorothy Norman is about to start a new magazine called, or to be called, Twice a Year. She has money. She is a rather beautiful and intelligent Jewess married to a typical young Wall St. broker. I like them both. He doesn't interfere with her. She wants to issue a magazine which will cover the world geographically, artistically, philosophically and morally. She is in no hurry. Her plan is to contact all those she wishes to use for her purpose and to set them to work—if she can. She will pay _ cent a word. At least that is what she told me. She wants me to do an article—which you will have a chance to see later in which I hope to God I shall finish with Eliot forever—so far as I am concerned" (*Pound/Williams* 194). Dorothy Norman was married to Edward A. Norman, whose father had been one of the founders of Sears, Roebuck.

Wilson: Edmund Wilson (1895–1972), American critic and novelist.

Einters: Yvor Winters.

Marshall: Margaret Marshall was literary editor of *The Nation*. Williams's only contribution to *The Nation* during 1938 and 1939 was the story "Above the River," *The Nation* 147:24 (10 December 1938), 623–24. Wallace C266.

post script: See the previous letter.

Evans: Robert Allison Evans.

372. ALS-2

41 W. 11 St

n.y c.

Monday Dec 12/38

Dear Bill:

If you can possibly come here this Thursday without inconveniences, do so – because I arranged for Basil to come that night, & René may possibly show up, too. Don't bother wiring if you're coming, but if you don't let me know by mail before then to the contrary, then wire sometime in the morning, yes – i.e. if you can't make it. Don't lose business on acc't of me, tho. Tues. Dec. 20th will be alright instead if you can let me know by Friday of this week, so I can adjust my usual program. And I'll try to get Basil down, too. Invitation to supper goes for Floss, too, if she wants to come, no need to warn me about that etc. My kitchen is a vest pocket affair and I'm not much of a cook, but I seem to manage. I hope it'll be this Thursday simply because it'd be nice to see you sooner, but as I say don't go out of your way.

I notice all the revived activity in yr. letter, & what I say is: fine, & leave it for conversation when I see you, instead of a letter. It wd. be an achievement to the public good if you became director of N.Y.P.W.A. Lit Project. Right you are about poetic form, & all the more right pon yr. poems. The Collected came Sat. morning and I've gone thru it. But all last week I found myself going thru the separate volumes – from one to the next to the next etc – if they weren't good I couldn't have done it at this time. Damn few writers to-day that get any time from me at all – but what struck me especially at this time is not only yr. eminent readableness which very few of us have, but the music – the total movement of each piece, as well as the detail, alliteration, working over of actual sound etc – & well we labor, Ezra labors, etc & we contribute sumpn, but there's yr. work and the sound, the noises, are the virtuoso's in the best sense of the word. In this respect, Al Que Qiere, goes up a coupla' notches in my estimation. At any rate, it seems that way after 10 years of having it around here. A thing like "A Prelude" is well nigh perfect. – I've looked thru Collected to see what omissions there were, & you can tell my why History & Artzybasheff are omitted when you see me. – As for the looks of the volume itself, it's a pleasure. Thanks.

Evans is out in Scranton, starting a mining venture of his own and hasn't been in town. But he should be here during the holidays and perhaps we <can> arrange a meeting – He's a very busy man, but I'll write him now to see what can be done.

So, see you soon
Yrs.
Louis.
[...]

Basil: Basil Bunting.
René: René Taupin.
Collected: *The Complete Collected Poems 1906–1938.*
Al Que Qiere: *Al Que Qiere!* (Boston: The Four Seas Company, 1917). Wallace A3.
Artzybasheff: Williams's poem, "Foreign" (*CP1*, 79–80).

373. ACS

[41 West 11th Street]

[Postmarked 12 December 1938]

Dear Bill:

I forgot to say my ap't is the front basement – don't go upstairs. You enter thru the "garden" gate, bell near the gate door, or rap on my window. Come early, if you can, 5:00, whichever night is convenient.

Louis.

374. TLS-1

9 Ridge Road
Rutherford, N.J.

Dec. 13, 1938

Dear Louis:

Tell what I'll do, I'll come in Thursday after office hours. I can make it by 9 or so which will give us at least two hours of talk before I have to trickle off again. Later on we can meet again. If I'm not there by 9 I'm stuck.

The P.W.A. or whatever it is has been dumped into my lap. I've about made up my mind to give it a fling. If it sinks me I'll just step out of it.

Did you see The Nation for last week? Or is it this week? There's a story in it by me. I disremember whether or not I ever spoke to you of the thing.

See you soon, Thursday evening if possible.

Yours
Bill

story: "Above the River."

375. TLS-1

[Rutherford, N.J.]

April 19, 1939

Dear Louis:

Thanks for the clipping which I had missed and which is very much to the point. It brings out, the speech does, just the feeling I wanted to emphasize between Mr. and Mrs. Washinton on that day. I'll use it when I get back to that job as I will if I live for I am determined to make those acts into a good play before I am through.

Before going on to anything else I want to tell you that the idea of the opera is never far from my mind. I have worked at it unconsciously all this while until now I have it much more clearly formed than ever it has been heretofore.

I know now very definitely what I want – something quite different from the rough libretto we once sketched. The outlines are more or less the same but very little more than the rough outline.

What I plan to do is to write a poem, short and simple. I'm really going to write it this time and let the stage people fight over it afterward. I'm going to give it the smell and the taste, the direction and the body as well as the movement – but I'm not going to fuss over things which the poet has, properly, very little to do with. I've even started to write it again – from the beginning but many other things have stopped me short.

Right now I'm up to the ears in the second volume of White Mule, the first five chapters either finished or all set to be finished. Partisan Review is bringing out Chapter II of the new volume this month. etc etc

Wish you would come to one of the dinners Ford seems to want to arrange for me – under the name which you've heard. Come as my guest. Cummings is to be the guest of honor next time if I can capture him. He'll be the guest of honor anyway.

We'll be getting together again, if you will, someday wait and see. Recently I've been of little use to anyone as far as the development of new ideas is concerned. I've had to work to keep alive – in my mind. Many things have contributed to it. And now Ezra is coming over. As Laughlin says, It must be a war. He hasn't written to me so I'm not planning to see him untul he invites it. Let him run for the Senate on the Fascist slate if he wants to/ Anyhow I'm glad you wrote. Thank you.

Yours

Bill

I've got several things I want you to see, such as the finished introduction to the book on my mother, as I simply haven't been able to do more than I've done in the past year. Communication has had to wait.

clipping: Not located.

those acts: In *The First President*.

second volume: *In the Money* (Norfolk, Conn.: New Directions, 1940). Wallace A21.

Chapter Two: "Back to the City," *Partisan Review* 6:3 (Spring 1939), 148–58. Wallace C271.

dinners: In February 1939 Ford Madox Ford founded a group called the Friends of William Carlos Williams. It met five times before disbanding in June 1939. See Mariani 424.

Ezra: Pound arrived in New York on 21 April 1939. Williams and Pound met in Washington, D. C., on 30 April. Pound also stayed one night (5 June) at the Williams residence.

41 W. 11 St

Apr. 24/39

Dear Bill

Twice a Year arrived as your gift to-day, my day off, so thanks. Part III of Against the Weather: interests me most as statement of your position. Since it's a matter of me, too, against the weather, I won't say any more, but let the enclosures reflect what light they can in the weather. You might, if the "A"-9 lends itself to it, read it in the light of your statement "of a time, when Moslem, Christian and Jew mingled, as it has been said, in one great fraternity of mirth and pleasure, whatever ends" etc. I have tried to get the "Donne mi priegha" to fluoresce thru the Marx, by letting the light of what it might all mean to us in retrospect fall on the matter and background of "Capital."

It's interesting to me now to read <u>Anew</u> 10 alongside yr. ¶ 4, p. 63. Written some time ago, as Anew 11, which has something to do with Dante, also.

So thanks again.

   Yrs

   Louis

Against the Weather: "Against the Weather: A Study of the Artist," *Twice a Year* 2
  (Spring–Summer 1939), 53–78. Wallace C272.

enclosures: Stanzas 1–3 of "First Half of "A"-9."

your statement: The statement is in this paragraph: "With the author of the Libro de
  Buen Amor, the fat Archpriest of Hita the same. His work was not war but love, love
  of God and love of women—almost indistinguishable to the poet though he made
  ample gestures both ways. But the *poem* was the thing—that was his good—as he
  confesses very clearly. He came, this amorous archpriest, of a time when Moslem,
  Christian and Jew mingled, as it has been said, in one great fraternity of mirth and
  pleasure, whatever ends each otherwise was also seeking. They mingled without prej-
  udice, a resemblance to the conditions of art" (58–59).

"Donne mi priehga" . . . Marx: "A"-9's first half is patterned on Cavalcanti's "Donna Mi
  Prega," but much of its vocabulary draws on Karl Marx's *Das Kapital* (in the English
  translation by Eden and Cedar Paul).

Anew 10: "What are these songs," *CSP*, 81. Composed 6 December 1938. Though unnum-
  bered in manuscript, the chronological sequence of the manuscripts of the poems in
  Anew indicates Zukofsky would have numbered this poem 10.

¶ 4, p. 63: "Dante was the agent of art facing a time and place and enforcement which
  were his 'weather.' Taking this weather as his starting point, as an artist, he had to deal
  with it to affirm that which to him was greater than it. By his structure he shows this
  struggle" (63).

Anew 11: "The rains, the rains." Composed 7 March 1939 and numbered 11 at that time. *CSP*, 92.

377. ACS

[Rutherford, N.J.]

[1939]

Ford Madox Ford is the name. May 2 . 7.30 P.M. The Downtown Gallery
113 W. 13th St
Bill

May 2: The penultimate meeting of the Friends of William Carlos Williams. Zukofsky
and Williams read from Williams's *Complete Collected Poems*. Williams also read
poems by Cummings. See Richard M. Ludwig, ed., *Letters of Ford Madox Ford*
(Princeton: Princeton Univ. Press, 1965), 318–19.

378. TLS-1

9 Ridge Road, Rutherford, N.J.

May 3, 1939

Dear Louis:

Everyone was plucking me by the sleeve as things were breaking up last night, I didn't know which way to turn. I saw the back of your head as I went out the door but as you seemed to be in animated conversation I simply left and let it go at that. I wanted to say a few words to Jim Higgins as he had come all the way down from Boston for the event and had asked me to have a drink with him. I needed it.

Thank you for reading the poems which you do extremely well, a good voice and a flawless sense of rhythmical values. The reason I took the book into my own hands was that those on my right kept urging me to read this one and that one whereas what I really wanted to do was to get to the newer pieces which we never did get to. I wanted to end the business.

Then, really to end it, I would have my little Angelina shit in the pan. Boy! was I surprised at how full of shit that small story was. Nothing for it then, I had to go on. That put them on their backs!

Well, what did you think of it? I'm glad you came and I hope you'll come out here for the next one. It's hard to know just what to do about my part in the affair. Certainly if I'm to read I'm not going to read my own things any more, not for a long time at least. It's no good that way. I've got to play up others whom I admire and the reading part of the program must be better regulated and much better prepared. We've got to do as they do in medical conference, someone will have to draw up an abstract of the case – select revealing poems or prose and lay out an ordered half hour or so of palaver – no more than that.

In my own defense I'll say I did not play to read my own things last night, they rang it in on me. Oh hell, I don't like being up front, as I said to someone else in another letter just a moment ago – this being a figurehead to the ship of state has the disadvantage that one gets slapped in the face by every wave we head into.

Ford, though, is all right. I admire his get up and go. It means a lot to him so that if I can serve him I guess I can take it. The season is lightening up for me medically speaking, I'll be looking you up soon.

> Yours
> Bill

Higgins: James Higgins, aspiring poet and later a magazine and newspaper editor. During the early part of 1939 he worked for New Directions in Boston. *New Directions in Prose and Poetry* 4 was dedicated to him.

Angelina: Possibly a reference to the unnamed child in "World's End" (first published in *Life Along the Passaic River*).

next one: The final meeting of the Friends of Williams Carlos Williams took place on 6 June 1939 at Williams's home.

379. ACS

[Postmarked Rutherford, N.J.]

[Postmarked 19 July 1939]
There's a book out by a Greek-Frenchman, Nicolas Calas, Foyers d'Incendie that takes the object up into its final place in the modern sun. Literary criticism that looks good so far. I'll lend it to you later.

> Bill

Calas: Nicolas Calas (1907–1988), *Foyers D'Incendie* (Paris: Les Editions Denoël, 1939). Williams became acquainted with Calas and translated some of his poems: *Wrested from Mirrors: Poems by Nicholas Calas,* trans. William Carlos Williams (New York: Nierendorf Gallery, 1940[?]). Williams also wrote an essay for a magazine Calas had hoped to publish but which never materialized: "Midas: A Proposal for a Magazine," *Now* 1:1 (August 1941), 18–24. Wallace C306.

[Rutherford, N.J.]

Oct. 2, 1940

Dear Louis:

The article or essay which I hope to send you tomorrow and called,The Poet in Time of Confusion,may still have "soft" spots in it, please tear into it and prune away anything you find unworthy or redundant or possible bad, poorly thought out. Naturally, I don't want to touch it unless I have to,but if you have anything to say do not hesitate to say it. One thing I've noticed in the past, too much indiscriminate cutting, important as it may seem in deatil, can ruin a piece by making it jerky. But cut if you think it important.

I've been in a quandry about this piece from another angle. You already have two things of mine for this issue, the letter in reply to your questionaire and the Lafayette thing. Don't you think it rather too much for me to come forward now with an eleven page essay?

Thinking these things I was faced with a request from Parker Tyler on behalf of another group wanting to start a magazine, a group of English and French Surrealistes who want an essay on the position of the poet in the "free"world today. Naturally I want to write such an essay for them. But it seemed quite as if I had foreseen their request in this piece that I had already written. So there I have stuck.

Mind you, this piece (if you want it) was written for you and it is yours. If you do not want it I'll give it to them. If you do want it I'll write them another taking my text from this piece and going on to develope it as I already have in mind to do. So there you have it. I am being completely candid with you, I want you simply to know mt mind. Just weigh the factors and make your decision to use or not to use the piece quite as you see fit, I'll be fully content either way. Naturally I hope you like the piece so much that you won't want to give it up.

As to future issues I'd vote against a translation from In the Am. Grain, it's been done before as, I think, Rene knows in a fat French magazine or quarterly called ? ? ? I have one in the attic. I think they did the Rales not the Poe. The Poe might not be so bad. I'd rather do something new for you. It's importing to be contemporary, hot, hard, immediate, unrelenting. We've got to boil or evaporate slowly and ineffectively. No, now, now!

Glad to be writing to you again. There's always plenty of work to do in writing and every occasion must be an occasion for us.

Yours

Bill

God damn it, I ruined the coffee percolator writing this lettter – all over the floor –

Shit

It <u>boiled</u> alright!

The Poet in Time of Confusion: "The Poet in Time of Confusion," *Columbia Review* 23 (Autumn 1941), 1–5. Wallace C307.

this issue: Zukofsky and Taupin planned to issue a magazine, entitled *La France en Liberté*, but it never appeared. Among the Zukofsky papers at Texas is a copy of the prospectus for the magazine, on the verso of a letter to Lorine Niedecker dated 7 August 1940. The prospectus proclaimed that "*La France en Liberté* will be the review of free France. It will be published quarterly, consisting of approximately 150 pages, the French text alongside of English translation, and English originals accompanied by French translations." The editorial board consisted of René Taupin, Ivan Goll and Louis Zukofsky. Among members of the advisory board were Ernest Hemingway, Richard Aldington, William Carlos Williams, Jules Supervielle and Albert Einstein.

Lafayette thing: "Under the Stars," the *University of Kansas City Review* 11:1 (August 1944), 26–28. Wallace C350. This one-act play is a dialogue between Washington and Lafayette. Zukofsky edited at least one draft of the play (see Baldwin and Meyers B116f).

a magazine: *View*.

Rene: René Taupin.

French magazine: Williams may recall the translation from *In the American Grain* by Raymond Queneau, "La Venue des Esclaves," *Mesures* 5:3 (15 July 1939), 372–77. Wallace T16.

381. TLS-1

[Rutherford, N.J.]

Oct. 3, 1940

Dear Louis:

Look it over, mark it up as you please and return it to me with whatever comments you wish to make. In this case I'm not going to be easily convinced – either way.

At the moment as you may imagine I'm looking forward with the usual trepidation to the appearance of the new White Mule as well as a pamphlet of new and old poems which will head Laughlin's new series, a thirty five cent item. Much will depend during the next year for me on what happens to In the Money. If the feeling veers this way I'm likely to go the other – or as it may turn out. I don't quite know what project to tackle next. I want to do a little thinking before I let myself in for another two year job. The Introduction to the book on Mother which will appear shortly in Twice a Year will have its influence on me also. If that arouses any interest I may go that way.

What I'd like to do would be to write a practical play or two this winter, just to feel my way a little further there toward a major production I've long had in mind. I don't mean the Washington piece either which must still wait – perhaps indefinitely. I don't know, of course, how much longer I have to live but I can't consider that, I'm proceeding on the plan of another twenty years of effort. If I croke before that or go gaga it will be just too bad.

Hope you like the enclosed, if not, say so. My best to your young wife whom I admire.

Sincerely yours
Bill

new White Mule: *In the Money* (Norfolk, Conn.: New Directions, 1940). Wallace A21.
pamphlet: *The Broken Span* (Norfolk, Conn.: New Directions, 1941). Wallace A22.
Introduction: "Raquel Hélene Rose," *Twice a Year* 5– 6 (Fall–Winter 1940, Spring–Summer 1941), 402–12. Wallace C295.
Washington piece: *The First President*.
young wife: Celia Thaew Zukofsky.

■ 382. ALS-3

1088 E. 180 St
New York

Oct 4/40
Dear Bill:
"The Poet in Time of Confusion" is very acceptable, and both René and I want it for the first issue in which we feel it will have special bearing.

As to cutting it, the older I get the less inclination I have for such things, give me the good, and leave me to my own work, and if a work hasn't enough good in it to retrieve the bad, of itself, what's the use? I think the "soft" spots in the piece are very apparent. I'd like it better without 'em. If you wish, read it over with the following suggestions in mind, and decide for yourself if the piece moves faster, and your meaning comes thru more decisively, is less repetitious – as a result:

(I assume you have a carbon copy, so I'm not troubling to return the original) pg. 6 <(read)> – Thus I would say to the artist, write to correct lies. How? [And <leave> the rest of the ¶ as it is]

(read) Nothing that prevents this can be good. [Omit the rest of this ¶ and all of the next paragraph.]

pg. 7 – omit "Make a contortionist" etc thru "it makes not the least difference."

That's all, and to me personally the first four pages are very fine, and the burden of the rest very worth saying.

O yes p. 9 – I'm sort of puzzled by the *syntax* of "Has not the Jewish race been the catalyser bringing every race to its apex of political productivity, now to be removed?" The meaning, however, is clear, I guess.

In any case, we'll take the piece as it is, if you don't approve my suggestions. And too bad – or good – if you have to write another for the other magazine. Don't worry about our giving too much space to you – we have the space, and besides the reply to the question raised is not a personal exhibition since it's part of a number of replies.

Received in the same mail with your MS. a letter from Laughlin about the prose volume I mentioned to you at Pearl River. He says: "It certainly ought to be done, but I just can't see how I can do it. This damn business etc – you can't GIVE books away – " Well, if he can't, who will – business ain't simple.

René tells me Floss isn't feeling better entirely. I hope she does soon. My wife thanks you for remembering her, and we both invite both of you to come out and see us when you feel like it. Let me know if you want to make it a definite date – and when.

All your new works appearing, our mag. when it does, are something to celebrate

———

So live long, plan another twenty years – because I suppose it's as easy to do that at 56 as at 36 – it ought to be, there's more practice.

> Yours
> Louis.

René: René Taupin.

first issue: Of the magazine planned by Zukofsky and Taupin, *La France en Liberté*.

other magazine: Nicholas Calas's proposed magazine, *Midas*.

prose volume: In the "Year by Year" section of Celia Zukofsky's *A Bibliography of Louis Zukofsky*, she indicates that *Sincerity and Objectification* was "once intended to be the title of a book" (49). This may be the volume referred to.

Pearl River: A town in southern New York State, near the border with New Jersey.

383. ALS-1

> 9 Ridge Road
> Rutherford, N.J.

Oct 6/40

Here are the pages in question. Are the changes as you intended?

Floss is still rather uncertain of herself but appears to improve from day to day.

When is the new mag. to appear?

> Bill

■ 384. ACS

[Rutherford, N.J.]

[October 1940]

[The card's printed message: "The Gotham Book Mart and New Directions invite you to meet William Carlos Williams on the publication day of his new novel[,] "In the Money[.]" The date: Tuesday, October 29th[.] The Place: The Gotham Book Mart, 51 West 47, N.Y.C. The Time: 4 to 6 P.M.]

Tho't you might be interested
　　Bill

■ 385. ALS-1

1088 East 180 St
New York City

Nov. 27/40
Dear Bill:

Thanks a lot for Twice A Year. To me, your mother's book is very moving. It is as I know her. And, to me again, it is among the the things most deeply felt that you have done. Anyway, my brother read it <u>all</u> – and he has to be nailed down to read anything for the last fifteen years. And the scheme of the book as you outline it is really brilliant – and even when the sentences are a little difficult, it's the way <u>you</u> speak. That somethin:

As soon as I hear from the Register of Copyrights and can release Celia's mimeographing of "A"-9, I'll send it to you. Your copy was set aside some time ago with 14 others for presentation. If I can sell the remaining 40 – well, I have the beginning of an audience.

René sees us tomorrow, so we may have more news about La France en Liberté. We contacted an out-of-town printer, but he has too many contracts already! I wonder if you know of a cheap printer, & if you do would you mind sending the address to René or to me.

Best regards to Floss the mater et al
　　Yours
　　Louis

Twice A Year: "Raquel Hélene Rose," Twice a Year 5– 6 (Fall–Winter 1940, Spring–Summer 1941), 402–12.
my brother: Morris Zukowsky.
"A"-9": First Half of "A"-9.
René: René Taupin.
La France en Liberté: The magazine that Zukofsky and Taupin hoped to produce.

9 Ridge Road
Rutherford, N.J.

Dec 1/40

Dear Louis:

I don't know a thing about printing or presses – Surely somewhere in New York City ought to be the best place to get work of this sort done. I have seen two small books recently done by The Black Faun Press – Prairie City, Illinois and Rochester, N.Y. I don't know whether or not their prices are high or low. I think James Laughlin would be a good man to ask about that.

I'll be very glad to have the copy of "A" when you finish it. I think you were wise to mimeograph it. That will be the beginning.

Best to you.
Bill

Black Faun Press: The *Cumulative Book Index 1938–1942* identifies it as "The Black Faun Press (Compass Editions), 121 Edgerton St., Rochester, New York. Affiliated with Press of James A. Decker." Decker would publish *55 Poems* in October 1941.

1088 E. 180 St
N.Y.C.

Dec 6/40

Dear Bill

I've sent "A"-9 to you under separate cover. I hope you enjoy it – tho I admit it's hard going. Nothing would please me more than to have you review it for Poetry or whatever, preferably a mag. that circulates or has standing; but if you're not in the mood to write a review or otherwise engaged, of course, you don't have to. I'm not sending out review copies, tho.

Best,
Louis

[Postmarked Rutherford, N.J.]

[Postmarked 8 December 1940]

As soon as I have received and read the poem I'll write you whatever I have to say, impromptu, about it. Then I'll let it soak in awhile and if anything important follows I'll write it out and send it to Poetry. I'm very curious to see how you have completed the work. You're right it's a tough assignment for any reader, I know that already – my objective in writing of the poem, among other things, will be to making such a reading assignment less severe for the next guy – if possible! So I go and sell two short ones to New Yorker. Maybe it's senility – maybe just spittin'.

Yrs
Bill

two short ones: Only one poem by Williams appeared in the *New Yorker* during 1941.
"The Hounded Lovers," 17:37 (25 October 1941), 41. Wallace C309. *CP2,* 66– 67.

389. ACS

[Rutherford, N.J.]

[December 1940]

I am somewhat confused, what relation does this section of "A" bear in relation to the whole poems as written & as projected? I'd like a specific skeleton outline of the whole if you can give it to me. It is hard going – unless it be read casually – which may be the correct way to read it. And I wish you'd ask René again to let me have the stuff of mine he is holding. I'd particularly like to see the Wash. Lafayette thing – as revised but also the article. Will you do this for me? Anyhow & small comfort as it may be the sun has turned northward again.

Yours
Bill

Wash. Lafayette thing: "Under the Stars."
Article: "The Poet in Time of Confusion."

390. ACS

[Rutherford, N.J.]

[December 1940]

I had, foolishly enough, forgotten about "A" in New Directions. Thank you for the information. No other word <from me> as yet about it for I really wonder how to read the poem. – or how to tell anyone how to read it. It has me stumped. For you do not consider human abilities or attention & application. you abandon all that. Well, we go on! I heard from Rene. Thanks

Bill

9 Ridge Road
Rutherford, N.J.

Mar. 31, 1941

Dear Louis:

Why not? I suggested that Poetry print your Canzon solo. Why don't you let them do so, I think it would be an outstanding event?

yrs.

Bill

~~I never tho't of writing an article for Poetry. Strange! because I enjoy reading the essays I see there. I'll see what comes up. do my best. I'm working on a play using verse (in part). Want to use a slab of it? Two or three pages?~~ Stupid ass! I wrote this for Dillon on the back of <u>your</u> letter. Sorry.

Bill

Canzon: *First Half of "A"-9.*

~~play using verse:~~ *Many Loves.*

Dillon: George Dillon (1906–1968), editor of *Poetry.* In a letter of 18 March 1941 to
   Williams, Dillon remarked, "It would be a pleasure to see the poem by Louis Zukof-
   sky. You seem to think that he may need some persuading to send it to us, and since I
   don't have his address, perhaps you will try to persuade him." On Dillon's letter,
   Williams wrote this note to Zukofsky: "Louis: I wrote praising an article in the last
   Poetry. I am so thoroughly sick of the metaphysical God-shit they flush on us that I
   couldn't help saying something about a man who at least knows plumbing. <u>W</u>" (Yale).

1088 East 180 St
New York

Apr. 1/41

Dear Bill:

I'm forwarding "A"-9 to Dillon at your suggestion. Thanks for mentioning me to him.

Have you had a chance to read "Paris" ('A'-10)?

We're coming to your reading April 10 – unless something unforeseen prevents us. I've got some tickets for the Evanses who say they'll be there, too.

It was like old times <u>having</u> you both here with us the other night – but you know that.

Yours

Louis

"Paris": First published in *Calendar: An Anthology of 1941 Poetry,* ed. Norman MacLeod (Prairie City, Illinois: James A. Decker, 1941), 8–20. Williams's poem, "The Yellow Season," also appeared in this volume.

your reading: Williams read at the Poetry Center of the 92nd Street Young Men's Hebrew Association.

■ 393. TLS-1

[Rutherford, N.J.]

April 3, 1941

Dear Louis:

The poem "Paris" appears to me to be the best of yours that I have seen to date, it has more eveness of unfolding, more pith and more metrical organization and uniformity than the other section of "A" that I remember also more subtlty and sobriety, more emotional impact. It is one of the few long pieces I know that I can call a poem – there aren't many. I enjoyed it greatly without understanding every detail to be sure and yet it did appear to me and impress me as a whole, one perfectly understandable ideogram which is the last significance of form. I especially appreciated the language and the use of speech contours and the word choice in building the metric – this alone gives the poem seriousness, I quite envy you your correct use of speech in making your meters, it is a rare gift – you have shown that you are learning to do this better and better so that here you show considerable facility in the technique – it doesn't matter where you learned it, it is the last answer to "free verse" which is a contradiction in terms.

Don't bother to come to my reading. Most of the stuff that I have to read is twenty and thirty years old, I am getting so that I dislike most of it, it is not important to hear it all once more – though I am always glad to see you.

I have been thinking, thinking, thinking what to do with my half written stuff if I should croak some time – as on this trip. It can happen. Not that it is really so important or that I think in terms of my "reputation". For that I give not a single damn – nothing, in all probablility, will happen anyway. – but I'd like somebody to check over the stuff and dig out anything that might seem to be of value. Maybe, after all, I'll make you my literary executor, if it wouldn't be too much trouble. I've thought of various people but in the end you are the only one that really knows what I've been after. You would have to restrain yourself a little on theoretical ground, no doubt, but you <u>would</u> at least know what to discard. Or would you? You'd have to be careful to leave in a few of the connectives, not make it too too objective. Who can tell?

Anyhow, your poem is a beauty, you are fast becoming the most important and neglected poet of our time and place. God how dull men are, how unwilling and vulgar. If a man should permit himself to do so he would very nearly despise nearly everyone on emotional and intellectual grounds – beginning with himself, no doubt.

> Yours
> Bill

"Paris": "A"-10.

this trip: Later that month Williams attended the First Inter-America Writers' Conference at the University of Puerto Rico, where he delivered "A Statement as to the Modern Basis of Poetic Form" (Yale).

394. ALS-2

> 1088 E. 180 St.
> New York

Apr. 5/41

Dear Bill,

Celia is playing the pyanny in the other room. If I follow the music – and I can't help it – I probably will take up too much paper saying what I can say to myself in a second. But I want this to follow yours of yesterday. That you should think of dying makes me feel like an undertaker whose smile is un-called for because life is black enough. Me your literary executor – what if the undertaker dies? I don't think either of us wants to tempt god or whatever you call him. Not yet.

I think perhaps I know what you want me to do with your "half written stuff" – and I'm willing whatever your conditions are. Would I know what to discard? That's hard to say – but as much as I know to date about my own stuff. Sometimes after several years – as the other day – I look thru a batch of poems and make some revisions, and then the next day maybe only one or two revisions stand up. Usually the original – if worth keeping – is the final choice. I think that's true of most work in which a guy is not merely a writer but saying something. If you let me do this job you probably understand that I wouldn't want to bother with the work of someone still learning 'how to write' or 'who would give his life to write' etc. We know that we learn all the time, or make mistakes or whatever, but the demarcation between imposition and necessity I take it is clear to us. It is only for that reason I think I know what you've been after. You see the reason I know is really no reason, if you would have it so.

The older I get, the less public notice I receive, the more skeptical I become about my own necessity. That leaves out thinking in terms of "reputation" altogether. Also I can say honestly I have no theory, not even about leaving out connectives. I suspect that if I live I shall be inclined to leave them in more and more. I am breaking my neck now to do it in a story. I wish it were done. But connectives can be impersonal, too, as you know. And the more impersonal one is the more personal one is as everybody doesn't know.

In the long run, what I've said above won't matter. I suspect, two people may be said to understand each other's work, aims, etc., by some indication they share in common totally removed from them. It's apparent sometimes in a chance remark about something, anything – as when you were here and re- marked about Jerry's unpractised landscape (like the early Am. prints on the 3rd floor of the N.Y.P.L.) – I like the tone of it. I've never heard anyone put it that way, but I had put it that way countless times to myself every time I looked at that part of the wall. What I mean is, neither of us was considering painting or giving a damn about aesthetics etc., but that such things are best casually a part of us – for better or worse. More understanding I can't promise you or anyone.

Decide when you wish about all this, and you can call on me here, Ruther- ford, wherever you say. I have few other commitments – almost none as a mat- ter of fact.

If you don't mind, we'd like to come to the reading. I know how you feel about people when they start cluttering around you – I feel the same – we don't like it or need it – it doesn't matter, make believe we're not there. And I don't have to tell you that most of your stuff does not sound twenty or thirty years old to me. Even if I'm wrong and you're right why should you worry. I prom- ised Evans I'd be there, so let it go at that. Maybe hearing you'll do us all good. Better than tuning in to the news anyway.

I meant "Paris" to serve that kind of purpose, but a dozen or more publish- ers have rejected it. When you come back from Puerto Rico (is that where you're going?) your praise will mean more for your being here. So to hell with croaking etc.

> Yours
> Louis

a story: Probably "A Keystone Comedy." The first of the surviving drafts is dated 19 Janu-
ary 1941.
Jerry's: Jerry Reisman.
N.Y.P.L.: New York Public Library.

[1088 East 180th Street, New York]

April 10/41

Dear Bill,

You were fine. Sorry I didn't get a chance to say so long and tell you so. But Bob Evans was driving me home, and I was anxious to get back, since Celia was alone & down with a bad cold. She had planned to come and insisted that I go.

Bob told me that you arranged for a walk in the park here. Fine. Let me know when, & I'll get in touch with Bob. Sat. or Sun. would be O.K. with us (that is Celia & me) – but if you can't make it a week-end when Celia is home, I'm usually free Fridays during the day, and I suspect Bob is.

I suppose you won't be able to make it till after your trip to Puerto Rico – so when you can.

Poetry took first half of "A"-9 thanks to you.

Bon voyage, & tell the Carribeans what we have & best to Florence

Yrs

Louis

the park: The park nearest the Zukofsky home was Bronx Park.

Poetry took: "'A'-9 (First Half)," Poetry 58:3 (June 1941), 128–30.

1088 E. 180 St

New York

Aug 25/41

Dear Bill,

We've been hoping Floss and you would come here for the walk in the park we talked about in the spring, but I take it you've been busy.

We've spent the summer here working as usual. The enclosure is one of the products – <originally> intended to be a short story, and I'm still working on it as such, part III to be completed. Now that I look over what there is of it, it appears to me material better suited for a novel. And I'm going to try to get one of the Houghton Mifflin Company's Literary Fellowships on that basis. Will you please write me a letter recommending me to them – if it's not too much bother – and send it to me so I can forward it with my application? The letter "may refer either to the applicant's character, or literary qualifications, or both." I'm enclosing "Ferdinand" in case you find anything in that to recommend me, but if for one reason or another you can't read it now or it doesn't interest you, just return it. Any thing you care to say to the publisher will suit me. I know it's a thankless task for you to write them, since I probably won't get the fellowship, but then if I don't try to get out of my rut I suppose I'll regret it. So thanks for your trouble.

Decker's <publication of my> "55 Poems" is still in press – two months late already, and I don't know how long he will take to finish the job. But it's on the way and as soon as the book is out you'll get a copy.

We trust you're all well, and anytime you can get around to see us please drop us a line and we'll be delighted.

Yours

Louis

P.S. We'll probably be away from home and looking for jobs in Washington Aug 30 to Sept 7, so if your answer comes here during that time, I'll reply when I get home, since it's no use complicating things by having mail forwarded. I need your letter of recommendation by Sept 12 the latest, so don't spend time writing a long letter – make it short and sweet. Again, lots of thanks.

Louis.

enclosure: Enclosure ("Ferdinand") lacking.
"55 Poems": *55 Poems* (Prairie City, Illinois: James A. Decker, 1941).

397. TLS-2

[Rutherford, N.J.]

August 26, 1941

Dear Louis:

Two letters from Ezra today written within weeks of each other but delayed by the hazzards of war. The first was an acknowledgement of a "boost" (?) I had given him in a small college sheet, Hika. More of this later. The second was a letter written as if there were no war at all and he at peace with his own mind waiting for the Germans to conquer Russia so that he, Ezra, might get papers again from Tokyo via the trans- Siberian railway. He said he expected it would be possible again, no doubt, in another week or so. This is something to amaze!

These letters were all the more affecting to me since I had just finished, for Decision, an attack upon Ezra as mouthpiece for Mussolini which I intended to be as destructive as I could make it. It will appear in September. I have instructed Klaus Mann to subjoin Ezra's letter to my article since, in a sense, it is an unconscious reply to it. I think you'll be interested.

All summer I have wanted to communicate with you but didn't do so for no reason at all. I wanted to tell you that I had finished a three act play and to send you the play for your amusement and the comments you might make. I'll still send it. I have six copies of it but all are out now. I am trying the producers first. The Theatre Guild have turned it down after a series of letters from an old classmate of yours named Gassner. He has been quite friendly but also very opaque in his replies to my questions about what he thought or they thought about the <u>verse</u> of the play. No reply. All he would say was that the prose parts were excellent but undeveloped and that the play would not be suitable for presentation to a general audience.

But something important has come of my connection with this Gassner. I met him again last week at Bread Loaf where I appeared as a guest speaker last Saturday evening. I read my poems with comments on literary form just as I had done at Harvard last February. Gassner was shy of me at first but (aside from commenting on my verse) spoke freely of other matters. Among such other matters was yourself. He spoke of you as one of his old friends whom he has tried to assist for years. At the moment, he says, he has a job with a publishing house which he would like you to have. If it come through he will communicate with you shortly. Take it for what it is worth. He says he always thinks of you and plans to land you something as soon as he can. What the hell? I urged him to not fail you.

I think a walk in the park will be more enjoyable in the fall than in June. When you get back from Washington write me again. I'll have much more time at my disposal in September and October than I have had on a year.

It looks as though my connection with Laughlin and his New Directions Press is coming to an end. I regret it in some ways but I can't tell you the relief it is to me in other ways to be on my own again. I don't think I could ever be happy under contract. I'd rather write and take a chance on publication wherever I can catch hold. But there are more reasons than that for breaking up with Laughlin imporant among which is his casual way of doing business. Once a rich boy, I'm afraid, always a rich boy. I'm sick of it. I cannot deny however that better offers from more responsible publishers have affected me. Laughlin's cavalier treatment of Miller and Patchen have something to do with the case.

Every word of your plan for the novel interests me. I read from beginning to the end without artificial urging and wait impatiently for more – which I do not want to see until the book shall be published. The style is unique in my experience and full of verbal and psychological felicities. Good obersvation, nothing pathologic, no heat of decomposition (not that this isn't permissable). I like the kid at once, you've made him live for me already. The projected Indian scene had better be convincing though. Sounds a bit phoney here, will require a master hand and no "imagination" if it's going to stand. Hope you did sleep with one and catch her lice. Bill Saphier (ever hear of him?) did once right in her father's tepee, said she was hot.

The letter you want is enclosed, hope it will do though I have no faith in my influence with publishers, they're upholding something far beyond my powers to influence. See the new little mag NOW, it's good. I'll send you a copy soon.

Whatever I write this winter will not be for "publication" thank the Lord. It'll be for writing. I'm already feeling my oats after having thrown Laughlin – not that he isn't my firend. He has done fine by me – but he's also been helped by me so I owe him nothing at all.

Floss and my mother kick along fine. The kids are on their own. Bill went crabbing in the meadows on Sunday and brought home a bagful. Remember me to the missus [...].

Yours
Bill

letters from Ezra: The first letter is printed in *EP/WCW*, 206–07. The second letter, dated 23 July 1941, is at Yale.

"boost": "Dr. Williams Cocks a Snook," *Hika* 7:7 (May 1941), 13, 27. Williams writes, "But in the case of many Americans Europe will always be the desired since it has always, and will always, assert the man, the one man, as the deciding apex of cultural development. To want and to get. I haven't the time to clarify it. I want to say Ezra Pound went to Europe to get personal recognition for his supreme genius. He wanted to rule because he was convinced he knew more than anyone else and so, by God! had a right. He still thinks so. Everything else, as he repeatedly asserts, is mere shepherding."

an attack: "Ezra Pound: Lord Ga-Ga!" *Decision* 2:3 (September 1941), 16–24. Wallace C308.

Mann: The son of Thomas Mann, Klaus Mann (1906–1949) was a novelist and essayist. He founded and edited the journal *Decision: A Review of Free Culture* (1941–1942).

three act play: *Many Loves.*

Gassner: John Waldhorn Gassner (1903–1967), teacher, critic, and author of numerous books and anthologies concerning drama. On 10 July 1941, Gassner wrote to Williams, "The undersigned, who happens to have been a classmate of Louis Zukofsky and Ted Hecht, has long been an admirer of William Carlos Williams' poetry" (Yale). "A"-21 is dedicated to the memory of Gassner and to Zukofsky's brother, Morris.

Bread Loaf: Williams spoke ("Bread Loaf Talk" — Yale) at the Bread Loaf Writers' Conference on 23 August 1941.

Harvard: Williams spoke on "The Basis of Poetic Form" (Yale) at Harvard University on 5 February 1941.

Miller and Patchen: Henry Miller and Kenneth Patchen.

Saphier: William Saphier (or Saphir), Roumanian-born poet and painter. His poems appeared in *Poetry,* the *Double Dealer,* and *Others.* He also edited and served as associate editor for *Others.*

NOW: Only one issue appeared. It printed Williams's "Midas: a Proposal for a Magazine," *Now* 1:1 (August 1941), 18–24. Wallace C306.

letter: TLS-1, dated 26 August 1941, from Williams to Houghton Mifflin Co.

Dear Sirs: This letter is in support of Louis Zukofsky's candidacy for a Literary Fellowship as offered by you toward the writing of a novel which he has planned and will submit to you in outline shortly. One has to be somewhat formal in a letter such as this.

Zukofksy has been one of my closest friends in the undertaking which we have faced with several others of our respective generations to write merely as well as we can and face the hazards on that basis. I don't know anyone who has progressed more in his prose, as shown by the synopsis of this novel he has shown me, than Zukofsky. It has an exceptional quality of excellence to my mind which you will not find duplicated anywhere. I am speaking now of the sheer writing. In addition to this I already sense the creation of a character, in his hero, full of appeal to the emotions and the intelligence. I like him.

Rather than to go any further I will close here by adding that Louis Zukofsky is a person of the rarest integrity in whom implicit trust can be placed that he will carry out his promises and stated intentions to the letter. I don't believe you will find in New York a man more suited for a fellowship such as you offer than he.

Sincerely yours

William Carlos Williams

398. ALS-3

1088 E. 180 St
New York

Aug 28/41

Dear Bill:

Your letter to Houghton Mifflin is a beauty and what you say about "Ferdinand" gives me courage. I'll complete it as a short story first, and then, if I'm lucky with the Fellowship application, will go on from that. Or rather, mentally I have been going on with the novel – part I would have to be overhauled completely if the thing is to be a novel. The question is, if I don't get the fellowship, whether I should write that novel or still another I have had in mind. At the same time, I've started on another short story which I think is better prose than what you've seen. Heaven knows I need the practice and it's damn near killing me. When I finish the two stories, it'll be a relief to get back to verse again – and there are two pieces of verse I'd like to finish before the year's over, if I'm going to be a contented man.

I get your meaning alright as to the Indian scene projected for <u>Ferd</u>. But, as a matter of fact, that Indian girl was one of the images that started Ferd. going. I never slept with her, but remember the face very well – there was no other face around for miles when we drove past her in the Arizona desert,

1932. On the other hand, I wonder how many novels etc start with an image. The point is, as you say, not to "imagine" anything – And since there's nothing personal about myself that I'm trying to confuse with Ferd., the sleeping won't matter. The point in all good writing is to get down what you are sure of and hide what you don't know – at least I imagine it is. But enough of that.

Thanks for sending Ezra's letter which I return. He seems a wee bit lonely between the lines – but why he should expect not to be, broadcasting for Muss. and writing for "Social Justice" – & expect civil life to continue under the circumstances beats me. I'm not surprised that he feels so balmy about the transSiberian being open again in a short while – or rather that he feels just a little inconvenienced. But then if you're an immigrant, and if H. James was (& by the way I don't think his father was an immigrant) a Russian must be the wild beast of Borneo. I wonder when Ez will realize the hole he's in – if ever. Things are happening so fast he may never get the chance. – I picked up his essay on James again, prompted by his letter. I wonder what he thinks of H.J.'s analysis of the Germans now. It's a damn valid piece that essay on James – And I can only conclude that the man has gone nuts – not merely "mad Hamlet" because we're living in a hell of a time & one won't even be able to say "here cracks a noble heart," when it gets him.

Funny coincidence about John Gassner – this is the second time I've heard he's been trying to assist me. I've been <out of> touch with him for years – but if he still remembers all the better, and thanks for urging him not to fail me. But I'll wait & see whether he'll get in touch with me. Yes, we went to school together and are old friends – but like his failure to comment on your verse, some things are just avoided when one has to get on in life. But he has a good head and is very kind at heart, and there's no reason why he shouldn't be where he is.

Yes, please send the play. The verse'll interest me very much – if only the producers would give enough of their time to get interested, too. Best luck with it.

"Better offers from responsible publishers." the Bread Loaf evening, the contribution to Sept. Decision etc are all good news.

I'll write you later in Sept and set a definite date or a choice of dates for you to come here.

[…]

Mine and the Missus' to you et al

    Yours Louis

P.S. Letter to Houghton's so good I'll have Celia type it over and you can sign several copies (!) to save yourself the trouble of writing another character reference for me if ever I need one in the future. If there's any objection you can tell me when we meet again.

>Best
>Louis

another short story: Probably "It Was."

two pieces of verse: Celia Zukofsky's *Bibliography* lists the following poems as having been completed in 1941: "No it was no dream of coming death"; "Strange"; "1892–1941"; "And so till we have died"; "In the midst of things"; "Guillaume de Ma-chault"; "Belly Locks Shnooks Oakie"; "Light 6, 8, 9, 10, 13, 14." The *Bibliography* also notes that "Light 11" was revised that year.

Ezra's letter: Not located.

"Social Justice": A weekly newspaper (1936–1942) published by Father Charles E. Coughlin. Donald Warren's *Radio Priest: Charles Coughlin, the Father of Hate Radio* (New York: Free Press, 1996) discusses the anti-Semitic and pro-Nazi sentiments of *Social Justice.*

essay on James: Pound's "Henry James" was available to Zukofsky either in *Instigations* (1920) or *Make It New* (1935).

the play: *Many Loves.*

399. ACS

[Postmarked Rutherford, N.J.]

[Postmarked 18 September 1941]

Let you know next week about the walk, possibly Oct. will be best. Floss' mother got hit by a car & broke her hip last Sat. eve. She is in hosp. you may guess what my own reactions are. Like to have you read my play some time. Bill

my play: *Many Loves.*

400. ALS-1

[Rutherford, N.J.]

10/1 [1941]

Sorry I didn't know you were in town Sat. eve. We weren't far & shd have like to have seen you.

The "walk" we've planned is for the weekend of 10th & 11th isn't that right?

Enclosed herewith is my shot at dear Ezra – he once, in his stupidity & awk-wardness almost put my eye out with the end of a cane. I hope this doesn't hit so high.

Maybe you let me have back the play & the mag back in a week express C.O.D.

>Bill

my shot: "Ezra Pound: Lord Ga-Ga!"

play & the mag: *Many Loves* and *Decision* (which contained "Ezra Pound: Lord Ga-Ga!").

▌ 401. ALS-2

1088 E 180 St

New York

Oct 3/41

Dear Bill:

Thanks for sending the play – which I'm reading now, the conception is splendid – and the mag – have read the article on Ez & he has it coming to him. I'll return both by express next Thurs. of Fri. so you'll have 'em a day or so later, with more comment if I have anything of value to say. – My usual routine has been broken into the last few weeks by several possibilities of jobs and the publication of "55 Poems" which has been one mess – So I don't know if I'm coming or going.

Sorry I didn't call up when I was in Rutherford last Sat. – I wanted to, but I was certain you'd be busy and didn't want to break in on your time. Forgive my diffidence, not my affections etc. I decided to go to Rutherford after I spoke to Floss over the phone, on the spur of the moment – wanted to do something else for a change than stay home etc.

Will you please let me know if you and Floss can come here the week-end of the 11th or 12th – either day will be alright. I'd appreciate it if you could let me know by next Sat. I understand that any date you make will depend on the contingencies of the profession, births etc – of course, but barring those, can you let me know?

Also if you've received "55 Poems" from Decker, which he was supposed to have sent you about two weeks ago? If not, I'll get after him. I suggested to him that you might want to write a blurb for the jacket (not ready yet) of the book. If you do, even a sentence or two would suit me fine. Thanks.

I enclose music to two of the poems in "55" – the music to Song 11 you have and have heard. Hope you like and enjoy.

> Yours
> Louis

the play: *Many Loves.*

the mag: *Decision* (which contained "Ezra Pound: Lord Ga-Ga!").

Enclosures: Music by Celia Thaew Zukofsky for "Happier, happier now" and "To my wash-stand."

[Rutherford, N.J.]

Oct. 6, 1941

Dear Louis:

Suppose we leave it this way, the day being clear Floss and I will break for your place – I think I can find it more easily this time – right after office hours on Saturday. This should be sometime between two and three o'clock. It won't give us a hell of a long time for a walk but we can at least go see the lions. And so on into the evening.

Sunday is too difficult. I have to work mornings anyway, Mother has to be disposed of and all that. Saturday Lucy can hold the fort. But if it rains Saturday call me up around 2 P.M. and we'll plan one thing or another that way.

No, I did not receive the poems from Prairie Press – or any other press. I remember you said you were forwarding them and so was on the lookout but nothing has arrived.

The war goes on. Today the latest is that Hitler is having one more go at the Russians and then, hit or miss, intends to call the war off and go on organizing Europe "according to plan". And what shall the rest of us do? It seems all the <more> poignant since I have been reading the Dean of Caterbury''s, The Soviet Power. He's an old man and I didn't like the way he acted toward Eddie the King and his Moll – but if you haven't glanced into that book, do it. To let such an enlightenment as Russia represents no matter how failingly be blotted <out> by the brutality of Nazidom would be the final disgrace. And yet, I'm not fooled. There are those in power everywhere who finally fear Socialism more than the Germans. Isn't this the history of the world?

How ever shall we expect to receive truly liberal support from Montague Norman and his England? The outlook is bad.

     Yours

     Bill

lions: At the Bronx Zoo, which was near the Zukofskys' home. See Florence Williams's
    letter of 1 November 1941.

Lucy: Lucy Wooton.

Prairie Press: The publisher of Zukofsky's 55 Poems.

The Soviet Power: Hewlett Johnson, The Soviet Power (New York: International Publishers, 1940). Johnson (1874–1966) was popularly known as "the Red Dean" because of his support for socialism and communism. In The Soviet Power (originally published in England as The Socialist Sixth of the World), Johnson argues that the future moral and material progress of the world depends upon following the example of the Soviet Union.

Eddie the King and his Moll: Edward VIII and Wallace Warfield Simpson.

Norman: Montagu Collet Norman (1871–1950), governor (1920–1944) of the Bank of
England.

■ 403. TLS-2

9 Ridge Road
Rutherford, N.J

Oct. 20, 1941

Dear Louis:

I read your book of poems through last night at one sitting, fairly carefully.
Some are very beautiful, some did not affect me, did not seem to come alive. I
made some notes which I will send you presently. If there is anything among
them you care to use for the dust jacket, do so. If you want me to try to place
the review somewhere (with added detail or otherwise) I'll do so. Do you
know of any review you'd prefer to have them in. What about <u>Poetry</u>?

I'm glad Stalin has decided to defend Moscow. Rumor persists that London
is not backing Russia as it should and that products our manufacturers are not
permitted to export they are having made in England for Eastern and South
American trade. They say Dunlop auto tires are a drug on the market in many
South American cities. Hard not to believe such tales – but the "sinister figure
of Montague Norman" continues to appear at major conferences.

Yours
Bill

P.S. The poems are much more impressive to me today than they were when
I glanced at them in manuscript several years ago which is all to the good. As I
remember some of them I couldn't make head nor tail of them. They are clear
now and effective – not all though. Sometimes they do not work. I still find the
notes to the Mantis poem more interesting and important than the poem
which is bad (not the poem, the situation).

What I wanted to say, though, was that the poems have improved by keep-
ing – in my eyes. In fact (as I said at the beginning) some of them, especially
the earlier ones are to me a permanent and exquisite contribution to our fund
of fine verse. It is stupid that they are not in all the anthologies, they will be.

book of poems: *55 Poems.*

notes to the Mantis poem: Williams probably refers to "'Mantis,' an Interpretation." *CSP,*
67–73.

404. ALS-1

[Rutherford, N.J.]

10/21/41

I send these notes as they are – not specific enough, pointing to individual instances – for you to look at & comment on.

Bill

Please read, use (if any use) & return – with or without comment.

notes: Enclosure lacking. The "notes" are a draft of Williams's "An Extraordinary Sensitivity," *Poetry* 60:6 (September 1942), 338– 40. Wallace C324. A copy made by Zukofsky is in the Zukofsky papers at Texas. After the conclusion of the essay, Williams continues,

Louis[,] This is a dangerous sort of writing for if it doesn't click, if it doesn't do the magic and arouse the reader or doesn't find one who is sensitive enough, trained enough and ready enough to place himself exactly in tune with it – or if, in writing it, the writer isn't instructed by deep enough feeling (as it sometimes happens here) it becomes a mere jargon and a reaching. Explicit (as contrasted with this: emphasis and codification) writing at least always makes sense. Here unless the sense is instructed the writing makes no sense too often. But explicit writing is so very often as it were a runner fastened to a cart and this, when it succeeds, is a runner free! that is wholly justified. But, as I say, it is difficult for the writer and the reader, and always dangerous, for to bore by an unsolvable obscurity is the worst of all writing. And when sense, even ploddingly, cannot solve a sentence because of lack of its parts – the fault cannot be said to lie with the reader. But to fly, we require a certain lightness and wings. HERE, at their best, we have them.

405. ALS-7

1088 East 180 St
New York

Oct 22/41

Dear Bill:

Of the 30 odd people (I don't mean the people <are odd> but 30+) who got my volume you are the only one who has committed himself about my verse – so far. I'm touched. Every one of them had at least 3 times as much time as you have (I should say "as you have not"?)

I've copied out two bits for the dust jacket. Let me know which you prefer – the first bit is from the notes, the second from the P.S. of the letter you sent the day before. Or shall we use them in that order, together? If O.K., I'll save you the trouble and send the "advertisement" (I've clipped them as it were for advertising value, but that's not all their value) to Decker myself, & maybe he'll get around to printing a jacket or announcement after all. I'm not too hopeful about his speed.

The notes are beautiful writing – so much so, so felt, that I see my character and intention in them. I wouldn't have them different. The red pencil, marking a word or two, questions only the possible ambiguity of meaning the words might have in your context. Leave them that way if you think they're clear. If not it's only a question of finding a word with the meaning <u>you</u> intend to replace the original. I don't see that you need to add anything to the notes, unless you want to – they're an excellent review of the work, as is. You might if you have the time give the poems another glance and just say to point your text, as you say in your letter "Some are very beautiful, some did not affect me, did not seem to come alive" and indicate which are which by title or number. It would help me and help your reader. – I <u>don't think</u> you should spend your time on more detailed comment, i.e. picking lines etc. They don't matter. All that does is that this poem stands or doesn't.

Since you have justly pointed out the chronology – I'm taking the trouble to copy out the exact chronology of the 29 short poems (not the 29 songs, which are later & were done in a period of 3 to 4 years). It may interest you & be helpful for critical reference as to maturity etc. – the point being I'm sometimes mature and sometimes not, depending on the success of the poem not youth or old age – like all poets. None of the poems <written> after June 1924 come literally under "student days and student excellences" (a damn good phrase to use in discussing "The" by the way) – . That is, almost all but 2 or 3 were written after I got my M.A. – and curiously enough those that <u>displease</u> me most now are not among the 2 or 3 "early" ones: the ones that make me <u>uncomfort</u>able <u>now</u> are on – pp. 27, 28, that damn word "gyre" on pg 30, pg 33, 47, 61 & 62 (because it's better than the subject). Well, enough of this.

If you can get the notes printed as review in "Poetry" it would give me great pleasure – but great pleasure. Or any other magazine you wish – I have no preference, except that it will give me greater pleasure if you get it printed in one that'll enable you to treat yourself to two neckties or whatever instead of one – no reflection on your neckties, just a reflection of my dude aspirations! Kenyon Review, Southern Review, New Republic, New Yorker, Nation, Yale or Virginia Quarterly pay more? But anyone that offers the least resistance and the least demand on your time ~~contacting it~~ to contact.

Well, it's a strange world with me still sitting here writing about poetry & all that's going on in the street as you say. Moscow and Leningrad hold. Let's hope for the miracle that they will throw the Germans back. No doubt Montague Norman wants our trade & we're cutting England out of S. America, too. Ever see two capitalists happy together except when they're putting something over on ~~each~~ one another etc etc.

For the Dust Jacket

I   An extraordinary sensitivity. Only the merely contemporary sloughed off and only the primarily beautiful and new (old: new) remaining.

II   A permanent and exquisite contribution to our fund of fine verse. It is stupid that they are not in all the anthologies, they will be.

(I quote your letter exactly under II – but the second sentence should probably be – for the purpose of a dust jacket: "The poems are not in all the anthologies, they will be.")

I'll use either I or II, or I and II, as you say.

L.

P.S. I'm coitenly drinking sweet cream in the above!

The next time I see you, if you're in the mood for 'em, I'd like to leave the play, collected essays, and text-book on poetry, all going back 5 years or more – but it's time somebody who counts looked at them.

Our best to you and Floss

Yours

Louis.

P.S. In re- Mantis you're probably right, the notes are "more interesting and important than the poem", but then the notes as you know wouldn't have been written but for the poem and your comment of that time. Anyway, the "poem" – I don't explain, any more than I dedicate the "notes" – but my secret dedications are always the better ones I feel – the "poem" is really a cantata & some day if music can be written to it, its entire intention may seem more worth while – I hope.

Chronology of the 29 Poems

Poem – Written
1 – Aug. 1925
2 – Jan 1924 – ("student days")
3 – June 1928
4 – Nov. 1928
5 – Jan. 1925
6 – July 1926
7 – Apr. 1926
8 – Oct 1928
9 – Apr. 1927
10 – Apr. 1925
11 – May 1926

12 – Feb 1924 ("Student days")

13 – Jan 1926

14 – Aug 1926

15 – Apr. 1925

16 – Sept. 1925

17 – Dec. 1924

18 – July 1924

19 – Oct 1925

20 – Dec 1925

21 – Dec 1925

22 – Jan 1928

23 – Jan 1927

24 – Nov 1923 ("Student days")

25 – Jan 1926

26 – June 1928

27 – Nov. 1928

28

& – Feb. 1929

29

pp. 27, 28: "Memory of V. I. Ulianov." *CSP*, 21–22.

pg 30, pg 33, 47, 61 & 62: Poem 3 of "29 Poems" ("Cocktails"); poem 5 of "29 Poems" ("Ferry"); poem 17 of "29 Poems" ("Cars once steel and green, now old'); "D.R." *CSP*, 22–24, 31, 38–39.

play: *Arise, Arise*. Its orginal version was completed in 1936.

text-book: *A Test of Poetry*, completed in 1940.

406. ALS-1

[Rutherford, N.J.]

10/23/41

Dear Louis:

Glad you liked what I said. Keep the enclosed if you want it. I sent the original to Poetry today.

Working away! its the only solution to anything – as far as I'm concerned.

Bill

enclosed: Enclosure lacking. Williams refers to his review of *55 Poems:* "An Extraordinary Sensitivity."

[1088 East 180th Street
New York]

10/25/41

Dear Bill:

The review is perfect now. I'll appreciate hearing if <u>Poetry</u> accepts it. Here's luck to us both!

I've sent Decker the blurb for the dust jacket, using extracts I and II (leaving out "It is stupid" for the purpose of the jacket) as per enclosure of the other day. I take it that's all O.K.

Met a wonderful person yesterday by accident, a young Hindu of 23, working for the Congress Party in India. Tell you about him when I see you

Do lots of work, and I hope I see you soon!

Yours,
Louis

wonderful person: Unidentified.
Enclosures: "1892–1941" and "*Anew* 10." *CSP* 81 and 91.

■ 408. ALS-1

9 Ridge Road
Rutherford, N. J

Nov 1/41

Dear Celia,

How about you and Louis having supper with us this coming Tues. Nov. 4th. If not convenient next Tues. a week, the Eleventh – being a holiday as well – might be better. If election day is O.K. just drop me a card.

It will be nice to see you <u>here</u>. Bill & I both enjoyed our walk in the Park – and <u>you</u>. Louis is a lucky man.

As a result of our brief inspection of the Rose Garden in the park – we, yesterday, planted 30 nice new plants – and will be expecting miracles of blooms next Spring!

Our best to you both – and looking forward to seeing you soon
– Sincerely yours
Florence Williams

walk in the park: Zukofsky quotes from this letter in his essay, "William Carlos Williams," but remembers the letter as coming from Bill, not Florence. Zukofsky also recalls, "That would be after the four of us had walked in the rose garden in Bronx Park during the worst of the war in 1941" (*Prepositions* +, 47– 48).

9 Ridge Road, Rutherford, N.J.

Jan. 19, 1942

Dear Louis and Celia:

I was disappointed and half ashamed having to send you that wire Saturday evening. I had hoped right up to the end to be able to make it – after promising you (and myself) to be there on the seventeenth. It was just not to be.

As a matter of fact we could have gone had we been endowed with prescience in detail; the baby didn't arrive until 5.41 Sunday morning but that was something I couldn't preascertain.

Not only that but I had a second case going on all the time, a stubborn session which kept me attentive until Sunday evening at 7.34! It was a hell of a night – and day, I spent the whole time in the hospital in my white suit wandering the halls, watching and sleeping in snatches.

I wanted to talk to you, too, about the Mary Colum scribble in Sunday before last times Books. Not so hot. Dense as turf smoke. Why in hell did she write it when she had not one word to say by way of intelligent communication. To have said nothing at all would have been far worthier.

Forgive us this once. I don't know what else to say. Next time it may be worse. I hope we didn't put you out too much or disappoint the others. I should have like nothing else better than to have met them

Mother is still in the hospital but her leg seems definitely to have healed. Ma Herman is starting to walk again. What next?

Our best to you both.

Bill

Colum scribble: Mary Colum, "The New Books of Poetry," *New York Times Book Review,* 11 January 1942, p. 5. Colum reviews, among other books, two published at Prairie City, Illinois, by James A. Decker: *Calendar: An Anthology of 1941 Poetry*—in which "Paris" ("A"-10) appeared—and Zukofsky's *55 Poems*. She remarks, "The author of 'Paris' throws out words loosely, repetitiously, and often pointlessly. In something like three-fourths of a page the word 'people' occurs eight times. Then there are geographical names thrown in in the worst manner of Whitman, the 'Salut au Monde' manner. Louis Zukofsky appears by himself in a volume entitled '55 Poems': here there are some pieces that can be read with pleasure, but for the most part they are eccentric expressions of some not very significant reactions of the author, several are neither more nor less than blague."

1088 E. 180 St
N.Y.C.

Apr. 9/42
Dear Bill,
How've you and Floss and all been?

Paul Brooks of Houghton Mifflin Co wrote me this morning saying that you had mentioned "a fine novel" I had, "partly written," and enclosing an application blank for their Literary Fellowship. Thanks a lot for keeping me in mind. But I'm in a quandary. The novel he refers to is, of course, the same project – "Ferdinand" – I submitted to them last fall along with your letter of recommendation. It was returned to me end of November with a letter signed by A. Christensen of the editorial dept., saying it had been eliminated from the contest, but that he would be glad to read it when finished. I don't know what to tell Paul Brooks. Perhaps the truth. As you know, the original intention was to have the piece be a novella – a long short story – and I'm quite satisfied with the form to-date. I've done about 15,000 words (you saw only half of these) and the thing is about two thirds from the end, as far as I can see its scope now as a novella. I can see where the subject differently turned could be a novel – and some of the writing, especially that of part 2 which you read would hardly have to be rehandled for that purpose. But it's impossible for me in my present circumstances to think in terms of the larger scope of the novel. With a year off and the backing of a fellowship I feel I could do it. As things are now, it's taking a dreadfully long time to finish the thing even as a novella. The closing date for the application is July 1st. I hope I can get the thing done as a long story by then. And I think I ought to tell Paul Brooks that I'll submit it to him as such by then, and if he sees a novel in it worthy of a fellowship, well and good – I'll revamp it. If not, perhaps he might want to consider it as part of another venture, a book of short stories – of different times, but related in outlook the way Flaubert's Three Tales are. I don't know that Houghton Mifflin has been considering short stories for their Fellowship Awards. But "Ferdinand" would make one; I have another, much shorter, completed; and still another about half done. <And there would be two others I have in mind to make up the book.> What do you think?

Not much to say otherwise. I've been in the dumps – Celia sick for a while, now my father and now myself again like last spring, but not so bad. I guess it's all that plus the gruelling stupidity of the job I have which doesn't leave the mind free for my own work and after no consolation or exhiliration in itself, that let me down. Well, I've tried for over two years now every gov't agency, private concern etc. where I might be useful in the "war effort" – as they call it

– and no go. No doubt I could have done a novel in the time wasted on that. Maybe the Army – if they can use my 110 lbs – will decide sooner that my brains are worth no more than $42 a month after 3 months training. Anyway my order no. in the last draft was 54.

The only good that came out of the League of American Writers' reading was that I met William J. Blake, the novelist, there. If not for him, the criticism would have been all averse, and the kind of averseness that obviously means to be nasty and petty. I had never met Blake before, but he stood up for me and bravely told 'em where to come off. Neither of the commentators I had picked showed up – you see.

I am sorry you weren't at the Poetry Center's poets' symposium on the war to hear me read Walt Whitman's <u>Respondez.</u> <u>En masse</u> the old boy had something to say, as you know – whatever our disagreement with his foibles etc. But <u>Respondez,</u> to me at any rate, is a perfect poem in itself – the kind of thing that an intelligence in our time ought to be willing to live and die for. Naturally, there wasn't one person in the audience – about a hundred people – who had heard of it.

Celia says, watching me write on, my goodness this looks like the Bronx home news. I guess it's being depressed which has started me off – the imbecilities in the world, the disaster in the Philippines, the ease with which everybody is watching the Russians fight etc.

If we're still here end of this month, what do you say about coming for dinner and a walk again? We were stranded in Times Square last Sunday evening – & if it had been an hour earlier I'd have called you up, & had you been free, taken the bus and come out. But everything is agin' us.

Well, yours as in the song Ramona – as the bloody cow says every night at eleven o'clock, before we hear what the latest news over wor is.

    All our best to you both

        Louis

Brooks: Brooks was Managing Editor of Houghton Mifflin.

Three Tales: *Trois Contes* (1877): "Un Coeur Simple," "La Légende de Saint Julien L'Hospitalier," and "Hérodias."

Blake: William J. Blake (1894–1969), American novelist. Author of *The World Is Mine* (New York: Simon and Schuster, 1938), *The Painter and the Lady* (New York: Simon and Schuster, 1939), *Elements of Marxian Economic Theory and Its Criticism* (Cordon: 1941), *The Copperheads* (New York: Dial Press, 1941), and other novels.

symposium on the war: The Poetry Center of the 92nd Street Young Men's Hebrew Association sponsored a series of readings and discussions under the title, "The American Way of Life." On 23 March 1942, four poets (Norman Macleod, Robert Goffin, Sheamas O'Sheal, and Louis Zukofsky) addressed the questions: "What has American poetry contributed to the democratic tradition? What is the American poet's responsibility in the present war?" See the *Y.M.H.A. Bulletin* 43:27 (30 March 1942).

disaster in the Philippines: The Japanese army completed its victory over United States forces in the Philippines on 9 April 1942, when General Wainwright surrendered the island of Corregidor.

411. ALS-1

9 Ridge Road, Rutherford, N.J.

4/13/42

Dear Louis:

Sent essential part of your letter to H.M. Co. – that relieves you of explaining to them.

I don't remember learning of the Poetry Center's Symposium on the war & should have greatly enjoyed hearing you read. I go about eratically – as time allows – being present when I'd rather be elsewhere & missing what I'd enjoy. It is my nature – hard to cure. Bill in navy. Paul waiting. I write a little. Please write again.

Bill

412. ALS-2

1088 E. 180 St, New York

June 18/42

Dear Bill:

Here is "Ferdinand", done as a long short story, which I am submitting to Paul Brooks of Houghton Mifflin, along with application for one of their fellowships: the project, to make a novel out of it.

The story itself looks better to me this morning than last night. I hope you think so, too.

I've been writing it under stress, unemployed (that is without a job) etc – which is no good. Who knows, maybe it is?

I still have the letter of recommendation you wrote for me to Houghton Mifflin when I submitted pp 1–21 of the present mss. to them last year. They require a letter of recommendation. Shall I send them that? Or since you've been in touch with Paul Brooks recently, isn't it necessary? Or do you think you had better write a new letter based on the entire story, & send that to me for forwarding? If you do write me a new letter, I'd be very grateful if I can have it by next Monday or Tues. at the latest. Thanks no end.

Celia and I feel very bad about not having been able to have Floss & you over again this spring. I won't trouble you with excuses – it was just one damn thing after another that prevented it. Right now, we're faced with the problem of getting out of this apartment by June 29. I haven't any idea where we'll be after Sept 1 – but between July 1st & Sept 1st we'll be with some friends near Lake George, where we've rented a cottage to live cheaply. I hope that by some miracle you can drive up there and drop in on us:

    c/o Huss Cottage

      Diamond Point

        Warren Co., N.Y.

I'll verify that address – anything might happen before July 1st, who knows I may get a job – when I hear from you. Meanwhile, write here.

We hope Floss & you and all are prospering.

      All the best

      Yrs

      Louis

P.S. The other story, in case you're interested, & want another slant on me as concocter of fiction – to hell with <it> all. <(wrote that last year)> No hurry to return either story. I'll pick them up sometime or sumpn.

some friends: Unidentified.

other story: Probably "A Keystone Comedy."

413. TLS-1

[Rutherford, N.J.]

June 19, 1942

Dear Louis:

The first six pages of the story make excellent reading, take a person right on into it with a real interest. I had to stop there but expect to go on at the first free moment. Floss will be reading it too. Haven't touched the other story yet.

Enclosed is a new letter to Paul Brooks, I don't think it necessary but we might as well send it. I'm dropping him a note besides.

I'm working on "Paterson" again and hope to have some pages of it in reasonable condition to be seen by the middle of summer, never can tell. Whit Burnett of "Story" is asking me for a group of poems – from past work – for an anthology. I'm getting it up for him. Laughlin (who has been dropped from the army for no reason at the time apparent) is bringing out my play of last year in New Directions. That's about all.

Haven't heard from Pound after my last blast but hear that he is trying to get back to U.S., God knows why. They'll lynch him. Maybe my source of rumor is cockeyed.

Paul plans to make me a grandfather by Aug. 7. Bill is somewhere in the Pacific area.

May you have a good rest at Lake George. Our best to Celia.

Yrs.

Bill

the story: "Ferdinand."

other story: Probably "A Keystone Comedy."

letter to Paul Brooks: Williams's letter to Paul Brooks, of Houghton Mifflin Company, 19
June 1942: "Dear Mr. Brooks: Let me again recommend Louis Zukofsky and his short
novel, Ferdinand, for your fellowship list. The script has been completely reworked
since you saw it last year, I believe you will find it excellent reading. There's no use, I
think, in going into further detail concerning Zukofsky as a writer. I believe in him
and feel convinced that he has a valuable contribution to make to American letters
today. With best personal wishes, Sincerely yours[,] W. C. Williams[.]"

Burnett: For the anthology *This Is My Best*, ed. Whit Burnett (New York: Dial Press,
1942), Williams chose "Daisy," "Primrose," and "Queen-Ann's-Lace" (*CP1*, 160– 62).
He also provided a brief statement, "Why He Selected Some Flower Studies." Wallace B40.

my play: *Trial Horse No. 1 (Many Loves): An Entertainment in Three Acts and Six Scenes*, in
New Directions 7 (1942), 233–305. Wallace C311.

414. TLS-1

[Rutherford, N.J.]

June 20, 1942

Dear Louis:

The plot's a good one, I think, for a carefully written philosophic novel. It
would have to be too well written to be popular,to make it a success. As it is, as
a short story,though for a person like myself it has the charm of compression
and occasional sharp sentence or paragraph, it would take a doughty reader to
stick it. Floss couldn't. No soap as a short story. Too sketchy.

Thus I'd say it's only chance is as a novel, full length. There there would have
to be an enormous elaboration of scenes, with reams of dialogue – each bit to
be carefully worked, with verisimilitude in locale and dialect, Boy! it would
take you five years. Maybe not, if you had a fellowship.

There isn't much dramatic action in spite of a few scenes of violence.

I like your characters, all of them. I think they are well imagined and stand
up pretty well – as far as I can see from your descriptions. I'm sure it would
take the strength of a Hercules to do the job as it should be done.

I'm returning the script herewith. I'm keeping the other story which I have not read.

Returning to the story as it now exists, you write better in some parts than in others. Occasionally you get stalled and fumble around without anything happening. For instance, after the first 6 pages there are several pages about the gardner which stop the mind completely. If you're going to jump as you do in other places you should have jumped there also.

Best luck. If you ever do the book as it should be done let me see it again – if you want to. I might be of some assistance technically here and there. I doubt that the Creeping Charlie is the same as the Wandering Jew. I think the Creeping Charlie is a true vine. In fact I know it is. But you are right in saying that the Wandering Jew and Comelina Virginica are the same.

Best luck
Bill

Creeping Charlie: *Sedum acre.* Wandering Jew is the name for various plants, but *Commelina virginica* is not one of them.

415. TLS-1

[Rutherford, N.J.]

June 21, 1942

Dear Louis:

All right it isn't a philosophic novel then. Perhaps you're right. In that case, God damn it, you've got to kill the old couple in the end . Who cares about "truth"? You've got a presumptive work of art on your hands; it's ridiculous to sidestep the situation in the way you have. Either you should kill everybody and follow through with the "truth" of the story as a story. Or else just don't do anything. Don't even have the hallucination of an accident but make them come out perfectly safely into a beautiful sunny green California valley and have a picnic lunch on the grass.

Your explanation makes the story more comprehensible to me but in that case a little tighter writing here and there, a little more care with the sentences, removal of hanging clauses and some play with the sentence structure to avoid monotony would be of great help. I didn't indicate anything because I wasn't ast but I saw several spots that needed touching. With more bruskness in going over, without transitional explanation, from incident to incident (as you have very well done for the most part) stronger <u>lines</u> in the composition would be indicated. It needs sharpness of compositional lines in several places.

What to do with the girl at the end is something of a problem. He might find himself wanting almost irres<is>tably to turn back to her but, after a struggle, going on. I certainly do not like the phantasm, the fantasy – which seems very definitely manufactured and anything but "true" at the finish.

I think the whole might easily be brought down to ten or at least eight pages less than it is by judicious clippong here and there throughout. Nothing like caerful snipping for the bringing out of the profile. Even a word cut will very often brighten a whole paragraph miraculously.

Wish you luck.

Bill

Your dope on the Creeping Charlie is absolutely correct and it ain't the Comelina Virginica. The correct name for the ubiquitous "Wandering Jew" or Comelina is Day Flower. What finer name than that? The blue is one of the finest blues in all our flowers . First in the morning the flower fades and is gone by noon – except in a very shady place.

416. ALS-1

c/o Thaew
513 Alabama Av,
Brooklyn, N.Y.

Sept 8/42

Dear Bill:

How are you, Florence et al?

We're back at Celia's ma's – address above – till the end of the month when we move into our new place in Brooklyn Heights which we rented today. You'll get the address when we're in it.

We'll be telling you the details of our hitch-hiking when we see you. Also about an excellent painter we discovered at Diamond Point, where he has terraced <by himself> a whole mountain that calls up photos of Taxaco, Mexico.

I got around to revising early "A", so that it stands up alongside of the later, and to writing an article on Guczul (the painter).

No news yet from Houghton Mifflin. When I hear from them either way – if you're still in the mood I'll take you up on the spots you thought would benefit by editing. I've noticed some myself since I last wrote you. – Did you ever get around to the other story?

What's new with your own work. What do you hear from Bill and Paul?

Celia's best and mine to you both

Louis

excellent painter: Dometer Guczul. A typescript essay in the Williams archive at Yale ("Guczul") notes that "He was born in 1886, at Temetes Kubin, Hungary, near the Roumanian and Serbian border, of Serbian extraction. After serving in the Hungarian army, he escaped to New York City, in 1913, where on the East Side he worked as a baker, his occupation in the homeland. He attended classes at the Art Students League from 1924 to 1926; motorcycled to the West Coast and back in 1924. He came to Hearthstone State Park, Lake George, in 1926, starting, as he says, his original work in 1927 and staying to do the backgrounds of his large paintings. From there, in 1937, he came to Diamond Point where he is known as 'Teddy' to the 150 inhabitants of the village. He has since terraced, landscaped, and planted most of a five-acre wooded mountain all by himself. His 'Gallery' of one small room, in a temporary wood cottage in which he lives, is on one of the lower terraces." This typescript is clearly a draft of Zukofsky's essay, since it closely resembles the one published in *View* and in *Prepositions*. I give the information about Guczul contained in the draft of the essay because it contains a few more details than the published version.

Enclosure: "Dometer Guczul."

■ 417. TLS-1

[Rutherford, N.J.]

Sept. 15, 1942

Dear Louis:

Where in hell that other story of yours has got to is more than I can say. I've looked for it in all the likely places but so far it hasn't turned up. It isn't lost, probably in the attic somewhere but I wanted to finish it before writing. Had to give that up.

I started to read it when you first sent it to me but didn't get very far, it seemed to me you were borrowing a style from the newspapers, quite consciously of course, and I didn't approve. Hell, I'll catch up with it after another search I am sure then I'll try to say something intelligent. Hope this wasn't a unique script.

Floss and I have remained home all summer. The only break occured when we went to Ohio to see the grandson. Yes, Paul has produced another boy, not a very big one but he'll grow if he has the authentic toxin in him. He was born August 3, Floss and I made the trip when he was two weeks old. It was marvellous to travel on a railroad train again, soldiers, sailors and everything. Sat up all night in a coach, around the Horseshoe Curve, through Pittsburg at night with the blast furnaces sending up infernal flames and sulphurous fumes, orange and brown. It's a hell of a world all right.

Bill is on some island south of the Equator and west of the Date Line, that's all we know. We haven't heard from him now in two weeks. I try not to think about it.

The summer, apart from those four days, meant only work to me. It has been bad enough but will get much worse soon. Many of the younger men in the profession are being called. Haven't written a line – aside from the blurb for Chas.Henri Ford , not one poem. I did though do some work on the Paterson thing but quit even that finally. Wish I could go on. I dreamed a play one night and jotted down the plot, the name and made sketches of one or two scenes. Someday, perhaps. A play in verse in one scene – but three acts for all that, a modern tragedy of the spirit.

I've been crawling under my office today collecting scrap, a hell of a dirty place to look for old pieces of iron pipe, old wire, anything at all. I got a throat full of muck – but what is that to what the kids are getting? I take a masochistic pleasure in whatever I can force myself to do.

Best to Celia. Floss is doing all right. My mother is just pooping along in the same sad way. If only she had her eyes so she could READ! Geezus what a fate.

    Yours

    Bill

other story: Probably "A Keystone Comedy."

the grandson: Paul Herman Williams, Jr.

blurb: Probably "Surrealism and the Moment," *View* 2:2 (May 1942), 19. Wallace C322.

Paterson thing: Eventually published as *Paterson: Book I* by New Directions in 1946. (Wallace A24)

a play: None of the manuscripts in the Williams collection at the University of Buffalo precisely match this description.

418. TLS-1

9 Ridge Road, Rutherford, N.J.

November 7, 1942

Dear Louis:

Whether you like or not take this letter today, Monday morning, November 9, 1942, and go to the editorial office of the New York Sun. Ask for Clayton Hoagland and tell him you are Louis Zukofsky. There may be a job for you with the Sun, though never so humble or Hoagland will definitely direct you to the office of a mutual friend in the publishing business – unless you object to newspapers and publishing houses as sources of revenue. Do me at least the favor of talking with Hoagland. If Monday morning is not a good time for you go Monday afternoon or Tuesday morning or whenever you can. The lead looks fruitful to me.

Your story has been found, right under my nose as I knew it would be found but I have not as yet had time to read it. It is bewildering how insistent my pursuers can be, they keep after me from morning until night and often into the night so that I am in constant dread of the phone.

But the news from Africa is cheering. In fact the news generally is cheering. If only we do not fumble the ball, if only our Congress can forget is innate stupidity and catch fire in their balls and not only their pants. So far all that seems to have been scared out of them is the shit. Maybe someone, somewhere will rise to the occasion and the rest will follow. I sometimes think that there is no longer a possibllity of spontaneous and generous action left in the human soul – outside of Russia. Perhaps the English have a plodding sort of virtue: but the real war as ever remains to be determined between England at its worst and most successful and Russia at its best: all the overflowing wealth of spontaneous generosity, the real wealth of plenty, of giving of plunging into virtue, the overwhelming wealth of life, not niggardly, a southern profusion – perhaps Mexico. The Indians have kept their blood preeminent, uncooled, relentlessly coursing, undefeated there.

The Russians and the Chinese are to me the hope of the world because they are continental peoples, they know the repose and placidity and abundant wealth, arctic and tropics, east and west. They are the true balance wheels of all peoples. The island peoples are too protective in their instincts. We need a genius that is not self protective, that flings everything magnificently wide to the winds for every seed they know will fall on the soil and grow. They don't have to be careful or sectional.

Shit. I'll write to Bunting. Enjoyed Tenaire and Zadkin with his pregnant blond. The supper was delicious, a good feast.

    Yours

    Bill

Sent your paper about the painter fellow to Jim Laughlin.

this letter: Enclosure lacking.

Hoagland: Rutherford residents Clayton and Katherine Hoagland had long been friends of the Williamses.

Your story: Probably "A Keystone Comedy."

news from Africa: On 7 November 1942, Allied forces landed in French North Africa.

Tenair: Yves Tinayre (1891–1972), French musicologist and singer. Zukofsky translated Tinayre's "Paraboles" (Texas) on 13 November 1941. A note by Zukofsky on the earliest extant draft of his poem, "Guillaume De Machault" states, "Orig. text given by me / Ives Tinayre Nov 4/41" (Texas).

Zadkin: Ossip Zadkine (1890–1967), French sculptor. Zadkine lived in the U.S. (principally in New York City) 1940–1945. Poem 25 of *Anew* is subtitled "for Zadkine." It is about Zadkine's sculpture, "La Prisonniére." *CSP*, 90.

your paper: "Dometer Guczul."

419. ALS-1

9 Ridge Road
Rutherford, N.J.

11/8/42

Got me, I don't know what it is. For a comedy there is no surprise, no suddeness, no unexpectedness – or not enough – to give it that change of direction or pace which brings laughter. It isn't swift enough or boastful then crushed, not relieved <u>enough</u>. a disconcerting switch. the hurry, fear, fright needs high lights – jerks, emphasis is lacking – to my taste. Needs a punch –
<u>W</u>

what it is: "A Keystone Comedy."

420. ACS

[Postmarked Rutherford, N.J.]

[Postmarked 9 November 1942]

It is <u>sad</u> enough to be a comedy so that one feels <u>enough</u> relief. It's that burst of relief that busts the bubble
Bill

421. ALS-2

202 Columbia Hts
Brooklyn N.Y.

Nov 10/42
Dear Bill,

Hi! The news from Africa is <u>news</u>! Suspected something like that would follow when the day after you were here Major Robert L. Crawford, New York officer Procurement District, A.G.D. 42 B'way, asked me to telephone him with reference to my application for commission in the Army. He wanted a man who could speak French without the <u>least</u> hesitation, who had a vocabulary including patois, argot etc etc. <and could understand everything <u>anyone</u> speaking French might spill on him.> I assured him I could fill the bill with a little practice, but no he wanted me to swear that I could do all he asked <u>immediately</u>. Naturally, I couldn't swear to that. He appreciated my honesty, & asked me to call him back in two weeks. So here I am tenser than ever – waiting for the end of those two weeks. I wish there were some way of hastening the decision – one way or another – but I take it there's no use prodding the army when the order is to wait. I have no idea & neither has the Major where the job would be. If it's out of the country, I should hate to leave Celia, but I can't see myself refusing to go once a commission is offered me. So cross yr. fingers or what? Maybe if I had said "Merde, alors!" at once, I'd have got the job!

Thanks for returning "A Keystone Comedy." I'll contemplate the corrections when I can think of such things again. The title literally meant to indicate the pace of some of the old slapstick movies of 1910 or thereabouts. Some of 'em as I recall it began very sad and slow & speeded up when it got to the mud-slinging. Your second card, I believe, understands the intention of the piece. No matter.

I'll send my prospectus on Guczul to Jim Laughlin – bless me.

Thanks for the lead to Clayton Hoagland whom I had met before. I saw him – nothing so far, but he'll keep an eye open he says, & will write a few people. He wasn't any too specific about <my seeing> "the mutual friend" who I understand works for Fischer Verlag. If by any chance, they're the firm publishing the Judaica Encyclopedia – I'm sure I could fit into some editorial position. I haven't been able to find out who the publishers of that encyclopedia are. Anyway, why should I object to publishing houses etc as source of revenue??

The only damn thing I object to in this world is waste. Neglect's part of that set-up of waste.

What you say about Russia & my Chinese blood-brothers – I've no doubt I'll be growing a pigtail by the end of my life – makes me feel less isolated. I'm very fond of one sentence in "Ferdinand" – "The Russian told him what the Chinese were doing."

You may remember that was almost at the end of the story.

Ours to you & to good news from Bill, Jr.

> Yrs
> Louis

P.S. We've a telephone now – so we're easier to get in touch with: Main 4–0766

news from Africa: See Williams's letter of 7 November 1942.
"the mutual friend": Unidentified.
Judaica Encyclopedia: No such publication seems to have appeared in the 1940s.
one sentence: *Collected Fiction*, 267.

■ 422. ALS-1

> 202 Columbia Hts
> Bklyn, N.Y.

Jan 24/42 [1943]
Dear Bill:
Felt like old times last night, even tho I didn't get around to say much. I enclose the translation of Bosquet. And two of my own recent squirts.

J. Q. Adams on astronomy etc is in "A"-8, <u>New Directions, 1938</u>, pg 27 from the beginning (since there are no page numbers in that no. of New Direct.).

The <u>Kermess</u> poem is good, alright, alright, so cheer up. And if the worst comes to the worst, and we won't be able to talk here, Floss is right, we'll go to Russia, or at least continue to live in the Russia of our imagination about which you said something over 10 years ago in another poem.

We'll have to get around to an evening here one of these weeks, but aside from that we have a phone now – Main 4-0766 and anytime you're in town – we'd be grateful no end if you'll call us up to make a day or an evening of it right there and then.

So, our best to yuse guys.

Louis

Bosquet: Alain Bosquet (1919–1998) (born Anatole Bisk in Odessa), Belgian poet who emigrated to New York in 1941. He enlisted in the U.S. army in 1942, serving subsequently in other branches of the government. In 1951 he settled in Paris to teach and write. The translation (signed by Zukofsky and dated "Dec 16/42") is headed, "(from 'L'Image Impardonnable' of Alain Bosquet)." Zukofsky's translation is titled "The need to have you": "It is midnight, hour that kills / great flesh and images, / bubbles show on our palms / to break open like flowers, / in us the groaning leper / attains the rain and the rainbow, / all things prepare for north winds: / our ranged eyelid, / our fingers that resemble obelisks / and our spinal columns / cartilage on cartilage / blooming with bites. / You are the sister of misfortunes, / you are the friend of distress / and at the bottom of your shoulders / are sparrows, caravans, / great faces become / marsh spiders, / but among your stars / you transfigure the sonata, / tall plumage, the water-cooler, / such a poem as moves, / an ocean for your birds, / a happy man like me, / too rich to express himself / and, under your curse / that lives to make me more mad, / a body, a criminal hide, / a body that will no more be fooled, / a body that will not live after itself." At some later date, this translation and another translation of Bosquet ("Pluck the cascade") were included in the typescript of a draft of *Anew.* Zukofsky's translation was published in *View* 1:3 (Spring 1943). A copy of Bosquet's *Le Vie est Clandestine* (Paris: Carrea, 1945) in the Zukofsky archive at Texas is inscribed by the author to Zukofsky.

recent squirts: "('One oak fool box': – the pun')" and "A Marriage Song for Florence and Harry." The first poem is headed "Anew 45," the second "Anew 47." Their final order in *Anew* was 14 (*CSP*, 84–85) and 30 (*CSP*, 93).

Adams on astronomy: John Quincy Adams is cited as referring to observatories as "Light-houses of the skies." "A," 71–72.

Kermess: "The Dance," *Palisade* 1:4 (Winter 1942), 66. Wallace C327. *CP2*, 58–59.

another poem: "A Morning Imagination of Russia," first published in the fourth issue of the *Exile* (1928). Wallace C122. *CP1*, 303.

9 Ridge Road, Rutherford, N.J.

Jan. 29, 1943

Dear Louis:

Glad you wrote as you did, I was moved to do the same,feeling much as you did,but couldn't find five minutes in which to sit down to it. Friends rely (is that a word?) on each other but often do not realize the measure of their indebtedness to each other until something happens to spearate them. Your appreciations always give me a feeling of renewed confidence in what I am about.

That may not be very well expressed, almost everything we say might have been better said, but I was glad to see you and Celia also. I have about me always a vivid sense of the tremendous creations that might be possible if only we can manoeuvre ourselves into a position where we are secure enough to attempt them. I've never felt secure, have no confidence in the world about me to give me the means to carry on. Oh well, I carry on.

I don't know how to bring out the music Celia has written for your words. Until I can get the sense of things tactically I can't say anything about them. Thanks just the same.

Anyhow we had a warming sort of an evening, the sort of talk that is full of eggs – I don't want to strain the figure. Livening – you've changed condsiderable since your marriage and may I say for the better? Maybe it's just age but just possibly it may be Celia. Perhaps a little self improvement has crept in. I wish I could write more and so do you. Maybe it's just as well that we don't have too much time for it. But I wish I could count on really soaking myself in the tasks we both enjoy, to bring out always more and more clearly the contemporary forms which embody that which both feel are the true aspects of our day. Maybe it'll happen. In that case we 'll have other talks back and forth.

Sincerely,

Bill

Looking your letter over again I find that I have neglected to comment on the enclosures. You gave me some reason for looking at Bosquet's work more carefully – but where in hell am I going to find the time. Here it is Friday afternoon and I'm likely to spend almost all of it answering letters and not all of any real interest to me. The thing is I don't know french well enough to get what the guy is after at the first reading – and that's all I ever have time for. I look and if I'm lucky I get something but most often I'm simply repelld by the difficulties. I see now what he's doing. Thanks for the critical introduction. He seems wordy, wanders on as I imagine most surrealistus are bound to. If you give yourself over to the unconscious you know as well as I that it's going to be repetitious to sat the least. Maybe a nugget will be turned up. And not that critical stops ans starts aren't evident but they're not acknowledged. We're to suppose that the poet is born perfect – if only he can loosen the neck of his bladder and piss it out. Sure, he's perfect piss – which does have for all that a critical value I suppose. I ain't completely convinced as yet that they're got anything much – nothing really characteristic. Neither has Patchen with his religiosity – and not that occasionally he doesn't raa ly turn up a nugget.

Your own poems, I don't know how you write them but I still think they need a freer verbalism, more loose playing with the words – I have difficulties, my mind won't wrap itself about them. Maybe Celias words will sone day do the trick for me I like the end of the poem from the place whre Mr Dooley comes in but I can't for the life pf of me connect it with the beginning of the poem.

The first stanza of your own small thing goes over but, again, I can't for the life of me bring the birds on the hedge into it. What were they doing, screwing – which they do so well? I don't mean to be flippant. No doubt you mean happy as a bird. I suppose I'm really thick – but then, all readers are – mostly. Maybe that's a comma at the end of the first stanza. Yes, that explains it. All right, now I get it but for that subject matter it needs more of a Herrick's, Mozartian finish, more embellishment, grace notes, tootling on the flute. Or am I mad and blind or just dull? I want more of a flare – flair? But at that I begin to like it.

  Bill

music Celia has written: By this date, Celia Zukofsky had set at least ten of her husband's
  poems to music. See Louis Zukofsky, *Autobiography*, 11– 41.
Mr Dooley: Finley Peter Dunne (1867–1936) wrote a series of books (1898–1919) featuring
  this character commenting on current events. Zukofsky refers to him in *Anew* 14,
  "('One oak fool box': —the pun')." *CSP*, 84– 85.
the birds: In stanza two of *Anew* 30, "A marriage song for Florence and Harry." *CSP*, 93.

424. ALS-2

            [202 Columbia Heights
             Brooklyn, New York]

Feb 1/43
Dear Bill:
Lets see if I can get this down on one sheet of paper. I don't want you to spend another Friday answering letters – I know what a drain on time that damn business of letter-writing can be.

First, you're right about Bosquet. No need for <u>you</u> to give any more time to it. I was merely pointing out that occasionally the man turns out a nugget, precisely because he's thinking about a matter in direction opposed to the unconscious and the Patchen kind of thing which takes ease of achievement on faith. – I translated the piece I sent you because it does that, & the man's in the army, but now he asks for more, & since he went ahead & translated some of "55", I'm bounden goddamnit etc.

Second, my own poems don't, of course, for the most part, <(i.e. except when I dream 'em – which is rare)> depend on the unconscious at all. What bothers you in reading them is probably syntactical understatement. As a matter of fact, I knew exactly what would appear unclear to you when I sent them. But I'll just have to take the risk I've been taking all along that if people learn to read me for the cadence, & the proper pauses, they'll ultimately understand all of the words, too. I mean <to have> a continuous meaning all right! The Marriage Song: Yes, there's a period after the first four lines. And a pause. And the next line is a guy saying half to himself "As the birds on the hedge", and a period, with all the implications you got out of it. And you say "At that I begin to like it". I wish you had got it the first time – for my sake. But you were right mentioning Herrick & Mozart. That's exactly what I intended – but streamlined 20th cent. All the grace notes are there, but the thing is so short they're also the notes of the poem. And the tootling, too, the variations. Anyway, that's what I intended – only one can't tootle an epithalamium on an extended line these days, as far as I can see. – The other poem, well, if you're not bored by it, we can talk about that sometime.

As I said, I don't want to take up your time unnecessarily, so I find myself shutting up about literature when I see you these days. That's perhaps to be regretted, because aside from answering an occasional question of Celia as to the meaning of this or that when she writes down the music to one of the songs I don't talk literature to anybody any more.

Which brings me to the real purpose of this letter – Sorry I've run on till now. But you say, "Friends . . do not realize the measure of their indebtedness to each other until something happens to separate them." and "that [I've] changed considerable since [my marriage] and may I say for the better." – You know, I remember the squabble of a few years ago and the reason it happened was that I felt you really didn't care to see me much, and well I never like to make a nuisance of myself if I'm smart enough to catch on. But everytime you hint at that business, as now, I feel that something else that I still don't know the first thing about escaped me and I still don't know what the hell the whole business was about. It troubles me – since there aren't many friends of the last ten years that have stuck as you have. And if I am better, maybe you can tell me why sometime – don't bother to in a letter – but when I see you here or wherever – because I don't see myself that way these days. Maybe that's why?

Oh, bosh, when you get here maybe you can listen to some of C's music, let it steal all the thunder <if it can!> etc. Best to you both

Louis

425. TLS-1

[Rutherford, N.J.]

January (imagine!)
February 3, 1943

Dear Louis:

I'm sitting here in my office this evening and of all things, without a patient to annoy me. It must be the moon. So I have been reading or have just finished reading for the first time your letter which arrived yesterday morning. I started it then but had to fly to the phone and then out the door yelling to Floss to stick the mail in the desk etc

If anything happened between us "years ago" for my part it was, if I remember anything at all – it was that I began to feel restless at your critical position, as I used to feel with Pound at times when he would press me too hard. I wanted to break away (probably from something inside myself) and felt, perhaps, that you represented certain critical restraints that acted as a check upon me. There is a certain meticulousness about your position that I respect, in you, but which doesn't agree with my particular kind of irritabliltiy after the first ten years. I wanted to get off on the loose and see what a different sort of treatment would do for me. Something like that.

Now that we've been plowing different fields for a time I feel better and more ready to listen to you again. When I say listen I don't mean that you ever asked me to take notes on any formal lectures, I mean only that I always listen to the thing that is my friend.

Do you know the story of the two Frenchmen attached to a caravan or a body of troops crossing the desert? They were the two officers in charge. One asked the other where he was going to station himself that day, front or rear. When the other had said the advance the first went to the rear. They were the best friends in the world but as the relator confessed, if he had had to remain near his friend that day he would have killed him before nightfall.

If fact I find that I really need your criticism.

The difference I find in you is that you are older and that the change, a change in appearance as well as mood, has made you – has widened your range rather than fixed you in a slot – perhaps inclined you to be more (critically) tolerant. Hell, you are riper. That's what I felt – what's the use of talking of such things when we can't work at them. I think you're less jittery, more on the ball – less waste motion. You don't jar me as you did – if you did. I think you're in a better position to do your job as a critic and a writer – if you ever get the chance. A steadier, slower look at the task, more clarity, consequently more insight. Your jaw is longer and steadier – you don't have to hold yourself so much in rein since you don't have to prove anything: description of some fictional person who might have existed under your name if eh hadn't been someone else. I gotta quit – forget it.

Take it easy, as they say. Been thinking of Pound again. A translator primarily, not at all original – full of verbal felicities, one of world's outstanding word-man. Could sling a romantic cadence better than those he followed. Never knew a thing about Shakespeare except the "pure beauty" of a few lines. Never had the vaguest sense of what made S. go and wouldn't have accepted it if he had known. In spite of which he's a genius of the first water. His Seafarer, the translations from the Provencal, even from the German; the long early Canto translated from a Latin version of the Greek – superb work.

And there's where we stick. "Beauty" to Pound is a very narrow thing, a cult and his words are the carefully selected words of a slender hand pointing minute points in a feild of interest.

He bitched his Chinese translation though, to make a Chinaman laugh. Really so. Once they could catch up with him he came out second best. He's always shifting, lest someone catch up with him, a fast mover. At last they've caught him in a position from which he cannot escape: let him translate the "beauty" of his present position and he might, just might, turn into the world's greatest tragic poet.

I must love to write – letters. Had one patient this evening, a ponderous, 65 year old Englishman. You've got to hand it to them. He actually scared me – like my father. A big, big fisted, slow speaking, red faced, H dropping Englishman from Birmingham – the town where my father was born. He came in as if the world were really his and he was destined to be tolerant of it, completely sure of himself, a bit out of breath, very polite but one of God's own chillen. Had been a gurad on an armored truck that takes money from one bank to another. Absolutely trustworthy, would die on the spot rather than have a penny lost. The ribs of the Empire. Gesus! what am I beside that magnificence. All you can do or could do would be to fuck it. I can now understand why Englishmen are buggers by nature, there's absolutle nothing else to do but take out a 3 ft tool and shove it up the man's ass. It would be like a crown on one's head to have been connected with so much empire.

     Yours
     Bill

Seafarer: Pound's translation of this Old English poem was first published in 1911.

early Canto: The first Canto.

Chinese translation: *Cathay* (London: Elkin Mathews, 1915).

426. ALS-2

[202 Columbia Heights
Brooklyn, New York]

Feb 9/43

Dear Bill:

Following up your last letter – some day I'd like to read a volume by you "on what made Shakespeare go". I suppose that "Many Loves" – at least as far as basic idea – offers one phase of such a volume.

Yup, I find myself going back every now and again to Ez's work, with the same reaction as yours. What you say in your letter about it makes fine criticism: "let him translate the beauty of his present position and he might, just might, turn into the world's greatest tragic poet." Well, at least into an important one, if not the greatest. The question is if there'll be any writing worth the name even 20 years after this war. Ez also mistranslated one line of deepest tragic significance in the Cavalcanti Canzone: Di sua virtu seghere ispesso morte – which he translated once: Often his power meeteth with death in the end". And again: "Often his power cometh on death in the end". What Guido was saying was "Its very power is often the source of death." Guido had an idea there – devastating in its understanding of love. Pound ornaments it with an image which changes the whole meaning, takes the tragedy out of it in the Greek or Shakespearian sense.

On the other hand, Dante's Vita Nuova has the same sense of tragedy objectified into one extended image, an image personifying <& embodying> every psychological emotion of love to the remarkable extent that, unwilling to tell the world more than it can understand on the surface, the poem has remained "pretty" to most readers since its inception.

À propos Ez's Chinese translations & what poets know about love – do you know Arthur Waley's translation of Yüan Chen's The Pitcher (779–831 A.D.) – not a remarkable translation, but nothing can kill the poem, which might have been written today, if we could – certainly the surrealists with all their study of the unconscious haven't felt it to that degree, or anywhere near it.

That poem has been "bothering" me a lot these days. Somehow I seem to remember you mentioning it somewhere, or something like "weeping (or wailing) at the well-head." I don't think I have the "Black winds from the north," no V in Spring And All, in mind.

Anyway, Confucius said, "Education begins with poetry, is strengthened through proper conduct (self-discipline) and consummated through music."

Damn my job etc – against that statement.

 Yours

 Louis

Cavalcanti Canzone: "Donna mi prega." The line "Often his power meeteth with death in the end" appears in Pound's *Guido Cavalcanti Rime* (Genoa: Marsano, 1932). The line "Often his power cometh on death in the end" appears in Canto 36. See David Anderson, *Pound's Cavalcanti: An Edition of the Translations, Notes, and Essays* (Princeton: Princeton Univ. Press, 1983), 173 and 180.

Waley's translation: In Arthur Waley's *More Translations from the Chinese* (New York: Knopf, 1937), 118–19. Zukofsky discusses the poem in *Poetry / For My Son When He Can Read* (*Prepositions +*, 3–11).

■ 427. TLS-1

          9 Ridge Road, Rutherford, N.J.

Feb. 15, 1943

Dear Louis:

Just finished reading your letter dated Feb. 9. I do that sometimes not wanting to be in the wrong mood for what I take to be a communication of a certain sort. Glad I waited, it's a good letter which, what with this zero weather, I have now found the time to take in: no one at the office at the moment.

I wish we might be able to live a life permitting the writing of books one for another, of that purpose at least – money or even critical fame no object. Just a book as a communication in full for one other person. It would be the only proper way to write a book. Should we ever arrive at that happy state I'll do you my book on Shakespeare. The amusing thing is that I've always wanted to do such a book. How did you guess it? The man is constantly in my mind, more than his writing – which is the wrong way about for a writer. But if I ever did such an indiscrete thing, being no scholar and the whole structure having to be invented out of whole cloth, it would have to be just for you. It's all mixed up with England, my grandmother and my own father's secret history – Mary Wolstonecraft, THE Godwin and that Williams who was drowned off the coast of Italy with Shelly. Sh. the country boy, buggered by Mi Lawd Fuck Em Young, the stage, innate genius, a world of delectable words dripping from the choisest crowd that ever attended a play and drank it down later, the "Younger Set" hanging about the theatre. S. himself having been taken over by an older woman, raped; raped the other way – losing his beloved son, and LOVE! L O V E ! the topic of the hour with Elezabeth a sour-pus with a hot twat filling the news

 What could pure loving Willie do but get himself a loving boy (confused in his mind with the male:female actress, Young, young! YOUNG – as they never are) pure as there is no woman to be got who is so pure. Reliving his own lost youth, writing feverishly. Jesus there's everything worth knowing. And the man getting old and worse, fashionable! How he must have run from it – to THAT: his revenge for everything. Revenge and bliss.

Did you hear about the WAAC who was sucked under a pier by a WAVE? So it goes.

Write again when you feel like it about whatever you're thinking about. I don't know the one about the pitcher but I'll get out my Arthur Whaley and look it up.

I see my namesake Oscar has a group in Poetry this week or month. I got what Celia said about his appearance but I assure her it isn't that that turns my stomach in him. I think he is pretentious as a poet and altogether too glib. What would be the use? After all one doesn't dish it out like oatmeal. If we're going to slop it around that way (although Lope de Vega did) we'd better take it out in reatiling a sand pit. I just don't like what he does – but I'll go read it. Oh I'll read it – and if I like it by ill chance I'll quit writing forever.

In fact just now when I'm getting together a book of unpublished verse for possible publication – I've got to keep away from such people as this Williams – or I'll have to give up my own project. Maybe he's that good. I hope not. Poetry (the Magot of verse) has given him first honors in this issue. I feel like puking - can't help it. Maybe he's really ggod.

> Yours
> Bill

Wolstonecraft: Mary Wollstonecraft (1759–1797), English feminist and author. Wife of
    William Godwin; mother of Mary Shelley.
Godwin: William Godwin (1756–1836), English social philosopher and novelist.
Williams: Edward Williams (1793–1822).
WAAC: Women's Army Auxiliary Corps. Established May 1942.
WAVE: Women Accepted for Voluntary Emergency Service. Established July 1942.
group in Poetry: Oscar Williams (1900–1964) published six poems in Poetry 61:5 (Febru-
    ary 1943).
Lope de Vega: (1562–1635), Spanish playwright, romancer and poet.
a book: The Wedge (Cummington, Mass.: The Cummington Press, 1944). Wallace A23.

202 Columbia Heights
Brooklyn, N.Y.

Feb 16/43

Dear Bill:

How did I guess that you wanted to do a book on Shakespeare? Because of what you've said about it in "Spring & All" etc. Anyway I said something about it a long time ago – in my essay on Am. Poesy in Jan 1934 issue of Symposium.

Yup – your method of handling such a book would be along my lines if I were to etc. I wouldn't, because I'm satisfied to read the text & say that's Shakespeare. One can, like Stephen in "Ulysses", get up a whole train of conjecture, very stimulating & based on the text – if one wishes to infer Shakespeare's person from what he seems to have understood – & then say one doesn't believe a word of it. On the other hand, I think you'll find full support for your WAAC-WAVE conjecture in "Twelfth Night." Viola don't go around in pants for nuthn in that play – the integrity of Shakespeare's cadence as to that matter commits him to such an "indiscrete" (yr. word) position as you conjecture. A guy doesn't write that way unless he knows. On the other hand a man doesn't have to bugger or be buggered to understand and know what Shakespeare did. – Or, hell, there are more things in heaven and earth than you or I, Horatio, etc. The trouble with writing such a book would be everybody would put you down as a bugger <ever> after. So fuck 'em before you do!

There's nothing, absolutely nothing in Oscar Williams – why let him worry you. Why even bother reading it?

Celia by some strange coincidence is being paid to play the piano at Union College (I'm not sure of the name) in Rutherford, this Sat. night – some function or other. I was thinking last night – before I got your letter – if you're free I could turn up to see you at <your> home about 8 and then meet Celia later at the train, because it'll probably be too late for her to turn up too. Anyway, if you're free, let me know. No, don't bother about dinner for me, we'll have eaten at home etc.

Our best to you both

Louis

P.S. The pretty letter paper is my sister-in-law's not Celia's.
Shakespeare.

my essay: "American Poetry 1920–1930," *The Symposium* 2:1 (January 1931). Reprinted in *Prepositions +*.

9 Ridge Road, Rutherford, N.J.

Feb.17, 1943

Dear Louis:

By all means come on Saturday, at your own convenience. I presume Celia is to play at the Fairleigh-Dickinson Junior College. that's the only college there is in Rutherford. Or it may be she's going to play at the Union School. Whichever it is why can't we hear her? If she prefers otherwise that's one thing or perhaps it's a private affair. But if it's public I'd enjoy being present, so would Floss and maybe some others. I'm not pressing this. Come on Saturday when you're ready, if you want to bering Celia with you early I'll drive her to her appointment when she is ready.

Nothing much else to report – except worries over the war.

Yours

Bill

9 Ridge Road
Rutherford, N.J.

March 3, 1943

Dear Celia:

I'm answering for Florence to say that we'll be there on Saturday as close to 6 o'clock as possible PROVIDED some gal doesn't go into labor too near that time. If that should occur I'll phone you as soon as I know we are definitel stuck. I think things will be all right.

I'll bring the TEST OF POETRY with me. It is a fascinating and important book. In fact it is so important to me that I feel that nothing else should be published, no other poetry until that appears. It is like a Chinese wall separating the civilized from the barbarian! I mean to say that most of it is slops, horrible slops and as abundant as slops.

Please tell Louis that I want the book. Mrs. Hoagland told me today that she would tuype it for me. I mention these things to say that the book is a landmark. Not that certain criticisms might not be validly advanced – but that is all of secondary importance. I'll never stop until the book is printed.

Yours

Bill

A TEST: *A Test of Poetry* (Brooklyn, N.Y.: The Objectivist Press, 1948). In a letter of 21 February 1943, Williams had brought *A Test* to the attention of James Laughlin. *WCW/JL*, 86–87.

431. TCS

[Postmarked Rutherford, N.J.]

[Postmarked 7 March 1943]

Lucky we didn't keep to our plan to go in through this soup: a maternity case is just starting now at 4.30 o'clock. What a day. inside and out! As I told you over the phone I'm starting to put the pressure on for your book wherever I can. It must first be typed in multiple, as least two more copies, then we'll see. A friend, you met him at I.B. Fisher or Fischer Co is interested but doubts that this is the time for it due to the undoubted lack of paper. Maybe by hitting at the top we may get through. Why not? More of this later.

My book of new stuff is shaping up, I should have the final (first copies) of the final group to go in by the middle of next week. More at that time

    Bill

your book: *A Test of Poetry.*
a friend: See Zukofsky's letter of 10 November 1942.
My book: *The Wedge.*

432. ACS

202 Columbia Heights
Brooklyn, N.Y.

[Postmarked 8 March 1943]
Mon.

Celia says dinner, here, March 20 (Sat.) is definite. So we hope nothing'll prevent Floss & you from coming about six, or as soon after is convenient. Thanks for the card, and please thank Kitty Hoagland for taking over the job of typing "Test of Poetry." I suppose if we knew someone with the bigger publishers, we cold put pressure on them, too, in this matter. But thanks again wherever you put it. I look forward to the Ms. of yr. new book whenever you're ready. – Our best, then,

    Louis

yr. new book: *The Wedge.*

433. ALS-1

[Rutherford, N.J.]

3/9/43

Could you, offhand, name a script or two, not your own, that you think deserves or deserve to be published?

    Bill

[202 Columbia Heights
Brooklyn, New York]

3/10/43

Dear Bill,

Scripts, not my own, James Laughlin could publish:

1) Lorine Niedecker has, or can gather, several volumes of poems
2) Basil Bunting's Caveat Emptor of which I have the ms, J. L. refused it a long time ago – it's better than the work of any Englishman he's published.
3) I'm sure it would surprise Charles Reznikoff if JIV ever thought of asking him etc
4) Bob Evans' Below the Grass Roots (poems); also a novel on the Pa. miners, the first part of which I read and thought very good. It wouldn't cost much to get out the poems, or the best of them, in the Poets of the Month series, & might give Bob who has been dying for over two years now some urge to live.

As for myself, I'm almost certain I sent him "Test of Poetry" – a few years ago – or that I at least mentioned it to him as something I had on hand. The enclosure – please return it – will explain the general attitude to me.

Therefore, I've no objection to his seeing "Test of Poetry" when it is typed, but I hope he understands that if he wants it he'll take it without any revision, and under contract, with an advance. If the last paragraph of his letter is worth anything, it might occur to him that some guys like me don't even have time to look at the sun or the snow in Bklyn (let alone Sandy, Utah), or can't think of having a kid without thinking first of having to feed him.

See what you got yourself in for trying to help! Best to you both & C's best

Louis.

Caveat Emptor: Bunting assembled this collection of his poems in 1935. Although he offered it to various publishers, there were no buyers.

Below the Grass Roots: This volume, as well as the "novel on the P[ennsylvani]a. miners" has not been published.

Poets of the Month series: A paperback series begun by New Directions in January 1941. Williams had been the first "Poet of the Month." Wallace A22.

enclosure: Enclosure lacking.

Sandy, Utah: James Laughlin had written to Williams on 6 March 1943 from Sandy, Utah, where he was skiing. See WCW/JL, 87.

[Rutherford, N.J.]

March 21, 1943
1st day of Spring!
Dear Louis:

Up betimes (about quarter to eight) to get going before someone gets me first.

Celia's music is something I could listen to for hours, the antithesis of all the shouting and spouting, distortion and clouding of words and phrases that is opera. The music holds the words in its amber, assists them to be seen. It calls for a kind of writing too. That's not all, either. I watched the phrasing and the alternation of phrasing – thinking of a long work, asking myself whether there was variety enough, resilience enough in the manner to give it range for such a tremendous gamut as Shakespeare demands. Could one sit through two hours and a half of it and still find invention enough to pole the jaded senses – or, by God, annihilate them if necessary? The answer, I think, from what I heard, is yes. There's plenty of art in the woman – the terminations of her phrases are full of variety.

No use going overboard with wild expectations, we've had enough of the bitter wine for that. But there is no reason why we should not look forward to more of this music. I confess I have had my eyes opened – again. Now I want to hear some of your own things sung.

We enjoyed the party and all that went with it. Just as soon as I am able I'll send you the tome of my new book of poems by express – the damned book has assumed the proportions of a tome – and ask you to slash it unmercifully. Not that I intend to take your advice holus bolus, I don't but I'd like you to indicate for me just how much could be cut from the script without hurting it, in fact I want you to help me get rid of the downright bad scribbles and the worst of the repetitious ones. Don't hesitate, go to town, cut the whole damned book out if you feel like it. If Celia has anything to say about the book and feels like sparing the time I'd like her opinion too. Just as she feels.

Laughlin's card enclosed. I don't know what to do about him. Nothing, I suspect.

As to the rest, for God's sake don't you go and get labor pains. Nobody knows the future, just nobody – except, of course, that we'll all be alike before very long. So take it as it comes. The old world can always use another. Best to you both.
    Bill

new book: *The Wedge.*
Laughlin's card: Enclosure lacking.

[Rutherford, N.J.]

March 27, 1943

Dear Louis:

Under separate cover I am sending the conglomorate of scripts of which I have spoken to you. It is obviously not a book. I don't want to burden you nor am I asking you to make a book of it for me. There is the idea of a book there as may, with good will, be inferred from the title. Perhaps a book will come of it in the end.

The first question I have to decide is whether to make a small select or a large inclusive collection. What I should like you to do if you have the time and inclination to do so is to brush over the miscellany and check whatever high points – or let them catch you – if there are any to be found. At the same time, if you will, I'd appreciate your indicating the things, and I know there are a number in this class, that you'd positively throw into the discard.

Don't make a labor of this. Don't even look at the mess if you have something better to do with your time. Floss and I are going out to see the grandson. We'll be gone a week. When I return I'll ask you to ship the script back to me when I shall hope to find a few red and black pencil checks here and there on the pages to indicate your opinion.

Naturally, if you want to tell me how the book should be constructed (now only slung together assways) that's up to you. I'll probably follow my own advices in the end anyway so don't waste your time.

Our best to Celia. I've dropped Laughlin a card telling of Evans' death and suggesting that he write to his widow for the scripts. What he'll do, if anything, I don't know but I thought that if he writes to Mrs. Evans it would be wise, if possible, for you to make a selection of the poems, sufficient for a pamphlet, etc That's all. I gotta go.

    Yours

    Bill

the title: Williams's first title for the manuscript was THE (lang)WEDGE.

grandson: Paul Herman Williams, Jr., born 3 August 1942.

Evans' death: Evans's letters to Zukofsky indicate he had been suffering from cancer for several years. At one point the typescript for *Anew* contained an elegy, "Robert Allison Evans" (Yale).

[copy in Louis Zukofsky's hand] Madison, Ohio

Mar 31/43

Here it is, the great American rolling mill, rolls you out flat, hot or cold, to desired thinness. Paul's workshop. A hyper-stimulated people, all look alike, fast eaters, polished like ball-bearings – and they do. Hope the litter and script arrived OK.

    Bill

(p.c. Republic Iron & Steel Company Mill)

Paul's workshop: Paul Herman Williams.

■ 438. ACS

[Postmarked Rutherford, N.J.]

[Postmarked 6 April 1943]

Home again Slightly the worse for wear but all in one piece for all that. Thanks for the card. No hurry about the script but when you can shoot it back, I'll take care of the postage later.

    Bill

■ 439. ALS-2

[202 Columbia Heights
Brooklyn, New York]

Tues Apr 6/43

Dear Bill,

Here y'are! Don't accept the detailed criticism in the manuscript unless it verifies your own misgivings, doubts etc. I've written in the MS. lightly so it can be erased & you can still use the copy.

There's a big book in it <(in size and more)> & if you mean it as summary, there's no reason why it shouldn't be an <u>inclusive</u> collection. As that, it arranges itself in my mind in an order along the lines outlined on the attached sheet. If you prefer to <be> more serious about the title, perhaps you might call it <(simply)> <u>The Language</u>. In any case, it's your summary of what you've done with, & to, it over some time – or in your life.

And if I change as to some of the criticism and arrangement offered here, after some months or whenever, you can blame it on <my> present state of affairs. The Board of Education surprised me (and the chairman of my department at the Brooklyn Tech H.S.) by appointing a duly licensed Lab. Asst in Physics in my place. So now I have to depend on day to day substitute work –

of which there may not be many days in the spring. My chairman had assured me the job would last thru June & probably go on thru next year. And I had banked on that – at least, well, as you know. Some fun, eh?

Etc. Lemme know what you think about all these jottings etc.

Our best to you both

Yrs

Louis

detailed criticism: Zukofsky's comments on the manuscript of *The Wedge*. The draft Zukofsky saw was titled THE (lang)WEDGE. Williams accepted Zukofsky's suggestion; he crossed out the title and wrote instead, "The Language."

attached sheet: Zukofsky divided the draft into four sections and listed the poems he suggested for each of the sections (Buffalo).

440. TLS-1

9 Ridge Road, Rutherford, N.J.

April 9, 1943

Dear Louis:

Thank you for your assistance, I have not as yet had time to check your work but from what I have glimpsed I can say at once that it is invaluable to me and I deeply appreciate what you have done.

I wish I could do as much for you. I have not even read the play , nor have I made more than a slight beginning on the work that will be necessary before the Test of Poetry can be brought to attention. I'm not forgetting.

The school situation you report puzzles me. I can't see why in bloody hell you can't find something congenial to do. Hoagland at the Sun, as an example, says he can't offer you the job of a copy boy and I suppose that is part of the picture. These are things I am powerless to cope with for you. I wish I knew an answer.

I'll work again at the book taking most of your suggestions I am sure and then ship you a copy for your amusement. Maybe it'll get published somewhere. I enclose stamps.

Bill

the play: *Arise, Arise.*

the book: *The Wedge.*

441. ALS-3

9 Ridge Road
Rutherford, N.J.

April 9, 1943

Dear Louis:

Excellent criticism, hard enough at times – but salutary. Hell, who's a poet? Christ knows no one is – mostly. I don't like snips of poems left alone on the page & sometimes its that or total discard unless some less worthy tissue is left to hold that up. A man can't be all eye, all tongue or all cocksure as are these bits. We'll see. I'll send you a copy of the script to glance at – as I say – & burn after if you don't want your rooms to be cluttered.

I enclose a card which may be the first step to something in Evans' memory. Please advise Mrs. E. – but as I say don't let her overplay the part. 15 or twenty of Evans best things might be enough.

I'm delighted that we've made a start.

W̲̲

a post card from Laughlin (<u>which I have mislaid</u>) says he is writing to Mrs. Evans for the script of Evans poems

442. TLS-1

[Rutherford, N.J.]

April 11, 1943

Dear Louis:

Without waiting to hear from you after my last scribbles I want to tell you that with your assistance I have succeeded in cutting 33 pages from the script I sent you to the great enhancement of what remains. It is now getting to be a book, one that I cannot read without a slight choking from the cumulative effect – almost as much from your arrangements of the individual pieces as from their separate virtues. I may make further cuts in the last section, perhaps five more items may fall before I am through. I deeply appreciate what you have done.

Friday and today I have been able to really sit down to the work for a few hours. I have adopted almost all your suggestions though not quite all. Almost all have resulted in improvements to the text. I have decided not to rearrange the long prose impovisations into lines. I have cut them here and there, worked over them where necessary and straightened out some of the typist's blunders but that is all. Also I have decided to go back to <the> original plan, not to group them but to use them between the formal verse groups as buffers. It will work all right that way, you'll see.

Now I've got to get to work and retype all that God damned mess again. I thought I was all set. There's hardly one piece that hasn't been altered in one way or another. What the hell? It'll just take a little longer. First I had to find the things, then get them in order, have them typed and now, after your friendly and decisive comments, I've got to go back to the grubbing again.

You really got to me that time. I've beeen troubled, upset, thrown off my balance – but instructed. I needed a good hot iron shoved into me for I was not a little lost. A splendid lesson. What will ultimately happen to the book is almost of no importance now. It IS A BOOK. I think even you will be surprised when the thing is finally put into shape. I'm going to dedicate it to you.

Bill

the script: The manuscript of *The Wedge*.

443. TLS-1

[Rutherford, N.J.]

Sunday afternoon [April 1943]

Dear Louis:

Have changed my mind for the third time, today I cut the book by about twenty three pages and that is final. So you won't have to do anything but put it in the drawer, at ease. I feel much better. I had almost to get a fever to do it – in fact I was helped by an article on gardening which said that the victory gardneers next year, it is hoped, will profit by their errors next year. That if you plant too much and have not the hardihood to weed out what you cannot use or that you have not the place for,the overabundance of no matter what you have growing is a WEED! Tear it up.

Had a nice letter from Bill Bird, show it to you some time.

And I sent a letter the other day to 102 Columbia Hts followed by another letter sent to 202 – Jesus Christ only knows where the first one went.

This cool weather has me nuts. I wanna.

Yours
Bill

In a few days, as soon as I have checked everything I'll send you my thing. Gonna read to this evening.

victory gardeners: During World War II, Americans were encouraged to plant their own vegetable gardens, called Victory Gardens.

letter from Bill Bird: Not located.

[Rutherford, N.J.]

May 11, 1943

Dear Louis:

I'm glad Maria Leiper followed up my suggestion as she did. May something come of it.

The work closed down on me again after my last communication so that for several weeks there was nothing for me to do but follow my practice. The book slumped and I had several changes of heart concerning it.

After considerable thought and the discovery of several poems which I had forgotten about, a decision to include several which I had rejected and a final determination to cut out the prose bits entirely the collection has been finally made up – after considerable effort. This was the sort of thing I wanted to avoid but I couldn't escape. If it doesn't involve heart searching and hard work nothing evolves satisfactorily. After I have made sure that I have a copy of everything I'll ship the book to Simon & Schuster. They'll probably reject it and then the game will be on.

I may want to ask your advice about the book as it has finally showed itself to be but that will come later. That is, if it is to be published I'll want to fine comb it before it goes to print and that is when I may ask you to look it over again. It's quite a different thing from the first huggle muggle I sent you.

I will now read your play. It's the first time I've fet that I wanted to read anything recently and return it to you with any comments I find I can make in a day or two.

I know Celia will appreciate and perhaps demonstrate the truth of a comment made by one of my older patients the other day to the effect that "the younger generation is putting up quite a front nowadays". I hope she keeps feeling fit.

     Yours

     Bill

Leiper: Leiper (b. 1906) had been an editor with Simon and Schuster since 1932.

The book: *The Wedge.*

your play: *Arise, Arise.*

[Rutherford, N.J.]

May 19, 1943

Dear Louis:

I tell you merely what I myself am attempting to learn, partly from you:

There is something exceptionally beautiful and fine about the play, which I am returning under separate cover, but it is almost lost in the lumber. Instead of moving in a lithe, spare and accomplished sequence of poetic episodes it stumbles and is lost among prosaic details of mechanism in which you have no aptitude and which have no place in a composition of this sort.

The good of the play lies only in certain speeches scattered through it and in the general poetic unfolding of the total conception which in the reading is only rescued by an analytic effort on the part of the reader which is not to be counted on.

Two thirds of the composition should be blue penciled. I'll tell you the same Virgil Thompson said to me when I showed him the libretto of the Geo. Washington piece. "What the hell do you know about the stage?" I confessed, "Nothing." And in your case I might add, What the hell do you know about music? I think, very little. You know something of the effects music achieves but that's all. Don't for God's sake imitate the Poundian stupidity in that Pound who can't know music and <u>therefore</u> keeps dragging it in.

In short, as Virgil Thompson said, "What are you writing?" "A poem." "Then for God's sake stick to that. Make it a poem pure and simple". If you must make musical notes that seem to you to be applicable and which, by the way, mean absolutely nothing to the reader, nothing unless <u>heard</u>, then keep them on a separate sheet for the possible stage production.

Omit all specific references to particular music, omit all but the barest stage directions, reference to curtains and even costuming. Omit them all – except on separate notes for possible production. You will then, as you yourself said to me recently, have a poem which, perhaps, someone familiar with the stage and music may be able to prepare for the stage. You will then be able to see what to cut, what should be in and what out; dull speeches without a single distinguishing word in them, by the doctor by the nurse and others, no point other than for the mechanical hitching up of a sequence which is false.

Read over what the Mother says, yoi will then get the cue to the rest.

The Attendants are not in character as negroes, not to me. Abd there is too much of them, too much of their speeches. They should be truly "attendants" almost completely silent or else really niggers. They belong all right but shd be, as you suggest, dancers.

In short the play should be cut drastically, removing everything but the most delicate and purest poetry to give a lightness, a rapidity that is lost here. Read, though I imply no comparison, this fantasy that is now a best seller, The Little Prince. You will get in that what – essentially – I mean. A mere touch should suffice. I stress, there is no comparison implied except in the quantity of material used to gain the effects.

For instance, all the opening scene of doctor, nurse could be cut to the one point, of How long have you been here? Five years. etc etc the same doctor? etc If that were brought out discretely with a touch perhaps of the relationship between the doctor and the nurse it would be all you need.

I know this is rather heavy handed criticism but it has to be so to cut loose what is you in your poems as in life. This play contains all your "faults" i.e. your virtues. It needs surgery. Your mind composes, you know, but you do not get it on the page. It just, often, isn't there – for a reader, escept he be a Sandow and even then he has to work too hard to retrieve it. You have no right to force that on anyone, you cant rightly expect it of one.

The bits you quote (perhaps you wrote them yourself) are startling the way they stand out. They are "realized", concrete, disparate. You do not "realize" your own virtues (here), you have them to a high degree but they are too knocked about, too bruised by their contexts to stand out as they should. You've got to make them clearer and more understandable, I wish you had a job.

     Yours

     Bill

The play: *Arise, Arise.*

Thompson: Virgil Thomson (1896–1989), American composer.

Washington piece: *The First President.*

The Little Prince: Antoine de Saint Exupéry, *The Little Prince* (New York: Harcourt-Brace and World, 1943).

Sandow: Eugene Sandow (1867–1925), renowned strongman and body-builder.

446. TLS-1

9 Ridge Road, Rutherford, N.J.

May 25, 1943

Dear Louis:

Whether or not what I say to you is worth a good God damn at least I'm pulling no punches. Same to you. Perhaps by kicking the bloody shit out of each other, if we're able, we may get a hell of a lot further than we ever have in the past. I don't for one moment enjoy being rubbed out by the publishing bastards and if by hook or by crook I could manoeuvre myself, by sheer ability, into making them print me I'd consider it a triumph. I see no good in high and lofty feelings of regret. I don't like it. I don't write to be pushed aside. I see no honor in being a "pure" artist who accepts defeat and the glorious isolation that comes with it. Nuts.

Well, Simon & Schuster turned me down also – with a few complimentary phrases to go with it. The strange thing is that if they had accepted my book I'd have been horribly disappointed. I'd have felt slightly disgraced in my own mind. Yet, I felt sick at the rejection. I'm going to send the book to every God damned publisher in the country before I'm through – you'd think there would be one who could find enough "paper" for it, especially so when you see what does get printed.

The older I get the more it stings me not to be in power, some sort of power, enough power to get done what I want done. It riles me to have to go on practicing Medicine with only a year left, a month or a week left perhaps before I'm deaf, blind paralysed or whatever it may be.

Did you see the Andrade article in the last issue of Poetry, or have I already spoken to you of that? It's good.

Well, so what? I could commit murder tonight if it would do any good. The principal of a school in a nearby town committed suicide by turnin on the gas because he had been caught committing sodomy. Geezus what a world . Many have been made princes for less. Poor guy. I tell Floss she's educated, enlightened, a flame in the dark because she has felt sad ever since the news came out today concerning the poor guy.

Well again. And so,

> Yours
> Bill

Andrade article: Jorge Carrera Andrade, "The New American and His Point of View toward Poetry," *Poetry* 62:2 (May 1943), 88–104.

447. ALS-1

[No return address]

May 28/43

Dear Bill:

The enclosure, if you wish to take it that way, a kind of reply to your last. No, I don't see no honor in being a "pure" artist – same like you – & don't write to be pushed aside.

Simon & Schuster's rejection of your volume makes me sick, too. But what can we do? They've got the power. If I had any money I'd start the Objectivist Press all over again & tell 'em to fuck a rubber duck – but if's don't help now.

Hope you have better luck with the book soon.

    Yours,

    Louis

enclosure: Enclosure lacking, but references in the following letter indicate it was a copy of Zukofsky's poem beginning, "You three:—my wife," (poem 42 of *Anew*). *CSP*, 99–102.

448. TLS-1

9 Ridge Road
Rutherford, N.J.

May 29, 1943

Dear Louis:

The best you have ever written, in my calm opinion. Most important for that, nearly as important because it seems to me to inaugurate a more explicit style in you. I refuse to criticis any man drastically until I can say something good about his work. But now I've got to say that much that you have written in the past, graphic as it might be, has been too broken, too unexplicit to bridge the gap between the writer and the reader, myself the reader. Not that I am a measuring rod or than anyone needs to approach me in his own mind. I believe, for all that that it was a fault. You were overimpressed by the theories of the objectivist approach. It was paralyzing, starving you, it made jerky, "hysterical" reading.

This piece flows as much of your poems do not flow. It has organic organization, word sequnce that is modled after speech. The mind may jerk from point to point, as may the eye, but speech is only as strong as its weakest link.

A specific criticism of the poem remains. To bring in the toes and the details of the morning toilet is excellent, full of proper pathos and justly in place. But I don't like the word "grouchy". That is not serious, not important and out of key. In fact even the "Okay! poet etc I don't like. In fact I don't like the sentence as a question. I'd be inclined to cut out both those stanzas. The rest of the poem is so very serious to moving, so correctly "placed" that those two stanzas stick out worse than a sore thumb.

A book of poems in that style and you'd be where you rightly deserve to be, at the top in recognition as well as merit. You have chopped yourself up for some reason, from starvation, from finikiness (at times) from a false arrogance which comes from weakness and nothing else. With a flow as of blood in the arteries that may have a pulse but isn't jerky and intermottent but steady and uninterrupted – you will produce a body of verse that a man of judgement and feeling will want to own.

Duell, Sloane & Pierce have the script (of my poems) now. There are encouraging signs. My best to Celia.

> Yours
> Bill

Why don't you send this poem to Partisan Review

Duell, Sloane & Pierce: A New York publishing firm founded in 1939.
Partisan Review: *Anew* 42 appeared first in *Anew*.

449. TLS-1

> 9 Ridge Road
> Rutherford, N.J.

June 4, 1943
Dear Louis:

A strange thing happened yesterday, one of those detached phenomena that might, on occasion, determine the future of the world. Here it is.

The postman delivered some mail. Floss went out to pick it up and found that it was just or appeared to be just a magazine in an envelope. As she took this out of the basket a card, which the postman must have dropped in there for his own convenience, fell out in the air. Floss saw it go and at the same moment thought she recognized your handwriting on it.

The card slid through the air and miracle of miracles entered the slit under the sill of the front door, not under the door but under the sill to the door and disappeared from sight, completely disappeared.

This morning I fished for it with a long knife but it is gone. We'd have to rip the whole bottom of the entryway out to retrieve it. Isn't that the damndest thing? The reason I write to you of it is that Floss thought it was your card. If so what the hell was on it? Was it about your new job concerning which we have already had a communication?

No word as yet from Duell, Sloan & Pearce.

> Yrs
> Bill

450. TLS-1

> 9 Ridge Road, Rutherford, N.J.

July 7, 1943
Dear Louis:

Nothing much to report. Duell, Sloane & Pearce turned the book down just as Simon & Schuster had done. I let it go at that. After a time I'll go over the thing, take out a few, add any that may have been written during the summer and perhaps try someone else. Perhaps I'll do nothing at all but wait until I get a lead somewhere.

Did you see the issue of a new magazine edited by Goll? Hemispheres, he calls it. He lives somewhere near you.

New Republic is publishing a small anthology of "modern" or at least recent American verse by certain selected poets, the selection being their own. I have been asked to contribute something for their approval. In other words, if they don't like it they won't print it. I sent them something that has been lying around unfinished for three or four years waiting for such an occasion. Something different from my usual line. If they return it I'll send it to you, if they print it you'll see it anyway.

Had a letter from Bill this morning, a letter written a month ago from his tropic isle. He's drinking water distilled from the sea topped off by the juice of green cocoanuts which he says is more delicious than that from the ripe fruit. He's living in a tent close to the sea. Recently (at the time of the writing of the letter) he had put through a night in a tent during a downpour, the lightning and thunder keeping pace with the tremendous pounding of the surf. Everything about the camp is drenched with salt spray to such an extent that they can never get their clothes to dry. He had to revaccinate his battalion or company or section or whatever it is. At about the same time the men were ordered on firing duty, a practice bout as I understand it. The rifle strap is pulled tight across the upper part of the left arm, exactly where the vaccination is made. He said none of the men complained.

Paul has been told that his credentials are satisfactory and to stand by for induction within six weeks. He hopes to go to Harvard for a three months course.

The work is somewhat lighter than earlier in the year so that at times I have an hour or two to myself for gardening or reading but, for the moment, there's little inclination toward composition.

We did get into New York with the Hoaglands to see the Pulitzer Prize play, The Skin of Our Teeth. It's surprising what those theatre guys get away with. But then there's always Edgar Guest.

Our best to Celia, glad you're working even if it isn't precisely as you'd like it.
    Sincerely
    Bill

new magazine: *Hemispheres* (Brooklyn, New York), was founded in 1943 and edited by
    Yvan Goll. Part of "The Clouds" appeared in the first issue (Wallace C332).
small anthology: No such anthology appeared.
something: Unidentified.
The Skin of Our Teeth: A play by Thornton Wilder. It won a Pulitzer prize in 1942.
Guest: Edgar A. Guest (1881–1959), English-born American author of popular verse.

[no return address]

Sept 5/43

Dear Bill

I see your last letter which I haven't answered is dated July 7. But I have 3 days off now, or rather 1 left. How have you both been and what do you hear from Bill & Paul?

Not much news. I am no longer "on trial" at the radio plant. All I've done is read radio & write about it. <u>View</u> may print my article on the painter Guczul. Not to forget that I once wrote poetry – I've collected the enclosed (1935–1943). If I can get around <to> it, I'll write the 4, or at the most 5, short pieces I want to add to this collection. But the order as you have it is pretty much as I want it. Celia typed an extra copy for you, so <u>don't</u> return it.

She's been alright except for a pain in her hip which makes it hard for her to walk. Probably a cold or a muscular sprain – or perhaps as she says she's reached the stage of having to sit and wait for the baby. She'll be seeing her doctor this week.

[. . .]

My nephew is in India. So now all of us have our eyes on the other side of the world.

The poems are for your pleasure if they can give it. If they don't, don't bother. No need to comment unless you're inspired etc.

What happened to your book?

Our best to you & Floss

Louis

radio plant: Hazeltine Electronics Corporation, in Little Neck, New York.

my article: "Dometer Guczul," *View* 3:3 (Fall 1943). Reprinted in *Prepositions +*.

the enclosed: Enclosure lacking.

nephew: Daniel Zukowsky (b. 1924), the son of Morris Zukowsky. He served as a military policeman in New Delhi from 1944 to 1946.

[Rutherford, N.J.]

Sept. 7, 1943

Dear Louis:

Thanks for the poems, I'll read them by and by and, as you suggest, write only should the mood be on me. I'm in no mood now for anything worth while, just dreggish (if that's a word)

No, Paul's not at Harvard but at the Cornell Naval Trining Station taking a four month course. He has his wife and baby with him or near him to state it more properly.

Floss and I took a short vacation toward the end of August but I didn't get the swimming I wanted, not in the quantity I wanted. But what I got was paradise. I love the salt water, I'd soak in it from one year's end to the next if I could vary my latitude at will.

The book has been to all publishers and has been rejected by all. Now at the end Laughlin is suggesting that I send it to him on the chance that he might still be able to do it. Why not? The main thing is to get it printed if possible, now.

Our greetings to Celia, I wish her an easy time as I'm sure she has a good man to take care of her.

I see Marsden Hartley died, poor guy. We may get up a testimonial group statement of some sort by those who knew him and admired his work. What good, now? But I suppose it might as well be done, please don't ever do it for me, Just forget it – or remember the few things we shared in private, a few beliefs or common admirations. Shit with memorials nand I mean just that, shit. Sometimes I don't think it will be long.

That's a hell of a cheerful note to end a letter on.

    Yours

    Bill

Maybe before I send my book to Laughlin I should let you see it – to extract the worst bits. No I don't want to bother you, you've done enough. I'll slap away at it and let it go at that. Sorry I even added this postscript. Forget it.

[Williams wrote across this letter in large script, "discount 60%."]

Hartley: On 4 September 1943, Williams wrote to Robert McAlmon, "Floss always, for some reason, looks at the obituary notices in the N. Y. *Times* every morning. Yesterday she found the name of Marsden Hartley" (*Selected Letters*, 216).

my book: *The Wedge*.

453. ALS-2

[No return address]

Sept 9/43

Dear Bill,

Alright, I'll discount your "It won't be long now" 60%. The other 40% – which tells me that by and large we'll all kick off one of these days ain't too fruitful a thought to produce a memorial. So you see you've got nothing to worry about. Besides I suspect that being the least bit immortal myself I wrote your memorial back in 1930 or thereabouts and that the world has since be-

haved as if I were my own memorial, so I've got you & you've got me comin'
and going – so you better resign yourself to long life. What other choice have
you?!

The postcards which you may want to show to someone else are amazing.

Aw shit, if we're dying at all, I guess it's for lack of good fellowship or as
Shakespeare might put it for lack of time.

Who'd have thought even five years ago that the American army would be
in Italy. By the way, if the Am. army has really landed in Genoa, that's not far
from Rapallo & Ez is in the Am. Army's arms? Unless he's escaped to "bar-
baric" Spain, or nootral Switzerland. Or "Ezra in Sweden" for the title of ???.
The comedy vies with the tragedy. I suppose Shakespeare could have written a
tragedy on the fall of Mussolini, with Ez. as a minor counsellor, but even that
would have been Richard the Thirdish.

That's about as far as my mind will carry me after a day's work in Little
Neck. We're all our age's little neckers. Phfut!

Send me your book if you want to – I won't be able to concentrate enough
on individual lines, but if there's a poem or two that might not come up to the
rest which I told you was good I'll say so. But please do exactly as you wish.

By the way, Celia finished one whole scene of Pericles & it's good – or did I
say so.

The best to you both & Celia's thanks for the good wishes to her

    Yours

    Louis

your memorial: "Beginning Again with William Carlos Williams (Postscript to 'Henry
    Adams')," *Hound and Horn* 4:2 (Winter 1931).

your book: *The Wedge.*

Pericles: Celia Zukofsky's music for *Pericles* was published as volume 2 of *Bottom: On*
    Shakespeare (Austin, Texas: Ark Press, 1963).

454. TLS-1

[Rutherford, N.J.]

Sept. 10, 1943

Dear Louis:

You called my bluff all right. I really want you to see the book as it now
stands – inflated! What I'll do is this, I'll send you a copy to keep, to file away,
to poke into from time to time. But I'll ask you to do me a favor, two things –
suggest a revised sequence for the poems and if you see any abortive attempts
or weak sisters please throw them out for me. No matter what the reason, don't
give any but suggest cuts if you feel that any should be made, whole poems this

time. Never mind the lines. Just say which you think had better be out to improve the book as a whole.

Haven't looked at your book as yet.

It wouldn't be fair to ask Celia to play her scene at this moment but I'm really very much interested to see what she has done with her transitions, really a fascinating project, as full of pleasure for the ear as well as meat for the mind. I hope to see a full dress performance of the work some day not too distant.

Keep up your strength, labors are exhausting to fathers and there's no joke about that Esquire notwithstanding.

  Sincerely
  Bill

the book: *The Wedge.*

your book: A typescript of *Anew.*

her scene: See the preceding letter.

Esquire: A sophisticated men's magazine that featured cartoons about adult life.

455. TLS-1

[Rutherford, N.J.]

9/11/43

Look Louis:

(sorry to intrude again) I think the book's got too much in it, too much of the same; as one friend (inexpert) said, It's monotonous, just like that.

Not to burden you, to make it more amusing to look over the script, easier I will do this: I'll strip the book down to what I consider the best pieces. I'll put these in the first part.

Following that will be the balance of the poems. Now, if there is any poem in the second lot that you think should absolutely be placed in the first group or replace one in the first group, indicate it – if you please.

Is the Frenchman around and would he sing, could he sing Celia's Scene? I am all for getting up an evening, a good, properly selected singer, Celia at the piano, a few people who should be admitted, Paul Rosenfled would furnish the piano and the room at his apartment . . I think it would be something.

I'm reading your book over the weekend. Delivered a baby between 3a.m. and 5.30 a.m. today then gave two anesthesias for tonsilectomies at 9 and 9.30. Just finished office hours for the afternoon now. Must go out in the yard and dig a little.

  Yours
  Bill

the book's: *The Wedge.*

one friend: Unidentified.

Frenchman: Probably Yves Tinayre.

Celia's scene: Celia Zukofsky's musical adaptation of a scene from Shakespeare's *Pericles*.

Rosenfled: Paul Rosenfeld (1890–1946), critic of literature, art and music. Author of *Modern Tendencies in Music* (1927), *Discoveries of a Music Critic* (1936) and other books. Williams contributed an essay, "A Poet Remembers," to the memorial volume, *Paul Rosenfeld: Voyager in the Arts*, ed. Jerome Mellquist and Lucie Wiese (New York: Creative Age Press, 1948), 154–57.

your book: A typescript of *Anew*.

456. ACS

[Rutherford, N.J.]

[Postmarked 17 September 1943]

I am keeping the script destined for you until I can make an accurate copy for my own use. The original copy is still going the rounds. Recently it came back from Farrar & Rinehart where it was looked at by a "Harvard man" who decreed that it was not good enough for publication. I'll answer Celia later, we'll see.

> Bill

script: The manuscript for *The Wedge*.

Farrar & Rinehart: This New York firm had published Archibald MacLeish, John Gould Fletcher, and Stephen Vincent Benét.

457. ACS

[Rutherford, N.J.]

[Postmarked 24 September 1943]

Script on its way to you: save the stamps for me if you don't want them & somebody hasn't stolen them before arrival. Cummington Press is bringing the book out, due next March. Let me know if you want to tear out & discard any of the verses.

> Bill

script: The manuscript of *The Wedge*.

Cummington Press: The Cummington Press, operated by Harry Duncan and Paul Williams, and located in Cummington, Massachusetts, published *The Wedge* on 27 September 1944.

9 Ridge Road,
Rutherford, N.J.

Sept. 27, 1943

Dear Louis:

[. . .]

Really, you have nothing to fear as long as you are in the hands of a good man – which is the case here. better for Celia and far better for the baby. Let us know the time & the place when the date arrives.

Forget the script. Thanks for returning the stamps. No great news other than that we've been asked to see Porgy & Bess tomorrow evening.

Our love to Celia. Tell her she'll be all right.

> Yours
> Bill

script: The manuscript of *The Wedge*.

Porgy & Bess: George Gershwin's opera had premiered in New York on 10 October 1935. A 1943 New York revival ran from January to the end of September.

9 Ridge Road,
Rutherford, N.J.

Oct. 5, 1943

Dear Louis:

Thanks you for your pains with the script. I have adopted all your suggestions and corrected all the errors you detected. I have deleted the poems entire which you found fault with, all except the Ford Madox Ford piece. In that I cut the first stanza, all except the first line,which has been left standing alone to the great improvement of the whole poem.

I have said nothing about your book of poems. I don't know what to say. Certainly they are cryptic in my eyes. I see that they are objects, unique objects, like shells on a shore of some land quite unknown to me, in most cases. As objects they have decided interest but what their significance can be, in most cases, is more than I can say. I am waiting to read them again, I'll read them several times before I make any definite comment. Certainly they are like nothing else, but what disturbs me most is the lack of emotional impact. I am repelled by the impenetrability of the words – or the words that just ain't there, to my ears. I don't know what the hell to say. Your poems make my own work <seem> juvenile, considered as constructions. I nevertheless come away baffled. Witter Bynner wrote practically the same thing to me relative to my own work. What the hell? Maybe you're the ultimate genius. Wish I had the answer. All I can say is that I like your style.

> Sincerely
> Bill

Ford piece: "To Ford Madox Ford in Heaven."
your book: A typescript of *Anew*.
Witter Bynner: American poet (1881–1968).

460. TLS-1

Oct. 24, 1943
Dear Louis:

Above all else congratulations on the birth of young Paul and that Celia has come through it without accident. I knew that barring the unforeseeable there would be no difficulty. Now it's over and – you'll have another ration book! Make good use of it.

What else is there to say? The back yard's full of birds and flowers, we've had no frost as yet: crysanthemums, cosmos, with goldfinches hanging upside down under the seed clusters eating the ripe seeds, a few late petunias, white throated sparrows, juncos, starlings, purple grackle and the ubiquitous passer domesticus – running all around among the dry leaves, dodging the grey squirrels even taking a bath where we've put water for them. There are still even a few roses. Tell your son, some day, that that was the atmosphere he was born into.

I've been working, spasmodically (frantically, late at night as I am able) on the revision of that long To All Gentleness which I acknowledge was in a fine mess as you saw it. It's better now. Thanks for not accepting it as it was. Also I've been reading Melville's Pierre. It's a messily written novel, badly addressed, but with some places in it that can't be overlooked and with an overall seriousness about it that is all but unique in American letters. I have to skip page after page a t times but it's a good book.

> Give our live to Celia.

> Yours
> Bill

birth of young Paul: On 22 October 1943.
ration book: Necessities such as food, shoes, tires, and gasoline were rationed during
   wartime. Coupons entitling one to buy them were issued in ration books.
To All Gentleness: "To All Gentleness" was first published in *The Wedge*. CP2 68–72.
Pierre: *Pierre; or, the Ambiguities* (1852).

461. ACS

[Rutherford, N.J.]

[1943]

[In Florence Williams's hand, with printed message: "GREETINGS"]
Bill & Florence Williams
We hope before the baby goes to college to get over to see him!

462. ALS-1

9 Ridge Road, Rutherford, N.J.

10/27/43

The reading, to about 100 people, went all right – in the deluge! a strange
world of strangers.

W

reading: Williams read his "Introduction" to *The Wedge* at the New York Public Library
on 26 October 1943. See Mariani 482.

463. TLS-1

9 Ridge Road, Rutherford, N.J.

January 3, 1944

Dear Louis:

For you and Louis a book which I am sure you'll enjoy looking into, a translation by a very distant cousin of mine Sister Felicia of the Episcopal Order of St Ann, a nun. But that I put in merely to amuse you. The real thing is the book itself and the superb job the gal made of it. I think it a masterpiece, a solid contribution to our American literature, beautiful language entirely our own – unsmirched by English but scholarly in the finest sense. Fun to read for the pious saltiness of the old Spaniard primarily of course, something noteworthy in itself with which we are not sufficiently familiar, 16th century Spanish lit.

Paul's at sea on a destriyer and Bill's still in the far Pacific. We have Paul's wife and 17 months old son here with us for a while. I hope you and yours are doing well.

Yours
Bill

a book: Luis Ponce de León, *The Perfect Wife*, trans. Sister Felicia, O.S.A. (Denton, Texas:
The College Press of the Texas State College for Women, 1943). Sister Felicia's name
before she became a nun was Alice Philena Hubbard.
Paul's wife: Virginia Carnes Williams.
17 months old son: Paul Williams, Jr.

9 Ridge Road, Rutherford, New Jersey

March 15, 1944

Dear Louis:

Floss was saying the other night she wondered how the little red-head was coming on and that she'd like to go over and see him sometime. I said I'd write and tell you.

Two weeks ago tomorrow night Bill and Paul were here together for supper. It was a wonderful thing to have the two of them at home again that way. The next day Paul left for Key West Florida to attend the Fleet Sound School for special training in what I believe to be submarine detection. He is a member of a destroyer crew and will have to join his ship again as soon as the school finishes with him. His wife and baby are here in Rutherford though not with us. Jinny is expecting another come August.

Bill returned after 20 months in the South Seas. He is 30 now, somewhat sobered by his experiences, a little bald but essentially the same. He said his greatest lack where he found himself stationed was good music on the radio. He had all the orchestras tuned in practically all the time he was at home, two weeks in all – I can't tell you how happy we were to see him again. He is engaged to be married to a navy nurse stationed in Pearl Harbor, a lovely girl. I hope the poor kids finally get together. Bill has gone again but this time no further than Camp Bainbridge in Maryland. We may see him frequently this spring.

I am working steadily day after day for longer hours than I like. No time is left for writing yet I do occasionally get in a swipe at the Paterson Introduction which I may finish in spite of everything this year – if I am lucky.

Floss keeps pretty well. You should have seen the difference in her after Bill and Paul returned. Paul had been on one trip in his ship to Africa, a terribly rough trip of which we haven't even now received the full details. Imagine Paul, a month out of school in control of a destroyer at night, jigzagging and keeping watch through a storm. He says the porpoises at first gave him heart failure, they approach the ship in exactly the manner of a torpedo then, just when the danger seems catastrophic they dive under the hull and come out the other side.

What a world these young men are seeing. The dark alleys of Casablanca while on guard duty expecting to be shot in the back by some Arab at any moment. Or the foul Melanesians washing, pissing, bathing in the same muddy water they take home to drink.

Yours

Bill

little red-head: Paul Zukofsky.

Jinny: Virginia Carnes Williams.

Paterson Introduction: Williams probably refers to *Paterson: Book I*. A few months later, however, Williams wrote James Laughlin that the title of *Paterson* as a whole would be *Paterson: Introduction* (*WCW/JL*, 105).

465. TLS-1

9 Ridge Road
Rutherford, N.J.

Sept. 11, 1944

Dear Louis:

Your note just arrived, I'll answer it at once, the only way for me. I note the new address, Floss and I will definitely run out to see you within the next few weeks. I note the phone address also, I'll call you first.

I go on writing though not what I'd most like to do i.e. work on Paterson, I haven't felt up to that . I did do some filing, to give it a name, even on that during my vacation in Connecticut early in July. That vacation was Paradise, pure and simple. I did nothing but move stones on the beach, chop wood and bathe. The bathing in salt water has always been my delight and my cure.

But summer back here in the office was Purgatory. I have felt exhausted; beginning to do better of late.

We are altering our second floor to make an apartment for Paul's wife, Jinny, and her two children. We have a one month old girl on the premises together with the two year old boy now. It is as it is, we enjoy the children – and Jinny also but it takes energy.

Bill is in the States as you may know, in a camp in Maryland. Paul is at sea.

As I said, I occasionally write a thing or two. A Cuban magazine, Origines, is printing one piece and Quarterly Review of Literature, Chapel Hill, is doing another. And, now that I think of it, some Canadian Literary Journal will probably bring out a third. Then a "new magazine" to be called Et Cetera, from Cleveland, Ohio, a mag whose policy is to select the personalities wanted and then give the selectee free rein – has asked me for a group which I have been scrambling to get together – about 8 poems, a year's work!

Most important along this direction is that the small book The Wedge will be out tomorrow. It has been plain hell to get it printed and bound. It was promised for last March. Finally a binder was dug up (by me) so that the infant will be born – or may be born. I'll send you a copy within a week, I hope – it has to go back to Cummington and from there be shipped back to me – then to you.

So there you are. Our best to Celia and the infant. We're really going to make it this time. We've had little inclination to go anywhere during the hot weather.

> Yours
> Bill

I don't feel proud of my writing of late.

new address: The Zukofskys had moved to 35-44 163rd Street, Flushing, New York.

Jinny . . . children: Virginia Carnes Williams, Paul Williams, Jr., and Suzanne Williams.

one piece: "The Bitter World of Spring," *Orígenes* 1:3 (Autumn 1944), 22-23. Wallace C351.
  CP2, 132-33.

Another: Although unidentified, this would have been included in "Summary of a Year's
  Verse" [15 poems], *Quarterly Review of Literature* 2:2, 89-99. Wallace C352.

a third: No Canadian journal published poetry by Williams in 1945 or 1946.

Et Cetera: This journal apparently was never published.

A group: This appeared in *Quarterly Review of Literature.*

466. TLS-1

> 9 Ridge Road
> Rutherford, N.J.

Sept. 23, 1944
Dear Louis:
Thought of you today and was half of a mind to dash madly out to see you. But such is my present estate that I dreaded what tonight and tomorrow <might> do to me if I did not remain here and conserve my energy. There's evidence for you of my sixty first birthday just past! It isn't that I would hurt myself but I have noticed that fatigue, excessive fatigue wipes the slate of my brain as if with a wet cloth, I am a blank. It depresses me beyond words. There's no use in my trying to do what I used to do in running around.

Besides I wanted to bring The Wedge out to you in my hand but, although it has been printed and bound and must be in the hands of its publisher for more than ten days I haven't even heard of it. Were it not that I had a friend at the binders remove a set a sheets and see to it that they were bound separately by hand I would not even know what the book looks like. It is very attractive. Floss has the one copy, if the others were lost in the hurricane this one copy will constitute the whole edition. It is a thought.

I feel better tonight than I did this afternoon when I was about ready to go to the hospital of the sewer I didn't care which. No reason that I can think of for it, just emptiness.

Meanwhile I had a letter from Paul telling of swimming off some tropical

Crusoe's isle, the water infested by sharks, barracuda and octopuses, a guard sitting watch with a rifle in hand to ward off the fish – but he and another had to go on along a shore beside a jungle too dense for penetration where they swam the clear green water of an inlet to a cave, thrashing through the water to frighten possible marauders – to gather shells on the beach beyond. Such may be war, at times.

I've gathered a small collection of poems produced this past year, I have nothing to do with them though one or two will come out – one in Cuba, at Havana in a mag called Origenes (origins) and another will be used by the gang at Chapel Hill. If I can get them copied I'll send you a copy. I sent one today (enclosed) to Malcolm Cowley of New Republic. He may take it – unless the head editor sees it and happens to be a Presbyterian or business man. What the hell. The next mag that asks me for something will have to print me as I demand or not at all. I want a prominent place and at least ten pages to myself. Otherwise, no soap.

When I think of going anywhere I get a chill. It may be neurasthenia but I can't help it. I dread making any trips away from home. I hope I get over it. No doubt I'm plain hog tired. It wouldn't be any wonder if I were.

    Yours
    Bill

hurricane: A powerful hurricane affected the Atlantic coast from Cape Hatteras to Long
    Island on 14 September 1944.
small collection: See the preceding letter.
one in Cuba: See the preceding letter.
another: "Summary of a Year's Verse."
(enclosed): "Threnody" was published as part of "Summary of a Year's Verse" in *Quar-*
    terly Review of Literature. CP2, 99.

                    Threnody

            The Christian Coin -
            embossed with a dove and sword -
            is not wasted by war,
            rather it thrives on it
            and should be tossed
            into the sea for the fish
            to eye it as it falls
            past the clutching fingers
            of children -
            for them to eye it
            and sing, join in a choir

to rival the land and set

coral branches swaying:

Peace, peace to the oceans,

the dread hurricane die,

ice melt at the poles

and sharks be at rest!

as it drops lost to its grave.

467. TLS-1

9 Ridge Road
Rutherford, N.J.

Sept. 27, 1944

Dear Louis:

Not this weekend but the 6th looks all right, we'll take a run over there that day come hell or highwater. We ought to be able to leave here early in the afternoon to get there after four or so. Glad to stay for supper, thanks, but please don't go to any unusual pains. Can't you open a can of sardines? Jezus! I forgot. No sardines to be had I suppose. All right, caviare, sour cream and champagne.

The Wedge! Again, Jezus! It's lost! Never has arrived at the publishers from the binders. I don't know what jinx is on that book but it's a beaut. If it really has disappeared permanently we'll have just 6 copies left of the whole edition. Here's hoping.But it's been over two weeks now and no word of it. I'll let you know by card if they find it.

Add to that that the combined White Mule-In the Money volume which Laughlin was bringing out is stalled at the binders by reason of the sheets having been lost in transit . Time marches ON!

Yours
Bill

I'll get hold of Reznikoff's The Lion Hearted though to tell the truth I didn't even know it had been published until you told me.

combined . . . volume: *First Act* (New Directions, 1945). Wallace A21b.

The Lion Hearted: Charles Reznikoff, *The Lionhearted* (Philadelphia: Jewish Publication Society of America, 1944).

■ **468.** ALS-1

35– 44 163 St
Flushing, N.Y.

Sept 30/44

Dear Bill:

Good, Celia and I look forward to seeing Floss & you Sat. the 7th (not the 6th, my error) about 4.

If you come in the car, go up Northern Blvd. to 162nd St where Northern Blvd joins Crocheron Av. We're one block up and down part of that block, 163 St, to your left as you turn off Crocheron.

If you take the train, it's the Port Washington line, L.I.R.R. Stop at B'way. and we're about a block and a half away

So, we'll be seeing you.

> Yours
> Louis

P.S. There are trains at 2:42, 3:12, 3:42, 4:32 from Li.I. Sta. (Penn Terminal)

■ **469.** TLS-1

9 Ridge Road
Rutherford, N.J.

Oct. 2, 1944

Dear Louis:

Sorry about the change of date. I keep forgetting that you can't get off Fridays. You see, on Saturday I'm stuck here in the office almost the entire afternoon. We'd better make it Sunday. I'll run over in the afternoon fairly early and in that case not stay for supper. It will be best that way. I'll phone you some evening later in the week.

They finally caught up with the book, I received my quota this afternoon and will bring one with me the weekend. I suppose there are trains out there fairly regularly on Sundays as well as week days. I'll try to get Floss to come with me though she's hard to move these days with the new baby in the house.

> Best
> Bill

the book: *The Wedge.*

[Rutherford, N.J.]

[1944?]

Louis:

This – keep it. or return

    Bill

    The League to Support Poetry

    327 W. 18 St

    NY, 11, NY

    Dorothy Hobson

    Alfred ?

League to Support Poetry: Unidentified.

9 Ridge Road, Rutherford, New Jersey

December 22, 1944

Dear Louis:

Well I'll be damned, that's an odd one – that you should end up in Towson, Md, of all places [. . .]. Did you ever meet my old girl friend Mrs. Heath? A big, buxom gal with a Baltimore accent. She's no friend now if I'm to judge by her manner, but if you remember her and wish to brave her wrath or whatever the hell her Methodist past may bring out – look her up at 404 W Pennsylvania Ave. Towson Md. She has a husband and daughter. At least she sent us a Christmas card. I don't particularly recommend the call unless you knew her – I've forgot. She may know some place you could find an apartment. If you do see her give her my humble greetings which may or may not be humble but may be so spoken of. Same to Jerry.

Yasus! the world does move along – to what heaven I do not say, to eternal life and to perfection if we belive the grouped preacherdom. It would be nice – and for anything to the contracy may be so. Also may be anything but so and we had better make up our minds. I have decided, not so. But whichever way it is tragedy seems to be excluded. What the hell has happened to tragedy? Nobody believes in it – but the balled and even they do not for they are all gourmands and eat instead of other. I suppose tragedy goes only with an artistocracy and really means loss of cast, the only real tragedy! I wonder.

I have just been reading a really amazing, I was going to say wonderful, poem by André Breton (translated by Edouard Roditi) in the current View – a very good number. It's the Winter issue and costs one buck. Do you want it? The poem is one of those rarities – something simple coming out of an insensate complexity of method which may be the authentic mark of genius – it is, at least, the first time I myself ever saw any genius in Breton – though I have read little of his writing. Anyhow it's a good poem. There are other good things in the issue – good criticism by Calas and others – and some shit as always. The mag is picking up.

Both Paul and Bill will be home for Christmas I hope and believe. Paul is now at damage control school in Philadelphia after which he rejoins his ship. Bill is still at the boot training camp at Bainbridge – careing for niggers mostly – a wonderful opportunity, in a humane way, for him. He likes them but isn't bewildered by their social position, pretty bad mostly. I write whenevger I get the chance. Today I am at letters. I did a couple of critical pieces for two poets – a beginner named Vazakas and on Rexroth's The Phoenix and the Tortoise – a good though unnecessarily long winded book. Good work is still rare and really – not easy to find.

It really takes a lifetime not only to do anything worth while but even to find what we want in others – one is so unsure, so tentative because of lack of opposrtunity to observe. And any decent intelligence is humble at core, too humble to want to make to brash an assertion in a fluid world. Finally a small amount of positive statement is possible.

The war's rising to a grand climax in Eisenhower's character and that means the character of our whole middle west. As an auto-glass mechanic told me the other day, The trouble with this god damned countty is that we're trying to glamourize the war. For Christ's sake they guys over there are gettin'n cut up. They're bleedin' and dying. This is WAR, he said. Few know what is going on. We oppose killing without knowing the meaning of death. We hate violence, explosions, persecution, dismemberment and the filth and squalor od it all without realizing that only by that can be get to a knowledge of saintliness, cleanliness, peace. Only in war is peace born.

Don't think me sententious, or that I am parading my insignificant moods. I believe that something in war is the thing that will make us over – may my intelligence or the better knowledge correct me if I am wrong. In tragedy a man is reborn not merely purged. One dies, crushed by a tank, blown to hell, in an ecstacy of fear or unconcern or "heroism". But he does it for all, that others may live. I believe it. For if we do not have this feeling of solidarity we are nothing. I am not excusing war or inviting it. . We've got to try to make it impossible.

BUT in the stalemat that has been prevailing in the European war the char-acter of America, of our men was allowed to be that of a sort of specialized mechanic – but now the man, as a man, is being terribly tested and you can't tell me that it isn't affecting every last human being in our country. We are waiting, waiting.' not to win so much as to see ourselves tested by a desperate Germany, a dangerous individual who may annihilate not one man or ten or twenty thousand helpless (mentally) soldiers but us, you and me, now. That's the crisis. We'll be different men after this crisis – win or lose. For we may lose.

This has brown to be a long letter.

    Yours
    Bill

Mrs. Heath: Louise Heath. Although I have not been able to discover much about her, it is clear from a letter of 27 August 1943 from Heath to Williams that at one time they worked together. She recalls, "I remember so well the glance or expression that told me that you too had caught the delicious humor or perhaps the pathos hidden in some shared adventure. And those jaunts of ours were adventures to me." In the same letter she noted that her recommendation of Williams's work to another doctor met with the rejoinder that "I was certainly no judge since I was so obviously infatuated with you. Apparently it must stick out all over me" (Yale).

wonderful poem: André Breton, "Full Margin" [trans. Edouard Roditi], View 4:4 (December 1944), 132–33.

Calas: Nicholas Calas, "Auden's Time Being," View 4:4 (December 1944), 144, 146. Calas reviews W. H. Auden's For the Time Being (New York: Random House, 1944), observing, "Nothing original, nothing personal to be found in Auden's apostasy; and by exchanging A Season in Hell for the works of the Danish preacher [Kierkegaard], he has not acquired in his art a single virtue that he could not have developed without surrendering to mysticism."

critical pieces: "In Praise of Marriage," Quarterly Review of Literature 2:2, 145–149. Wallace C354. "Preface," Quarterly Review of Literature 2:4, 346–349. Wallace C361. The first of these is on Rexroth, the second on Vazakas.

472. ALS-1

                9 Ridge Road
                Rutherford, N.J.

[Zukofsky's notation: "Jan. 45"]
Please return "the Works" at your early convenience.
    Bill

"the Works": Probably "In Praise of Marriage" and "Preface."

[Rutherford, N.J.]

[Zukofsky's notation: "Jan. '45"]
This is the only copy I have at the moment.

629 Murdock Rd
Baltimore 12 Md.

Jan 23/45
Dear Bill,

I like your criticism much more than the examples of the verse you pin it to
– but pinning it to something is generous, too. At least it makes one feel that
something is continuing to happen. Anyway, I read the last page of the piece
on Vazakas several times after 12 hours at the plant yesterday – because it made
me feel like writing again.

You're right about the Breton piece in <u>View</u> – not all of it, but enough of it
has sparkle and passion. I'm holding on to <u>View</u> for a while to look thru more
of it.

      All the best, Celia's, to both of you
      Louis

piece on Vazakas: "Preface."
Breton piece: See Williams's letter of 22 December 1944.

35– 44 163 St
Flushing, N.Y.

Apr. 30/44 [1945]
Dear Bill,

We've been back since March 10th and I guess it's just inertia, overtime, etc
that keeps <me> from getting down to writing you. Too bad, since there ought
to be a lot to say in these historic times. I wish I could be happier about the fu-
ture than the enclosed. Maybe the future'll make it seem nonsense. In that case
we'll all be happier. Anyway, it's the end of an era. The dynasts are crumbling
again. Wonder where E.P. is after yesterday in Milan.

For the rest, Celia & I are tired, tho she's managed to do more Pericles. The
kid's beautiful: it walks, it talks & so on. <u>He</u>'s deservedly tired at the end of a day.

I take it you received the reviews, View etc which you sent while we were in
Baltimore?

How are you, Floss, the sons etc?

>Yours
>
>Louis

Enclosed: Enclosure lacking. Probably section 2 of "A Song for the Year's End," the earliest surviving manuscript version of which Zukofsky dated 16 April 1945. A typed draft of "A Song for the Year's End" is in the Williams papers at Yale. *CSP,* 111–12.

Milan: Benito Mussolini was executed by Italian partisans in Milan on 28 April 1945.

View: Williams had published "Paterson: The Falls" in *View* 3:1 (April 1943), 19. Wallace C330. *CP2,* 57–58.

476. TLS-1

>9 Ridge Road
>Rutherford, N.J.

May 8, 1945

Dear Louis:

Have been away for a few days. When I returned I found your letter with the poem enclosed, "the best he has ever written" says Floss with which I thoroughly agree. It moves, it is.

Our best to Celia. In spite of many difficulties there will still be a life for us in the days to come.

I wonder whether or not you have heard of the death of Joe Hecht. The poor Kid was in camp in Texas when, last January, he contracted Scarlet Fever. In spite of the best of care, as verified by Ted's brother who flew there to look into the case, things went wrong. The kid died last week. He was buried in Arlington Cemetary in Washington with full military honors. An interesting touch was that Rabbi Silverman of East Rutherford assisted at the ceremonies.

Almost at the very moment of the funeral I was recording a reading of my poems at the Library of Congress. More of that another time.

>Yours
>
>Bill

poem enclosed: "A Song for the Year's End."

Joe Hecht: The son of Ted and Kate Hecht.

a reading: Williams recorded a large number of his poems at the Library of Congress on 5 May 1945. Wallace F2.

9 Ridge Road
Rutherford, N.J.

Aug. 27, 1945
Dear Louis:

The wars having officially ended I begin to look around again and the first thing I notice is that I have lost your address – unless you have returned to this address from Baltimore on the chance of which being true I send this letter.

Drop me a line to say you are alive.

Yours
Bill

■ 478. TLS-1

9 Ridge Road
Rutherford, N.J.

Aug. 31, 1945
Dear Louis:

Don't tell me you're going into the Real Estate business! Jayzus! 's the best news I've heard in a long time.

We'll be seeing you this fall sometime or other but as yet we're hardly more at liberty to move than we've been for the past three years. Bill and Paul are both in the Pacific area and are like to be there for a good many months to come. Jinny and her kids are here with us as you know, lively as ever. But we'll manage. At the moment I'm planning to take my sensation starved daughter-in-law to Joe Gould's Birthday Party, Sept. 12th somewhere in Greenwich Village . It's a more or less open affair, why don't you come ? It'll be advertised somewhere or other before long.

I disagree with you on there being little beside my scribbles in the recent Literary Quarterly. I very much admired Rene Taupin's article. But where is that guy ? Do you have his address . Or do you disagree with me ? And why ? I think what he said was important.

Yours
Bill

Real Estate business: Perhaps a reference to Louis and Celia's plans to purchase a home at in Brooklyn.

Jinny: Virginia Carnes Williams.

Joe Gould's: Joseph Ferdinand Gould (1889–1957), notable Greenwich Village Bohemian.

My scribbles: "Summary of a Year's Verse" [fifteen poems], *Quarterly Review of Literature* 2:2 (1945), 89– 99; "The Fatal Blunder," 125– 26; "In Praise of Marriage," 145– 49. In

"The Fatal Blunder," Williams contends that T. S. Eliot misunderstands the significance of "place." "Obviously when Mr. T. S. Eliot in *Ash Wednesday* says—I'm sure he says it somewhere, he must have siad it somewhere since it constitutes his obvious fault—Here it is, *The place is always and only place / And what is actual is actual . . . only for one place.* —When he says a thing like that we know he must be either mad or asleep.

"If anything could be farther from the truth of experience or learning or philosophy or religion, since Mr. Eliot wishes us to take him most seriously on that score, I must confess my inability to find it." After further discussion about one's relation to place, Williams concludes, "We live only in one place at a time but far from being bound by it, only through it do we realize our freedom. Place then ceases to be a restriction, we do not have to abandon our familiar and known to achieve distinction but far from constricting ourselves, not searching for some release in some particular place, rather in that place, if we only make ourselves sufficiently aware of it, do join with others in other places."

Taupin's article: René Taupin, "The Supremacy of Lyricism," *Quarterly Review of Literature* 2:2 (1950), 127–32.

479. ALS-1

35– 44 163 St
Flushing, N.Y.

Sept 7/45

Dear Bill:

I doubt if I'll be able to get to Joe Gould's party. So have a good time there and give him my best wishes.

René hasn't been in touch with us for two years or more, but I guess he's still in Pearl River, and a letter c/o the French Dep't, Hunter College should reach him.

His article in Literary Quarterly is eloquent, intelligent history of literature etc, but I was thinking of poetry when I failed to mention it. Anyway, what he says was said better under our joint names in "Le Style Apollinaire," English aboriginal in Westminster Magazine (georgia) back in 1934 or thereabouts – 3rd installment, the pages on <u>Etc.</u> – said more truthfully & I'm afraid I'm still the only one who thinks said with more fun, which has its pernt, too.

I still prefer to linger over your "scribbles" even if they're not always successful – prefer the human to the humane, except as against the inanities of instruction book writing, my job – the humane is always easier.

Oh, well, hope the boys come home soon & we'll see each other.

> Yours
> Louis

P.S. I'l let Celia tell you about the real estate when she sees you – she knows how to make it funny.

article: "The Supremacy of Lyricism."

pages on Etc.: Louis Zukofsky and René Taupin, "& Cie," *Westminster Magazine* 23:1 (Spring 1934), 7– 46. The "Notes on Contributors" for this issue stated that "The second and concluding installment, Chapter III, of *The Writing of Guillaume Apollinaire* appears in this issue of the magazine. A commentary 'on aesthetics, considering his (Apollinaire's) own and all previous ones of consequence and breaking 'em down including his own to repeat in a kind of stretto the material of the first two chapters.'"

your "scribbles": "In Praise of Marriage" and "Preface." Wallace C354 and C361.

480. TLS-1

[Rutherford, N.J.]

Dec. 19, 1945

Dear Louis:

While sitting here waiting to be called from the hospital – between now, 9 p.m. and morning – for a maternity case let me write you a note of appreciation for your card just received. It's a good card, I was glad to receive it. Thank you.

We don't see each other much these days, perhaps it's just as well as far as our writing goes. Each of us has his own talent or style or genius which, I think, is best developed without too great friction with other talents. Best for us not to bother too much about the other. At least I find that I am freer when I'm not concerning myself with what someone else, even a good friend, is doing. The theme of the song you have written and Celia has put to music shows you too need no advising.

That leaves common friendship which I hope we may enjoy again in a guiet way one of these days – by spring perhaps.

I've been pretty busy writing, I suppose because I've been so busy working at my trade that I had to write more to make up for that. I know I've spoken of the Paterson thing whenever I've written during the past yar. It's in the page-proof stage now but we're held up as it often happens by a detail which should be resolved before many weeks. Thus Part I should be out by – shall we say the ist of March?

Various small magazines have things of mine they plan to use. One of them, Harvard Wake, should be out soon – a new thing I'm interested to see.

My typist finished my play last evening – a prose thing concerning middleage love and disaster. It could be interesting if played – if you guess what I mean. Fred Miller whom you may remember having met (this son-of-a-bitch of a phone has been ringing for hours – I almost said wringing!) sent me a quotation from Stendahl which said, in substance, that he had always wanted to write a play but had never done so because of the neccessityfor so much assinine manoeuvering to get it produced.

Anyhow there is now a new play.

Paul is home and released from the Navy for whatever may come of it. His wife and two kids have been with us for more than a year. They'll be moving on in a matter of months. Bill being a doctor and without dependants has not been released. On the contrary he'll be at sea again by Monday bound for Tokyo I presume.

One thing I believe we have in common, Louis, we have both been excluded from Aiken's Comprehensive Anthology of American poetry. That, perhaps among other things, gives the book a distinction it would not otherwise have had. It's an odd but persistent characteristic of man as an animal that he for the most part despises anyone who has done him a favor – that is the sole reason I can give for Aiken's behavior in my case. Shall we not one of these days get up a timeless anthology of our own, I think we could develope something startling – with though and great care that is. If only we had the leisure. I helped Aiken to the lips of two of his wives -

Floss is well and my mother is going along. She shd reach 89 the evening before Christmas. The other day, with a malicious villain's look to her face, she told me that the daughter of the very kind and efficient English woman who cares for her is going to have a baby! Her whisper was dramatic and low. You wait and see, she said madly. The girl is unmarried and quite flat bellied as far as I can see, quite unaffected and simple in her manner. But SHE'S GOING TO HAVE A BABY! said the old woman maliciously. Hard to kill huh, that wish.

And Ezra! Did you see my article in P.M. about a month ago? I have an extra copy if you haven't seen the symposium. What a nut. I'm afraid he's really insane.

Best to Celia (I haven't had her music played as yet but shall have Charlotte play it when she comes on Sunday) and to Paul.

> Yours
> Bill

Kenneth Rexroth
> 692 Wisconsin St
> > San Francisco, Cal.
was asking after you (in a letter) the other day.

the song: Possibly section 3 ("Heart too human") of "Sequence 1944– 6." Its earliest sur-
   viving draft is dated by Zukofsky 7– 8 September 1945. *CSP,* 110.
Paterson thing: *Paterson: (Book I).*

Harvard Wake: A collection of nine poems by Williams appeared under the title, "The Peacock's Eyes." The *Harvard Wake* 5 (Spring 1946), 80–82. Wallace C365.

my play: *A Dream of Love.*

Fred Miller: Miller, a short story writer and poet, collaborated with Williams on an unfinished novel, *Man Orchid,* the typescript of which is at Yale.

Aiken's Comprehensive Anthology: Conrad Aiken and William Rose Benét, eds., *An Anthology of Famous English and American Poetry* (New York: Modern Library, 1945). Aiken selected the American poets.

two of his wives: Aiken married his second wife in Williams's home in 1930. An Aiken letter of 16 May 1937 to Williams indicates how Williams helped with the third wife. In the letter Aiken explained that in order to obtain a divorce from his second wife he needed a copy of the 1930 marriage certificate, which Williams was to obtain from "the Rutherford Town fathers" (Joseph Killorin, ed., *Selected Letters of Conrad Aiken* [New Haven and London: Yale Univ. Press, 1978], 215).

article in P.M.: "The Case for and against Ezra Pound," *PM* (25 November 1945). Reprinted in *Ezra Pound's Poetry and Prose: Contributions to Periodicals.* Lea Baechler, A. Walton Litz, and James Longenbach, eds. (New York: Garland, 1991) 8: 255–65.

Charlotte: Charlotte Herman, Florence Williams's older sister.

■ 481. ALS-2

[No return address]

Xmas 1945

Dear Bill

Today's greetings to all of you – I'm sorry Bill had to ship out again.

I'm glad you liked the song on the greeting card, especially since this year's net total of writing amounted to five short poems and the enclosed fragment which I haven't been able to finish, let alone have typed. Keep it as an indication of what I think about these days when I have time to think – or sense, or feel. There's lots I want to write. Taking care of the output of eight writers turning out 3000 pages of crap for the Corps of Engineers is no excuse for not writing my own work. I'll get back to it sooner or later – or what's the use – too bad we can't move from our crowded 3 rooms to the house in Brooklyn before June 1st – the judge has decided.

I'm glad you're writing – that means less of a vacuum. . Lack of mutual advising doesn't bother me either – if I ever advise it's the desire to have what's good around one rather than – and that I suppose turns back on oneself and the sum total is friendship anyway. I'll get a lot of friendship out of "Paterson" (is all of it done or only part I?), your new play, the pieces in the magazines, when you send them to me. The only thing I miss is the stimulant of seeing you and talking.

I'm certain I'd write more if the possibility of publication drove me to it. Stendhal's reason for not writing a play applies all around. Decker takes so long it's hopeless. Duncan of Cummington is so impressed by Test of Poetry, tho he can't afford to do it, he's not returned the ms. after repeated requests during the last two months. I can't afford to lose the ms. Is there any way you know I can get him to return it?

About other writers: I don't remember having met Fred Miller though I heard a lot about him from Oppen once. It's over 15 years I've seen Rexroth – thanks for the address. Curiously enough I <also> heard about him <recently> through Stephen Seley who wrote "The Cradle Will Fall." Seley worked several weeks for my company – it was nice to have a guy with integrity around for a while. He's since quit to do another novel for Scribner's: He has a lot of talent. I told him to send you the book I mention – it's about his New Jersey family, & I thought you'd be interested. Maybe he will – tho he doesn't care for the book anymore and doesn't see why you should be bothered.

I saw the symposium on Ezra and I see that he's been adjudged insane. It's a mad way out – typical of our time: glib psychiatrists, willing judges etc. As far as Ezra is concerned it doesn't make any difference, I suppose. As an old friend I hate to think of him suffering, if he is (I doubt it), but he was certainly willing to see millions suffer <while he> ranted. Personally, it's just as well Norman didn't use the enclosed typed letter – please return it – after persuading me to send him something – his excuse, the symposium had already gone to press. He did manage to cut the word "patronage" out of his article.

Saxe Commins exclusion of Ezra from Aiken's anthology is a shitty business. Maybe he had something to do with excluding you – and poor achin' Aiken had nothing to do with it? As for me, as you said once, he's not in the anthologies, but will be. But before we meet in the other world,

A Happy New Year – and let's get together as soon as we can – an offer still stands "call up and say you'll come." Paul's [sic] a big fellah but still not big enough to bother other people with – so we stay at home. Celia's best to you & Floss.

> Yours
> Louis

the song: Possibly section 3 of "Sequence 1944– 6."
five short poems: Celia Zukofsky's *Bibliography* lists these poems as having been com-
　　pleted in 1945: "A Song for the Year's End" (parts 1 and 2); "Light" (part 4); "Sequence"
　　(parts 2, 3, and 4—original versions). *CSP*, 111–13, 116–17, 109–10.
enclosed fragment: Enclosure lacking.
new play: *A Dream of Love.*
Duncan: Harry Duncan.

Seley: Stephen Seley (b. 1915), novelist. Author of *The Cradle Will Fall* (New York: Harcourt, Brace, 1945).

another novel: *Baxter Bernstein: A Hero of Sorts* (New York: Scribner's, 1949).

the book: Apparently this remained unpublished.

symposium on Ezra: "The Case for and against Ezra Pound."

Norman: Charles Norman (1904–1996), American poet and biographer. Norman expanded his *PM* symposium and published it as a booklet (1948) and as a longer book (*The Case of Ezra Pound* [New York: Funk and Wagnalls, 1968]). Both editions contained Williams's and Zukofsky's statements about Pound.

enclosed typed letter: Enclosure lacking. The letter is in the Zukofsky papers at Texas. It is dated 14 November 1945.

My dear Mr. Norman: You may quote me as follows: My dear Mr. Norman: Your use of the word patronage to describe my relationship with Pound is not accurate. A concern for my work is what happened. I should prefer to say nothing now. But a preference for silence might be misinterpreted by even the closest friends. Knowing my convictions, Pound, I am sure, does not look to my defense of him, any more than I would look for his defense of me if our positions were reversed.

When he was here in 1939 (?), I told him that I did not doubt his integrity had decided his political action, but I pointed to his head, indicating something had gone wrong. When he asked me if it was possible to educate Coughlin, I retorted, Whatever you don't know, Ezra, you ought to know voices. This exchange of frankness was accepted tacitly by both of us as a dissociation of values above personal bickering.

He approached literature and music at that depth. His profound and intimate knowledge and practice of these things still leave that part of his mind entire. The heavy-footed and the stupid will never see the truth of his essay "Mediaevalism". Those who seek publicity from his predicament will never know the worth of Canto I or Canto XIII, or of –

> Sun up; work
> Sundown; to rest
> dig well and drink of the water
> dig field; eat of the grain
> Imperial power is? And to us what is it?
>
> The fourth; the dimension of stillness.
> And the power over wild beasts.

Or the weight of "Anyone can run to excesses", or the fact of "Who even dead, yet hath his mind entire".

Those who in this country effectively supported the cause Pound foolishly broadcast have not been brought to justice.

I never felt the least trace of anti-semitism in his presence. Nothing he ever said to me made me feel the embarrassment I always have for the "Goy" in whom a residue of antagonism to "Jew" remains. If we had occasion to use the words "Jew" and "Goy" they were no more or less ethnological in their sense than "Chinese" and "Italian".

I remember an animated cartoon which pointed up human brutishness over which both of us could still chuckle. He may be condemned or forgiven. Biographers of the future may find his character as charming a subject as that of Aaron Burr. It will matter very little against his finest work overshadowed in his lifetime by the hell of Belsen which he overlooked.

Yours,

Louis Zukofsky

Very sincerely

[Zukofsky's notation] "Suggested revisions to Charles Norman Aug 26/48 but preferred not to publish any of this."

Among the revisions Zukofsky suggested (which were mostly deletions) was the substitution of "some politicians" for "Coughlin." The letter also contains an appended comment in Williams's hand: "See the opening of A Wakefield Nativity for much of Pound's early style. Christ! The guy never told his sources but sucked up everything loose & let it be thought his own—that sort of thing is pure shit."

exclusion of Ezra: Bennet Cerf decided to exclude Pound from Conrad Aiken's and William Rose Benét's *An Anthology of Famous English and American Poetry* (New York: The Modern Library, 1945). In March 1946, however, Cerf changed his mind, allowing twelve poems by Pound to appear in the second edition. See Julien Cornell, *The Trial of Ezra Pound* (London: Faber and Faber, 1966), 112–15. Saxe Commins (1892?-1958) was for many years a senior editor at Random House. In Charles Norman's *PM* article, "The Case for and against Ezra Pound," Commins says, "Random House is not going to publish any fascist. As a matter of fact, we don't think Ezra Pound is good enough, or important enough, to include."

you said once: At the conclusion of Williams's review of *55 Poems*, "An Extraordinary Sensitivity." Reprinted in *Something to Say*.

Paul's: Paul Zukofsky.

9 Ridge Road, Rutherford, N.J.

Dec 28, 1945

Dear Louis:

I've go to tear off ten quick letters on this my afternoon off (shd have been in quotes). Hence the shortness of this – and those to follow.

Glad to hear from you. Your letter to Norton was by far the best of all those contributed on the subject. But what good whould it have done to print it? It was beyond the level of the occasion, including my own contribution. In fact what you wrote is so good I'd like to have a copy of it for my own collection. It reveals you yourself at your best . It is the very best statement upon all the issues involved in the case. I positively felt ashamed of myself because of some of the things I had written about Ezra.

No use to go further. I admire you and that's that. I have a friend, a patient of mine in Passaic, who looks very much like you. I told him about you today. "French, I suppose?" was his answer. A really good guy.

For me in that letter you settled the Jew-Goy question forever. It'll never occur to me again.

You also said in a few words all that could and should be said about Ezra's poetry, its great excellence – when it is at its best – the finest poetry in many ways that has ever been written in our language. You have done not only Ezra a great service there but the rest of us also.

For I confess to long periods of obtuseness about critical values. I seem to descend into my nerves and my nerves frequently trip me. When I see clearly what is portrayed before me I recognize it without supporting argument. But too often I am inclined to rush over the writing without stopping to study the detail. Not always but often. Again, I say, I admire you.

Not that you don't muddle yourself up in your own secretion yourself at times! But when you do manage to hit, you hit beautifully on the mark.

I'll write to Cummington and do what I can to shake What's His Name loose.

Do you want to see the page proofs of the Paterson or would you rather wait for the book. It's up to you, the proofs are here now.

I've sketched in the other three parts of the Paterson in fullest detail, only the finishing waits – and the time to do it in. Could be finished in a month or two: next on my calendar now the play is done. See that too if you like – but privately.

We'LL be seeing you as soon as can be. Best to all.

Bill

Norton: Charles Norman.

What's His Name: Harry Duncan.

the play: *A Dream of Love.*

■ 483. TLS-1

Jan 13, 1946

Dear Louis:

I have made the copy, thanks. Letter enclosed.

Enclosed also is a line from Cummington in reply to a letter from me asking about your script. Keep it or toss it into the discard.

Here's something new : Paul has found himself a job with Abraham-Strauss in Brookly ! It's what he has always wanted to do, sell thing to people, give them what they want at a reasonable price – or know why it can't be done. AS – or A.S. has , apparently, a top reputation in the trade. Paul went after the job and won it on his own merits – got the highest IQ ever found among the store's applicants by the way. How he did that is more than I know.

But where in hell is he going to live with his wife and two children? He may stay here for a while but Floss has to have a break soon, the sooner the better . Shall he buy a house in Rutherford?

At about this stage I thought of you. When you leave the place you are now in (in June?) will it be available for rerenting to Paul ? Or, better, will you not have in June an appartment in your own building for rent ?

These questions are perhaps somewhat academic today but I shouldn't feel satisfied if I hadn't asked them of you.

Regarding PATERSON, no use my sending you the messy script since the book itself will be out so soon – so Laughlin tells me . It'll be a rather handsome affair according to Laughlin, he says the press will be running it this week. If that is true you'll have your copy shortly.

The play is in process of being copyrighted, I have resolved not to let it go out of my hands until I know where I stand – probably a senseless gesture but it has been set down as a rule at the moment so forgive me. You'll see the damned thing as soon as anybody if you're still interested.

Glad your printer has come again to life.

Best luck

Bill

enclosed: Enclosures lacking.

Cummington: The Cummington Press.

Paul: Paul Williams.

PATERSON: *Paterson: Book I* was published on 1 June 1946.

the play: *A Dream of Love.*

your printer: James A. Decker.

484. TLS-1

9 Ridge Road
Rutherford, N.J.

1/20/46

Dear Louis:

The Wakefield Mysteries is a 14th century English play I came across in a collection recently. Very primitive and very "modern" for that reason. Quite astonishing to me in some of its particularizations – as an or a tirade by one of the shepherds – shepards – against wives in general and his in particular. his own.

Should your Brooklyn apartment be available any time in the future let me know what you're asking for it.

Paul goes to work tomorrow,

It's cold.

Yours
Bill

Wakefield Mysteries: One of the Wakefield plays, "The Second Shepherd's Play," contains the speech Williams describes.

Paul: Paul Williams.

485. TLS-1

9 Ridge Road, Rutherford, N.J.

March 26, 1946

Dear Louis:

Wonderful! Metrically I can see at once that it is the only adult verse being written today. It carries on the best of Pound's discoveries (perceptions no less yours than his) as he has not been able to carry them on. It carrys out the things that kick in my mind as I have not been able to carry them out. Celia is in it for you and has been a tremendous help in giving you continuity, a musical sequence which you have not always had. But the basic movement is yours. Really wonderful to me to get that new, magnificent feel of the line.

When I look at the St Whatever-it-is- Perse and his astonishments I want to wet my pants. Even my darling e.e.c. resorts too much to the infantile in his metric. But a line! a line that is variable and that flows with feeling, musically and yet retains the measured qualities (and quantities) of a line. I do not find it (aside from the early Pound) anywhere else than in you, at your best. And this new work appears on first glance to be you at your best.

I feel warmed and happy over this, a real renewal, an actual coming out of the heaviness of a war that is more a war than the Churchills will ever know, an actual springtime, actual, not merely left to the plants and the stars. I'm glad you've kept on. Beautiful, really.

No use telling you to be patient, just be patient with me. I'll soon be sending you the Paterson thing, it ought to be out in April. The play is still at the agency so that at least it has not been returned to me as yet. Oh, and I sold a long poem to New Republic, four pages long. I hope they use it. The title, RUSSIA. Bill's more or less out of the Navy and home. Paul's working. We'll be seeing you, believe it. I'm going to write a review of your book; more of that soon.

Congratulations

Bill

adult verse: Williams refers to the newly published volume of poems by Zukofsky, *Anew*
(Prairie City, Illinois: James A. Decker, 1946).

Perse: Saint-John Perse, the pseudonym of Marie-René-Alexis St.-Léger Léger
(1887–1975), French diplomat and poet.

e.e.c.: Edward Estlin Cummings.

Paterson thing: *Paterson: Book I.*

play: *A Dream of Love.*

long poem: "Russia," the *New Republic* 94:17 (29 April 1946), 615. Wallace C369. *CP2,*
144–46.

Bill's: William Eric Williams.

Paul's: Paul Herman Williams.

review: "A New Line is a New Measure," *New Quarterly of Poetry* 2:2 (Winter 1947–48),
8–16. Wallace C392. Reprinted in *Something to Say,* 161–69.

486. ANS

[1946]
Make any suggestions that may occur to you.

Bill

[Zukofsky's notation: "re 'Relique of the Farm' 1946"]

Relique: An early draft of Williams's short story, "The Farmer's Daughters."

[Rutherford, N.J.]

[Zukofsky's notation: "Mar 31/46 re—Anew"]

Keep these notes – if you want to – to be returned to me after I get through saying (what's on my mind).

I feel very reluctant to writing a criticism of the book (tho' I will – in time.) Let me unfold. as I am able -

I'll send more as I write more. I'll go on till I haven't any more to say – as far as I know then ask the stuff back & make what I can of it.

Individual poems are more illuminating than others – but I'd have to go back to the beginning of everything I have spent a life on to say all I'd wish to say.

It is truly a dawn or the beginning of a dawn for me. & the most vicious hatred of others. I can't express my furious detestation of almost everyone writing today. Not all – but the most.

But that's nothing. Forget it.

Bill

these notes: Several drafts of Williams's comments on *Anew* are among the Zukofsky papers at Texas.

[Rutherford, N.J.]

April 3/46

Dear Louis:

Page 6 – hasn't been lost. I just guessed at the correct sequence. There ain't no page 6.

All right, I'll finish it up—may take me a couple of weeks to get down to specific poems, which I intend to do, to say <u>precisely</u> what I mean (if I can get it all in—ought to be a book if I say all I want to say, about the spareness of the verbal means, the necessity to <u>read</u> in order to understand and not just schmear over the page. One must go, necessarily slow in order to go. Impossible to escape reading. O.K. to reject reading—but not escape.)

I don't know about not touching a word – what about the casual beginning? What about a better order in the ideas? Oh well. I suppose you're right. It'll be printed somewhere at my present rate of acceptances.

Saw the <u>Russia</u> today in galley proofs. Shd be out in two weeks at most. Glad you enjoyed it. Fun to see if I get any comebacks. Probably not. They'll say, "Oh just a poet. Don't have to take him seriously." It's the modern technique.

Here's some more – perhaps repetitious. Please number the pages in your own sequence for me.

I enjoy the book more every time I read it.
>Yrs
>Bill

book: *Anew.*

489. TLS-1

[Rutherford, N.J.]

Apr 5/46
Dear Louis:

Finis, for the moment. Perhaps more detail later but not for the moment. If I rewrite the whole the connecting links appear as I go.

I've been writing to Ezra who has become somewhat pathetic realization of what he has done. I enclose his lates letter because of its mention of you -and others. He is almost infantile in his reliances and lack of realization. I told him of mother's present condition but of her loyalty of Ezra as an "artist" in distress. Poor mother. She asks everyone for word about Ezra – as she often mentions you also and wants to know what has become of you.

Please return E's letter promptly as I want to keep everything he writes to me in these latter days. Poor stupid guy.

Well, there it is. He was "the dawn" for all of us in many ways, a really great literary genius in my opinion. Too bad he had to let himself be led astray by baser ambitions than those he so beautifully embodied at times. He just didn't know what it was, really, all about. And yet he practices the best – at times.

Nothing new otherwise.
>Yours
>Bill

latest letter: Among the Zukofsky papers at Texas is a copy of the letter Pound wrote to
Williams. "Dear Bill: You can't xpect me to conduct a polemic from inside a mad
house. Zuk, however, might know what became of Bunting. Cataklasm!! Compre-
nez?? I know mostly who's alive and who's dead = but no news of Bunting or of
Nancy Cunard. Yr Ez[.]"

490. ALS-1

[No return address]

Sat Apr 6/46
Dear Bill
I'm numbering the pages –
What I mean about not changing a word – you've plumbed so much about

my intention in general – which is all of poetry etc – I don't want to stop that. Or you've got a <u>head</u> such as no other "mind" thinking about such things to-day, which is all important to me, & no doubt to a coupla' others.

If you do get down to specific poems it'll be especially enlightening to me – & if then you want to cut down to a review, that's o.k. but I still think all of it should be, as is, a separate thing – the review a much lesser thing – the other the result of a much greater aim – the review after all for a little fart of a volume even if we say it compassionately.

> Yours
> Louis

volume: *Anew*.

491. TLS

[Rutherford, N.J.]

April 8/46

Dear Louis:

All right about the head, <my head> I hope so. The thing is how to make it operative for our purposes on a crescent scale, I've never been able to solve that one. All I've ever sought to date is to find a base, like oyster spawn hanging to a rock in a strong current. I've had to base myself as best I could, as you know the same. But how to maintain an adult life – and GROW! Grow into the physical world and be a "success". Damn it why not? We have much to displace in the world.

We've got the old Pound stuff, a beginning, but not a very saleable beginning. We've got you, Niedecker (I agree – more of that soon, but limited as you are not) some of my stuff but damned little else to bank on. Eliot is still our enemy and ALL the universities without exception. And the french influence today unless we can find some new strain there which I doubt. You'd be surprised at some of the Irish (the "communists", especially one Leslie Daiken).

Isn't there really someone with money? I mean it seriously. We really might start a magazine but without real money it's impossible. It could,now, have a clear, invincible and EXCLUSIVE editorial policy that would knock their eyes out. Oh boy! how I should like to work on that

Daiken: Leslie H. Daiken (1912– 64), Irish-born businessman and author. Williams reported to Pound in a letter of 6 April 1946 (*EP/WCW*) that Daikin had sent him a copy of his book of poems, *Signatures of All Things* (1945).

[Rutherford, N.J.]

[1946]

Dear Louis:

After you've perused the enclosed, no hurry, send the bunch of sheets back to me. I'll have a corrected (spelling) copy of the thing made returning to you the original and a carbon.

Then I'm going to condense it all as a review of the book with some additional words (I think) on the one poem I have picked as the best. It'll all be printed somewhere.

You saw my preface to Vazakases forthcoming book (by Macmillan) in the Quarterly review. Vazakases poems are interesting to me for the reasons stated there. They are nothing like your work – which is truly lyrical in the sense of being song-like. But you both fit into the larger scheme – quite apart from your relative excellences as poets which I refrain from attempting to pass judgement upon. I should be incapable of doing so.

I see a brilliant critical opportunity ahead of us but doubt that we shall be able to seize it.

Beside you at your best, who knows how to sing? I find nobody, no one with an understanding of what it means to invent a musical phrase that is fresh to the ear. Almost all work I attempt to apprais or enjoy positively revolts me – my own, generally speaking, included. Vazakas is musical but you, hard as you are to find (I can't always find you in your work) make songs.

This isn't praise in the vulgar sense and I hope you do not find it fulsome – I believe you see what I am aiming at as you are very certainly comprehend, when you speak of a little fart of a book, that not a great deal has been realized by you yourself. But it is there.

Well, we go on – I wish at least that PATERSON would get bound and be released.

     Yours,
     ` Bill

enclosed: Enclosure lacking. Clearly notes by Williams regarding *Anew*.

one poem: *Anew* 42: ["You three: — my wife,"]. *CSP*, 99–102.

my preface: "Preface," *Quarterly Review of Literature* 2:4, 346– 49. Wallace C361. The first publication of Williams's Introduction to Byron Vazakas's *Transfigured Night* (New York: Macmillan, 1946).

PATERSON: *Paterson: Book I.*

9 Ridge Road, Rutherford, N.J.

4/30/46

Dear Louis:

I'll take care of the application form for you (Columbia – teaching) later this p.m.

I'm going up for a herniotomy this evening, they'll do me tomorrow at 8 a.m. I don't know what else – a wild letter from Ezra saying he's having trouble remaining lucid! I'm afraid he's really bad. poor boob. well –

Yours

Bill

wild letter: In a letter of 26 April 1946, Pound commented to Williams, "My Main spring is busted" (*EP/WCW*, 226–27).

■ 494. ALS-1

[Passaic General Hospital, Passaic, N.J.]

Tuesday [7 May 1946]

Dear Louis:

I can't remember whether or not I <told you I> was gong to the hospital for a herniotomy. Well, here I am a cutté now rather than a cutter. The leisure is a delight even tho' the discomfort isn't. Wish I didn't have piles.

While here I've been reading steadily, among other things <u>Anew</u> again and <u>New Goose</u>. The advance can't be anywhere else than in the <u>Art</u>, in the work that's been done & is doing with the metric. Everything else is second thought if not second rate.

There just isn't <u>much</u> that can be done. The fight is selective & the perceptions rare. But by the narrow entrance to the secret (for I come to believe it is a secret) enormous transformations can be made.

The changes are in the <u>poetry</u> – as no one seems to remember – not even Ezra any longer – the possible changes in poems are in the <u>making</u> of the poems.

It is all completely simple & almost impossible to explain to a class. They just can't see it – But to make new poems by the new means is our test. pragmatists all – or nothing but hot air.

Bill

New Goose: Lorine Niedecker, *New Goose* (Prairie City, Illinois: James A. Decker, 1946).

[Passaic General Hospital, Passaic, N.J.]

Wednesday [8 May 1946; Zukofsky's notation: "R'cd May 14/46"]

Dear Louis:

I've got it – the first few paragraphs of your critique. The rest is just a matter of wearing the thing down – from the draft you have already seen. This is going to be *good:* as it will go (necessarily) unnoticed – Thank God. Give us a little privacy.

This minute a week ago I was on my way to the O.R. (operating room) to be sliced. Lots of amusement in it all. I've had fun (hope I haven't busted out any sutures these last few days)

The marvellous thing is that I've been imprisoned – <u>away from</u> distractions and at physical rest (if not ease). I have reviewed & replotted my entire life with the greatest satisfaction to myself you can imagine.

And what do you think my inspiration has been – that enabled me to discern the real character of your work? Billy the Kid! believe it or not: the desperate bandit of the old South West – who had killed a man for every year of his life – unfortunately no successful poets among them.

I've read much else, of course –

I guess that's all.

As soon as I get home I'll slap the stuff I have on you into a whole – have it typed & send you the originals & a <fine> copy as promised. . We'll get it published where ever you want it published, just name your spot & I'll land it there, me, Billy the Kid (62½) See if I don't.

    Bill

                      9 Ridge Road, Rutherford, N.J.

P.S. I wrote the enclosed while still confined in the hospital – and misplaced it among various stray papers.

Home now – shaky but – up.

    Bill

Billy the Kid: William H. Bonney (1859–1881). The famous outlaw was born in New York City.

enclosed: Enclosure lacking. Possibly drafts of Williams's review of *Anew:* "A New Line is a New Measure."

[Rutherford, N.J.]

May 18, 1946

Dear Louis:

Home now (tho' not fully active) I have had a chance to look over the pages I sent you piecemeal concerning your book. I was amazed to see how much I had written – a new first page has been added.

I can't digest, revise and realign that mass. It will have to stand as it is – with some minor cuts and corrections, of course, where typographic errors have occured.

Then what? I think I have the answer.

First I'm going to entitle it simply: Notes on Zukofsky's recent book of poems, ANEW. Then I'm going to have it printed as it stands, they've got to do it, in a new magazine of the arts – Iconograph. This is now a printed (instead of a mimeographed) mag the first issue of which has appeared recently. I have subscribed but haven't yet seen the format. It sounds good.

Next, since it would be difficult to start a magazine of our own now we'll have to form a phalynx using Iconograph as our medium (whenever we can pry our way into it) and pound, pound, pound home what we have to say. I may be wrong but this mag seems to offer us our best opportunity to get going. At least we can have an objective, a temporary objective and hammer at it as we may.

It may even offer Celia an opportunity. It wants to print musical scores. I don't know what money they have but it sounds like something, as I have said. More of this later.

Now I'll put what final touches I'm able to put on your notes – quote the one poem #42 entire and shoot for the mark.

    Yours

    Bill

I'll send stuff soon.

Iconograph: Nothing by Williams or Zukofsky appeared in this magazine.
Poem #42: ["You three:—my wife,"]. *CSP*, 99–102.

9 Ridge Road, Rutherford, N.J.

5/20/46

Dear Louis:

So be it. I'll make a concise extract of the 19 pages – say five or six pages – and send it to the Times – & so on along the list.

The Iconograph proposal stands.

I'm working again and feeling fit.

As soon as I can get copies made I'm sending Celia a "Choral" for her to look at. It is called <u>The Pink Church</u>. & celebrates the "pink" – one of God's noblest creatures.

   Yours
   Bill

the Times: The *New York Times* did not publish any comments by Williams about *Anew*.

The Pink Church: "Choral: The Pink Church," *Briarcliff Quarterly* 3:3 (October 1946),
 165– 68. Wallace C374. *CP2*, 177– 80. On 22 May 1946 Williams sent a typed copy of
 "Choral: The Pink Church," with a note saying, "Keep it if you like. Could music be
 made for it?" Celia Thaew Zukofsky set the poem to music within the next two
 months.

498. TCS

[Rutherford, N.J.]

[May or June 1946]

Impossible to abridge yr review properly and retain the loose character of the style and the meaning – so I wrote another review in more succinct terms. I'll type this out now, let you have a copy and send it to the T's Book Section as a starter. Please tell Celia there's no obligation to put the Choral to music, all I wanted to know was whether or not the thing sounded in her ears as though it <u>might</u> be material for music. Nothing more. Nice day today. Paul and Bill have gone fishing. I've been meeting and hearing from several new irish writers through Kitty Hoagland who is doing an irish anthology "1000 Years of Irish Poetry". But if you ever happen to stumble on Scribner's latest, "A Little Treasury of Modern Poetry" edited by O. Williams – look into it and die – of laughing. What a sell!

   Bill

Choral: "Choral: The Pink Church."

Paul and Bill: Williams's sons.

"1000 Years of Irish Poetry": Kathleen Hoagland, ed., *1000 Years of Irish Poetry; The*
 Gaelic and Anglo-Irish Poets from Pagan Times to the Present (New York: Devin-Adair,
 1947).

"A Little Treasury of Modern Poetry": Oscar Williams, ed., *A Little Treasury of Modern*
 Poetry (New York: Scribner's, 1946).

9 Ridge Road, Rutherford, N.J.

June 7/46

Bulletin

We're going away for a week for a little visit. Be back June 16 or so.

The critical piece is being typed for me by Kitty Hoagland – in two continuous parts, like a freight train of two cars. The first may be detached as desired, a shorter part continuous with the second to which it is as Chaucer's prologues are to his tales. I'll have it for you week after next.

I'm taking no trouble, it's an opportunity.

The Choral was sent to Partisan Review with considerable curiosity as to whether they'd be smart enough to refuse it on dialectic grounds. They smelt a rat and welched, to my amusement – said they'd print it but not now! They had already too many committments respecting poems – though, of course, not of the excellence of my work. I told them to print it not later than the fall 46 issue or to return it at once.

If and when Celia finishes the music (I feel guilty as hell about taking up her time for that) I'm gong to suggest to Laughlin or some one else that the Choral with music be published in some form, as a large size, music size, pamphlet or as may be possible with a view toward some sort of performance. Maybebe Iconograph – if they really are what they say they are – and have some money.

I sent you a copy of Paterson by book post which may be the reason why it has been so slow in arriving; judging from the experience of friends living even as near as Passaic it takes four days by book post to go three miles. It'll get there in the end or let me know! Hope you like something of it as I know you will.

Mother (90 the day before Christmas this year) was in good mystic form yesterday: she told me that she now understand that the "other world" and "what we call the world around us" are one. Her friends talk to her very intelligently and pleasantly every day, her friends, that is who have died but who are constantly about her. It is a very casual world, the way she presents it, very matter of fact and very comforting. I was thrilled to have her tell me of her discoveries. She has great sympathy for Ezra and feels very sorry for him. She has so much to give, apparently!

Yours

Bill

Choral with music: Eventually Williams's wish was partly realized. *The Pink Church* (Columbus, Ohio: Golden Goose Press, 1949). Wallace A29. In this edition, Celia Zukofsky's music was published with the text of the poem.

[Rutherford, N.J.]

June 21, 1946

Dear Louis:

Here's the works. There are two parts as you see – the first, the shorter, is for the bastards (generally speaking), those who would print a notice grudgingly, perhaps. The other is for some such magazine as Kenyon Review – or any other which you might prefer. Both are parts of a whole; perhaps Kenyon (John Crowe Ransom) would use both. Briarcliff Quarterly would use them both I am sure.

I am sending you both originals and carbons. I have made a few corrections. If you see others to make go ahead and make them. I'll keep the originals for the time being.

Either you send the reviews here and there in my name (filling in the heading in the usual book-review style as you see fit) or send the first script back to me and keep the yellow sheets and I'll do the canvassing.

I think the reviews are important. I think they are as important – taken with two or three of your poems – as the 1913 Armory show was to painting. In fact my own opinion that the whole complex of the work and thought initiate a completely new era in the making of poems. The writers will catch on, shall we say? in 1976 (the new American Revolution!) I hope I'm there. No I don't. Sorry. Too old by then.

So let's see if we can place anything. Oh yes, and insert the quote by impagination and asterisk.

Best luck, I'm working on the Choral. Partisan Review accepted it for re-mote publication. I refused. It's now with Kenyon Review. In each case I have mentioned Celia's music. A recital at Town Hall with chorus and perhaps part of the Pericles. I wonder if we could get away with it. Ask Celia whom tp approach for the actual choral singing. The New Friends of Music?

Harper's Bazaar has accepted two new poems ($75.00) The Nation has taken one. etc etc I'm all over my operation.

Best luck

Bill

the works: Williams's comments on *Anew*. Several drafts of the review ("A New Line is a New Measure") are in the Williams archive at Buffalo.

Ransom: John Crowe Ransom (1888–1974), poet and critic. Ransom edited the *Kenyon Review* from 1939 to 1959.

Armory show: The International Exhibition of Modern Art at the 69th Infantry Regiment Armory in New York City, held in February and March, 1913.

the Pericles: Shakespeare's play had been set to music by Celia Zukofsky.

two new poems: "The Usurers of Heaven," *Harper's Bazaar* 2819 (November 1946), 391.
Wallace C379. This was the only poem printed by *Harper's. CP2*, 109–10.

The Nation: "A Unison," *The Nation* 163:23 (7 December 1946), 649. Wallace C382. *CP2*,
157–58.

■ 501. ALS-3

[30 Willow Street
Brooklyn, New York]

June 22/46
Dear Bill,

I'm glad you're going strong again.

Enclosed are the originals emended lightly in pencil. If you don't agree, I'd prefer not to see the first part printed – because frankly I don't see the point of laying myself (and you, too, for that matter) unnecessarily open to the "bastards." Even as emended I don't suppose there's any use trying to pass off the first part to the newspapers or weeklies, as I proposed originally, as a review – they won't see it as such. Unless you change the last sentences of this part to read: "So I wrote the foregoing notes on these poems:" and follow that by quoting 41 (if you like it well enough) and 42. That is, for the newspapers etc, it's well to assume that you didn't write the second part at all. – But as I said I doubt if there is any earthly use trying to market the first part at all.

If you agree to the emendations, I'll appreciate it if you do the canvassing. I'm a bastard for imposing, but it's no use I'd just feel too sick at heart trying to make the rounds myself. If you do the canvassing and agree to the changes, try both parts on Kenyon Review first. I might as well tell you that Mark Van Doren who I believe is associate editor of Kenyon thought <u>Anew</u> "entirely successful" – I sent him a copy since I needed a<n academic> reference and I thought I might as well show him my worst and best side. If Kenyon rejects you, why not try Sewanee – Tate surprisingly thought "Ferdinand" a fine story (tho its length prohibited his acceptance) – so maybe he'll be favorably disposed. If he isn't, try anybody you think will take it, tho as I said we might as well try a magazine that has more circulation than an offshoot of a college. (That's between us; and since there have been no other reviews and won't be as far as I can judge, what's the use of bogging us further.)

You'll notice that I inserted – "see poem 41*", on page 1 of the NOTES, and that I'd like you to quote that poem at the end of your NOTES (again if you like it well enough): that is, Celia as such means nothing to anybody, but Celia of the poem does. Or as I said to her after I showed her your letter saying she'd influenced my music or something to that effect – "he's partly right, but all wrong."

And on the whole you have as you say written something important, and maybe it's a shame it'll be wasted in my connection – tho I agree with you, unhappy as I feel not having been able to write more poems like 42 – the poems you'd like to see – as to the significance of the whole complex of "Anew" – or I wouldn't be bothering you now at all. (On rereading I note a lot of <u>at all</u>'s in this letter.)

I hope Kenyon takes the Choral. About Celia's music – you'll have to do the canvassing again, I'm afraid, if you intend a recital in Town Hall. We'd like it – and I believe we could even get away with it – but we don't know anyone to implement it – but no one. Anyway, you ought to hear the music <first> and by the time I answer your next we ought to be able to set a definite date for that.

By the way – whose quotes at the opening of the "Notes" – very good. There's also some penciling on p. 16 of 'em – which ain't mine.

> All the best
> Louis.

P.S. I'm returning both "originals" and carbons – since I'm softie enough to still want the <u>very</u> originals. Etc.

PSS: Enclosing 2 sets of poems – please return what you don't use.

41 and 42: "After Charles Sedley" (*CSP*, 98–99) and ["You three:—my wife,"] (*CSP*, 99–102)

Tate: Allen Tate (1899–1979), poet and novelist. Tate edited the *Sewanee Review* from the summer of 1944 to the fall of 1945. On 21 July 1946, Tate wrote Williams that he would probably publish Zukofsky were he still editor of the *Review* (a copy of the letter in Zukofsky's hand is among the Zukofsky papers at Texas).

2 sets of poems: Enclosures lacking.

502. ACS

[Postmarked Rutherford, N. J.]

[Postmarked 25 June 1946]

1st quotation – Winston Churchill – anent the proposed new Parliament bl'd'g.

2nd quotation – Arthur M. Schlesinger Jr in The Age <u>of Jackson.</u>

Glad you like these.

> Bill

1st quotation: Williams's draft of "Notes on Zukofsky's Recent Book of Poems—Anew" began with two quotations: "We shape our buildings and afterwards our buildings shape us" and "They cherished a set of values in discouraging times when the values seemed impossible of realization. In later days other men would come along, abler in devising means for the end, but supported by the fact that these men had kept the end steadily in sight. By refusing to yield an inch . . ." (Buffalo).

9 Ridge Road, Rutherford, N.J.

June 25, 1946

Dear Louis:

Of course, I'll take out anything you want me to, you know that. But I had to write the thing as I wrote it, no holds barred – even though I felt certain you'd object – and that you'd know I knew I could only write from my own partie pris (is that the way to spell it?)

I can see what you mean relative to Celia, she's right – you don't need her music. Campion, huh? O.K.

I'm sending the stuff to Tate (whom I wisely or not detest) I'm sending it to him first – on general principles.

Original copy of script enclosed, it's yours.

One thing sure, if we can get the Choral prominently printed and with a strong reference to the music (no immediate hurry about that) we can move toward a public performance somewhere, which will lead to other things or so I hope.

Yours
Bill

Campion: Thomas Campion (1567–1620), English physician, poet, and composer.
Choral: "Choral: The Pink Church."

[Greenport, N.Y.]

[Postmarked 5 July 1946]

Here (Greenport, L.I.) over the 4th loafing again – think<ing> from present evidence of what life happily has been and must be again if man is to continue his assinine career: sunlight, fresh air, clean water, flowers and thriving vegetation. – until Sunday

Bill

9 Ridge Road, Rutherford, N.J.

July 26, 1946

Dear Louis:

Prying apart the granite minutes – the enclosed shd prove of interest to you. I suppose you'd better return it for filing. Haven't as yet had a chance to propose a call on you. Briarcliffe Q. is bringing out a special issue, a special

Williams issue, this fall. I've sent Vivienne Koch the article in question – telling her she may cut if necessary (but I want to see the proofs).

Ransom returned the Choral – says he prefers me in a different mood (as if there are two moods to a man, the ass: why doesn't he tell the truth and reject outright or the opposite?) So I have plans either to let Ted Weiss use it in his issue of Literary Quarterly three removes from now or, preferably perhaps, to let Laughlin use it in his annual (ND) with the music.

Ezra still writes out of his pedagogical fixation to me what to read. what a pathetic fool is now being revealed. God gives genius to children for the most part – and leaves them, apart from their genius, children.

Floss and I are going to the wilds (?) of Western Massachusetts for much of August. I want to read, walk aroundand perhaps work on the play.

Yours as ever
Bill

enclosed: Enclosure lacking. Possibly Tate's letter (21 July 1946) to Williams indicating
    that he would have published Williams's comments on *Anew* had he still been editor
    of the *Sewanee Review*.
Williams issue: *Briarcliff Quarterly* 3:2 (October 1946).
Koch: (1911–1961), educator and critic. She was married to Norman Macleod from 1935 to
    1946. Her critical study of Williams is *William Carlos Williams* (Norfolk, Connecticut:
    New Directions, 1950).
Weiss: Theodore Russell Weiss (b. 1916), poet and co-editor of the *Quarterly Review of
    Literature* since 1943.
Ezra still writes: In a letter of 10 July 1946, Pound asked, "How 'bout ole Fordie? Didja
    learn anyfink from 'im?" (Buffalo).
Western Massachusetts: The Williamses stayed in Charlemont, Massachusetts. Mariani
    530.

506. TLS-1

9 Ridge Road, Rutherford, N.J.

Monday [29 July 1946]

Dear Louis:

No card from Celia – as yet. We couldn't come anyway, not at the moment. What we will do and what we have planned to do is to reserve our visit until we have the time for it during the last two weeks in August.

Our plan is as follows, we are going away for a two weeks rest. After that we are coming home but not to work. Instead we are planning to spend ten or twelve days here and there visiting those friends we have wanted to see but have found ourselves unable to visit during the past year. We hope it will be convenient for you to let us come then. One advantage will be that we'll be completely free, barring other visits, to come when it is most convenient for you – and we shan't have to rush away to rest up against the morrow.

What you've said about Paterson is to the point and well said – almost unsaid! just left to be obvious. I'm sure Koch will use it – she'd better use it!

Glad you communicated with Tate. I also have never seen him. I had a good letter from Wyndham Lewis the other day. Ezra suggested that I at least study Ford Madox Ford's style. "You can at least <u>try</u> to improve yourself" is what he actually said. His uninformed presumptions make him pitiable. Once he asked me if I had read the Athenian Constitution. I think the word was "constitution". I lied and said, yes – more out of irritation than for any other reason. Perhaps that illustrates his worth, to badger others into doing the things which he does not perform as he should. I think he very definitely is dappled rather than evenly colored from his faulty reading.

I'm happy over Celia's occupation with her music for my Choral, very happy. To have that performed adequately would shake the world as far as I'm concerned. And poor Paul Rosenfeld, who might have helped us, dead. Did you ever read his <u>Boy in the Sun</u>? It was a beautiful (in the sense that a girl's summer dress is beautiful) novel. I wonder if poor Ezra would ever take the time for that?

I think I'll send you a story I wrote the other day, it's one of my best but unpublishable, so I'm told, by reason of its libelousness. Read it and keep it for me until I see you.

I'm taking the play with me on my vacation in order to revise and prepare it for a professional typing job. After that! ?

Best from Flossie.

    Yours

    Bill

letter from Wyndham Lewis: Letter not located.

Ezra suggested: Letter not located.

Choral: "Choral: The Pink Church."

story: See the following letter.

play: *A Dream of Love.*

9 Ridge Road, Rutherford, N.J.

9/12/46

Dear Louis:

We've been home a couple of weeks, time enough for me to rise again through the leaves – like the new – rather full – moon last night. At last I've got again to my correspondence.

I presume you received the story about the thin girl who was shot to death and have kept it for me as I suggested. The case is still pending and the story perforce since we'll have to see first what they're going to do with the guy.

Besides, the story is yet to be "written", all I have down so far is the bones of it – as you may have noticed.

We had a quiet sort of vacation walking about in the woods and fields but the weather was vile, too cold and rainy for full delight. I was glad to get back and to work again.

Would next Wednesday be a possible evening for us to drop in on you? This weekend comprises combined birthday celbrations for two of us and the following Friday will be taken up with a family wedding. Then the maternity cases start! Tell us how you stand. We can phone you. Keep the story till I call for it.

Nothing new on the piece I wrote for Tate – at least that Tate saw. Vivienne Koch still has it – and says nothing. I begin to wonder about the woman, she is holding too many things of mine without report. I presume there are good reasons for her failure to report but it is inconvenient for me.

I wrote one poem all summer – which I am holding for future use when the occasion shall arise. The play of which I probably spoke to you last year is still under construction: the agent said it wasn't long enough etc so I wrote a new (additional) act, to be Act I. Now it's ready to be retyped by me incorporating certain changes and emendations throughout all the acts (a slow 3 finger process) after which it goes to the professional typist, then to the agent, then to another agent (after the first turns it down.) then to Laughlin and then . . hell only knows. It's a serious piece of work which, of course, means that its chances are slim for getting on B'way. I'll be glad to be through with it as it has occupied much of my spare time for the past two years, off and on, to the exclusion of many things such as the company of certain of my friends. It takes it out of one.

Floss and I have been reading, for the first time much to my shame, Ford Madox Ford's World War I novels. They are magnificent.

Celia probably knows that Briarcliffe Quarterly wants to use some or all of her music to my Choral in their next issue. At least I hope she gave her consent to their using it.

Best from us all
Bill

Dorothy Pound is here, insists Ezra is "innocent" – technically he'll be hung or shot – but I imagine they'll stretch a point and release him soon.

thin girl: Eleanor Musgrove Britton Mark, an old friend of Williams, had been shot to death by her husband in June 1946. See Mariani 529. The story she inspired is "The Farmer's Daughters," *Hudson Review* 10:3 (Autumn 1957), 329–52. Wallace C541.
birthday: Williams's birthday fell on 17 September.
one poem: Unidentified.
play: *A Dream of Love.*
agent: Unidentified.
World War I novels: *Some Do Not* (1924), *No More Parades* (1926), *A Man Could Stand Up* (1926), *Last Post* (1928).
Dorothy Pound: She had arrived in the United States on 6 July 1946 and soon took up residence in Washington, D.C.

508. ALS-1

9 Ridge Road
Rutherford, N.J.

9/29/46

New Republic has bought this for publication "soon". Damn them, why not now, today.

W

this: No contributions by Williams appeared in the *New Republic* between 1947 and 1954.

509. TLS-1

9 Ridge Road, Rutherford, N.J.

10/2/46

Dear Louis:

Again for your private ear (until next Friday after 4 P.M.) for at that hour, October 4, 1946, I am to be hung about the neck with a hood of some unknown color by the University of Buffalo and clept LLD! Nobody knows of this for I was asked for obvious reasons not to let the news get into the hands of the newsmen until after the event.

It's the hundredth year of the founding of the university and a big time for them since they have never given any honorary degrees. They offered me the honor which I at first refused since I do not lay much importance to such gestures and do not feel that I deserve that title. I asked for a Litt doctorate if they insisted on doing something but they said LLD was the highest honor they could give and that they were giving it to scientists and other scholars alike. What could I do?

So Floss and Bill and I are leaving by train tomorrow night – between maternity cases. Such a business! I thought it might amuse you to be told of the thing in advance.

We'll really be seeing you anon. It looks now as though with this past I'll be a little freer again.

> Best to all
> Bill

510. ALS-1

> 30 Willow St
> Brooklyn, 2, N.Y.

Oct 19/46

Dear Bill,

From Bunting:

"Please ask Bill Williams to convey to Dorothy that I will do anything for Ezra that may be in my power: but that I don't think there is anything in my power. Let her have my address and tell her my mother often wishes to hear from her. We cannot help Ezra by asserting his literary value. In fact, the only defence likely to go down with a tribunal would be, that he was so easily tricked & outwitted by Fascists of high position who ministered to his unfortunate appetite for flattery: and I daresay that would be too humiliating for him to own to. Otherwise, so far as I can see, they must endeavour to prove him mad: an untrue defence, but it could easily be supported from his eccentricities."

Basil Bunting

242 Newburn Rd

Throckley, Northumberland

England

Now that I've copied it – I don't know but what Basil doesn't want me to convey more than the first two sentences. Let's say those.

I suppose you've seen September "Poetry" – I suppose what it amounts to is: Dillon <etc> is dead, let the virtuoso live, if we're going to be heroick about it. The tragedy in the whole affair is that Ez can no longer teach us – tho there are, say, six lines in the portion of the canto held at a depth worthier than virtuosity. As I said a long time ago – it's a sad world anyway, not many of us will get out of it alive.

We all have colds, and I suppose you're treating everybody in New Jersey for 'em – I guess that's why you still haven't come over.

Yours

Louis

September "Poetry": See George Dillon, "A Note on the Obvious," *Poetry* 68:6 (September 1946), 322–25. Dillon discusses whether Pound should be published, in view of his wartime radio broadcasts and political beliefs. Dillon argues that Pound, "an important, though frequently mad, writer," should at least be allowed to publish his poems.

the canto: "From *Canto LXXX*," *Poetry* 68:6 (September 1946), 310–21.

As I said: In "Poem Beginning 'The.'"

511. ACS

[Rutherford, N.J.]

[Postmarked 10 January 1947]

Script rec'd. as usual the time in which to read it – carefully, is at the moment lacking. Was in hospital again for a recurrence of hernia making it urgent to work at top speed to catch up on old business. Best

Bill

Script: "Poetry / *For My Son When He Can Read.*"

512. TLS-1

[Rutherford, N.J.]

Januray 26, 1947

Dear Louis:

I have just finished reading through, for the first time, your "Poetry"; it is in yourbest tradition and explains, though it does not clarify, the "cuts" that make your verse what it is. It would be, as it stands, a very necessary preface to the publication of your complete poems or if not this, which you may be preserving for a special purpose, at least something containing what this contains. Your style though simple is, as you must know by this time, hard, hard to follow, the matter of it difficult, in spite of an extreme simplicty, to grasp. I have great difficulty in forming concrete images from your – some of your clauses and sentences.

Yet the whole is clear, as clear perhaps as you want it to be – in order to preserve a music which is as much part of the meaning as anything else and without which no explicitness would be explicit. That's for the reader to struggle with.

It just so happens that yesterday while I was in the attic hunting insanely (in the sense that I was unable to find what I wanted) for a story I wrote several years ago and which was printed and has disappeared! I dug up your poems, the book containing the beginning of "The" and started to read, uncomfortably as I was seated and kept on reading till I had finished that bit. It was good, good in an unusual way.

It was good as music, as measure and as a consciousness of a new measure. It looked in fact as though it would be useful to me in my contual but recently renewed studies of measure and what measure implies in poetry. You state that beautifully in this essay. You use the knowledge beautifully in that poem. The two make a whole.

Not that you represent all that I am after, nor that I sense completely all that you are after. After all, why should either of us be the other. But there is definitely a common ground which is our common inheritance of poetry, its basic importance to us – that unites us. You say this well also in the essay and it is of the essence for us – uniting our differences.

I am continually irritated by my own wars with other men as well as by their self seeking. Nobody sufficiently writes to make us at least tolerate each other. But the good in poetry is a common good, not a sentimental one and not a proprietary one for any of us. At least science has nothing of that. I am glad that in your way you point out that poetry should not have it either. That there should be a measuring (not just a measure).

In a sense you don't say anything new in this essay, "anew" yes and so new to

(10 hours elapsed – during which your letter of this morning has arrived)

Back to the essay: I had been thinking and writing (private papers) of Ezra's encounter with Chinese poetry – thinking that at that very point his deterioration began due entirely (tho' the inclination was already in him) to his turning from <u>sound</u> to pronunciamentos. He from that moment imagined himself Kung or equated himself with all wisdom and, by that failing against which all poets must guard themselves went straight to hell.

     Bill

"Poetry": "Poetry / *For My Son When He Can Read.*"

book containing: *55 Poems* (1941).

private papers: Published posthumously as "A Study of Ezra Pound's Present Position," *Massachusetts Review* 14:1 (Winter 1973), 118–23. In the essay, Williams remarks, "Of his Chinese studies—or from that time on, perhaps—he went astray. The thing is that for us and for him Chinese poetry has never 'sounded.' He lost track there, I am afraid. Either we cannot or at least have not been able to 'hear' Chinese poetry and so it cannot be of any use to us in Pound's old, earlier sense or in my present sense. Pound's insistence on Kung and his importance are all on the soundless idea, on the character. Perhaps that is the precise spot where he went astray—thinking of Kung and his ideographs" (120–21).

513. ALS-1

1/27/47

I'm fine, more secure physically than I've felt in ten years. Work is hard. Laughlin has given me the green light on the next installment of Paterson but I'm having trouble working myself free for it.

Bill

next installment: *Paterson (Book II)* (Norfolk, Connecticut: New Directions, 1948). Wallace A25.

514. TLS-1

9 Ridge Road, Rutherford, N.J.

June 8/47

Dear Louis:

Did I tell you, I've forgot, that I have been invited to <be> and I am going to be an adviser at a literary conference at the University of Utah in July? I have to give one formal lecture. In it I want to refer to that poem of Whitman's which you have mentioned to me of late which is not always included in his collected works.

Give me the name of that poem, will you?

The topic upon which I shall speak will be, Our formal heritage from Walt Whitman. That isn't exactly the wording but something like that. We're going to drive out in my old (reconditioned) Buick with my sister in law as co-pilot. Floss, of course, will be the passenger.

I finished Paterson Book II the other day – good in spots but still not satisfactory. It runs to about sixty pages. If I hear from Laughlin some day it will go some day to the printer and be printed some day and some day appear between covers – perhaps next spring or fall or what the hell.

Yours
Bill

literary conference: The conference was held on 7–18 July. See Mariani 545– 49.
that poem: See the next letter.
The topic: Williams's final title for his lecture was "An Approach to the Poem." It was
    published in *English Institute Essays, 1947* (New York: Columbia Univ. Press, 1948),
    50– 75. Wallace B54.

515. ACS

30 Willow St, B'klyn 2, N.Y.

[Postmarked 9 June 1947]

Dear Bill:

Whitman's <u>Respondez</u>. I understand that Holloway's latest ed. of W's Leaves includes it. Must be a case of extra-sensory perception of you in Utah and me at Colgate this summer that caused it. I've been invited, too; as Asst. Prof. to teach Shakespeare & Eng Renaissance. I note what you say about Paterson II. Maybe ten years from now the Mormons'll be singing C's music to your Choral. Bon Voyage – best to all

Louis.

Holloway's latest ed.: Emory Holloway, ed., *Leaves of Grass* (Garden City, New York: Doubleday, Page, 1924). Holloway included "Respondez" in all of his editions of *Leaves of Grass*. The poem first appeared in the 1856 edition of *Leaves*, but Whitman excluded it after 1876.

Colgate: Colgate University, in Hamilton, New York.

C's music to your Choral: Celia Zukofsky's musical setting of Williams's poem, "Choral: The Pink Church."

516. ACS

[Rutherford, N.J.]

[1947]

Thanks for the information. I'm delighted to hear of the Colgate job. Maybe in another year if Bill takes over at that time we'll get young again. Best.

Bill

Colgate job: See the previous letter.

Bill takes over: William Eric Williams.

517. ACS

[Rutherford, N.J.]

[9 September 1947]

I'm to read the address I gave at Utah this Wednesday (tomorrow) Faculty Club, Columbia U., 400 W 117 St. N.Y.C. 8 p.m. – guests appear to be welcome – if you wish.

Bill

the address: "An Approach to the Poem."

518. TLS-1

[Rutherford, N.J.]

September 23, 1947

Dear Louis:

I have searched the house through, for the past hour, looking into every file and drawer, even into my sacred trunk but I cannot find your "Poetry". I remember having the script but feel sure it was returned to you for I have never yet lost a writing that has been entrusted to me – so far as I know. If I can think of another place to look I'll do so but so far, no luck. I hope you have a third copy.

You ask what's doing. Sam Kootz asked me to write 1000 words for a book to contain reproductions of paintings he is now exhibiting. I wrote the 1000 words which will appear, if he carries out his scheem, in book now scheduled for Christmas.

I'm sorry about the essay. Try to recall what happened. Didn't you ask me to send it to someone else at one time? I have't seenit here for at least two years as far as I remember. I'm sure it was either returned to you or sent elsewhere, perhaps to Laughlin. These things bother me.

    Sincerely

    Bill

I found "A" part 1 in my trunk.

your "Poetry": "Poetry / *For My Son When He Can Read.*"
1000 words: "Woman as Operator," *Women: A Collaboration of Artists and Writers* (New York: Samuel M Kootz Editions, 1948). Wallace B51.

519. ALS-2

9 Ridge Road, Rutherford, New Jersey

March 9/48

Dear Louis:

I'm still in bed, it's about a month now of it, but I hope to be allowed to be up this week sometime, at least in a chair. I've not been idle of course, rather the opposite as far as reading is concerned. It's been a great treat on that score. I haven't read so much in so short a time since I got fuzz on my belly.

If you like the article we sent you and shd want more of the same say the word & I'll get a few extra copies of it for you. I still think the poem I quoted is a beauty & for very sound theoretical reasons, you'll hear more of that another time. For I'm invited to speak at a conference again this year but at the U. of Washington in Seattle this time – in July. I'll send you my principal thesis as soon as I write it. It will refer among other things to that poem of yours.

I don't know whether you saw the February Partisan Review, it contains a few selections from Paterson II which ought to be out any day now – but I've been saying this for a month.

Your new "love" theme interests me greatly – but do get to work on it, don't let it lag. I'll be waiting.

Kate Hecht baked me a swell pumpkin pie this week or was it last week? – made from the last pumpkin brought home form their farm. It was delicious.

Just rec'd a copy of <u>Life Along the Passaic River</u> translated into french in Lausanne, paper bound. It looks interesting. I hope they make a few bucks on it for their trouble.

– & Spring is all but here! I hope I don't bust a gut welcoming it. See you sometime. Love to Celia & the Kid.

> Yours
> Bill

Among other things including some Chaucer, I read Freud's The Interpretation of Dreams. What a marvelous (but technical) book! Also Santayana's The Last Puritan. Good but slow. Also read Wilson's Axel's Castle; Short Stories of Frank O'Connor, Auden's Poems – dabbled in Untermeyer's Anthology; Christ Stopped at Eboli <by Carlo Levi> (1935) The Marble Cliffs, a new New Directions book & much else. Now well into Chapman's Homer's Iliads. Wonderful moments. Have made some notes on Paterson III & IV, enough to have mapped the completed poem. Here's hoping I can use them to effect when they let me use the typewriter again. I hear from Ezra, brief jottings, from time to time. He's apparently well and in good spirits as far as I can tell.

still in bed: Williams had suffered a heart attack in mid–February.

article we sent you: Probably "A New Line is a New Measure."

poem I quoted: In "A New Line is a New Measure," Williams quotes *Anew* 42.

conference: See Mariani 561– 65. Williams's "principal thesis" was "The Poem as a Field of Action." It appears in *SE*.

February Partisan Review: "From Paterson: Book II," *Partisan Review* 15:2 (February 1948), 213– 16. Wallace C398.

"love theme": Probably a portion of *Bottom: On Shakespeare*, which Zukofsky had begun in 1947.

translated: Jean Vermandoy, trans., *Passaic, Passaic!* (Lausanne, Switzerland: Abbaye du livre, 1948). Wallace T5.

among other things: Sigmund Freud, *The Interpretation of Dreams* (1900); George Santayana, *The Last Puritan* (1935); Edmund Wilson, *Axel's Castle* (1930); Frank O'Connor (Williams may refer to *The Common Chord* [New York: Knopf, 1948]); W. H. Auden (In a letter of 25 May 1948 to Babette Deutsch [*Selected Letters*, 264– 65], Williams reports he has read *The Age of Anxiety* [New York: Random House, 1947],

SL, 264); Louis Untermeyer's anthology, *Modern American Poetry* (1919) went through eight editions; Carlo Levi, *Christ Stopped at Eboli* (New York: Farrar, 1947); Ernst Juenger, *On the Marble Cliffs* (Norfolk, Connecticut: New Directions, 1947).

520. ALS-1

9 Ridge Road, Rutherford, N.J.

March 15/48

Dear Louis:

I read your theme with the greatest interest. It's good but difficult, really tough going for the mind unskilled in the techniques of abstruse thought. For myself nothing excites me more than hard thinking, close attention and the real work of getting down on top of a difficult thinking job. But it took all I had.

And yet its simple! I realize that and necessary to a mind intent upon finding out a right way in the world especially the world of the poems. There is no other way than this, too, I acknowledge that. It is salutary to thought – but it's still tough. Got to be, I guess. I enjoyed it. Let's have more.

I wonder who'd print it? I'd like to show it to Eric Bentley some day. Meanwhile I return it: read.

I'm getting on but still a bit shaky.

Get hold of a mag, called Touchstone, 17 E. 42nd St & send them 50¢ for their 2nd & last issue!! Do it at once as I have an article in it I'd like you to see – the thing is likely to become a rarity now that its going out of print.

> Best to all
> Bill

your theme: Probably a portion of *Bottom: On Shakespeare.*

Bentley: (b. 1916), British-born American critic, translator and playwright. Author of *The Playwright as Thinker* (1946).

an article: "VS," *Touchstone* 1:3 (January 1948), 2–7. Wallace C397.

521. ALS-2

Hotel Chalfonte-Haddon Hall, Atlantic City, N.J.

April 6/48

Dear Louis:

Almost two months now and I'm still not working: just made up my mind this morning while taking my salt "tub" in this luxurious hotel that until the small wound on my right shin I got kicking snow away from the front of my stalled car in February finally looks normal again I ~~won't~~ shan't be cured. It still looks an angry red.

We have been here at Atlantic City for not quite a week. It's <just> the place for wounded veterans and I'm much improved over the way I was even ten days ago. Oh well, I didn't croak, that's the main thing. Wish I could give a little of this to stupid ol' Ezra little as he deserves it in some ways. Still I'd like to see him escape what might very well might be meted out to him finally.

You saw perhaps that the Academy of Arts & Sciences gave me their poetry prize this year. Marianne Moore is to make the speech of bestowal some time in May. That was another reason for staying alive if that isn't putting it a little too strong.

That Mag. Touchstone was a failure. My piece was in the *third* issue of which they sent me one copy before they folded up & have not so much as answered my letters since. Too bad – but that's what happens. I hope I don't jinx the Academy of arts & Sciences or spavin poor Marianne.

Of course I go on writing, just can't stop. I did the opening passage of Paterson III while here and finally worked out an outline for what I'll say at Seattle in July.

That outline had me stymied. I had voluminous notes (which usually come first with me) but no satisfactory framework on which to hang them: no bones. Now I got de bones. So it goes.

Best to Celia and the kid, wish you all all the luck that's decent to have.

Bill

poetry prize: The National Institute of Arts and Letters awarded the Russell Loines
Award for Poetry to Williams and Allen Tate. The prize was bestowed on 21 May 1948.
Mariani 559– 61.

outline: Of the seven drafts for "The Poem as a Field of Action" at Buffalo, one is dated
"Atlantic City—April 6– 9."

522. ALS-1

30 Willow St.
Brooklyn 2, N.Y.

April 7/48
Dear Bill:
Felicitations! Yes, I saw the announcement of your award in Sat.'s Times, proving that virtue is its own reward. Just stop worrying! Your attitude about your health has to be that of a friend once told by an evangelist he was going to die: "That's strange, it has never happened to me before." You may remember twenty years ago, when I first met you, you were feeling blue, and I prophesied some good etc. I'm a prophet in these things.

I didn't know you were consultant of poetry in English for Lib. of Cong. Do they pay? I wonder what your duties are.

I'll get hold of <u>Touchstone</u> 3 somehow, sometime. Brentano's said they had never heard from them after 2nd No. One copy! Yes, Cronos wrote last week to tell me they'll be sending me <u>one</u> copy of <u>Poetry: For My Son</u>, which has finally come out. I haven't received it yet. Are you a subscriber? If not, I'll order a few copies and send you one, since you're in it. Let me know.

What's Ezra bothering you about now? I wonder if the guy who was going to edit his early letters ca 1928, ever got around to it, after troubling <me> for a collection which he never picked up. People always get scared of decency.

All the luck to Paterson III. You don't say whether II is out.

My teaching job is deadly, in one way – the time I have to put in correcting papers, theses etc – some of 'em running into 100 pages. I might as well have been a doctor. I hope I can rest up this summer – I get so tired I feel drugged. Like glass in the eyes.

[...]

You might as well hold on to the stray copy of the poem, enclosed, I wrote last year; the jotting on the same piece probably goes back six years. Found it by accident the other day and it seemed funny enough, about as funny as our time.

Best to Floss & all. Get well.

Louis

announcement: "Jersey Physician Wins Loines Award for Poetry," the *New York Times* (3 April 1948, p. 6). "Dr. William Carlos Williams of Rutherford, N.J., physician, poet and author, has been chosen as the recipient of the Russell Loines Memorial Award for Poetry, Douglas Moore, president of the National Institute of Arts and Letters, announced yesterday. The award derives from a fund established in 1924 by friends of Russell Loines to perpetuate his memory by according recognition to an American or an English poet. Dr. Williams, who recently was appointed as a consultant of poetry in English by the Library of Congress, in 1926 won the Dial award of $2,000 for 'services to American literature' and in 1931 won the Guarantor's Prize awarded by Poetry. His twelve published poetical works include 'Sour Grapes,' 'Adam and Eve and the City' and 'Broken Span.' He has also published eleven volumes of prose. The award will amount to $1,000 and will be presented on May 21 at the Academy auditorium, 632 West Fifty-sixth Street."

consultant in poetry: Robert Lowell had urged Williams to take up the post (in the fall of the year) of Consultant in Poetry at the Library of Congress. Williams accepted the offer in late January. Mariani 560.

<u>one</u> copy: "Poetry / *For My Son When He Can Read*," *Cronos* 2:4 (March 1948), 22–30.

the guy: Possibly Douglas Duncan Paige, editor of *The Letters of Ezra Pound 1907–1941* (New York: Harcourt, Brace, 1950).

stray copy: Enclosure lacking.

30 Willow St
Brooklyn 2, N.Y.

[Postmarked 27 May 1948]

Dear Bill – "Just to say" I enjoyed what you had to say about "the Eliot" in Four Pages – run by Confucius himself? I notice you girded your loins the other day (last page of N.Y. Times) – so I hope you're really better. Not feeling so hot myself this week – bad cold, aches. I suppose you got my note at Atlantic City – nothing that required immediate answer, something about your job with Lib. of Cong. All the best. Celia's too – Louis.

what you had to say: "With Forced Fingers Rude," *Four Pages* 2 (February 1948), 1– 4. Wallace C399.

Confucius: Ezra Pound.

last page: "Writers, Artists Win $1,000 Grants," the *New York Times* (22 May 1948, p. 16). The article remarks of Williams that "Dr. William Carlos Williams received the Russell Loines Memorial award of $1,000 for poetry. The Rutherford (N.J.) physician, poet, novelist, essayist and author of short stories, who more than two decades ago helped free American poetry from some of its inhibitions, is now consultant of poetry in English to the Library of Congress."

[30 Willow Street
Brooklyn, New York]

June 7/48
Dear Bill

"April is the Saddest Month" is, of course, a good poem. I thought it might have to do with T.S.E., from the title, but he's not in that part of the zodiac. So what were people shocked about?!

I've read Baxter Bernstein, and am going on into Firdausi – a punk translation but enough to make out . . . It's pleasant in a sense to have "The" etc quoted in a serious book – tho it <(the book)> could have been funnier and more serious – especially good in the Inez, beggar, and Johnnie Mae episodes – but after 20 years I shrug my shoulders: what's good about style is that the "attempt at" doesn't show thru. But that's everybody's job – so why criticize. Incidentally, the "selected eggs" couplet in Baxter is not mine – I had merely quoted it to Serly on one occasion. If anyone cares – I say this for the record. The curious will be curious as to what kind of gazelle am I, and then be disillusioned – as were Scribners recently who wanted to see me and? my poems. I told them I didn't care but it would be nice if they'd help me celebrate my 25th anniversary as poet, published poet, and Wheelock said "almost 26th to be exact" out of the year 1910 or ten years earlier. But, of course, they won't. I suppose I have about ten years to wait yet.

So I should be on "A" again in Lyme. And a good summer to you two.
> Best
> Louis

good poem: "April Is the Saddest Month," *Imagi* 4:2 (Summer-Fall 1948), 1. Wallace C409. *CP2*, 117.

Bernstein: Stephen Seley, *Baxter Bernstein: A Hero of Sorts* (New York: Scribner's, 1949). Baxter Bernstein is a young, aspiring writer. The novel is set in New Orleans during November, 1941, and in Mexico City in April and May 1942. Selected phrases from "Poem Beginning 'The'" frequently drift through Bernstein's consciousness.

Inez: *Baxter Bernstein*, 66–81.

beggar: *Baxter Bernstein*, 91–92 and 144.

Johnnie Mae: *Baxter Bernstein*, 155–56 and 171–84.

"selected eggs": "Now, too, between his legs ('Oh, what are those between your legs?' Louis Zukofsky had inquired), hung his dark-brown curly head ('Why, two fresh-selected eggs'), to which, like shame, the blood rushed as he said to himself that he must be degenerating, must be prematurely becoming a tenth-rate Baron de Charlus," *Baxter Bernstein*, 119–20.

gazelle: "And about the only kind of thing that he could learn to understand without being hit between the eyes was the kind of thing that his friend Louis Zukofsky, a gazelle, once said to him: 'It's a sad world, anyway. Not many of us will get out of it alive . . .'" *Baxter Bernstein*, 3. Zukofsky is also referred to as a gazelle on the novel's final page (239).

Wheelock: John Hall Wheelock (1886–1978), poet and editor. Wheelock was an editor at Scribner's from 1926 to 1957.

Lyme: Lyme, Connecticut, where the Zukofsky family vacationed that summer.

■ 525. TLS-1

[Rutherford, N.J.]

June 26, 1948

Dear Louis:

Dorothy Pound's address enclosed. Write to her asking her to question Ezra on the details you are interested in. She may give you the information you need. Or she may say nothing at all. She has abnegated whatever independant thought she ever had in order to make herself his rubber stamp. Or rather his mouth-piece. I have discovered no evident of independant thought in her in years. It can be annoying. It can be annoying when the evidence points to a sane person making herself the mouth-piece of another's insanity. Or perhaps she's just English.

But it infuriates me that the shits of the world, where I include Ezra in some of his moods (not all) should block you in your valuable idea of using their work to help an appreciation of them. Of course it is to vomit to think of the publishers and their demands for "royalties" at all times – regardless of the quality of the demand for the work their copyrights cover.

You have helped me, even finalcially, in the past. I'd be glad to contribute twenty five to fifty dollarstoto help you and to help Celia in her puspose to help you get out your very valuable book. It would be no more than just for me to do so. Count on me.

The news about the theatre is this: I have the two plays of which you know. (1) Trial Horse #1 and (2) A Dream of Love. The first came out in one of the New Directions annual anthologies several years ago. The second is to appear as an issue of Pharos, a mag Laughlin brings out now and then. This play I have somewhat revised, printed (I have a few advance copies) it looks pretty good.

Now during the last month or two, ever since the Loines Award in fact, I have been receiving all sorts of attention (in a small way) from strangers. Among such strangers have been people wanting "to bring out my plays". There are 3 offers for one or the other of the plays. All are professional "non-profit" groups whose names mean little – but all New York sponsored. Oh well, oh well, oh well. That's that. Let's hope there'll be some fire after the smoke clears up. I'll let you know.

Ger after Dorothy and pay the God damned royalties if you must. I'll help.

Best

Bill

Enclosure: A leaf from Williams's prescription pad: "D.P. 3211—10th Place S.E. Washington D.C. Say that I gave it to you."

your valuable idea: Zukofsky sought permission from various poets to include their work in *A Test of Poetry* (New York: Objectivist Press, 1948). On 18 June 1947, Zukofsky wrote to Ezra Pound, asking his permission to quote from various works (Lilly). Pound declined to permit the quotation of any of his poems in *A Test.*

Pharos: James Laughlin's magazine was titled *Direction.* Williams's play was published in the sixth issue (1948). Wallace A27.

[30 Willow Street
Brooklyn, New York]

June 28/48

Dear Bill,

Thanks, thanks. I've written Dorothy to say that if Ez. does not wish me to include him, I won't tho with regret – and that if I do not hear from them by this Friday, to save her the nuisance of writing, I'll assume their answer is <u>no</u>. Celia called New Directions & we know definitely that Ez. has the copyright to his works.

Thanks for offering to help financially, Bill – but we wouldn't feel right taking it. Let it be for <u>Dog and the Fever</u> if & when – that book means a lot to me, takes me back 20 years when I first came out to Rutherford.

But you can help with a sentence about <u>Test</u> for the jacket – you remember Celia asked, no doubt an oversight you haven't sent it. Fadiman (I think I told you he was crazy about the book a few years ago & tried to market it, but even he couldn't) has given us a good blurb. I haven't heard from Mark Van Doren who has been friendly and decent, especially about C's <u>Pericles</u>, but he may be who knows where -he's involved in many things, and if we don't hear from him – Fadiman's blurb & yours will have to be enough. The printer is cheap, all others ask twice as much and more, but he must have the Ms right away, i.e. when he's free in the summer. I hate to bother you for another blurb, but as you say those things count – "ever since the Loines Award" etc. If we suffer long, we smile automatically etc.

Another thing you can do, tho' you've already given it – write out a sentence granting formal permission, just in case there is ever any trouble you don't anticipate now – i.e. L.Z. may quote in his <u>A Test of Poetry</u> any of my published work – signed W.C.W. I'm asking <u>everybody</u>.

Going back to Ez, I propose, if he says no, since there are gaps in the volume, to use instead quotes from Paterson I, or some of 'em, included in my unpublished review of it, <which you saw.> If the volume were written today from scratch, they'd be in, in any case, but it represents more than criticism to me, so much of what things were in 1934 & you know my persistent loyalties etc. Besides the volume has a plan I can't break into without having to re-write it all – & it so happens <certain> quotes from <u>Cantos</u> can be replaced very pointedly by <some from> Paterson I. I haven't seen Paterson II – but, in any case, I'd have to think fast & fresh if I wanted to use some of that – & I'm swamped what with summer school, & thinking of pertinent substitutions for Ez's Homer, Propertius etc etc, and of telling the Royalties gang of pubs. where to come off re – Emily Dickinson etc.

Yup, I hope the professional theater <u>acts</u> for you. I might be able to look at "A Dream of Love" as soon as the mess here is cleaned up.

Incidentally, ~~I may that~~ Celia, the kid & I, may be seeing the Kinnings <this Wed.> in Rutherford <or stet> ~~one of these days~~ – my, own, inclination, of course, is to phone you when I get there & if you're free to say hello for a few minutes before <we> ~~going~~ to the Kinnings – but please be frank if it's too much of a strain on you – I know Floss & you have gone thru plenty – - please <say> so – <u>we won't feel hurt, if you can't.</u>

So if you can let me know about all this by Wed – I'll stop rushing you.

Incidentally I forgot to say I cleaned up the questions & prose of <u>Test</u> a bit – and Part II opens with your blurb for "55" (no reference to "55", of course, in this case) and a quote from an honest guy, Michael Faraday. But let the printed text surprise you.

  Best
  Louis.

<u>Dog and the Fever</u>: William Carlos Williams and Raquel Hélène Williams, trans., *The Dog and the Fever* (Hamden, Connecticut: Shoe String Press, 1954). Wallace A39.

sentence about <u>Test</u>: Williams's sentence: "There is no test for poetry, barring this test, available to our present world—save in the minds of a few experts" (Wallace G3).

Fadiman: Clifton Fadiman (1904-1999), American critic and author. He had first become acquainted with Zukofsky when both were students at Columbia University. "[Fadiman] has, I believe, a great respect for Zukofsky—they were at college together," *Selected Letters of Charles Reznikoff*, Milton Hindus, ed. (Santa Rosa, California: Black Sparrow Press, 1997), 113-14. Fadiman's "good blurb" was, "Ingenious and amusing. More important, this goes to the very heart of poetry and in so doing, becomes a test of the reader's own mind and imagination."

unpublished review: I have not been able to locate the review Zukofsky refers to. The "Notes on Paterson" (1946) at the Harry Ransom Humanities Research Center (Booth E19) are just that—a few brief jottings.

Kinnings: Leslie Kinning was an art director at Techlit, a company Zukofsky had worked for in 1946. Kinning resided in Rutherford, New Jersey.

your blurb: Part II begins with this quotation from Williams: ". . . only the primarily beautiful and new (old:new) remaining."

quote from an honest guy: This passage from Faraday follows the quotation from Williams: "You will find many pencil marks, for I made them as I read. I let them stand, for though many receive their answer as the story proceeds, yet they show how the wording impresses a mind fresh to the subject, and perhaps here and there you may like to alter it slightly, if you wish the full idea, i.e. not an inaccurate one, to be suggested at first; and yet after all I believe it is not your exposition, but the natural jumping to a conclusion that affects or has affected my pencil."

Seattle, Washington

Thursday

July 22/48

Dear Louis:

Getting through my week of "teaching" here at the Convention – & still alive!

Professor Perrin gave the key-note speech on the opening night, a good speech & a good man. I spoke to him of you. He remembered you well and was anxious to know how you were getting on. He seemed genuinely concerned, as much as to say, "I like the guy but I'm worried about him." I told him of your book. He liked that.

This is a "far country" all right but, dumb as their politicians may be the run of the people is/are first rate.

Best to Celia

Bill

Convention: See Mariani 561– 65.

Perrin: Charles Perrin. I have not been able to discover how he knew Zukofsky.

your book: *A Test of Poetry*.

[Postmarked Rutherford, N.J.]

[Postmarked 27 August 1948]

I spoke to Norton over the phone & told him I'd go in as my scrips originally stood without deletions. He said he would make it clear <u>where</u> my scrip was written. Mail books today.

Yours as ever

Bill

Hope you saw the last <u>"Accent"</u>? Quotes you on Pound

Norton: Probably Charles Norman, whose *The Case of Ezra Pound* (New York: Bodley Press, 1948) contained statements about Pound by Williams and Zukofsky. The book was published on 1 October 1948.

"Accent": Robert M. Adams, "A Hawk and a Handsaw for Ezra Pound," *Accent* (Summer 1948), 205–14. Early in his essay, Adams writes, "In 1930 Louis Zukovsky [*sic*] inspected the first twenty-seven Cantos and found them 'closely related in method and spirit to the kind of ideation found in Dante's *Divine Comedy*.'" Adams found the passage in Zukofsky's essay, "Ezra Pound" (*Prepositions +*, 75).

[Rutherford, N.J.]

Friday [3 September 1948]

Dear Celia:

Life permitting, how about next Wednesday evening? We can, I think, make it then. Then or Friday but Wednesday would be best for us. And many thanks. I'll bring the books.

      Best luck

      Bill

If I don't hear from you we'll come Wednesday getting there as near 6 p.m. as we may.

      <u>W</u>

the books: The following letter indicates that at least one of the books was the recently published *The Clouds*. Williams's presentation copy of *The Clouds* in the Zukofsky papers is dated "9/8/48[.]"

■ 530. TLS-1

[Rutherford, N.J.]

Sept 12/48

Dear Louis:

Many thanks for the letter with the specific citations of lines and poems you enjoyed. I was very much interested in what you selected and what you passed over – not, I understand, that your selections were mean to be exclusive. I'm glad you liked the little Flossie poem as well as the one to Suzanne – and also the one about the "red-wing blackbird" which was, I suppose, autobiographic.

We enjoyed our visit, more I think than ever before. The violin playing was a high light. And how fast they grow! In a few years it'll be Town hall at the very least. At least that is my hope. The compliment of his First Symphony (Number 7!) if it was meant to be favorable to me, is very thrilling.

School will give Celia a chance to do more composition. I was conscious that we didn't get to speak of Celia's music. I wanted to say something but the time lacking it appeared to me best to forget it. Some day (when Bill is practicing and I have more time to myself) we've got to have an evening together with no other topic appointed for consideration than Celia's music and what she is doing with it. I want to hear. And we must plan some performance. Maybe when I'm in Washington! Maybe something can be arranged – if I go to Washington next year.

I'll be looking for A Test before Christmas.

      Best all around

      Bill

Flossie poem: "The Flower," first published in *The Clouds. CP2*, 152–53.

one to Suzanne: "Suzanne," first published in *The Clouds. CP2*, 150.

"red-wing blackbird": "The Red-Wing Blackbird," first collected in *The Clouds*. Its only previous publication was in the *New Leader* 30:9 (1 March 1947), 12. Wallace C385. *CP2*, 163.

Bill: William Eric Williams.

Washington: Williams hoped to be able to take up his appointment as Consultant in Poetry to the Library of Congress in 1949.

531. ACS

[Postmarked Rutherford, N.J.]

[Postmarked 13 September 1948]
The writer was Vivienne Koch.
And what to do with all this. Nice space left on the card?

Bill

532. TLS-1

[Rutherford, N.J.]

Sept. 15/48
Dear Louis:

This is the Aegeltinger story (on a dirty sheet ofpaper) When my brother and I commuted to Horace Mann High School in 1899–1903 (leaving Ruth. at 7 A.M. daily through Friday) we'd take the Chambers St. ferry, then the 9th Ave L for 116th St.

At about Desbrosses St. a New York gang would get on the train and join us. Aegetltinger, who was in our class, was frequently among them. He was a big rather soft guy whom we all recognized to be a mathematical genius. We'd be slaving over our algebra, sometimes winning, sometimes losing – after hard work for an hour or so. We all waited for Aegeltinger.

We'd show him the problem – which he hadn't even looked at the night before and he'd do it in his head in about 30 seconds. It was wonderful to us.

Well, Aegetltinger also played football and when he went to Columbia he got to be captain of the Varsity – or if not captain he became very popular as a player and everybody knew him. He graduated as an engineer and set up an office in New York. He was very successful but for some reason started to drink and drank so heavily that he completely ruined his business and himself.

At this point my informer, a Mr. Goss enters the story. Mr. Goss lived in Rutherford and went to our church. My brother got his first job from Goss who had an office on the 22nd floor of the St Paul Building on Park Row. I had completely lost track of Aegeltinger but one day Mr. Goss said he'd have to lookup Aegetltinger as a had a particularly tough piece of figuring he'd have to face and he didn't know anyone else in N.Y. who could do it so well.

Aegeltltinger, I said, I used to know a man named Aegeltinger. It turned out to be the same man. He was well known among the engineers. First they'd have to find him – in the back of some saloon where he'd been drinking for a week. Then they'd send him to a hotel, sober himup, give him the job to solve, pay him and – away he'd go back to drinking. That's all.

I meant Washington, D.C. – but that's at leat a year away – if I take it up, which is not at all certain at this time. But I'm not through with C. by any means. I've got my ears pointed, I'd especially want to work on a summer porject I have in mind – which may or may not work out: a U. of Rochester (N.Y.) business. More of that at another time.

> Best
> Bill

There are still a few (very few) Aegeltingers in the N.Y.C. Telephone directory. He's probably among them.

Aegeltinger: Williams's poem about this man was originally titled "April 6," *The General Magazine and Historical Chronicle* 47:4 (Summer 1945), 220–221. Wallace C356. Subsequent printings of the poem were titled "Aigeltinger." It was the first poem in *The Clouds. CP2*, 123–24.

summer porject: I have been unable to determine what Williams intended with respect to the University of Rochester. The project appears not to have been realized.

533. TLS-1

[Rutherford, N.J.]

Sept. 15/48

Dear Louis & Celia:

I told Mother this afternoon of Paul's playing of the violin. She was highly amused and interested, could hardly believe it true. I had to show her the size of the fiddle and show her how he stood and bowed. She was very much taken by the story. Finally she said, My compliments to the father and mother. So that's what I'm sending you.

> Best
> Bill

Paul's: Paul Zukofsky.

[Rutherford, N.J.]

Constitution Day [17 September] 1948

Dear Louis:

Happy Birthday (my own); what's the different? Thought you might enjoy the enclosed greeting.

Maybe Celia will set it to music – notice the slow nostalgic line.

Best

Bill

enclosed greeting: "Turkey in the Straw," *CP2*, 231. In a subsequent letter (September 1948) to Celia Zukofsky, Williams commented, "No, I guess I didn't exactly mean the same tune as Turkey in the Straw—but after that nature. Please don't waste your time for, after all, I have no clear conception of what sort of music it might make. All I have in mind is a contrast between a residual sensuality and the romantic dreams of youth: both, however, somehow related" (Maryland).

■ 535. ALS-2

[Rutherford, N.J.]

9/30/48

Dear Louis:

It is a wonderful book, I have a feeling of awe at being in such places – such a place seems to restrictive.

Really a magnificent achievement – to get such clarity and depth of feeling and such conviction into so small a space.

I have never felt the meaning of the poems so convincingly presented – really there is something so clean. So sweet smelling about this all – the whole book that it is saintlike to me in the most profanely beautiful way I can imagine –

———

Mother said to me yesterday – I have been philosophizing all afternoon (she sits alone there in her room for months and years at a time – & was very clear in her statements then) – all afternooon and I have come to the conclusion that this life is worth nothing at all.

———

Such serious, if demented statement, has the same quality to it as your book, this book. It has the total dedication of absolute statements. Frankly I am amazed at the finality of almost all of your prose comments. I have never in my life seen anything like it – like that, of that nature – even tho' I say it has the same quality as poor Mother's near-raving.

Bill

wonderful book: *A Test of Poetry.*

536. TLS-1

Sunday Oct 4/48

Dear Louis:

I feel terribly flattered and uncertain by your inclusion of so many short pieces of mine in such an amazing combination with the poems of all ages – so inexplicably effective in its secret meaning: I can't find out the whole meaning. I am still and always shall be very much upset by this. I see the good that is in what I have done – but a sort of bedazzlement takes hold of me. Can it be as good as that or has Louis out of his love and knowledge so arranged things that he has put me up where many another might do as well or better? I don't know. I hope for the best.

You have succeeded so astonishingly in <u>making</u> something – this book, in itself such an elevated composition, all in one, that actually is a sort of heavenly collage (Colage?) that brings out the good in great and poor – in itself as great as the greatest.

I want to say that the book still comes to me in a cloud. I can't quite make it out, why it is so good – as great as any one of the contents.

And it makes Shakespeare, for instance, humble – it takes him out of the vulgar context (by the slightest examples, a few bits of his work) and brings Shelly (at his best) up to him and yet takes Shakespeare down (in some of his sonnets which I have always suspected) and Shelly in some of his lyrics down too beside the weakest. Then up with them again.

I am trying to show a something which is the book itself, an excellence of measure which carries all these things as if they were on a wire, strung to meet a certain exalted meaning or existance rather, a "live wire" holding them together in a garland. It ought to be known, this book, in the old fashioned way as "a garland".

But suppose it had been composed by someone else, someone to whom I was unknown (I don't think <u>any</u>body else could have composed it but you – and that's t he answer) But suppose someone else had composed it and left me out. Would I have in the first place ever have read it? And if I had would I have believed in it?

I don't know. In fact the book is you and it is magnificent so my question does not need answering – doe'nt exists (as Dora Marsden would have said) I am still in a daze.

Oh yes, and send me five copies to give away. Check enclosed.

Best

Bill

this book: *A Test of Poetry*.

Marsden: (1882–1960), British feminist, editor and author. Williams published some of his early poetry and prose in Marsden's *New Freewoman and Egoist*. For a discussion of Williams's interest in Marsden, see Bruce Clarke, *Dora Marsden and Early Modernism* (Ann Arbor: Univ. of Michigan Press, 1996).

537. TLS-1

[Rutherford, N.J.]

Oct. 16 or so [1948]

Dear Louis:

I wish you had been at the Y.M.H.A. last Thursday or the Thursday just past – when I gave the first of my four lectures on "the new measure" – which is supplanting the Saintsbury english foot. I didn't speak very well but among other things I read various examples of the "american stroke" the expanded foot and what it implies (I'm beginning at last to understand what is taking place myself).

Among other things I read your long poem about the three who are your closet friends – the one I admire so much and think so important as a landmark in wath is going on. It is a very valuable piece of work and one which you yourself have not sufficently exploited.

Well, at the end during the question period (and there was some young professorial face that was white with anger at my statements) Parker Tyler spoke and spoke well from the floor. The point of this letter is that he pointed out your poem as the only one that bore out my presentation convincingly. It is true, it is a striking piece of new work.

I want to go on with my exposition of the new practice (I avoid all mention of "theory"). It accumulates in my mind gradually with accretions forming every day now. I must get it down for it resolves a liftime of thought – and practice.

Bill has at last, day before yesterday, been given his license to practice medicine in New Jersey after surmounting whole thickets of Red Tabe – a most disgraceful exhibition on the part of the State Examiners; a struggle that has had me close to murder since last March – the sonsdof bitches. It is all but incredible what has been taking place with delay, lies, carelessness and indifference.

But it is over now and I am free to die as I please from now on. It is all his, all the kid's. I am extremely happy for I know what he is and I know him to be good in no mean way.

(Breakfast)

Brahms' First Symphony is on the machine (we're trying out a new needle: it works fine) This is an instance when the first work was the greatest, Brahms 1st is, I think, the best.

I got Celia's music but haven't had a moment in which to try it as yet. Patience.

> Best
> Bill

P.S. My mind's a sieve.

four lectures: Williams wrote to Celia Zukofsky in September 1948, "I am to give a lecture at the 92nd St Y.M.H.A. Thurs. Oct. 14th one of four lectures on 'the new measure' tho' the first one is entitled A Few Hints Toward the Enjoyment of the Modern Poem" (Maryland).

Saintsbury: George Saintsbury (1845–1933), British literary critic and historian. Author of *A History of English Prosody from the Twelfth Century to the Present Day* (3 vols., 1906–1910) and *Historical Manual of English Prosody.*

your long poem: *Anew* 42.

Tyler: (1907–1974), poet and film critic.

Bill: William Eric Williams.

538. ALS-1

[Rutherford, N.J.]

Oct 20/48

Dear Louis:

I wrote Jim mentioning Ferdinand again & telling him that I'm sending him a copy of Test which I'm doing now.

You might care to see his reply.

> Best
> Bill

Jim: James Laughlin.

Test: *A Test of Poetry.*

539. ALS-1

11/14/48
Dear Louis:
It moves a little.
 Bill
Please return the letter.

the letter: Enclosure lacking.

540. TLS-1

[Rutherford, N.J.]

November 19, 1948
Dear Louis:

I got such a sharp barking at by Floss when the music Celia wrote for my BEAUTIFUL song came back that I've never had it played for me. Not serious on Flossie's part, just a momentary flash of anger, that I had, actually "kissed her while she pissed" I guess. "Aren't you ever going to grow up"? is the way she phrased it. Clever of her, what?

We'll get to the muisc, have it played at Christmas as a carol perhaps.

She and I are going to Washington today, to hear the great Eliot tonight at the Library of Congress. I thought I might as well and with Bill here it is the first plum we have reached for and picked – or planned to pick.

Decided this motning with fog outside the bedroom window that I might as well believe in a future life. Why not if it makes the mind lively? All the crooks and hidden-evil-wishers <so> yodel and scream in public of their new found catholicity (with a c (l.c.)) that there should be a *scatalogical correction somewhere. I feel better already.

<Wrong word: I meant to say – relating to catalogues (see reverse)>

Me ma is wonderful on the subject, the only difficulty being that all her re-venants are such nasty bastards. I don't know why she bas to pick such skunks. She says they want to "hurt people" but she can't say why. Pour sould, being unable to see or hear or walk she has invented the most marvellous assembly of mitches and whore-masters to entertain her. The other day is a was an endless column of Mexican cavalry riding bareback "to show us how they ride" There's a war on between Mexico and the U.S. . you know. She tells you all about it

The guy's name is Bob Wetterau, an employee of thr Pickwick Book Shop in L.A., a swell egg.
 Best
 Bill

Funny as hell, when I looked it up (still don't know the correct word) but
scatology means the study of the excrement of fossil fish to determine identities.

beautiful song: "Turkey in the Straw." Celia Zukofsky dated her music for the poem 6 Oc-
tober 1948.

Eliot tonight: Robert Lowell introduced Williams to Eliot that night. Mariani 572.

Bill: William Eric Williams.

Wetterau: Williams met him in May 1940, when Wetterau (1911–1972) managed the book-
store at Pennsylvania State University. Williams had come to read at the university.
Wetterau was interested in promoting Williams's work, as he indicated in a letter of 21
June 1950: "I just reminded Bennett [Cerf] that about 10 years ago I suggested WHITE
MULE for Modern Library. . . ." (Yale).

541. TLS-3

[Rutherford, N.J.]

February 23, 1949

Dear Louis:

Some interesting things to tell you about – a letter's almost as good as a visit
anyway – sometimes better since the talk is by turns.

I finished Paterson III an hour or two ago. That's a relief. Perhaps I ought to
go right on to Book IV but it scares me a little – for various reasons. When I go
into the composition stage I go a little nuts and have to count on irritability,
bad dreams, horrible moments of depression, for what? A few moments of
heavenly exhilleration when I think I'm king of the world. But with age these
flights are not as convincing as formerly. They are, though, as much fun as ever
– if I can take the exhaustion they entail.

So maybe I'll start IV and maybe I'll lay back and drift awhile. But I bet I'll
start it – damn it. The bait is that when I finish that I'll be through, THROUGH!
That'll be the day. Ugh, I guess I'll have to do it. At least I can START. Once the
thing is embplaced, divided into its 3 component parts and very roughly laid
out maybe I'll be able to rest until fall, We'll see. So, that's that.

Laughlin in in Switzerland skiing. That means he won't get Pat III to the
printer before May, I suppose. That in turns means that it won't be out till fall.

But that wasn't what I first set out to tell you. I was reading Ez's Active An-
thology and I discovered something. I know I'm pretty slow at getting into new
work, really new work and digging its guts out, its why? and wherefores? What
I discovered was that I've developed tremendously in the last 15 years as a
reader, I mean. My taste has developed so that (as I discovered) I can't read
anything but the sort of work represented in the Active Anthology, your work
for instance, Basil's work and some of the other work presented there. I

discovered that there is a necessity to that work that isn't apparent at the time it is written. Time has to pass before we KNOW that we HAD to write that way. Our instincts were far ahead of our knowledge – or my knowledge at least. I must say I never felt so inclined to admire Ezra's perceptions as I do today having witnessed what he did in that work, did as a piece of criticism.

Of course he couldn't make a book of what didn't exist. He had to take what there was. And we assisted in producing what was there to take. But when one realizes how haphazard most anothologies are, how vulgar and blind – his anthology of 1933 emerges as a work of genius. I realized all that as I read.

And to come wholly clean let me tell you how I came to pick up the anthology – which, I believe, I have never read carefully before this. This guy in Galveston, Texas, the publisher of 4 pages came to me through Ez asking if I would lend him the Active Anthology for his purposes whatever they are. Ez had told him that the only copy in the U.S. was probably in my hands (is that true?)

So I hunted around, found the book on my shelves and was about to wrap it up when Floss caught me. What are you doing? sez she. Sending this book to Texas, sez I. Oh no you're not, sez she. O.K., sez I. But why not. Because you'll never see it again, sez she. Maybe you're right, sez I. I know I'm right, sez she. Oh well sez I, I doubt it but I'm willing to check first, sez I. etc etc and with that I sat me down and began to read with the astonishing results noted.

Your work came off very well. The thing is we need to know how to read (as Ez would say) in order to GET what the newer way of writing calls for. One has to loosen the attention more, has to go perhaps more into a different region than that which most reading asks us to enter. When we do that the unique pleasure which that sort of writing insists on – comes though and posesses us to our enormous gain. That is, at least, what I got.

There'll be a back kick on my writing from that, you wait and see.

Ez, as you must have noticed, got the #1000 award from the fellows of the library, the Bollingen prize. Quite a pother it kicked up. I was away Sunday so althought the papers called up in the afternoon they failed to get me. Thank goodness.

The day being fime I dragged Floss with me to Princeton – by car (to Newark) and train, I don't mean that she wasn't willing but she wouldn't have urged me if I hadn't been up to it. Kenneth Burke was giiving a cocktail party for no reason that I could see. He's been at the Institute for Advanced Studies on a fellowship (4 mos) in order to finish his new book on Rhetoric. It was fun. Not a bad gang. I met John Berryman whom I liked and a few others. Saw Malcolm Cowley again, a very staid gentleman now and his very pleasant and cordial wife. I talked my head off – to the birds and beginning forsythia flowers. We had fun.

As we had to wait 50 minutes before getting a train for Princeton from Newark Floss and I walked around 3 downtown blocks in Newark near the station. It must be the lowdown district of Newark for we ran into 5 Sunday afternoon bums that really hurt. I can't have anything to do with tramps. I can't take it. What in hell is one to do? Become a bum oneself? I can't see any other answer. Anything else is a complicated lie. These men in their 40s or so, big broken nosed wrecks either out to be taken out and shot or be sheltered and fed and loved, God damn it. It distresses me more and more as I get older. I fell dirty and cowardly. I can only avoid looking at them.

The only two reasonably bearable people of that group that we looked at were two young colored lads. They had their belongings in newspapers under their arms and at least they were young. They could function. One of them even looked into the window of an empty show, using it as a mirror to arrange his fedora.

I'm an I wonder what the hell I am writing about when I see people like that. And if it had been women! the equivalents of such men I know I should have cried – I did see one a month or two ago as we were driving out of the Hudson Tube. She was standing on the corner of 40th St just near where the cars from Jersey disgorge from the tube. It was horrible – a sick, deathly sick piece of female filth and rags – practically falling apart. I didn't know what to do. Nothing to do but look. We don't connect the right things together.

And Feb. 23 we have two crocuses in bloom and a dozen snowdrops – to match your blue grass.

We're going to Yaddo for a month this summer – in July I guess.

Have you got a copy of the Active Anthology? Let me know. If there's one around I won't feel so bad about lending mine.

I hear fairly regularly from Ez, sometimes only a card but once in a while he scribbles up a page or two – almost illegibly. Nothing to tell. He is said to be working on translatinoms from Kung but he never says anything to me about it.

Floss and Bill are sending up praises daily for the mild winter O me too.

Glad the kid's in the school orchestra. He'll be leading it by Easter.

Best to Celia.

And for God's sak go on and finish "A" and whatever else. It's necessary to do so.

     Best
     Bill

Paterson III: *Paterson: Book III* (Norfolk, Connecticut: New Directions, 1949). Wallace
    A30. Published 22 December 1949.

Active Anthology: Ezra Pound, ed., *Active Anthology* (London: Faber and Faber, 1933).
    Williams contributed fifteen poems to the anthology. Wallace B21.

your work: Zukofsky was represented in Pound's *Active Anthology* by "Poem Beginning

'The" and "A" 5–7. These versions of "A," however, were later revised by Zukofsky. It is unclear whether Williams saw the revised versions until they were published in "A" 1–12 in 1959.

Basil's work: Bunting's poems in *Active Anthology* were: "Villon," "Attis Or, Something Missing," "How Duke Valentine Contrived," "They Say Etna," [Yes, it's slow, docked of amours,], [Weeping oaks grieve, chestnuts raise], [Molten pool, incandescent spilth of], "The Passport Officer," [Fruits breaking the branches,], "Chomei at Toyama," "The Complaint of the Morpethshire Farmer" and "Gin the Goodwife Stint."

This guy: Dallam Simpson (also known as Dallam Flynn), American poet and publisher (b. 1925 or 1926). Williams's essay on T. S. Eliot, "With Forced Fingers Rude," was in the second issue of Simpson's periodical, *Four Pages* (February 1948).

Bollingen prize: Pound was awarded the Bollingen Prize for Poetry on 19 February 1949. The award proved highly controversial.

new book on Rhetoric: *A Rhetoric of Motives* (New York: Prentice-Hall, 1950).

Berryman: American poet (1914–1972). Berryman was then the Resident Fellow in Creative Writing at Princeton University.

Yaddo: This artists' and writers' community is located at Saratoga Springs, New York.

translatinoms from Kung: Pound's work was published as *The Classic Anthology Defined by Confucius* (Cambridge, Massachusetts: Harvard Univ. Press, 1954).

the kid's: Paul Zukofsky.

542. TLS-1

[Rutherford, N.J.]

March 1/49

Dear Louis:

Yes, the Pisan Cantos are not all gold by any means, much of it is trash – but there IS a music that <u>perhaps</u> saves all of it. (Tho' who's gonig to pronounce the chinese characters so the thing can BE music) When I first looked at the Cantos and began to read I had to quit. It put me to sleep, dull as heel. Later I found better going. I wrote to Ez at the tiem amd told him I couldn't get past p. 18. – Wall, he replied, you never could read more than 18 pages of anything since I knew you. – which may be true.

The Non ti fidar piece is more congenial to me than the Xenophanes. I have to read things a long time to really get them – and then only at times and with luck. To readmodern verse that is modern verse one must watch and wait sometimes a long time. But sooner or later the chaff is blown away and ONLY the modern, the really modern, remains.

March always means the beginning of the year for me

    Best to you all

    Bill

Pisan Cantos: Published by New Directions on 30 July 1948.

he replied: Letter not located.

Non ti fidar piece: Zukofsky's poem, "Non ti Fidar" (*CSP*, 123–24).

Xenophanes: Zukofsky's poem, "Xenophanes" (*CSP*, 123).

543. ALS-1

[Rutherford, N.J.]

Apr. 8/49
Dear Louis
Here's this. Best to the violinist et al (whoever al is)
    Bill

this: Enclosure lacking.

violinist: Paul Zukofsky.

544. ALS-1

[Rutherford, N.J.]

6/1/49
Saw your name on the 1st page of a new novel sent me gratis from Scribners. Baxter Bernstein Seley.

    The enclosed may or may not interest you.
      Bill

new novel: Stephen Seley, *Baxter Bernstein: A Hero of Sorts* (New York: Scribner's, 1949).
    See Zukofsky's letter of 7 June 1948.

Enclosed: Enclosure lacking. Zukofsky's reply indicates it was Williams's review of the
    Pisan Cantos, "The Fistula of the Law," Imagi 4:4 (Spring 1949), 10–11. Wallace C425

545. ALS-1

[30 Willow Street[
Brooklyn, New York]

Fri June 3/49
Dear Bill,
    I told Steve Seley you'd probably write me that you've seen my name in a book etc – good, I'm glad you got it. I haven't read it yet – except for parts of the original ms – but will have time to do so now – I hope!

    Thanks for *Imagi:* a good note on Pisan, and I agree with you. That I had read very carefully last Xmas and there's a lot in them one couldn't see at first glance from single Cantos published in magazines.

A letter from Basil after visiting Meshed with his young Persian bride and the Sanctuary there "done in mirror work", along with two poems not weaker in gusto. He seems to lead an enviable life tho he says all the American journalists descended on him more or less together after he came back to Teheran.

We've arranged to spend August in Lyme, Conn., with meals served and a one room cabin, toilet (important!) screen porch <all to ourselves,> and even a swing for the fiddler, for what seems dirt cheap. Is Lyme anywhere near your place – I forget the name. Maybe if Paul gets the lady who owns the farm to drive us we'll meet in the ocean etc. Or you can drive up the estuary where we are.

      Best and to Floss et al

      Louis

P.S. I note the reference to April is the saddest month (in Imagi) – I wanna see that!

letter from Basil: This letter of 28 May 1949, from Teheran, is in the Zukofsky papers at
    Texas. The two poems are not with the letter.

fiddler: Paul Zukofsky.

your place: In West Haven, Connecticut.

the reference: "April is the Saddest Month." Williams sent Zukofsky a typed copy of the
    poem, which Zukofsky noted as received on 6 June 1949. At the bottom of the type-
    script, Williams wrote, "We'll not be at the shore but on a farm in Buffalo –Lyme
    sounds marvelous. Best luck for a good summer. Bill[.]"

546. TC

[Rutherford, N.J.]

[July 1949]

A Dream of Love goes on <Tues> at Hudson Guild Playhouse, 436 W 27th, July 19 for 2 or 3 weeks (Chickering 4–0795) $1.20 – $1.80, Sat Mat. half price, via "We Present" a young company off-Broadway, nice professional kids – as innocent as day!

Maybe you're on vacation at Lynn or Lime of wherever. Tho't I'd better let you know at least where hent.

      Best

547. ALS-1

30 Willow Street
Brooklyn 2, N.Y

Oct 19/49

Dear Bill,

We've been back, of course, but rushed cleaning up here after 3 months shut-down and the lack minded perfessor starting the ack-adam-dick year. I could never find a notice in the papers in Old Lyme about A Dream of Love. So I've wondered if it had any success. So how are you both? And not by way of prelude to what I'm going to ask –

Could you consider talking to my poetry class – I'm giving one, using A Test. Talk on anything or read anything. There are now 15 in the class, all interested – most of them have had me in other courses i.e. required courses in the last three years. This is an elective course. It is not that I'm trying to save myself some work – but I think they ought to hear another voice besides mine.

Don't consider it, if you don't want to.

But if you do, the hitch is the hour. They meet Mondays 9:50 A.M. That's early. I could arrange a special session on <a> Tuesday 11:40 A.M., which visitors could attend. That would give you a larger audience than 15 – probably most of the school and all of the English faculty. Which do you prefer if you can make either? Of course, the Institute won't pay. But we can run off as soon as we're thru and spend the afternoon here – lunch etc – make a day of it with Floss too. That is, Celia and she can talk here while we "work".

> All our best
> Louis

P.S. Set your own date, if – except Election Day (we shut down)

548. TLS-1

[Rutherford, N.J.]

Oct. 23 (Yes, it is) 1949

Dear Louis:

The rotting is going along nicely in this compost heap, we shall soon have some ripe soil. As to speaking for you, the flies will buzz if you stirr them (are there 2 r's in stir? No.) As far as I can tell Monday at 9.50 would be all right for me but I'd better come home afterward to be here by 1 o'clock. (You see the rotting is still tempered by caution.)

I speak at Brandeis on November 2. Bill gets married on November 10. Thanksgiving is ? Suppose we make it the 14th. Election Day is on Tuesday!

Mother died a week agao (I always (frequently) add an a to "ago") She curious little thing that she was simply went to sleep. Whether or not I could have "saved" her by giving penicillin the week before is something I have debated in my mind ever since her death. So that, in effect, I "killed" her. In her coffin her features were astounding, an Egyptian princess.

Paterson III will be out in November together with the biography by Vivienne Koch. The Botteghe Oscure woman, the Princess di Bassiano (nee Biddle) is bringing out a new poem of mine in the November issue of her mag – I hope (she doesn't like some of my buffo touches but I think she'll come through).

Glad to hear about A. Recently in looking through my files I came across a copy of some part of the poem for which I think you asked earlier during the year. If you will tell me what it is that you wanted returned I'll verify my findings and act accordingly.

The play was not a success save with my inner conceits. I learned a lot from the performance and learned how very difficult it must inevitably be for a playright such as myself to get a play performed, a difficult play, as he has conveived it. It is almost an impossiblity. In this case the cast was wretchedly chosen or ill-chosen, the room in which the play was acted (a basement) was wholly inadequate for the purpose and the heat of summer, 97 at the back of the place, made the whole an intolerable, insufferable torment. Yet parts of the show were good. ALL the subtlties were lost, irreparable lost in the scramble to get through the evening. I attended the opening performance and never returned.

Patchen, your neighbor this summer, called me up one evening, long distance, to salute me - for no reason at all. I was surprised.

Another company of players may produce my other play during thw winter in an adequate theatre. I'll keep you posted. Best

    Bill

speak at Brandeis: Emily Mitchell Wallace observes that "Brief Note on a Recent Talk," *12th Street* 3:1 (December 1949), 27, is "probably" about the Brandeis lecture. Wallace C435. Williams spoke at Brandeis University on 2 November 1949.

Bill gets married: William Eric Williams married Daphne Spence on 19 November 1949.

biography: Vivienne Koch, *William Carlos Williams* (Norfolk, Connecticut: New Directions, 1950).

Princess di Bassiano: Marguerite Chapin Caetani (1880–1963), Duchess of Sermoneta. Wife of Roffredo Caetani (1871–1961), Prince of Bassiano and 17th Duke of Sermoneta. One of her sisters was the wife of Francis Biddle, who had been the U. S. Attorney General when Ezra Pound was indicted for treason. In 1948 Marguerite founded the Italian literary journal, *Botteghe Oscure*, which was edited by Giorgio Bassani.

new poem: No poem by Williams appeared in this issue of *Botteghe Oscure*.

The play: *A Dream of Love.*

Patchen: Kenneth Patchen (1911–1972), American poet. Patchen lived in Old Lyme, Connecticut (1947–1951). Williams had reviewed Patchen's *The Journal of Albion Moonlight* in 1942: "A Counsel of Madness," *Fantasy* 10:26 (1942), 102–07. Wallace C310. Reprinted in *Something to Say.*

[Rutherford, N.J.]

Oct 28/49

Dear Louis:

It was the 14th wasn't it? I won't go by car but go in with my son Paul who has to be at A & S at 9 so he'll get me, surely, to your abouts before 9.30 I suppose.

But I can't, really, stay for lunch or for anything once I am done – except to pow wow with you for a while if you can get off.

We shan't discuss origins.

    Flub dub

    Bill

[Zukofsky's notation, in reference to the last sentence, "Shortly after his mother's death."]

the 14th: Williams lectured to a group of students at the Brooklyn Polytechnic Institute

    on 14 November 1949. A summary of his talk, in Zukofsky's hand, is at Texas. Five

    typed pages of a "Brooklyn Lecture: Notes for a lecture at the Brooklyn Institute of

    Arts & Sciences" are in the Williams archive at Buffalo.

Paul: Paul Herman Williams.

■ 550. TLS-1

[Rutherford, N.J.]

Nov 1/49

Thanks Louis:

It is beautiful, in one of your lucky moods. I have sent it to Laughlin with your letter. But it will stand by itself, without me or a dedication to me. If he cannot or will not use it, send it elsewhere for publication – or as you see fit.

To Brandeis tomorrow. Tell you about it later.

    Best

    Bill

[Zukofsky's notation: "Re – _W._"]

It is beautiful: Section III of "Chloride of Lime and Charcoal" is "W." *CSP*, 127.

■ 551. ALS-1

30 Willow St

Bklyn 2, N.Y.

Fri 4 Nov 1949

Dear Bill:

Glad you liked _W_. And thanks for sending it to J.L. – tho that wasn't my real intention. But if he does use it along with any project of yours I'd be delighted.

I don't see where else he'll use it – i.e. can use it. If not, I'll send it somewhere – Lord knows where – in time. The <u>W</u> stays: that's my pleasure.

Your calendar: Polytechnic Institute of Brooklyn, 99 Livingston St., Monday, Nov. 14, 9:50 A.M. I can't make out from your letter whether Paul's driving you in or you're both going the hard way. In any case, he probably passes Poly on the way to A&S, ~~in any case~~. Nearest west side subway station to Poly is Borough Hall. Since he has to be at A&S at 9, it would probably be better not to waste time looking for Willow Street but, to meet <me> at the school – just a few blocks, downtown, from A&S, at 9. I'll wait for you just inside the street doors of 99 Livingston; or if it's cold, in the lounge: entered by the next pair of doors – leather covered, nail-studded, I believe, with round (?) windows, like the entrance to a yelegant bar that's degenerated. The description is probably not like the thing but my usual feeling. If this ~~is~~ arrangement is satisfactory, no need to write me. If you think of a better meeting place, let me know.

Yes, we shan't discuss origins. Never fear!

If you meet me at 9:00 we can pow wow till 9:50. And after the affair we'll beat it <u>alone</u> and let happen as your mood is. If you remember to look in-a-hurry when you're done, I'll look in-a-double-hurry.

And note my address is not Maple Street tho there's a maple not a willow in front of the house. Yours Oct 28 just reached me – I guess by this time the letter carrier has mastered poetry and knows I'm a Heights figger.

    As ever
    Louis

■ 552. ACS

                                                    [Postmarked Rutherford, N.J.]
[Postmarked 17 November 1949]
    a good group. I'll send them to the woman at once. Let you know what happens – unless she writes direct.
    Best Bill

group: The poems of *Some Time*.
the woman: Probably Princess Marguerite Chapin Caetani.

553. TLS-1

Monday [28 November 1949]

Dear Celia:

Thanks for the bid to supper but, if you don't mind, I think we'd better postpone it for a while. Bill's still away on his vacation (did I say?) I mean his honeymoon, serving the race, I suppose. Papa's more than swamped as a consequence taking into consideration the mind he has : possessed (looks funny) by dreams.

It was a true pleasure to write about you as I did for the Gug, maybe we'd better wait for a celebration until you get their accolade, then cheer. Or don't you trust them? We'll be seeing you soon.

> Best luck all around
> Bill

Bill's still away: William Eric Williams.

the Gug: Williams recommended Celia Zukofsky for a Guggenheim Foundation Fellowship. Williams noted, "I have been privileged, from time to time, to be present when parts of Celia Zukofsky's Pericles have been performed by piano and voice in her home. I was astonished at the possibilities discovered in this really extraordinary achievement." A copy of his letter (19 November 1949) is at Texas.

554. AC

[On "Republican National Committee" contribution receipt form]

[Rutherford, N.J.]

[December 1949]

Pa Hermann used to specialize in things like this (printed matter I mean)

[Zukofsky's notation, "12/27/49 Re—Botteghe Oscure acceptance"]

Pa Hermann: Florence Williams's father was a printer.

555. AL

[Rutherford, N.J.]

[After 27 December 1949]

My God! said Floss when she first saw it.

Yiddish!

it: See William L. Lawrence, "New Einstein Theory Gives a Master Key to the Universe," the New York Times, 27 December 1949, p. 1. The article reproduces a portion of the typescript with the caption: "The principal equations in the Einstein text which may offer important clues to the major mysteries of the cosmos."

■ 556. ALS-1

[On a pamphlet]

[Rutherford, N.J.]

1/11/50

This was intended to be in the form of a newspaper clipping. oh well.
    Bill

This: A pamphlet advertising an exhibition of paintings by Pablo Picasso at the Louis
    Carré Gallery. Headed, "Picasso Sticks Out / An Invested World," the text is by
    Williams. Wallace D5.

■ 557. ALS-1

[30 Willow Street
Brooklyn, N.Y.]

Jan 14/50
Dear Bill

"So be it." Let us talk. ~~This~~ "Reading and talking" says something like the Picasso "news" item.

Paterson III came from N.D. – at your request? I've just finished it. What counts is I don't care anymore about the "meaning". You "owe" no one "double" – especially, "the tin roof . . . lifted like a skirt." "Unapproached by symbols" etc

    When do we see you?
        Louis

"Reading and talking": The earliest extant draft of Zukofsky's poem, "Reading and Talk-
    ing," is dated 10–11 January 1950. *CSP*, 127–29.
"owe" . . . "double": Not a quotation from *Paterson*.
"tin roof": See *Paterson* (1992), 122.
"Unapproached": Not a quotation from *Paterson*.

■ 558. TLS-1

[Rutherford, N.J.]

Jan. 27/50
Dear Louis:

Has the enclosed poem which you sent me some weeks or months ago ever been used? I find it an extraordinary one and should like to have young Cole use it in his forthcoming All America issue. In any case please return it as I do not want to lose it.

Perhaps you have something else which you consider as good which he could use.

Something has let loose the furies of communication upon me, I am deluged with letters – Which I cannot avoid answering so tht I have no time to do anything else. But I want to get on with some composition.

That Italian princess has not sent me her latest Bottegh Oscure – tho' it has been printed, so I am told. I wish she'd make haste – as my grandmother used to say.

I can hear the buzz of time.

> Best
> Bill

Go see the Clee show at Modern Museum – a <u>must</u>.

poem: Williams probably refers to "Reading and Talking," but the poem which appeared in Thomas Cole's magazine was "As to How Much." *Imagi* 5:2 (issue 13), 17. *CSP*, 130. The earliest draft of "As to How Much" is dated 1 February 1950.

Cole: Thomas Cole. *Imagi* 13 was devoted to "Mid-century American Poetry." Williams contributed "Moon and Stars" and "The Girl." Wallace C442. *CP2*, 222.

Italian princess: Princess Marguerite Chapin Caetani. Zukofsky published three poems (under the collective title, "Some Time") in *Botteghe Oscure* 5 (1950), 375–80: "Chloride of Lime and Charcoal," "Non Ti Fidar," and "Some Time Has Gone." *CSP*, 124–27; 123–24; 107.

Clee show: The Museum of Modern Art's retrospective of the work of Paul Klee extended from 20 December 1949 to 14 February 1950.

559. TLS-1

[Rutherford, N.J.]

February 8/50

Dear Louis:

Good boy. You have a sense of shall I say seriousness? Most would say "humor". And you've sent a first rate poem – we ARE coming on, you wait and see. Your recent things, the short ones (so far) enthrall me and make me believe.

I sent no other of your poems to Cole (editor of IMAGI, Muhlenberg College (Senior Year) Allentown? Penna.) I thought it best not to mix things up. So that I am doubly glad to have this. I'm posting it tonight.

– and tomorrow you'll see my puss in Time Mag, with a baby before me. Look it up. I wonder what's up? Won't last, can't last at this rate unless they make me Charley Chaplin.

I don't know what in Hell has happened to the Princess. Maybe she's dead.

She wrote me before Christmas that this issue of her mag would be delayed but I presumed that that would mean no more than a month's delay at most. But this! it begins to look serious. However she has paid me for my contribution – and plenty. Someone in Washington said there had been a strike in Italy – a post Office strike. Too much for me. All we can do is to wait hopefully.

Best
Bill

first rate poem: *As to How Much.*

Time mag.: "Poetry Between Patients," *Time* 55:7 (13 February 1950), 94. This review of
   Paterson, Books I and II, and *Paterson: Book III,* is accompanied by a photograph of
   Williams examining a baby in his office. The review is favorable, but notes a "humor-
   lessness and awkwardness that makes Williams the Dreiser of U.S. poets."

the Princess: Marguerite Chapin Caetani.

my contibution: "The Desert Music," *Botteghe Oscure* 8 (1951), 310–22. Wallace C453. *CP2,*
   273–84.

▓ 560. ALS-2

[30 Willow Street
Brooklyn, New York]

Feb 20/50

O Bill!

A billet-doux, duleis, duleis! Or do I mean dolce, dolce? The princess took half of the group – to appear in April – and sent a check for $150. Celia called me at the Institute about it, prefacing the news with "don't faint." I didn't but am still smiling: that's more than I've earned by <u>poetry</u> – since 1929 when the first things first appeared in The Dial till now – in 21 years. I have reached my majority?

I've written her recommending Celia's <u>Pericles</u> – at least a scene of it, saying you heard it and were moved. Says my enterprising wife – that's an awful lot of lines Shakespeare wrote; and she ought to pay for my lines and Shakespeare's too.

[. . .]

In the same mail, Cole's acceptance of the lyric. I'll write him – and since the <u>Oscure</u> acceptance frees "Marry" I'll ask him about that. I'm glad Ez is still perking. The "All America" issue prolongs the smile.

I'll bestir myself when the cold moves off and see if I can find a copy of this number of Oscure you're in. Will you be in the April issue?

So: thanks. There are so many things we need after spending a hundred on doctor's and dentists' bills since Xmas – the $150 is a windfall. We still need beds in Old Lyme etc. And – but – forgossakes when are Floss and you coming so we can celebrate. Let's make it the first signs of warm weather. Okay?

> Louis

"Billet-doux" – no respectable male envelop to hand.

half the group: "Chloride of Lime and Charcoal," "Non Ti Fidar," and "Some Time Has Gone."

Institute: Brooklyn Polytechnic Institute.

Celia's Pericles: Celia Zukofsky's musical setting of Shakespeare's *Pericles.*

"Marry": Perhaps part two of "Que J'ay Dit Devant": "Marry or don't." *CSP,* 113–14.

"All America" issue: *Imagi* 13. The contributors to this issue were: E. E. Cummings, Ezra Pound, Marianne Moore, Wallace Stevens, Williams, Jaime de Angulo, Francis Berry, Pearl Bond, Virginia Carnes, Thomas Cole, J. C. Crews, Louis Dudek, Lora Dunetz, Charles Edward Eaton, Albert Herzing, David Ignatow, Walter H. Kerr, Audrey McGaffin, Earl Mohn, Philip Murray, Charles Olson, Dachine Ranier, William Jay Smith, Marvin Solomon, Ruth Stephens, and Zukofsky. Virginia Carnes was Williams's daughter-in-law.

561. TCS

[Rutherford, N.J.]

[1950]

The issue of Botteghe Oscure finally came through – a beauty. What must it cost!? If only that money could be spent "wildly" enough and HERE. What couldn't we do with it. I don't suppose that anyone here will see this issue.

But I think you are now assured that she is not "dead" but will bring along an April issue as she orignally planned.

Cole (Imagi) is extremely pleased with your contribution to his "All America" issue soon to appear. It is Ezra's idea. There'll be some good things in it – very good: Stevens, Cummings, Marianne, you, me – as a backbone to which the rest will be attached.

> Bill

"All America" issue: See the previous letter and Williams's letter of 27 January 1950.

562. TLS-1

[Rutherford, N.J.]

Monday [10 April 1950]

Dear Louis:

You guessed it, I've been overwhelmed with obligations. (There goes the # % bell now, at 9.52 p.m.) (some ointment to put on a lady's ass-hole for hemorrhoids – which, by the way, I had neglected to send earlier: it is always our own fault!) (We breathe)

What size violin is it now? He is amazing. I have half planned a concert for him with a five year old pianist, a little girl who also plays her Bach by reams. What is to become of us? We must soon talk of this seriously.

No. They couldn't give Celia her award. I went to my first "banquet" with the fellows of the Institute. It saddened me. Action is the last word they can know.

But I am being approached by a big commercial publisher who wants to take me over. Laughlin cannot give me a living. These people say they can. What am I to do? But not the poems, I will not give them the poems.

I suppose the only chance we'll have to see you will be at Lime now. I'll write again soon. This just to acknowledge your last.

> Best all around
> Bill

concert for him: Paul Zukofsky.

her award: Williams recommended Celia Zukofsky for a grant from the National Institute of Arts and Letters.

Institute: Williams had been elected a member of the National Institute of Arts and Letters in January 1950.

commercial publisher: Random House.

563. TLS-2

[Rutherford, N.J.]

April 13/50
Dear Louis:

Poor old man, I know what you mean and, by God, there's not a thing to say, absolutely nothing. Sometimes I think what passes for religion in our lives is as close to blasphemy as blasphemy itself. The only thing that man can do for man in the world is to warm him when he is cold and feed him when he is hungry – profusely, generously. We never do it. We ourselves are so threatened by our immediate surroundings that we become cowards and niggards even when we most want to give.

But I can't believe in their stupid original sin. That's just the excuse for offenses. All anyone could do, I say it again, is as primitive people do, to close in about the dying and give them ourselves, to make them feel us near them.

Maybe it is impossible. If we spend ourselves too carelessly we'll die too and quickly. But we needn't stand off as if we didn't know what was going on – without our neatness and hygiene.

We'll come over and have a talk some evening. I don't know when exactly it can be, right now I'm upset by my uncertainty over the Laughlin business. I get my books out and they are well printed, I believe also in what New Directions is doing, establishing all sorts of foreign reputations here, giving us a view of such men as Valery etc etc. But it does seem hard not to get money out of what I write. I could use it and it does not seem in itself a cirse that I should have it if I can get it by decent means.

And yet there does seem to me some subtle curse about it. Somehow I'd be much more comfortable as I am, writing and getting along fairly comfortably. I'm really afraid of money – even the comparatively little money that at best I am being offered now. I feel as if I'd be better off without it. I don't want to change my status.

Lord knows what's going to happen. One thing is sure. Bill is taking over much of mt practice of Medicine. I am making less at that now than I have made in the last twenty years or more. If I do not piece out my income with some sort of earnings by writing I shall have to retire more and more into my shell as I go along. Reputation becomes a joke under such circumstances. But then maybe the prospect of living no more than another five years, if that, will give me the peace I desire. Even to say that has its false aspect. What the hell do I know about it? Just go along is best. Monet might give me ideas. The only thing I could use it for would be to give it away.

We'll be seeing you soon.

Best

Bill

Not to seem to want to be mysterious, Random House wants me to sign a contract to let them publish the collected short stories, about 40 of them, the autobiography and the next book in the White Mule series. And I 67 in September! It's attractive in some ways. Laughlin to keep the poems.

poor old man: Zukofsky's father, Pinchos Zukofsky, died on 11 April 1950.

Laughlin business: James Laughlin felt that if Williams left New Directions for Random House that it would be an act of ingratitude. See *WCW/JL*, 180–84.

Bill: William Eric Williams.

30 Willow St.
Brooklyn 2, N.Y

Apr 15/50

Dear Bill:

Yes, come over and talk – any evening except Tues and Thurs. when I teach from 8–10. A phone call is notice enough – so you can make it at the spur of the moment to suit yourselves. Celia can always make a pie – she's discovered it's one of the few things she does that keeps Paul quiet watching.

It makes me sad that at this day you have to worry about income. I know what you mean when you say: "The only thing I could use it for would be to give it away." The amount given away always rises with one's "status" and "reputation." Those who really have it play dumb. Five thousand dollars – and at that advanced in gradual stages! – seems mighty little for three books. Is that what they call giving someone like yourself an income? My inclination is to say retire, as you say, more into your shell, for the sake of health, peace of mind etc. But I suppose that's no good either – one keeps young they say doing the things one did when younger. And then I suppose my inclination is pure self-ishness – to keep you alive as my father used to say "till 120 and then ask Him for more," for the simple reason that as far as my world is concerned it would be pretty paltry without you. You know the friends I listed in <u>Cronos</u> 4 I guess it was – and you're the only one I see.

Original sin? From the point of view of hindsight – from the heap of swin-ery about us – I guess it's as good an explanation of the heap as any. My father who believed <u>Genesis</u> was inspired no doubt believed the story – but if I'm to do him justice I should say from the point of view of foresight of what hap-pens to man when he becomes a pig. He never really bothered me about my lack of piety since I was thirteen or younger. I'm sure he must have thought the negress I saw weeping as the hearse passed the synagog on Wed – She must have talked with him often as she cleaned there, he was always the first to arrive and the last to go – as pious in her way as he was.

So: don't be upset. "Just go along is best." See us soon.

All our best to you & Floss

Louis.

And without
Spring it is spring why
Is it death here grass somewhere
As dead as lonely walks

As living has less thought that is
The spring.

Spring it is spring why
Is it death grass somewhere
As dead as walks
As living has less thought that is
A spring. And without.

Dear Bill

Wrote this on Apr. 1st. Must have sensed something of the 11th tho my father was still well last Sat. That is, I <u>did sense</u> it, but unwilling to admit it worked it out to hide it. You might as well have it – since it's not likely to appear anywhere for another five years.

Louis.

friends I listed: Louis Zukofsky, "Poetry / *For My Son When He Can Read,*" *Cronos* 2:4
(March 1948), 22–30. In this essay Zukofsky cites lines by Bunting, Pound, Williams,
Niedecker and Reznikoff. Reprinted in *Prepositions +.*

And without: *CSP,* 131.

565. TLS-1

[Rutherford, N.J.]

April 15/50

Dear Louis:

This morning I read again your piece on <u>Poetry in the Modern Age</u> (after seeing <u>Chaplin's,City Lights</u> last evening), it does treat of the poem in the modern age – thus somewhat defining the modern age, making it come alive <u>because</u> the poem is shown to be alive in it.

You are always difficult for me, as for others, but for the best of reasons: that you make every step in your argument self proving. There is nothing explained about the explanation, as you ably point out.

Obviously the piece is too good for <u>Poetry</u>. It sticks out of that mood like a sore thumb. It is in a different, much simpler, more difficult class of writing. It requires work on the part of the reader. Readers like connectives and replies to elementary questions which you ignore. It is difficult to follow you but the difficulty becomes the answer you're seeking. It is in the ability to solve the difficulty that the answers lie.

An intimate friend of mine, a man of my own age, died last night just sitting in a chair talking with friends. What you write refers to the difficulty of get mind around events like that. Most can only take it up formally in thinking of his wife, his recent deal in purchasing a new home for her, the date of the funeral, how kind he was, how wrong abput so many things, how he hired a bus each year and took the ladies from the Old People' Home in Hackemsack each year to Radio City, dinner in N.Y.C. etc – but no one is moved by this death to think of death. Consequently they cannot <u>act</u> in any fgeneral way against "death" as a factor in our lives, their general concept of their lives by considering death as a thing in itself. The international situation as confronted by death, the racial, the social – complete blank. They don't know and they don't seem able to feel. They are gievn to death in their minds to such a degree that they are dazed by it and made impotent.

We speak of – glibly of death and the poem not realizing what we are talking about, neither is apprehended – but both (in your difficult) sense are of the same nature.

Few can make that transit from their lives to the poem or to death. That's whay your writing is hard to know. Nothing is topical in it.

It's a thoughtful article well written and designed to be read by saints, literate saints. All you do is like that but gets you no reward that can be measured except by standards – which do not operate about us.

> Best
> Bill

your piece: Zukofsky's review of Vivienne Koch's *William Carlos Williams*, "Poetry in a
Modern Age," *Poetry* 76:3 (June 1950), 177–80.
friend of mine: Unidentified.

■ **566. ALS-2**

> [30 Willow Street
> Brooklyn, N.Y.]

Apr. 17 [1950]
Dear Bill,
And your friend, too – as Lear would say.

It does me good thinking you can read my review after seeing Chaplin's <u>City Lights</u>. I've been wanting to see it again. The greatest artist of our time I suppose. I never succeeded in getting past Hollywood mail barriers 1936 or thereabout when I sent him my essay on him. I suppose he'll die without reading it – people liked it but wouldn't publish it. It's in a <ms. of> collected essays or what which will probably never appear in this life either. Wut n 'ell!

I'm glad you say what you say about the review because my saintliness worried me in this case. I wanted to help you in a practical sense as well as say – I mean sum up your worth, briefly, for me, for you, for our kids if they ever learn to read etc. And I'm not "practical" as you know. As for sticking out in Poetry, that doesn't bother me. For all I care about that end of it, the more priapic the better. (I see the dictionary says Priapean, so be it). Shapiro accepted it & said it would appear in an early issue, & wonder of wonders asked for no changes, but wondered whether he might use another title. So I asked what he had in mind, but no word from him as yet. What I had in mind in my title was Poetry (i.e. you) in a <u>A</u> Modern <u>Old</u> Age (like the anthology of Ciardi you reviewed yesterday). They're all so old in their thirties (yes, I agree Roethke, what I've seen, is thank god an exception) – it's like the "neatness" of modern furniture everybody buys when they're furnishing "modern". What a bloody world! All the more reason to be happy when <u>Time</u> (of the time as it is & so inevitably I suppose revealing ~~the~~ its best & worst) does for you in its repeated notices of <u>Paterson</u> what it does. I wonder who the guy back of that good deed is: just so I can give him my tacit blessing whenever I come across his name in print or hear it spoken.

I'll look up the <u>Poetry</u> review of <u>Paterson</u>. I see you're reading it this Thurs. at the Poetry Center – but I would have to teach that night. All the luck – by this time you're not "nervous" – for a full house.

    Yrs.

    Louis

my review: "Poetry in a Modern Age."

my essay: "*Modern Times.*"

Shapiro: Karl Shapiro.

anthology of Ciardi: John Ciardi, ed., *Mid-Century American Poetry* (New York: Twayne, 1950). Williams's review was "Voices in Verse," the *New York Times* (16 April 1950), section 7, pages 6, 28. An earlier and somewhat different draft of the review appears in *Something to Say.*

Roethke: Theodore Roethke was represented in the anthology.

567. ACS

[Postmarked Rutherford, N.J.]

[Postmarked 11 June 1950]

Bot. Oscure (april) has not yet arrived. Don't worry about it, it'll get here – tho 2 mos late.

up to my ears in letters by the ton. Bill

[Rutherford, N.J.]

Sunday [Zukofsky's notation, "Ea. summer 1950"]

Dear Louis:

There's no proper way of answering you except to say that I've been uncon-scious for the last month. It's been too much for me to keep alive. I haven't read Ferdinand, I will any minute but I haven't done it yet. I've been trying to read my nun cousin's The Names of the Lord by Fray Luis de Leon in the transla-tion, at which she has been laboring for years.

This has been my year of awards and I'm having a time, as I have told you, with Laughlin. It began with a simple request which I made of him to release the rights to the short stories. It has whipped itself up into what may end in court. And that isn't all by any means.

Louis, please brush all this aside. It will right itself within a short time. If we get anywhere near Old Lime this summer we'll drop in – and I promise you I'll write again soon.

Have a good and profitable summer.

> Best
>
> Bill

The mother of the little <5 year old> Bach playing piano virtuoso and pa-tient of mine has asked me several time to ask you to let her have the accompa-niments of your son's violin pieces that she may practice them up during the summer looking toward a concert next fall. If Celia approves all you need do is tell me what pieces they are, the proper key etc etc and I'll get them for the kid.

Ferdinand: "Ferdinand" (second half), *Quarterly Review of Literature* 5:4 (November 1950).

nun cousin's: Sister Felicia (Alice Philena Hubbard).

Names of the Lord: Fray Luis de León (1528–1591), *De Los Nombres De Cristo* (Salamanca: 1583). This is a treatise, often in the form of philosophical dialogue, on the reasons why certain names belong to Christ. It appears that Sister Felicia's translation was never published.

[Rutherford, N.J.]

Quatorze Juillet / 50

Dear Louis:

Glad to see Botteghe Oscure has arrived. You do yourself proud. Glad of it.

We're headed for YADDO for 2 weeks. Who knows? Hope I can work. Pater-son IV . .

Doesn't look as though we'd get up Connecticut way all summer. Certainly noy before August 15.

Hope you keep well and the same for Celia and the savage.

Our little Suzanne just had her appendix out. Was quite sick. The thing that impressed her most was being haled forth into the night at 3 A.M.

> Best
> Bill

How is Patchen? I was very much moved last year to have him phone me long distance – and to learn later that he has been seriously ill.

Yaddo
Saratoga Springs
N.Y.

Will drop you a card now & then –

YADDO: Williams stayed at the artists' and writers' colony from 15 July to 2 August.
Suzanne: Suzanne Williams, the granddaughter of Williams and Floss.

570. ALS-2

P.O. Box 164
Old Lyme, Conn.

July 15/50

Dear Bill:

We hope Suzanne's well again – sorry to hear what happened.

Have a good time in Yaddo.

I've felt pepped up these last <2> days writing some "A"-9 – after 4 weeks of aching like an old dog, post-virus contracted in the city. I don't know what youth Ez is referring to, but I felt the climacteric. The local doctor helped me, so I'm better.

If I guess right Ez's reference to "Z." has to do with my reference to H.J. in my review of V.K's book on you: I was thinking of the American Scene – in which somewhere in his visit to the South the "bright chick in resplendent plumage" (wonderful!) magnanimously sees a negro – but naturally flutters impressed by a new kind of animal: no simultaneous immediate sympathy for it as in your jungle – but there's a parallel perception for the rendering of the thing.

[. . .] I hope you do get up to Conn. Any – some – time – we'll be here at least till Sept 15. I have to be back by the 18th, perhaps Celia will stay on a week or so after. It would do us all good for Floss & you to come here.

I've passed on your greetings to the Patchins. Kenneth's about the same, so we see each other when & if our pains permitting, not too often. Paul, of course, is the only one who pays no attention to it and seems as far as I can gather to have been adopted by Mrs. P. etc–

Hope we'll be seeing you

Best

Louis

Ez's reference: In the Zukofsky papers at Texas is a copy in Zukofsky's hand of a letter of 8 July 1950 from Pound to Williams. In this letter Pound remarks, "dunno az z.-unnerstan' awl yer le'r (ties?). Henrietta one bright chick—wot will flutter above our tombs in resplendent plumage."

my reference to H.J.: Zukofsky wrote, "And of Lucretius' 'Spring goes on her way and Venus,' and the same new life that followed later in Dante, and some Villon, and Chaucer's own rooster, and Anonymous English, and Shakespeare ('the clatter and true sound of verse'), and, well, the Jamesian perception of Williams' *The Jungle*." "Poetry in a Modern Age," *Poetry* 76:3 (June 1950), 180. In *The American Scene*, James comments at various points on African Americans, but the only such remarks associated with a jungle are those in chapter 14 ("Florida"). James notes that his hotel is surrounded by a jungle, which one can penetrate "by means of a light perambulator, 'of adult size,' but constructed of wicker-work, and pendent from a bicycle propelled by a robust Negro. . . ." Leon Edel, ed., *The American Scene* (Bloomington and London: Univ. of Indiana Press, 1968), 449–50. Zukofsky's quotation regarding the "bright chick" I have not found in *The American Scene*. He seems to be simply citing Pound's letter.

your jungle: "The Jungle," *CP1*, 241–42.

Paul: Paul Zukofsky.

■ 571. ALS-1

30 Willow Street

Brooklyn 2, N.Y.

[September 1950]

Dear Bill:

I'm back in the salt mines. I guess you never got to Essex. How are you, Floss, and all?

Poetry that printed the first half of the double canzone has rejected the second. You might as well look at it – no one else will for a long time I guess. Please return it. Celia's too busy with Paul Vivaldi Veracini to make extra copies at the moment. I hope Random's come along with its obligations

All the best

Louis

salt mines: The English Department of the Brooklyn Polytechnic Institute.

Essex: Essex, Connecticut.

Poetry: "'A'-9 (First half)," *Poetry* 58:3 (June 1941), 128–30.

Veracini: Francesco Maria Veracini (1690–1768), Italian composer and violinist.

Random's: Random House.

572. AL-1

[Rutherford, N.J.]

10/10/50

Dear Louis:

Do you want it printed? I'll get it printed. But you want money for it, I suppose. I enjoyed the last 3 stanzas as more than the first – but its well worth the difficulty of reading.

(immediately after reading poem)

[Zukofsky's notation: "A-9 Second Half"]

573. TLS-1

[Rutherford, N.J.]

Saturday eve [Zukofsky's notation, "Oct 14/50"]

Dear Louis:

Floss and I leave next Thursday evening for a 5 week tour, you might say, of the country! Say it over again and it amounts to this:

I have been asked to give 3 weeks of reading and talking, one week each, at the U. Washington, Reed College and the U. of Oregon,beginning Oct 23. They pay me $1500. for the stint. A five day week in each case. Pray for me.

From there we'll go to visit Charlotte, Flosses sister in Los Angeles, for a week. Then to El Paso to see Bob McAlmon for a couple of days, New Orleans to please Floss and then home.

I enclose a letter from Dahlberg which maybe you'd better return to me. His Flea of Sodom (I have an extra copy you can have) is tough but impressive. I'm reviewing it but so far I haven't had the time to really weld into one the voluminous notes I've made on it (only 12 pages to be truthful) .

The canzon is excellent. I can get it printed if you say so. Why not send it to Dallam Simpson, the editor of 4 pages? At least let him look at it.

> Dallam Simpson
> Congress Heights Station
> Box 6974
> Washington, D.C.

Couldn't see you this summer, just couldn't. I had leagal matter pending with Laughlin, had to get a lawyer. It was tough. Yet I did go to Yaddo (for free, you can understand that) and did little else all summer.

I confidently hope and expect that from this moment out, if I survive this winter, I'll be much more my own master and see much more of my close friends than has been possible in all my life heretofore.

Best to ~~Cynthia~~ Celia and the kid.

>Yours as ever
>Bill

next Thursday evening: They left on 19 October 1950.

letter from Dahlberg: Edward Dahlberg (1900–1977), novelist and essayist. Williams probably refers to a letter of 13 September 1950, in which Dahlberg recounts his difficulties getting published and expresses admiration for Williams's work (Yale). For a selection of Dahlberg's letters to Williams see *Epitaphs of Our Times: the Letters of Edward Dahlberg* (New York: George Braziller, 1967), 177–206. Williams included a letter from Dahlberg in *Paterson*. When Dahlberg reviewed Williams's *Autobiography*, he concluded, "Williams writes that he always has been a liar, and always will be. But a man at sixty-eight is too old to lie. Williams not only hides people who are not successful, but he altogether conceals his own gifts. He has lost his true memory and has become a weathervane admirer. His feelings for the gifts of Josephine Herbst and Louis Zukofsky are very ardent in private, and yet in this book he does little more than prattle about Josephine Herbst, and is not even gallant enough in his hasty mention of Louis Zukofsky to assert that he started the Objectivist movement to which Williams himself belonged. He has become mellow, which is another word for moldering." "The Art of Concealment," *Samuel Beckett's Wake and Other Uncollected Prose*, ed. Steven Moore (Elmwood Park, Illinois: Dalkey Archive Press, 1989), 276–78.

Flea of Sodom: *The Flea of Sodom* (Norfolk, Connecticut: New Directions, 1950). Williams's review appeared posthumously. "The Flea of Sodom," *Edward Dahlberg: American Ishmael of Letters*, ed. Harold Billings (Austin, Texas: Roger Beacham, 1968), 55–62.

canzon: Second half of "A"-9.

a lawyer: James F. Murray.

■ 574. ACS

El Paso, Texas

[Postmarked 22 November 1950]

Over this bridge lies tequilla – at 5¢ a short & T bone steaks at 75¢ with soup & coffee thrown in. I shall miss them all. Off for N. Orleans in 15 minutes.

>Happy Thanksgiving
>Best Bill & Floss

[Rutherford, N.J.]

[1950]

My "negative component" is working fine today: forgot how to spell Brookli(y)n. Sent the canzon to Simpson of "4 pages" but have had no word from him since. Yea, I'm home. We had a good hard working trip of it; no desire to stay out there. I'll never catch up with my mail, never: therefore this card. . The publicity you saw was not of my choosing but since I consented to it I'm still culpable. I'll be sending you the poems soon as I can pack and address a copy. (Note: 6 of the better poems were omitted from the book through an error on my part – was practically out of the house on my trip west when I corrected the galleys but failed to check, count by count) They have me working on an autobiography, to be finished by March 1/51. Best to you all.

    Bill

canzon: Second half of "A"-9.

publicity you saw: Not located.

the poems: *The Collected Later Poems* (Norfolk, Connecticut: New Directions, 1950). Wallace A31.

my autobiography: *The Autobiography of William Carlos Williams* (New York: Random House, 1951). Wallace A35.

[Rutherford, N.J.]

[1950]

(2) Laughlin is making up a "signature" of 16 pages, more less, to contain the omitted poems only half of the original sheets having been bound. These additional pages will be bound in with the book when and if the presently bound copies are exhausted. If current purchasers want the added sheets they may obtain them without cost from New Directions or any book store that has them,without cost.

My best to Chas. Reznikoff. I'll buy his book re. th Jews of Charleston the first time I am conscious again.

    Luck with your comic. Best Bill

"signature": As Hugh Witemeyer notes, "The accidental omission of ten poems from the first binding of *Collected Later Poems* was first noticed in December 1950 by Babette Deutsch. . . . A section of eight leaves entitled 'The Rose' (pp. 233– 45) was printed separately for insertion into the bound copies" (*WCW/JL*, 204n).

Jews of Charleston: Charles Reznikoff, *The Jews of Charleston* (Philadelphia: Jewish Pub-
   lication Society of America, 1950).
your comic: Unidentified.

■ 577. ALS-1

30 Willow Street
Brooklyn 2, N.Y.

Ja 29/51

Dear Bill,

Just to say I'm taking time off – as much as I can <from the wilds (let's not
omit that)> – re-making "Make Light of It" & "The Collected Later." I won't
bother you with criticism, since you're probably steeped in the autobiography.
But I'll say this if I stand back some times from the verities of the stories, as I
suspect you do – the verities are not things they can make light of. Which
means the poems are for me, instead of talk where there isn't any, along with
good music as I read while I overhear Paul play his fiddle, things to show when
people don't see etc. Alright I'm a damned saint – as you said once – since
there'll be a world it'll catch up with the prose to check on what they fouled up.
But the poems are nobody's record.

   I wrote Laughlin for the extra omitted 16 pages or so – but haven't heard.
Maybe my copy has them bound in?

   And here's a poem to read. Reference to Bk X of The Republic (myth of Er.)
Much as Plato annoys me I think he knew where the hell the Idea (1) came
from. If he didn't this is telling him – I hope the irony gets across in the "he-
roic" opening six verses etc etc.

   All the best to all – Louis

"Make Light of It": *Make Light of It* (New York: Random House, 1950). Wallace A32.
"The Collected Later": *The Collected Later Poems.*
autobiography: *The Autobiography of William Carlos Williams.*
Paul: Paul Zukofsky.
myth of Er.: *Republic* 10: 614–21. Socrates relates the warrior Er's vision of how souls
   choose their lives for the next cycle of regeneration.
poem: "Pamphylian," *CSP,* 133.

578. ALS-4

[Rutherford, N.J.]

Monday [30 April 1951]

Dear Louis:

a beutiful poem (in Tomorrow) one of your most coherent (in my ears) and best to date. It shows construction, it shows work it is made (out of words) the words are put together to make it. So few poems are made of words.

My God will they never learn? They think the meaning makes the poem, they never seem to comprehend that it is the words that make the poem tho' they have been quoting Shakespeare for 400 years. They never learn anything. It is largely due to the esoteric writing of aristotle and to the text books that carry it on – I begin to think that Aristotle is the arch-criminal of the ages

But <by> today you would think we would have learned at last that a poem is made, made, made A thousand examples a day (literally) show we have learned nothing. We have learned nothing.

It was an excellent poem, shows you are getting more freedom of thought into the way you use your words. I'm proud of you. The poem stands out.

Bill

beautiful poem: "Air," *Tomorrow* 10:9 (May 1951). *CSP*, 132–33.

579. TLS-1

30 Willow St.
B'klyn 2, N.Y.

June 13, 1951

Dear Bill,

I hope you're well. We're going to Old Lyme on Sunday and if you get to Conn. I hope you'll be able to see us there. We'll be in the phone book.

I'm writing this in behalf of Edward Dahlberg. Please don't ever tell him I've written this. He is impetuous, no doubt, but a hard life has made him bitter. And generous too, let's not forget this. My school has no more teaching for him. I wish he could find some means to assure him over the summer. I write to you, not because I feel you can do anything we'd like to see done, but on the chance that maybe, maybe you know of something – a grant, summer teaching or something like that, or more permanent.

Some months ago you sent me a letter he wrote to you asking whether you could do something about me. You know of course that I did not prompt that letter, and that I feel in no way as he does about myself. There is no telling what with the moral almost prophetic outlook that he has about the quality of a man's work arising out of the man in this country – beset as it is with evils, you and I know of – to what extent he will take up an unrequested fight in my be-half, when that fight as I tell him concerns me personally not at all. He can and yet cannot understand this resignation of mine. It is hard for him to see what you and I mean to each other. It is hard for him to see that I can dissociate the fact that I cannot get printed, let us say, from the fact that my friends ought to do something about it. I know that they would if they could. And even if they wouldn't, I'd assume that they would. Whatever he said about you in the arti-cle in Tomorrow is beside the point. I feel it is honest as he sees it. I wish he hadn't said it. The Flea of Sodom has some great writing in it. It's that we want to save. He's read parts of a new novel to me which are even better. And I feel like a dirty plutocrat having a job and knowing that he hasn't.

He confided in Celia recently and told her not to tell me that he wrote you again in my behalf. I can't of course stop him or betray Celia's confidence! But what's the use going on in this vein. I like the guy a hell of a lot and whatever he said about me and he didn't tell Celia what it was, and I hope he didn't hurt your feelings – let's see what we can do for him.

All our best to Floss.

Yours,

Louis

[In Louis Zukofsky's hand] P.S. Celia's typing – since she had the typewriter out. I'm still writing long hand. Country address: Library Lane, Old Lyme, Conn. Best Again

Louis

[In Celia Zukofsky's hand] P.P.S. I'm not proud of this typing tho L. seems to be – he gives me honorable mention I see. All our best to you & Floss. C.

article in Tomorrow: "My Friends Stieglitz, Anderson, and Dreiser," *Tomorrow* 10 (May 1951), 22–27. Reprinted in *Alms for Oblivion* (Minneapolis: Univ. of Minnesota Press, 1964). Dahlberg writes, "Williams was . . . himself a ravine and cold-water man. Williams was a provincial pill-satchel man of Rutherford, New Jersey. He was a doc-tor perhaps because he looked all his life for human staples for direct potato-and-apple people, with simple arithmetic morals and plain salt and pepper in their acts. Art people today have not honest bread, pear, and chicory or grass in their vices, deeds, and souls, and Williams, the genius of *In the American Grain,* had as much loose water in his nature as there was in Stieglitz."

new novel: Possibly *Diary of a Social Man*. Charles DeFanti notes in *The Wages of Expec-tation: A Biography of Edward Dahlberg* (New York: New York Univ. Press, 1978), that this unpublished novel "may date from the mid-1940s, but may have been written as late as 1952" (170n116).

wrote you again: Letter not located.

[Rutherford, N.J.]

June 19, 1951

Dear Louis:

I share your feeling over Edward Dahlberg. I don't pay any attention to his attacks, no doubt I deserve them; I admire both him and his writing and will do whatever I can to help him.

It should be possible for me to get some money for him in the form of a grant from The National Institute of Arts and letters. I'll write to them today and find out what can be done. I won't mention your name either to them or to him. As soon as I find out how the situation lies I'll tell you and tell you what they say to me. By the way, have you got his address handy? If not I'll look around, New Directions should have it – I have heard that he's driven that office to distraction with his insistences.

We'll be at the shore in Connecticut sometime in the early part of July. While I'm there I'll drop you a card te ling you when we'll drive up to see you at Lyme, it should make a good day's. Besides, this time, we'll come!

Best luck for a happy summer.

I was the Phi Beta Kappa poet at their Literary Celebration at Harvard yesterday. It's been something for which I've been preparing for months. My cerebral accident almost spoiled the party. But by dint of persistence I was able to write a "15 minute" poem and recite it. The atmosphere was semi-ecclesiastic, a hall hallowed by thradition and my poem was low (high). They seemed pleased.

I still write with difficulty as my frequent erasures will testify.

What shall I do with my future? I am stumped.

> Yours
> Bill

celebration at Harvard: Williams read "The Desert Music."
cerebral accident: See Mariani 629.

P.O. Box 188
Old Lyme, Conn.

[Postmarked 21 June 1951]

Thurs

Dear Bill,

Writing in a hurry at the P.O. to speed matters, just having read your letter. Dahlberg's address: 39½ Washington Square So., N.Y.C. It would be wonderful if N.I.A.L. would etc. – Do, do, come out to see us. Phone Lyme 4-7362. If you forget it, information will give it to you – we didn't get into the phone book. Congratulations on the Harvard ΦBK Poem! We'll be seeing you. All the best & to Floss –

     Louis

N.I.A.L.: The National Institute of Arts and Letters.

582. ALS-2

P.O. Box 188
Old Lyme Connecticut

June 21/51

Dear Bill:

Answering what I did not answer on the rushed card at the post office. You ask what shall you do with your future. I don't know whether you want it answered. Back in 1928 one summer day, with Floss away in Geneva if I remember, you asked the same question, "stumped" more or less, and you've always managed to answer it. I said you would – it's a mood. No use answering it in the "next" world if it's going to be different from this. But I'm going to say in A-12 or 13 – probably say – unless I change my mind: in any world of two living, touching animate things there are saints and bastards at once; if there were only one <animate thing> it wouldn't matter. Here you say you still write with difficulty after the "cerebral accident" and I'm going to bother you with writing. And if I didn't and thought only of your health, I'd be a bastard anyway – considering how many years you've given to writing. Maybe A-11, which I'm copying out for you, says all I've said in this paragraph better – if you can get into the long hand.

Anyway, what shall you do with your future? I suppose you can't stop any short poems. They always crop up. And a "15 minute" poem, like your Harvard one, is not exactly short. I take it Paterson IV finishes that – I haven't seen it. And you've finished the autobiography – if announcements are correct? And "White Mule"? What about your mother's book including the Spanish translation? I don't know your other immediate commitments – but when you're thru with them there is one thing I should like to see you do: a W.C.W. Poetics or whatever you want to call it. Do you still have the pages of the one you started I should say at least 10 or 12 years ago with the stuff of "A"-8 as a springboard. I have a copy somewhere in my files at home. "A"-8 is a good start for it. Neglect, modesty & such has nothing to do with the facts. If we want to explain rightly, what you started let's say in 1915 or perhaps earlier and what broadened into Objectivists Anthology about 1930 is the "new" we achieved in our lives.

Obviously your <N.Y.> Times reviewer (believe me, I've nothing against him as a living creature – or don't I have to ask you to believe < – I don't>) just has no insight into the poetics of Paterson. You're the best man to explain it – along with whatever else in our time's prosody – & that's the only one that will last, I'm confiding in you, no use looking for somebody who'll call me arrogant – makes a confluence that'll bear what'll come after. If I couldn't say this to you honestly, I'd stop writing right now – I mean whatever "A" is to get done this summer. In this Poetics as I see it ought to be: you, me, Bunting, Niedecker, E.P. (tho it's time some one read the dedication to Obj. Anthology where I isolated the difference between him & us – for better or worse), & whoever else <in Obj. Anth.> has gone on in the last 20 years. Dahlberg, if o whose long melodic line, <is> not "prose" – for anyone charitable enough to see under or thru the blast of metaphor, which I feel he'll be reducing given a chance. In any case, in this Poetics there would not be the Harvard anthologists who include you out of deference, not insight, Bill. Other contemporary inclusions are in "A Test of Poetry." I don't think I've missed anybody. You needn't – to make the analysis simpler – include our imitators – yes I'm beginning to see some, especially of you. Use whatever you can find that makes sense as <general> background in enclosure (Poetry 1951) & go on from there in detail, mentioning names that count from your point of view & citing examples. What a wonderful book it would make! I don't want to do it, because as I say you'd do it better right now. Twenty years from now I might – may – have equal effect. You'll note I've changed the date on my essay written early in 1950 1949. It's been rejected by a dozen mags, often with praise – I stand no chance.

Please return the essay to me after – as soon as you've read it – maybe I can think of another place that'll reject it again. Keep A-11.

And, of course, more pressing than any future project is your immediate & future health.

> All our love
> Louis
> P.S. Hindemith & Schoenberg
> did it for music –
> why not W.C.W. for poetry!

"15 minute" poem: "The Desert Music."

mother's book: *Yes, Mrs. Williams* and *The Dog and the Fever.*

W.C.W. Poetics: See the note to Zukofsky's letter of 15 March 1937.

Times reviewer: Richard Eberhart, "A Vision Welded to the World," *New York Times Book Review* (17 June 1951). Reprinted in *William Carlos Williams: The Critical Heritage.*

dedication to Obj. Anthology: "To / Ezra Pound / who despite the fact / that his epic discourse / always his own choice of matter / causes him in his Cantos / to write syntactically almost no two lines / the consecutiveness of which / includes less than two phrases / 'And doom goes with her in walking, / Let her go back to the ships / back among Grecian voices.' / himself masterly engaging / an inference of musical self-criticism / in his Fifth Canto / (readers can afford to look for the lines) / is still for the poets of our time / the / most important."

Harvard anthologists: Unidentified.

enclosure: Enclosure lacking. See the following letter.

Hindemith & Schoenberg: Paul Hindemith (1895–1963), German composer, theorist and teacher. Author of *A Concentrated Course in Traditional Harmony* (1943), *Elementary Training for Musicians* (1946), and *A Concentrated Course in Traditional Harmony II: Exercises for Advanced Students* (1948). Arnold Schoenberg (1874–1951), Austro-American composer. Author of *Models for Beginners in Composition* (1942), *Structural Functions of Harmony* (1948), *Style and Idea* (1950), *Preliminary Exercises in Composition* (1963), and *Fundamentals of Musical Composition* (1967).

▰ 583. TLS-1

9 Rudge Rd. Rutherford, N.J.

June 22, 1951

Dear Louis:

Very moving. I will keep the poem and read it again. You are best when you talk to the small circle, those who you want to have understand you explicitly. That enforces a simplicity which you sometimes strain when talk to a vaguer public.

I return the Poetry (1951). It is a move towrd clarity, white as bone long bleached in the sun. I know how hard it is to buy readers for that work. How you tried The American Scholar? Have you tried Botteghe Oscure? Have you tried Kenyon Review?Even such magazines as some of the smaller southern quarterlies: Montevallo Review, Alabama College, Montevallo, Alabama is a new and very promising enterprise (Robert Payne). There are also the Atisona Quarterly and the New Mexico Quarterly, The University of New Mexico, Box 85, Albuquerque, N.M.

We'll call you up sometime in July.

> Best
> Bill

the poem: "A"-11.

Poetry (1951): An essay, published as "Poetry (1952)," *Montevallo Review* 1:3 (Spring 1952), 49–54.

Payne: The editor of the *Montevallo Review*.

[Rutherford, N.J.]

July 6, 1951

Dear Louis:

Is Patchen still up there? If so, act as my agent, will you? Give him the enclosed check, not from me but from an unknown friend. At the same time (after you have read it) show him the enclosed letter but don't let him have it. It is mine and I want it for various reasons which you <will> understand.

If you can't find Patchen just put the whole business aside for me when I come up to see you week after next. Keep the letter in any case against my visit when I will pick it up. You might, if you want to, drop me a card saying you've received it.

It's wonderful to know there are such men as this McIntryre about us in the country. For the major phenomenon of the day in our blessed country is that hidden away in all corners there are such unapparent people. It is our business as men and as artists to believe in their existence, to have faith in their latent power and to work for them, to write for them with all the perseverence and power we have. When we are in doubt we must thing only the best we are capable of, for these men can't be fooled. They count on us to make good. They are not a coterie but the best grain of all running through the foul rot,of "they" whom McIntyre speaks of. Think of his predicament: having to serve, with his devoted carcass knowing all along that in order to reach the objectives he cherishes he has to work through such shits. That's faith and courage. And farsightedness.

Korea seem quieting down. It's at least something.I feel ashamed that I haven't had more part in it.

　　　　Yours
　　　　Bill

enclosed letter: Enclosure lacking.

McIntryre: Unidentified.

Korea: *Make Light of It* had as its dedication, "For our troops in Korea."

201 Ocean Ave.
West Haven, Conn.

July 17 (Tuesday) / 51

Dear Louis:

We plan to see you Thursday, this week. We'll get there, with Susie our grand daughter, at about one o'clock after lunch and stay till about 5 o'clock when we have to leave to visit someone else for supper nearby. It's the only way we can make ends meet.

That's the story.

In the cottage next to us in this most inconspicuous place and most undistinguished in the world I spoke to a woman who lent me W.H.D.Rouse's The Odessy. Her husband whom I have not yet met is a professor of Greek and Roman Civilization at the U. of Chicago. Thus the world goes. We can't escape.

She's an Irish Catholic, she reports his opinion as "intellectually" interested in her beliefs. We had a good talk. She does not write. I introduced Floss.

See you Thursday.

> Best
> Bill

a professor: Livio Catullo Stecchini, author of *Athenaion Politeia: The Constitution of the Athenians* (Glencoe, Illinois: Free Press, 1950). In a letter of 23 July 1951 to Kathleen Hoagland, Williams discusses Stecchini (*SE*, 306–7).

586. TLS-1

[201 Ocean Avenue, West Haven, Connecticut]

July 30, 1951

Dear Celia and Louis:

You must have had a time. I'm glad we didn't all come together in one grand slam, Patchen, Dahlberg and ourselves. That would have been something, the little house would have bust its seams. As I grow older I have come to realize that courtesy (and logic) in our person-relationships with others is something never to be realized. Especially among the intellectuals roughshod discourtesy is the rule.

Our vacation at the shore is now at an end, we return home today. We have both had a good rest, as far as the weather would allow, but I got no writing done. The feature of my time here was the trip to Bread Loaf. We drove up taking two days to it and by good fortune had good weather. The talk went fairly well, the students seemed apathetic but that may have been due to the speaker. As a matter of fact I should not speak of those attending the session as "students" since that give the impression that they were undergraduates: they were mostly teachers seeking their M.A.s. I don't think many of them knew what I was talking about. The instructors, however, were a good sort so that the informal get together in the "barn" after the formal reading really warmed up. We drove home on Thursday in one leap.

We surely laughed over your description of your experience with Dahlberg. Floss said, Celia is all right! But it is t o bad that we have to go through with that sort of thing im the name of culture. There is very little we can do about it.

Your boy Paul is a remarkable performer of the violin and he seems healthy and vigorous besides. We enjoyed hearing him play and wish you both all sorts of joy from his future successes. It is hard to say, of course, but it looks both from his skill and evident intelligence that he will go far. At least he has made a wonderful start. Musically I have one regret associated with our visit, that we didn't speak of your Pericles setting. I tell everyone about it but so far have had no leads looking toward a production. But that's an old story with me.

Best luck for you both, the summer is now no more than half gone, have a good rest and get lots of work done.

> Sincerely,
> Bill

Bread Loaf: The annual summer writers' conference in Vermont, founded in 1926.
Pericles setting: Celia Zukofsky's musical setting of Shakespeare's *Pericles*.

587. ALS-1

> P.O. Box 188
> Old Lyme
> Conn

Aug 6/51

Dear Bill,

Yes to the Foreword of your Autobiography. Don't let me miss publication date as I did Paterson. If a free copy adds up beyond means and piles a chore on a few hundred others let me know and I'll order from the publisher. [. . .]

I was going to copy out some of A-12 – a longish adaptation of Lucretius I think will interest you – by way of answer to the Foreword in kind – touching things you say in it. But I'm in too much of a stew to finish before the vacation is over – approaching typed page 30 and not half done or just about, I spill over as I go – and besides you'll find final typing or print easier to read. So just this:

> Nor do diverse songs
> Stop flaying, wet salt savours
> Into the mouth, eyes
> Not a whit deceived,
> There in the spots light is

And shade, nor do eyes
Know <u>the nature of things,</u>
Do not accuse the eye
Of this fault of the mind.

All our love to you and Floss
 Yours
  Louis

some of A-12: "A"-12, 166.

■ 588. ALS-2

> 30 Willow Street
> Brooklyn 2, N.Y.

Sept 30/51
Dear Bill

I've been reading your Autobiography – as relief from getting into the grind of the academic year. I've told my chairman, the dean, and my colleagues that you mention Bklyn Poly – it flatters them, I hope to the extent of adding to the sales of the book.

I didn't quite get thru with all of A-12 – but finished 65 pages of it. Not more than 10 to go to the end, I should judge, probably less once I get organized. Sitting up late alone – after a hundred pages of your book <i.e. Part I – tho' I find myself reading all thru as the "subject" strikes me when I thumb pages> – I turned to A-12 again last night. And on page 58 I found myself reverting to your book in way of:

> Easy to distract—
> Thought cannot will to hold on to a hand
> Nor the assailed hand remember straight,
> So easily driven on all hands
> The mind is not free to remember or forget
> Anything the opened hand feels.

Let it stand or rather serve as a criticism of what your book's "thought" and form mean to me.

I hope you've not been worrying about the future – i.e. that you're prospering. Incidentally, the local Womrath did not have your book in stock – maybe Random ought to see that <they> do.

If you're in the mood to see us let us know. All the best to Floss & you from C.
 Yours,
  Louis.

Bklyn Poly: "At the Brooklyn Polytechnic Institute a class of men showed arresting inter-
est in verse construction when I showed them something of its mechanics and ex-
plained the rationale governing my proposals for making a comprehensive change
from the older modes," *Autobiography*, 311.

page 58: "A"-12, 225.

Womrath: A chain of New York area bookstores.

589. TLS-1

9 Ridge Road, Rutherford, N.J.

December 19, 1951

Dear Louis:

I've just been reading over your 'A'-11 in the just arrived Botteghe Oscure. I
get its music better than its sense, as always, but, as always, the dignity of the
love is there. I get that, though for me the tortuousness of the diction is a diffi-
culty which I must always find foreign; to you, perhaps, necessary. I accept it.
It is effective.

What I do not understand is that the Princess has not, as she has done in the
past, paid me on the apperance of my own contribution to this issue of her
magazine. Has she paid you?

This Christmas has been complicated for us by the very welcome presence
of my son Paul and his family. They have sold their house without waiting to
provide themselves another. So here they are, little Paul from school for his
mid-winter vacation ~~from school~~ and all. You can imagine!

Yesterday, or was it the day before? I finished the first draft of my novel
which I have been writing for the last three months for Random House. Prac-
tice being what it is, practifcally nil, I pushed the work through at top speed.
Now comes the real work, the rewriting.

Best to you all
Bill

your 'A'-11: "'A'-11," *Botteghe Oscure* 8 (1951), 326–27.

Princess: Marguerite Chapin Caetani.

my own contribution: "The Desert Music," *Botteghe Oscure* 8 (1951), 310–22. Wallace
C453. *CP2*, 273–84.

my novel: *The Build-Up* (New York: Random House, 1952). Wallace A37.

30 Willow Street
Brooklyn 2, N.Y

Dec. 21/51

Dear Bill:

The Princess paid on acceptance, so I hope she pays you soon.

I'm glad you're on the novel – if you are, that is, happy about it. Are you less worried about a living than you were last summer? You don't say. Your family Xmas reunion – well, once a father, as we know, alwus, all ways.

About A-11 – I'll take the praise, in season. I suppose "The Desert Music" will also be charged with 'tortuousness' of one kind or another. I always intend my diction in the most literal and colloquial sense and let that < – its> rhythm – find its measure. The hart or the heart should bound from bringing some unlike and more like things together – that is, some intellective, but more seeing and hearing words for their definitive sense. I don't intend fuzz of "symbols" ever. But one takes one's chances in printing A-11 as I did – showing off the measure (line, rhyme, stanza). The slick at these things will not find their slickness – & say I fall short of music, rather than what you say. Whereas those who expect me to speak will not pause or pulse at the right time expecting, despite themselves, to read me like a Rossetti ballate. <not that this hasn't merits, but it's something they've got used to – & different from what I do!> But the point in printing it that way is precisely to show off the difference. Your printing

painted
hardihood   a screen
etc

has pretty much the same technical consequences. One takes one chances that it'll be easy for someone else to see that a rather individual, even analytical but unadorned speech is meant to end up in music. Whatever other point it has. [. . .]

    Happy New Year to you & Floss & all formally
      Louis

Princess: Marguerite Chapin Caetani.

[Rutherford, N.J.]

Jan 6, 1952

Dear Louis:

I just read your A-1 over again this morning, it's still difficult, hard for me to follow it – since I must try to follow it. Sometimes, in spite of my best efforts I fail. It isn't like some work I've been looking at by Norman Macleod that Golden Goose is about to publish as a booklet. His nouns and verbs are ~~are~~ completely disoriented from normal sequences. They are ungrammatically (at times) placed in arbitrary juxtapositions as "stops" about which hover or float or stand certain overtones which offer a secret language which, if the reader is able, make sense. It is difficult in another way from your way. Modern poems are a trial and a burden to a man.

The Princess has neither paid me nor answered my letter asking her what she is about. Perhaps I shall hear later. But if I do not hear from her, in other words if she intends a deliberate slight, I shall tell you.

Paul and his family are living with us for an indefinite period while he straightens himself out on the sale of his property and the repurchase of another place. It is trying but little Paul goes back to school in Massachusetts Tuesday. We can get along with the others. All this, since you mention my finances, does not make me inclined to feel at ease. I have to live close in order to be ready to assume responsibilities which may prove heavy. It is all very well to say that if I dispose of all my property I can exist for ten years, somehow, somewhere – but that is not something to look forward to with any joy. And I might conceivably live more than ten years.

But let that drop. I have not written a poem for a year (save that one) and not like to write any. On the other hand I'm reading more, all sorts of things, modern mostly but older work as well. It has done me good to meet members of the National Institute of Arts & Letters, to dine with them and take part in their discussions: there's nothing there save individually when you can find it. It has made me a wiser and a sadder man. But I have been able to round out my own concepts as against them. If I survive I may have learned something at the end of another year.

But the unhappiness of my grandchildren is of more moment than all that. I pity the young – and their parents. It is horrible. To say that they need love is idle. Where are they going to get it? They are not going to get it and that is flat. And time is running out.

Yours

Bill

some work: Norman Macleod, *Golden Goose* (Columbus, Ohio: Golden Goose Press, 1952).

The Princess: Marguerite Chapin Caetani.

Paul: Paul Herman Williams.

little Paul: Williams's grandson, Paul Williams, Jr.

that one: Probably a reference to "The Desert Music."

592. ALS-1

30 Willow Street, Brooklyn 2, N.Y.

Jan 8/52

Dear Bill:

I don't see why the Princess should intend deliberate slight – but if we wait, all things – or some rather – become apparent, in time. So-o-o for our worldly and unworldly state, complaint, whatever. I suppose we feel better if we pay no attention to it. Too bad I realize it's harder to do than not – but

What etc – why don't you and Floss tell us what week-end night (incl. Friday) you'd like to come over for dinner. All our best

Louis.

Princess: Marguerite Chapin Caetani.

593. TLS-1

[Rutherford, N.J.]

Feb 4, 1952

Dear Louis:

A slave to "the novel" (which I am writing) I have not overlooked your invitation to visit you which we shall do in time. Called on the Hechts last evening and had a good round of conversation about poetry, Vermont and teaching school in Newark.

Thought you might be interested in the enclosed. Inaccuracy is the bane of our lives: "all sonnets, . . . are exactly the same" is NOT the same as saying, "all sonnets mean exactly the same thing", which is my dictum.

No use returning the piece.

Floss and I may, probably shall go south this month. I'm going to drive it. So that if you get a card from Sarasota from us one of these days you will not think we've gone mad a capitalist. Maybe we'll change our minds and spend a week in New York instead.

The sun comes up on the morning to the <u>left</u> of the house in our rear instead of to the right of it. Thus I measure my days.

Yours

Bill

"the novel": *The Build-Up*.

the enclosed: Enclosure lacking. Williams's comment suggests it was a review of—or
essay on—his poetry.

594. ACS.

[Hotel New Weston, New York City]

[Postmarked 21 February 1952]

We changed our minds. We're spending our "Winter vacation" <?> in N.Y.
(Hotel New Weston) this week & next. I'll call you up early next week to ask
when we may come of an evening for a visit. This, at the Frick Museum, is for
all time, annihilates time as far as poor mortals may. Been to shows etc. Best to
Celia & the Kid. all very thrilling. Best

Bill

This: Titian's *Man in a Red Cap* in the Frick Collection.

595. ALS-1

30 Willow St
Brooklyn 2, NY

Nov 5/52

Dear Floss and Bill

- And vice versa, considering there's no protocol when all I want to say for
all of us is you were wonderful to us yesterday – and that you yourselves are
wonderful etc. So there's all the more reason to <u>urge</u> you to get to Washington,
D.C. as you planned – and to forget everything else to get there. Don't worry
about anyone.

Bill, I heard from the Princess Caetani, this morning – and I hope you did at
the same time. She's taken two out of four selections from A-12 I sent – a Chi-
nese bit and a Spinoza bit – and promises spring publication. If and when
you're up to it and want a typed preview, I'll be glad to send it. But just let me
know you're improving right now.

All our love to you both,

Louis

Washington, D.C.: Williams wondered how his health would be affected by taking up his
appointment as Poetry Consultant at the Library of Congress.

two out of four: Not published in *Botteghe Oscure*.

596. ACS

[Postmarked Rutherford, N.J.]

Nov 16/52

Dear Celia & Louis – Everything going fine. We were so delighted with your visit and with Paul's playing. An altogether fine day. – Can't tell you how much we have enjoyed "Unforgotten Years". So much so that Bill have given it as one of the three books he has enjoyed reading this year – for the Herald-Trib. Xmas Book list – Planning to go to Wash. D.C. early in Dec!

Our best to you all – as ever. Floss

"Unforgotten Years": Logan Pearsall Smith, *Unforgotten Years* (Boston: Little, Brown, 1939). A passage from this memoir is briefly referred to in "A"-13. See Ahearn, *Zukofsky's "A,"* 145– 46.

597. ACS

[Rutherford, N.J.]

[December 1952]

[Printed greeting: "Wishing You the Joys of the Holiday Season"]
[In Florence Williams's hand:]

Our best to you all
Bill & Floss

598. ALS-2

[30 Willow Street
Brooklyn, New York]

Jan 11/52 [1953]
Dear Bill:

Dee-lighted with your Bollingen! We hope the rest of the news is as cheerful.

I'm all of a dither myself working to get the rest of the Bottom: on Shake-speare out of my mind and onto paper.

Paul's been invited to play at New Haven with the symphony orchestra there – I think it's the Philarmonic, conducted by one Harry Beman Feb. 21. One of their concerts for kids – more I don't know myself. I'll have to write one of these days to find out the hour, where etc. He'll play the Mozart you heard.

All the best and to Floss – let's hear – from us all.

Yours
Louis

Bollingen: Williams and Archibald MacLeish had been awarded the Bollingen Prize in
Poetry.

Paul's been invited: See "Nine-Year-Old Violinist Performs at Woolsey Hall Concert," the
New Haven Register (22 February 1953), p. 3. This brief article notes that Paul played
the first movement of Mozart's *Concerto Number Three*, and that he "was besieged by
autograph seekers after his performance."

599. TLS-1

9 Ridge Road, Rutherford, N.J.

Jan. 16, 1953

Dear Louis:

As toward the end of I PALLIACHI, the comedy is played out: My appoint-
ment to serve as consultant in poetry at the has been revoked. I have received
no salary all these months but have been paying rent on an apartment for all
that.

No use calling names.

Congratulations on Paul's appointment to play at Yale. I wish him all suc-
cess as he deserves – if genius ever deserves the success that comes to <it.>
May the Poweres that Be be kind to him.

Louis, you have always been a good friend, the best, and Celia has been a
good friend to both Flossie and me also, maybe a new life is starting.

If with time, as they say, I shell recover a reasonable use of my faculties,that
is all I shall ask. Let's hope for the best.

Keep well.

> Your friend
> Bill

I PALLIACHI: Ruggerio Leoncavallo's (1858–1919) opera, *I Pagliacci* (1892) ends with the
words, "La commedia è finita."

my appointment: In a letter of 28 February 1953, Florence Williams told the Zukofskys
that her husband "was fine when we went to Washington early in December—but
that Communist business knocked him out completely. He just wilted and within a
few days—was just not the same person" (Texas).

600. TLS-1

[Rutherford, N.J.]

8/27/53

Dear Louis:

I just lost, or misplaced, the piece of sponge rubber I keep in my pocket
or near it upon which to exercise my fingers. In my present condition it

constituted a major tragedy! By this your are to grasp the state of my mind – and soul.That I found the offending article again, by my own initiative, doesn't alter the case except philosophically, the damage had already been done.

But we are tricked by the sonority of our writing into saying what we do not mean – if we ever mean what we say. Thorsten Veblin, who had no vestige of a literary style, is the only writer I know that escapes being lulled to sleep by his own periods. He really thought to a purpose and wrote down what he thought and his style is atrocious, you cannot read him without a great effort. No doubt that is what he intended.

This makes little sense coming after my first paragraph but in the total non-sense of the times it has a certain pertinance.

When and if you get the chance before your classes begin come out some afternoon and see me . There's nothing much to communicate but it would be a pleasure to hear what you are doing with yourself these days. I go along much as I have been doing today . It is strange to see the menand women getting rich, many of them, and buy large houses with lakes and woods adjoining and to realiza that I too might have had such things in my reach had I applied myself to the task of getting them. I was interested in other things. Not all, of course, have succeeded so well in life as I picture it but it is amazing over the span of the last twenty years how the world has changed. Thorsten Veblen's "leisure class" categories have extended far afield. Every plumber is a rich man.

I had a letter from E.P. yesterday, rather a long one for him recently. It was the same old assumption of superiority over us all which we have become accustomed with the same bad spelling we are familiar with which comes, though we did not in the past suspect it that he knows no better. He is a wild romantic masquerading as a classical scholar. He is an unfortunate man now but one who has loyal friends who may yet save him. I wish him luck. His endurance under thae trials that he has been through is phenominal and due to what must be called his strength of mind but also, I think, his egotism and insensitivity. He has a hide like a rhinocerous, really.

Come out and see me if you get the chance. I hope the summer has passed pleasantly.

     Best
     Bill

Veblin: Thorstein Veblen's (1857–1929) best-known work is *The Theory of the Leisure Class* (1899). Passages from other Veblen works appear in "A"-8.

letter from E.P.: Letter from Ezra Pound not located.

601. TLS-1

10/17/53

Dear Louis:

Sorry you've been ill, hope you'll be better soon. I return Bunting's letter as you asked me t. The CURRICULUM VITAE I have sent on to Norman Pearson at Yale who as far as I know is more likely than any one else to be of assistance. I sent him also Bunting's address on the chance that he want to communicate direct with him.

Take care of yourself. That goes also for Celia.

    Sincerely,

    Bill

[In Florence Williams's hand] Dear Louis – I've had some sort of virus myself – unless it's just plain fatigue. Now that Bill is better – I guess I'm letting go a bit and feel the need for <u>rest</u>. But, we'll get over to see you before too long. It will be a pleasure.

    Best to all—Floss

Bunting's letter: A letter of 28 September 1953, from Throckley, England, among the Zukofsky papers at Texas. Bunting indicated his want of gainful employment and asked Zukofsky to spread the word among his friends and colleagues that Bunting was willing to move to the United States to obtain suitable work.

602. ACS

[December 1953]

[Printed greeting:] "Wishing You the Joys of The Holiday Season"

With our love—

    Bill & Floss

We haven't been able to get over to see you. – I have been under the weather with the bug that bit you. – and am taking an extra long time to get back on my feet! – Bill is improving steadily and we'll surely get in to see you before <u>too</u> long.

    As ever -

    Floss

30 Willow Street
Brooklyn 2, N.Y.

Sun., Mar. 14/54

Dear Bill,

I spent yesterday with "The Desert Music and other Poems" (thanks for sending it) "the full meaning of it all" assuring to me what I know of you – and assuring the succession of the poems as a group, from the first taken from Paterson to the last definition of their music: 'shed of a shape close as it can get to no shape'. And nevertheless, or rather so the skill stays.

I felt closest to "To Daphne and Virginia", "The Yellow Flower", "Deep Religious Faith", the beginnings of "The Garden" & "Work in Progress" (pp 37, 45 thru 50), and the Theocritus.

The Idyl is lovely (sound lovely if you wish with the tone of Floss whenever she uses that word of something – it has that way always struck me as final). And since we're talking I might as well say I've a hunch as to the measure that keeps this group together: starting with your "old" idea that it's the words that make the poem, that alone can get things said, they're (the words) are activated out of you in groups of four – whatever they are, e.g 3 articles and a noun, or a countless variation of the grammar of speech, but always in groups of four – a measure hovering over the visual <stepped-down> three-line stanza – breaking the stanza and the line as convention; but so pointing them out over and across the groups of four <words> as their measure. Do I make myself clear? If I do, it ought to be explained to the National Inst. of Arts & Letters. How does one get in, become a member, by being voted in? Who proposes? Here's a bid. Just so you can [sic] say sainthood never asked. I won't <ask> anyone else – nor do I see myself inclined to approach anyone else on that score in the next ten years. And I don't know how the bid has followed out of what I've said about your measure – except that feeling sometimes leads to a desire for practical action. A force don't push unless it's pushed: Newtonian! Personal references enclosed for the nomination, if the opportunity happens with ease. Anyway, I've asked. It's done. It's over.

Getting back to Idyl – I wonder if you've thought of doing the rest of that it, Thyrsis' song. I'm curious <too> whether you worked with the Greek before you – since the three of us here spend about 5–15 minutes of Paul's school day trying to catch some Greek. The pleasure of being able to recognize something in the Iliad on the basis of the little grammar we have is a pleasure.

It'll be official spring next Sunday. When are you both coming over?

Regards,
Yours
Louis

Desert Music: *The Desert Music and Other Poems* (New York: Random House, 1954). Wallace A38.

the Theocritus: "Theocritus: Idyl I (A Version from the Greek)." *CP2*, 268–73.

references enclosed: Enclosure lacking.

Thyrsis' song: Thyrsis is the shepherd who sings in Theocritus's first idyl. Williams translated only a portion of the poem.

604. TLS-1

9 Ridge Road, Rutherford, N.J.

June 24, 1954

Dear Louis:

Your fairly recent letter reminds me that we have a long postponed date to visit you in Brooklyn. Let explanations go out the window. You say you are making no plans to go away for the summer. If there is enough of us left to make the trip may we come over some convenient afternoon during next week – not Thursday – and chew the fat a while?

I have a pencil drawing of an angel blowing a horn by Ben Shahn on which appears in a matted green script , preceeded by an ornate initial P , a verse from the bible praising God for his manifest blessings. It is fastened to the wall before my eyes where I can see it every day merely by lifting my eyes.

Best luck
Bill

Ben Shahn: (1898–1969) Russian-born American artist. Williams had met Shahn in June 1950. Williams refers to him in Book Five of *Paterson*.

605. TCS

[Rutherford, N.J.]

[1954]

Tuesday not the other , my retainers inform me, is my bad day.
Cheerio
Bill

606. TLS-1

9 Ridge Road, Rutherford, N.J.

June 26, 1954

Dear Louis:

The weekend of July 4th is impossible for me. So once again let us postpone this epochal meeting until a later date. Have a good vacation and get as far from the scrape of a fiddle string as your conscience permits – or do you believe after all that your muse thrives on just that fare? Best to Celia and his nibs but remember that you yourself are not a violin player. I heard a good report of a poem by you from Ignatow who says he will publish it later in the summer.

Best
Bill

his nibs: Paul Zukofsky.

a poem: "From 'A'-12," the *Beloit Poetry Journal* (5:1), 1–3. The selection begins: "In the eighth month / In the second year of Darius / I saw by night—// Thru running manes of Leaves of Grass[.]" It concludes: "The fire roared, quieted to light."

Ignatow: David Ignatow (1914–1997), poet. Ignatow was the guest editor of the Whitman Centennial Issue of the *Beloit Poetry Journal* issue in which Zukofsky's selection from "A"-12 appeared. Ignatow discusses Williams and Zukofsky in *The One in the Many: A Poet's Memoirs* (Middletown, Connecticut: Wesleyan University Press, 1988).

607. TLS-1

9 Ridge Road, Rutherford, N.J.

June 29, 1954

Dear Louis:

Fine! We'll be over Friday afternoon come Hell or low water. It is thrilling to hear of your sion's plans for the summer and yours along with him. The best of luck to you all. We'll leave here in mid afternoon and should arrive at your house sometime around 4 o'clock. See you then.

Best
Bill

plans for the summer: The Zukofsky family made a cross-country trip that summer.

608. TLS-1

9 Ridge Road, Rutherford, N.J.

July 27, 1954

Dear Louis:

We received, yesterday, your letter written enroute telling of your son's playing at the mental hospital for Ezra. It was a wonderful thing to think of and for your son to perform. God I wish I had been there but I'm afraid I would not have been able to control myself but would have wept all over the place. The comment it makes on our age is devastating. I am glad you spoke of it. Congratulations all around.

You know how unsatisfactory it is for me to attempt to get around but as soon as you return from your trip and get settled again give me a chance to make good on my promise to come over and spend an afternoon and evening with you.

Best to all. Your friend,
Bill

son's playing: The Zukofskys visited Pound on 11 July 1954. See David Gordon, "Zuk and Ez at St. Liz," *Paideuma* 7:3 (Winter 1978), 581–84.

---

609. ALS-1

[On letterhead of the St. Francis Hotel,
San Francisco, California]

Aug 5/54

Dear Bill & Floss,

Your note of 27 July here on our arrival. The enclosures which – telepathy or what have you – anticipated it – ought to immortalize, or again what have you, hymn-ort-alize us for a while – in the American Grain. Paul & I are tape-recording for the FM channel here = to WQXR, NY – i.e. KPFA. I hear you will, too. The Patchens insisted on it, among other contacts – they've been very kind. We continue to Oregon first thing next Tues. morning. [. . .] And, of course, we'll see you back home – only stay well both of you.

The map shows the route that goes with the signature to the poem. Keep it – if you wish – i.e. keep both.

C's best, P's–&
as ever yrs.
Louis

enclosures: Enclosures lacking.

tape-recording: On 6 August 1954 Zukofsky recorded "The Judge and the Bird," "Spooks' Sabbath," "Little Wrists," "Reading and Talking," "George Washington," "The World Autumn," "I walk," "Catullus 8," "To Zadkine," "Glad they were there," "Machault," "'A'-11," "A-9 (second half)," and "On Valentine's Day to Friends."

map: Enclosure lacking.

the poem: Enclosure lacking.

610. TLS-1

9 Ridge Road, Rutherford, N.J.

Aug. 9, 1954

Dear Louis:

Your Odyssey unfolds with Telemucus at the bow, ha! oddly enough. When written after your return it should make interesting reading. The incident of the San Francisco recording might all under the Sirens' singing etc etc. No matter it is all very interesting. Have a good time on the rest of the trip. Regards to your present hostess.

Summer here has been hot and dry but today it is raining blessedly. As I sit at my machine I am thinking how blessed it is to spend a lifetime in pursuit of a style in both prose and verse which if we never achieve it has enlivened many otherwise dull hours for us.

Take care of yourself; we'll be over to see you soon after your return.

Sincerely yours
Bill

present hostess: Lorine Niedecker, whom the Zukofskys visited in Fort Atkinson, Wisconsin.

611. ALS-1

on the "Coast Daylight", S.P
gaviota-soledad Calif.

Aug 31/54

[Text of "William Carlos Williams alive!" Subsequently designated as part 5 of "Songs of Degrees" (*CSP*, 148–51).]

P.S. of course it shouldn't be printed in columns but consecutively. The train I was on was two hours late arriving – so I wrote 10 hours[.] P.Z. dozed off. This is the first clear copy I've made – no time to do one for myself.

S.P.: Southern Pacific.
P.Z.: Paul Zukofsky.

30 Willow St
Brooklyn 1, N.Y.

Sat [Postmarked 11 September 1954]

Dear Bill & Floss:

Just to ask how you've been and to say we're back – I've nursed an infection in my foot for the past two weeks. Better now, the school opens Monday. Let us know when you feel like coming over.

> All our best
> Louis

the school: The Brooklyn Polytechnic Institute.

■ 613. TC

[Rutherford, N.J.]

[1954]

Flossie broke a small bone in her ankle two months ago and has not been able to walk on the street since. She is somewhat better now but still imobilized. Or should I spell it "immoblized", same thing. I'll be there alone on the date set, if I don't get lost in the subway.

> Bill

■ 614. TC

[Rutherford, N.J.]

[1954]

Make it a week from Friday, Oct. 1, about four in the afternoon. I'll come alone as Floss is still unable to bear her weight on her ankle. See you then. Sorry you have been ill.

> Bill

■ 615. TLS-1

9 Ridge Road, Rutherford, N.J.

Oct. 2/54

Dear Louis:

We had a good time with our talk and I at least listeng to Paul and his fiddle. Very good. The boy has a long row to hoe and he'll have to sweat copiously in the course of it. Best luck to him.

Celia did me a great service in looking up my "sforza" for me, I'll send her the poem in which I use the term as soon as I can copy it out. I enjoyed my supper. It was fine of you all to guide my doddering steps through that subway maze at the bus termeinal.

Will you please copy out for me, from your memory, that anecdote about Socrates and Plato and Alcibiades about the old, it is no doubt one of the treasures of the ages and I am not familiar with it.

I'll come over again when Florence can be with me sometime during the winter. Take care of yourself.

Best Bill

my "sforza": Williams refers to a detail in "The Drunk and the Sailor": "The nerve-tingling screeches / that sprang // *sforzando* / from that stubble beard[.]" The poem was first published in *Journey to Love* (New York: Random House, 1955). Wallace A41. *CP2*, 305– 6.

anecdote: See the following letter.

▮ 616. ALS-2

30 Willow Street, Brooklyn 1, N.Y.

Oct 4/54

Dear Bill:

Glad you wrote – now we know you're home. If C and I looked worried about you, however, it wasn't you – you looked fine. That's just us. We dodder too often ourselves, and worry about each other the same way. No reason to impress others with it – as a kind of carry-over, or what?

The Alcibiades confession from Plato's <u>Symposium</u> – about five pages before the end of it – might as well condense Plato: (Alcibiades starts off:)

"Socrates, are you asleep?" No," he said. "Do you know what I am meditating?" "What are you meditating?" he said. "I think," I replied, "that of all the lovers whom I have ever had you are the only one who is worthy of me . . And I should certainly have more reason to be ashamed of what wise men would say if I were to refuse a favour to such as you, than of what the world, who are mostly fools, would say of me if I granted it." To these words he replied in an ironical manner which is so characteristic of him: – "Alcibiades, my friend . . truly you must see in me some rare beauty of a kind infinitely higher than any which I see in you . . . if you mean to share with me and to exchange beauty for beauty, you will have greatly the advantage of me; you will gain true beauty in return for appearance – like Diomede, gold in exchange for brass. But look again, sweet friend, and see whether you are not deceived in me. The mind begins to grow critical when the bodily eye fails, and it will be a long time before you get old."

Should be read in context tho. The drama is what counts. And since the Symposium is only about 50 pp. long, if Floss can get over the speeches of the very nice Greek boys at the beginning of the dialogue, I'm sure both of you will enjoy Eryximachus, the doctor, and Aristophanes' myth of how many loves (!) came to be – as well as the bit I've quoted here. Try it: you probably have Plato on your book shelves – if not, a good selection is the Viking Portable Plato – And there are paper book edtns. of Symposium plus for 50¢ or less.

We'll be glad to get the poem including "sforzando" or?

And, when Floss can come – we hope she's better – come over as you say – or if you prefer we come to Rutherford when it's easy enough for you both, say.

> All our best – and take care of
> yourself – yourselves etc
> Louis

Viking Portable Plato: *The Portable Plato*, Scott Buchanan, ed. (New York: Viking, 1948). the poem: "The Drunk and the Sailor."

617. ACS [Printed message: "Season's Greetings"]

[Rutherford, N.J.]

[December 1954]

[In Florence Williams's hand:] Hope we can get t-gether before long. My ankle is just about well – so Bill decided to get some attention & sprained his three weeks ago! –

Happy New Year! –
F. & B.

618. TLS-1

9 Ridge Road, Rutherford, N.J.

2/19/55

Dear Louis:

I'm not very bright as you perhaps have long since found so that I have always had difficulty in following your poems – just as I have difficulty in understanding what Rosalie Moore is saying. "Thru running manes of Leaves of Grass" came therefor as a great light into your method and I will be more understanding in future, I'll get out the opening pages of "A", which I have, and tackle it again. It is not easy for me. Hope for the best.

I wasn't able to hear Paul when he performed, whenever it was, though I should have liked to. I hope he did well. I go along as usual impatient of death.

Flossie is reading to me the autobiograohy of a Scotchmen named Edwin Muir which someone, probably the publisher, has sent me. Do you know his poems? Seems to be a good guy.

Spring is almost here. We have been invited to go to Florida for a two week visit. I hear two cats making love in the yard – or fighting, the same thing. Best.
Bill

Rosalie Moore: (1910–2001), poet. Her poem in the *Beloit Poetry Journal* Whitman Centennial issue, "Reunion for Walt Whitman," followed immediately after Zukofsky's selection from "A"-12.

"Thru running manes. . . .": Zukofsky's selection from "A"-12, published in the Whitman Centennial issue of the *Beloit Poetry Journal.*

Muir: (1887–1959), British poet, essayist and novelist. Williams refers to *An Autobiography* (1954).

Florida: Willliams and his wife flew to Florida in the middle of March for a two-week vacation.

619. TC

[Rutherford, N.J.]

[1955]

By mere chance we heard Paul play his fiddle last night, it sounded wonderfully able. I can't say more since we didn't tune in till the program was almost over. Too bad we didn't realize what was going on until too late – tho' this may have been the concert you had written me about earlier. What was he playing, we missed the announcem_ent?

We've been to Florica for the last two weeks visiting a friend. Flew down.

Congratulate P. for us, he's coming up in the world. Best to you all from Floss & me.
Bill

620. TLS-1

9 Ridge Road, Rutherford, N.J.

April 22, 1955
Dear Louis:

How did Celia make out with her medical exam? Keep me posted for I have been worrying about her ever since your last letter.

Haven't had a chance to enquire about her and you since I flew out to Chicago for a reading at the Art Canter. It went well but as a result I'm tuckered out; not as young as I was.

Let me hear from you about Celia.

> Best
> Bill

Chicago: From April 13–20, Williams had been away undertaking readings at the Art
Center and at the Writers' Workshop in Iowa City.

---

621. ACS

San Francisco, California

5/20/55

[In Florence Williams's hand:] Having a fine trip. Bill is doing very well –
and his audiences seem to like him very much. Having fine weather – which
helps a lot. Hope Celia is O.K. Love to all – Bill & Floss.

fine trip: "Then, beginning May 7, he began a three weeks' reading tour of the West
Coast. . . . The trip began at Washington University in St. Louis—for which he re-
ceived $500—and then he and Floss made trips to the university of Washington, Seat-
tle (May 13–14), where they stayed with Roethke this time, then San Francisco State,
Berkeley, San José, Santa Barbara, UCLA, and, finally Riverside on May 31. For each
reading Williams received $150. From there they flew on to Santa Fe, New Mexico, to
visit with Winfield Townley Scott and his wife. On June 5, four weeks after they had
begun, the Williamses were back home" (Mariani 688).

---

622. TLS-1

9 Ridge Road, Rutherford, N.J.

June 27, 1955

Dear Louis:

Saluti! The kid's good – as you know. Even over last year the authority of
his playing has made vast strides. It was a pleasure for us yesterday to hear
him over the air. Hope we live long enough to hear him on the concert stage
after he has been playing a man's size fiddle for a number of years – though
from <what> came over the air yesterday there isn't much to be added to his
accomplishmentes.

How is Celia? From what Kate said to Floss over the phone last week she
isn't too well but the bugaboo of a serious abdominal operation seems to have
been escaped.

Take care of yourself. We have scarcely recovered from our trip to the coast
. When we have we'll be talking of coming over to see you some afternoon.
Let's hear from you when you have anything to tell me.

> Sincerely,
> Bill

9 Ridge Road, Rutherford, N.J.

Oct. 27 , '55

Dear Louis:

You must be sick of asking me to come over and see you when I never come. Cheer up, I go nowhere. Last spring I did go on a long trip to the coast by plane , we'll talk of that when we finally get together which we must do before the too cold weather or one of us croaks. It's not easy for me to tear myself away but before Christmas I'll be getting Floss and we'll be making the trip to Brooklyn – you'd think it was to the moon yet Paul makes it every day! It must be the mind that baulks or invents difficulties.

We didn't hear your Paul play a week or two ago, we don't own a television, we could all have gone to Bill's house but at the last minute I learned that he and his family had been incited here. I was mad but Floss had so arranged it without thinking of the music and so it had to be. Did he do well? No matter what he played , I'll hear him the next time if I have to hear him alone. Not that Floss isn't interested, she is; it was just an unfortunate concatenation of circumstances.

Rexroth, I think it was, was telling me the Ferlinghetti (that guy in San Francisco) is planning to bring out the whole of "The". At least someone is to bring it out. That will be an overdue event I'm looking forward to with keen interest. I've always had difficulty with that poem, having the affection I have for you, that has bothered me no end. It is no doubt the fault of my slowwittedness that the difficulty has occurred. It is not from lack of trying. In any case it will be a relief to have the poem printed as a whole, I find that I have to get my hand all the way round a subject to understand it, when I do get my hand round it it often becomes clear to me. Also a completed text that my eye can see on the page is of great assistance to me. I look forward to the appearance of a completed text.

I had a letter from the Ezra upraiding for something I know nothing about. It seems you had sent him a letter that concerned his old man, Homer L. Pound. In the course of his letter (just a scrawl) I gathered with difficulty that you had sent ol' Ez an excerpt from an article or book I had written (years ago) quoting something the elder Pound had said or written about Cavalcanti. Jesus Christ! I have never pretended to know anything about Cavalcante and have not as far as I can recollect ever written anything about him.

Don't get excited or think that I have been upset. The only reason I mention the circumstance is that our friend seems to take it amiss so that if you can clarify my mind on the subject I'd be grateful to you.

I've been asked to do an obituary notice for Poetry on the death of Wallace Stevens. I sent it off yesterday – 2500 words. Also a magazine, Arts, it used to be Arts Digest, commissioned me to do an article on Brancusi for an early issue – 3000 words. I sent the corrected galleys off on Monday. I'm going to Buffalo to give a reading on the 9th. After ahat we'll come out to see you.

Jinny's mother died this week in Ohio. She of course flew out to the funeral. We're waiting to see what her mood is when she returns. We've been seeing to the care of the children during ~~in~~ her and Paul's absence.

What the hell else was I going to tell you? It's gone now.

> Cheerio
>
> Bill

Ferlinghetti: Lawrence Ferlinghetti (b. 1919), poet and publisher. Founder (with Peter D. Martin) of the City Lights bookshop in 1953. City Lights began publishing books in 1955. City Lights did not publish Zukofsky, but did reprint *Kora in Hell* in 1957. Wallace A4b.

letter from the Ezra: A letter of 24 October 1955 from Pound (Yale). In a subsequent letter (27 October 1955) Pound explained that "Yr / error re / me yole man wuz in a privik letter to I fergit whom which has been printed in theEz / Snooze Letter by them californias." (Yale). Pound referred to a short article by John C. Thirlwall: "The Quality of Mercy Was Not Strained: A Footnote Followed by a Letter," the *Pound Newsletter* 8 (October 1955), 22–23. Wallace D11. In the article, Thirlwall printed a letter of 19 January 1943 from Williams to Babette Deutsch. In this letter, Williams writes, "He [Pound] was at the University of Pennsylvania in 1902, '03, '04 and in 1905 was banished by his father to the sticks for general insubordination of what quality I don't know, probably nothing more than refusing to do anything but what he pleased to do in his classes, perhaps spending more cash than the old man could give him." The letter is reprinted in *SL*. Zukofsky had sent Pound an issue (or issues) of the *Quarterly Review of Literature* containing contributions by Williams. In "Williams' Letter," *Quarterly Review of Literature* 5:3, 301 (Wallace C441), Williams praises the *Review*'s Pound issue (5:2), then notes: "But of it all, and it is important and all excellent, nothing surpasses the wonder of Ezra's two translations from Cavalcanti." The sonnets reprinted in the Pound issue were sonnets 7 and 16 from *Guido Cavalcanti: Rime* (1932).

obituary notice: "Comment: Wallace Stevens," *Poetry* 87:4 (January 1956), 234–39. Wallace C515.

article on Brancusi: "Brancusi," *Arts* 30:2 (November 1955), 21–25. Wallace C513.

Jinny's: Virginia Carnes Williams.

[30 Willow Street
Brooklyn, New York]

Oct 29/55

Dear Bill:

Okay! think of the phoenix or the sparrows and call up and come in November. Both of you.

I sound silly <to myself> – considering you have your hands full with Paul's children. I'm sorry to hear of Jinny's mother's death. But the older we get what is there say.

Never mind missing Paul's concert. He played well, yes, and a week of congratulations by phone etc followed. But you'll hear him – [. . .] Remember we've arranged it with God for you to come to Carnegie.

I'm puzzled by Rexroth's telling you that Ferlinghetti will do <u>The</u>. ??? First I heard of it! I met Ferlinghetti in S.F. in 1954 by accident – Paul, he & myself all broadcasting or tape recording over Berkeley station. He introduced himself & subsequently asked me to recommend him for a Gugg. Fellowship. Which I did & he recently sent me his book to thank me tho he didn't get the grant. But not a word of printing me – and I haven't asked. Maybe you can clear up the rumor for me.

I'm equally at a loss about the Homer L. Pound – Cavalcanti incident. Mebbe if I saw Ez's scrawl I could figure it out. I seem to remember vaguely that you had a note in Quarterly Review of Lit. – of where was it? – on the verse line of one of Ez's Cav. Sonnets. But the impression persists that you praised it. I dunno.

I hope your contribution to Poetry appears in the same issue with a recent poem <of mine> they've accepted – so I'll have company. It'll be nice to see the Brancusi article.

Have a good trip to Buffalo & come back & see us.

> Our love to you
> & Floss
> Louis

his book: Lawrence Ferlinghetti, *Pictures of the Gone World* (San Francisco: City Lights, 1955).

you had a note: See the previous letter.

your contribution: "Comment: Wallace Stevens."

recent poem: "The Guests," *Poetry* 87:6 (March 1956), 346– 48. *CSP,* 153– 54.

Jan 18th [1956]

[In Florence Williams's hand:] Hi! As of to-day – our new telephone no –
WE-3-1496 – Hope you all are well and busy – Best to all

    Bill & Floss

■ 626. TLS-1

9 Ridge Road, Rutherford, N.J.

Jan. 30/56

Dear Louis:

Still alive, believe it or not. Our sources of information have not been so
optimistic about you and Celia. In fact they have been most alarming about
her. I hope they have been exaggerated. I hope she's better now.

Why don't you come and see for yourself? I can almost hear you say. Around
the Christmas holidays would I know be a good time but it was impossible to
tear myself loose – as it is now. In fact until after the middle of February when I
have a poetry reading at the Lauter Piano Company! I will not feel free to move.
At that timeI'll call you on the phone, when the weather promises to be fine,
and ask Celia if we can't come over perhaps some Sunday afternoon.

I had a call from Jack Thirlwall saying he had a letter from Norman Pearson
telling him that Yale has just acquired a file of our letters which Jack had
thought were lost. He is going up this week to look them over. He is a most ef-
ficient collector of my letters imaginable, good luck to him, I don't think
they're worth it.

I have a picture post card on my desk sent to me by a friend, a woman living
in Brasil now, whom I met in the nut house when I was there. It shows four old
musicians walking poorly clad in the snow from left to right between – or ap-
proaching a village no doubt somewhere in Europe. They are all scrunched
togeter their instruments in their hands trudging along. I mean to keep the
card there a long time as a reminder of our probable fate as artists. I know just
what is going on in the minds of those white haired muscians.

It is a miserable day today. I have at the moment nothing to do but sit her
typing this letter to you. When I see you we'll find something to say about our
lives. Love to Celia from us both. I presume young Paul is growing up fast. My
own grandchildren are going their various ways as children do, poor kids, if
they can hook onto something as Paul has done to his fiddle they are lucky .

    Best luck

    Bill

poetry reading: Williams read on 14 February. The piano company was in Newark.

Thirlwall: John C. Thirlwall

nut house: Hillside Hospital, in Floral Park, New York. Willliams was treated for depression from 21 February to 18 April 1953.

■ 627. ALS-2

30 Willow Street
Brooklyn 1, N.Y.

Feb. 1/56

Dear Bill:

Celia and I hope you will call up when the weather's fine – that should be about Easter week when we'll all be free again and <u>well</u> I hope. No use talkin' about ills – we're sick all right and what with Paul's schedule we just crawl along as fast as we can: [. . .].

We think about you – and, of course, know winter's no time for you to be visiting. I've had the most god awful arthritis myself – that I don't even bother to tell anyone about[.] Paul's appearances – all requests <u>we</u> have to go thru with not to offend. The good in it: he can now face any audience. Perhaps you heard that he played in Newark at the Mosque Theatre last Sat. morning with Thomas Scherman's Orchestra, a Mozart festival program for kids. To get away from the milieu C & I went up to the last row of the empty second balcony and of course we were pleased and reassured when we could hear every note very beautifully of his first fiddle part in the quartet version of Eine Kleine Nacht-musik. Later, Griffith of the Foundation that sponsored the concert asked Scherman's <business> manager to look for us – we were hurrying out – and well he had only the highest praise, I suppose. Too bad, he said, Paul hadn't a concerto to play & show off solo – but he listens to 3000 auditioning fiddles a year – & there's nothing like that kid's playing. On the strength of which we had grilled hot dogs at the Penn. terminal in Newark.

———

Your letters – what I sometimes thought would happen has happened. No use talkin' again. The lesson to me, never store anything anywhere* if you think you'll want it again some day –

*especially with family

    All our love to you & Floss

    Louis

P.S. And let's all stay alive, by all means! There's our work to do – QRL will even be printing some things – for nuthin' as usual!

Scherman: (1917–1979), conductor. Founder (1947) of the Little Orchestra Society, which performed concerts in the greater New York area.

Griffith: Mrs. Parker O. Griffith (ca. 1878–1960) established the Griffith Music Founda-
    tion in Newark in 1938. She was its president until its cessation in 1959.

some things: "All of December toward New Year's" (*CSP*, 143–44); "Reading and Talking"
    (*CSP*, 127–29); "From 'A'-12," *Quarterly Review of Literature* 8:3 (April 1956), 190–98.

628. TLS-1

9 Ridge Road, Rutherford, N.J.

Feb. 2/56

Dera Louis:

In Newark! I would have given something to be there. But I had it coming to
me. Never do it again no matter how neglectful I have been. I feel as if I had
lost a friend. I would have loved to have heard him.

We even had a brainstorm and on the spur of the moment just hopped a
bus and went to the Civic Center to see Marceau, the French mime, last night.
We succeeded in getting about the last seat in the house, no better, but it was
worth it. Alone on that enormous stage in his pierrot's suit, with chalked face
and a red flower in his fool's cap, without a word spoken and only a minimum
of tinny music he held that audience and me spellbound. As an example of
what he did his first number was entitled – WALKING. He walked, without
moving from one place, for about five minutes. You wouldn't believe that a
man could hold your interest in such a performance without moving from
that place.

We're not going to wait for the good weather, rheumatism or no rheuma-
tism we're coming to see you in the next 2 or 3 weeks. I'll call up first.

    Bill

Marceau: Marcel Marceau (b. 1923), French pantomimist. His first U.S. performances
    (September 1955) were widely acclaimed. He appeared a second time in February 1956
    at New York's City Center.

629. TC

[Rutherford, N.J.]

[1956]

I've got to write, a definitive note, on OBJECTIVIST POETRY. Won't you sit
down, and in a few words, give me a definition to compare with my own. Be-
tween us we ought to be able to give a stranger a good impresson of what we
mean. Maybe you've done it already, in that case just give me the chapter and
verse so I won't have to bother you any further.

Floss said she enjoyed the concert and that the kid and his piano pal were
worth the whole show. I had my hands full that night but it went off, for me

also, very well. We'll call up some night soon and make a date for a visit. Love to Celia. Best.

Lookinf forward to hearing from you. No hurry.

Bill

definitive note: Williams contributed notes on "Free Verse" and "Objectivism" to the *Encyclopedia of Poetry and Poetics,* Alex Preminger, ed. (Princeton: Princeton Univ. Press, 1965). Wallace B95.

630. ALS-3

[30 Willow Street
Brooklyn, New York]

Feb. 27/56

Dear Bill:

Objectivist Poetry = <equals> poetry – and that's that. A poem has an <u>expressed</u> shape, form, love, music (or what other word have you?) And that goes for a poem in any time, for any time – granted the other guy knows the language. Otherwise nothing is said, the "poem" so-called is empty, misshapen. It ought to be the same when we're all – not we but the deluge <is> – buzzing around in interstellar space. Only heavens knows what words if any they'll be using to make up the shape, and the order (movement) another indissoluble aspect of it.

Tell the "stranger" if you must that L.Z.'s poetics is in:

1. <u>Sincerity and Objectification</u> (Poetry, Feb. 1931) especially part II pp 273–276
2. <u>An "Objectivists" Anthology</u>. The Preface 1932
3. <u>Poetry, For My Son</u>, Cronos II 4 1948
4. <u>A Test of Poetry</u> N.Y. 1948 London 1952
5. <u>[A Statement for] Poetry</u> (the words in brackets were omitted from the title by mistake) Montevallo Review I, 13 1952.

Notice that I try to say it differently each time – so as not to bore – but after all I'm saying the same thing. Also in the <u>Bottom: on Shakespeare</u> (New Directions 14, 1953) and as it continues, still unprinted.

But I hope in every poem I've done – best said that way, <u>embodied</u> – to read so you can <u>see</u> and <u>hear</u>.*

Maybe quote this letter to your "stranger" – my mind is not on it, my being is it, tell him.

So call up when you can. All our love to you both

Louis

* Of course, I assume a world where one speaks and looks – ~~in a sense~~ alto-

gether different from a world in which oscilliscopes dont look tho they <u>show</u> and geiger counters count but don't show up etc etc – but why complicate it!

P.S. You say don't hurry but if I don't it would come down to "who cares" – and one cares so much. So I've hurried.

Louis

631. TC

[Rutherford, N.J.]

[March 1956]

Once more ye laurels and once more ye myrtles ever seer – what the hell is the correct name of that woman living in Wisconsin, I think, "Loreen Nedicker", or something like that? She used to write some damned good Objectivist poems, had a small book of them published. Her name, please – you are the only one who will remember it.

Thanks for sending me the note on the Objectivists – I couldn't use much of it but thank you again, never the less. It is for a new encyclopedia of the art of poetry which is being compiled by a group in NYC. More when I myself know more of it. Tell me when your spring vacation is on that we may come over at that time. W.

632. TCS

30 Willow St.
Brooklyn 1, N.Y.

[Postmarked 15 March 1956]

Dear Bill: The name you want is LORINE NIEDECKER. Hope the compilers spell it right now they have it.

Easter vacation: first week in April. We're not sure <just now> we may not have to go away again. So will you please phone us then – the calendar gets so crowded it's easier sometimes to make it at the spur of the moment than to plan.*

All the best & to Floss
from all Louis

*The remove of them adverbs is a case in <u>pernt</u> – as who used to say? L.

who used to say: Perhaps Bert Lahr (1895–1967), comic actor on stage, screen, and radio.

■ 633. TLS-1

9 Ridge Road, Rutherford, N.J.

April 1, 1956

Dear Louis:

I have just subscribed to Jonathan Williams' Author's Edition of your new book of poems. Congratulations. It's wonderful that this man has tome along in our lifetimes, mine at least since my life expectancy grows rapidly less with every year. I firmly believe that with the nutty experimentation due before long to have evaporated from our systems (necessary as it was to break down stodginess) a great dawn is soon to burst above American letters.

Our trip to Brooklyn has to be postponed again. On Wednesday we fly to Puerto Rico for another reading at the university there. I'll write you from there and plan (again) to come over to Brooklyn in May! Best to Celia and the brat.

Best

Bill

new book: *Some Time* (Stuttgart, Germany: Jonathan Williams, 1956). Celia Zukofsky's *A Bibliography of Louis Zukofsky* notes the "Author's Edition of 50 by Dr. Cantz'sche Druckerei, Stuttgart-Bad Canstatt, Germany, autumn 1956 designed and published by Jonathan Williams as Jargon 15." Williams (b. 1929), poet, essayist, and publisher, founded the Jargon Society in 1951.

Puerto Rico: Williams and Floss spent ten days there, and Williams read at the University of Puerto Rico.

■ 634. TLS-1

9 Ridge Road, Rutherford, N.J.

Nov. — (imagine!)

Sept. 20/56

Dear Louis & Celia:

After we have returned from Buffalo early next month we're coming to see you some afternoon when it is convenient for you – which I shall ask you to name. I have written to Paul as you'll probably see. It is a noteworthy occasion to which we plan guests, don't you interfere.

Congratulations on Paul's success. As for ourselves we have been nowhere this summer but instead have enjoyed our own back yard hobbling between the flowers as we were able and believe me I mean hobbling. My long short story as been finally accepted by Hudson Review for publication next spring and I have had other small successes but we can talk about when I see you. Meanwhile all hail to Paul (and his mother) for his success as a violin vrtuoso.

Best

Bill

long short story: "The Farmer's Daughters," *Hudson Review* 10:3 (Autumn 1957), 329–52. Wallace C541.

635. TLS-1

9 Ridge Road, Rutherford, N.J.

Oct. 20, 1956

Dear Louis:

The time for our visit is drawing near. Shall we come next Friday or Saturday and at what time? I suggest about mid afternoon or about 4 p.m.

Another matter we'll have to get straightened out: we'll come armed with a blank check for which, when it is filled out of course, we want to buy 5 tickets for Paul's concert. Tell us us where to sit if we haven't already waited too long. If it would be convenient for you to get the tickets for us that yould be all to the good. In any case we'll talk it over with you when we see you.

You must be experiencing many of the thrills and the headaches which I hope you will be in for on many future occasions of this sort for many years to come. Bear up, it's no skin off your ass but the younger generation will have to take the brunt of the beating for which they are made. They're younger and they can take it.

See you this coming week as soon as we get the word.

> Best
> Bill

Paul's concert: Paul Zukofsky's Carnegie Hall debut on 30 November 1956.

636. ALS-1

[30 Willow Street
Brooklyn, New York]

Nov 15/56

Dear Bill:

Mainly to thank you for Dazai's The Setting Sun, which came from ND two days ago. I wanted to say thanks at once, but delayed thinking I'd have a chance to read it first. But between papering the house (we're almost thru!) and school papers I haven't been able to get further than turning pages for the feel of the book. And how spare and delicate "our" realism (European etc realism!) works out here. But I intend to have enough time over Thanksgiving to read it thru and we'll talk about it. And damn the rush of everything – it's not just the skin off one's rear as you say – one needs a baseboard!

I finally got around to telling EZ about the pleasure of your visit after neglecting him for a month.

Otherwise everything is fine – especially the virtuose – and we're just tense thinking how close it is to seeing you back stage.

All the best to you
and Floss from
Celia & Paul
&
Louis

The Setting Sun: Osamu Dazai, *The Setting Sun,* trans. Donald Keene (New Directions, 1956). "Osamu Dazai" was the pseudonym for the Japanese writer Tsushima Shuji (1909–1948). His book, originally published in 1947, is about the effects changing times have on an aristocratic Japanese family. *Paterson: Book V* mentions "Osamu / Dazai and his saintly sister."

telling EZ: Letter not located.

■ 637. ALS-1

[30 Willow Street
Brooklyn, New York]

Sat Dec 1/56
Dear Bill and Floss

It was brave of you – and sweet – to wade thru that crowd last night. I must have sounded half cracked speaking to you and anything but myself, but I've had the grippe all week, and a running fever last night, and the last thing I wanted to do is to get near enough to pass it on. As a matter of fact, I'm waiting for the doctor now so he <can> give me a shot or two to get rid of that fever.

Babette Deutch called this morning – outraged by the Times critic doubting Paul's musicality. I felt like Harry Truman <about Margaret> myself at first reading thru the review. But on the whole I suppose the dead have to say the living must grow into their own shapes and forms – or what distinguishes mulch? And on the whole I guess the critic meant to be kind.

But we'll be seeing you – and we'll have the fun we should have over it.

All our love
Louis

[In Paul Zukofsky's hand:] Dear Bill and Floss, In the Tribune I'm a "pianist" and play "Hinemith," so it's all a myth.

Love,
P

Times critic: Harold C. Schonberg, "Paul Zukofsky, 13, Heard in Recital," the *New York Times* (1 December 1956), 17.

Harry Truman: Margaret Truman, President Truman's daughter, had embarked on a
    singing career in the late 1940s. After the music critic of the *Washington Post* com-
    mented adversely on one of her performances, the President wrote an angry response,
    which was published by the *Post*. See Margaret Truman, *Harry S. Truman* (New York:
    William Morrow, 1973), 502.

Tribune: "Pianist, 13; At Carnegie Hall," the *New York Herald Tribune* (1 Dec 1956), 7.

638. ALS-1

[30 Willow Street
Brooklyn, New York]

Fri <u>breakfast</u> [28 December 1956]

Dear Bill and Floss,

Just read – all of us read – the Times' item on the prize – over let's see, toast,
and let's see ("Mary Jane" – orange pineapple with cherries) a Xmas gift – so
our trio extends greetings again for a very happy New Year.

And this ought to please you, too. Paul has his own violin at last – i.e. a Kloz
still being evaluated for the "floater" we'll have to get for it – at Wurlitzer's. The
wife of a famous faculty member of ours whom I don't know – Dr. Ernst
Weber – gave it to him after hearing him at the concert. Was her father's, a fa-
mous German doctor, Eserich, who got <it> as – Xmas present in 1879. Old
Choimin fiddle ca. 1700 – and while not worth thousands, is worth some hun-
dreds, so as far as that concert went we're successful financiers.

Take care of yourselves and come and hear it.

Love
Louis—& C & P

Times' item: Emma Harrison, "William Carlos Williams Wins Poets' Academy Prize of
    $5,000," the *New York Times* (28 December 1956), 23. This article about Williams re-
    ceiving the prize from the Academy of American Poets included comments by
    Williams about his writing ("All my life I've never stopped thinking. I think all writing
    is a disease. You can't stop it.") and about his poor reception in Britain ("I don't speak
    English, but the American idiom. . . . I don't know how to write anything else and I re-
    fuse to learn.").

Kloz: The Kloz (or Klotz) family were renowned German violin makers. Some of the
    more important members were Matthias (1656–1743), Aegidus (1675–1711) and Sebas-
    tian (1696–1767).

"floater": Supplemental insurance.

Weber: Ernst Weber (1901–1996), Austrian-born electrical engineer who emigrated to the
    United States in 1930.

9 Ridge Road, Rutherford, N.J.

June 16, 1957

Dear Louis:

You move like a basketball player, all over the lot in the twinkling of an eye! I wish you the finest possible summer abroad. As for the move to the apartment, I think it's a good one and just down the block so that you don't have to get used to a new neighborhood.

– There is of course not time for us the see you before you go – nothing much to say if we did have the time. The trip down the Mississippi we did take won't compare with your coming trip abroad. I still haven't had the time to go over your book of poems as I'd like to but that can wait.

Take care of yourselfand the same for Celia and Paul. They gave me anorher nice party at Brandeis U. last week. Come back to us refreshed in spirit and see as much as you can of London, Paris & Rome – nothing much to hope for any more from Moscow, a stone hung on a rope round our necks.

Sincerely yours

Bill

summer abroad: The Zukofsky family toured England, France, and Italy in the summer of 1957.

down the Mississippi: Williams and Floss took passage on the *Delta Queen* for a three week trip down the Mississippi in late June and early July, 1957.

book of poems: *Some Time* (Stuttgart, Germany: Jonathan Williams, 1956).

Brandeis: Williams was honored at a "Poetry Program" at Brandeis University on 7 June 1957.

135 Willow Street
Brooklyn 1, New York

Sept. 22, 1957

Dear Bill,

To say: we're home and have at last read your June letter. We've not sat down yet in the new apartment, so the tale of Europe will keep for when we see you: except this, after all the noise of the rest of the continent, in Bern and Lucerne the flowers and the quiet constantly reminded us of Floss's love of Switzerland.

The phone by the way is the same Main 5-2848. We hope both of you can make it soon this fall and are having a good time all around.

I almost forgot: while we were unpacking and arranging the phone rang twice – some friends all hepped up about a broadcast with Mike Wallace (whom I had never heard of) in which you said I was your friend. That goes for me too – whatever else is bothering everybody else about that broadcast. Not to feel hate in your voice, whatever off hand remark one may make about this or that trait of a people or sect – is reassuring enough for me. Neither did we like all the French, all the English, all the Italians, all the Jews, all the Swiss for that matter! we met this summer. Just two Episcopalian ministers in mufti we met in Perigeux who treated Celia to Chartreuse verte and it didn't bother her ulcers! I just took a sip <of hers> to keep holy – I'm not telling what the revds. had before.

> Love from all of us
> Louis

broadcast: Columbia Broadcasting System reporter Mike Wallace interviewed Williams
> for his television program, Nitebeat, on 4 September 1957. See Mariani 714.

641. TC

[Rutheford, N.J.]

[1957]

Glad you're back and had a good time abroad, "good" to be interpreted as variously as you may find possible. We'll be in to see you just as soon as you give us the word that you are ready to have us.

As to that broadcast: I am waiting to receive the disk-record (which we have long since orderedand paid for) which we will bring to you that you may see for yourself how much "hate" was in my voice. Nuts for them all. As usual.

Lots to talk about – if only I could talk. I trust Paul and Celia benefited by the trip physically and in spirit as did you and feel rested.

> BILL

642. TC

[Rutherford, N.J.]

[1957]

Friday Oct. 18 toward 4 in the afternoon will be about right. We may have snow or sleet by then but we'll have to chance it. If you have other ideas as to the time let us know. Must keep at my correspondence so . . But want to tell you I started a thesis on you but had to abandon it temporarily because of lack of time to pursue the thoughts involved; will return to them and it in the next couple of months. No hurry, 'twill wait without loss of timeliness. See you later.

> Bill

thesis: Probably "Zukofsky," first published as an end note to Zukofsky's *"A" 1–12* ([Kyoto, Japan]: Origin Press, 1959), 291–96. Wallace B83. Reprinted in *Something to Say*.

■ **643. TLS-1**

9 Ridge Road, Rutherford, N.J.

Oct. 15, 1957

Dear Louis:

We'll be there Friday around 4 – with the RECOR! and the beginning of the article which I hope to write as soon as I have a chance to think about a little longer.

Things are happening at a rate accelerated far above normal and I am not always able to keep up with that as I formerly did.

Best to the family
Bill

article: See the previous letter.

■ **644. ALS-1**

135 Willow Street
Brooklyn 1, N.Y.

Oct 19/57

Dear Bill and Floss,

The smart thing would have been to order a cab in the first place and so warded off the rain last night. But who can be smart? Are you all right? And were my directions to the bus all right?

You can see why Paul is sometimes impatient with me. Just the worrying kind!

We had a wonderful evening – not often we have so much to say.

Have a good flight West and back, and we'll see you again soon, and here – like my old man used to bless guests – I'll invoke a blessing – only it can't be translated: al-be all right: meaning something like, ~~meaning something like~~ "It's marvellous that one can really say it's all right."

Love from all of us
Louis

flight West: Williams and Floss spent much of November in California. See Mariani 718.

[Rutherford, N.J.]

[1957]

Card received. Just back from our flight (from the Devil!) across the mountains at 25,000 feet back home!

As soon as I get my breath you'll hear from me again, in about a week I imagine when we'll discuss the picture among other things – also what I have done with "A".

    Bill

picture: Unidentified.

■ 646. TLS-1

9 Ridge Road, Rutherford, N.J.

Dec. 10/57

Dear Louis:

Flossie has gone over this for me for mistake of spelling and obvious grammatical bloomers or bloopers but if you will go over it from your own viewpoint and pencil it it as you find it necessary I'll be grateful

This is a unique copy. If Celia will make me a carbon duplicat with yor additions and deletions and let me have it I'll be very much obliged. So unless you throw the whole thigg out you are ready to submit it to your publisher friend who may thus be st to start on the book.

Drop me a card to tell me when you can come out here. We have multiple engagements during the holidays but since you will have freedom from your classes then we won't have any difficulty hitting on a date. Drop me a kine.

    Best
    Bill

publisher friend: Emanuel Navaretta (1913–1977), a building contractor who in early 1957
    had indicated to Zukofsky that he hoped to publish "A" 1–12. In a letter of 22 October
    1957 (Yale), Navaretta asked Williams to write a preface for the volume.

■ 647. ALS-4

135 Willow Street
Brooklyn 1, New York

Dec 12/57

Dear Bill,

Here it is – Celia has to type fast or she won't at all – and thanks. It's a fine piece – and I mean fine, some of your best perception. What moves me is that without having seen most of A-12, you've struck on so much that is in it, and without having read my stuff on Shakespeare you have come so close to what (who can help it?) I hint about myself in those – by now – reams.

As for pencillings on your original: I started out by putting in a lot of commas, since you were typing fast, and have ended by ~~putting~~ <taking> 'em all ~~back~~ <out> again except maybe one – the professor's totem fear of the (it makes me sick to use the word) "run-on" sentence <u>deflated</u>. Because your meaning is so continuous that <u>it has to run on.</u> All other changes of a word here and there are chiefly matter-of-fact as I know them – and which you're not expected to remember. Quite frequently I've pencilled your original and had Celia type out the original in her copy, because I prefer it intuitively to my questions.

I might as well take up all my mullings and changes one by one – the references are to the pencillings on your original.

> Page 1—lines 2 and 3: no reason why it shouldn't stay as it is—sounds more like Bill Williams
> —same ¶ <u>moved</u> by instead of <u>associated with</u> (that's that <u>the fact</u>)
> Page 1—¶ 2 <u>sometimes</u> instead of <u>avowedly</u>: matter-of-fact. I never avowed it, but Ezra is taken up in the poem—not the <u>Cantos</u> (I feel modern, like an atomic pile compared to his <u>beauty</u>)—but the <u>How To Read</u>, and apart from that monument of good sense, "differences", and friendship (A-8)
> Page 2—line 2 after <u>handled</u>, the one comma I've stuck in, I've retained: take it out if you want to.
> Page 2—¶ 2 You typed <u>affective</u>. I hope you meant that, because that's what I'd like (not <u>effective</u>—but I'm curious to know which)
> page 2—same ¶—last sentence—you were typing very fast: my substitution of <u>in</u> for <u>but</u> is the quickest way I see of making sentence sense out of it.
> page 2—second line from the bottom—<u>monodic</u>. You mean a monody, as I infer from <u>chant</u> on the next page, and not a <u>monotone</u>. At least I hope so. If you don't like my word—do as you please.
> page 3—line 2: <u>irrelevance</u> instead of <u>impertinence</u>—I'm getting to be a gentle old man myself—maybe onc't, but in Paris last summer, I could look at some impressionists <work> and be moved by the sentiment.
> page 3—the coils of the professors etc the date I stick in etc, all <a> matter-of-fact change: I never really felt I was in their coils, I might

have been shy of 'em and lived with my own poetry—and yes I
wrote for the others whom I respected. But you know one of 'em
professors has even come around to write me he's read Some Time
six times and expects to find more in it. One never knows!

The same ¶ in part conventional—also a matter-of-fact change—all
kinds of verse in "The"

The same ¶ I omit To deny at the beginning of the sentence. I missed
that fast typing after several readings, and didn't catch up with the
not to be denied at the end of the sentence <(which would make the
sentence meaningless)> until I was proofreading Celia's copy. Which
nobody can deny!

The same ¶. Satyric. Please leave it that way—the typing gods are on
our side even if it's a misspelling for satiric.

Pg. 3—last ¶ you mean reprinted (not copied?) arouses instead of
raises, but change back again if you wish: raises sometimes means
arouses and is the more unusual word.

Pg 4—line 2—I've omitted the few words—are they necessary?—makes
your sentence, its thought, more beautiful to me.

Pg 4—¶ 3: Celia's copy retains a "modern" Jew. Maybe you want to omit
that word "modern" which always makes me feel the "conservative"
and "reform" synagog—my father as human being is too much in
me for me to feel comfortable with that, or a universal Jew. But again
do exactly as you please.

And the end of this ¶: I omit "20 c. of our Lord," and substitute this
time. Something in the cadence even after omitting the repetition of
man in that line (which ain't successful) leads me to think that some
pigheads will infer from it that I'm an apostate and you an idolater.
Consult Floss about this, before you return it. I've consulted Celia,
who says let him say what he wants. I agree if you don't think it runs
the risk of being stupidly misinterpreted.

Page 4 ¶ Your typing error mords for words gave me the idea for the
addition like mordents. It's sure Zukofsky-ish but I've a mystical
feeling it's just right for the context, but again leave it out if you
wish. Anyway, thanks for The Farmer's Daughters. I read it this
evening to Paul's running the hi-fi playing Bach's Goldberg
variations played by Landowska and the prose ran on—the
paragraphs ran on like a lot of mordents themselves. And whenever
I can hear music these days and still read I know the reading
<matter> is right. Ditto the piece for American Scholar. Both among
your best—and a new strain in them too.

Page 5 -line 2—another matter-of-fact change and I guess you don't
need <u>At least</u> opening the next ¶.

So that's that. What a letter – sorry for the scrawl and the length. But I want
you to do exactly as you want to.

My publisher has not been in touch. I guess he's busy with his own business.
And you know me – I don't like to prod. You'll probably hear from him, no
doubt, and can then send him the copy as you finally decide. Or, if you prefer,
I have another carbon I can send him, as and when you want me to, saying it's
what you've asked me to do.

We'll be glad to come out to Rutherford any time you say between the 22nd
and the New Year if it'll spare you the hazards of winter etc, and you want it
that way this time. We have no commitments right now, so not to run the risk
of a conflict with some other engagement, could you let us know soon. On the
other hand, if you're going to be in town and it'll be less of a chore, or more
exciting for you, to come here, let us know when you want to come. So you
have all the choices and decisions.

> All our love and to Floss
> Louis

Here it is: Zukofsky's corrections and suggestions regarding Williams's essay on Zukofsky
intended for publication with "A" 1–12.
stuff on Shakespeare: *Bottom: On Shakespeare.*
one of 'em: Mark Van Doren.
The Farmer's Daughters: First published in the *Hudson Review* 10:3 (Autumn 1957),
329–52. Wallace C541.
Landowska: Wanda Landowska (1878–1959), Polish keyboard player and composer. She was
particularly renowned for her harpsichord performances of the Goldberg Variations.
piece for <u>American Scholar</u>: "Faith for a Complex World," the *American Scholar* 26:4 (Au-
tumn 1957), 453–57. Wallace C537.
publisher: Emanuel Navaretta.

648. TC

[Rutherford, N.J.]

[December 1957]
Thanks for the note. Come out on the 27th in the afternoon and stay to sup-
per, come after the middle of the afternoon so we can have a talk.

Glad the notice for the book will do, thanks (said <u>that</u> twice) – no matter.
Celia transctibed your comments so that I was able to revise the thing satis-
factorily. I'll had it to you for his nibs, the impressarion, when I see you. We've

been talking together bbot S. long enough so that we ought to have reached a common understanding long since.

> Best
> Bill

S.: Shakespeare.

▪ 649. AL-1

[135 Willow Street
Brooklyn, New York]

Dec. 28/57

Dear Bill,

To go on talking after last night (as if I haven't talked enough!) I wasn't wrong at all when I said don't worry, rest, and go on to Paterson 21. What's to prevent you, considering your theme is ~~your theme is~~ Here / is not there – and this is Paradise.

But first: the pages on me for "A" are now poifick – as my brother-in-law would say. Thanks again. (Celia says, this ain't a blurb you wrote, but an intelligent statement.)

I've read Paterson V 3 times now – a good part of it aloud to Celia who sends her greetings with this: without going back to reread the other four books, my impression is that this book V is the most constructed (in the poet's sense of the word) of them all. The image of the unicorn is most fortunate and holds the contrapuntal material together – so that I never feel a symbol, but the whole poem at once as it moves, or tho it moves. As you say: she whom I see. And the last four words of the poem are a great stroke, rounding out everything as I remember it of your poetics in the other 4 books, rounding out the note from Symonds in book I. Indelible passages – I might as well tell you, as old friend, what I'll continue to thumb the printed pages for: p. 1 – the four lines beginning "the angle of a forehead; p 3 – "Paterson, for the air; pp 4–5 Jo's letter (who's he?!); p6 – "in a field . . . stars – and again as you come to the flowers, page after beautiful page at the end of the third section, which is so poised, it has, of course, no end.

Anything contra? a few lines here and there <especially in the beautiful flower passage pp 33–39> of what musicians call "passage" material – but good enough for nobody else to take exception to, & they really don't bother me; and if the "profanity" is sometimes compulsive it's after all your gentle thought for the young. So: nothing contra.

You might just look thru the copy I return for typing errors which I've marked very lightly in pencil you can erase, in the right hand margin, &

sometimes where I wondered if ~~you intended~~ the typist goofed up your origi-
nal sense:

p 7. (spelling) lov_eliness

p 7. get the bottom? Not _to the bottom, or _at?

p 10. vulgarassaing?

p. 20. Symphone_—not _y? at the end?

p. 26. Miriam? & not Mary?? spelling es pos_esed

What else? Just curious: whose quote beginning II before the Sappho?
Damn dignified "Sapphics" you did. Too bad I didn't have that for "A Test of
Poetry": compare the versions I discuss on pp. 55–56 in that book. Might also
interest you that the lines in Some Time: I am crazy about you

> I feel
>
> sick—

are my "modern" version.

pages on me: Williams's essay, "Zukofsky."

brother-in-law: Which of his three brothers-in-law Zukofsky refers to is uncertain.

Paterson V: Williams had sent a typed draft of *Paterson: Book V* to Zukofsky.

Symonds: *Paterson* (1992), 40.

Jo's letter: *Paterson* (1992), 208. "Jo" was Josephine Herbst.

quote beginning II: *Paterson* (1992), 215.

lines in *Some Time*: Part 2 of "Sequence 1944–6" (*CSP*, 109).

■ 650. TC

[Rutherford, N.J.]

[1957]

There are several slips the stenog made but I can't blame her: my original
typing as LOUSY! Thanks to your careful check, for which I am profoundly
grateful, all textual errors are being corrected. thanks. I don't know as yet who
will accept the thing – if anyone. No more Patersons, this is the last. Much
more to say but not now.

The comment of Sapphos style is from a Greek student, professor of Greek
at Haverford. I must acknowledge his assistance in the text of the poem itself,
a shameful neglect: many thanks, I'll do it.

You cheer me up in your comments, especially about the Unicorn and "the
last four (lines?) or words". We'll be seeing you.

BILL

Greek student: Levi Arnold Post (1883–1971), Emeritus Professor of Greek at Haverford
College.

651. TC

[1958?]

Books recd. Glad you included Celia – and Floss & me – in your theme. I had not seen it to date or any mention of it: I must have seemed very "dumb" to you when you spok of Shakes'e. How the h. I had the instinct to inclyde C. in my recent piece I do not know – exceppt it was so evident that you owed her so much. Fine of JohnathinW. to print notice of you and the include your "notes". Only goes to show how vigorous is the "modern movement", it <u>will</u> be seen. Now to the reading. May take us months. Meanwhile thanks for expediting the exemplar: Paterson 5 much improved in my final revisions, don't see how you tolerated the penultimate inanities.

BILL

books: Probably *Some Time* and *Black Mountain Review* 6 and 7. *Black Mountain Review* 6 contains Zukofsky's "Songs of Degrees" (which includes three valentine poems for Celia and "William / Carlos / Williams / alive!"), 15–25. It also contains "Bottom: on Shakespeare: Part Two," 119–57. *Black Mountain Review* 7 contains "Bottom: on Shakespeare: Part Two (continued)," 95–133.

my recent piece: Williams's essay, "Zukofsky." Williams notes that "To some extent Louis and Celia must be taken as an identity when their lives are weighed," *Something to Say*, 266.

JohnathinW.: Jonathan Williams, the publisher of *Some Time.*

652. TCS

[January 1958]

Thanks for the invite but it's beyond us to make that trip for many months to come even to meet a friend as close to us as B.D. It's amazing how we dread the trip and with how good a reason when you consider the circumstances, those we meet on the tubes seem to have the faces of the damned.

I'll be sending you soon the text of Pat. 5 to resann in a day or two to see what I have done to it mainly part or book 3. Please return it so that I may send it further before the release. Love to Celia from us both. Keep me posted on the progress of "A".

Bill

B.D.: Babette Deutsch (1895–1982), poet, novelist, critic and editor. She discusses Williams's poetry in *This Modern Poetry* (New York: W. W. Norton, 1935) and *Poetry in Our Time* (New York: Columbia Univ. Press, 1956). In the second work she refers to Zukofsky, but misspells his name: "For a time he [Kenneth Rexroth] and Williams were associated with the little circle of self-styled objectivists headed by Louis Zukov-sky, epigones of the imagists" (91).

653. TLS-1

9 Ridge Road, Rutherford, N.J.

Jan. 23/58

Dear Louis:

Here's the finished script – apart from some possible final minor textual final corrections. The latter 5 pages of Book 3, substituting an entire new letter for that that there before, and <a> rewritten end to the poem, are the principal thing I should like to call to your attention.

When You have finished with it shoot it back to me so that others may see it. Thanks. orry we don't feel up to making the trip to the city.

> Sincerely yours
> Bill

finished script: Of *Paterson: (Book V)*.

654. TC

[Rutherford, N.J.]

[1958]

Don't worry about my changing anything as essential as the last 4 words which you pointed out for me (so helpfully) toward the end of that poem. The thing I did change was the beginning only of Book 3, clarifying dirst 5 lines and giving them the punch that had, inexplicably, been lost in the final transcription. You'll be proud of me when you see the result: amazing even to my own eyes.

Final arrangements for the printing are going ahead at hurricane speed.

> BILL

655. TLS-1

9 Ridge Road, Rutherford, N.J.

March 3/58

Dear Louis:

I am going carefully through your book SOME TIME, poem by poem; so far I have got through just CHLORIDE OF LIME AND CHARCOAL – thinking all the time or more accuarately lifting my eye from the page almost at every line to retire into my thoughts to consider what the author can have been about to have written a book so stripped of all reference to the ordinary course of English poetry.

The effect in this book of lyrics is startling: there is nothing that the thought can attach itself to in these poems by way of reference: either you must accept what the author has set down as making up an authentic poem or throw out his entire conception. It is clean, one way or the other.

Either this is a poem or not a poem:

> There when the water was not potable
> etc etc

- that is <a> perfectly discrete group of lines, intimately related to an object and with a moral implication and possed of rythmic relationship within themselves which is not facile or related to the usual musical relationship. In that it resembles the constructions of Bach who is the poet's avowed musical master who was in turn influenced by the music of the Hebrew psalms in the Bible.

See also:

> How sweet is the sun, etc

I'll finish my reading, it is difficult for me, but when I have finished with this book so violent has been the wrench from my usual reading, casting such a light <on> what I have been used to, that I don't that I shall ever be able to enjoy usual English verse again.

And there are other matters related more to the sense of the text in many cases which come up for study.

William Carlos Williams

There when: The first line of "Chloride of Lime and Charcoal." *CSP*, 124.
How sweet: Lines from "Chloride of Lime and Charcoal," part I, section 3. *CSP*, 125.

656. TLS-2

9 Ridge Road, Rutherford, N.J.

Mar. 5/58
Dear Louis:

Get over your cold but I know only the sun can have any influence with that, so as in all else we miserable humans look always exclusively to the sun. Early in April we'll make a date for our visit. We like Babette, have her there too.

having finished SOME TIME and got half way thru your article in BLACK MOUNTAIN REVIEW 6 I have to finish that before I will have anything worth your reading. I'm still puzzled by anything but your simplest propositions. When your construction becomes in any way complicated I am left flat on my back gasping for air. No light.

In fact to date what I get from you is a refusal to be trite. Rather than to fall in with the usual dead poetic patterns you prefer to be utterly unintelligible. In THAT you succeed admirably!

But the positive thing about that is that you never and I mean never relent. One has the impression that if this man would relax and relent a moment he has something to say which it is important for us even thrilling for us to hear but he WILL not compromise. It is utterly simple, as simple as daylight itself or water or a flower – and he has the retiring modesty not to want to appear to force it on us. The rare instants when he permits himself to speak with complete directness is as sunlight around the edges of clouds. You are obstinate but I don't blame you except – that your friends also are defeated when the others go down. What can we do, what else can we do, as artists facing an inimical world? Without opposition perhaps we should not exist at all.

Why haven't you heard from your backer? I still have his address somewhere in my files. I'll look it up and write to him, he should not be allowed to get away with that. Don't worry I won't be rough. I'll do it.

> Best
>
> Bill

P.S. Not a word about MANY LOVES, I doubt that the production is going ahead. Paterson 5 however will be sent to the printer within the next few days. J. has been occupied with a very careful study of the text for corrections I might have missed, spelling and a restudy of the meaning in all instances, minor but important revisions involvig in some instancesthe deletion of short sequences. E.P. wanted his letter revised, something I had not forseen, much to my amusement. What could I do?When the final text is in, momently, we should have something which will resist attacks from every quarter.

Meanwhild a new photo of me had to be taken, now done. Other publicity involving articles with illustrations in ART NEWS and (without illustration) THE NATION. I know bothing about the details.

> Bill

Babette: Babette Deutsch.

your article: "Bottom: on Shakespeare: Part Two."

your backer: Emanuel Navaretta.

his letter: *Paterson* (1992), 215–16.

articles: "Tapestries at the Cloisters," *Art News* 57:3 (May 1958), 28. This excerpt from *Paterson: (Book V)*, begins, "The figures / are of heroic size," and concludes, "out of it if you call yourself a woman," *Paterson* (1992), 231–34.

Mar. 6/58

Dear Bill,

Good. Don't forget our date here early in April – and I'll vow to cough less in anticipation. (Must be so: the last 8 words of the previous sentence now my ears hear 'em as I inspect do sound like a cough held back. The choys of the pote!)

What's "The Swivel hipped Amazon" a preview from? Do you want it back? Gives both C. & me a good laugh. And, by the way, it's a good clue to reading Bottom in Black Mtn. Rev. – if you read it as the product of a pliant breed not forcing any thing on one, but presenting, as much as it can, everything around a thing, without, if possible, cluttering: instead of a pat answer to philosophy, to show up how swivelhipped it is. So I proceed in prose as I do in "A": I show & come back to it, & show something related, & come back to both <etc> – but always (I hope) saying it's neither the pat answer nor philosophy that makes or sees anything solid-like. What's in BMR 6 & 7 is getting to be only a small part of what I have & have yet to do: and I'm getting fed up, because the only philosophy that counts is poetry anyway.

—

Wish I could write to your producer! As for my backer, I'm not worried what you'll say – after all he rushed you for the preface; I can't understand his silence to me, when he's told Jonathan Williams, he'll come out of his present halt & do it – except I suppose embarrasment of not meeting a promise, but then he ought to know I'd understand that etc & just call up to find out how I am or sumpn.

One of these days I'll be as clear as mud to the world, took a great time for the world to become mud.

Forgot to say Sorrentino of Neon asked me some time ago to contribute to No 4, & sent previous issues including yours to E.P. (January or Jukowsky – very good!). Ez. doesn't write, wonder if he saw it? (I didn't until about two weeks ago). Anyway, Sorrentino wrote again & asked for stuff for No 5 – tho 4 ain't out – & has taken bits from the 85 pp of 12th movement of "A" – so we'll see which Eyetalian makes home first – Sorrentino or Navaretta or both fumble & leave Jukowsky in the bleachers.

       Love from all

       Louis

P.S. Glad Pat. V is moving!

Not a word about "A" yet. I'll let you know if and when. And your theatre group?

Don't tell me this is going to be another case of summer's not the season, so next winter.

Nowt else, as Ez used to write –

Tell Floss that Tobler box <u>was</u> wonderful – every bit of it*

    All our love to you both

    Louis

*They ought to advertise it: Swiss Toblers <u>SOO</u>the ulcers! (<u>It's</u> a fact!!!!)

Amazon: "The Swivelhipped Amazon," the *Grecourt Review* 1:2 (December 1957), 14. Wallace C548. *CP2*, 425–26. Later Williams retitled this poem "Mounted as an Amazon." The offprint Williams sent is among the Zukofsky papers at Texas.

producer: Julian Beck (1925–1985), painter, producer, director, and actor. In 1947 he and his wife Malina founded Living Theatre Productions.

my backer: Emanuel Navaretta.

Sorrentino: Gilbert Sorrentino (b. 1929), novelist, poet, editor and professor. He edited *Neon* from 1956 to 1960. Zukofsky's poem, "A Valentine," appeared in *Neon* 4, 11. *CSP*, 164–65.

yours to E.P.: "To My Friend Ezra Pound," *Neon* 2 (1956), 8. Wallace C514. *CP2*, 434.

▉ 658. TCS

[Rutherford, N.J.]

[1958]

The little poem was published in a Smith College undergraduate magazine last fall. They sent me "a million" copies. Want some? I don't know what to do with 'em. Glad you like it and have some use for it.

    Bill

little poem: "The Swivelhipped Amazon."

▉ 659. TCS

[Rutherford, N.J.]

11 of April D.V. as my distant cousin used to write, will be all right, weather permitting. If I don't have to bring my head along , so much the better since I'm not too certain of it nowadays.

Aint this weather something "out of this world" – the only excuse for it! Gragh!!

    Bill

cousin: Sister Felicia, O.S.A. (Alice Philena Hubbard).

[135 Willow Street
Brooklyn, New York]

May 21/58

Dear Bill,

What in Nell! Why should I keep it a secret from you when you can keep it a secret from them (just dawned on me!). It's the enclosure <you might as well have the original> to appear in The Nation, I guess May 31, with the <u>Paterson V</u> fête. The craziest thing is that the literary editor, Nathan Rosenthal, called me up the same afternoon I got that unexpected wire from San Francisco to come and teach and read, and asked me – The Nation – asked me – to do it. That we should live to see that day! I can't fathom how it all happened.

I read proof of it yesterday. So I guess it's true.

Went at it right away, of course, with a thousand papers etc lying around to be done – & with Celia standing over me for two days quite sure I was going about it the wrong way.

Well, it'll appear without that first ¶ which I couldn't resist despite Celia's objections – but we'll all agree by now, it's better for all of us it's out. The other emendations in red represent Hatch's request for clarification, which I handled 1 -2 – 3 over the phone to Hatch's satisfaction. He was very nice about it – and I said nothing about the first ¶.

About coming out to see you – we'd love to. How about this coming Sunday or Monday May 25 or May 26? After that I'm swamped with school exams for a week. Paul, too – he has one on Decoration Day at 5:15 P.M., for example.

———

And after that the only possibility is June 3 – because after that we better get our bones together for the trip on June 10.

———

So: Sunday or Monday May 25 or May 26 or Tues June 3? Just drop us a line.
Love from all
Louis

a secret: In a letter of 7 May 1958, Robert Hatch, literary editor of *The Nation,* told Zukofsky that Williams would not know that the selections from *Paterson: Book V* to be published in *The Nation* would be accompanied by Zukofsky's and Rosenthal's articles about Williams.

enclosure: Enclosure lacking.

original: "The Best Human Value," *The Nation* 186:22 (31 May 1958), 500–02. Later included as part of "William Carlos Williams" in *Prepositions +.*

Rosenthal: M. L. Rosenthal (1917–1996), poet and professor. He was the poetry editor of

The Nation. See his *The Modern Poets* (New York: Oxford Univ. Press) 1960 and *Our*
Life in Poetry (New York: Persea Books, 1991) for discussions of Williams and Zukofsky.

wire from San Francisco: This telegram of 30 April 1958 is from Ruth Witt-Diamant, Di-
rector of the Poetry Center at San Francisco State College, and is in the Zukofsky
papers at Texas. The terms of the appointment required Zukofsky to teach a five-hour
lecture course, hold three conferences a week for gifted poetry students, and give two
readings. The six weeks of his residence were from 23 June to August 1.

first ¶: In the typescript made from Zukofsky's autograph manuscript, the first paragraph
was as follows: "This is, as you will find out, for the nation. Or, as you have found out,
for several nations. What for? A celebration of your life and poems" (Texas). Al-
though Zukofsky wrote to Williams that the first paragraph would be deleted, this
copy of the typescript, corrected by Zukofsky, indicates the first paragraph should
stand. With slight alterations, this paragraph was kept for *The Nation* and for
Zukofsky's essay, "William Carlos Williams."

Hatch's: Robert Hatch, literary editor of *The Nation.*

Paul: Paul Zukofsky.

661. TLS-1

9 Ridge Road, Rutherford, N.J.

May 23, 1958

Dear Louis:

Very kind of you to write as you did . I havn't had time as yet to absorb it
thoroughly, can't catch up with my reader on short notice. It was splendid of
Hatch to to give you the nod, and you to get to work on the assignment with-
out delay on spite of papers to grade etc etc

The June 2 visit will be better for us than the earlier date – and this is why I
am hurrying with this that you may get it by tomorrow.

Time passes and pisses on us all,is one of my favorite aphorisms – in this
case fortunately untrue.

Best
Bill

662. TLS-1

[Rutherford, N.J.]

May 29/58

Dear Louis:

Sandwiched among a dentist's appointment and yesterday's long call from
an intimate friend recently from Italy (everything takes time) I have finally got
time to have Floss read me your letter from the Nation – and your personal

accompanying it. I'll write you at once, I am not sure of the arragements we can make about the date of your coming visit, but you'll hear from me by early next week.

Your inimitable letter is all that I could wish it. To be startd by a quotation from Hume, though I have never read a word from him, makes him intimate with me, and you at the same time my close intimate: so we grow closer together as we grow older.

Not to waste others' time has always been an object of us both – it has been that which has contributed most to our styles. Nuf said.

Thank you for the intimacy of your letter and for the love which it breathes. Good luck. We must at any cost keep the world at bay.

> Affectionately
> Bill

your letter: "The Best Human Value."

663. ALS-2

[135 Willow Street
Brooklyn, New York]

Sat. June 7/58
Dear Bill,

The enclosure a solitary carbon. There are three others III to V, but I haven't a typed copy. Sorry I didn't bring 'em along yesterday – but after all we came for you not for me. You'll see them in the fall. If you want to tell me how good or how bad these are, do so in a postcard to the SF address Floss filed so carefully.

Let me know if you don't find that copy of please and I'll send you another when we get back – or in any case let me send you another anyway, please. I'd do so now, but it means a trip to the P.O. in the rush of packing.

Have a good time this summer – & say Bon Voyage to Ez & D
Our love to both of you & the fambly*

> Louis

*I hope little Paul's finger is better pronto.

enclosure: "Gaius Valerius Catullus," I-III, inscribed, "translated by Celia & Louis Zukofsky / to Floss & Bill / for June 6/58 / was a wonderful day[.]"

Bon Voyage: Ezra Pound was released from Saint Elizabeths Hospital on 7 May 1958. In a letter of 20 May 1958, Pound indicated to Williams he hoped to "spend my last night on these rockbound shores in yr/ paternal establishment// (EP/WCW, 316). Ezra and Dorothy Pound stayed at the Williams home June 28–30. See the following letter.

little Paul's: Paul Williams, Jr., Williams's grandson.

9 Ridge Road
Rutherford, N.J.

July 14/58

Dear Zukofskys –

Well – the famous Ezra has come & gone. – We survived – but it was quite an ordeal. – Ezra terribly jittery – Dorothy uncommunicative – she looked very tired. They were driven up here by a young man – Dan Horton – his wife and along in the party a young woman Marcella S____? I can't remember her last name! She went along to Italy with them. She & Ezra have just completed a text book for Junior College age students of Poetry from Confucius to E. E. Cummings. When I asked – why stop at E.E.C. – I was informed that there were no poets after that! Ho-hum! We had them all five over night – in the hottest spell of weather so far this summer. – Ezra sat around in a pair of shorts and an open shirt – or minus the shirt most of the time.

Bill found that he couldn't talk to Ezra – and sat around looking quite unhappy. I was glad when they left. We did manage to keep all reporters & photographers away – The phone rang madly for two days before they arrived – as word came from Washington that Ezra was on his way here. – We had the pleasure of meeting Omar. A charming young man – with both feet on the ground. He came down from Boston & had supper with us.

Hope you are enjoying S.F. David Wang writes that he has seen you & thinks you all are tops.

Enjoy the rest of your stay. We'll be thinking of you as you wend your way homeward and will forward [sic] to having a good talk fest when you return.

Our love to you all –

As ever—Floss

Wang: David Rafael Wang (1931–1977), American poet. Wang wrote Williams on 10 July 1958 that he "Saw the Zukofskies tonight. Louis read at the Art Museum in the War Memorial Building. Among those present were Vincent McHugh [. . .], Jess Collins [. . .] and Mike McClure" (Yale).

Apt. 8B – 55 Chumasero Drive
San Francisco 27, Calif.

July 16/58

Dear Floss and Bill,

What a sweet, good letter you wrote us, considering the conjunction (if you get what the poet-in-residence-implies) of your ordeal and the heat of the

East. I was reluctant a bit to absorb all the story as David Wang told it, but the Mormon sure teaches 'em culture fast. The young lady's name is Span – who was sent at Kung's or is it Yen's behest to us to be eddicated, as one of the two Marigolds. You remember our story? If not, it must keep for our talk fest in September. I'm – O-o-o-o as that popular fat comedian used to say about a year ago – just too innocent and preoccupied a guy to let loose just now.

But what happens to Confucius, what happens to the Root? to the Mean? What happens? We ourselves feel as popular as Zen here, and whereas San Francisco before our advent – every day and hour of the week, we are so popular – whereas S. F. until now was a city of Montague and Capulet poets – we brought peace so that all factions attended my museum reading. The result: invitations from everybody – we've never had such a calendar, and nice as everybody is we wanna be on the train again.

We've had visits with the Rexroths, Patchens, Duncan and so on, Ruth taxies us constantly – and we carry your regards wherever we go.

People whom I last saw thirty years ago turn up – like George Oppen's sister, who was nine when I last saw her, and since George is in Mexico City, our trip to Mexico may turn out more surprises.

They'll keep, just both of you keep well. Paul takes refuge in his fiddle, Celia in that she ain't a poet and has no wishes and aspirations except, as ever,

> our love to you all,
> Louis

P.S. We leave Aug 2 & expect to be back by Sept 10 the latest, and will be in touch.

Mormon: Probably Ezra Pound.

Span: Marcella Spann, co-editor with Pound of *Confucius to Cummings* (New York: New Directions, 1964) and author (as Marcella Spann Booth) of *A Catalogue of the Louis Zukofsky Manuscipt Collection* (Austin, Texas: The Humanities Research Center, 1975).

Marigolds: Marcella Spann and Pansy Pinkston. In a letter of 24 December [1956?] Pound wrote E. E. Cummings that these "teXas marigolds have survived several months in yr/ gorful city" (*EP/EEC*, 389). In a letter of 29 December 1956, Zukofsky wrote to Pound that, "by this time Marcella & Pansy eager out of Texas must be reporting about the three fragiles from B'klyn . . . (Yale).

fat comedian: Possibly Jackie Gleason.

Duncan: Robert Duncan.

Ruth: Ruth Witt-Diamant, director of the Poetry Center at San Francisco State College.

Oppen's sister: June Oppen Degnan (b. 1918), publisher of the *San Francisco Review.*

Paul: Paul Zukofsky.

666. TC

[1958]

It makes me gd mad to have to pay 3¢ for a penny post card. Wish I could stop writing entirely. Glad you're back, see you sometime but not at once apparently. We're going to our shack at the shore, be there till the 30th., will write you again after that.

Pat. 5 not out yet, won't be out till Sept. 17 which I may already have told you. The Pound visit went off as scheduled without publicity. Not a reporter was allowed to get to him. One unforseen feature, we fell in love with Omar. A real person and charming besides. The old boy furiously jealousy of him whatever his parenthood. A man to be cultivated. Best to the family I understand that yours readings went well.

Bill

Pound visit: Ezra and Dorothy Pound stayed at the Williams home June 28–30. See Florence Williams's letter of 14 July 1958.

Omar: Omar Pound (b. 1926), translator, scholar, and lecturer.

667. ALS-1

135 Willow St
Brooklyn 1, N.Y.

Sept 4/58

Dear Bill,

We take it you're home by now, and perhaps free, so let us know if you feel like coming here or what? I say perhaps free because I hope what I saw in the Times a week ago or so is true: Oct 19 premiere of <u>Many Loves</u>. So maybe you're not free. But I hope the date's true – we have it down on our calendar.

To <u>Pat 5</u> on the 17th!

The horses have been sort of glad to be browsing home, before the <winter> drudge – Whao! Soon, soon.

But I've finished a longish poem – despite the fact that my delaying publishers are still not moving – in fact, just silent. But we expect it.

All the best & to Floss

Louis

Oct 19 premiere: The Living Theatre production of *Many Loves* did not open until 13 January 1959.

longish poem: "4 Other Countries," *CSP*, 171–99.

delaying publishers: Emanuel Navaretta.

9 Ridge Road, Rutherford, N.J.

Sept. 6, 1958

Dear Louis:

I'm much interested in your new "long" poem; long? When you get time let me see a copy of it. You guessed it, we can't come out now. We'll have to wait until God knows when. But the play, if it comes off has nothing to do with it, just our inability to get about. We can do it as an emergency but it does take it out of us without house to house to house transportation.

Pat 5 was handed to me by the postman this morning. I am satisfied as far as I can see. It might have been better but then it might not have been written at all which might have been best. A man never knows. Apparently the itch to produce is still in me, I seem to think it is important that I go on – as best I can.

What the Hell has happened to your architect, builder friend? Maybe the costs have discouraged him. It must be getting near the time for Paul's next Carnegie Hall appearance. Godd luck to him. I go plugging along, rather dejectedly at times. Love from us both to Celia.

Affectionatly yours

Bill

"long" poem: "4 Other Countries."

the play: *Many Loves.*

builder friend: Emanuel Navaretta.

135 Willow Street
Brooklyn 1, New York

Sat. Sept ~~18~~<no the 20th!>/58

Dear Bill

Pat 5 here today – and this is my fifth reading of it with no diminution of pleasure, and with more insight here and there where before perhaps I was not quick to an occasional concise syntax. I've not noticed any reviews, tho you said you made some. So I feel confirmed in my previous judgments – I saw few, if any revisions necessary. I am especially aware this time of the adagio effect of the beginning two pages as it is picked up again later: "Paterson has grown older." <"A flight of birds etc> Lovely how speech there – speaking – slows down to music.

These lines which I jotted down while reading the MS., which I intend to use for my continuing Shakespeare sermon – I didn't say so before – well, I'm glad they're still there, because if you had left them out it would be harder to give the source. Now the book's out, it's simple to credit them to Pat. 5. The lines:

> and saw,
> Saw with their proper eyes
>
> ———————————
>
> which is she whom I see
> and not touch her flesh?

Thanks no end for the book and the inscription!

I hope you had a good rest at the Sheelers – I meant to say hello to Charles after Floss introduced me to his wife, but somehow got lost in what was, after all, your party.

Let us know when you're free and we'll arrange to come out. In any case, you'll be hearing again from us shortly – that copy of the poem you asked for.

> All our love to you & Floss
> Louis

"Paterson has grown older.": *Paterson* (1992), 227.

A flight of birds: *Paterson* (1992), 227.

Shakespeare sermon: *Bottom: On Shakespeare.*

Sheelers: Charles Sheeler and his wife had hosted a birthday party for Williams at their home near Tarrytown, New York. Mariani 742.

■ 670. TC

[Rutherford, N.J.]

[1958]

As far as the play is concerned, forget it. If it ever comes off I'll be surprised. I have no confidence in the group whatever, their reliabilit of their ability. The're great talkers playing a shifty game as far as I can see to involve me in the finance of the game. Makes me think of Ezra. I'm not at all eager to be a play-right at my age. I'll keep you posted.

> W.

the play: *Many Loves.*

the group: The Living Theatre.

[Rutherford, N.J.]

[1958]

It'll take a couple of days at least, early next week at most before I can get to you new stuff. It looks fascinating. Good for you. That's the way, if you can't get ahead one way, try another – really it has a good feel to it, I'm crazy to know what you have been up to. Affectionately

Bill

stuff: *Barely and Widely*.

■ 672. TLS-1

9 Ridge Road, Rutherford, N.J.

Oct. 15, 1958

Dear Louis:

I've had another stroke and have been laid up more or less completely for the last couple of days, confined to my room, Floss more than ever, has becom the man of the family. But more immidiately I've had to give up all my engahements including one to read in Baltimore the first week in November at a poetry festivan at Johns Hopkins which breaks my heart.

I am typing this with my left hand to show that I still have that left. Nothing more to be said at the moment. Take casr of tourself.

Affectionately yours

Bill

■ 673. TLS-1

9 Ridge Road, Rutherford, N.J.

Oct. 23, 1958

Dear Louis:

I don't care if I never write another line and hope not to do it after Floss has just read me the 4 Other Countries which she has just finished reading me and at her own request reading it over again. That is a pleasure I never hope to live through again – and when I looked over her shoulder to see the pages as she was and saw those quatrains unrolling before her – my mouth literally fell open at my own amazement. I mean it,I'm going to stop writing forever unless and until I can somewhat imitate you as you have written this poem – and that's not to be. I am warmed at this poem to the roots of my being. That poem is a miracle to me which I have been slow to accept , for that is the second time that you have sent it to me: dumkopf that I have proven myself to be.

Celia has my thanks for her devotion and ability to observe and assess what she saw and that is not a simple thing. I know it because I too have been a poet.

It's not all in the technique though much of it is as we know. But the address to the task, your reticenses what you have elided from the text and what, at the same time you have chosen to includ – I hate to say it – marks you for the genius you are, in this poem – but that's enough. You have come through this once. I will hold you to this for the rest of my life. And as I say I hope never to write a word gain, a word of poetry, as long as I shall live. There is enough in this poem to occupy me for years or according to my determination forever.

You can talk deprecatingly about what you have shown here but I know better, grant me that. It goes into the whole field occupied by your contemparies. The lyricism in contemporary, through your knowledge of musc with Paus's music continually dinning it in your ears . . I'm gettin tire. I'm going to quit. I have not half covered that points that need to be mad. No one will belive what I have set down, leastwise you yourself. It doesn matter, I believe it and will continue to believe it to my dying day.

> Devotedly
> Bill

674. TLS-1

9 Ridge Road, Rutherford, N.J.

Nov. 10, '58

Dear Louis:

Read and return to me this important letter.

Take care of yourself, I'm trying my best to do the same, sometimes a tough job to keep my spirits up. Such letters as this are a great help to me.

> Best
> Bill

important letter: Possibly a letter (6 August 1958) from Cid Corman in which Corman discusses measure and rhythm (Yale).

675. ALS-2

135 Willow Street
Brooklyn 1, New York

Nov 12/58

Dear Bill,

Thanks for showing me Cid's letter. He's so dogged honest – it's hard to find anyone like him but once in thirty years.

I don't know whether I told you that we first met him in Florence two years ago – or it's almost that, that 1957 summer in Europe seems longer off than that. We walked all thru the city with him the few days we were there, and he's the guy who took us to San Miniato so we could look down on the "Flower" from the other side of the Arno – I write about in Barely & Widely. A wonderfully restful afternoon I shall always remember. – He's a solid poet too. And as loyal to the poem – and us – as you can make 'em.

It's in friends like that that it all pays off.

A kind note from Norman Pearson about my book – he ordered a copy & I dedicated it to – or rather inscribed it to him – I liked his face when I met him at your party.

And I have to give a talk on "Obscurity in Modern Poetry" for a forum some colleague has been running at Polytech – So I'll tell him or rather them – if they turn out in all their scientific obscurity that we at least mean to be clear and most often are, and that we even write about their concepts sometimes because we're interested & that the same courtesy ought to be extended to us: at least interest in what we say.

So be patient and continue improving.

Love & to Floss
Louis

the "Flower": Florence.

I write about: In the last poem of Barely and Widely, "4 Other Countries."

kind note: Pearson's letter of 9 November 1958—in which he calls Barely And Widely "a
very good book of poems"—is among the Zukofsky papers at Texas.

your party: See letter to Williams of 20 September 1958.

"Obscurity in Modern Poetry": Not located.

676. ALS-1

135 Willow Street
Brooklyn 1, New York

Thanksgiving Day, 1958
Dear Bill,

And we hope Floss and you are having a cheerful day: so much for the wish-bone.

The nearer Paul's concert draws the more Celia's lost in chores. Having to run off today she asks me to thank you for selling 2 Barely & Widely (the first orders in some time) to Miss (?) Solt of Indiana and Mrs. Bullock of New York, both of whom mentioned you as daimon. My thanks with hers, Bill.

I keep forgetting when I write <you> some of <the> things I've had on my mind to tell you since June, when we went West, what happened there and so on – but that'll keep for talk. Nothing much really, but some pleasant stories.

But in case you've wondered about "A" and my innocence as to its state at the time of your birthday party at Laughlin's – well, this is between us, the fact was nothing <As I found out after I got tough – Since I felt like a fool and <i.e. must have appeared like> a liar when you told me you had heard it was at the printer's – And all I could say was I hadn't heard, when you had.> was happening at the time. An estimate of printing costs finally came in last week, but there's been no decision yet as to whether the "publisher" will go thru with it. As I say and I must hold you to it for my pride and comfort this is between us – don't mention it to anyone & don't certainly urge the "publisher." Some day I'll tell you the fantastic involutions of this deal viva voce. All I can say is I hope your chance of production with your theatrical folk now seems more certain. Have you heard?

I mustn't forget the enclosure. I told your namesake J.W. about your letter – and since all Williamses are loyal to me he came up with this Parson Weems little sermon which he's sending out with his own flyers for Jargon press. Nice, eh?

So there are thanks to give all around you see.

> All our love to you & Floss,
> Louis

Paul's concert: Paul Zukofsky's recital at Carnegie Hall on 10 February 1959, at which he
    played works by Bach, Stravinsky, Glazunov, and Wieniawski.
Solt: Mary Ellen Solt (b. 1920), poet, critic and professor. Editor of *Dear Ez: Letters from
    William Carlos Williams to Ezra Pound* (Bloomington, Indiana: Frederic Brewer, 1985).
    Her first article on Williams appeared in 1960. She first met Zukofsky in April 1958.
    The Zukofsky papers at Texas contain numerous letters from her.
Bullock: Marie Leontine Bullock (1911–1986), civic activist. President of the Academy of
    American Poets, 1939–1986.
"publisher": Emanuel Navaretta.
J.W.: Jonathan Williams.

■ 677. TCS

[Rutherford, N.J.]

[1958]

It still goes on getting later and later – con amore Still writing when the mood with a good kick in the behind permits it – though the clouds from a befuddled brain have first to be swept away. Heard a late concerto by Bartok over the radio last week which gave me a thrill. If I find the energy I may send you this week a new poem which may interest you. Best to Celia. Bill concerto: Either Béla Bartók's *Concerto for Orchestra* (1943, 1945), *Third Piano Concerto*

(1945), or *Viola Concerto* (1945), which was completed by Tibor Serly.

new poem: Unidentified.

678. TLS-1

9 Ridge Road, Rutherford, N.J.

Dec. 6, 1958

Dear Louis & Celia:

Wish I could promise to be with you for the concert but I'have to pass that up this time.

This is just to ask you when I was at your house this summer or about that time I spoke of having writtn a poem involving a repulsive Negro. It was really on that trip that I saw him. I may have slipped a copy into the envelope – but I don't think so. No harm in asking. I sent it to some publisher of one of the San Francisco magazines. It has completely disappeared and the name and address of the magazine along with it. I confidently thought I would be able to retrieve the poem from the mag itself but it may never have appeared.

Don't bother about it unless I sent you the poem in a letter.

Take care of yourself and may Paul do well in his concert.

Sincerely yours

Bill

the concert: Paul Zukofsky's recital at Carnegie Hall in February 1959.
a poem: "The Drunk and the Sailor."

679. ALS-2

[135 Willow Street
Brooklyn, New York]

12/8/58

Dear Bill:

I see our letters have crossed. But about the poem about the Negro – I've looked & can't find anything. Wasn't it the one you asked Celia about – the meaning of the word sforzando? If that's the one I should say that was on the trip you came alone one afternoon & we took you back to the bus terminal – & that wasn't last summer but I'd say late spring of 1957 when <we> were still at the old brownstone down the street. If that's so, I believe I've seen that poem in print somewhere, but I just can't remember where. Maybe even in a volume of yours. No help to you, but just goes to show what the poem means to us, that it has nothing to do with provenance, as they say, – or its dissemination, but the instant of living it. I hope I've the right poem in mind – may help you to find it.

<u>You</u> take care of <u>yourself</u>. You're coming to the concert in Feb. – I tell you <u>I</u> <u>know it</u> – don't ask me how – but the older I get the more I trust visions, or what you will, in these matters.

And besides Floss has the right idea. This time the weather's gotta be good! Love from all of us
Louis

the poem: "The Drunk and the Sailor."
the concert: Paul Zukofsky's recital at Carnegie Hall in February 1959.

■ 680. ALS-2

135 Willow Street
Brooklyn 1, N.Y.

Jan 11/59
Dear Bill:

All the luck with the reviewers Tues. the 13 – that's our lucky number, no kiddin'. after the newspaper strike & the delays at last an announcement – today's <u>Times</u>, but they would pick a Tues, the night I teach (moreover a final exam this week) to open. I'll just have to make it some balmy Sunday matinee – my back's been relentless, all I can do is just make it to school. Finally gave in & went to the doctor yesterday – as I suspected arthritis or sciatica of the aging, the one comfort of being assured it's not my "prosperons" gland as the doc jested.

I learned from the N.Y. Post reviewer or rather reporter who's coming over tomorrow to interview me as grandfather Beatnik that he's after you or has been for the same reasons, as great-grandfather of the Beats – which is the best news yet from you as it means I take it you're up to it. So I'm more confident than ever you'll be making Paul's concert – tickets etc to reach as soon as we have 'em, probably end of this week.

As much as the Post interview takes up time etc, nice of Allen Ginsberg to think of us. It's funny how things like that make the people in my Institute realize they have a poet around who adds a bit to the publicity they are always seeking – when my work that's been available to them over 12 years now hardly ever exacts a peep from 'em. But it takes years to do anything for 'em with one's <u>own</u> capacities: there's even a <u>glimmer</u> of a prospect that I might get them to start a magazine that would plant Brooklyn as the seat of culture that the publication of Leaves of Grass there in 1855 foresaw. I said a glimmer! Probably take somebody to push me into the Nat. Inst. of Arts & Letters before they are completely overwhelmed by my – o my – stature – petrification – as men of letters etc. But they have been amusingly respectful these days –

We'll talk about it one of these balmy spring days after Paul's Concert – that has chasing our tales, I mean tails – it ain't easy being a sponsor of music, end so on.

> Love to you & Floss
> take care of yourselves
> both – & from
> Celia & Paul
> Louis

newspaper strike: The major New York daily newspapers did not publish from 12–29 December 1958 because of Newspaper and Mail Deliverers Union strike.

an announcement: "Many Loves—Tuesday at the Living Theatre. A comedy in verse by William Carlos Williams. Opening night curtain: 7:45," the *New York Times* (11 January 1959), 2:1.

Post interview: I have been unable to find any such article in the *New York Post* issues for January 1959.

Institute: Brooklyn Polytechnic Institute.

glimmer of a prospect: In the margin opposite these lines, Zukofsky wrote, "Between us all this!"

681. ALS-3

[135 Willow Street
Brooklyn, New York]

Jan 21/59
(Celia's Birthday)
Dear Bill,

Here's 4 more tickets for the same box – that ought to make a good party. Lucky I thought of it – Columbia was supposed to send you that many, but goofed as they say.

The Coupons <Each one is good for 2 (two) seats> are for the grocer, the baker, etc <or poor poets & friends> – if they redeem 'em early enough they ought to get good seats for 'em.

Will phone Mrs. Bullock or the Acad. of Am. Potes tomorrow – thanks for telling me – I might as well be in Alaska.

& to amuse <you> the latest, greatest intellexshule haiku – this one for all the cows, & may they never know sciatica

> Love to you both Louis

haiku: "Hi, Kuh." *CSP*, 214.

682. TLS-1

9 Ridge Road, Rutherford, N.J.

Jan. 23, 1959

Dear Louis & Celia:

Anent tickets for my play, Many Loves,you know where the theatre is, your lumbago permitting, go any time you can including any Sunday matinee, tickets will be waiting for you at the box-office. You saw the notice in this week's New Yorker, the 24th. It is apparently going well.

If Paul can go along or Celia go with him if Louis cannot make it he'll be more than welcome, it may serve to divert him and ease the burdens he is now carrying.

Sincerely,

Bill

[In Florence Williams's hand:] and a million thanks for the tickets for Paul's recital. We <u>will</u> get there – but I doubt that we'll get back stage as we did last time. Bill is too shaky for that. Best of luck and do if you can – get to the play – Love to you all –

Floss

the notice: Donald Malcolm, "Off Broadway," *The New Yorker* 34:49 (24 January 1959), 74–76. Malcolm found *Many Loves* "a thoroughly amiable effort to entertain; not even its overagainstness was stern." He concluded that the play succeeded "as an exercise in entertainment" but not "as an exercise in dramaturgy."

683. TLS-1

9 Ridge Road, Rutherford, N.J.

Feb. 9 [11], 1959

Dear Celia & Louis and Paul:

I simply at the last minute was not up to it, it would not have been possible for me to go in and return on the bus at the late hour involved – and we could not find anyone at the moment to lend me the use of their car.

So that there is nothing left for me but to acknologe my defeat, another defeat in the mounting field of defeats that I have had to accept of late. The report of the concert in this mornings Times is unconvincig but laudatory when it spoke of Paul's technical accomplishments. Which is I suppose as much as can be expected of a child of sixteen. The critic, whoever he was, recognized at least that. Only time can fill in the gap of the years.

But that cannot make up to me for my not having been there to hear for myself, the report of one's own ears is the only possible reply to the critics. Paul has now taken his place in the ranks of the virtuosi about New York. He no longer can be classed as an adolescent. After a few year's rest, I presume he'll have to take his place among the originals with a style of his own, untaught by any teacher whom he is presumed to be copying. That will be the final test. All the rest has been no more than preliminary.

Nevertheless, I am disheartend not to have been able not to attend the concert.

> Sincerely yours
> Bill

report of the concert: Eric Salzman, "Paul Zukofsky, Violinist, Plays: 15-Year-Old Offers Bach, Stravinsky and Glazunov in Carnegie Hall Recital," the *New York Times* (11 Februrary 1959), 11.

684. TLS-1

[Rutherford, N.J.]

March 6, 1959
Dear Louis:
Pretty little book, nice international gesture. Hope you're well.

> Best
> Bill

[Zukofsky's notation:] re – Il Fiori (Scheweiller Milan, Italy)
little book: *Il Fiore è il Nostro Segno, Poesie di William Carlos Williams,* trans. Cristina Campo (Milan: Vanni Scheiwiller, 1958). Wallace T38.

685. TCS

[Rutherford, N.J.]

[July 1959]
Glad to hear from you that your trip to Mexico turund out well – and that you are satisfied to be at home again. Come mid afternoon, the 3 of you, Aug. 9 and stay for an early supper. Floss insists on this. We'll look over the poems I have, not much, including the CALYPSO. I'm now engaged in writing a play (just to keep busy) encouraged by my old offbroadway success. My head is seething as usual with new ideas. I do my best to keep up with them if they will only let me SLEEP! Recently I am doing better with that also. While it lasts I realize that I am luck to have my writing to keep me occupied, God be praised. Love to Paul and Celie. Till Aug. 9 then. Looking forward with lively expectation to seeing you. Your old friend,

> Bill

trip to Mexico: The Zukofsky family and George and Mary Oppen drove to Mexico, leav-

ing Brooklyn on 29 June 1959 and arriving a week later. On 16 July the Zukofskys flew
back to New York. The journey is recalled in Mary Oppen's memoir, *Meaning a Life*,
and in Zukofsky's poem, "Jaunt" (*CSP*, 210–13).

CALYPSO: Either "Calypso," *Hudson Review* 9:4 (Winter 1956–1957), 485–87 (Wallace
 C526) or "Puerto Rico Song," *The New Yorker* 33:30 (14 September 1957), 94 (Wallace
 C545). Subsequently retitled "Calypsos I–II." *CP2*, 426–27.

A play: Possibly *The Cure*, which Williams had begun in 1952.

success: Williams probably refers to *Many Loves*, not *A Dream of Love*.

▨ 686. ALS-2

135 Willow Street
Brooklyn 1, N.Y.

July 25/59

Dear Floss and Bill,

 Thanks for the invitation. Would Saturday afternoon – or say what time –
August 8 be a good day for you? We pick the week-end, thinking we'll escape
the week-day crowds, but it can be any day between Aug 3 and 15 as you say,
only let us know so it won't conflict with at present non-existent arrangements
– but then something always comes up even if we don't look for it. Because yes,
we're glad to be home, comfortable or otherwise!

 You in your collar and Bill as you say – I just hate to say it, but I won't con-
sole you, mad as I feel about all this age pack sagging on all of us – because
we're coming despite it (not because of it) – sure of good company. To resig-
nation and giddiness – what? It's all a pretty good joke after all.

 Love from all of us,* we'll be talking.

  Louis

*I take it the three of us won't be a troop – but you say, if it's too much
strain all at once.

——

 Sure Bill's stuff in March <u>Poetry</u> was <u>fine</u>. And someone mentioned the Ca-
lypso poem in New Yorker, but I missed that so I'll read it in Rutherford. Tell
him, more power to his left!

invitation: In a letter from Florence Williams dated 23 July 1959.

Bill's stuff: "Some Simple Measures in the American Idiom and the Variable Foot" [nine
 poems], *Poetry* 93:6 (March 1959), 386–91. Wallace C569. *CP2*, 418–23.

Calypso poem: "Puerto Rico Song."

[Rutherford, N.J.]

Aug. 10, 1959

Dear Louis:

Just got my call to go to the hospital. Before I go I want you to have this poem on which you helped me so much for you to have is as your own.

See you next week.

> Affectionately yours
> Bill

poem: "The Parable of the Blind." *CP2*, 391.

688. TLS-1

9 Ridge Road, Rutherford, N.J.

Aug. 18 [12], 1959

Dear Louis:

Today or tomorrow I have to go in to the N.Y. Hospital for an operation during which it will be determined whether or not not I have a malignancy in a form possible of successful of operative attack. In other words, if it is or is not a benign polyp.

It's sort of hot weather for such a job but it cannot wait. So here goes. Call up Flossie tomorrow night and she'll give you the lowdown on my progress. Hope for the best. Love to Celia and Paul.

> Cheerio
> Bill

operation: A malignant tumor was removed from Williams's rectum. Mariani 750–51.

689. ALS-2

135 Willow Street
Brooklyn 1, N.Y.

Aug 12/59

Dear Bill:

Just to wish you an easy time of it and quick recovery! Sunday was wonderful for all of us and there'll have to be other Sundays like it – without the over-hanging worry, of course.

I phoned and spoke to Floss yesterday, as you know, and I'll be calling her again. And she'll let me know when and if you feel like a visit – either at the hospital, or as I hope, soon, at home – or both. We'll be in touch, so just get

well, and don't worry – because anybody who's capable of those Breughe
pieces etc just <u>has to</u> get well.

I'm reading your mother's book with great pleasure for the intimacy it
makes present – I can hear both of you speaking. <This ain't just "reading.">

It's sort of hard to end this note – well, –

> Love from all of us.
>
> Louis

P.S. <u>For Floss</u> – the photographer is late with his dewollopments, tomorrow
he says. So I'll probably be calling you for good news & telling you I sent the
snapshots in a day or so. And take good care of yourself,

Love

Louis

And to both of you – please let me know if there's anything you'd like me to
do that'll help.

> L

Breughel pieces: The sequence of poems, "Pictures from Brueghel."

mother's book: *Yes, Mrs. Williams* (New York: McDowell, Obolensky, 1959). Wallace A45.

690. TCS

[Rutherford, N.J.]

[1959]

Please send me Cid Cormans Japanese <address> I'd like to tell him what
has happened to me – and have misplaced the address.

Nothing additional has happened to date, still waiting for my appetite to re-
turn. A short letter Dorothy P. saying that Ezras translation of the Greek play
has been a great success somewhere in Germany – Munich perhaps. I have al-
ready forgot the details.

> Affectionately
>
> Bill

Cid Cormans: Cid Corman (b. 1924), poet, translator and publisher. Publisher of *"A"* *1–12*
(Kyoto, Japan: Origin Press, 1959).

short letter: Not located.

Greek play: *The Women of Trachis* was performed in Eva Hesse's German translation in
Berlin (premiering 9 May 1959) and Darmstadt (12 December 1959).

[135 Willow Street
Brooklyn, New York]

Fri Sept 11/59

Dear Bill,

Gees! back at the typewriter! But take it easy! Anyway, I told you I was a good prophet: those new x-rays must have been O.K.? Tell me at your leisure or when you can stand a visit.

Family sent you some of those candies you seemed to like before you left for the hospital – to anticipate Sept 17 & many happy returns – and to play with your appetite, all we need is calories anyway. So enjoy 'em.

The address you want is

CID CORMAN

C/O IBUKI NOBUKO

52 KITA HIYOSHI-CHO

IMAKUMANO, HIGASHIYAMA-KU

KYOTO, JAPAN

That takes a day to write in itself.

Cid will definitely do "A" 1–12, expects it out by New Year. He's a good guy. And your piece on me will be in the book, of course, but both of us agreed to have it close the book – a kind of postlude after another one I once wrote for Paul "when he can read" in 1950. And so not a "preface." You share the book with me. You'll be on the title page and contents page, of course – only thing is we have to find a word that will say what I say here concisely – i.e. with a ? by W.C.W. Any ideas?

Ezra's success with Women of Trachis – I take it – cheers me. Maybe it'll pep up his health. I'll write him but he doesn't answer except to fight about economics etc – & I've nothing to fight about – so I won't disturb him.

So keep improving.

Celia's still nursing the African violet leaves Floss gave her for roots – takes time!

School starts Monday & I still have some to go before I finish the particular section of the Shakespeare book I've been working on all summer – which only required re-reading all the works again.

Love to you both from all

Louis

Sept 17: Williams's birthday.

your piece: "Zukofsky," in "A" 1–12 (Kyoto, Japan: Origin Press, 1959).

find a word: See Zukofsky's letter of 23 December 1959.

Ezra's success: See the previous letter.

Shakespeare book: *Bottom: On Shakespeare*.

■ **692.** TLS-1

[Rutherford, N.J.]

Oct. 13, 1959

Dear Louis:

"To the next 50 years". Don't return this script.

Take care of yourself.

Bill

By the way, Floss is now reading The Guernamentes to me – that ought to take all winter. W.

this script: Williams's introduction to *The Complete Works of François Villon*, trans. Anthony Bonner (New York: Bantam Books, 1960). Wallace B84. The copy Williams sent is in the Zukofsky papers at Texas.

The Guernamentes: Marcel Proust's *Le Côte de Guermantes* (1920–1921). Florence Williams most likely read to her husband from an edition such as *The Guermantes Way*, trans. C. K. Scott Moncrieff (New York: Modern Library, 1952).

■ **693.** ALS-1

135 Willow Street

Oct 16/59 Brooklyn 1, N.Y.

Dear Bill:

Thanks for the unique carbon of <u>Villon</u> – it'll be here if ever you need it. It's solace for me to – speaking of the "next fifty years" – to be able to go on looking at the infold-outfolds of your mind these days, even if typing slips here and there distract me, but only for the moment. The editors I know will put in the commas etc. But I refuse to share in their trepanning – for my pleasure. One after all writes what one knows and cares for – and it's oneself outward (Villon one incident). The best of this essay is summed up, is <u>you</u>, on pages 9 & 10 versus "seekers" after effects.

Well – here's something <u>temps jadis</u> (from a sequence of last February or so, you haven't seen) in Chaucer's – Villon's "tradition", when English was still French:

> Fiddler Age Nine
> (with brief- and violin- case)
> Sir Attaché Détaché
>
> ——

The last word if you'll remember your early lessons plays on a way of violin bowing (to rhyme with hoeing): detached.

And here's another, when French was translated into American:

For

Four tubas

or

two-by-four's.

Well, again well, if one of these crisp blue autumn days you feel up to company, call up. I have Tuesdays off this term, presumably, tho they have a way of arranging faculty meetings that day. But in any case call up & we'll try to make it either there or here or midway as suits you.

> Be well both of you.
> All of us,
> Louis

unique carbon: See the previous letter.

sequence of last February: "I's (Pronounced *Eyes*)." *CSP*, 214–17.

For: Also part of "I's (Pronounced *Eyes*)."

694. ACS

135 Willow Street
Brooklyn 1, New York

Dec 23/59

Dear Bill and Floss,

The red to supplement the holiday greetings – and for this unusual communiqué: Cid has just sent me very pretty and bound in red ONE copy by air mail of "A", and there you are occupying pp 291–296 "with (I quote from the title page) "a final note by WCW." As soon as the first shipment arrives – probably not until well on in January* I'll be sending you your post new year's present. – love from all – Louis

*Let's keep this between us until the boat arrives!

Cid: Cid Corman, publisher of the Origin Press edition of "A" *1–12*.

9 Ridge Road
Rutherford, N.J.

Feb. 15, 1960
Dear Celia:

Thirlwall sent me the enclosed card, please send Louis' book. I'd like to have it. Unless Louis doesn't want me to for some reason.

We're heading toward Florida, finally, on the first of March for a month to be with the Kenneth Burkes, not to live with them but to live near them.

What's doing with Paul, it must be approaching the time for another concert.

Give Louis my best.

> Love [in Florence Williams's hand] (from me too) –Floss
> Bill

[in Florence Williams's hand] Bill's nuts! Of course you want him to have it. F.H.W.

card: Enclosure lacking.
book: "A" 1–12.

135 Willow Street
Brooklyn 1, New York

Feb 16/60
Dear Floss,

Bill's, I guess, told you I talked to him over the drat phone before my arthritic departure to the academy this morning. So let's be gallant all around: he wrote to Celia & I write to you. And have fun with the enclosure both of you.

Naturally the U.S.A. distributor – who's at the moment sitting with a wet headband, a familiar costume by now for her migraines – naturally she wouldn't send you an announcement such as is meant to tell people that "A" is out & if they're interested in poetry they can pay $5 for it.

You got your announcement in red ink on a postcard Xmas - you were the first to get <it>, and I assumed since I didn't hear from you that you weren't up to writing and there's a time when even cheer isn't cheer. And if Bill wants to think that for some reason I don't want him to see "A" - who else does he think is so uppermost on my mind that I think ought to see it instead? "Nuts," as you said, covers it. As for paying for it, haven't we <you & us> all done enough of that all our lives.

Tell Bill again if he by any chance missed what I was saying over the phone to him – there were only 200 copies printed of this edition, that those I am paying for, about a hundred, are taking time to come from Japan; that poor Cid out there has been a one man sacrifice to this job; that he sent me the <u>one</u> copy for myself by air mail, <which cost him $3 to send & I've tried to foot <u>some</u> of the postage> but all the others must come by boat, or we'll never stop paying for having written a poem. (And a damn moving one he tells me; by this time it makes no difference to me except I have <u>one</u> handy copy from which to go on); that neither the U.S.A. distributor, Celia nor Paul have copies; that they & you & Bill will get them when the next shipment, in the bosom of the Pacific or maybe now in some orifice of the customs, arrives. Of the 24 that came Celia <u>had</u> to dispose of (no use worrying you with why <they were bought up by colleagues at Poly, libraries etc – unavoidable when you earn your bread & butter there> – well to give one reason, if she didn't no one would ever know that Bill even wrote a preface. And you know what a ready audience I have. They're just <u>dead</u> – not dying to read L.Z.

So take it easy – tell Bill I've waited for his books too in the past – & never doubted but that he wants me to have them. And if we start doubting now – don't worry I won't – I better call quits. They think the Russians let Pasternak down? They ought to give a thought to their native son – your friend – who could rave like Timon but just doesn't.

Paul's fine – tho he had a bad cold – finishing his diploma course at Juilliard. No dough for another concert so soon. But no hurry. The Z's are at least patient.

> Love from all of us
> Louis
> [In Celia Zukofsky's hand] Me too, love, Celia

the academy: The Brooklyn Polytechnic Institute.

enclosure: Enclosure lacking.

distributor: Celia Zukofsky.

Cid: Cid Corman.

Poly: The Brooklyn Polytechnic Institute.

Pasternak: Boris Pasternak (1890–1960), Russian poet and novelist. In October 1958, he was awarded the Nobel prize in literature, but adverse criticism in the Soviet Union moved Pasternak to decline the honor.

9 Ridge Road, Rutherford, N.J.

Feb. 17, 1960

Dear Louis:

A commedy of errors, forget it – as I sez. I only wanted to protect you against financial loss. I chose a stupid way, apparently, of going about it. I hope the mails from Japan don't go astray. Really wonderful of Cid to take the burden of the task on his shoulders.

I find my mental processes much retarded nowadays.

Affectionately

Bill

Cid: Cid Corman.

■ 698. TCS

[Rutherford, N.J.]

[1960]

Just in time. I'll get floss to read it to me in Florida – it looks impressive. sorry you have had so much trouble getting to it. Haven't they made a beautiful book of it! It's amazing!Celia must be proud.

We are going near Tampa where the Kenneth Burkes are spending the winter to to escape the rest of the winter. We have rented a bungalow right on the beach with supply stores just a stones throw away – we are told. We're going to fly.

Take care of yourselves. We'll see you when we return.

Bill

it: "A" 1–12.

■ 699. ACS

Englewood, Florida

3/9/60

[In Florence Williams's hand:] Hi! Bill says he'll write when he has his typewriter. Kenneth Burke is reading your book.

Nice down here – but not too warm! –

Best to all –

Bill & Floss

your book: "A" 1–12.

700. TC

[March/April 1960]

Glad to have heard from you, been thinking of you it was cold in Florida bup we am used ourselves picking up shelves. not too pleasant in the driving wind most of the time, we would have been lost without the Burkes to take us about the waterfront whenever they could find the time for it. The jet and helikopter were marvelos, they whisked us about the cities of our flights like enormous souless presences which they are bearing us in their bellies, we and our trivial businesses. It will take some time before we waken from the vision. Thhoug as soon as I have recovered from being without a typewriter for a month, a frightful handicap which only slowly I am beginnint to recover from. I horrible experilence. Best to Celia and Paul. Sorry about your cold. Maybe I shall never again be normal.

> Bill

701. TLS-1

9 Ridge Road, Rutherford, N.J.

April 14, 1960

Dear Louis:

It worries me that I have not heard from you. <you> told me that you were suffering from a cold for I know it knocks you out at this season of the year. I hope you are quite well, that it has not left you with any of its bad effects. Drop me a line.

The winter in Florida without a typewriter was not such a good idea. I all but ~~but~~ forgot where the keys were on the board, really. It gave me a fright.

I'm slowly getting control of myself again but I'm getting so far behind on my writing that I'm about ready to quit. In fact if it weren't for Floss to read to me I feel as though I might as well quit the game. Seriously.

But don't you get sick on me. It's probably too late for <me> to attempt to keep pace with your writeing. I can't do it any more.

I just want to be assured that you're not ill.

> Affectionly yours
>
> Bill

It's my memory, even my mind, which is a fear that is faliling me.

W.

135 Willow Street
Brooklyn 1, New York

April 15/60

Dear Bill,

Never fear – you can't kill a Polack or even a distant kinsman of him – I'm –
we're our usual selves: it's just as you said in the hospital last summer 'It's hard
to imagine one can get so tired.' Or as Celia said a minute ago "For one hour's
standing up to etc, you're fit to go bed for three days': the you're of herself. Or
once in three months I gather enough energy to ~~press~~ go to the tailor to press
my pants – the 106 pounds of impact in 'em doesn't require any more frequent
grooming. We're all right, really, don't you worry.

Mary Ellen who's coming over today to talk about her book on you and her
own work – anyway as your friend and mine – will report no doubt in detail
when she sees you, and probably – I hope – make off with the impression that
we're even chipper.

When your card came the other day I had just had about 18 hours of a day
of school, making up for a week away from it, and it didn't occur to me that
my card that preceded it, mainly for Easter greeting, would bother you. So I
took yours as an answer that merely said what had happened in Florida – since
Floss said you would write from there ~~you would write~~ when you could type at
home. As I said, I didn't know you were back till Mary Ellen wrote me. And I
had no Florida address to write you ~~in Florida~~ there that the Dean at Poly had
given me a leave of absence for the week of Mar 27, insisting I go and hear Paul
play in Memphis; & it so happened that someone asked me if <I might be
passing thru Washington> I could read <at the Jewish Center> for nothing as
usual, but it served to satisfy my conscience, since Poly was mentioned on the
program; so I did. Aside from the hole in one's pocket that fame always brings
us, everything went very well – hackclaim! etc – but I had started out with a
cold that just went deeper and deeper – and after a week of Southern feasting
C & P came down with ptomaine. So you see why I just sent Easter greetings.

Which brings me to the crisis of your typewriter. Your letter of Apr. 14
shows almost no errors. And if you will please let me be the doctor – since I'm
the only poet of our time, who fair as he has tried to be to the un-progress of
science, has never missed a typewriter – there is no crisis! And as for stopping
to write, I am really waiting for a time when – and that's not hard to imagine
having gone thru what we have – life, and that is the poem, will be no poorer
even when poetry is not being written. Because that's when it's written, and
even literally gets written down.

So you take care of yourselves, you and Floss, and we'll be talking.

> All our love
> Louis

Mary Ellen: Mary Ellen Solt.

her book: This planned work was not published.

Poly: The Brooklyn Polytechnic Institute.

■ 703. TLS-1

9 Ridge Road, Rutherford, N.J.

June 22, 1960

Dear Louis:

The school year having presumably ended how are you going to spend the summer and what is Paul planning to do with himself?

I tried to get you some cash from The Institute of Arts & Letters at their distribution of grants this spring for "A" but did not succeed. The son's of bitches!

Right now I'm in the middle of terminating my connections with McDowell Obolensky. I'm going back to New Directions for the last time, making a clean sweep of it, plays and all. A volume of the new poems will be turned over to them later in the year.

It occurs to me that you may be interested in seeing what I have to show with corrected texts, not much but it's all I have.

If there is anything new you have to show me in recents months and Celia has the time to copy them ship them on.

> Affectionatly
> Bill

get you some cash: In April 1960, Williams wrote to Louis Bogan (Chairman of the Committee on Grants for Literature) recommending Zukofsky for a grant.

McDowell Obolensky: The publishers of Williams's *Selected Letters* (1957) and *Yes, Mrs. Williams* (1959).

volume: *Pictures From Brueghel.*

135 Willow Street
Brooklyn 1, N.Y.

June 23/60

Dear Bill:

Good to hear as always. I assume you have your hands full so I don't swamp you with curryspundense.

Yes the school year has ended – and since they're investing several millions in a graduate center out on L.I., it ended for most of us, including me naturally, without a raise for next year. They smile at me like Mona Lisa with love, telling me how proud they are of my publications, my work with the kids' magazine there on poetry, but I'm still not a full professor.

Thanks for prodding the Institute of Arts and Letters for me, all the more because I didn't know about it and had not to ask you. Our successes are alike with the Mona Lisa's. Sure "some cash" would help – but it's not the cash so much as the prestige of a grant from or an election to the Institute that would impress the President and Trustees of my institute. They always need the word of someone else for goodness. But no use complaining – if Whitman were there today as he's always there for me when I pass the ashcans under his plaque a few blocks away from here, if I take a longer walk to Poly, he'd probably still be an instructor.

So finances is the reason why we'll stay here all summer, Paul too, since we're a one man foundation for two arts, stinting again for a Carnegie concert next February. We better do it, only by coming back again stronger and stronger, and again and again, if necessary, will virtue bend the ear of business. And it is the only way the public that knows of him will remember.

He's OK, and what have I to lose while I can still work? He got his diploma from Juilliard a few weeks ago, probably their youngest graduate ever, will go on with graduate studies in music and academic subjects towards an academic degree. He might as well have it for what it's worth.

We're <(C & I)> as the young Englishman said in a funny British film we saw years ago fragile – like argyle, 's the way to pronounce it – but that's not unusual.

I hope the change to N.D. works out for the best for you – and sure I'd be glad to look at the new work.

Any chance of you and Floss getting here? It's a long summer even if dedicated to poetry. Or I can make it up to you, if you're up to it.

Sure, I've new things to show – Celia* has just finished typing the Shakespeare – 553 pages of it – but how can you manage that monument from under which I still haven't risen – if "A" proved too had – I could read a bit of either to you but unless I became your permanent reader etc etc

    All our love to you both

        Louis

    *(it just made me sick for her sake to watch her – never mind, my dictating)

kids' magazine: This student publication was called *Counterweight*.

young Englishman: Ian Carmichael (b. 1920), who played private Stanley Windrush in the 1956 British film, *Private's Progress*. When reporting for sick call, Windrush says he is feeling "fragile."

N.D.: New Directions Publishing Company.

Shakespeare: *Bottom: On Shakespeare*.

◼ 705. TLS-1

9 Ridge Road, Rutherford, N.J.

June 25, 1960

Dear Louis:

Sooner or later I'll have a report for you on the situation in the Institute. it's bound to break before too long.

You're right, if I have difficulty with "A" which I have, there's no use my pushing my luck with the later work – the difficulties cannot be other than of the same sort. My eyes do not permit my pushing them further – as if mere seeing would help: I see too much as it is.

As far as my own verse is not much, in quantity, just a phrase or two – it can wait. I was struggling wity SOME TIME just now but I still like the Shakespeare sequence speaking of Coventry and the scenes about SRatford-on Avon beast, musically and from the viewpoint of the variable foot the best.

A good summer keep well.

New Directions is bring out 4 plays, the extant 4 plays in the fall.

    Yours

    Bill

Institute: The National Institute of Arts and Letters.

Shakespeare sequence: "Stratford-on-Avon." *CSP* 210–13.

4 plays: *Many Loves and Other Plays: The Collected Plays of William Carlos Williams* (Norfolk, Conn.: New Directions, 1961). Wallace A47.

■ 706. AL-2

135 Willow Street
Brooklyn 1, New York

6/27/60

Dear Bill,

It occurs to me, to make things easier re – "A" – <u>when</u> you're up to it, don't force it – Start with page 156 and see if you can read the next 10 pages consecutively. Then <u>stop</u> and <u>skip</u> to page 232 and read let's say thru page 243. And after that if it moves you you ought to be able to continue to the end. Never worry about starting from the beginning again. The whole poem has a structure (don't tell the fools – my life's the nearest thing to it) – but that's my affair, yours is to get pleasure out of it. And gosh if that Institute isn't Madam Tussaud's they ought to be moved too if they read it the right way.

You both have a good summer too – the best from all
    Love

page 156: The corresponding pages in the University of California Press edition (1978) are
    150– 60 ("And awoke afraid" to "—And the telephone teaches"). Pages 232– 43 in the
    Origin Press edition have for corresponding pages in the California edition 226–37
    ("Then what the mind sees" to "The lover of wisdom").
Institute: The National Institute of Arts and Letters.

■ 707. TLS-1

9 Ridge Road, Rutherford, N.J.

June 28, 1960

Dear Louis:

Give me a tip so I can put my hand on the the passage on the Stratfor on Avon bit – was it in POETRY or some other magazine or magazines? I seem to remember as appearing in 2 places. But where? It is probably safely put away in the attic but that doesn't do me any good unless I can put my hand on it when I want it.

I'll get Floss to help me with the page by page study of the "A" text. Sorry to be so dense. I'll report later on the Institute matter. I'm going to ask Marian Moore's assistance, at once.

    Best
    Bill

Avon bit: "Stratford-on-Avon," *Poetry* 92:3 (June 1958). The poem also appeared in *Barely*
and *Widely. CSP*, 166– 68.

Institute: The National Institute of Arts and Letters.

708. ALS-3

135 Willow Street
Brooklyn 1, New York

June 29, 1960
Dear Bill,

My 'first steps' to "A" in yesterday's note seems to cross yours of the same
day. I didn't mention the Stratford-on-Avon, because I thought you were mix-
ing it up in your mind with my book on Shakespeare – but more specifically
because I was thinking of what is evidently bothering you – your inability to
get into "A" – and why should you be bothered if I can help. But by gosh you
weren't confused about the Stratford poem, remembering more than I had
forgotten: it has appeared in two places – 1) Poetry for June 1958 and 2) the lit-
tle book of mine in my handwriting, Barely and widely that Celia published –
remember? and which you liked so much for the long poem in it, 4 Other
Countries.

The "matter of the Institute" (quoting you) comes down to: you can't kill
two Polacks – like my back (acting up again today) back on my Bach ("A"-13 –
it is going on). I keep on worrying about the strain on you of taking up, as they
say, the cause – but I better trust Floss in this matter; the more active you are
the better, & if it (my un-situation) bothers you you might as well have it out
and off!

The older I get the more I fall back quietly on my work for solace and don't
expect miracles for another how many years, if – from society. But that's the
wrong attitude too, noble (? no – bull) to myself as it is. At least half of the
truth is that society has no right to have buried good work ever since the Ob-
jectivists Anthology and before – for about 35 years, and if we let them they'll
even bury the work of those who like yourself appeared in that Anthology and
made their impress. For as you know the literary market works like all of our
society by whims and fashions – and that the good gets out at all is God's whim
along with his others. A case in point: all the work of the young (some not so
young) makes me shrug my shoulders, when I see them first beginning to do
what I did in my first book 55 Poems (some of the contents going back to
1924). And there are anthologies 1945–1960 of The New American Poetry etc
when no one so much has bothered to think of publishing a collected short
poems of me. Sure I can go on and work despite all that – despite the latest
printed rejection slip as this morning from the Hudson Review of <two of>

my Catullus translations – most of the time I refuse to bother – but I thought they're so damn interesting from the point of view of the play of sound and passion – I might as well. But to be resigned <u>only</u> to work <u>can</u> bury us, and as you know ultimately our society also.

———

My <u>Bottom: on Shakespeare</u> is another matter. It is the kind of work that Marianne Moore, if she wants to assist you in the matter of the Institute should be able to impress them with, ~~even~~ especially with its scholarship and, damn it, vast range of it. It is 553 pages long, and as Cid Corman whom in our mutual isolation I've shown bits of it, as much as I can copy in my hand at a time in a letter to sate his curiosity, put it neatly the other day: "the <u>weight</u> of it, it must be a classic." And I tell this to you <only>, Bill, I'm sure it is despite the weight. It is the <u>Biographia Literaria</u> of our time, and the music, the <u>intel-</u> <u>lective music</u> of it – on which I worked 15 years is something Coleridge had <u>no</u> <u>inkling</u> of. And I'm sure I'm <u>not</u> crazy. I'd be willing to lend Marianne a copy of the ms if she'd like to see it.

By the way the bit of it in Folio, which if it were not for Mary Ellen Solt would never have appeared, she's a good woman and a friend to both of us, is only a mit <will do for a bit at that> of mint sauce in the vast form of the whole thing. (Look at it Spring 1960 Folio – <u>you're mentioned in my piece</u> – I can send you a copy if you don't have it.)

Anyway, after Celia finished typing page 553 of it – we looked at each other as if to say what now! that we're out of the heap, it's only a monument over us.

One gets desperate – so I wrote James Laughlin who was very friendly at your 75th Anniversary party – and friendship if anything can always break down what I imagine people think my aloofness – and asked James if there was any institute like the Bollingen that might, might undertake the publication of <u>Bottom: on Shakespeare</u> – and he thought they <i.e. <u>Bollingen</u>> might very logically (he himself had been impressed by the first pages of it in New Direc- tions no. 14, but it's gone a long way since that preamble); and he told me to write Miss Van Gillmor. I have, but no answer yet.

My what a letter – I've tried to make it legible not to tire you out. I better stop. Love to you both for reading it from all of us Louis

The New American Poetry: Donald M. Allen, ed., *The New American Poetry* (New York: Grove Press, 1960).

in Folio: "All eyes," *Folio* 25:2 (Spring 1960).

first pages: "Preface & Part I," *New Directions* 14 (New York: New Directions, 1953).

Van Gillmor: On 23 June 1960, Zukofsky wrote Vaun Gillmor, an assistant editor with the Bollingen Foundation, bringing to her attention his "long manuscript on Shake- speare." She replied on 30 June 1960 that the Foundation was already heavily committed to various publishing projects and that it would be pointless for him to submit the manuscript.

709. TLS-1

9 Ridge Road, Rutherford, N.J.

June 30, 1960

Dear Louis:

When I first got my hands on your "A" I was on the way to take the plane for Florida. As it happened I was planning to meet my philosopgher friend Ken Burke there. I made up my mind since I would not be able to read your poem for at least a monthe (Flossy at once got down to work and read it to me but it was to much for us both) to turn it over the Ken at once.

That hound of the words read it the same evening and returned it to me at once. Half lit as he often is after a sleepless night, I got the impression that he did not much like it – and decided not to bother you with my own reactions while trying to get used to the Florida climate.

Reading the poem over more than a month later together with the notes elucidations you have given me prompts me to include his letter written in Florida with his own. Read what Burke has to say to you and let me have the letter back that I may preserve it for Yale with my own correspondence.

I feel better having got this matter off my chest. I can rest better now.

I'll continue to work on the Institute matter having got a reply to my letter to Marianne this morning, a bear for promptness, this gal. Hope this allergy doesn't keep you down for too long.

   Sincerely yours

   Bill

his letter: Burke to William Carlos Williams, 11 March 1960. This three-page letter about "A" 1–12 is in the file of letters to Williams at Yale.

710. ALS-5

135 Willow Street
Brooklyn 1, New York

July 1/60

Dear Bill,

Gosh, Kenneth Burke's letter on "A" is a surprise! O many thanks for sending it. Sure you should feel better for sending it.

It is an oynement unto my wounde – said Chaucer the joker – an ointment to my wound – wound up sometimes as one can get in utter isolation. And had I not seen it – never seen Burke's letter, how horrible to think I'd have gone on to my father's (Father's <rather>) bosom etc unabsolved of not even paying so much as thanks, via you for the present, for his very generous act of a <u>most</u> careful reading of me. I do feel grateful to him. Besides I don't see where you got the impression that he did not like "A". As I read his letter it's full of praise. Better it's <u>analysis</u>. And if he takes exception to pp 112–117 (the double canzone <u>transliteration</u> and <u>transposition</u> into "my time" of Cavalcanti) <u>I can't blame him</u> for the impediments <u>I</u> put in my way out of sheer pigheaded stubbornness loving a noise that made sense almost 700 years ago, and an ascetic belief I guess that if you're faithful to it even a noise <u>then</u> <at that time> still has a vestige of sense for us today.

I'm returning his letter to you. Celia has made a copy of it – is that OK with you? Because I value it – for ourselves. Not to show to anyone tho I'd love to, with your permission to Cid Corman (o what a lousy deal he's getting in S.F.) – it would be balm to him too – the first intelligent criticism of "A" <since publication> anybody took the trouble <u>to write down</u> – gosh, if it appeared as a review somewhere <u>or rather just as is, a letter to you</u>, it would speed the dissemination of what is in the poem by 10 years.

I'd like to thank Burke myself, if you approve, Bill, – in a letter – bless his Irish (any kind of drink included – and if drink makes my nose brittle and I can feel just as gay without it, I'm sure what he says about T.S.E. doesn't apply to me, at least not in this case.) So if you agree I should write him – and it would be a short note but sweet – please send me his address. I've no right to intrude on him – I met him only once ca. 1936 in the days of Legions of Am. Writers when only legion met legion – but obviously he'd be one of six possible readers of my Shakespeare book – as things stand now. No luck with Bollingen – their funds they write <committed> reserved for Jung, Valery, Coleridge, Mellon Lectures (sic). Don't even want to look at it!

Since you're rootin' up Sodom <etc> in this Institute Matter – I promise <not> or rather feel I should not thank Marianne – since you may not want her to know you told me. But again if you approve, or want me or maybe you <to> send her a copy of "A", I'd be glad to do it direct (from here) or via you.

It may not be so, but I always got the feeling that I interrupted her work by sending her mine – so, & since "A" is $5 out of my pocket, I didn't this time. Besides, she's always so righteous about these matters – I better <u>not</u> act unless you say.

And <u>thanks</u> again
    Love to you & Floss
    Louis

Chaucer: See line 7 of Chaucer's poem, "To Rosemounde."

if he takes exception: Burke to Williams, 1 July 1960, "But jeez, if you don't consider
   pp. 112–117 absolutely hideous, then prithee learne me!" (Yale).
lousy deal: In a letter of 25 June 1960, Corman reported that Ruth Witt-Diamant had of-
   fered him $200 to teach a seminar for 16 weeks in the following spring.
what he says about T.S.E.: Burke to Williams, 1 July 1960, "And I was saying how I loathed
   Eliot in his later phases, not for his religion but for his advertising of it" (Yale).

711. TLS-1

9 Ridge Road, Rutherford, N.J.

July 2, 1960
Dear Louis:
Ken's address is: Kenneth Burke
                  Andover, N.J.
- I'm writing to him that he'll be hearing from you.

Send a copy of the letter to Cid for his information. The reason I did not send the letter earlier was I thought you might be sensitive about his reference to you as a Jew, stupid of me. I don't see so good any more – actually and metaphorically. The fault is now corrected, forget it Floss couldn't understand why I did not send you the letter in the first place.

Through Mack Rosenthal whom I shall see shortly I'll see if I cannot get Ken's permission to print his letter to me in the ~~New Republic~~ Nation or elsewhere.

I'm still that much good at any rate.
       Best
       Bill

Cid: Cid Corman.
his reference: Burke's letter of 11 March 1960 contains this passage: "I was saying yes-
   tiddy that the guy is good insofar as (a) he can let it roll out nachurl and (b) he's en-
   tangled with the problem of beginnings (as every good Jew shd. Be, if he begins with
   Genesis)."

[135 Willow Street
Brooklyn, New York]
Same place as per enclosure!
on poesy.

July 5/60

Dear Bill,

A copy of my letter to Burke with this – as far as my eye could copy straight – the errors in this copy crossed out to be exact.* <*with respect to the original where I wrote straight because I wasn't copying> Thanks again, I'll send a copy of Burke's letter to Cid, and ask him to return it, so if you succeed in getting it printed Cid can look at it afresh.

Ah don' min' being called a Jew if anybody finds it a well-meaning and useful distinction (aint you called me one in that Note to my edition of 200 "A"s – snack-bar lingo = eggs) any mo' than ah'd min' being called an Amerikanski by an honest Russian, but if a Chinese or a genuine African called me that then I might grieve because it shouldn't yet be in their vocabulary or terminology unless they are already oxcidentals before their time.

Take good care of yourselves and keep in touch. And thanks again.

Love from all
Louis

Cid: Cid Corman.

enclosure: Zukofsky's copy of his letter to Kenneth Burke.

Louis Zukofsky
135 Willow Street
Brooklyn 1, New York
July 5/60

Dear Kenneth Burke:

Bill Williams has just let me see the letter you wrote to him about my poem "A" – dated 3/11/60. Your most careful reading of the poem meant a great deal to me, and I must thank you for it. This is it, then: thanks.

May I send you a copy of the book? You might ask why <don't> I just send it instead of asking. But on one occasion when a critic unexpectedly liked my prose and I sent him a volume of poems as thanks, the answer was, "Please!" No reason why I should even think of that incident in this case, since your analysis of my poem impressed me mostly as praise. But the world being what it is I have supposed from then on that any work at any time might be a distraction to anyone else. So: I'll feel happier if your answer is "yes."

Sincerely yours,
Louis Zukofsky

9 Ridge Road, Rutherford, N.J.

July 12, 1960

Dear Louis:

Since you positively forbid me to pay for getting you out to Indiana and I have no one to whom to turn for assistance I'll have to let the project go.

Jack Thirlwall has offed to accompany <me> on the plane, bearing his own exense, Mary Ellen will find us some convenient place in which to bunk up, she has already mentioned one on the Campus.

I would have liked you to be at the lecture to hear what the gal has to say, notes are unimportant, a reprint of the lecture will be furnisherd me later which I can let you see.

It's coming in a little over 2 weeks, I bet she's getting nervous. Wish you could have (break during which your phone call has just come in) come but we'll have to make the best of it.

> Affectionatly
> Bill

Indiana: Williams and Thirlwall traveled to the University of Indiana at Bloomington to hear Mary Ellen Solt lecture on 27 July 1960. Her subject was "William Carlos Williams: The American Idiom."

■ 714. ALS-1

[135 Willow Street
Brooklyn, New York]

July 20/60

Dear Bill,

Just wrote Burke that I'm sending you a copy of his letter (above) to reinforce the fact that your responsibility, if you still want to "carve" a review and can manage to publish it, is to Burke. So do as you please.

All Z best ever,
> Louis

copy: Zukofsky's letter was written at the bottom of a copy of Burke's letter of 11 March 1960. In his letter, Burke said he would be willing to be quoted in a review by Williams, if the review met with Burke's approval.

9 Ridge Road
Rutherford, N.J.

Aug. 9, 1960

Dear Louis:

Look at this and when you are through with it let me have it back. It was written for a prof at the Hun school at Princeton who is writing a book on aural poetry who is, I think, going to use it tn there.

I've been trying to find, as usual, one of your latest which gets me (I'll find it pretty soon) it must be incomprehensible to the ordinary reader, alternate passages from a musical notation of music and verse. Jutifiable?

Hope you're keeping on top of the weather.

Affectionately

Bill

this: A draft of Williams's essay, "The American Idiom." Published in *Fresco* 1:1 (1960)
15–16. Wallace C579

a prof: Thomas Edward Francis of the Hun School at Princeton. No book of his—either
on poetry or any other subject—appears to have been published.

one of your latest: See the following letter.

135 Willow Street
Brooklyn 1, New York

Aug 10/60

Dear Bill

Oak for this gospel to the Hun. Thanks for letting me see it. I did some proofreading lightly in pencil as you'll note - so you won't fail in English by way of getting over American. If they read liberally "<u>having to do</u> with 'the Establishment'" you've got a point, but if they take it as an <u>absolute</u> statement they'll accuse you of blaming it <u>all</u> on the Church of England or the Presbyterians in Scotland. (That's the dictionary meaning of <u>the Establishment</u>). And that way neither Shakes. nor Marlowe conformed unless they got into trouble with the censor. All the "dirty" words in Shakes - for instance "By cock you are to blame" (Hamlet) - are now interpreted blasphemously by professors only. They will say <u>cock</u> meant Christ or the Rooster that crowed etc. But the Elizabethan audiences must have known immediately what was responsible for Ophelia's madness. Well, for all the Establishment even Mr. Eliot sins sometimes, tho naturally he puts the unestablished words into Lou's or May's mouth. (Waste Land etc)

Lou's very appropriate – I'm working on A-13 now. You can't kill a Polack.

I'm at a loss to guess what of my recent work you're looking for – but maybe you mean JAUNT which appeared in Poetry February 1960.

So! take care of yourself

Love from all to you & Floss

Louis

proofreading: Williams's draft of his essay, "The American Idiom."

JAUNT: "Jaunt," *Poetry* 95:5 (February 1960), 296– 99. *CSP* 210–13.

717. ACS

135 Willow St
Brooklyn 1, N.Y.

Aug 18/60

Dear Bill

Thanks for the copy of Am. Idiom. OK!

I'm immersed in A-13 – not the Establishment exactly – I guess once you start it never stops. Trying to get thru with it before we go up to some friends in Old Lyme on Aug 31 for a week – and the year's grind starts after that.

Love to you & Floss

Louis

Am. Idiom: Williams's essay, "The American Idiom." The copy Zukofsky refers to is a finished draft, with the typed note:

Aug. 17/60

Louis:

This is for you.

Bill

718. TLS-1

135 Willow Street
Brooklyn 1, New York

Oct. 15, 1960

Dear Bill,

The University of Texas Press has asked me to edit a volume of letters whose contents, from various correspondents, is covered by the following preface.

Preface

Hamlet's <u>Let be</u> might speak for omissions from the
originals of these letters, and also for what is here in the
order it was received over nearly forty years. <u>A man's life's
no more than to say "One"</u> while the various perception—of
a time perhaps—remains.

L.Z.

March 21, 1953—May 1, 1954

There will be no other editorial comment.

May I have your permission to select and print from whatever of your let-
ters I have - at the latest by Nov. 15, so I can give the Press a list of the names of
correspondents.

Regards and thanks,
    Yours,
    Louis Zukofsky

■ 719. TL-1

9 Ridge Road, Rutherford, N.J.

Nov. 9/60
Dear Louis:

Witness this, enclosed. I suppose now the book will never appear. Please re-
turn this letter - they didn'h have the guts to publish what I had written.

Sorry you're not feeling up to getting out here with Oppen. Better luck next
time.

Best

[Zukofsky's notation:] re- Whitman photo pub. Ziff-Davis

this, enclosed: Enclosure lacking.

the book: In April, 1960, Louis Zara had asked Williams to write an essay for a proposed
    edition of *Leaves of Grass* to be illustrated with photographs. The project was delayed,
    however, and the edition not published until 1971. See Mariani 757–58.

135 Willow Street
Brooklyn 1, New York

Nov 12/60

Dear Bill,

I read the enclosure with anger, without reading the sender's signature. But my eye then side-glanced below it, to the left, at the typist's "LZ/es," and for a split second, can you beat the absent minded prof. I'm every now and then, wondered what I had to do with it! Ah well, they'll probably do it in time but they delight in being editors, showing business "sense," if not authority. Rather than let it hurt you, let it slide like water off a duck's back. Besides even if they don't publish it, don't they know that someone will? You should have no doubt about that by this time.

George Oppen called this morning to tell me how much he and Mary enjoyed seeing you again. Whatever my health, not much to feel chipper about, I'd have gone along to clear my head and rest my nerves, but <as> I said in my card my school sprang that unexpected faculty meeting – and one has to go to these things – bread and butter. I suppose I could have played sick, but even justifiable lies disturb me – foolish to be that way – but!

Some news for you – but before it slips my mind: I was shocked when George told me that you said Cid read all of "A" to you – is it possible? – taking two hours. Endurance! My! You understand, I hope, much as I value his faith <in me> and affection, I'd have stopped him after 15 minutes if I were there. Cid told me how happy he was to see you again and I got the impression that he read "from "A" – because you had asked him <I assumed>, I had nothing to do with it – but two hours of it! That's a fantastic ordeal to put you thru but evidently you've endured. Sorry if it tired you!

Which works in with the news: The Library of Congress via Eberhart finally asked – after hearing Cid read from "A" in Washington, they were impressed – for a tape recording of my voice reading my poetry. I had it done here, and was duly worn out by the effort. I'd have gone to Washington if I could afford <it> – but money's very tight with Paul's concert coming Feb 3. Mary Ellen Solt will be coming to N.Y. for it and maybe this time, since she'll be seeing you, Floss and you can make it with her along. I hope so! There's a lot of time yet, so we'll figure it out – anyhow and of course you're invited.

Also: Poetry Center, Toronto, sponsored by Canada Council has invited me to read next Sat. Hope the check for the flight arrives in time. The fee itself (i.e. for the reading) – well, I'd have refused to read in N.Y. for it – seeing I can afford to be poor if I'm left alone, all that counts after all is the work done – but Ray Souster who runs the readings sounds like a good guy, I couldn't refuse. I fly alone – much as it would be nice to have C & P get away from the grind. But we can't do it. It'll be strange being a thousand miles from home, even if <only> overnight. The last time was during World War II when I had that defense job in Baltimore – ~~I don't think~~ Paul was not quite a year old at the time.

So much to think back on – maybe it shapes up –

Dec. Poetry will print two extracts from the Shakespeare. I take it you get the mag. If not, let me know and I'll send a copy.

Take care of yourselves, both of you

Best all around from all

Louis

LZ: Louis Zara. See the note to the previous letter.

Mary: Mary Oppen, wife of George Oppen.

Cid: Cid Corman.

Eberhart: Richard Eberhart (b. 1904), poet. Consultant in poetry at the Library of Congress 1959–1961 and 1963–1969.

Paul's concert: At his third Carnegie Hall recital, on 3 February 1961, Paul Zukofsky performed works by Brahms, Bach, Saint-Saens, Piston, Webern, Satie, and the Rossini-Paganini "Moses-Fantasy."

Souster: Raymond Souster (b. 1921), Canadian poet.

two extracts: "From 'Bottom: On Shakespeare,'" *Poetry* 97:3 (December 1960), 141–52.

721. TLS-1

[Rutherford, N.J.]

Nov. 14/60

Dear Louis:

You make me feel much better about being turned back in my attempt to place my introduction about Whitman, my advancing years mame me feel that there is not enough time for me to put my ideas over. Your words reenforce my courage. I can now "take it" with better grace.

Cid Korman did us bothe a favor by his reading of "A" to me, I was not able to do it nor did I have the insight to demand it of others. His persistence won the day, it was a pleasure for me to hear it – far simpler than I had ever envisioned it and more lyrical than I was ever able to envisioned it.

Also to Cid goes the honor of the invitation to Washington for the permanent recording – I'll write at once to Dick Eberhart to do all he can to smooth out the way for you. At once! It does take a man recently from Japan to be linguage-free or untramelled to see his opportunity and seize it. It was quite a stunt for him to read the poem from beginning to the end , but both Flossie and I really enjoyed it. and it got better as we progressed. It is the opening of new territory that is the important thing. When the ear is not ready for the advance there is no possibility of its taking place. Cid Corman/s ear was clean from being used to hearing nothing but Japanese so that it was ready to hear our own language when it was presented fresh to us.

I can't understand any thing else by the experience. A new poet is a man who presents a reading as if it is being spoken for the first (and last) time.

– You are right to take the trip to Canada on your own. Read slowly and with as much assurance as you can muster, but slowly, repeating a phrase if you have to to put it over. Almost everyone is ready to listen if they can only understand what is being said.

There's much more I could say.

We'll be at Paul's concert in February.

> Affectionately
> Bill

■ 722. ALS-1

> 135 Willow Street
> Brooklyn 1, New York

Nov. 21/60

Dear Bill,

Before I run off to school – forgive the haste. It isn't necessary to write to Eberhart, he already has the recorded tapes which I made here. <u>Between you and me</u>, I didn't tell him I couldn't afford a trip to Washington, just that I would expedite it all here – and I have and he's acknowledged receiving the tapes.

So! as Ed Wynn used to say I hope this saves you the trouble of writing.

> Love to you both
> Louis

Wynn: Born Isaiah Edwin Leopold (1886–1966), actor and comedian. His career spanned vaudeville, musical comedy, radio, cinema, and television.

■ 723. TLS-1

> 9 Ridge Road, Rutherford, N.J.

Jan. 7/61

Dear Louis:

Bill's birthday.

Thanks for the concert tickets if I am still "alive" due to this winter's immobility. But I am sure we'll make it.

Nothing much to tell you. It moves, slowly as usual.

  Affectionately yours,

  Bill

Bill's: William Eric Williams.

tickets: For Paul Zukofsky's Carnegie Hall recital on 3 February 1961.

724. TLS-1

         9 Ridge Road, Rutherford, N.J.

Feb. 1/61

Dear Louis:

Trouble. I don't know whether or not I will be able to get in to Paul's concert. I'll not know for sure until the last minute. Meanwhile things must stay as they are pending some laboratory. I'll keep you posted.

At the same time I must ask you for 2 extra tickets for the concert if you can let me have them for my physician, who is taking care of me in Rutherford, himself an accomplished violinist ~~that~~ who has played with the Cincinatti orchestra. What can I do but play up to him.

I've not been doing so well recently. The cold weather has been ~~has been~~ hard on me. A new slant in the treatment may help me. I'll let you know during the next few days.

  Affectionately yours

  Bill

[In Florence Williams's hand:] We'll be at the concert – with Mary Ellen but will not attempt to see Paul back stage afterwards. That would be to much for Bill to undertake.

Best of luck – and we're as excited as if it were <u>our</u> son! –

Love to all

Floss.

Mary Ellen: Mary Ellen Solt. As it turned out, the Williamses did not attend.

725. ALS-1

         135 Willow Street

         Brooklyn 1, N.Y.

June 8/61

Dear Bill,

Don't answer now, but I just want you to know that in working on my index to the Shakespeare (which is no god damn good for bursitis and migraines, but which the printing division of the Humanities Research Center at the University of Texas has scheduled for publication in the spring of 1962) I just made out a card for Williams, William Carlos, and that alphabetically you're between <u>will</u> (as in will-power) and <u>Winter's Tale, The</u>. That settles it: it's a good sign for all of us – the older I get the more I trust in "signs." What else is there to trust in, we're gonna have some luck sometime – between <u>will</u> and that Shikes play where everything turns out miraculously happy!

So just you and Floss take care of your selves – and as I just told Floss <over the phone,> you'll live to be as old as your mother and healthier, and if in July you want to see us, just let us know and C & I'll be glad to be away from <u>this</u> – I mean what we're going thru now – no comment!

Love to you both Louis

the Shakespeare: *Bottom: On Shakespeare.*
C: Celia Zukofsky.

726. ACS

[Printed greeting: "With many good wishes for Christmas and the new year."]
[December 1961]   [Rutherford, N.J.]

Bill is not doing so well – depressed – and unhappy – I've been too rushed to keep in touch – but I know you understand.

Trust all is well with you all –
Affectionately
Floss

727. ALS-1

160 Columbia Heights
Brooklyn 1, New York

6/9/62
Dear Bill and Floss,

Thanks for <u>Pictures</u> and the inscription – and the handwriting on the envelop, too. Floss. I come back most this time to "The Dance" and "Fragment" of the new things – perhaps because my brother-in-law died last Sunday (my poor old sister and her one son, to console?), and again to "Theocritus" and the end of "Asphodel."

Comes down to as you say in Exercise No. 2 – or something like it, in the city there are no "close" neighbors, or more.

The editors who print me these days as usual without pay tell me, or write me rather, that you get the magazines – so you know more or less what's happening – "serving art," with or without blue jays.*

Take care of yourselves – we're trying to do the same.

*i.e. Some Simple Measures
          Love from all of us
          Louis

Pictures: *Pictures from Brueghel.*
"The Dance": "The Dance (When the snow falls)," *CP2*, 407–08.
"Fragment": "Fragment (as for him who)," *CP2*, 401.
brother-in-law: Al Wand. See "Atque in Perpetuum A.W.," *Poetry* 101: 1 & 2 (October–November 1962), 143. *CSP*, 231–32.
"Theocritus": "Theocritus: Idyl I (A Version from the Greek)," *CP2*, 268–73.
"Asphodel": "Asphodel, that Greeny Flower," *CP2*, 310–37.
Exercise No. 2: "Exercise No. 2," *CP2*, 415.
blue jays: "The Blue Jay" is poem 4 of "Some Simple Measures in the American Idiom and the Variable Foot." *CP2*, 420.

728. ACS [Printed greeting: "Season's Greetings and Best Wishes for a Happy New Year."]

[Rutherford, N.J.]

[December 1962]
Dear Louis and Celia—
We haven't much <u>pep</u> these days – Bill failing rapidly – and I have difficulty with my neck. – So be it.
We speak of you and wish we could be free to come & go as we did formerly – but – You are not forgotten – Your are treasured friends.
Hope all is well with you – and that Paul is getting some recognition!
          Our love to all of you
          Bill & Floss

[William Carlos Williams died on 4 March 1963.]

Appendix A

An Unsent Letter

ALS-4

[135 Willow Street
Brooklyn, New York]

Thanksgiving Day 1957
Dear Bill:
This has been on my mind since you showed me the few pages of your criticism of "A."

I was moved by your grasp of its poetic means: what I always want to be its means, if I have done well. That is: the clean statement – no matter what one's personal interests, leanings, refinements, excesses, abstentions, historic subjects, and so on are at any time – that does not impose a lie on the incontrovertible fact that because the statement is clean it compels only thru the construction in its music. In this sense, I do not have to tell you, the poem has no subject but the poem.

So: for all my interest in Marx when I wrote "about him" in "A", I held then, as I hold now, that for me as poet unassociated with party, what was valid in him was of the same matter that goes into the construction of the poem. For this reason, I wrote New Directions about the contributors note on me in the 1938 Annual (it said: The work published in this issue is the eighth section of his long poem called "A", an epic of the class struggle) – there's epic, but no epic of the class struggle. That may not be verbatim, but that was the substance. I was put out at the time by the wording of the note because of the untruth. I suppose I had no reason to be. It never convinced any practicing Communist that I followed "the line." Most of them thought I was all mixed up, a few even labeled me "fascist," tho one conservative reviewer annoyed by the fact New Directions pages weren't numbered decided, because I took up so many of them, that I was a Stalinist.

What has this to do with 1957? Emanuel Navaretta will be asking you for your preface to "A" 1–12, which he wants to publish in March 1958. Now, I have warned him that those who do not read the poem carefully may call me "Communist," tho that is not at all the case, as you may see when you read it. My intention is to let analysis of all I have felt and known come thru the clean impact of the statement, historical, personal, or otherwise, as it affected times and people, and find its music. That way – apart from accomplishment, and oh if I could say the same about that! – I'm no further along in civilization than Homer (in a different setting), insofar as I can make out, and Whitman (in a little later one) who say: What have you, you can have peace, love, but look at the mess, even the well-intentioned that went wrong – but the music is still all right.

The point, though, is: if I am misread, you might get involved in an attack on a "Communist." There's no criticism of "A" I'd rather have than yours, but before you finish what you've started, without perhaps thinking along the lines of this letter, do make sure that you have considered carefully the practical consequences to yourself. That's the last thing I want to do – involve you, tho I think (who knows perhaps foolishly) I could defend myself by pointing to context of the poem, if ever any accusations do come up.

LZ

[Zukofsky's notation: "never sent Bill was too ill and I decided to let the poem speak for itself."]

Appendix B

Extracts from Letters of
William Carlos Williams to Louis Zukofsky

[As Zukofsky's letter of 28 September 1932 indicates, the following compilation was meant for a Williams issue of *The Lion and Crown*. The issue, however, never appeared. Zukofsky appears to have sent Williams an autograph copy, but I have not been able to locate it. The typescript represents deletions from the letters by a sequence of six hyphens. It also silently corrects William's typographical errors and some of his spelling. In several instances the typescript silently altered words. For example, the last paragraph of the letter of 28 March 1928 was condensed. Also, in the letter of 2 April 1928, Williams had referred to "flaws" when discussing Zukofsky's early poetry; the typescript changed this to "plans." Readers who compare the versions here with the versions presented elsewhere in this edition will notice other slight changes.]

March 23, 1928

My dear Zukofsky:

By "human value" I suppose Ezrie means that in his opinion I can't write. Dammit, who can write isolated as we all find ourselves and robbed of the natural friendly stimulae on which we rest, at least, in our lesser moments? But undoubtedly the old ant-eater didn't mean anything at all other than that he'd like me to make your acquaintance, and you mine.

So you are responsible for Exile now. Is that so? Come over to this suburb some Tuesday, Friday or Saturday evening for a country meal and a talk and explain to me what all has taken place in "the center" while I have been rusticating. I'd like greatly to see you since you come with an introduction from my old friend. But do call up since I am a laborer and my time must be arranged to fit the advent of a guest. I have a good cook. What do you like especially to eat?

Yours,

W. C. Williams

Dear Zukofsky:

Neither am I of "the center". Lucy just likes to know what people especially fancy when she cooks for them so as to be sure, if possible, to please them. Nothing elaborate here.

Unfortunately I will not be at home this Saturday evening. What about Sunday? I am coming in to the Philharmonic Concert. Perhaps I could meet you between half past five and six somewhere in the city and you will have supper with me there.

It is funny that I am being interviewed – at five o'clock by some stranger at the Park Central Hotel – I didn't exactly catch his name over the phone. Could you not rescue me there at 5:30? Drop me a note here or just arrive there and ask for me at the time stated above.

> Yours,
> W. C. Williams

April 2, '28

Dear Zukofsky:

Yes, yes. You have the rare gift. As with everything else there are plans – the tripping rhythm – but not always the tripping rhythm – just sometimes. It spoils the adagio effect. It is noteable that the lines have such an excellent internal necessity that they must be read slowly. It is thoughtful poetry, but actual word stuff, not thoughts for thoughts. It escapes me in its analysis (thank God). There are not so many things in the world as we commonly imagine. Plenty of debris, plenty of smudges.

This has been a pleasure, i.e. the reading of your poem. You make me want to carry out deferred designs. Don't take my theories too seriously. They are not for you – or for you, of course, or anybody.

I'd give my shirt to hear the Matthaus Passion this week but I doubt if it can be done. If I do get there in spite of everything, I'll cast an eye around for you.

But you work's the thing. It encourages me in my designs. Makes me anxious to get at my notes and the things (thank God) which I did not tell the gentleman. Thanks for the supper. As soon as work lightens a bit for me here in the suburbs, I want you to come out . . . I congratulate Pound on his luck in finding you. You are another nail in the . . . coffin. Damn fools.

Easter 1928

Dear Zukofsky:

Was the Matthaus' Passion well sung? I wish I could have been there.

What meeting you meant to me was at first just that Pound had admired your work. I was amazed to see you, nothing like what I had imagined. Then just reticence.

I did not wish to be twenty years younger and surely I did not wish to be twenty years older. I was happy to find a link between myself and another wave of it. Sometimes one thinks the thing has died down. I believe that somehow you have benefited by my work. Not that you have even seen it fully but it proves to me (Christ, God Damn this machine) that the thing moves by a direct relationship between men from generation to generation. And that no matter how we may be ignored, maligned, left unnoticed, yet by doing straightforward work we do somehow reach the right people.

There must be an American magazine. As I have gotten older I am less volatile over projects such as this (a magazine) less willing to say much but more determined to make a go of it finally – after I am 70 perhaps . . . Perhaps it will crystalize soon.

  Williams

               April 27, 1928

Dear Louis:

Your Cummings is good, brief criticism . . . Is that your own about philosophy, the "dreampistol"? Wonderful if it is, and fine anyway. I hope it is yours.

The poems are nowhere up to the poem "The". I like a line here and there but they do not get going. But I'll read them again.

. . . Just now I have the novel again in my hands going over it finally before it will be sent to the printer. I am just dolling it up, . . . etc.

  Williams

               May 19, 1928

Dear Louis:

Did I mail you the right letter or did I put my wife's letter into your envelope? I had a queer feeling after the things had dropped into the box.

  . . . Williams

               May 12, 1928

Dear Louis:

 . . .

I must confess that I wrote to Cummings inviting him to spend a day with me. He came, a week ago. I told him no one else would be here. It's just as well. I left him alone most of the time: a real New Englander, not I but he.

———

Saw "Strange Interlude" last night . . . he is so god damned rotten that he is good. . . . And he knows the things that save him from realism. I wonder if he does. He will some day if he doesn't now.

> Williams

May 17, 1928

. . . The novel . . . oh well, I can't quite bring myself to throw the thing away though I wanted to do so after you had left.

. . .

Yours,

> Bill

June 25, 1928

. . . the book looks about as presentable as I can make it. I cut out a lot about <u>the Rhine!</u> Which should give you a special pleasure.

> So long
> Bill

July 5, 1928

Poems are inventions richer in thought as image. Your early poems even when the thought has enough force or freshness have not been objectivized in new or fresh observations. But if it is the music even that is not inventive enough to make up for images which give an overwhelming effect of triteness – as it has been said. The language is stilted "poetic" except in the piece I marked.

Eyes have always stood first in the poet's equipment. If you are mostly ear – a newer rhythm must come in more strongly than has been the case so far.

Yet I am willing to grant – to listen.

> Bill

July 12

Dear Louis;

. . .

I finished the "Henry Adams" yesterday before breakfast. It interested me greatly both as an introduction to the life of an American of extraordinary significance to my way of thinking – which is not putting it half firmly enough – and as the work of another American – Oh hell, my mind is thick this morning. I enjoyed your work. All through the reading I came upon lines of real distinction – without attempting to analyse them just now. To me your thesis shows a grain and selective power of thought which is unusual – Christ! what in hell am I saying? And it is true besides. Anyhow I liked your work. It impressed me. You seemed to hold the damned subject up from the table as a whole with clean hands. That's the gist of your power to me. I don't feel any . . . smell, would be better. You have power that is real, penetrant and (so far) flexible enough not to crack irritably the way the thing usually does in the people I have to do with most often.

Anyhow I read the thesis.

Drop me a line.

> Yours
> Bill

July 22, 1928

Dear Louis:

. . .

God know where one meets in N.Y., a stupid place. Let's start a sidewalk cafe. Is it the dirt or the weather or what that would make it a failure? Marianne is willing but she suffers from the terrific weight of indifference under which all labor in these here United States just as we do. I am glad she has accepted your poems. All the good that comes from such a success is, however, the cash you will pocket. The Dial is about as dead as a last year's birds' nest. One must believe in spiders –

July 18, 1928

Dear Louis:

Certainly the "Lenin" outdistances anything in the earlier book of poems as the effect of a "thing" surpasses all thought about it. It is the second poem of yours that I like, the first being the long one. In some ways this poem is your best work (that I have seen). It has the surging rhythms that in itself embodies all that is necessary to say but it carries the words nevertheless and the theme helplessly with it. The word "continual" at the end is fine.

It is this, the thing that this poem is, that makes you what you are today – I hope you're satisfied! No doubt it is the underlying theme to me of whatever feeling we have for each other – It seems to me surely the contra-bass for everything else we may do. If there is not that under our feel (though I realize that you are speaking of a star) then we cannot go on elaborating our stuff.

Sometimes though I don't like your language. It probably is me and not you who should be blamed for this. You are wrestling with the antagonist under newer rules. But I can't see "all live processes", "orbit-trembling", "our consciousness" "the sources of being" – what the hell? I'm not finding fault. I'm just trying to nail what troubles me. It may be that I am too literal in my search for objective clarities of image. It may be that you are completely right in forcing abstract conceptions into the sound pattern. I dunno. Anyhow, there you are.

I will say that in this case the abstract, philosophical-jargonist language is not an obstruction. It may be that when the force of the conception is sufficiently strong it can carry this sort of thing. If the force were weaker the whole poem would fall apart. Good, perhaps. Perhaps by my picayune imagistic mannerisms I hold together superficially what should by all means fall apart.

. . .

    Yours
    Bill

               October 18

. . . virtue exists like a small flower on a loose piece of earth above a precipice. And isn't it a fine day.

    Yours
    Bill

Appendix C
Zukofsky's Editing of the "Working Copy" of The Wedge

As Christopher MacGowan explains in his notes concerning *The Wedge* for his edition of Williams's *The Collected Poems of William Carlos Williams: Volume II, 1939–1962* (New Directions, 1988), Williams "originally envisioned a more comprehensive arrangement than the published version of this book, to be titled at one stage, 'The (lang)WEDGE: A New Summary.' His initial conception was to combine a number of forms, including improvisations from the 1920s, prose, and excerpts from his play *Many Loves*—as well as many poems from the *Detail & Parody for the poem Paterson* and *Broken Span* arrangements. With the assistance of Louis Zukofsky, WCW revised and rearranged the poems, cut down the material, and finally eliminated the prose—although adding an introduction based upon a talk he gave at the New York Public Library on 26 October 1943 . . . " (454). On 27 March 1943, Williams wrote Zukofsky that under "separate cover I am sending the conglomorate of scripts of which I have spoken to you." The conglomeration survives, with Zukofsky's penciled comments, among the Williams papers at the State University of New York at Buffalo. Neil Baldwin and Steven L. Meyer's descriptive catalogue of the Williams manuscripts at Buffalo number the collection of scripts D6(c) and describe it as a "working copy." They further remark, "It consists primarily of originals, while Williams kept the carbons himself. The manuscript has suggestions for revision and corr[ection]s. by Louis Zukofsky—nearly all followed—and a 2 pp. (recto & verso) letter with final comments" (201). The letter Baldwin and Meyers refers to is Zukofsky's letter of 6 April 1943.

The version of *The Wedge* that Zukofsky commented on, therefore, was one of a sequence of versions. Yet his interventions were crucial, for, as Baldwin and Meyers further remark, "The result of Zukofsky's influence can be gauged by the compactness of the final manuscript compared to the earlier arrangements" (202). One form Zukofsky's influence took was his summary comments on poems he thought should not appear in the collection. Sometimes he was blunt. "The Halfworld" drew a brief, emphatic "<u>No</u>." Williams removed the poem. "Gothic Candor," Zukofsky found "rather sentimental." Out it went. "I'm indifferent to this one," he comments regarding an eight-line poem beginning "a woman's breasts for beauty." Williams responded by crossing out the poem with a large X. After inspecting "The Unknown," Zukofsky found it wanting: "The first 3 and the last 3 lines of the coda are all I see in this; no use you doing a thing of the female poetess variety better." So "The Unknown" was unused in *The Wedge*. It was enough for Zukofsky to say of "Fertile" that "The thought's rather arbitrary" for Williams to excise it. Of "The Sisters" Zukofsky wrote, "I don't think this is successful—it isn't clear to me how the last couplet comes in—but it 'could be.'" Despite Zukofsky's hope that something "could be" done to improve the poem, Williams dispensed with it. "IMPROMPTU: The Suckers, 1927" was present in the typescript, but after Zukofsky found one phrase "awkward," wanted "a better word" at another point, and finally wondered "?who" the poem referred to at still another place, Williams seems to have been given pause. (The poem persisted into the next draft of *The Wedge*, but not as far as the published book.) Even a poem Williams had published as long ago as 1917—"History"—failed to pass muster when Zukofsky was dubious: "I dunno, but I still feel about this as I used to: there is some of your finest writing here imbedded in a discursive form which still doesn't form a setting. <Or perhaps just that –that there is a setting is the trouble> I think it's one of those things one has to live over again in re-writing—give it a year or a day when you can feel it again & the form'll drive in on you."

The "working copy" of *The Wedge* shows that Williams tended to jettison poems even when Zukofsky merely expressed doubt about their form. The manuscript Zukofsky examined contained numerous lengthy prose poems (Williams called them "improvisations"). Zukofsky did not suggest taking them out, but he did find their form as prose problematic. Of one of these, "Thatpoemjayjay," Zukofsky observed, "OK, but I wonder whether it wouldn't fit it in better, in a volume of poems, written out as lines rather than one prose stream. It's solid enough, & doesn't really need to call attention to JayJay's (James Joyces') device." He offered much the same advice for another prose poem, "Wellroundedthighs": "This means less to me than Thatpoemjayjay—but in any case, this too might gain in clearness written out as a poem in the line lengths indicating the sense." Zukofsky sounded the same note with the prose poem "THEESSENTIALROAR": "OK, I'd break this up into verse lines, too." Even when Zukofsky sounded a bit encouraging, as he did when commenting on the prose poem "The Runner" ("This can be chiseled down & written out as verse"), Williams evidently saw little point in recasting the prose poems as poetry. Perhaps he was discouraged by Zukofsky's comment about still another prose poem, "THICKCAKE": "Writing this out in verse lines would make it clear and show you where it ought to be cut, if –." Williams may have been reluctant to recast the prose and still have the job of cutting before him. None of the prose poems appeared in the next draft of *The Wedge*. It should be noted, however, that Williams was ready to adopt some of Zukofsky's suggestions for adjusting the lines of his poems. When Zukofsky remarked of "Raleigh was Right" that, "I think if you would realign this so that the lines end on the spoken cadence rather than a metrical one, the really new pattern of speech in it would be shown off better. Anyway, it's a good poem," Williams did reshuffle the line endings.

Williams rarely kept a poem when Zukofsky expressed doubt. One of the poems in the typescript, "An Exultation," drew two negative comments. The lines, "as she did, to send up thanks to those who / rain fire upon you," prompted Zukofsky to say, "ain't exactly what you want to say? The Miltonic note annoys." Further on, the lines, "they cannot comprehend / have worked this cleansing mystery upon you," have next to them Zukofsky's observation that, "allright as 'exultation,' but a bit too theosophical for me."

One of two exceptions to this exclusionary rule is "The Bare Tree," which Zukofsky found "Good," but added, "I imagine tho it would be more effective as speech in a play." The other exception is "The Semblables," in which Zukofsky found only a slight fault: "Good, but a little rhetorical here and there, especially pg 2."

Zukofsky's comments of general approval were rare. If he saw nothing wrong with a poem, he was usually silent. Of "The Dance" he simply wrote, "very fine." "The Forgotten City" drew the observation, "I like this very much." He was slightly more forthcoming about the second poem in the typescript, "Catastrophic Birth," which he found, "Very interesting. Kind of a modern Koholeth." These three poems remained part of *The Wedge*.

Zukofsky's scrutiny of the poems in the typescript went beyond summary comments about the poems. He offered advice in greater detail. For example, the position of the preposition "in" in the sixth line of "The Storm" ("south of the city shines in" [*CP2*, 86]) was determined by Zukofsky's noting that it "would sound better on that line" than it would where Williams had it initially, at the beginning of line seven. In the second stanza of "A Vision of Labor: 1931," Zukofsky bracketed a passage thusly

—by the edge of the sea! the shore
exploded away—{but in this case   *confusing* [Zukofsky's notation]
a bomb of construction,}
the sewer going down six feet inside

Williams substituted "constructively" for the bracketed phrase. Zukofsky's summary comment, however ("A lot in this. But could be more explicit—ordered. I see where the "depression" (above) could really fit in. But it should apply both to Rome and your Vision—in the text.") did not move Williams to drastically rearrange or rewrite the poem.

Upon inspecting a poem entitled by Williams, "The Rose in Time of War," Zukofsky bracketed "in Time of War" drew a line to the space between lines one and two, and commanded, "insert here!" When *The Wedge* was published, the title of the poem had indeed been truncated to "The Rose," and the second line was "in time of war" (*CP2*, 74). Similarly, a poem titled by Williams "The Winnah!," with its first line, "You were pure as snow," caused Zukofsky to comment, "I'd make the title part of the poem—and cut out <u>You were</u>." When *The Wedge* was published, the poem had been retitled "The Aftermath" and the first line now followed Zukofsky's direction: "The Winnah! pure as snow" (*CP2*, 84). The following lines in "Writer's Prologue to a Play in Verse" drew Zukofsky's attention.

> a book, inside the mind, natural
> to the mind as metals are to rock
> to be dug out and laid in their purity
> before you—if you will open

Zukofsky observed in the margin opposite the first two lines, "this and what follows rather a confused series of metaphors." The published version of the poem shows that Williams reworked the lines.

> It isn't masculine more than it is
> feminine, it's not a book more than
> it is a speech; inside the mind, natural
> to the mind as metals are to rock,
> a gist, puppets which if they present
> distinction, it is from that hidden
> dignity which they, by your leave,
> reflect from you who are the play. (*CP2*, 61–62)

The most numerous alterations suggested by Zukofsky pertain to "Burning the Christmas Greens." In the typescript, the line concluding stanza eight is, "white deer as if they had been." Zukofsky bracketed "as if they had been," and offered three possible replacements: "as if they were," "as though they were," and "as if they walked there." Williams adopted the first suggestion, but recast the line so that "were" became the first word of the following stanza. Of the sixteenth stanza, Zukofsky commented, "Is the cadence there? Commas would help." He also drew a line to the word "even" and called for, "a better word to make the line & verse move." Williams took corrective action, as we can see by comparing the typescript and published versions of the stanza.

In the jagged flames green	In the jagged flames green
to red instant and alive. Green!	to red, instant and alive. Green!
even the memory burnt away.	those sure abutments . . . Gone!
Those joists of winter's	lost to mind (*CP2*, 64)

Williams achieved the final form of the stanza by combining two consecutive stanzas from the typescript version. Here is the stanza following the one above, with Zukofsky's comments in italics.

dark towers from whose	*a little ornate albeit*
roofless perches the birds	*Shakespearian. I'd make this*
invite the music of storms,	*simple like the rest*
those sure abutments. Gone!	

Clearly the condensation of the two typescript stanzas owed much to Zukofsky's doubts about them. Williams also removed, at Zukofsky's suggestion, the phrase "we silent" in stanza 17 (in the typescript the phrase comes immediately before "Black / mountains . . . " (*CP2, 64*). At the end of "Burning the Christmas Greens," Zukofsky wrote, "Brush up the last page & the poem's one of your best."

Williams sometimes rejected his editor's advice. When he turned to "A Sort of a Song," which eventually Williams placed first in the collection, Zukofsky wrote: "Just the 4 lines—the rest is embroidery." The difficulty for the reader, however, and perhaps a difficulty for Williams, is that it is unclear to which four lines Zukofsky refers. In any event, Williams chose not to condense the poem. Similarly, when Zukofsky saw the fifth stanza of "Paterson: The Falls," he bracketed "I am the Resurrection / and the Life" and commented, "The sound of this ought to develop the historic idea more precisely than what follows." The published version, however, retained the phrases.

On occasion Zukofsky's suggestions seemed to assist Williams as he worked toward still further revisions. In the typescript Zukofsky received, the second stanza of "Paterson: The Falls" ran this way:

Begin; the middle of some trenchant
phrase, some well packed clause,
picked for the place. Then . .
answer! This is my plan.

Zukofsky bracketed two words and briefly commented.

{Begin;} the middle of some trenchant   *Don't repeat yourself* [Zukofsky]
phrase, some well packed clause,
picked for the place. Then . .
{answer!} This is my plan.

Williams took his advice about the two words, but realigned the lines so that in the published version the phrase, "in the middle of" became attached to the first stanza, while the second stanza became:

some trenchant phrase, some
well packed clause. Then . .
This is my plan. 4 sections: First,
the archaic persons of the drama. (*CP2*, 57)

Similarly when Zukofsky asked, "is the syntax clear?" of these lines in "Writer's Prologue to a Play in Verse": "strange, unnatural to the world, / that suffers the world poorly, is[,]" Williams kept the words but recast the lines so that in the published version we find: "something strange, unnatural to / the world, that suffers the world poorly, / is tripped at home, disciplined at" (*CP2*, 60).

For another account of how *The Wedge* relates to Williams's and Zukofsky's poetics, and particularly how it relates to their overall careers, see Neil Baldwin's essay, "Zukofsky, Williams, and *The Wedge:* Toward a Dynamic Convergence" in *Louis Zukofsky: Man and Poet,* Carroll F. Terrell, ed. (Orono, Maine: The National Poetry Foundation, 1979), 129–42.

Bunting, Basil (1900–1985), British poet. In 1930–1931, Bunting visited America, where he
met Zukofsky. Zukofsky reviewed Bunting's first book, *Redimiculum Matellarum* (1930)
in *Poetry*. In the "Objectivists" issue of *Poetry*, Zukofsky published section three of
"Attis: Or, Something Missing." Zukofsky also included poems by Bunting in *An "Objec-
tivists" Anthology* (1932). Bunting discusses Zukofsky's poetry in *Basil Bunting on Poetry*.

Dahlberg, Edward (1900–1977), American novelist and essayist. Dahlberg first made his
name with his fictionalized autobiography, *Bottom Dogs* (1929). In the same year he
became acquainted with Williams. Much later, in 1948–1950, he became friends with
Zukofsky while they both were teaching at Brooklyn Polytechnic Institute. A selection
of letters from Dahlberg to Williams appear in *Epitaphs of Our Times* (1967). In the
same volume, in a 1957 letter to Isabella Gardner, Dahlberg gives a lengthy summary of
his relations with Williams and Zukofsky.

Hecht, S. Theodore (1895–1973), Polish-born American educator. Hecht met Zukofsky
when both were students at Columbia University. Hecht taught in the New York city
school system during the 1920s and early 1930s, but then took a position with the New-
ark public schools. While he was employed by the city of Newark, Hecht and his wife
Kate lived in Rutherford, New Jersey, with their two sons. Williams became the family
physician for the Hechts.

Niedecker, Lorine (1903–1970), American poet. She began corresponding with Zukofsky
in 1931, after seeing the "Objectivists" issue of *Poetry*. She did not meet him until 1933,
when she visited New York. In September 1936, Jerry Reisman and Zukofsky visited her
in Wisconsin on their return from the West Coast. In the summer of 1954 the Zukofsky
family visited her in Wisconsin. The final meeting between Niedecker and Zukofsky
occurred in 1968 when he, Oppen, Rakosi, and Reznikoff participated in a conference
on the Objectivists at the University of Wisconsin. Her "The Poetry of Louis Zukof-
sky" in the *Quarterly Review of Literature* (April 1956) was one of the earliest studies of
Zukofsky's work.

Oppen, George (1908–1984), American poet. He first met Zukofsky, Tibor Serly, and
Charles Reznikoff in New York in 1928. In 1929 Oppen and his wife Mary went to
France, where they settle for three years. Here they began publishing books under the
imprint of the Objectivist Press. They issued *An "Objectivists" Anthology*, Williams's *A
Novelette and Other Prose*, and Pound's *ABC of Reading*. They returned to New York,
where they lived from 1933 to 1937, at first in Brooklyn Heights, not far from Zukofsky.
In 1934 Oppen published his first book of poems, *Discrete Series*. Williams reviewed it
in *Poetry*. This review, "The New Poetical Economy," is reprinted in *Something to Say*.

Pound, Ezra (1885–1972), American poet. Pound and Williams had been acquainted since 1902, when both were students at the University of Pennsylvania. Pound arranged for the publication of *The Tempers* (1913) in London. During the next four decades, both men often reviewed works by the other. Williams discusses his relations with Pound at greatest length in his *Autobiography*. The relationship between the two poets is also detailed in Paul Mariani's *A New World Naked* and Hugh Witemeyer's *Pound/Williams: Selected Letters of Ezra Pound and William Carlos Williams*. Pound's connection to Zukofsky is most extensively treated in Barry Ahearn's *Pound/Zukofskky: Selected Letters of Ezra Pound and Louis Zukofsky*.

Reisman, Jerry (1913–2000), American businessman. Reisman and Zukofsky met in 1929, when Zukofsky was working part time as a teacher at Stuyvesant High School, where Reisman was a student. During the 1930s, according to Zukofsky, Reisman was his "best friend." A collaborative poem, "After *Les Collines*," appears in *An "Objectivists" Anthology*. In 1936 they traveled to Mexico and the West Coast, returning to the East by way of Wisconsin, where they visited Lorine Niedecker. Zukofsky encouraged Reisman to write, but Reisman's interests were in the sciences and mathematics. It was Reisman who helped Zukofsky with the mathematical and scientific material in "A"-8 and "A"-9. Zukofsky was employed by Reisman's company, Techlit Consultants in 1946 and 1947, but their friendship ended at that point.

Reznikoff, Charles (1894–1976), American poet and novelist. Zukofsky's early essay, "Sincerity and Objectification: With Special Reference to the Work of Charles Reznikoff," was an important component of the "Objectivist" issue of *Poetry*. Along with Zukofsky and George Oppen, he helped establish the Objectivist Press, which published his *Jerusalem the Golden* (1934) as well as *In Memoriam: 1933* (1934) and *Separate Way* (1936).

Serly, Tibor (1900–1978), Hungarian-American violinist and composer. A viola player in the Cincinnati Symphony, the Philadelphia Symphony, and the NBC Symphony, Serly also composed songs, a viola concerto, a symphony, and other symphonic works. At some point in the late 1920s he became friends with Zukofsky. Through Zukofsky he became acquainted with Williams and Pound. During the mid-1930s Serly became interested in composing the music for Williams's opera, *The First President*. Eventually, however, Serly found himself unable to do so.

Taupin, René (1904–1981), Franco-American critic and teacher. In *L'influence du symbolisme français sur la poésie américaine (1910–1920)* (1929), Taupin ranked Williams, with Pound and Eliot, as the three most important living American poets. Taupin emigrated to the United States in 1930, where he made his living as a professor of French. He met Zukofsky in New York, and met Williams through Zukofsky. Zukofsky's translation of Taupin's essay on André Salmon appeared in two issues of *Poetry* (February and March 1931). Zukofsky also translated an essay on Eliot by Taupin, "The Classicism of T. S. Eliot," which appeared in *The Symposium* (January 1932). Zukofsky's "The Writing of Guillaume Apollinaire" was translated into French by Taupin and published in Paris in 1934 as *Le Style Apollinaire*.

Winters, Yvor (1900–1968), American poet and critic. Winters' negative review of Taupin's *L'influence du symbolisme français sur la poésie américaine* in *Hound and Horn* 4:4 (July–September 1931), 607–18, prompted Zukofsky to compose a reply. (This in turn elicited a response from Winters. The editors of *Hound and Horn* proposed to print the exchange, but never did. The page proofs that were sent to Zukofsky are now at the Harry Ransom Humanities Research Center in Austin, Texas. In 1932, Winters expressed his opinion of Zukofsky to Lincoln Kirstein in this fashion, "Our own generation, and the kids who are coming up, seem to be divided more or less clearly between those whose intellectual background is incomprehensible to the older men and who therefore remain largely meaningless to them, and those who imitate them feebly and flatter them in numerous ways (Zukofsky is the most shameless toady extant) and who are therefore praised by them," *The Selected Letters of Yvor Winters*, R. L. Barth, ed., 195. In a letter of 18 August 1932 to Williams, Winters remarked, "You ought to know better than to let an ass like Zukofsky revise your best poems in public" (Yale). Williams published a poem by Winters, "Chiron," in *Contact* 1:3 (October 1932), 49. Winters discusses Williams's poetry in *Primitivism and Decadence* (1937) and in "Poetry of Feeling" (collected in *Yvor Winters: The Uncollected Essays and Reviews*).

Firdausi, 395
Fischer Verlag, 310
Fitts, Dudley, 78, 85, 87, 122
Five Groups of Verse (Reznikoff), 31
Flaubert, Gustave, 299
Flea of Sodom, The (Dahlberg), 433
Fletcher, Frances, 120
Fletcher, John Gould, 87
Flores, Angel, 149, 158
Folio, 526
For the Time Being (Auden), 353n
Ford, Charles Henri, 24n, 307
Ford, Ford Madox, 216, 239–241, 268, 270–271, 381n, 382–383
"Forty-leben days gone by," 259
Forum Magazine, 14, 179n
Foster, Harvey N., 140
Four Pages, 395, 410, 433, 435
Four Seas Company, 65
Foyers D'Incendie (Calas), 271
France en Liberté, La, xx, 273n, 275–276
Francis, Thomas Edward, 532
Frank, Waldo, 214–215
Franklin, Benjamin, 52
Freud, Sigmund, 391
Frick Museum, 451
Friends of William Carlos Williams, 268n, 270n, 271n
Front Page, The (Hecht and MacArthur), 20
Frost, Robert, 253
"Full Margin" (Breton), 351, 352, 354
"Fundamental Disagreement with Two Contemporaries" (Rexroth), 135, 137

Gassner, John, 285, 288
Gielgud, John, 240n
Gilady, Dr. Ralph, 177
Gillmore, Vaun, 526
Ginsberg, Allen, 506
Gleason, Jackie, 497n
Godwin, William, 318
Goffin, Robert, 300n
Goldberg, Isaac, 43
Goldberg Variations (Bach), 483
Golden Goose (Macleod), 449
Goll, Yvan, 336
Goss, Mr., 402–403
Gotham Book Mart, 276
Gould, Joe, 26, 356–357

Green Horn, 235
Gregory, Horace, 178
Griffith, Mrs. Parker O., 470
Griffith Music Foundation, 470
Guczul, Dometer, 305, 310, 337
Guest, Edgar, 336
Guermantes Way, The (trans. Scott Moncrieff), 514
Guggenheim, William, 34

Hamerton, Philip Gilbert, 111
Hamlet, 240, 532
Hansen, Harry, 178–179
Harcourt, Brace, 158
Harper's Bazaar, 377
Hartley, Marsden, 142n, 232, 237–238, 338
Harvard Advocate, The, 178, 180, 219
Harvard University, 285, 336, 439–440
Harvard Wake, 358
Hatch, Robert, 493–494
"Hawk and a Handsaw for Ezra Pound, A" (Adams), 400n
Hays, H. R., 211
Hazeltine Electronics Corporation, 337n
Heath, Louise, 351
Hecht, Joe, 355
Hecht, Katherine, 46n, 211–212, 391, 450, 465
Hecht, Theodore, 46n, 211–212, 224, 233, 450
Hegel, Estelle, 180, 183
Hemingway, Ernest, 53, 175, 273n
Hemispheres, 336
"Henry James" (Pound), 288
Herbst, Josephine, 157, 159, 485
Herman, Charlotte, 359, 388, 433
Herman, Paul, 62, 419
Herman, Nannie, 131, 190, 289, 298
"Hero, The" (Moore), 129
Herrick, Robert, 313, 314
Herrman, Eva, 3–4
Herrmann, John, 48, 157n
Higgins, James, 270
Hika, 286n
Hiler, Hilaire, 180, 182, 216
Hillman, 34
Hillside Hospital, 469
Him (Cummings), 30n
Hindemith, Paul, 441
Hitler, Adolf, 291

195–198, 211–212, 222, 234–235, 237–
238, 243, 248, 266, 275–276, 286, 290,
291, 297, 299, 301–303, 305–307, 311,
315, 321–322, 325, 333, 337–338, 344–
347, 350, 355, 361, 365, 381–383, 385,
388, 394, 399, 401, 408, 410–411, 414–
415, 419, 426, 431, 433, 438, 440, 444–
446, 448, 450, 452, 456, 461–466, 471,
478, 481, 483, 487, 492, 494, 500–501,
505, 507, 509, 511–514, 518–520, 522,
524–525, 527, 529, 533, 535–536, 539; on
Ezra Pound, 496
Williams, Jonathan, 474, 487, 491, 504
Williams, Oscar, 319–320
Williams, Paul Herman, 33, 88, 108, 159,
216, 235, 254, 301, 303, 306, 326, 336–
337, 344–348, 352, 356, 359, 365, 367,
375, 414, 417–418, 447, 449, 467–468
Williams, Paul Herman, Jr., 306, 325, 344–
346, 447, 449, 469, 495
Williams, Suzanne, 346, 350, 431, 443
Williams, Virginia Carnes, 344–346, 356,
365, 423n, 467–468
Williams, William Carlos (WCW):
ailments, 74, 169, 373, 392, 453, 469,
501, 511, 519; ancestral history, 171–172;
attic, 71–72; Charles Reznikoff, 31, 50;
comments on Louis Zukofsky's
works, 4–5, 7–8, 11, 13, 18, 25–26, 30,
37, 63, 67–68, 78–81, 89, 135, 202, 244–
247, 250–251, 278, 292, 303–305, 313,
321, 331–332, 334, 340, 342, 364, 366–
368, 371, 386–387, 392, 404–406, 421,
427, 442, 449, 463, 488–490, 501–502,
523; Consultant in Poetry appoint-
ment, 393, 401, 403, 453; *Contact* (sec-
ond series), 101–146 *passim;* the *Dial,*
12; Ezra Pound, 15, 36, 162–163, 180,
212, 215, 218–219, 232, 241, 284, 286n,
289, 316, 359, 364, 369, 372, 382, 393,
397, 410–412, 454, 498; *First President,
The,* 131, 153–245 *passim;* Guggenheim
recommendations for Louis Zukof-
sky, 47–48, 258n, 259n; history of po-
etry, 233, 370; Houghton Mifflin rec-
ommendation for Louis Zukofsky,
287n; medical profession, 51, 164, 186,
298; modernism, 32, 412; Nathanael
West, 103; nature, 33, 343, 346, 380;
public appearances, 142, 233, 237, 270,
406, 439, 444, 465n, 531; publishing
plans, 27, 42, 55–56, 58–59, 65–66, 85,
100, 146, 154–159, 165–168; René
Taupin, 123; Richard Johns, 35, 70;
Shakespeare, 143, 235, 318–319; Surre-
alism, 312–313;
works: "Above the River," 265n, 266;
"Adam," 226n; *Adam & Eve & the
City,* 223n, 226–228; "Advent of
Today," 239n; "Against the Weather: A
Study of the Artist," 264, 269;
"Aigeltinger," 403n; *Al Que Quiere,* 17,
40, 266; "The American Idiom," 532–
533; "An American Poet," 257; " An
Approach to the Poem," 388n, 389n;
"April Is the Saddest Month," 395, 414;
"Asphodel, that Greeny Flower," 539;
"The Attack on Credit Monopoly
from a Cultural Viewpoint," 234;
"The Auto Ride" (*see* WCW, works,
"The Right of Way"); *The Autobiog-
raphy of William Carlos Williams,*
xviii, 425, 435–436, 440, 445–446;
"Back to the City," 268n; "The Basis of
Poetic Form," 286n; "Birds and Flow-
ers, I–II," 58, 62n; "The Bitter World
of Spring," 346; "The Black Winds,"
220, 317; "The Blue Jay," 540n; "The
Book of Prosody," 249–252, 440–441;
"The Boticellian Trees," 74, 81n, 105,
130n; "Brancusi," 467–468; "Bread
Loaf Talk," 286n; "Brief Note on a
Recent Talk," 416n; *The Broken Span,*
273; "Brooklyn Lecture: Notes for a
lecture at the Brooklyn Institute of
Arts & Sciences," 417n; *The Build-Up,*
425, 447–448, 450; "Calypso," 509 (*see
also* WCW, works, "Calypsos I–II"
and "Puerto Rico Song"); "Calypsos
I–II," 510n; "Cancion," 223–224; "The
Catholic Bells," 151; "The Centenar-
ian," 152n; "Child and Vegetables,"
64n; "A Chinese Toy," 228; "The
Clouds," 336n; *The Clouds,* 401n; "The
Cod Head," 98n; *The Collected Later
Poems,* 435; *Collected Poems 1921–1931,*
95–100, 102, 105, 148, 149n, 166–170,
173–175, 176n, 177, 179–180, 183, 194;
"The Colored Girls of Passenack, Old
and New," 90; "Comment:

Rivers," 70n, 72–73; "On Gay Wallpaper," 15n; "Our (American) Ragcademicians," 149n; "The Parable of the Blind," 511; *Passaic, Passaic!* (trans. Vermandoy), 391; "Paterson," 52, 127, 130, 151, 23; *Paterson*, 254, 256, 302, 307, 429, 441, 445, 456, 486 (*see also* WCW, works, "Detail and Parody for the Poem Patterson"); *Paterson: Book I*, 307n, 345–346, 358, 360, 364–365, 367, 371, 382, 398; *Paterson: Book II*, 388–389, 391, 398; *Paterson: Book III*, 391, 393–394, 409, 415, 420; *Paterson: Book IV*, 391, 409, 430, 440; *Paterson: Book V*, 476n, 485, 487–488, 490–491, 493, 498–500; "Perpetuum Mobile: The City," 225; "Picasso Sticks Out / An Invested World," 420; "Pictures from Brueghel," 512; *Pictures From Brueghel*, 521, 539; "The Pink Church," 375–377, 379–383, 389; "The Poem as a Field of Action," 393n; "A Poem for Norman Macleod," 222; *Poems*, 77–78; "The Poet in Time of Confusion," 272, 274–275, 278; "A Poet Remembers," 341n; "Poetry," 253, 254n; "Portrait of a Woman in Bed," 81n, 130n; "Postlude," 81n, 130n; "Preface," 352, 354, 371; "A Prelude," 266; "Proletarian Portrait," 220; "Puerto Rico Song," 510; "Rain," 35n; "Raquel Hélene Rose," 273, 274n, 276; "The Raper From Passenack," 213n; "The Red Wheelbarrow," 146n, 260; "The Red-Wing Blackbird," 401; "The Right of Way," 220; "Robert McAlmon," 111n; "The Rose," 228; "Russia," 367–368; "St. Francis Einstein of the Daffodils," 43, 226n; *Script* (*see* WCW, works, *Collected Poems 1921–1931*); "The Sea-Elephant," 62; "Sea-Trout and Butterfish," 65n; "Sluggishly," 151; "Some Simple Measures in the American Idiom and the Variable Foot," 510, 540; "The Somnabulists," 39, 115, 119–120; "Song," 152n; *Sour Grapes*, 43; "The Source," 15n; *Spring and All*, xiii, xix, 6, 19, 28n, 30, 40, 91, 100, 317, 320; "A Study of Ezra Pound's

Present Position," 387n; "Summary of a Year's Verse," 347n, 356; "Sunday," 65; "Surrealism and the Moment," 307; "Suzanne," 401; "The Swivelhipped Amazon" (*see* WCW, works, "Mounted as an Amazon"); *The Tempers*, 33, 261n; "Theocritus: Idyl I (A Version from the Greek)," 456, 539; "This Florida: 1924," 103n, 173; "Three Letters," 111n; "Threnody," 348–349; "To," 75–76, 92; "To All Gentleness," 343; "To a Mexican Pig-Bank," 220; "To an Elder Poet," 228; "To a Poor Old Woman," 199, 220; "To a Wood Thrush," 228; "To Be Hungry Is To Be Great," 220; "To Daphne and Virginia," 456; "To Elsie," 40, 49; "To Ford Madox Ford in Heaven," 342; "To My Friend Ezra Pound," 491; "To the Dean," 213n; "Tree and Sky," 152n, 220; *Trial Horse No. 1* (*see* WCW, works, *Many Loves*); *Tribute to Ezra Pound*, 85–87, 93–94, 100–101, 102n, 106–107, 117–118, 121; "Turkey in the Straw," 404, 408; "Under the Stars," 272, 273n, 278; "Unnamed: From 'Paterson,'" 228; "The Usurers of Heaven," 377; "View of a Lake," 220; *A Voyage to Pagany*, 7–8, 10, 16, 20, 35, 61, 161; "VS," 392–393; "Water, Salt, Fat, etc.," 113–114; *The Wedge*, xv, xxi. 319, 322, 324–330, 333–335, 338–341, 342, 344n, 346–347, 349–350; *White Mule*, 77, 82, 135, 141, 146–149, 151–152, 155, 175–176, 178, 187, 212, 241, 248, 254–256, 349, 409n, 440; "*White Mule* Versus Poetry," 256; "The Wind Increases," 220; "The Wind Meaning" (*see* WCW, works, "The Black Winds" and "The Wind Increases"); "Wind of the Village," 252n; "With Forced Fingers Rude," 395, 412n; "Woman as Operator," 390; "Work in Progress," 456; "*The Work of Gertrude Stein*," xv, 35, 38–43, 45, 47–50, 52–53, 112–113, 115; "The Writers of the American Revolution," 229–231, 234; "The Yachts," 212; "The Yellow Flower," 456; "The Yellow Season," 280n; *Yes, Mrs.*

Williams, William Carlos, works *(continued)*
  Williams, 240, 257, 268, 273, 440, 512;
  "Zukofsky," 479, 481–484, 487, 513, 530,
  541
  and World War II, 291, 306–308, 336, 345,
  348, 352–353
Williams, William Eric, xxi, 43, 88, 104,
  130–131, 138, 169, 172, 177, 232, 235, 286,
  301, 303, 306, 310, 336–337, 344–346,
  352, 356, 359–360, 367, 375, 385, 389,
  401, 406–408, 411, 415, 419, 425, 466,
  537
Williams, William George, 171–172, 316
Wilson, 179
Wilson, Edmund, 50, 264, 391
Wilson, T. C., 217n
Winters, Yvor, 110, 112, 141, 147–148, 264
Winter's Tale, The, 235, 539
Witt-Diamant, Ruth, 494n, 497, 529n
Wollstonecraft, Mary, 318
*Women: A Collaboration of Artists and
  Writers* (Kootz), 390
Women of Trachis, The (trans. Pound),
  512–513
Wooton, Lucy, 3, 6–7, 291
WOR, 243, 300
Wordsworth, William, xiii
"World's End," 271n
WQXR, 459
Writer, The, 256
Writers Extant. *See* Objectivist Press
Writers Publishers. *See* Objectivist Press
Wynn, Ed, 537

Yaddo, 411, 430–431, 434
Yale Quarterly, 294
Yale University, 469
Yale University Press, 207
Young, Kathleen Tankersley, 47

Zabel, Morton Dauwen, 87, 151, 184
Zacharia, Zachy, 17, 21
Zadkine, Ossip, 308
Zara, Louis, 534n, 535
Zhukovsky, Vasily Andreyevich, 212
Zukofsky, Celia Thaew, xxi, 288, 299–302,
  303, 305, 306, 309, 312–314, 319–322,
  323–324, 330, 337–343, 346, 350, 354–
  355, 358–359, 361, 366, 374–375, 377–
  383, 389, 391, 393, 395, 397–399, 401,

403–404, 407–408, 411, 415, 419, 422,
  424, 426, 430–431, 434, 438, 445, 451,
  453, 455, 458, 461–462, 464–465, 469–
  470, 472, 474, 478–479, 481, 483–485,
  487–488, 493, 497, 502–505, 507–509,
  511, 513, 516–521–522, 524–525, 527, 529,
  533, 535–536, 539
Zukofsky, Louis (LZ): comments on and
  edits works of William Carlos
  Williams, 40 59–62, 73, 78, 90, 95–96,
  137, 189–192, 266, 272–275, 281, 325–
  330, 339–340, 342, 354, 378–379, 395,
  446, 456, 481–486, 491, 510, 532, 539;
  Edward Dahlberg, 437–438; Ezra
  Pound, 37–38, 288, 317, 339, 354, 361,
  362n, 385, 513; *55 Poems,* 293–295; in-
  vites William Carlos Williams to lec-
  ture at Brooklyn Polytechnic, 415, 418;
  Kenneth Burke, 527–530; modernism,
  38, 77, 86, 487; *An "Objectivists" An-
  thology,* 106; Objectivist poetry, 472;
  on his own work, 313–314, 428–429,
  448, 491, 514–515, 524, 541–542, 526;
  proposes William Carlos Williams
  write a *Poetics,* 440–441; prosody, 224,
  249; public appearances, 300, 497,
  520, 535; publishing plans, 52, 55, 57,
  76, 111, 144, 273n, 299, 323, 333, 504,
  513, 533–534; Shakespeare, 320; Soviet
  cinema, 19;
  works: "A," xv, 15, 24–25, 26, 38–39, 42,
  44, 47, 52, 71, 78–79, 125, 245–246, 256,
  259, 269, 305, 396, 411, 441, 463, 481,
  485, 488, 491, 521; *"A" 1–12,* 480n, 484,
  504, 512n, 513, 515–518, 523–525, 527–
  528, 530, 535–536, 541–542; "A" 1–2, 19,
  449; "A" 1–7, 81n, 135; "A" 3–4, 100; "A"
  5–6, 126, 128; "A"– 6, 75n; "A"–7, 75n,
  76–77; "A"–8, 241, 243–247, 249–250,
  257n, 258, 259n, 278, 440, 454n; "A"–9,
  261n, 269, 276–279, 431–433, 435, 459n,
  528; "A"–10, 279–280; "A"–11, 440–441,
  447–448, 459n; "A"–12, xix, 440, 445–
  446, 451, 464n, 482, 491; "A"–13, 440,
  452n, 525, 533; "Air," 437; "All of De-
  cember toward New Year's," 470;
  "American Poetry 1920–1930," 67, 73,
  78, 320; "& Cie," 357; "And Looking To
  Where Shone Orion," 63n; "And with-
  out," 426–427; *Anew,* 340, 342, 366,

Zukofsky, Louis, works *(continued)*
Reznikoff," 80, 472; "Some one said, 'earth,'" 13n; *Some Time,* 418n, 474, 478, 483, 486, 488–489, 495, 523; "Some Time Has Gone," 421n; Song 4 ("29 Poems"), 26n; Song 9, 116n, 129n, 136; Song 10, 116n, 129n, 136; "A Song for the Year's End," 355n; "Songs of Degrees," 460n; "Song theme to the last movement of Beethoven's Quartet in C-sharp minor," 13n; "Spooks' Sabbath," 459n; "A Statement for Poetry," 442, 472; "Stratford-on-Avon," 523–525; "Tall and singularly," 80n; "tam cari capitis," 13n; *A Test of Poetry,* 259–260, 295, 321–323, 327–328, 361, 397–400, 404–407, 415, 441, 472, 486; "This Fall 1933 / American Banknote Factory," 217n; "Thru running manes of *Leaves of Grass,*" 463; "To My Wash-stand," 145n, 290n; "To such of one body as one mind," "3/4 time (pleasantly drunk)," 217n; "To Zadkine," 459n; "Two Dedications," 30n; "A Valentine," 492n; "W," 417–418; "What are these songs," 269; "William Carlos Williams," 297n, 493n; "William Carlos Williams alive!" 460n; "The World Autumn," 459n; *The Writing of Guillaume Apollinaire,* 159, 161, 183, 357, 358n; "Xenophanes," 412

World War II, 292, 300, 309–310, 339

Zukofsky, Paul, xxi, 343–346, 354, 359, 361, 391, 393, 399, 401, 403, 411, 413, 424, 426, 430–432, 434, 436, 445, 451–453, 456, 458–460, 463–466, 468–471, 474–480, 483, 493, 497, 499, 502–503, 506–509, 511, 513, 516–517, 519–522, 535–538, 540

Zukofsky, Pinchos, 125, 299, 424, 426–427, 480, 483

Zukowsky, Daniel, 337

Zukowsky, Morris, 125, 276, 286n

Printed in the United States
80862LV00006B/46-72